TADATOSHI FUJIMAKI

Maybe some of you have noticed... I'm talking about the little pictures above these comments. They actually form a flipbook story, starting back in volume 1.

And in that story, I get smacked down and beat up, but I keep on fighting. I don't mean on the outside. On the inside. Heart. That's what matters most.

That's totally the reason I included these the whole time...

Not.

—2014

Tadatoshi Fujimaki was born on June 9, 1982, in Tokyo. He made his debut in 2007 in *Akamaru Jump* with *Kuroko's Basketball*, which was later serialized in *Weekly Shonen Jump*. *Kuroko's Basketball* quickly gained popularity and became an anime in Japan in 2012.

BASKETBALL

29 & 30

SHONEN JUMP Manga Edition
BY TADATOSHI FUJIMAKI

Translation/Caleb Cook
Touch-Up Art & Lettering/Mark McMurray
Design/Julian [JR] Robinson
Editor/John Bae

KUROKO NO BASUKE © 2008 by Tadatoshi Fujimaki
All rights reserved.
First published in Japan in 2008 by SHUEISHA Inc., Tokyo.
English translation rights arranged by SHUEISHA Inc.

The stories, characters and incidents mentioned in this
publication are entirely fictional.

Printed in the U.S.A.

Published by VIZ Media, LLC
P.O. Box 77010
San Francisco, CA 94107

10 9 8 7 6 5 4 3 2 1
First printing, December 2018

viz.com

shonenjump.com

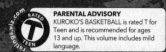

PARENTAL ADVISORY
KUROKO'S BASKETBALL is rated T for
Teen and is recommended for ages
13 and up. This volume includes mild
language.

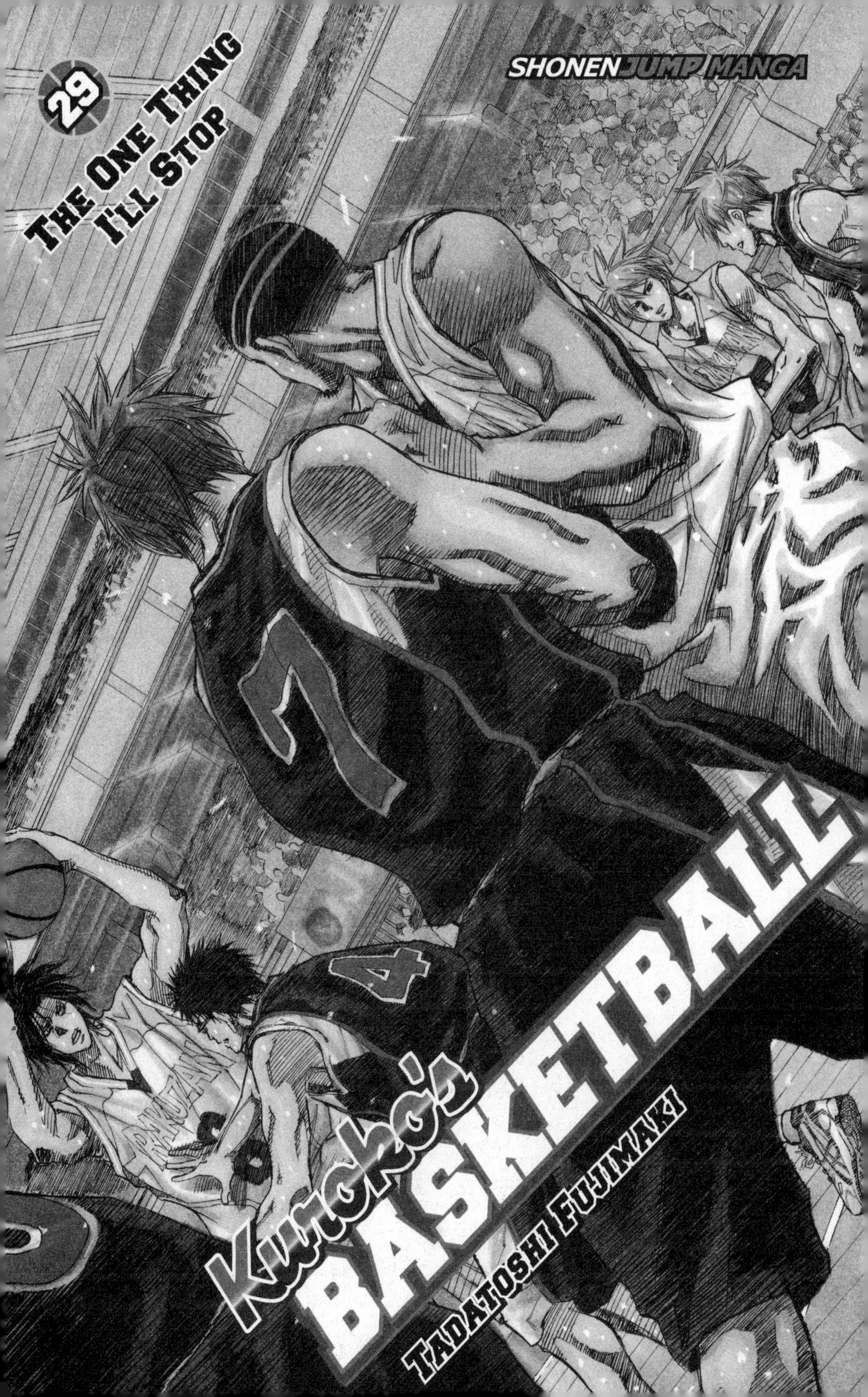
SHONEN JUMP MANGA
29
THE ONE THING I'LL STOP
Kuroko's BASKETBALL
TADATOSHI FUJIMAKI

CHARACTERS

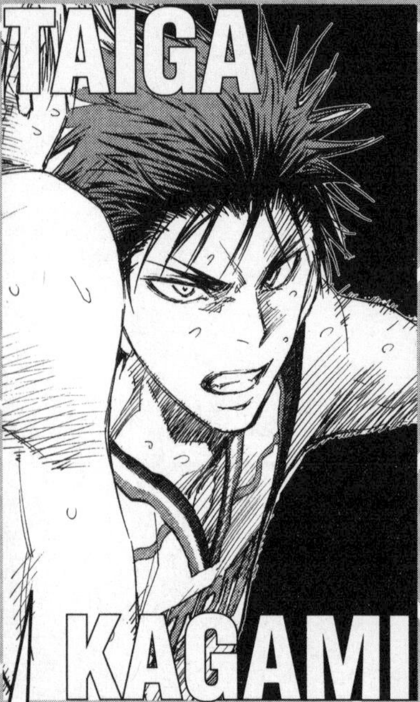
TAIGA
KAGAMI

A first-year on Seirin High's basketball team. Though he's rough around the edges, he's a gifted player with a lot of potential. His goal is to beat the Miracle Generation.

A first-year on Seirin High's basketball team. Gifted with a natural lack of presence, he utilizes misdirection on the court to make nearly invisible passes.

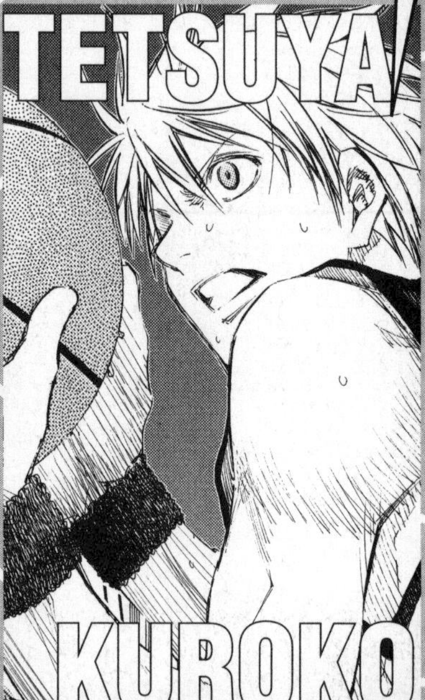
TETSUYA
KUROKO

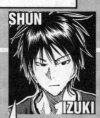

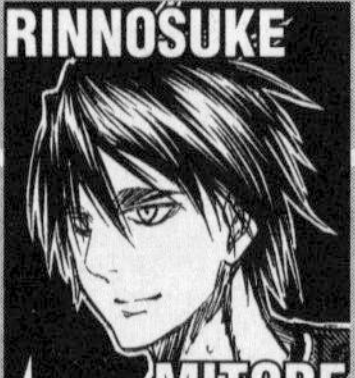
RINNOSUKE
MITOBE

A second-year on Seirin High's basketball club. A strong and silent type whose height makes him the right man to play center.

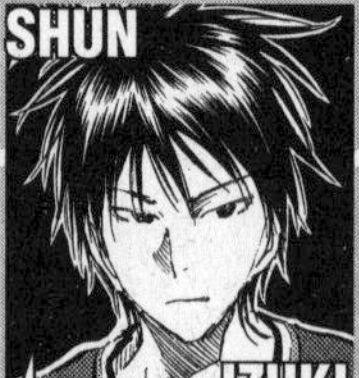
SHUN
IZUKI

A second-year on Seirin High's basketball club. He controls the flow of the game with his wide field of vision.

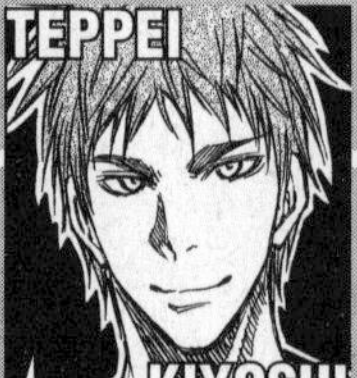
TEPPEI
KIYOSHI

A second-year on Seirin High's basketball team and the club's founder. He was hospitalized but returned shortly after Inter-High.

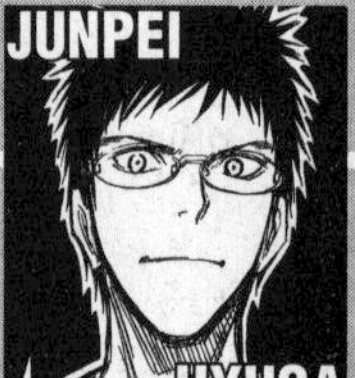
JUNPEI
HYUGA

A second-year on Seirin High's basketball team. As captain, he led his team to the Finals League last year despite only playing first-year players.

KUROKO'S BASKETBALL

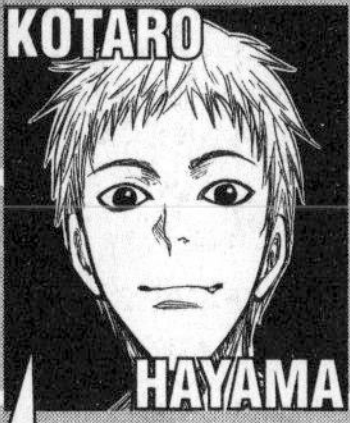
KOTARO
HAYAMA

A second-year on Rakuzan High's basketball club and one of the Uncrowned Generals. Rakuzan's easygoing small forward is the life of the party.

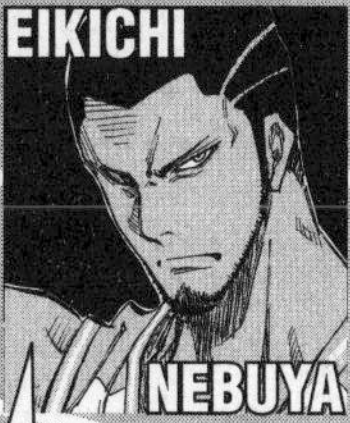
EIKICHI
NEBUYA

A second-year on Rakuzan High's basketball club and one of the Uncrowned Generals. As the team's powerful center, he specializes in battles of strength.

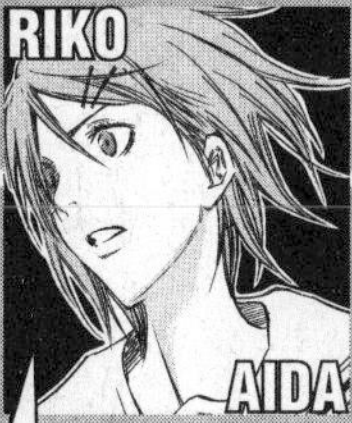
RIKO
AIDA

A second-year and coach of the Seirin High basketball team.

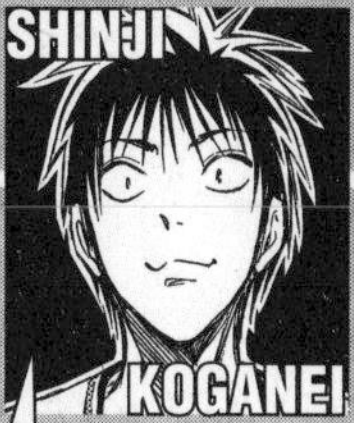
SHINJI
KOGANEI

A second-year on Seirin High's basketball club. His sunny disposition keeps the team in high spirits.

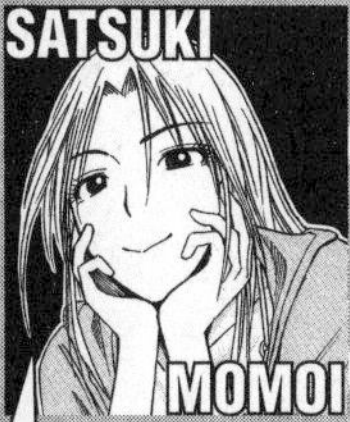
SATSUKI
MOMOI

A first-year who is To-oh's basketball club manager. She has extensive scouting reports on every high school player.

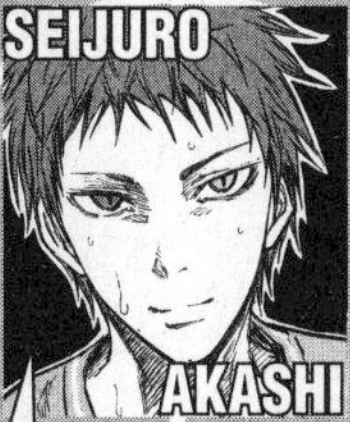
SEIJURO
AKASHI

Captain of the Miracle Generation during his time at Teiko Middle and the current leader of Rakuzan's ferocious team.

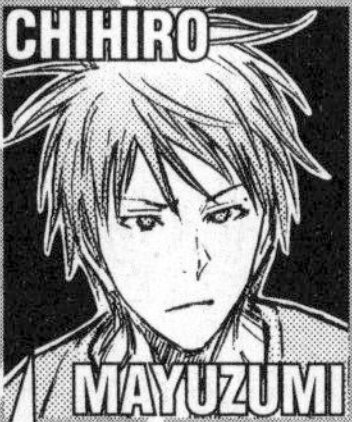
CHIHIRO
MAYUZUMI

A third-year on Rakuzan High's basketball club. He's the only third-year starting member, though his stats are all exceedingly average.

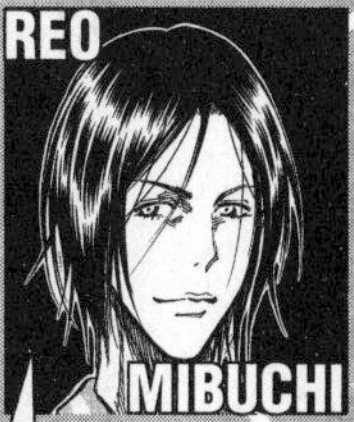
REO
MIBUCHI

Rakuzan High second-year and one of the Uncrowned Generals. His three-pointers make him a formidable shooting guard whom Akashi trusts implicitly.

Teiko Middle School is an elite championship school whose basketball team once fielded five prodigies collectively known as "the Miracle Generation." But supporting those five was a phantom sixth man—Tetsuya Kuroko. Now Kuroko's a first-year high school student with zero presence who joins Seirin High's basketball club. Though his physical abilities and stats are well below average, Kuroko thrives on the court by making passes his opponents can't detect!

Aiming for the Winter Cup title, Seirin has beaten one Miracle Generation member after another to reach the final match against Rakuzan, led by Akashi. Kuroko loses his trademark invisibility early in the game, and Seirin's in a pinch when Rakuzan's new phantom sixth man steps up just when Hyuga gets into foul trouble. But now that Kuroko's got his power back and Kagami's in the zone, the game's outcome is uncertain!

STORY THUS FAR

TABLE OF CONTENTS

255TH QUARTER: **DO MY PART!**

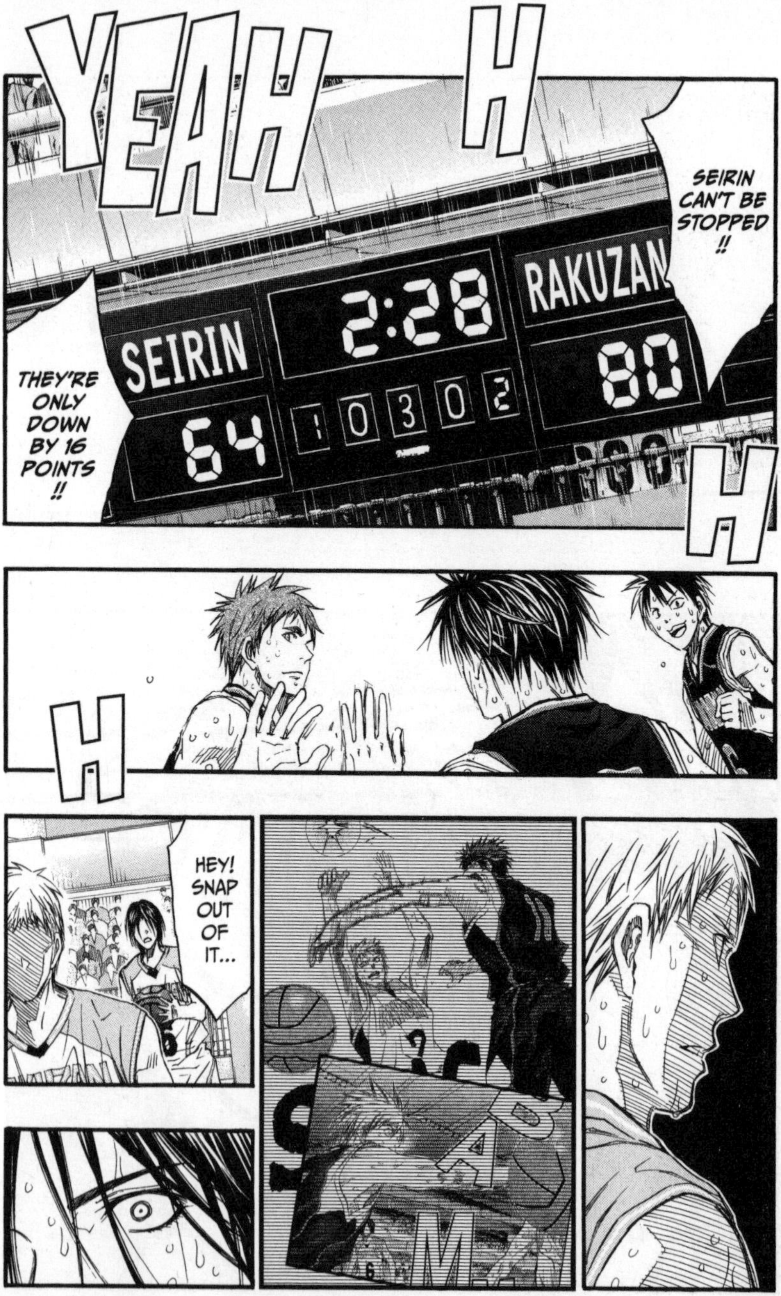
YEAH
H
SEIRIN CAN'T BE STOPPED!!
RAKUZAN
2:28
80
SEIRIN
64
THEY'RE ONLY DOWN BY 16 POINTS!!
H
H
H
HEY! SNAP OUT OF IT...

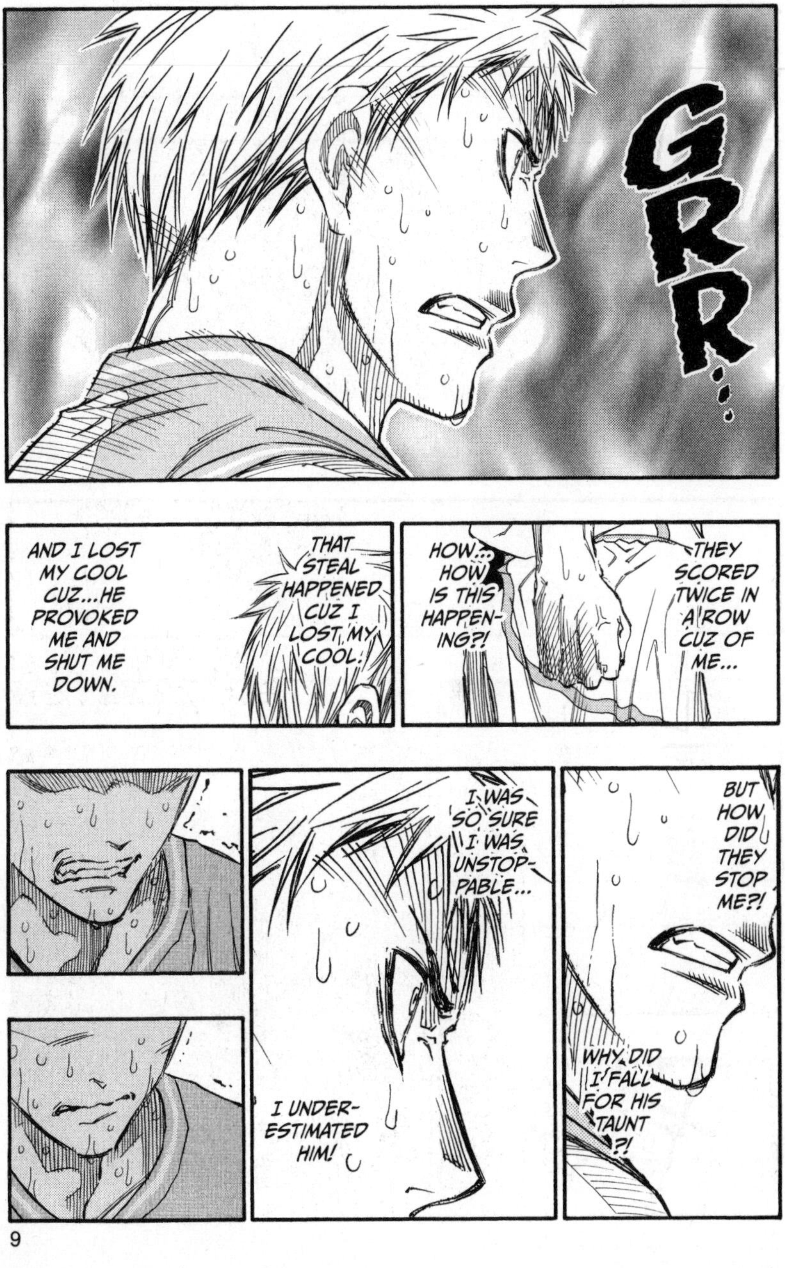
GRR...
THEY SCORED TWICE IN A ROW CUZ OF ME...
HOW... HOW IS THIS HAPPENING?!
THAT STEAL HAPPENED CUZ I LOST MY COOL.
AND I LOST MY COOL CUZ...HE PROVOKED ME AND SHUT ME DOWN.
BUT HOW DID THEY STOP ME?!
WHY DID I FALL FOR HIS TAUNT?!
I WAS SO SURE I WAS UNSTOPPABLE...
I UNDERESTIMATED HIM!

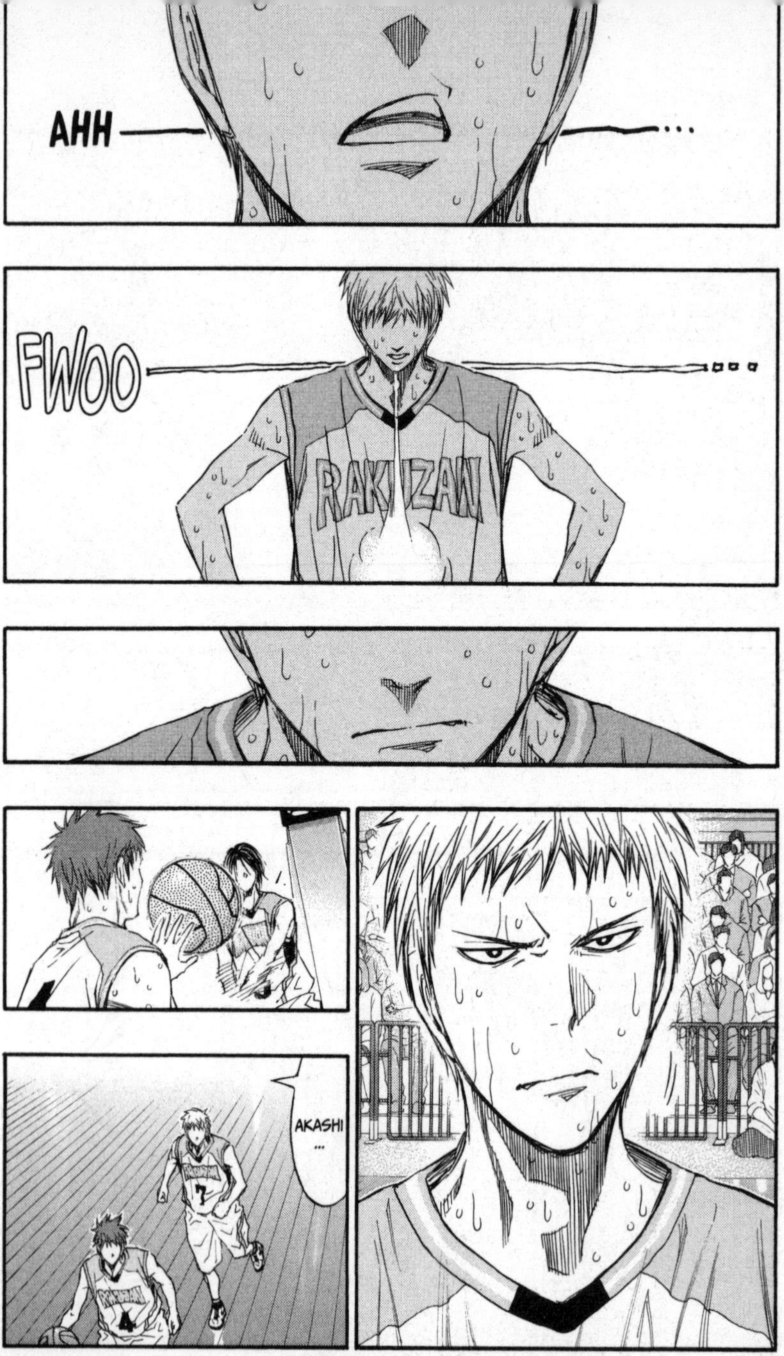
AHH—…
FWOO—…
AKASHI …
RAKUZAN

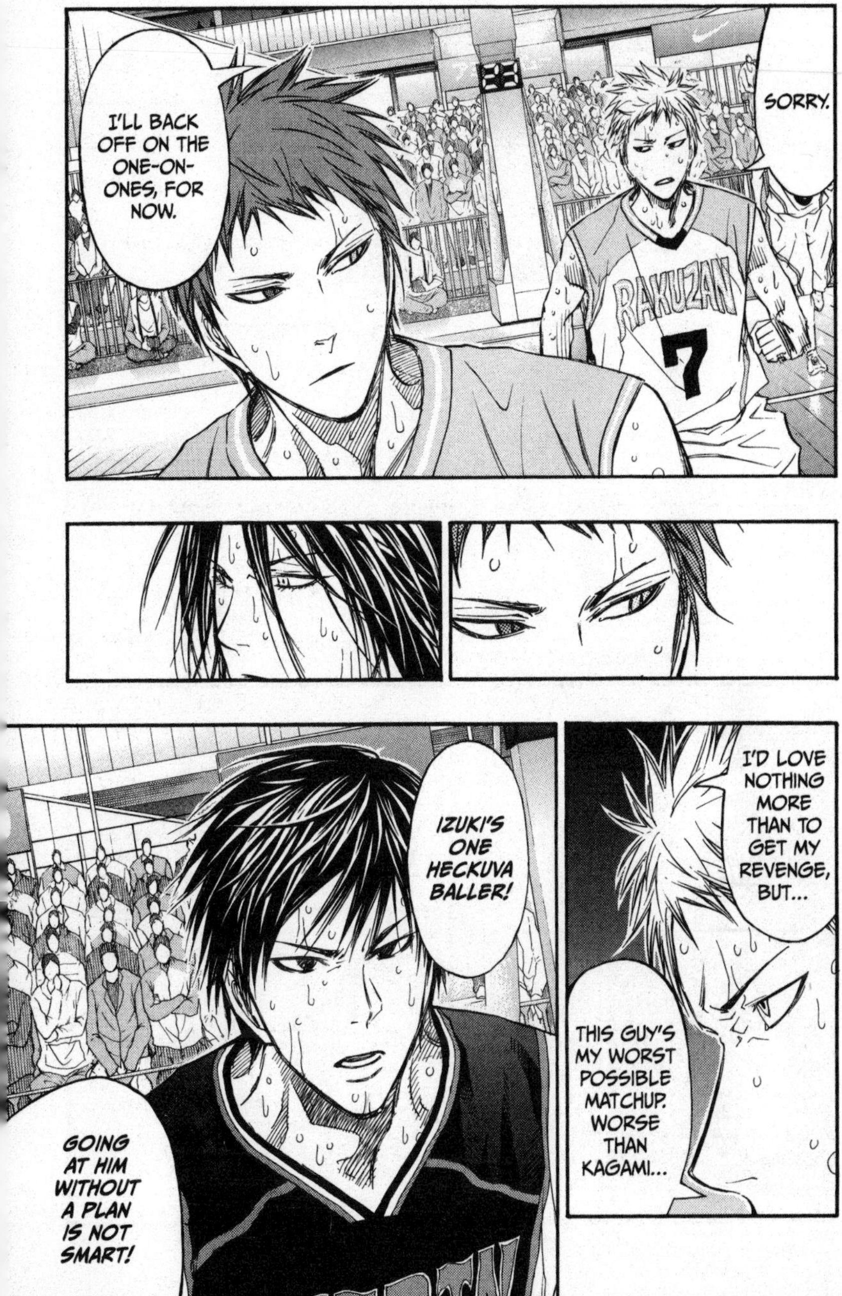
SORRY.
I'LL BACK OFF ON THE ONE-ON-ONES, FOR NOW.
I'D LOVE NOTHING MORE THAN TO GET MY REVENGE, BUT...
THIS GUY'S MY WORST POSSIBLE MATCHUP. WORSE THAN KAGAMI...
IZUKI'S ONE HECKUVA BALLER!
GOING AT HIM WITHOUT A PLAN IS NOT SMART!

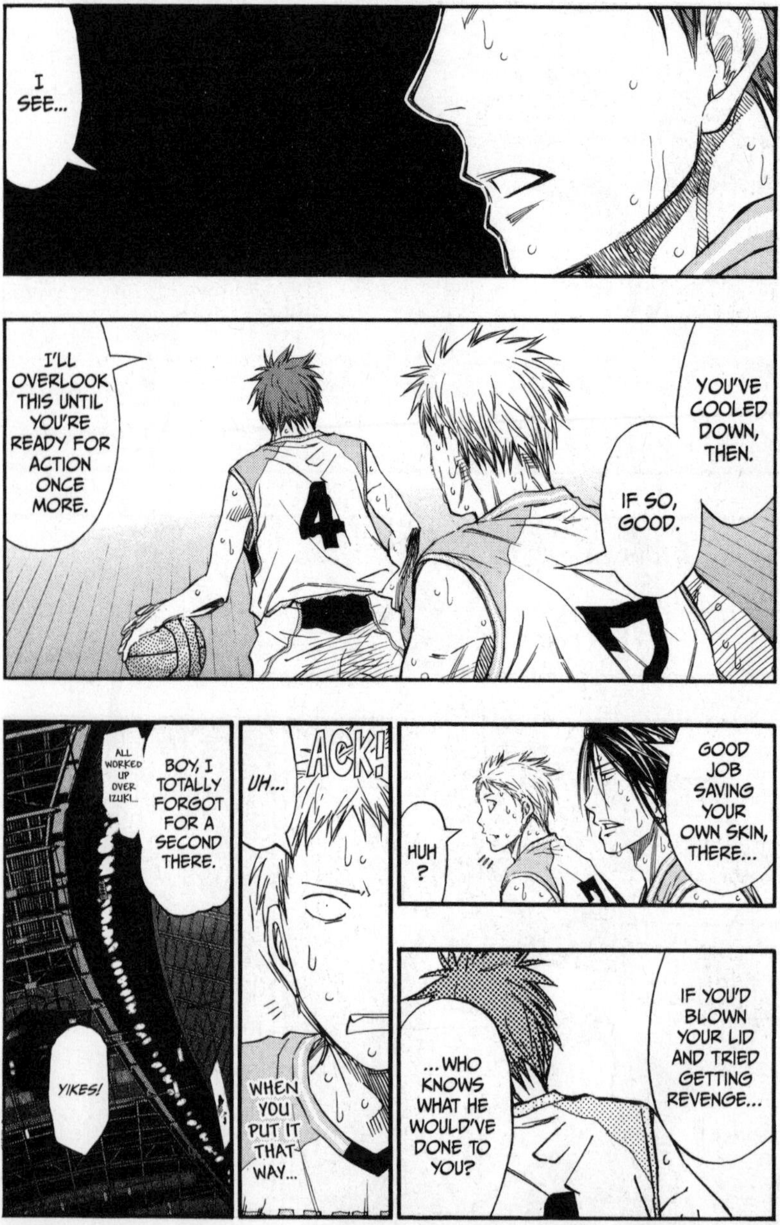
I SEE...
YOU'VE COOLED DOWN, THEN.
IF SO, GOOD.
I'LL OVERLOOK THIS UNTIL YOU'RE READY FOR ACTION ONCE MORE.
GOOD JOB SAVING YOUR OWN SKIN, THERE...
HUH?
IF YOU'D BLOWN YOUR LID AND TRIED GETTING REVENGE...
...WHO KNOWS WHAT HE WOULD'VE DONE TO YOU?
ACK!
UH...
WHEN YOU PUT IT THAT WAY...
BOY, I TOTALLY FORGOT FOR A SECOND THERE.
ALL WORKED UP OVER IZUKI...
YIKES!

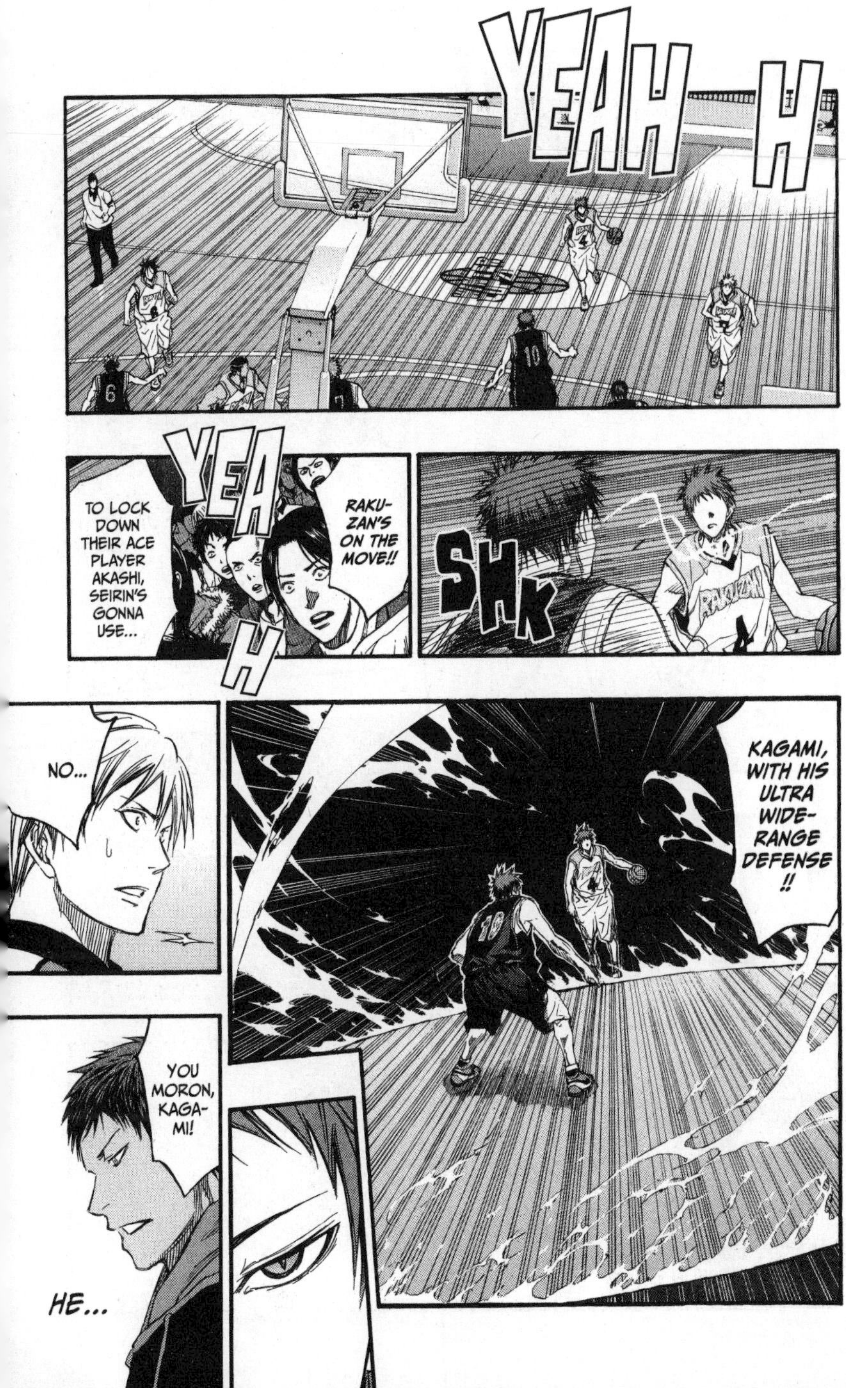
YEAH-H
SHK
RAKU-ZAN'S ON THE MOVE!!
TO LOCK DOWN THEIR ACE PLAYER AKASHI, SEIRIN'S GONNA USE...
YEAH-H
KAGAMI, WITH HIS ULTRA WIDE-RANGE DEFENSE!!
NO...
YOU MORON, KAGA-MI!
HE...

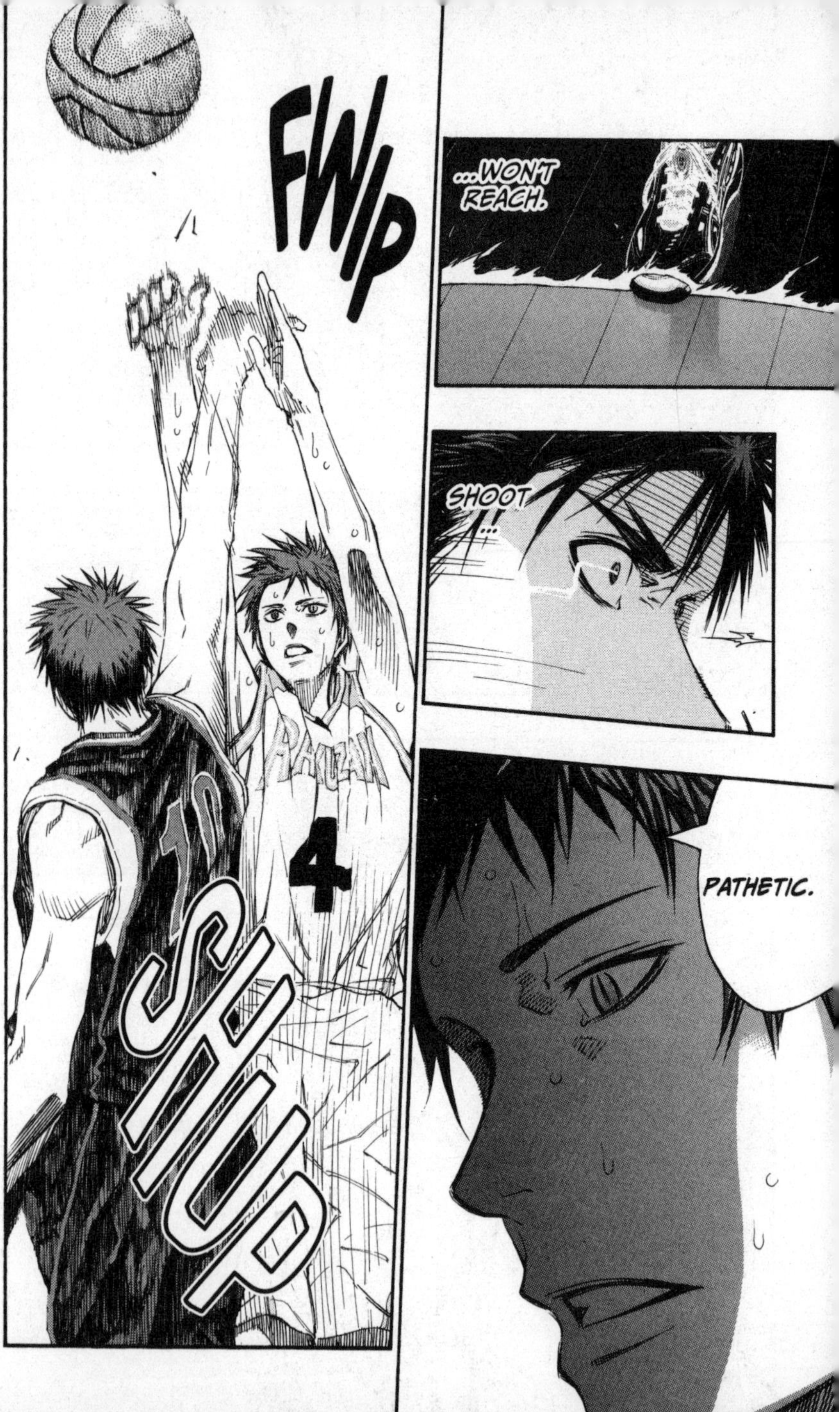
...WON'T REACH.
SHOOT...!!
PATHETIC.
FWIP
SHUP

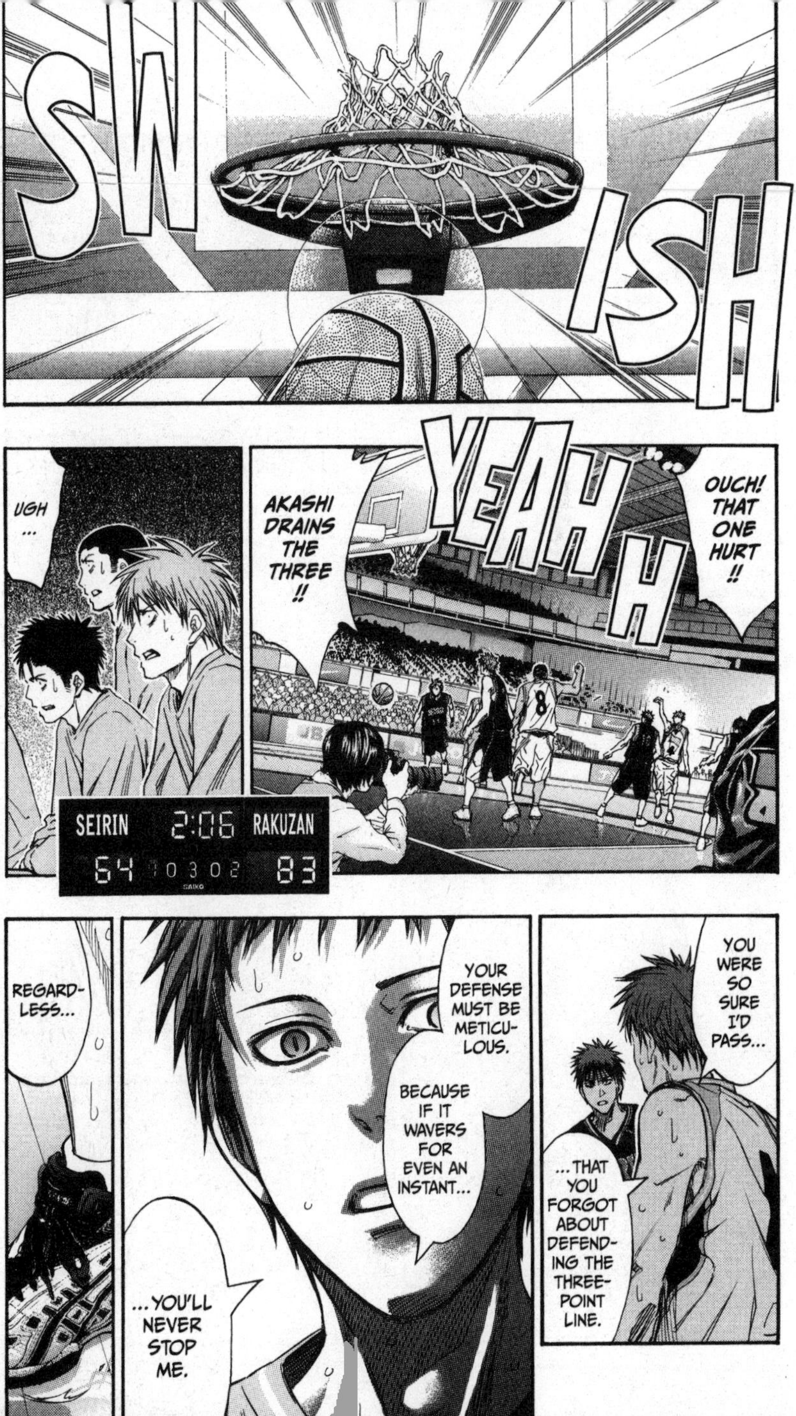
SWISH
OUCH! THAT ONE HURT!!
YEAHH
AKASHI DRAINS THE THREE!!
UGH...
SEIRIN 2:06 RAKUZAN
64 83
YOU WERE SO SURE I'D PASS...
...THAT YOU FORGOT ABOUT DEFENDING THE THREE-POINT LINE.
YOUR DEFENSE MUST BE METICULOUS.
BECAUSE IF IT WAVERS FOR EVEN AN INSTANT...
...YOU'LL NEVER STOP ME.
REGARDLESS...

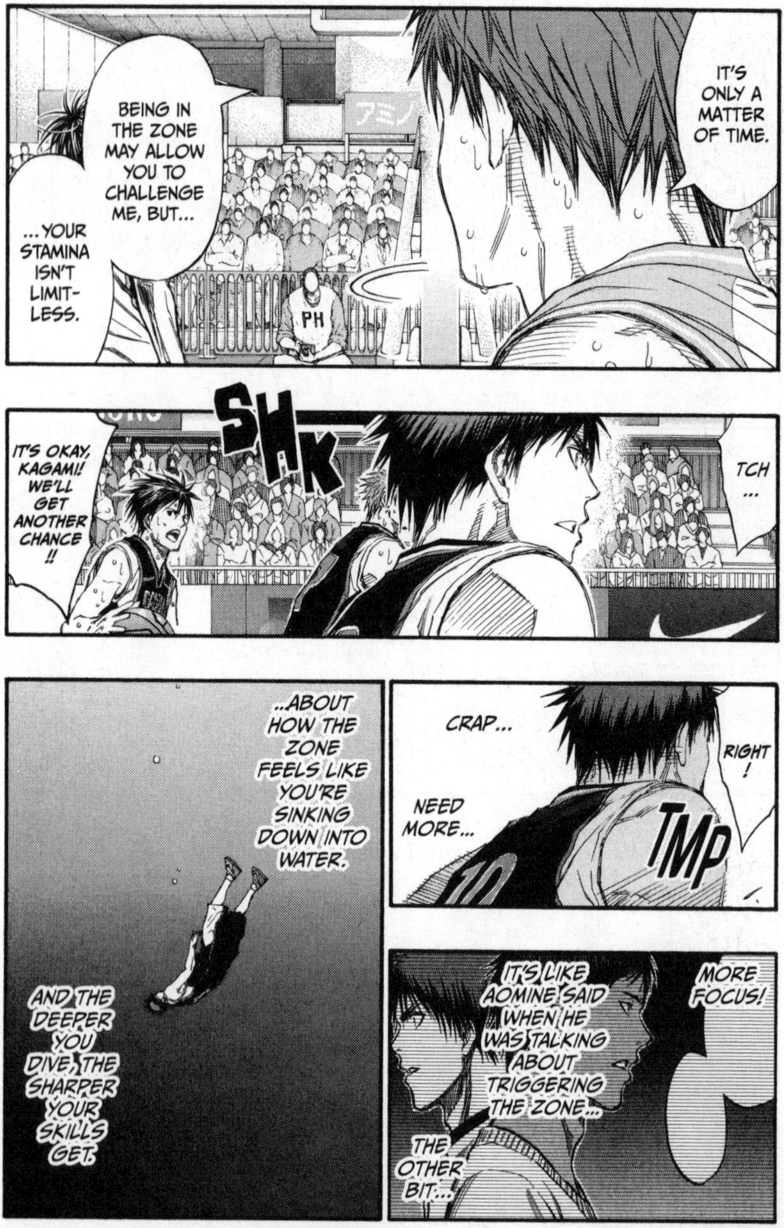

BEING IN THE ZONE MAY ALLOW YOU TO CHALLENGE ME, BUT...
...YOUR STAMINA ISN'T LIMITLESS.
IT'S ONLY A MATTER OF TIME.
TCH ...
SHK
IT'S OKAY, KAGAMI! WE'LL GET ANOTHER CHANCE !!
RIGHT !
CRAP...
TMP
NEED MORE...
MORE FOCUS!
IT'S LIKE AOMINE SAID WHEN HE WAS TALKING ABOUT TRIGGERING THE ZONE...
THE OTHER BIT...
..ABOUT HOW THE ZONE FEELS LIKE YOU'RE SINKING DOWN INTO WATER.
AND THE DEEPER YOU DIVE, THE SHARPER YOUR SKILLS GET.

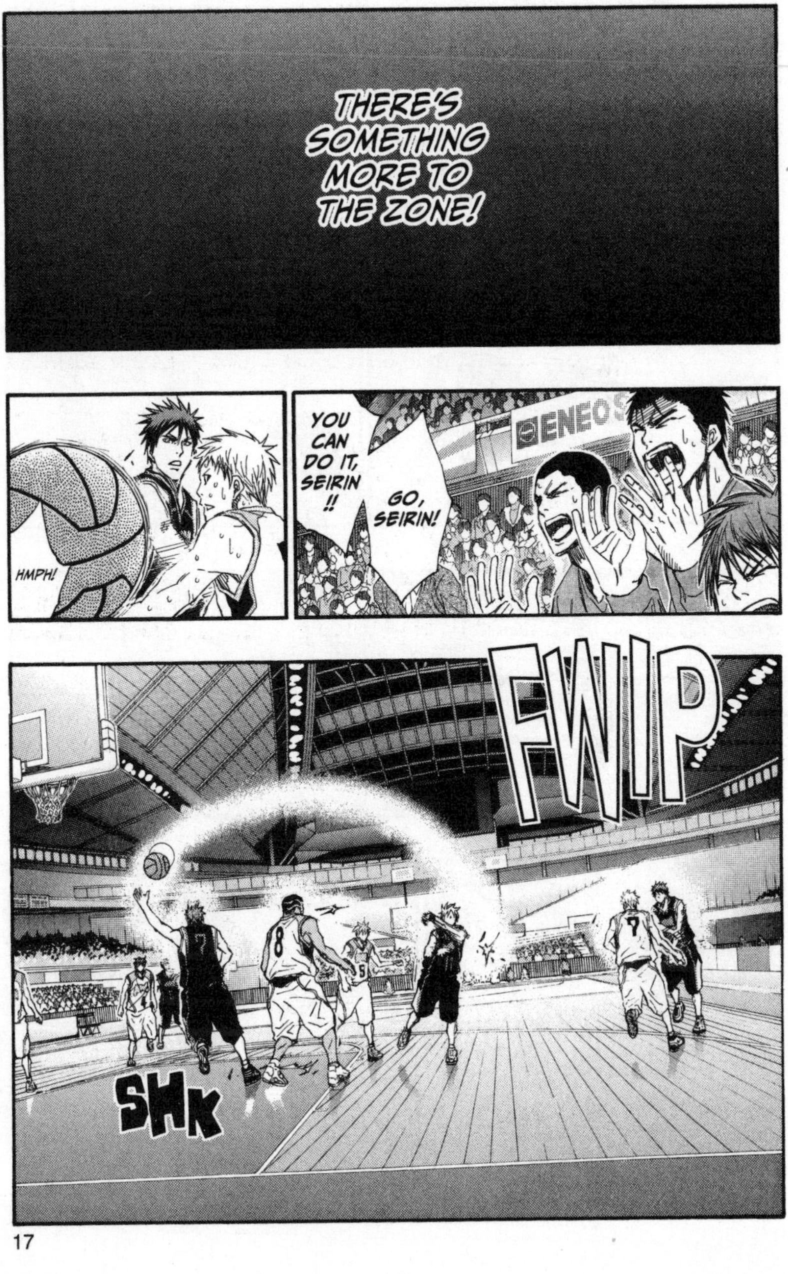
THERE'S SOMETHING MORE TO THE ZONE!
ENEOS
GO, SEIRIN!
YOU CAN DO IT, SEIRIN!!
HMPH!
FWIP
SHK

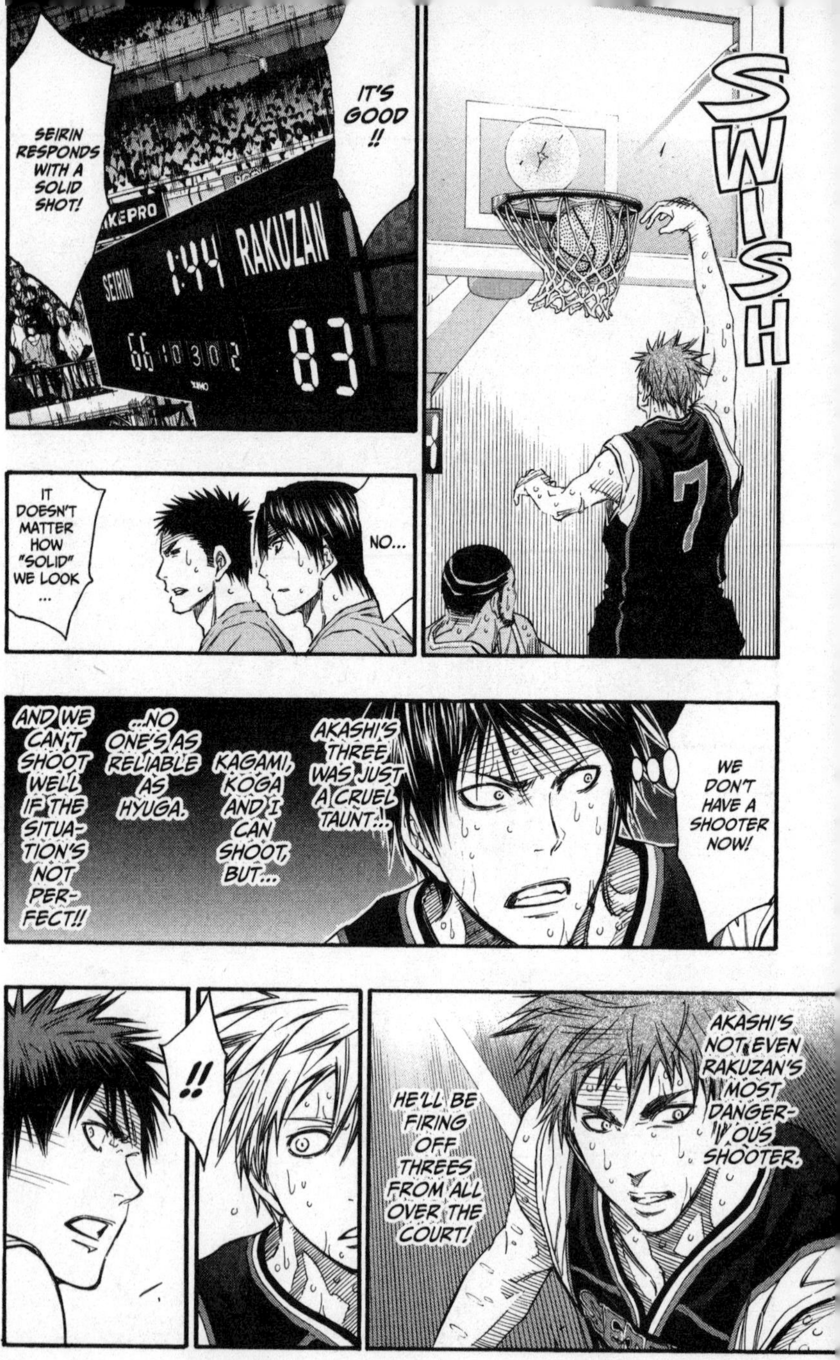
SWISH
IT'S GOOD!!
SEIRIN RESPONDS WITH A SOLID SHOT!
SEIRIN 1:44 RAKUZAN
66 83
NO...
IT DOESN'T MATTER HOW "SOLID" WE LOOK...
WE DON'T HAVE A SHOOTER NOW!
AKASHI'S THREE WAS JUST A CRUEL TAUNT...
KAGAMI, KOGA AND I CAN SHOOT, BUT...
...NO ONE'S AS RELIABLE AS HYUGA.
AND WE CAN'T SHOOT WELL IF THE SITUATION'S NOT PERFECT!!
AKASHI'S NOT EVEN RAKUZAN'S MOST DANGEROUS SHOOTER.
HE'LL BE FIRING OFF THREES FROM ALL OVER THE COURT!
!!

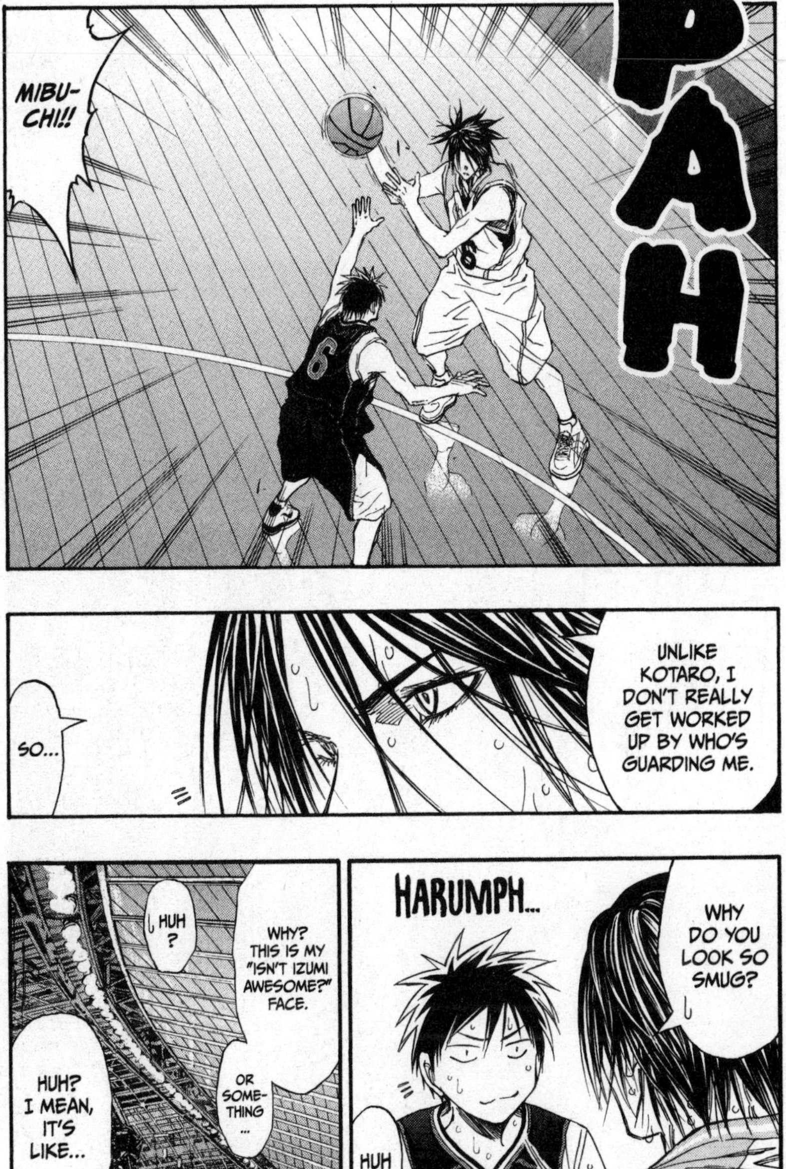
PAH
MIBU-CHI!!
UNLIKE KOTARO, I DON'T REALLY GET WORKED UP BY WHO'S GUARDING ME.
SO...
WHY DO YOU LOOK SO SMUG?
HARUMPH...
HUH?
WHY? THIS IS MY "ISN'T IZUMI AWESOME?" FACE.
HUH?
OR SOMETHING...
HUH? I MEAN, IT'S LIKE...

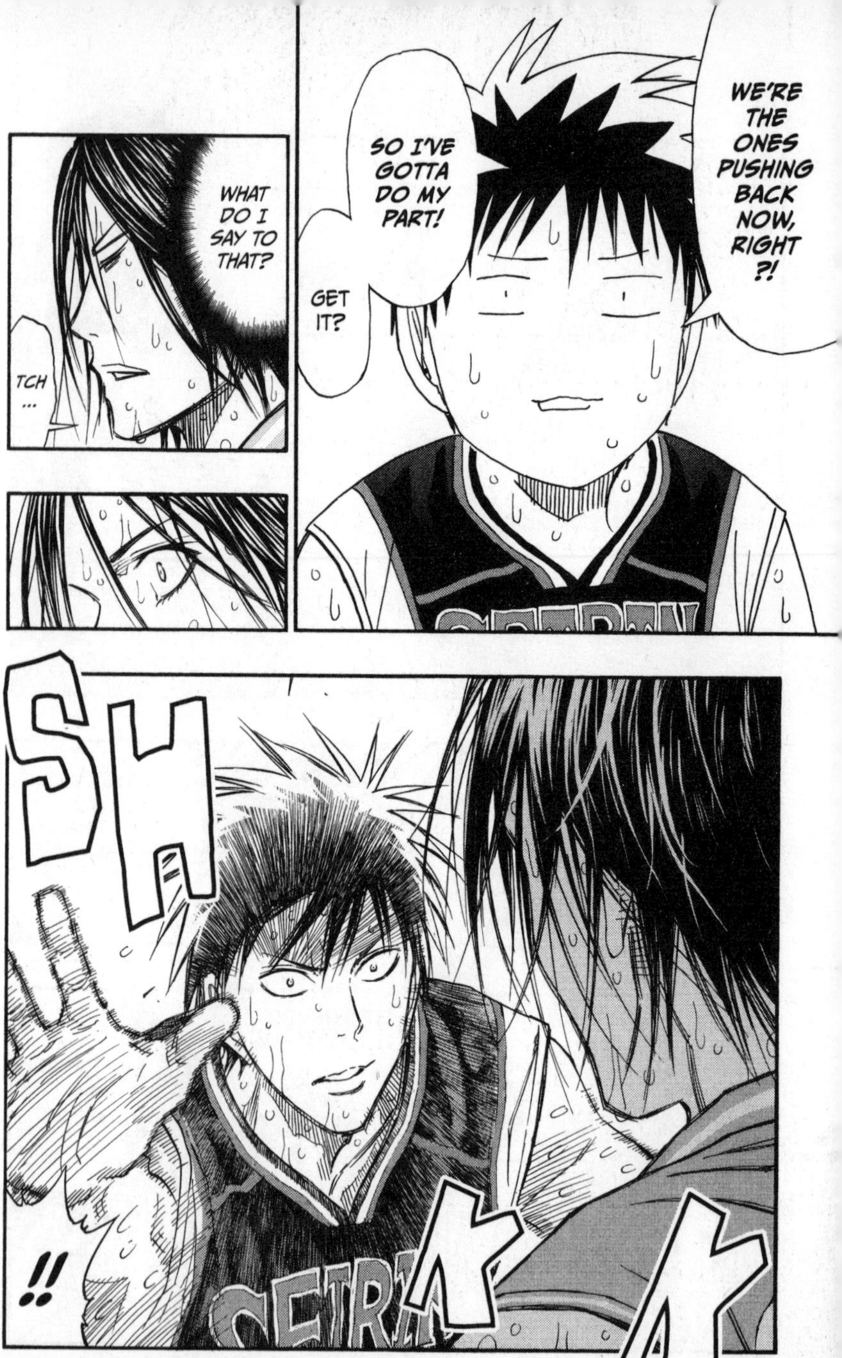

WE'RE THE ONES PUSHING BACK NOW, RIGHT?!
SO I'VE GOTTA DO MY PART!
GET IT?
WHAT DO I SAY TO THAT?
TCH ...
SH
!!

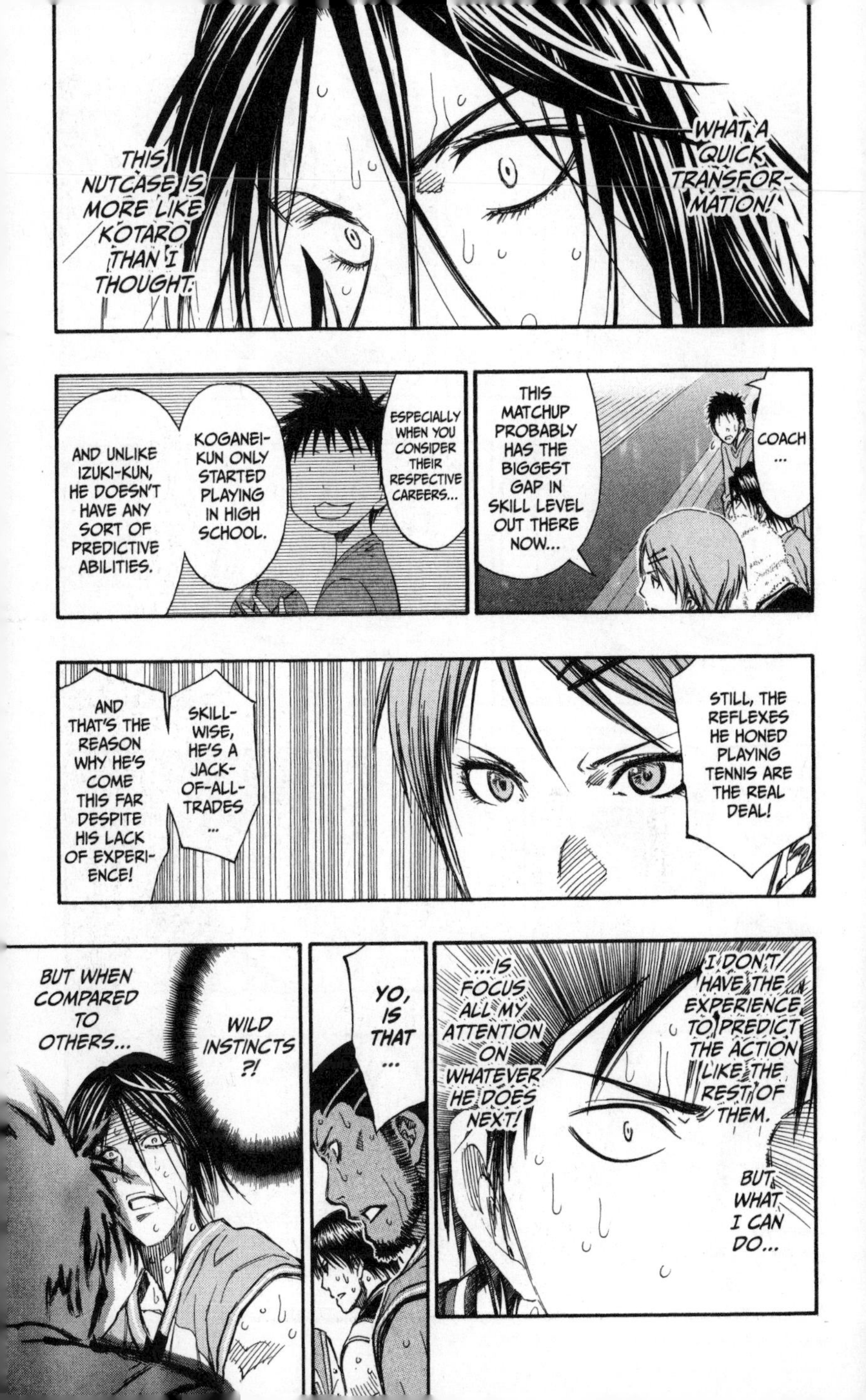
WHAT A QUICK TRANSFORMATION!
THIS NUTCASE IS MORE LIKE KOTARO THAN I THOUGHT.
COACH...
THIS MATCHUP PROBABLY HAS THE BIGGEST GAP IN SKILL LEVEL OUT THERE NOW...
ESPECIALLY WHEN YOU CONSIDER THEIR RESPECTIVE CAREERS...
KOGANEI-KUN ONLY STARTED PLAYING IN HIGH SCHOOL.
AND UNLIKE IZUKI-KUN, HE DOESN'T HAVE ANY SORT OF PREDICTIVE ABILITIES.
STILL, THE REFLEXES HE HONED PLAYING TENNIS ARE THE REAL DEAL!
SKILL-WISE, HE'S A JACK-OF-ALL-TRADES...
AND THAT'S THE REASON WHY HE'S COME THIS FAR DESPITE HIS LACK OF EXPERIENCE!
I DON'T HAVE THE EXPERIENCE TO PREDICT THE ACTION LIKE THE REST OF THEM.
BUT WHAT I CAN DO...
...IS FOCUS ALL MY ATTENTION ON WHATEVER HE DOES NEXT!
YO, IS THAT...
WILD INSTINCTS?!
BUT WHEN COMPARED TO OTHERS...

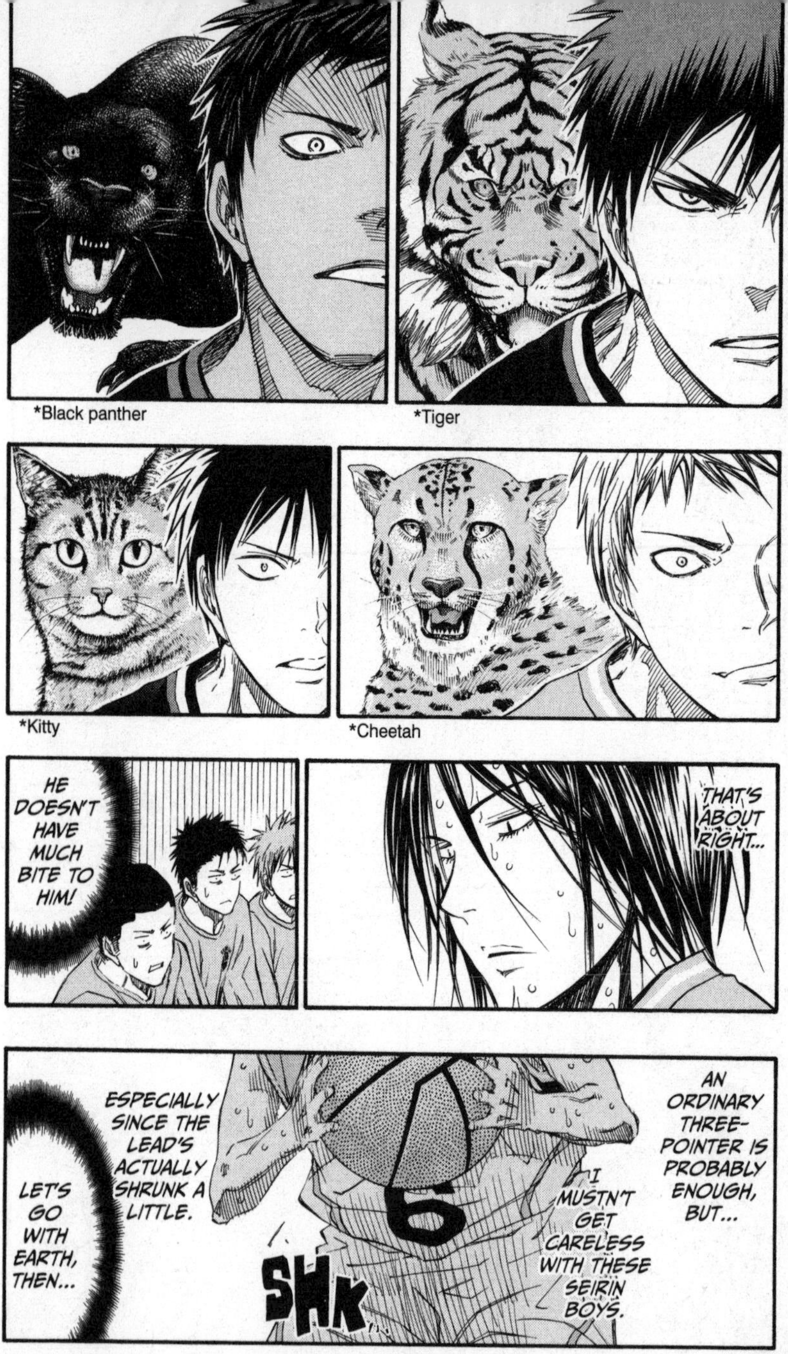
*Tiger
*Black panther
*Cheetah
*Kitty
THAT'S ABOUT RIGHT...
HE DOESN'T HAVE MUCH BITE TO HIM!
AN ORDINARY THREE-POINTER IS PROBABLY ENOUGH, BUT...
I MUSTN'T GET CARELESS WITH THESE SEIRIN BOYS.
ESPECIALLY SINCE THE LEAD'S ACTUALLY SHRUNK A LITTLE.
SHK
LET'S GO WITH EARTH, THEN...

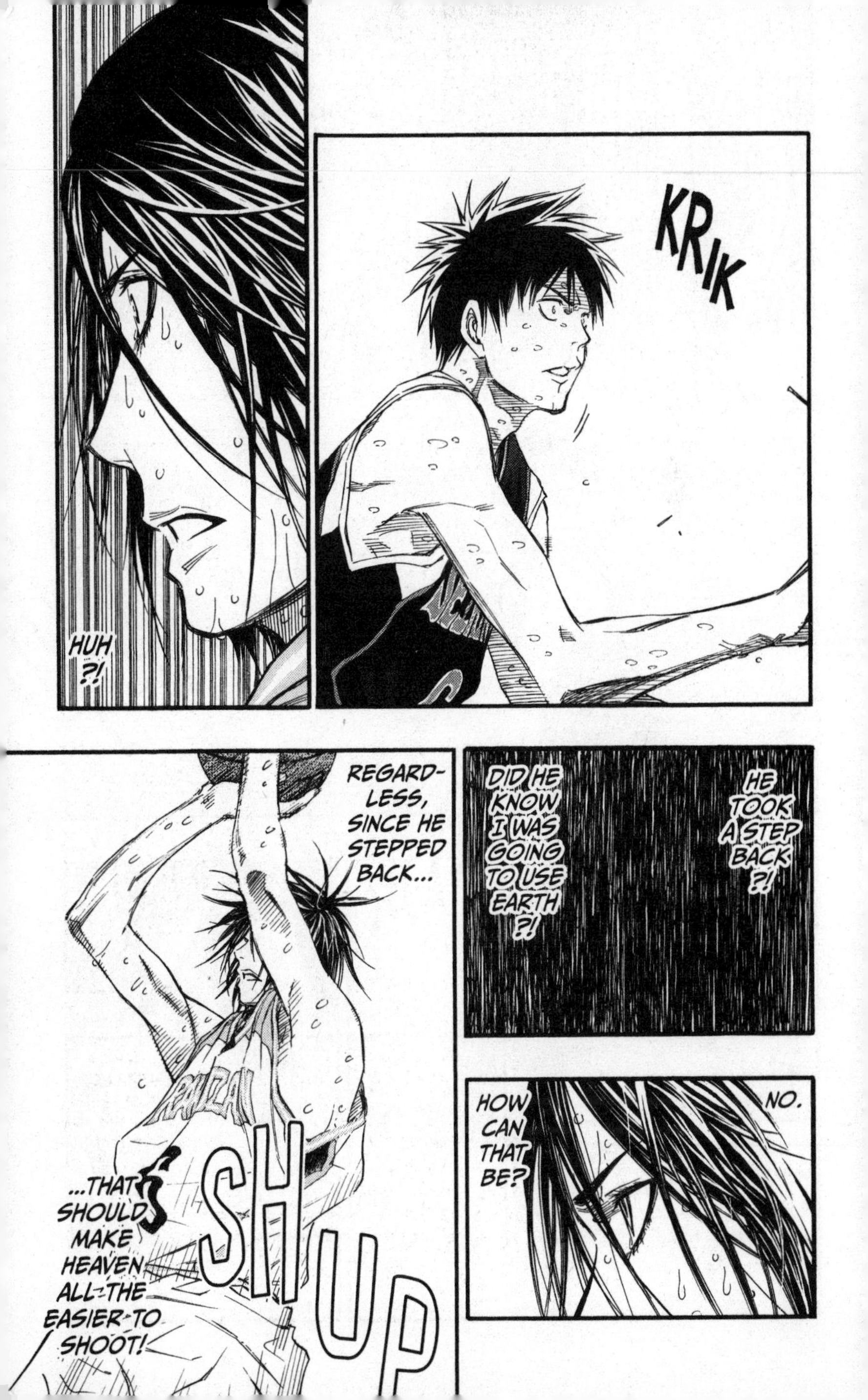
KRIK
HUH?!
HE TOOK A STEP BACK?!
DID HE KNOW I WAS GOING TO USE EARTH?!
NO.
HOW CAN THAT BE?
REGARDLESS, SINCE HE STEPPED BACK...
SHUP
...THAT SHOULD MAKE HEAVEN ALL THE EASIER TO SHOOT!

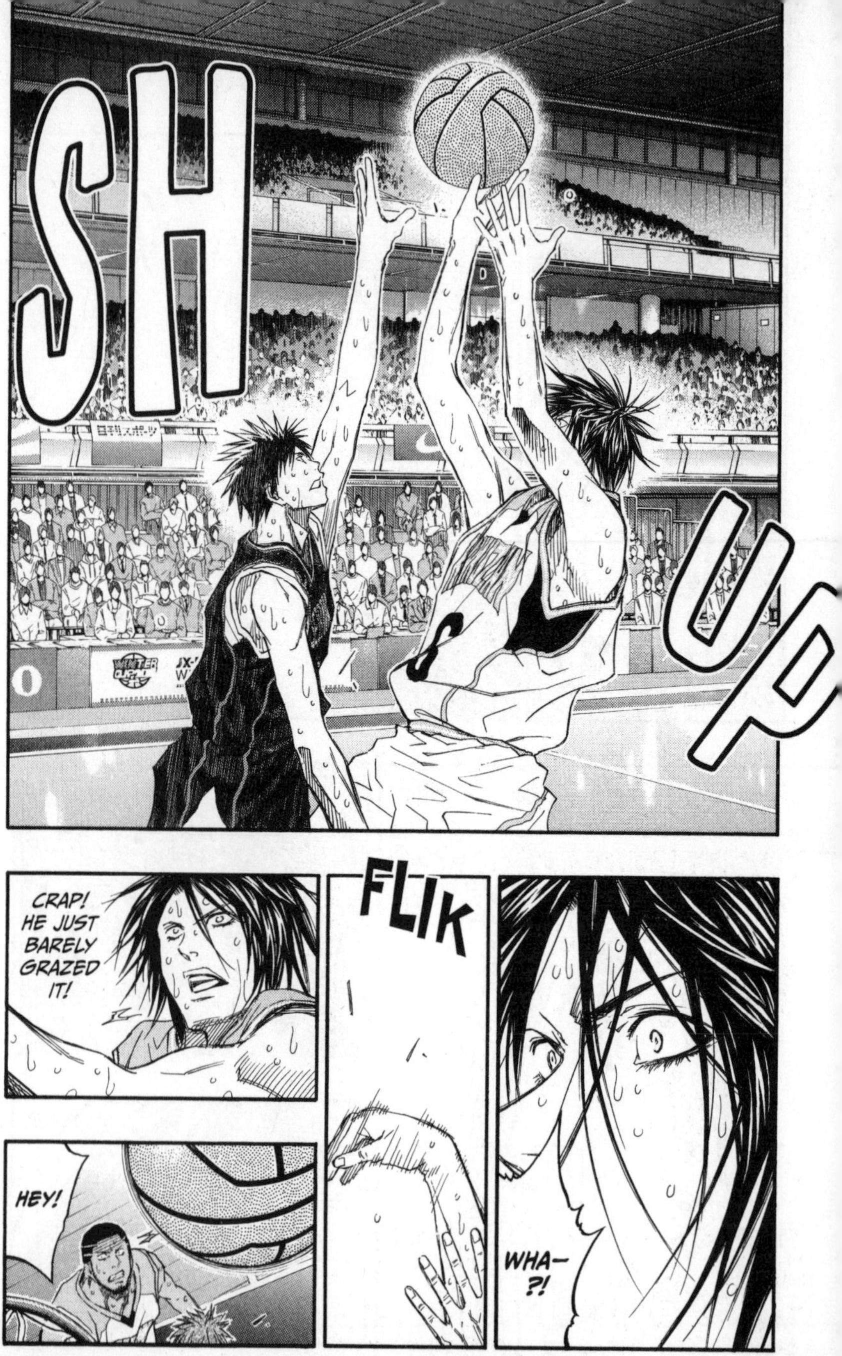
SH UP
WHA—?!
FLIK
CRAP! HE JUST BARELY GRAZED IT!
HEY!

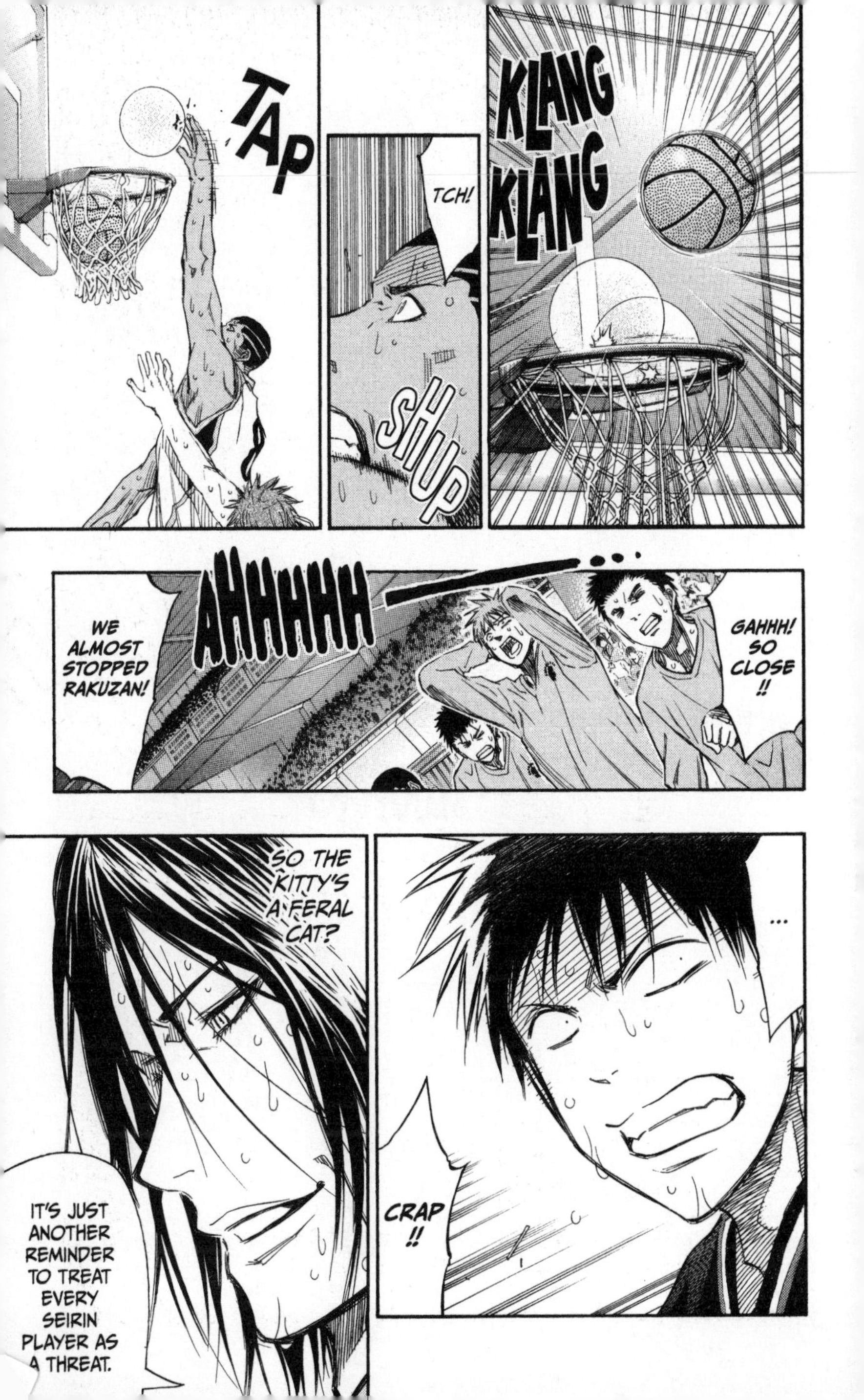

KLANG
KLANG
TCH!
SHUP
TAP
AHHHHH—...
GAHHH! SO CLOSE!!
WE ALMOST STOPPED RAKUZAN!
...
CRAP!!
SO THE KITTY'S A FERAL CAT?
IT'S JUST ANOTHER REMINDER TO TREAT EVERY SEIRIN PLAYER AS A THREAT.

KUROKO'S BASKETBALL BLOOPERS

TAKE 3

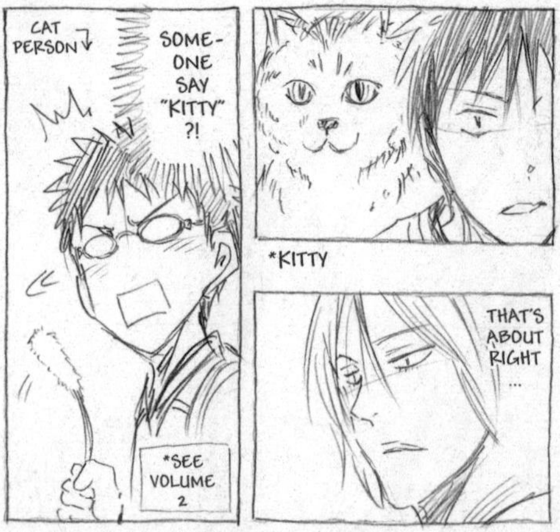
*KITTY
THAT'S ABOUT RIGHT ...
CAT PERSON
SOME-ONE SAY "KITTY" ?!
*SEE VOLUME 2

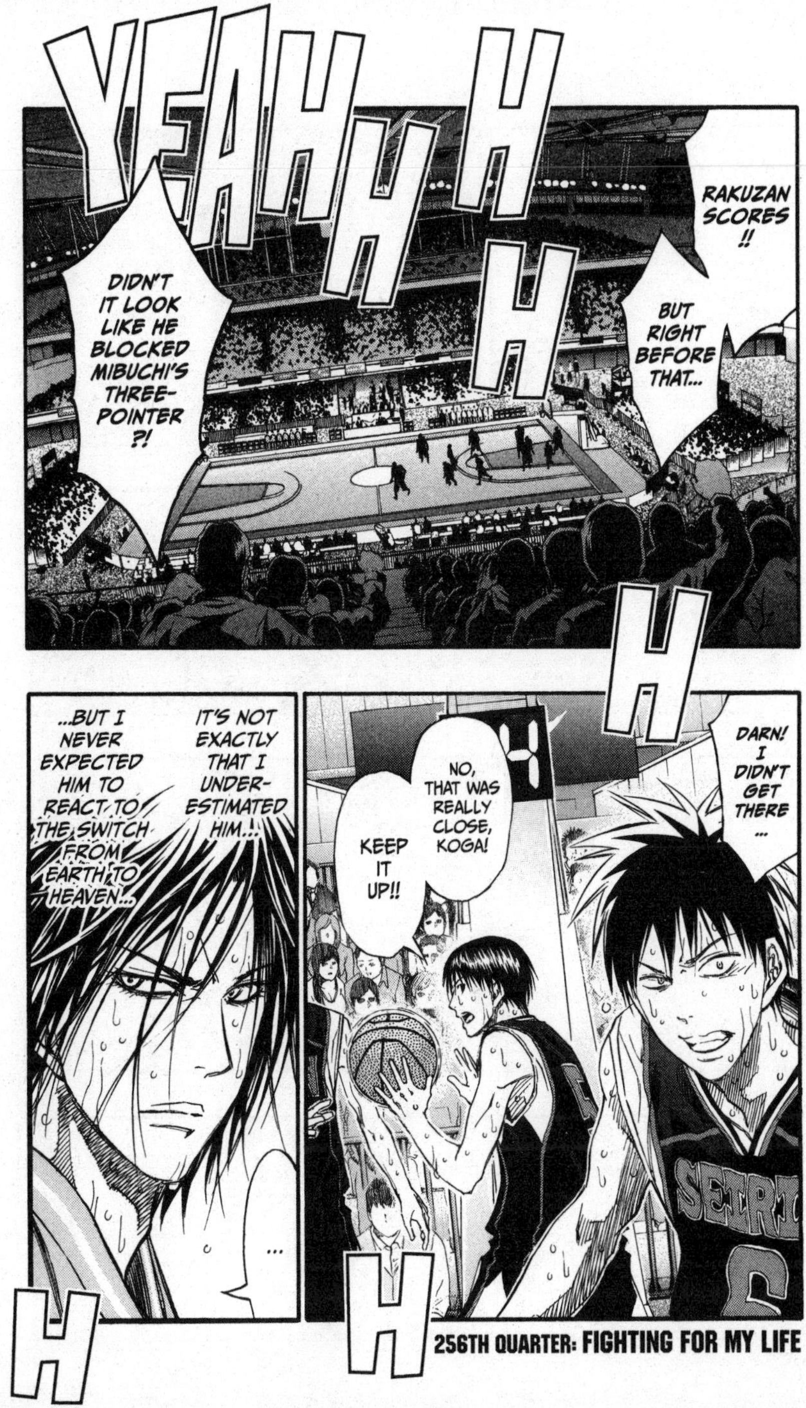
YEAHHHHHHH
RAKUZAN SCORES!!
BUT RIGHT BEFORE THAT...
DIDN'T IT LOOK LIKE HE BLOCKED MIBUCHI'S THREE-POINTER?!
DARN! I DIDN'T GET THERE ...
NO, THAT WAS REALLY CLOSE, KOGA!
KEEP IT UP!!
IT'S NOT EXACTLY THAT I UNDER-ESTIMATED HIM...
...BUT I NEVER EXPECTED HIM TO REACT TO THE SWITCH FROM EARTH TO HEAVEN...
...

256TH QUARTER: FIGHTING FOR MY LIFE

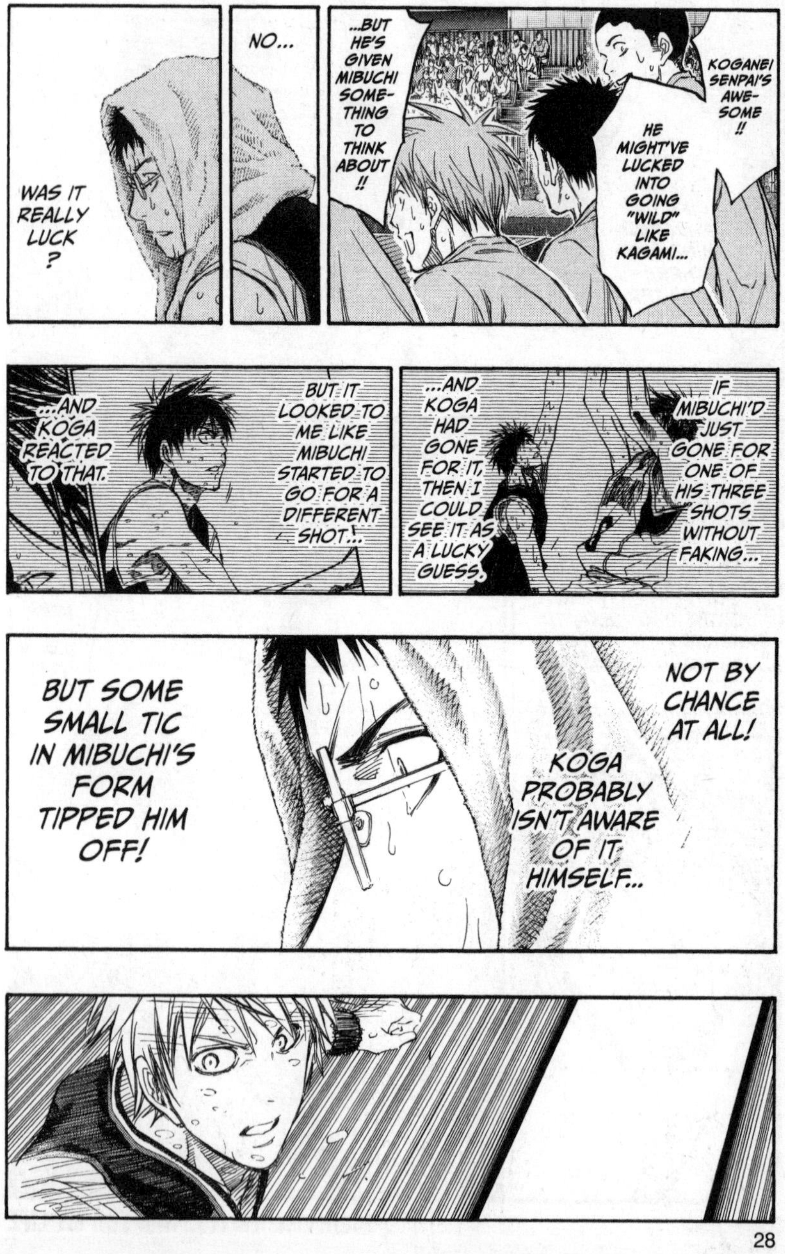
KOGANEI SENPAI'S AWESOME!!
HE MIGHT'VE LUCKED INTO GOING "WILD" LIKE KAGAMI...
...BUT HE'S GIVEN MIBUCHI SOMETHING TO THINK ABOUT!!
NO...
WAS IT REALLY LUCK?
IF MIBUCHI'D JUST GONE FOR ONE OF HIS THREE SHOTS WITHOUT FAKING...
...AND KOGA HAD GONE FOR IT, THEN I COULD SEE IT AS A LUCKY GUESS.
BUT IT LOOKED TO ME LIKE MIBUCHI STARTED TO GO FOR A DIFFERENT SHOT...
...AND KOGA REACTED TO THAT.
NOT BY CHANCE AT ALL!
KOGA PROBABLY ISN'T AWARE OF IT HIMSELF...
BUT SOME SMALL TIC IN MIBUCHI'S FORM TIPPED HIM OFF!

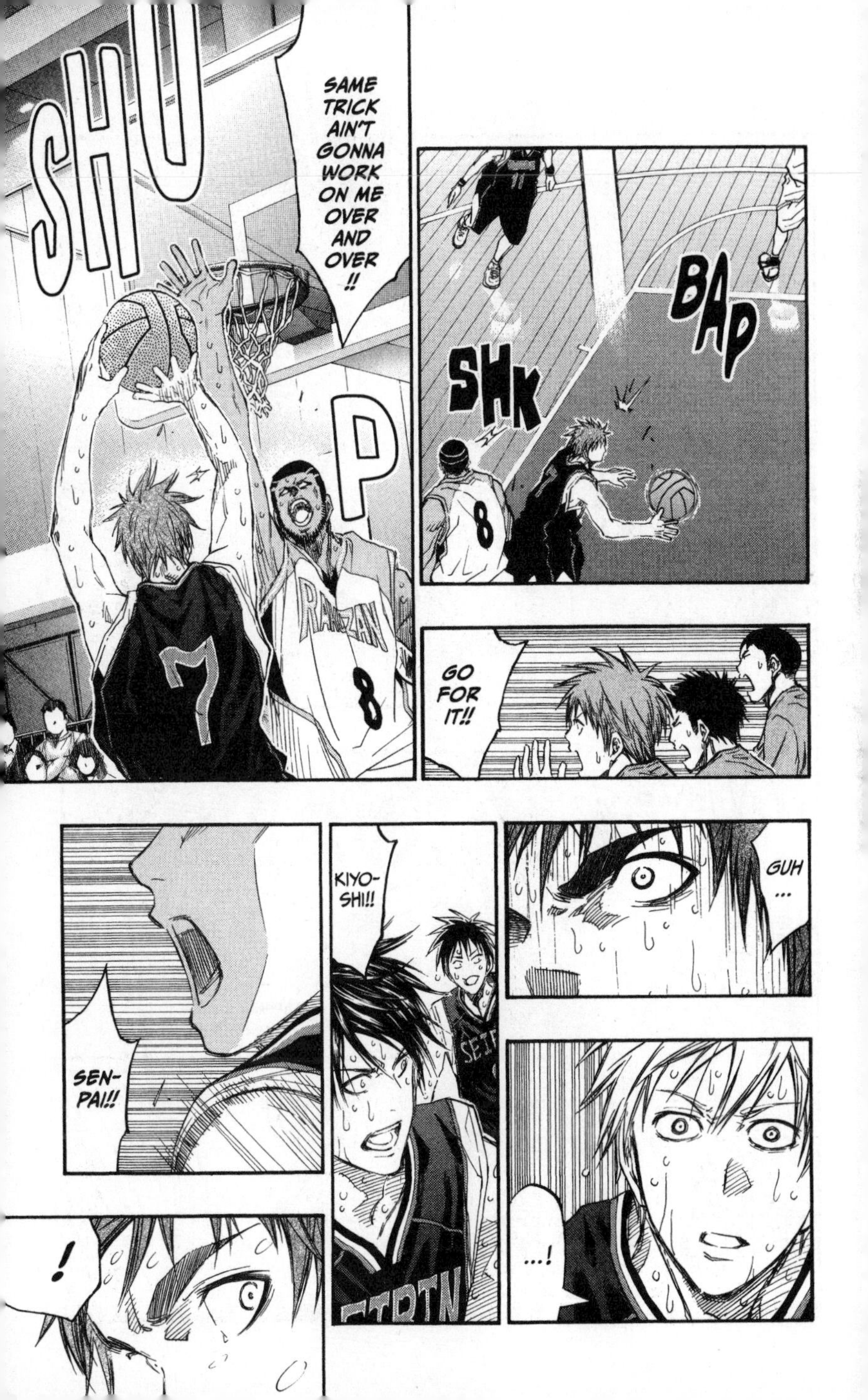
SAME TRICK AIN'T GONNA WORK ON ME OVER AND OVER!!
SHU
P
BAP
SHK
GO FOR IT!!
GUH...
...!
KIYO-SHI!!
SEN-PAI!!
!

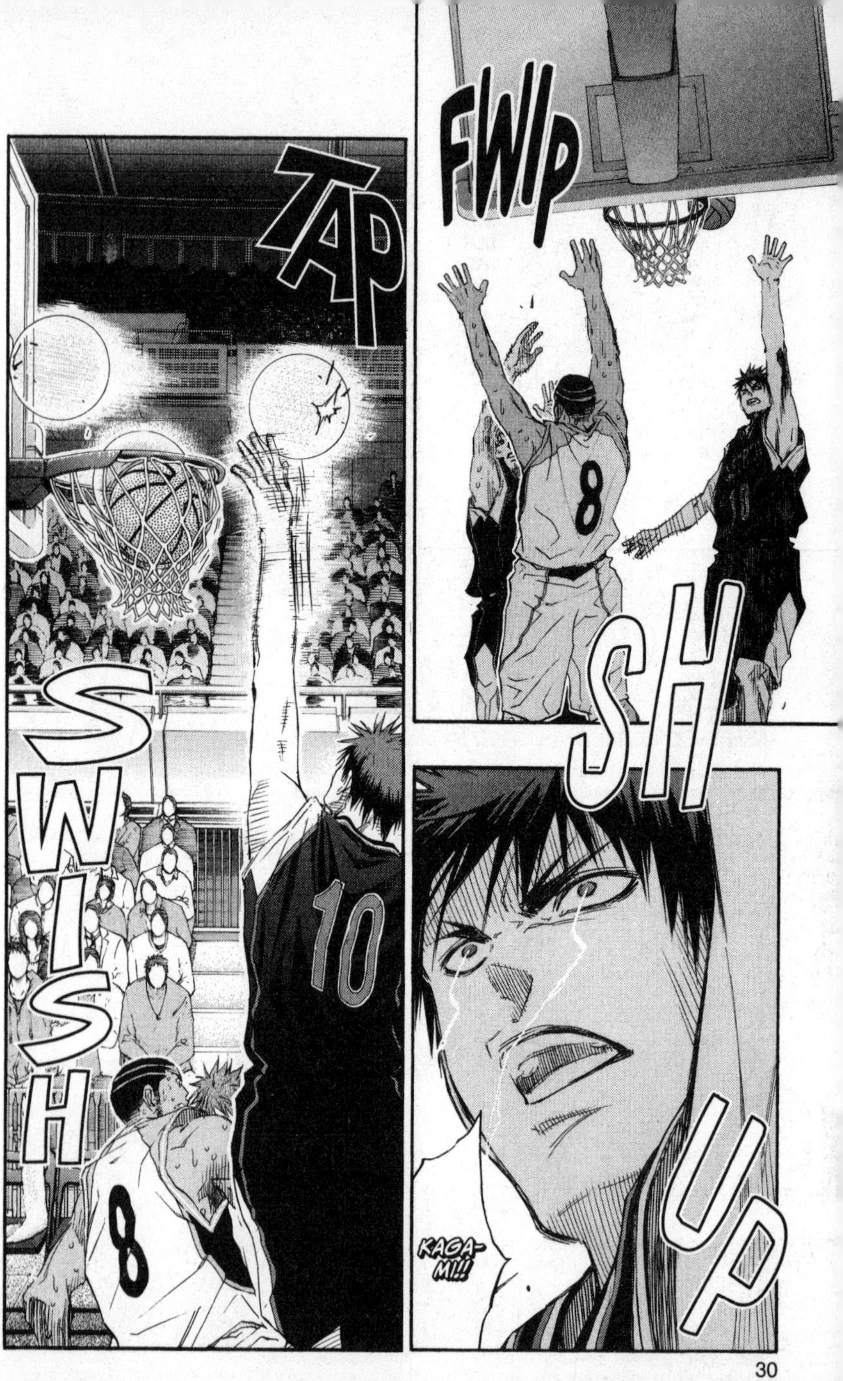
FWIP
SHUP
KAGA-MI!!
TAP
SWISH

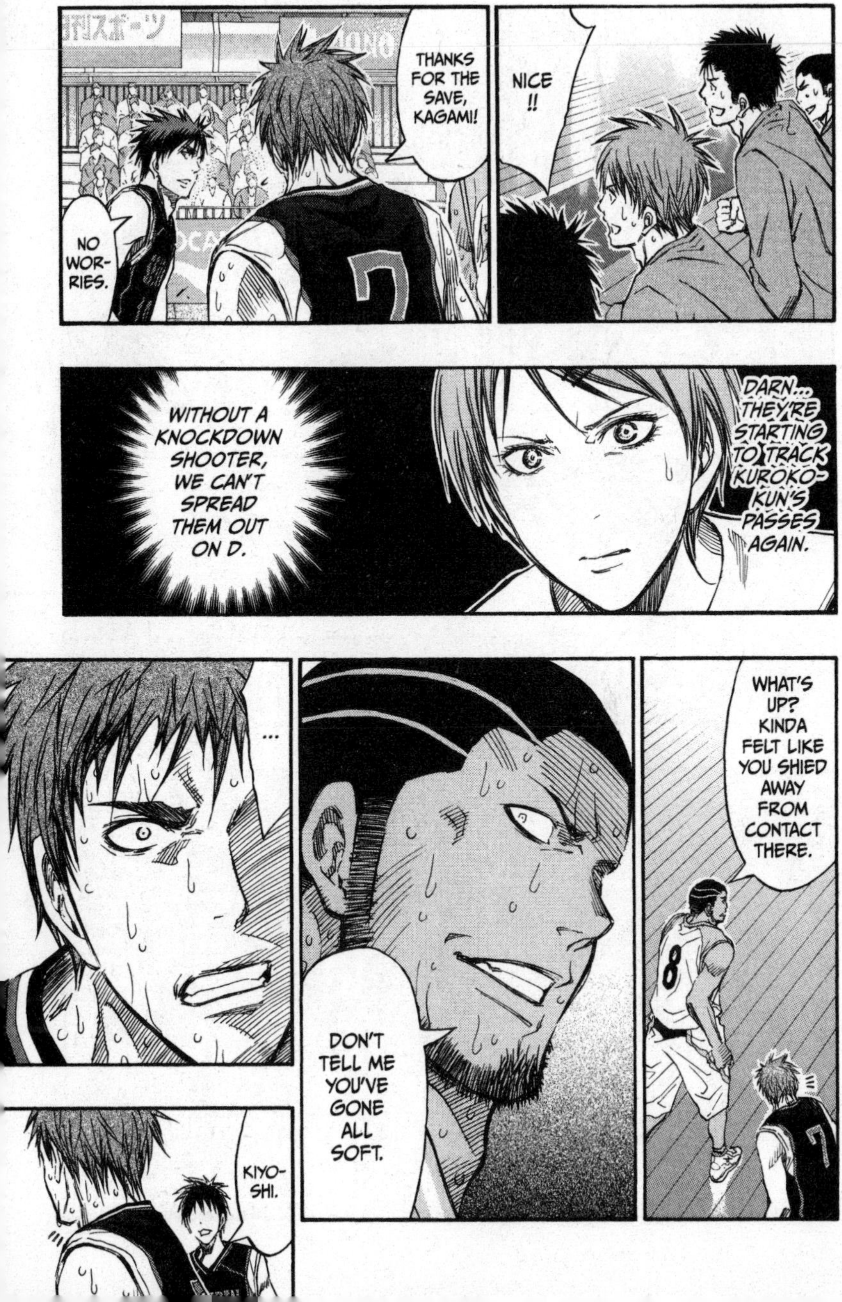
NICE !!
THANKS FOR THE SAVE, KAGAMI!
NO WORRIES.
DARN... THEY'RE STARTING TO TRACK KUROKO-KUN'S PASSES AGAIN.
WITHOUT A KNOCKDOWN SHOOTER, WE CAN'T SPREAD THEM OUT ON D.
WHAT'S UP? KINDA FELT LIKE YOU SHIED AWAY FROM CONTACT THERE.
DON'T TELL ME YOU'VE GONE ALL SOFT.
...
KIYOSHI.

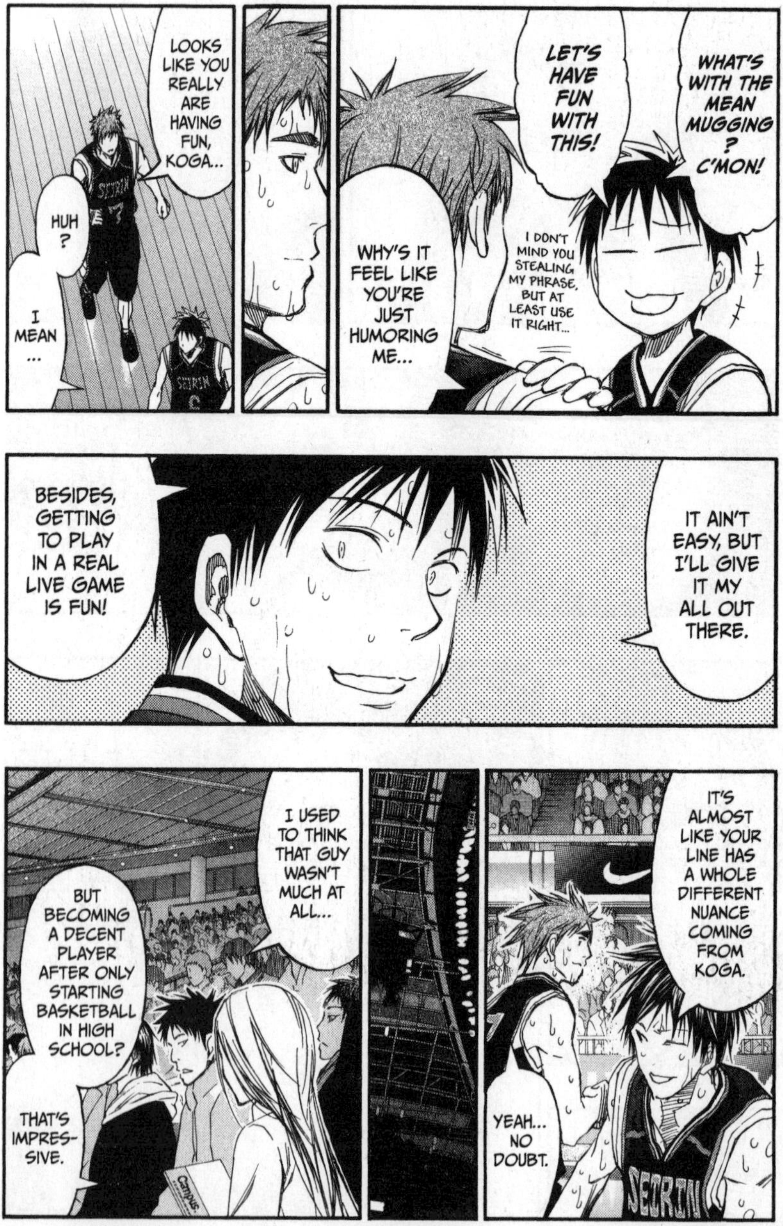
WHAT'S WITH THE MEAN MUGGING? C'MON!
LET'S HAVE FUN WITH THIS!
I DON'T MIND YOU STEALING MY PHRASE, BUT AT LEAST USE IT RIGHT...
WHY'S IT FEEL LIKE YOU'RE JUST HUMORING ME...
LOOKS LIKE YOU REALLY ARE HAVING FUN, KOGA...
HUH?
I MEAN...
IT AIN'T EASY, BUT I'LL GIVE IT MY ALL OUT THERE.
BESIDES, GETTING TO PLAY IN A REAL LIVE GAME IS FUN!
IT'S ALMOST LIKE YOUR LINE HAS A WHOLE DIFFERENT NUANCE COMING FROM KOGA.
YEAH... NO DOUBT.
I USED TO THINK THAT GUY WASN'T MUCH AT ALL...
BUT BECOMING A DECENT PLAYER AFTER ONLY STARTING BASKETBALL IN HIGH SCHOOL?
THAT'S IMPRESSIVE.

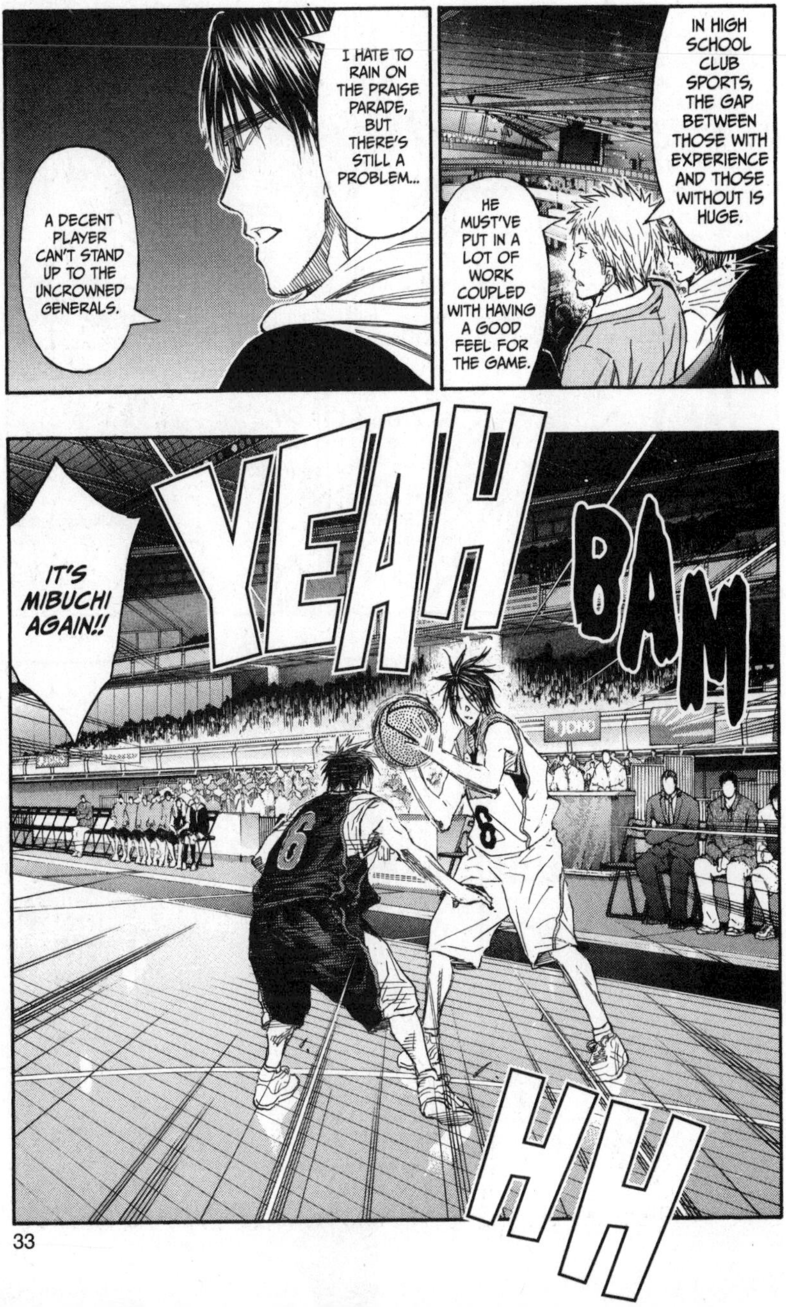
IN HIGH SCHOOL CLUB SPORTS, THE GAP BETWEEN THOSE WITH EXPERIENCE AND THOSE WITHOUT IS HUGE.
HE MUST'VE PUT IN A LOT OF WORK COUPLED WITH HAVING A GOOD FEEL FOR THE GAME.
I HATE TO RAIN ON THE PRAISE PARADE, BUT THERE'S STILL A PROBLEM...
A DECENT PLAYER CAN'T STAND UP TO THE UNCROWNED GENERALS.
BAM
YEAH
HH
IT'S MIBUCHI AGAIN!!

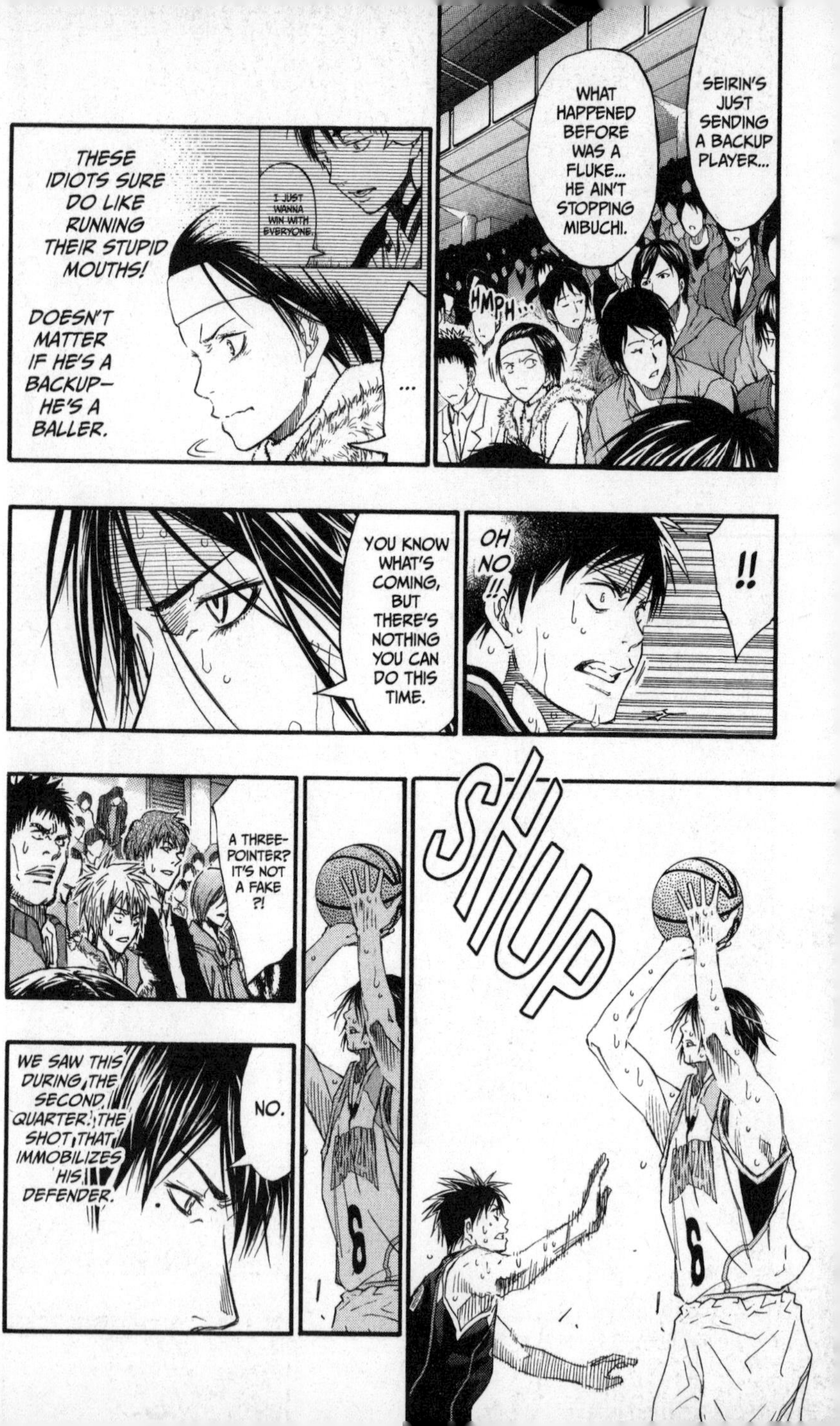
SEIRIN'S JUST SENDING A BACKUP PLAYER...
WHAT HAPPENED BEFORE WAS A FLUKE... HE AIN'T STOPPING MIBUCHI.
HMPH...
I JUST WANNA WIN WITH EVERYONE.
THESE IDIOTS SURE DO LIKE RUNNING THEIR STUPID MOUTHS!
...
DOESN'T MATTER IF HE'S A BACKUP— HE'S A BALLER.
!!
OH NO!!
YOU KNOW WHAT'S COMING, BUT THERE'S NOTHING YOU CAN DO THIS TIME.
SHUP
A THREE-POINTER? IT'S NOT A FAKE?!
NO.
WE SAW THIS DURING THE SECOND QUARTER. THE SHOT THAT IMMOBILIZES HIS DEFENDER.

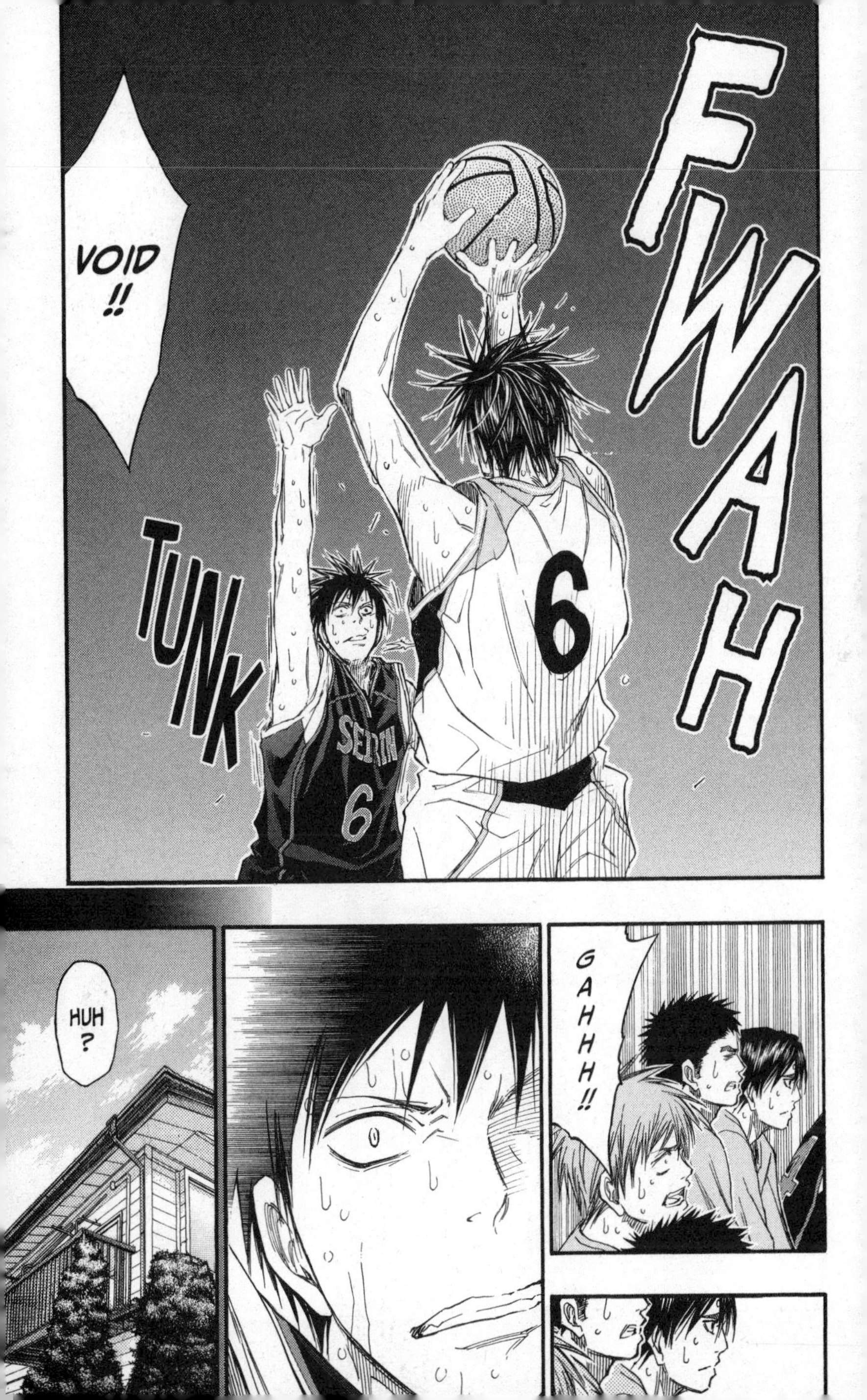
FWAH
VOID!!
TUNK
SEIRIN
6
6
GAHHHH!!
HUH?

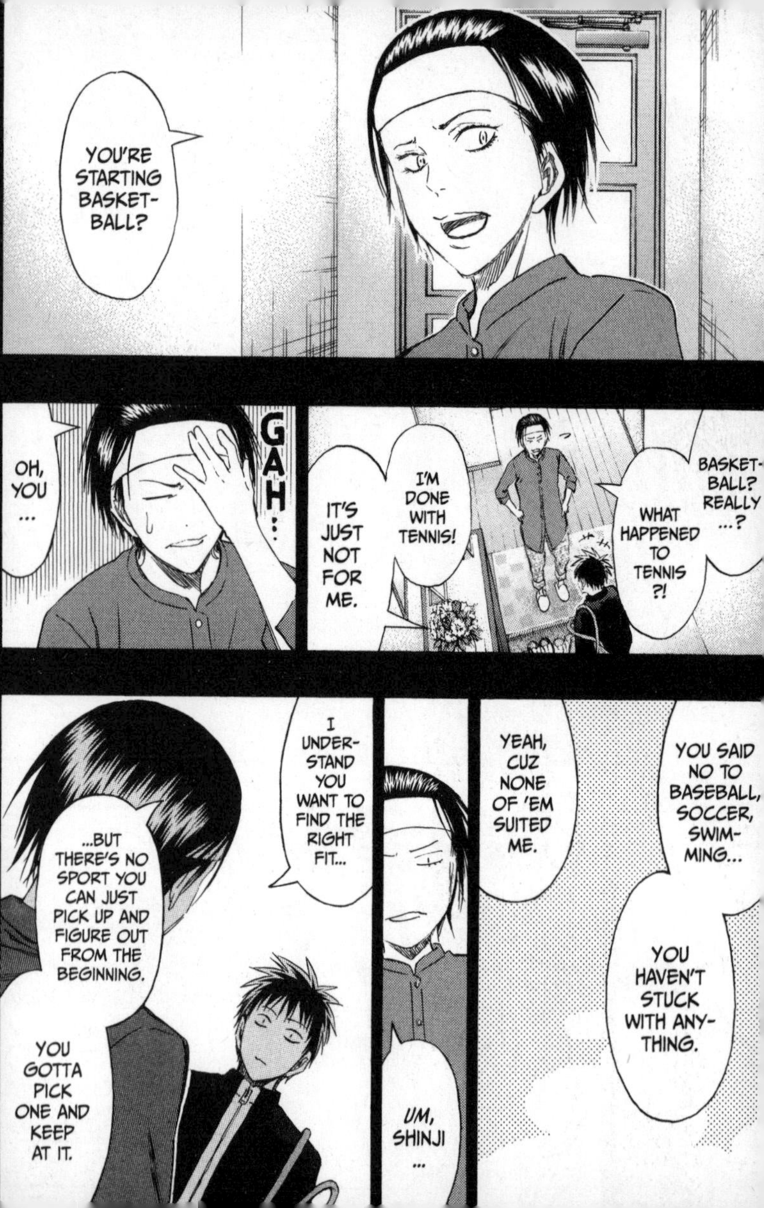
YOU'RE STARTING BASKET-BALL?
BASKET-BALL? REALLY ...?
WHAT HAPPENED TO TENNIS ?!
I'M DONE WITH TENNIS!
IT'S JUST NOT FOR ME.
GAH..
OH, YOU ...
YOU SAID NO TO BASEBALL, SOCCER, SWIM-MING...
YEAH, CUZ NONE OF 'EM SUITED ME.
YOU HAVEN'T STUCK WITH ANY-THING.
UM, SHINJI ...
I UNDER-STAND YOU WANT TO FIND THE RIGHT FIT...
...BUT THERE'S NO SPORT YOU CAN JUST PICK UP AND FIGURE OUT FROM THE BEGINNING.
YOU GOTTA PICK ONE AND KEEP AT IT.

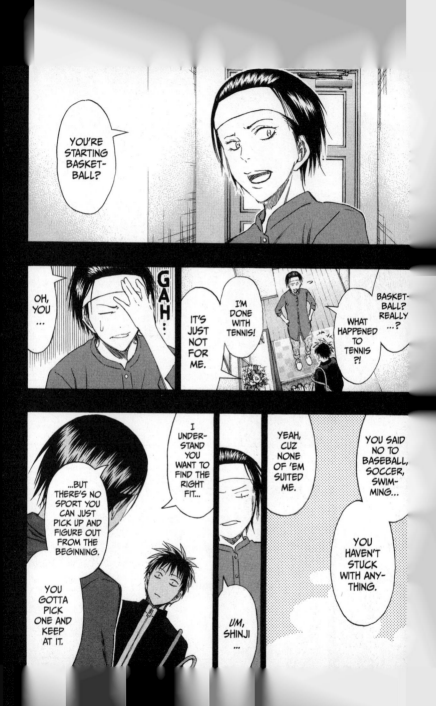

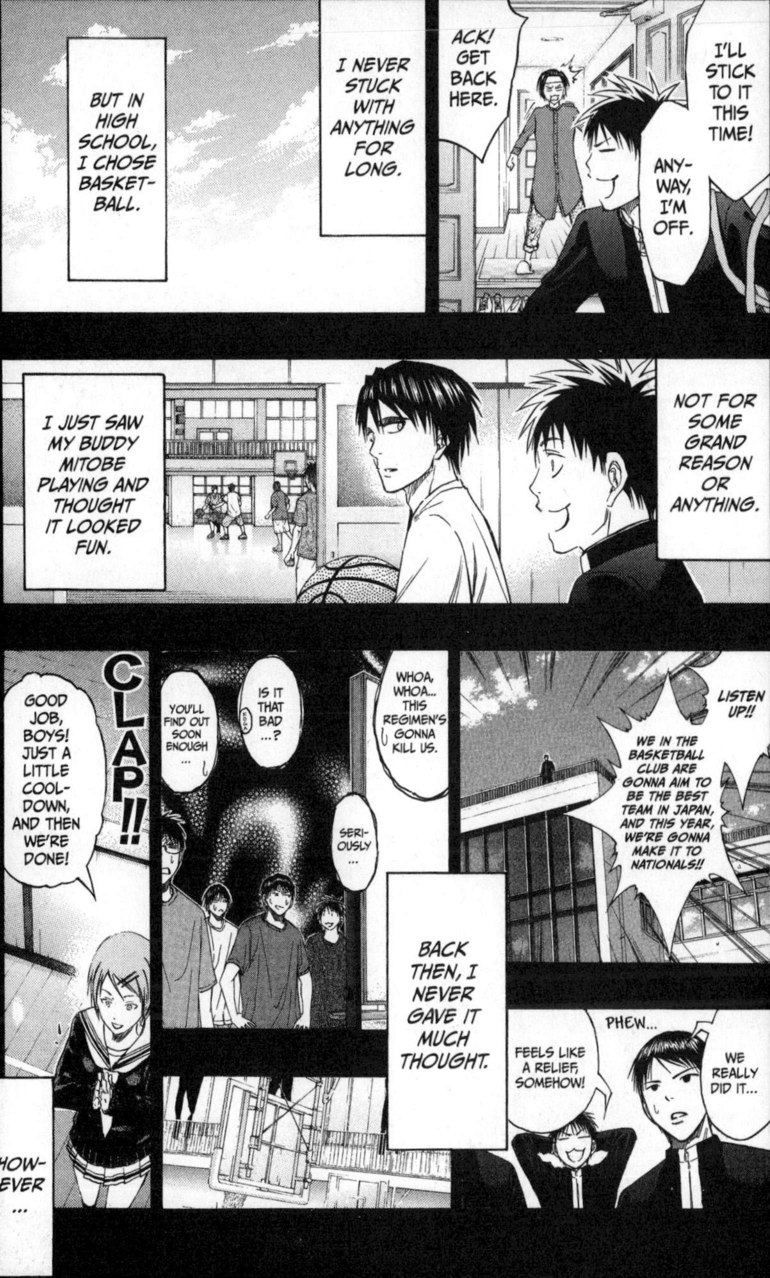
I'LL STICK TO IT THIS TIME!
ACK! GET BACK HERE.
ANY-WAY, I'M OFF.
I NEVER STUCK WITH ANYTHING FOR LONG.
BUT IN HIGH SCHOOL, I CHOSE BASKET-BALL.
NOT FOR SOME GRAND REASON OR ANYTHING.
I JUST SAW MY BUDDY MITOBE PLAYING AND THOUGHT IT LOOKED FUN.
LISTEN UP!!
WE IN THE BASKETBALL CLUB ARE GONNA AIM TO BE THE BEST TEAM IN JAPAN, AND THIS YEAR, WE'RE GONNA MAKE IT TO NATIONALS!!
WHOA, WHOA... THIS REGIMEN'S GONNA KILL US.
IS IT THAT BAD ...?
YOU'LL FIND OUT SOON ENOUGH ...
SERI-OUSLY ...
BACK THEN, I NEVER GAVE IT MUCH THOUGHT.
WE REALLY DID IT...
PHEW...
FEELS LIKE A RELIEF, SOMEHOW!
CLAP!!
GOOD JOB, BOYS! JUST A LITTLE COOL-DOWN, AND THEN WE'RE DONE!
HOW-EVER ...

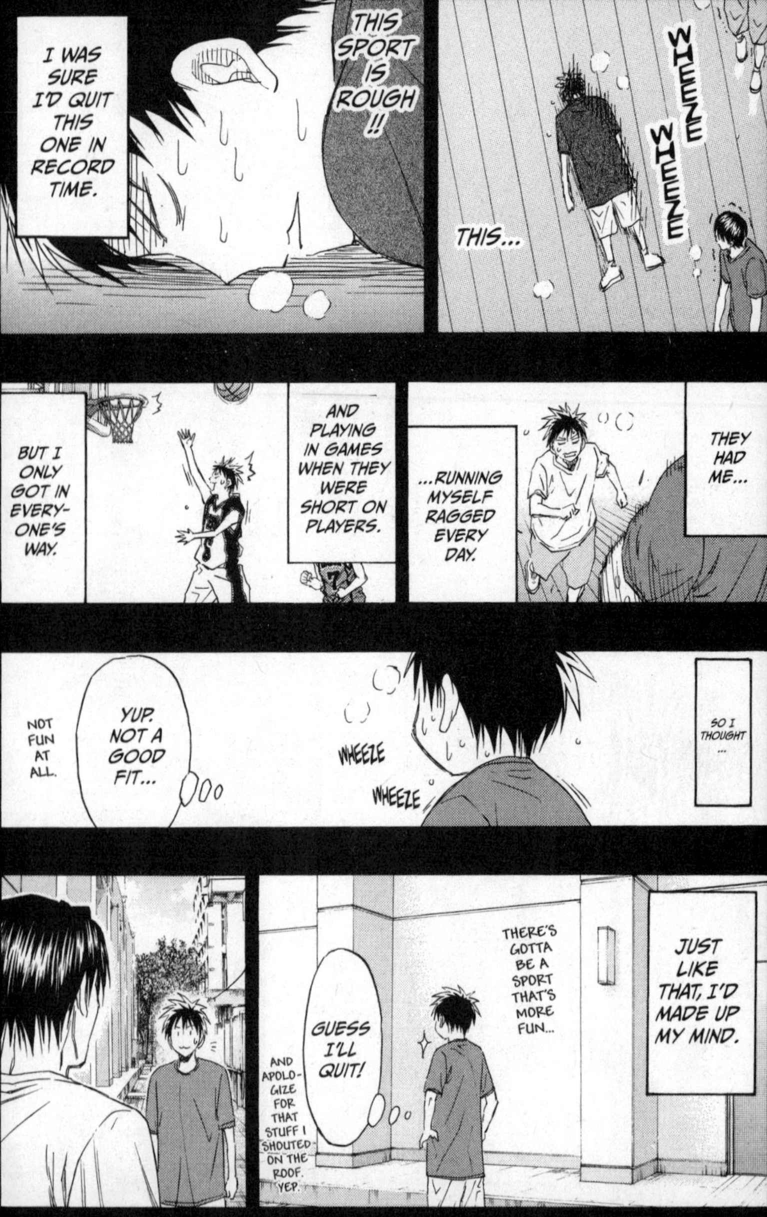
WHEEZE WHEEZE
THIS...
THIS SPORT IS ROUGH!!
I WAS SURE I'D QUIT THIS ONE IN RECORD TIME.
THEY HAD ME...
...RUNNING MYSELF RAGGED EVERY DAY.
AND PLAYING IN GAMES WHEN THEY WERE SHORT ON PLAYERS.
BUT I ONLY GOT IN EVERYONE'S WAY.
SO I THOUGHT...
WHEEZE
WHEEZE
YUP. NOT A GOOD FIT...
NOT FUN AT ALL.
JUST LIKE THAT, I'D MADE UP MY MIND.
THERE'S GOTTA BE A SPORT THAT'S MORE FUN...
GUESS I'LL QUIT!
AND APOLOGIZE FOR THAT STUFF I SHOUTED ON THE ROOF. YEP.

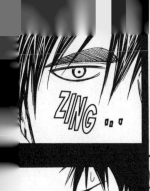

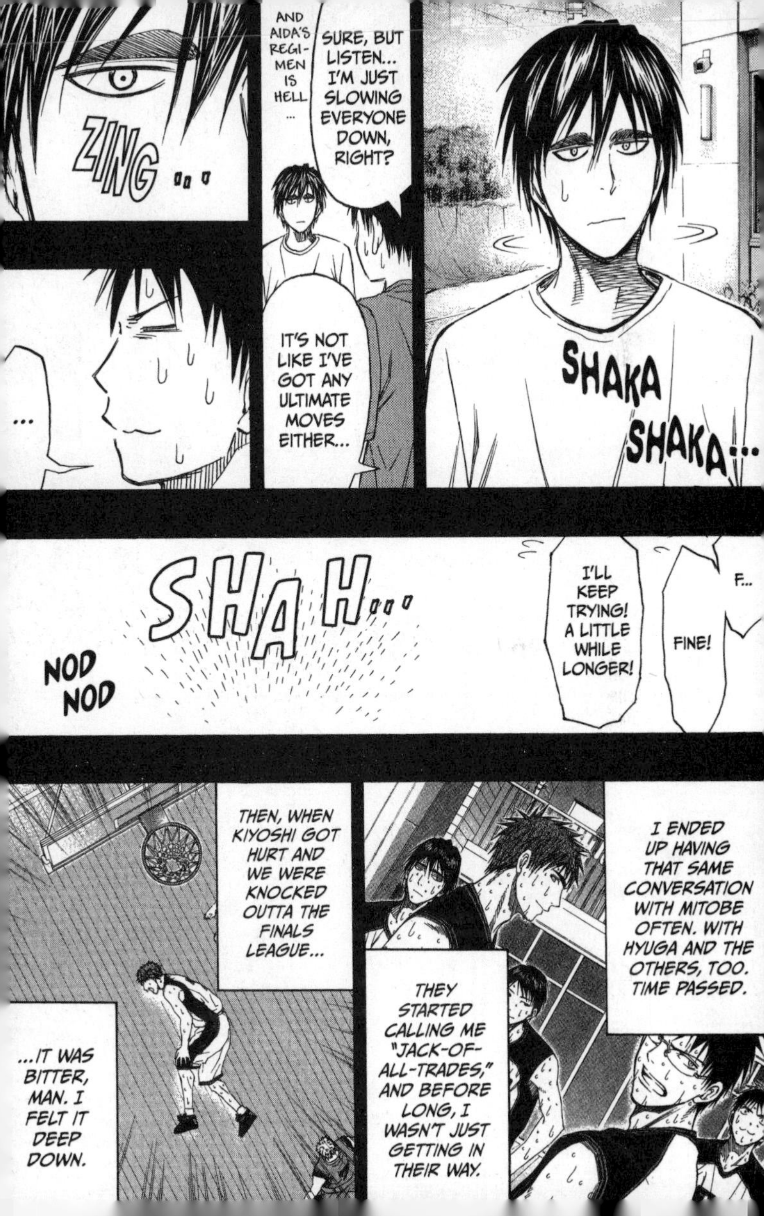
SHAKA SHAKA...
SURE, BUT LISTEN... I'M JUST SLOWING EVERYONE DOWN, RIGHT?
AND AIDA'S REGI-MEN IS HELL...
IT'S NOT LIKE I'VE GOT ANY ULTIMATE MOVES EITHER...
ZING...
...
F... FINE!
I'LL KEEP TRYING! A LITTLE WHILE LONGER!
SHAH...
NOD NOD
I ENDED UP HAVING THAT SAME CONVERSATION WITH MITOBE OFTEN. WITH HYUGA AND THE OTHERS, TOO. TIME PASSED.
THEY STARTED CALLING ME "JACK-OF-ALL-TRADES," AND BEFORE LONG, I WASN'T JUST GETTING IN THEIR WAY.
THEN, WHEN KIYOSHI GOT HURT AND WE WERE KNOCKED OUTTA THE FINALS LEAGUE...
...IT WAS BITTER, MAN. I FELT IT DEEP DOWN.

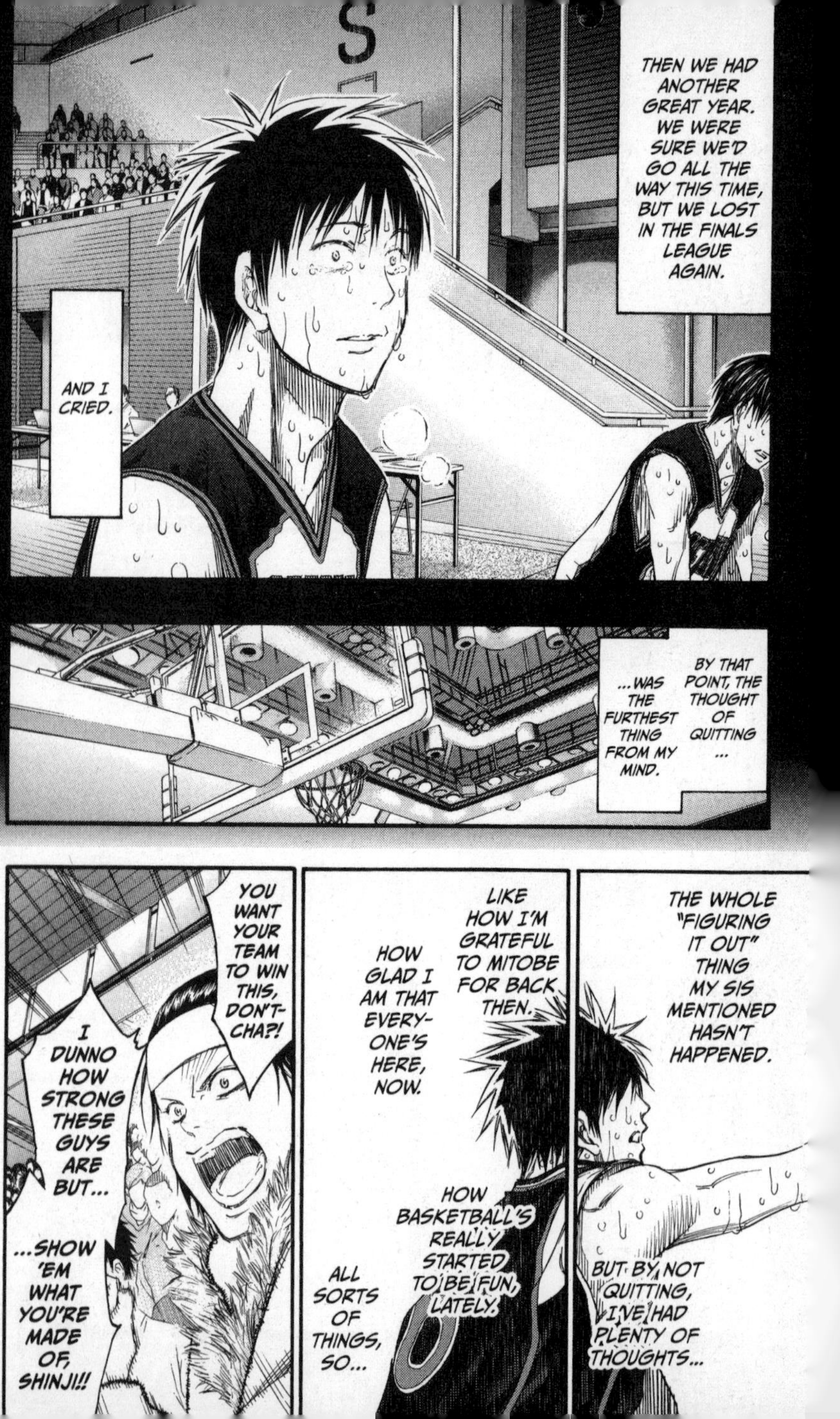
THEN WE HAD ANOTHER GREAT YEAR. WE WERE SURE WE'D GO ALL THE WAY THIS TIME, BUT WE LOST IN THE FINALS LEAGUE AGAIN.
AND I CRIED.
BY THAT POINT, THE THOUGHT OF QUITTING...
...WAS THE FURTHEST THING FROM MY MIND.
THE WHOLE "FIGURING IT OUT" THING MY SIS MENTIONED HASN'T HAPPENED.
BUT BY NOT QUITTING, I'VE HAD PLENTY OF THOUGHTS...
LIKE HOW I'M GRATEFUL TO MITOBE FOR BACK THEN.
HOW GLAD I AM THAT EVERY-ONE'S HERE, NOW.
HOW BASKETBALL'S REALLY STARTED TO BE FUN, LATELY.
ALL SORTS OF THINGS, SO...
YOU WANT YOUR TEAM TO WIN THIS, DON'T-CHA?!
I DUNNO HOW STRONG THESE GUYS ARE BUT...
...SHOW 'EM WHAT YOU'RE MADE OF, SHINJI!!

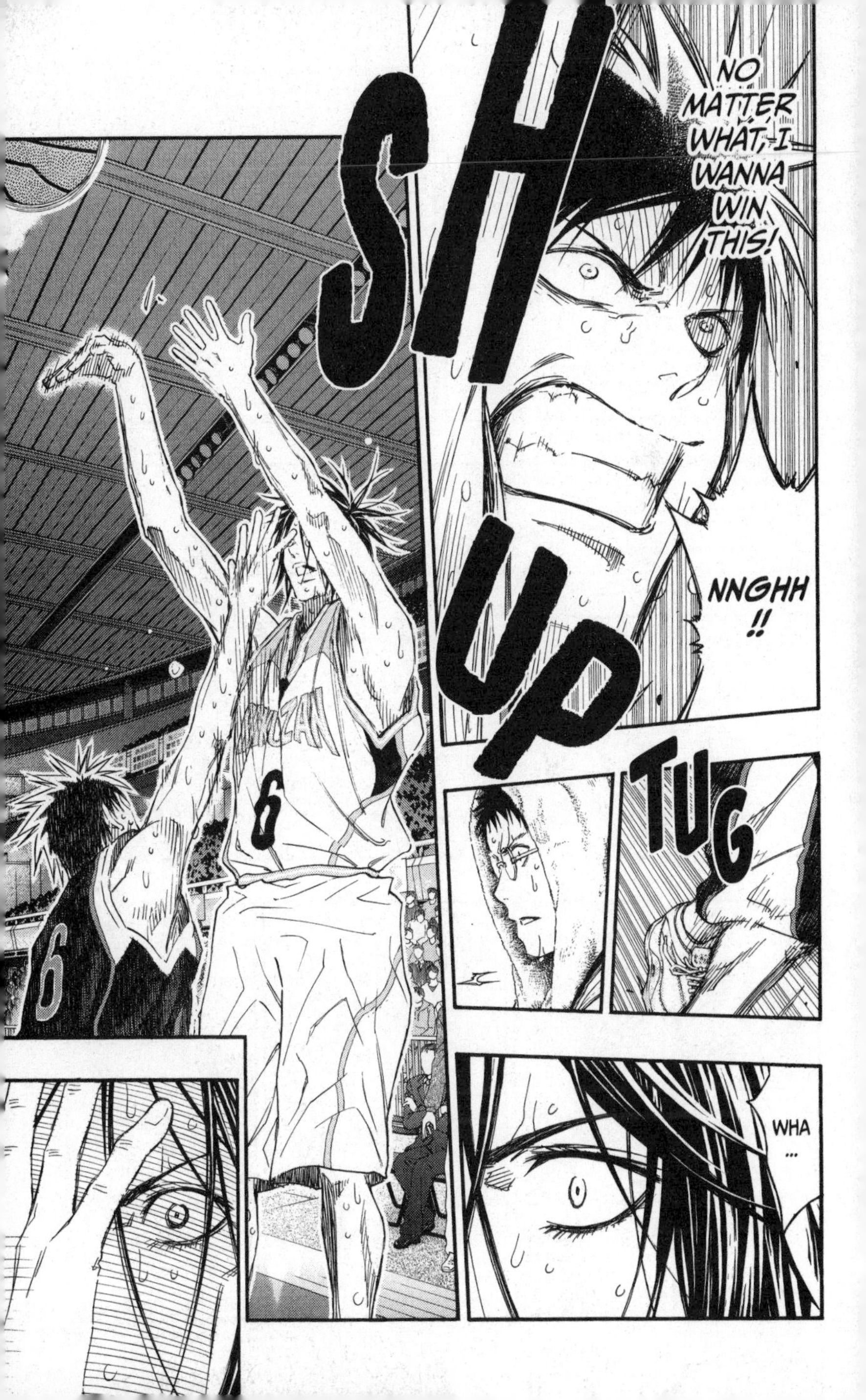
NO MATTER WHAT, I WANNA WIN THIS!
NNGHH !!
SHUP
TUG
WHA ...

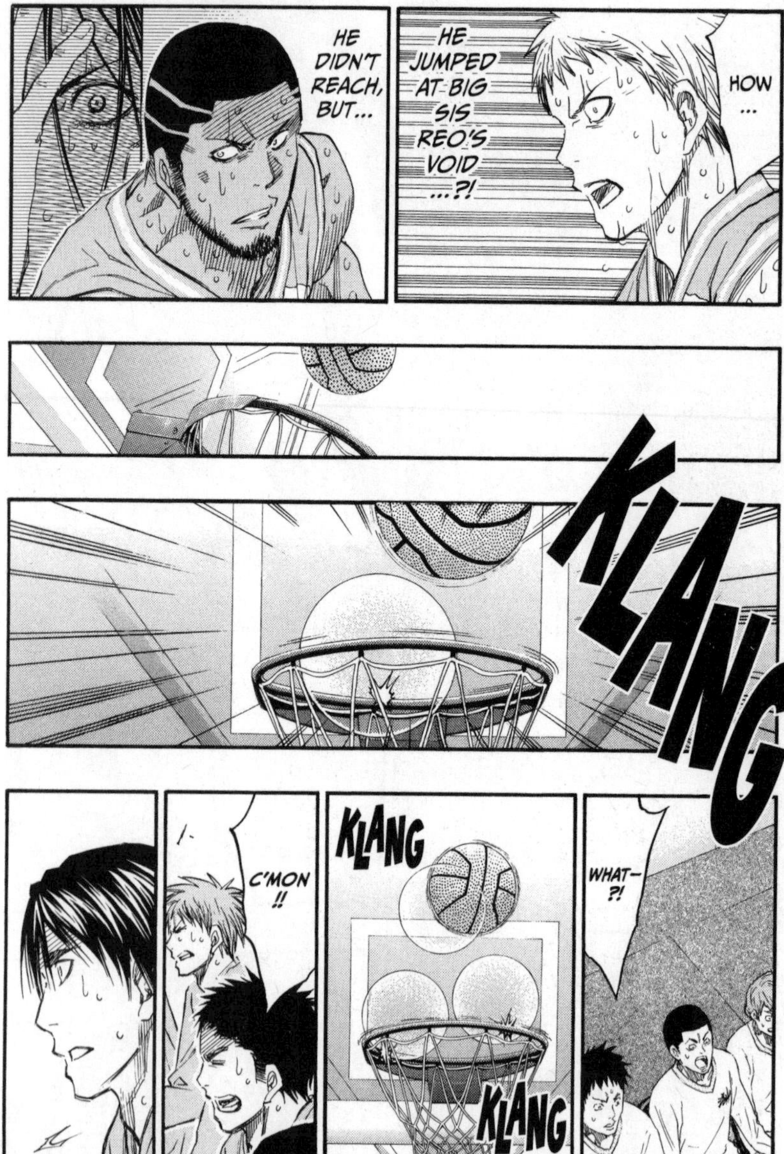
HOW ...
HE JUMPED AT BIG SIS REO'S VOID ...?!
HE DIDN'T REACH, BUT...
KLANG
WHAT— ?!
KLANG
KLANG
C'MON !!

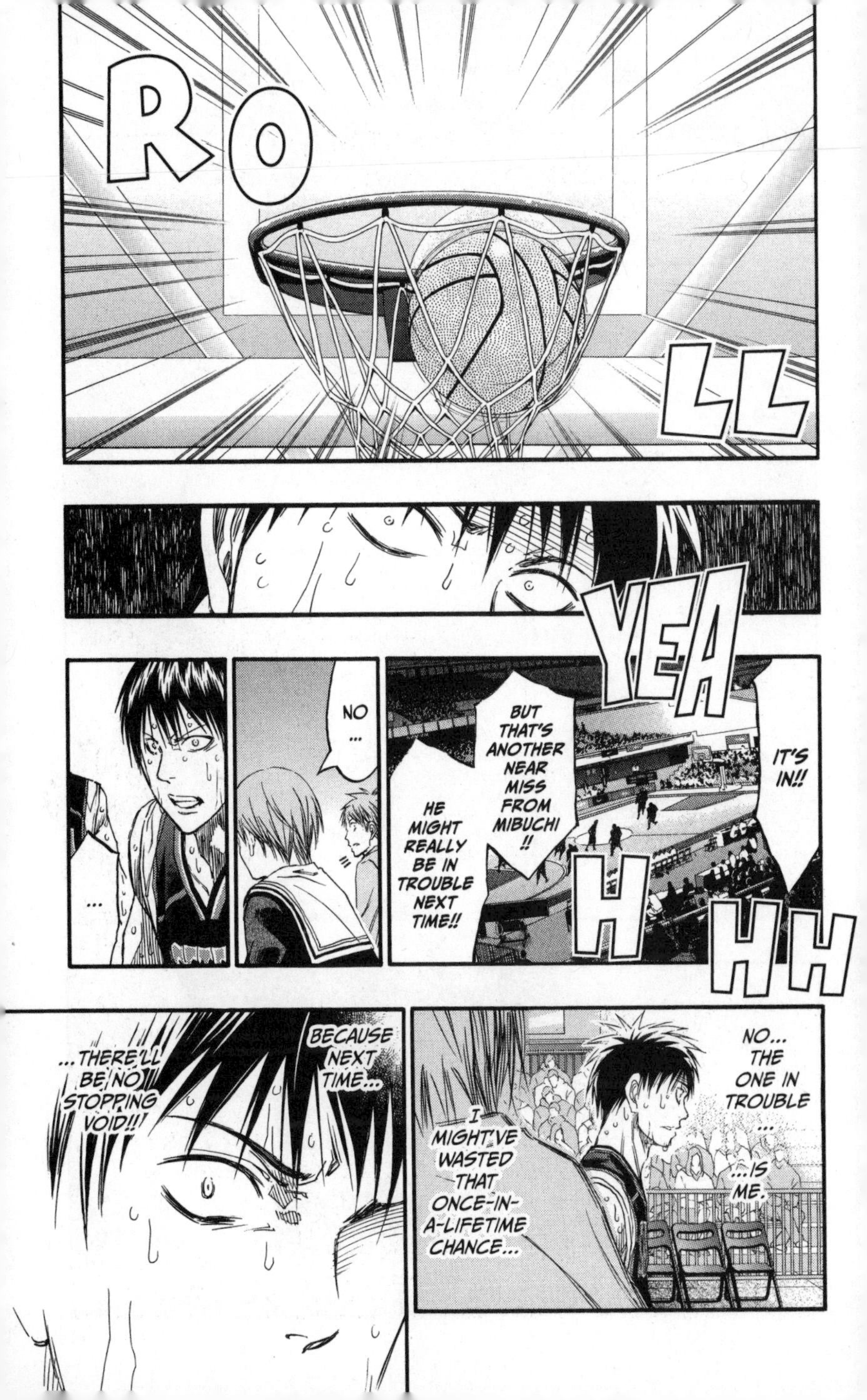
ROLL
YEAH
IT'S IN!!
BUT THAT'S ANOTHER NEAR MISS FROM MIBUCHI!!
HE MIGHT REALLY BE IN TROUBLE NEXT TIME!!
HHH
NO...
...
NO... THE ONE IN TROUBLE...
...IS ME.
I MIGHT'VE WASTED THAT ONCE-IN-A-LIFETIME CHANCE...
BECAUSE NEXT TIME...
...THERE'LL BE NO STOPPING VOID!!

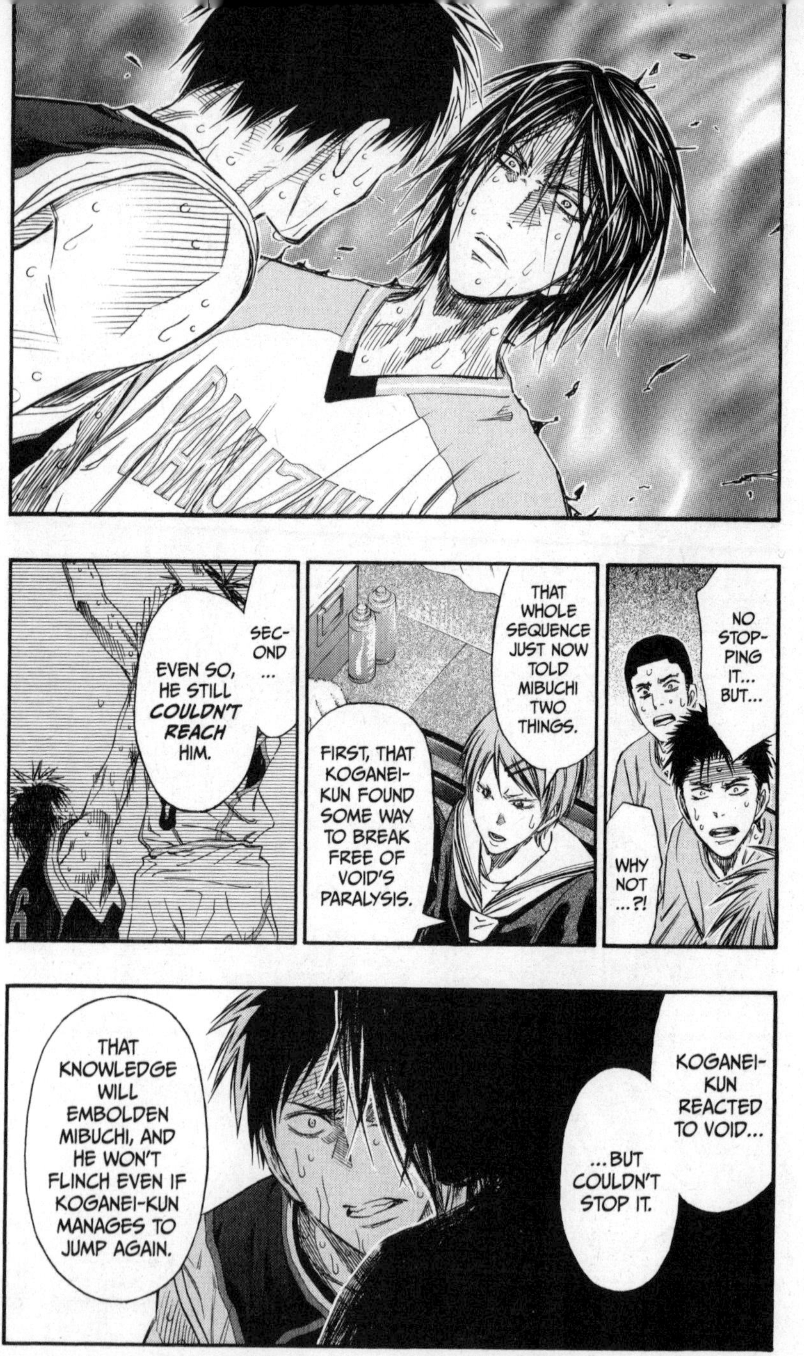
NO STOPPING IT... BUT...
WHY NOT ...?!
THAT WHOLE SEQUENCE JUST NOW TOLD MIBUCHI TWO THINGS.
FIRST, THAT KOGANEI-KUN FOUND SOME WAY TO BREAK FREE OF VOID'S PARALYSIS.
SECOND...
EVEN SO, HE STILL *COULDN'T REACH* HIM.
KOGANEI-KUN REACTED TO VOID...
...BUT COULDN'T STOP IT.
THAT KNOWLEDGE WILL EMBOLDEN MIBUCHI, AND HE WON'T FLINCH EVEN IF KOGANEI-KUN MANAGES TO JUMP AGAIN.

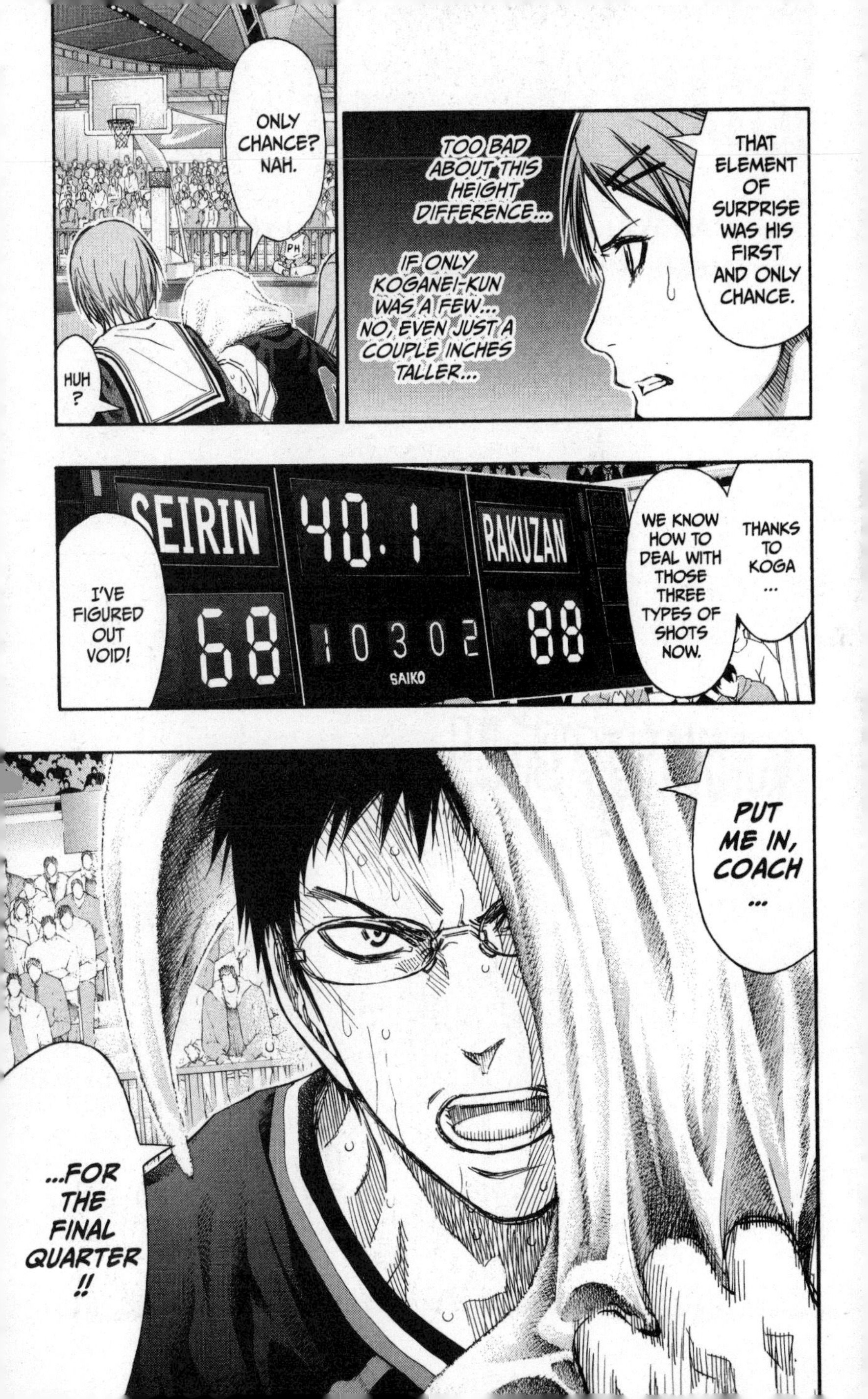
THAT ELEMENT OF SURPRISE WAS HIS FIRST AND ONLY CHANCE.
TOO BAD ABOUT THIS HEIGHT DIFFERENCE...
IF ONLY KOGANEI-KUN WAS A FEW... NO, EVEN JUST A COUPLE INCHES TALLER...
ONLY CHANCE? NAH.
HUH?
THANKS TO KOGA...
WE KNOW HOW TO DEAL WITH THOSE THREE TYPES OF SHOTS NOW.
RAKUZAN
40.1
SEIRIN
88
1 0 3 0 2
68
SAIKO
I'VE FIGURED OUT VOID!
PUT ME IN, COACH...
...FOR THE FINAL QUARTER!!

KUROKO'S BASKETBALL Q&A

W/ HALFWAY-DECENT ANSWERS

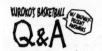

Q. CAN YOU LIST OUT EACH SEIRIN TEAM MEMBER'S FAMILY MEMBERS?

(ASTER from NAGASAKI PREFECTURE)

A. KUROKO→ FATHER, MOTHER, GRANDMOTHER
KAGAMI→ FATHER ONLY
HYUGA→ FATHER, MOTHER, LITTLE BROTHER
IZUKI→ FATHER, MOTHER, BIG SISTER, LITTLE SISTER
KIYOSHI→ GRANDFATHER, GRANDMOTHER
KOGANEI→ FATHER, MOTHER, BIG SISTER
MITOBE→ FATHER, MOTHER, FIVE LITTLE BROTHERS, THREE LITTLE SISTERS
TSUCHIDA→ FATHER, MOTHER, LITTLE SISTER
RIKO→ FATHER, MOTHER
FURIHATA→ FATHER, MOTHER, BIG BROTHER
KAWAHARA→ FATHER, MOTHER, BIG SISTER
FUKUDA→ MOTHER, TWO BIG BROTHERS

KUROKO'S BASKETBALL BLOOPERS

TAKE 5

ZING
...
F...
FINE!
I'LL KEEP TRYING! A LITTLE WHILE LONGER!
SHAH
NOD NOD
SERIOUSLY NO CLUE HOW THAT AMOUNTS TO A CONVERSATION.
HOW-EVER IT HAPPENED, GLAD YOU CHANGED YOUR MIND, KOGANEI-KUN!
BECAUSE WITHOUT YOU, WE'D HAVE NO WAY OF COMMUNI-CATING WITH MITOBE-KUN!
RIKO WAS RELIEVED FOR TWO REASONS.

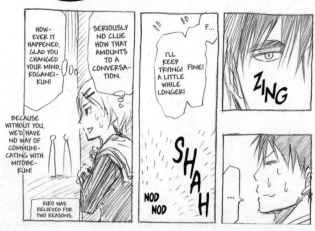

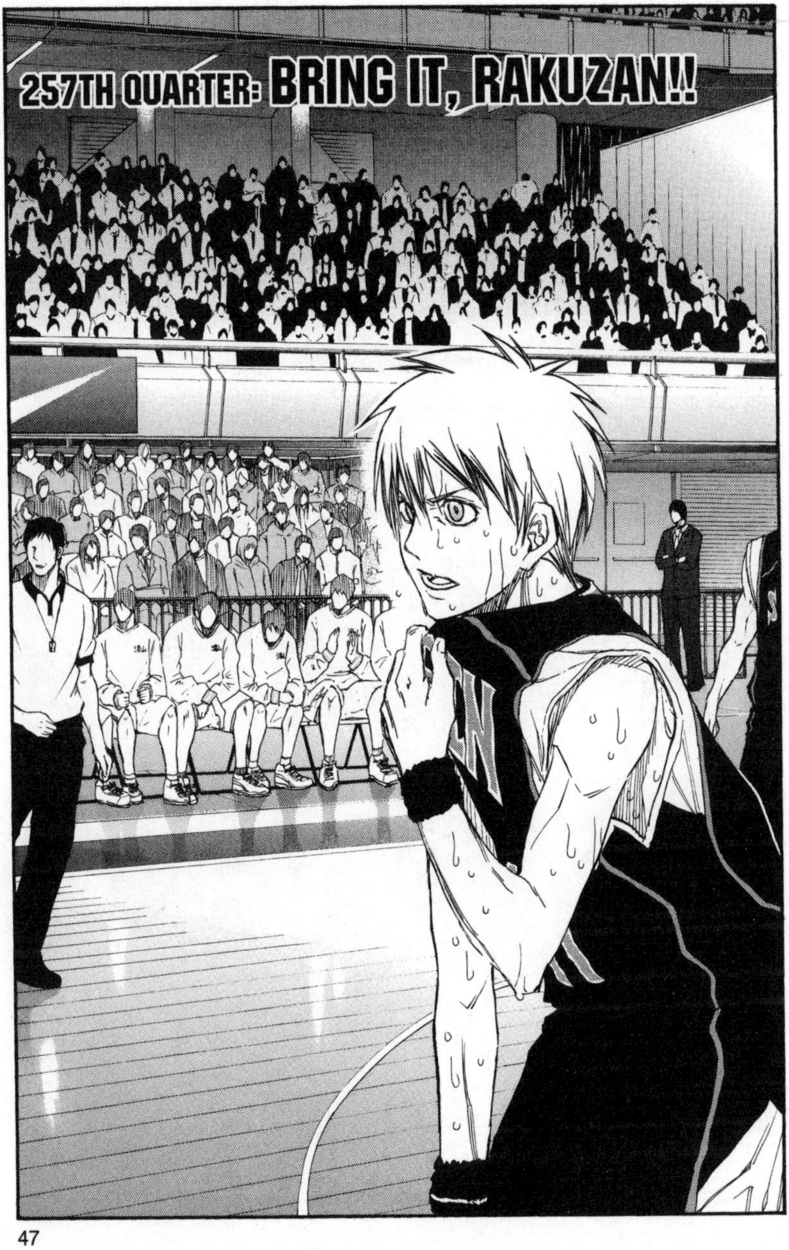
257TH QUARTER: BRING IT, RAKUZAN!!

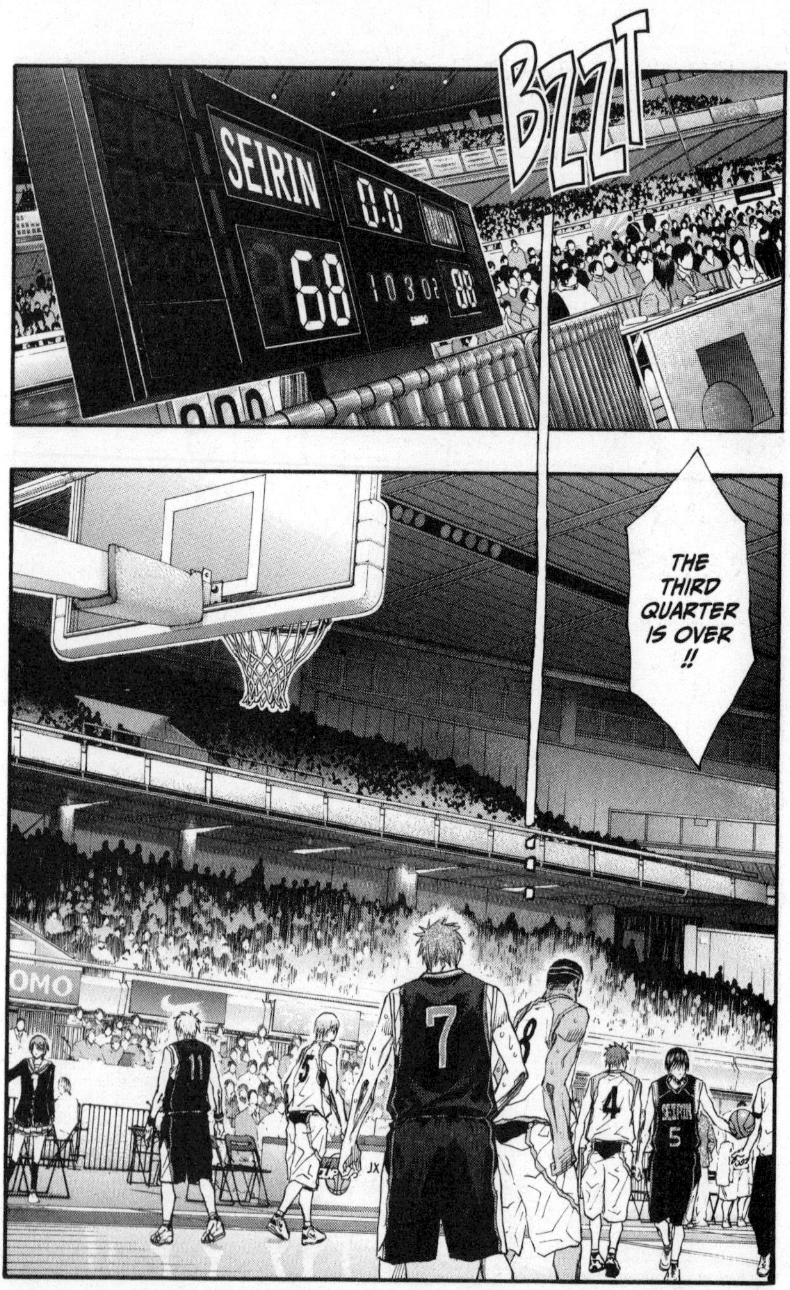
BZZT
SEIRIN
0.0
68
88
THE THIRD QUARTER IS OVER !!

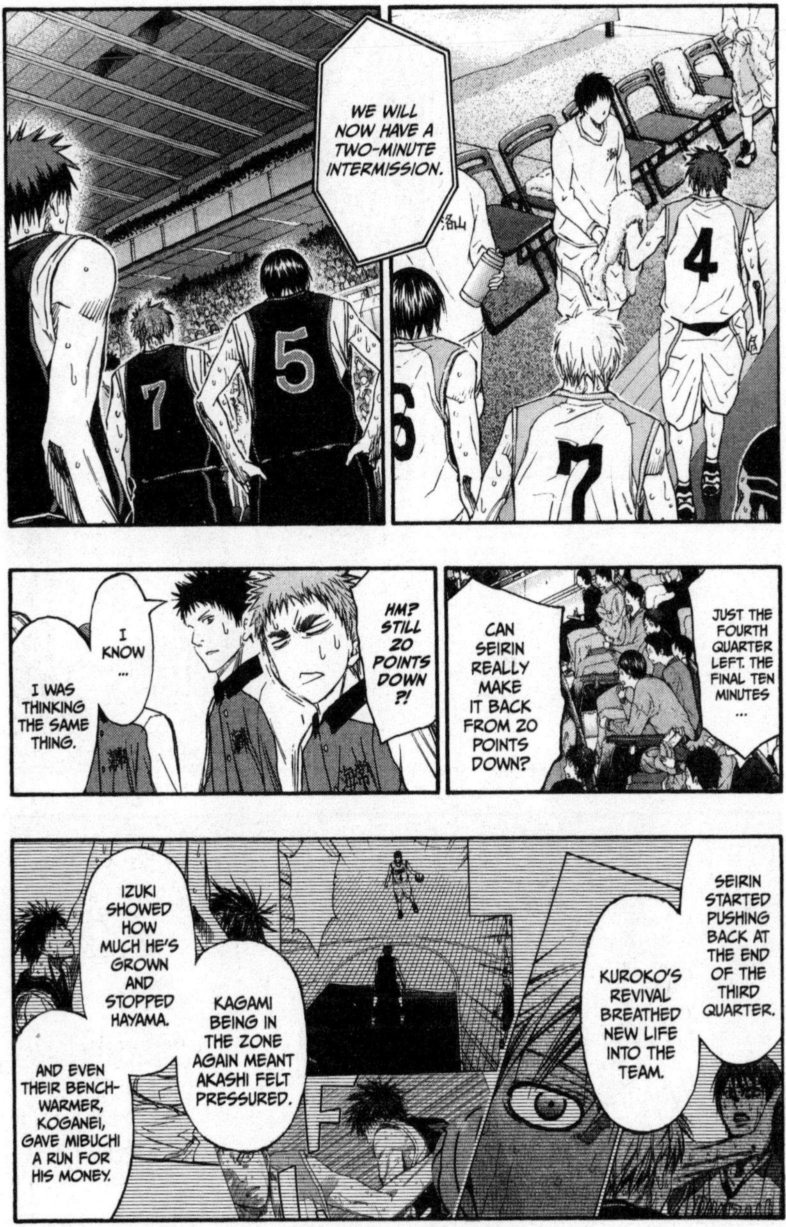
WE WILL NOW HAVE A TWO-MINUTE INTERMISSION.
JUST THE FOURTH QUARTER LEFT. THE FINAL TEN MINUTES ...
CAN SEIRIN REALLY MAKE IT BACK FROM 20 POINTS DOWN?
HM? STILL 20 POINTS DOWN ?!
I KNOW ...
I WAS THINKING THE SAME THING.
SEIRIN STARTED PUSHING BACK AT THE END OF THE THIRD QUARTER.
KUROKO'S REVIVAL BREATHED NEW LIFE INTO THE TEAM.
KAGAMI BEING IN THE ZONE AGAIN MEANT AKASHI FELT PRESSURED.
IZUKI SHOWED HOW MUCH HE'S GROWN AND STOPPED HAYAMA.
AND EVEN THEIR BENCH-WARMER, KOGANEI, GAVE MIBUCHI A RUN FOR HIS MONEY.

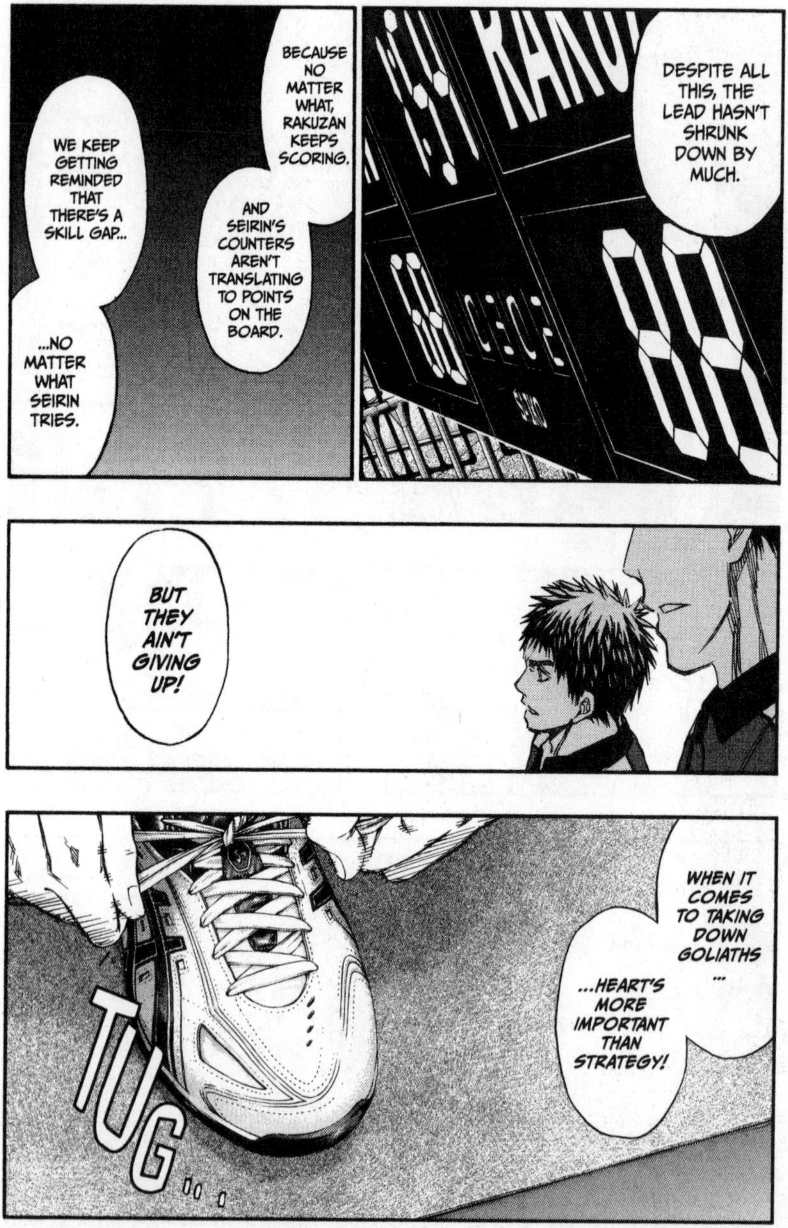
DESPITE ALL THIS, THE LEAD HASN'T SHRUNK DOWN BY MUCH.
BECAUSE NO MATTER WHAT, RAKUZAN KEEPS SCORING.
AND SEIRIN'S COUNTERS AREN'T TRANSLATING TO POINTS ON THE BOARD.
WE KEEP GETTING REMINDED THAT THERE'S A SKILL GAP...
...NO MATTER WHAT SEIRIN TRIES.
BUT THEY AIN'T GIVING UP!
WHEN IT COMES TO TAKING DOWN GOLIATHS ...
...HEART'S MORE IMPORTANT THAN STRATEGY!
TUG...

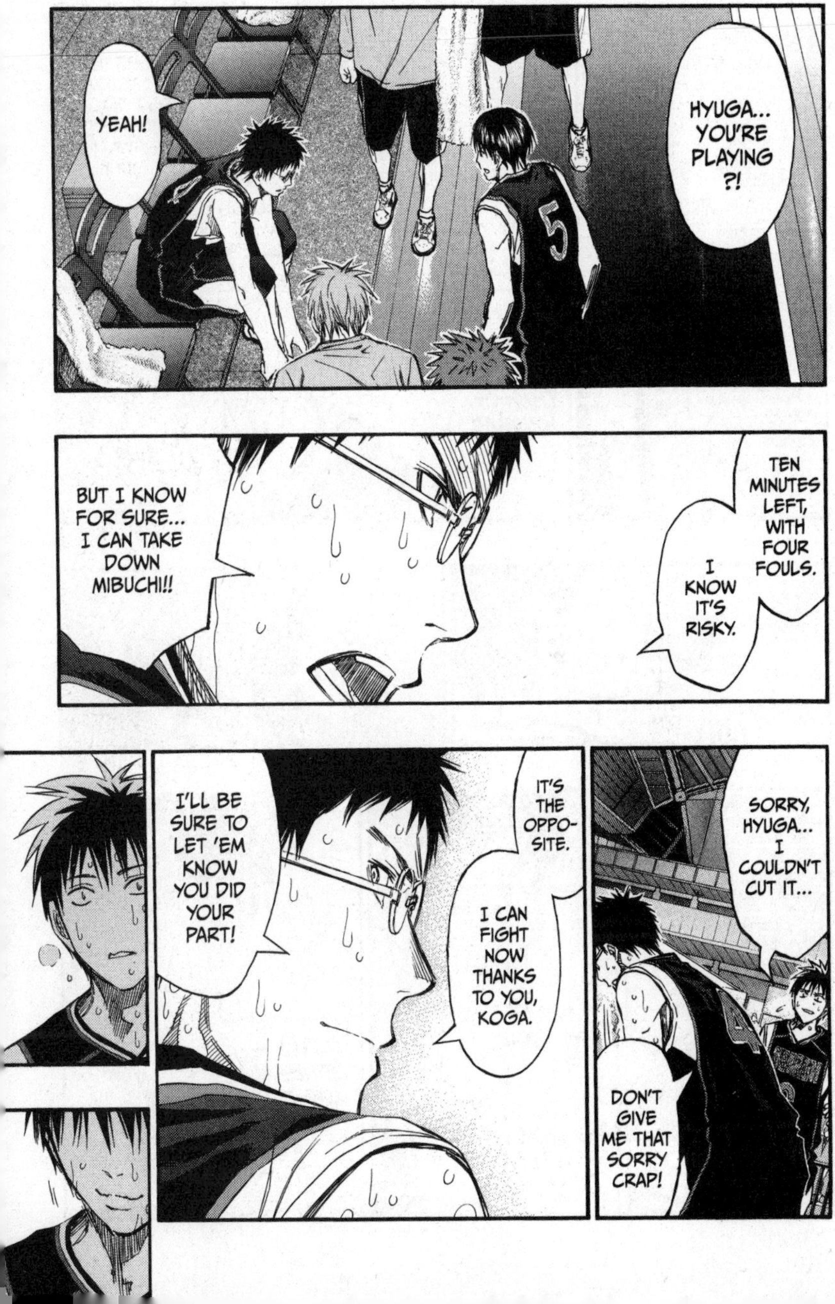
HYUGA... YOU'RE PLAYING ?!
YEAH!
TEN MINUTES LEFT, WITH FOUR FOULS.
I KNOW IT'S RISKY.
BUT I KNOW FOR SURE... I CAN TAKE DOWN MIBUCHI!!
SORRY, HYUGA... I COULDN'T CUT IT...
DON'T GIVE ME THAT SORRY CRAP!
IT'S THE OPPO-SITE.
I CAN FIGHT NOW THANKS TO YOU, KOGA.
I'LL BE SURE TO LET 'EM KNOW YOU DID YOUR PART!

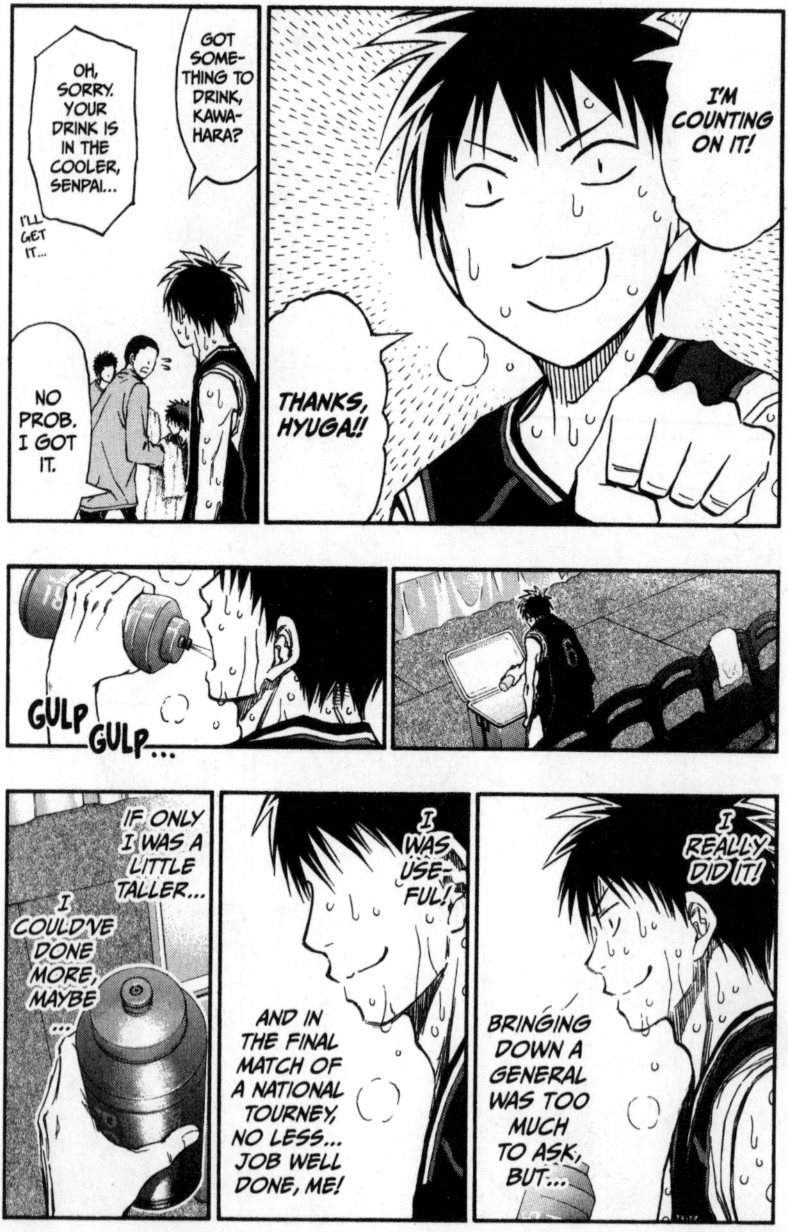
I'M COUNTING ON IT!
THANKS, HYUGA!!
GOT SOMETHING TO DRINK, KAWAHARA?
OH, SORRY. YOUR DRINK IS IN THE COOLER, SENPAI...
I'LL GET IT...
NO PROB. I GOT IT.
GULP GULP...
I REALLY DID IT!
BRINGING DOWN A GENERAL WAS TOO MUCH TO ASK, BUT...
I WAS USEFUL!
AND IN THE FINAL MATCH OF A NATIONAL TOURNEY, NO LESS... JOB WELL DONE, ME!
IF ONLY I WAS A LITTLE TALLER...
I COULD'VE DONE MORE, MAYBE...

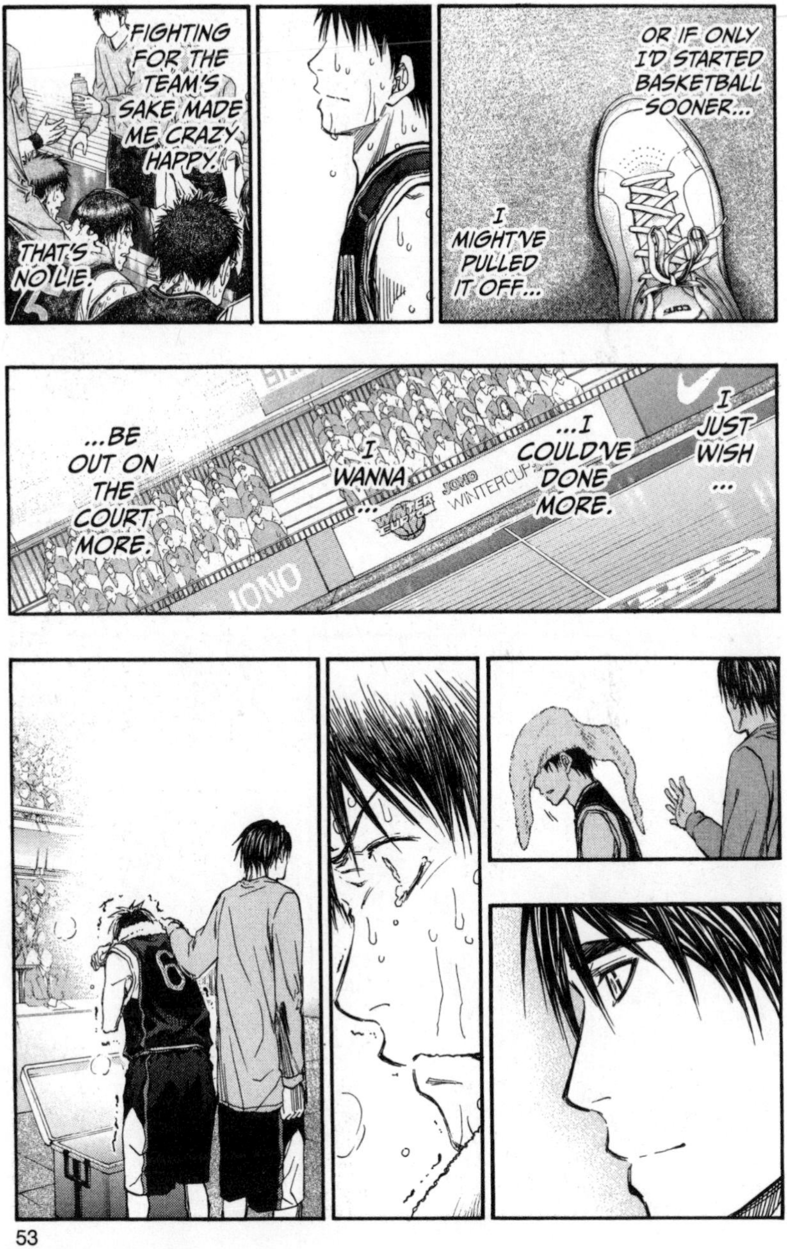
OR IF ONLY I'D STARTED BASKETBALL SOONER...
I MIGHT'VE PULLED IT OFF...
FIGHTING FOR THE TEAM'S SAKE MADE ME CRAZY HAPPY.
THAT'S NO LIE.
I JUST WISH...
...I COULD'VE DONE MORE.
JOMO WINTERCUP
I WANNA...
...BE OUT ON THE COURT MORE.

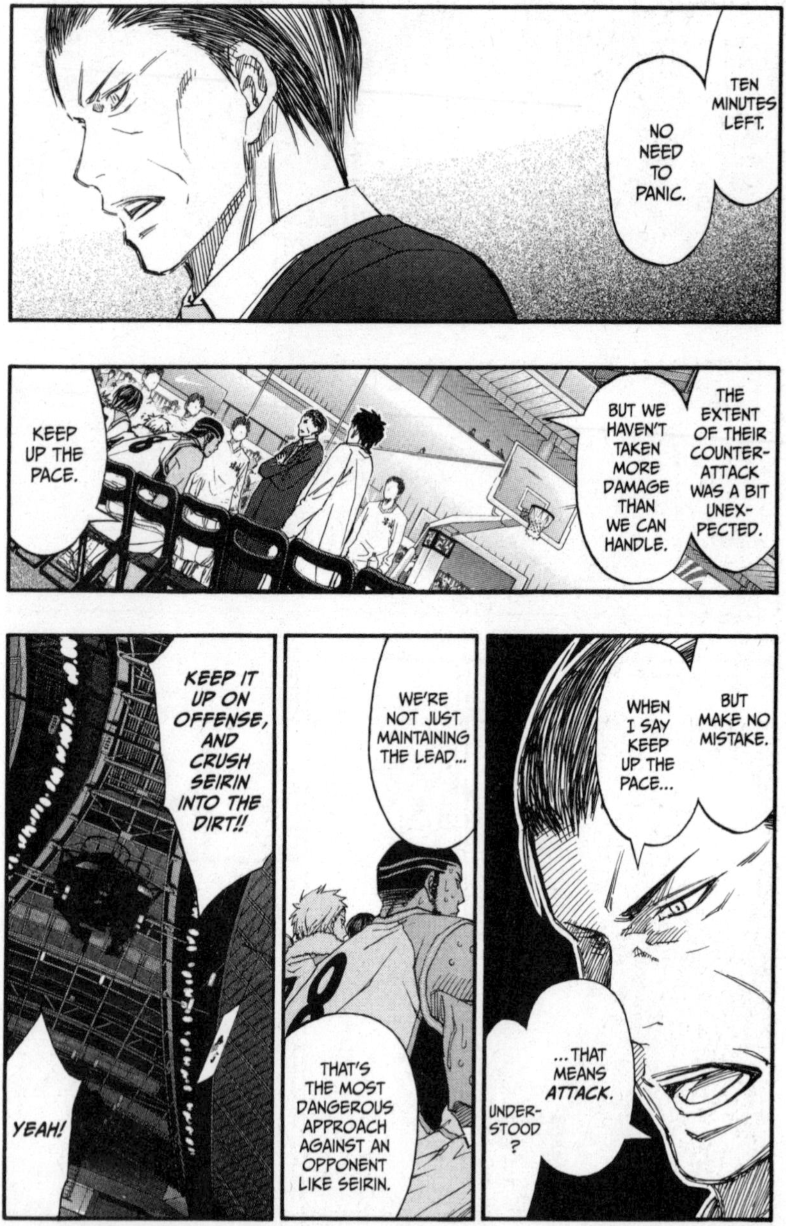
TEN MINUTES LEFT.
NO NEED TO PANIC.
THE EXTENT OF THEIR COUNTER-ATTACK WAS A BIT UNEXPECTED.
BUT WE HAVEN'T TAKEN MORE DAMAGE THAN WE CAN HANDLE.
KEEP UP THE PACE.
BUT MAKE NO MISTAKE.
WHEN I SAY KEEP UP THE PACE...
...THAT MEANS ATTACK.
UNDERSTOOD?
WE'RE NOT JUST MAINTAINING THE LEAD...
THAT'S THE MOST DANGEROUS APPROACH AGAINST AN OPPONENT LIKE SEIRIN.
KEEP IT UP ON OFFENSE, AND CRUSH SEIRIN INTO THE DIRT!!
YEAH!

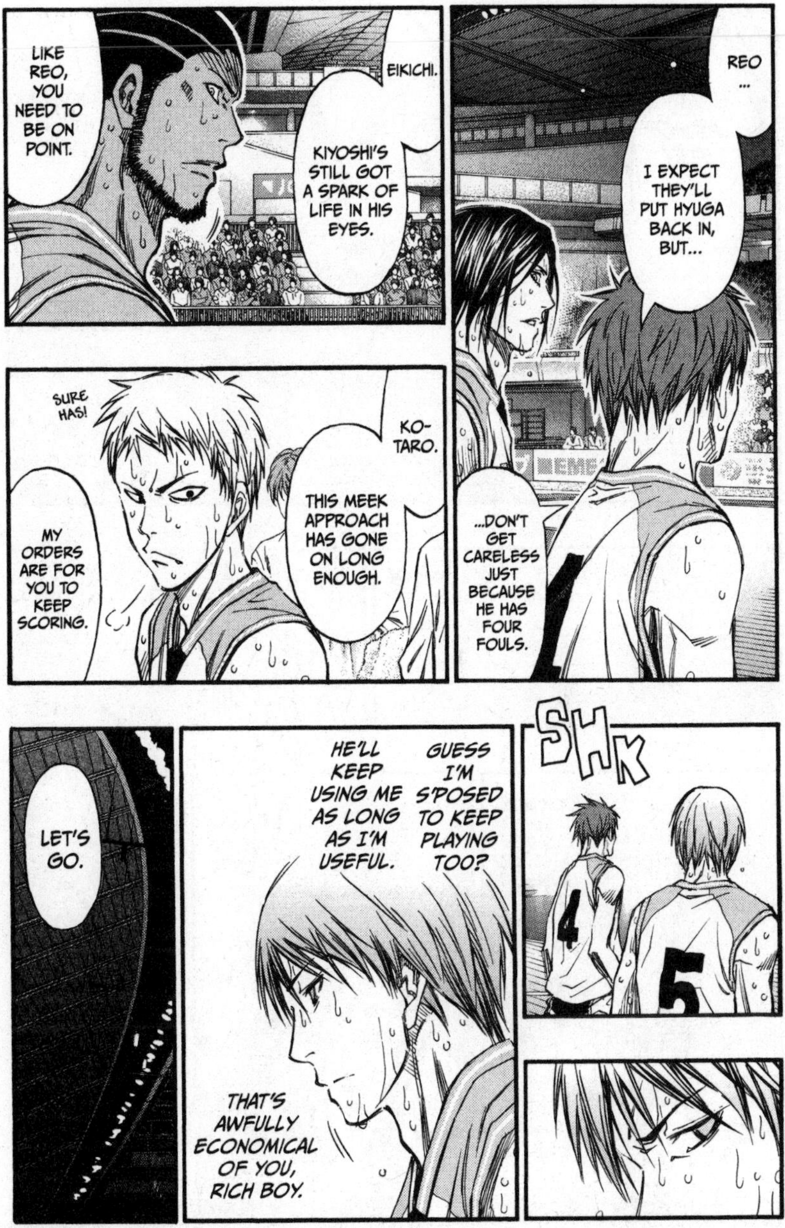
REO ...
I EXPECT THEY'LL PUT HYUGA BACK IN, BUT...
...DON'T GET CARELESS JUST BECAUSE HE HAS FOUR FOULS.
EIKICHI.
KIYOSHI'S STILL GOT A SPARK OF LIFE IN HIS EYES.
LIKE REO, YOU NEED TO BE ON POINT.
KO-TARO.
THIS MEEK APPROACH HAS GONE ON LONG ENOUGH.
SURE HAS!
MY ORDERS ARE FOR YOU TO KEEP SCORING.
SHK
GUESS I'M S'POSED TO KEEP PLAYING TOO?
HE'LL KEEP USING ME AS LONG AS I'M USEFUL.
THAT'S AWFULLY ECONOMICAL OF YOU, RICH BOY.
LET'S GO.

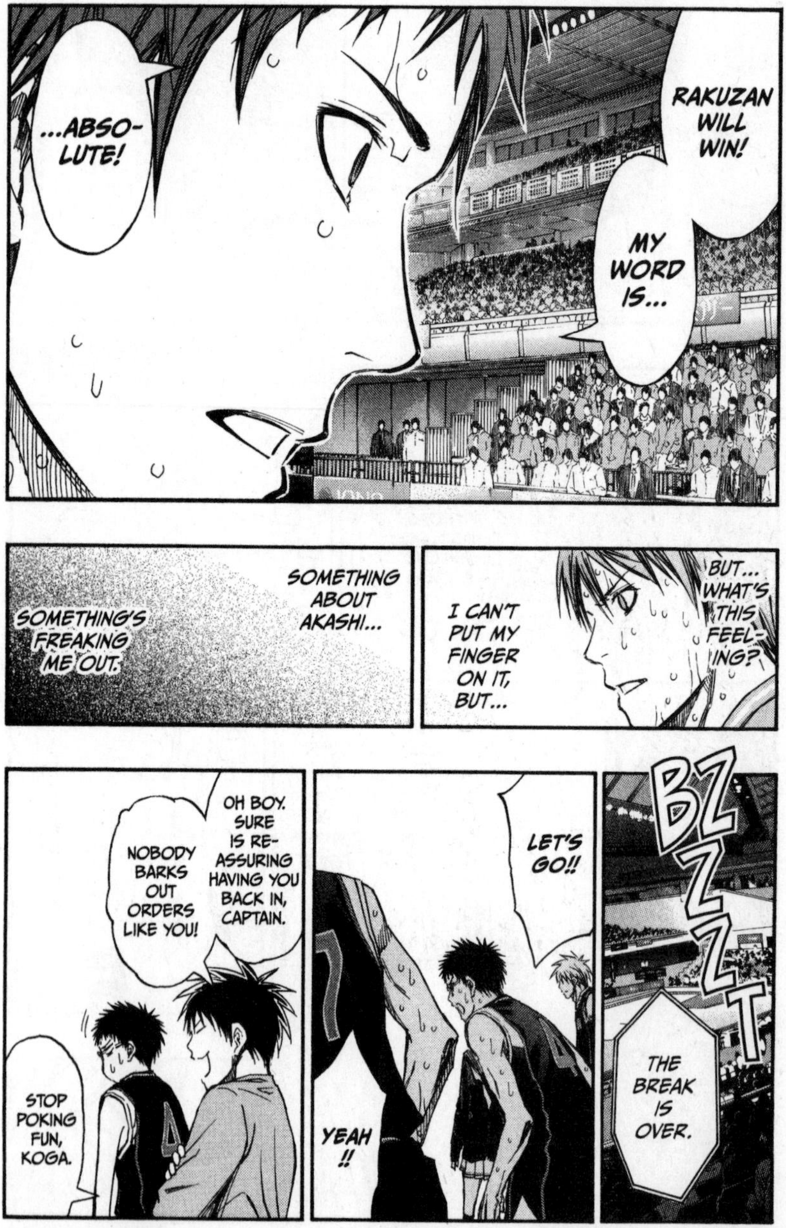

RAKUZAN WILL WIN!
MY WORD IS...
...ABSO-LUTE!
BUT... WHAT'S THIS FEEL-ING?
I CAN'T PUT MY FINGER ON IT, BUT...
SOMETHING ABOUT AKASHI...
SOMETHING'S FREAKING ME OUT.
BZZZT
THE BREAK IS OVER.
LET'S GO!!
YEAH !!
OH BOY. SURE IS RE-ASSURING HAVING YOU BACK IN, CAPTAIN.
NOBODY BARKS OUT ORDERS LIKE YOU!
STOP POKING FUN, KOGA.

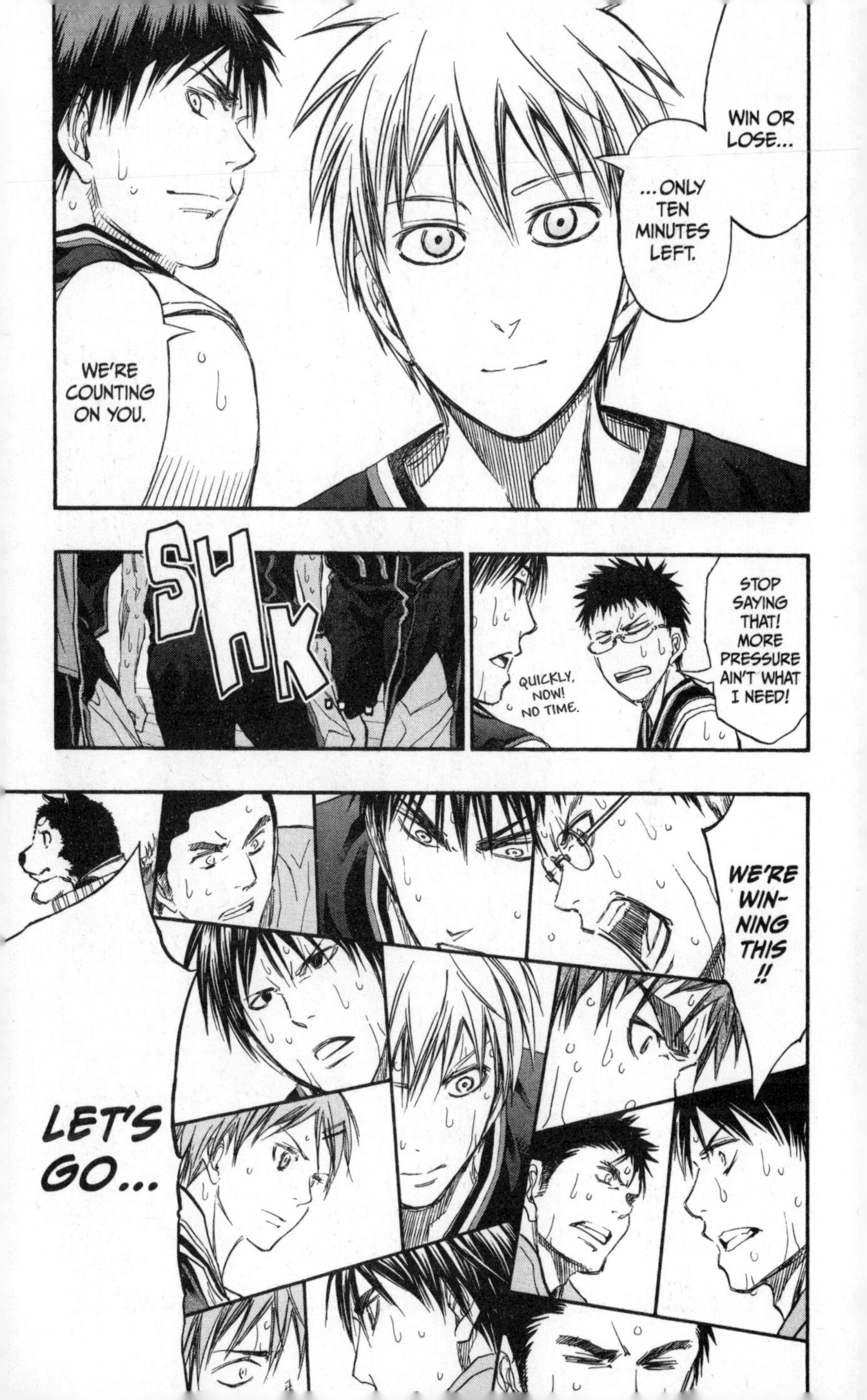
WIN OR LOSE...
...ONLY TEN MINUTES LEFT.
WE'RE COUNTING ON YOU.
STOP SAYING THAT! MORE PRESSURE AIN'T WHAT I NEED!
QUICKLY, NOW! NO TIME.
SHK
WE'RE WIN-NING THIS!!
LET'S GO...

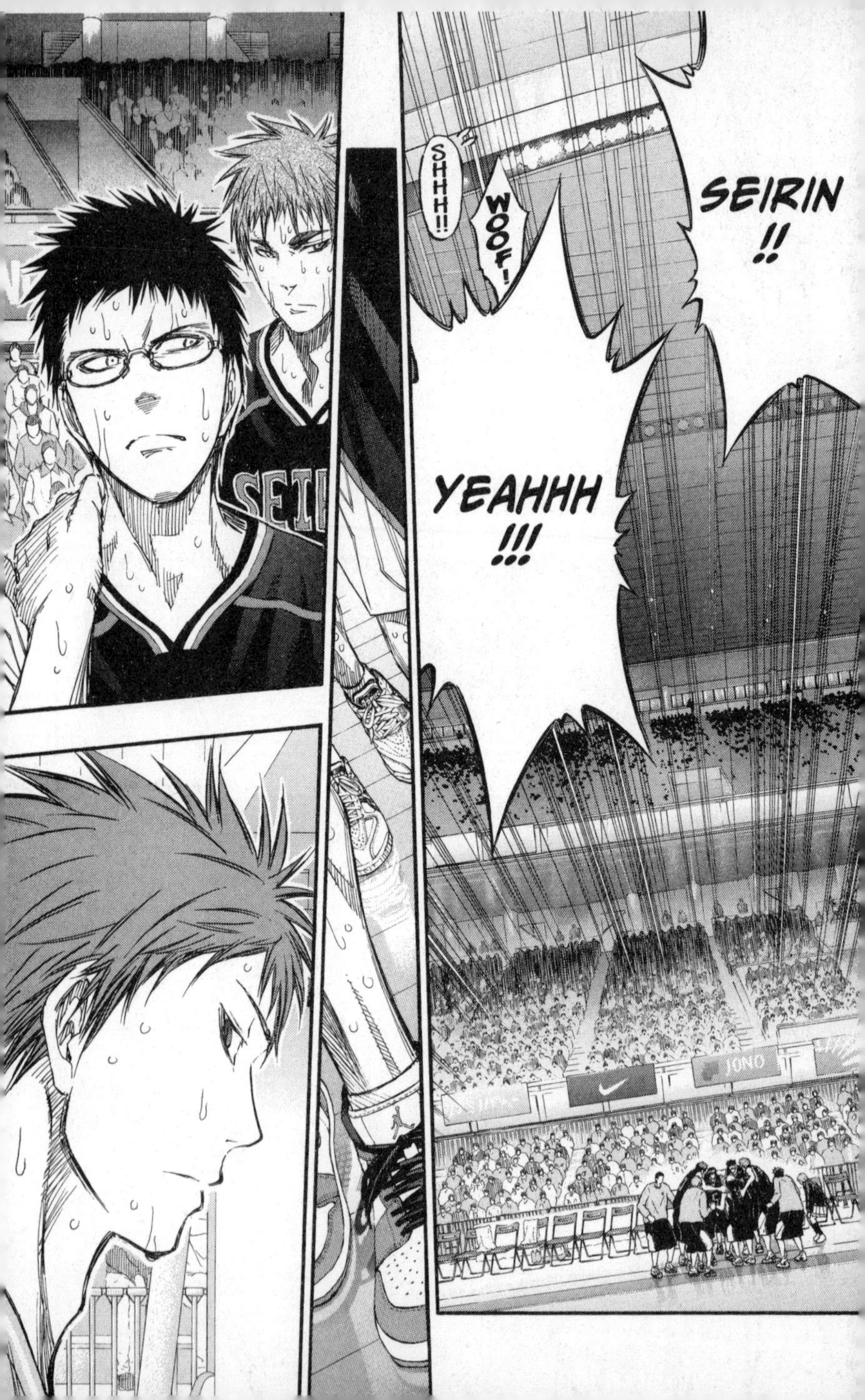
SEIRIN !!
YEAHHH !!!
WOOF!
SHHHH!!

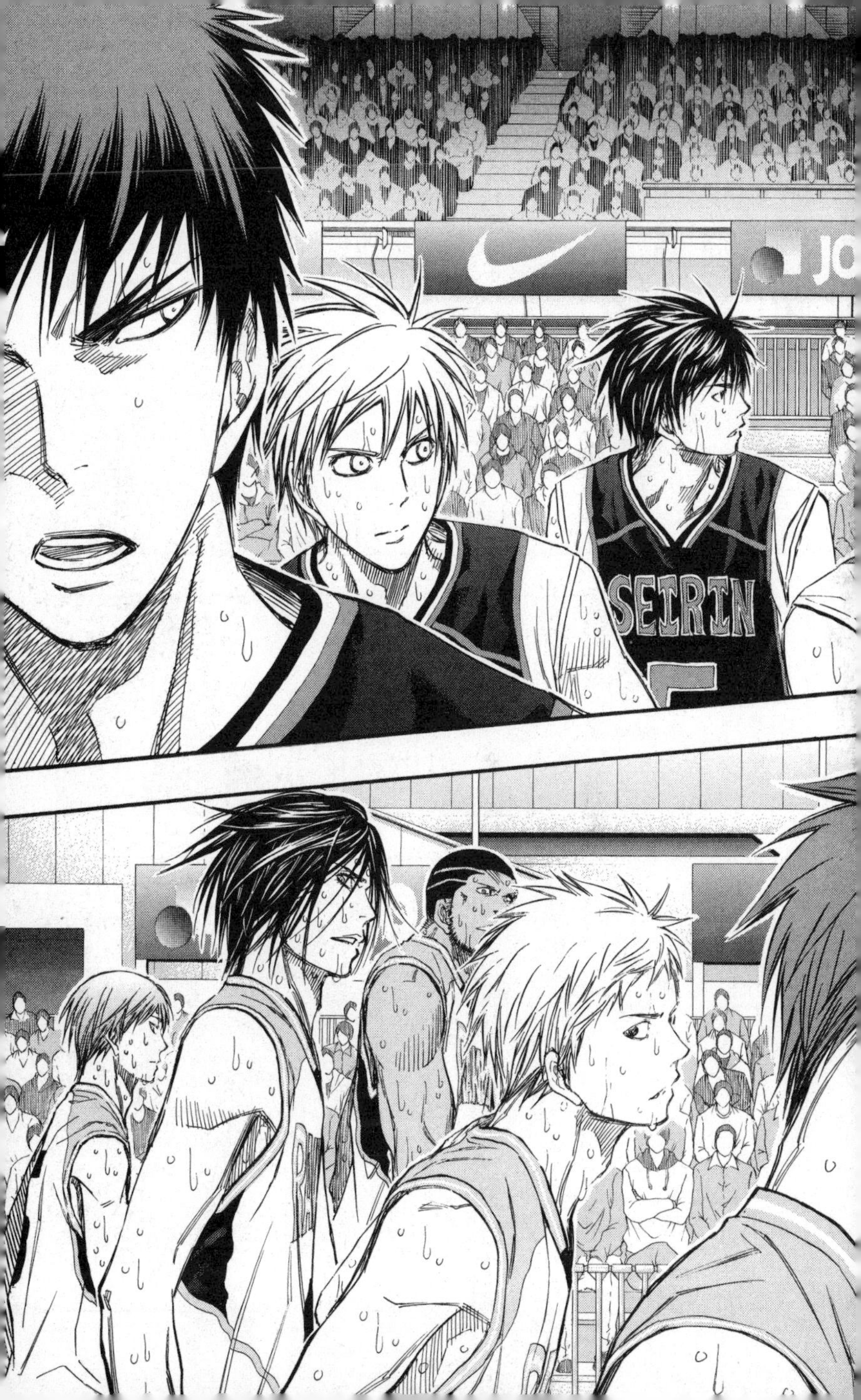
SEIRIN

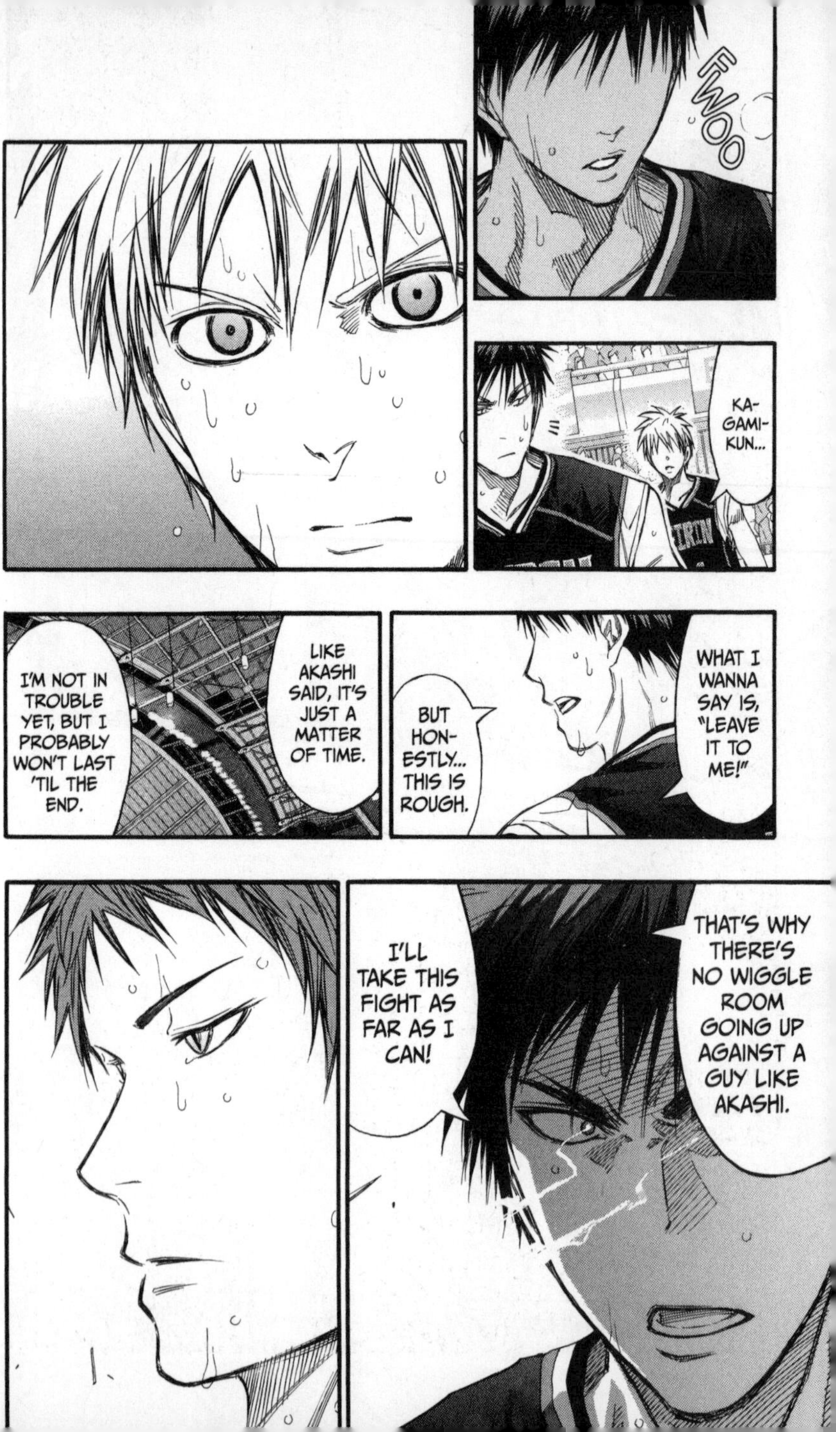
FWOO
KA-GAMI-KUN...
WHAT I WANNA SAY IS, "LEAVE IT TO ME!"
BUT HON-ESTLY... THIS IS ROUGH.
LIKE AKASHI SAID, IT'S JUST A MATTER OF TIME.
I'M NOT IN TROUBLE YET, BUT I PROBABLY WON'T LAST 'TIL THE END.
THAT'S WHY THERE'S NO WIGGLE ROOM GOING UP AGAINST A GUY LIKE AKASHI.
I'LL TAKE THIS FIGHT AS FAR AS I CAN!

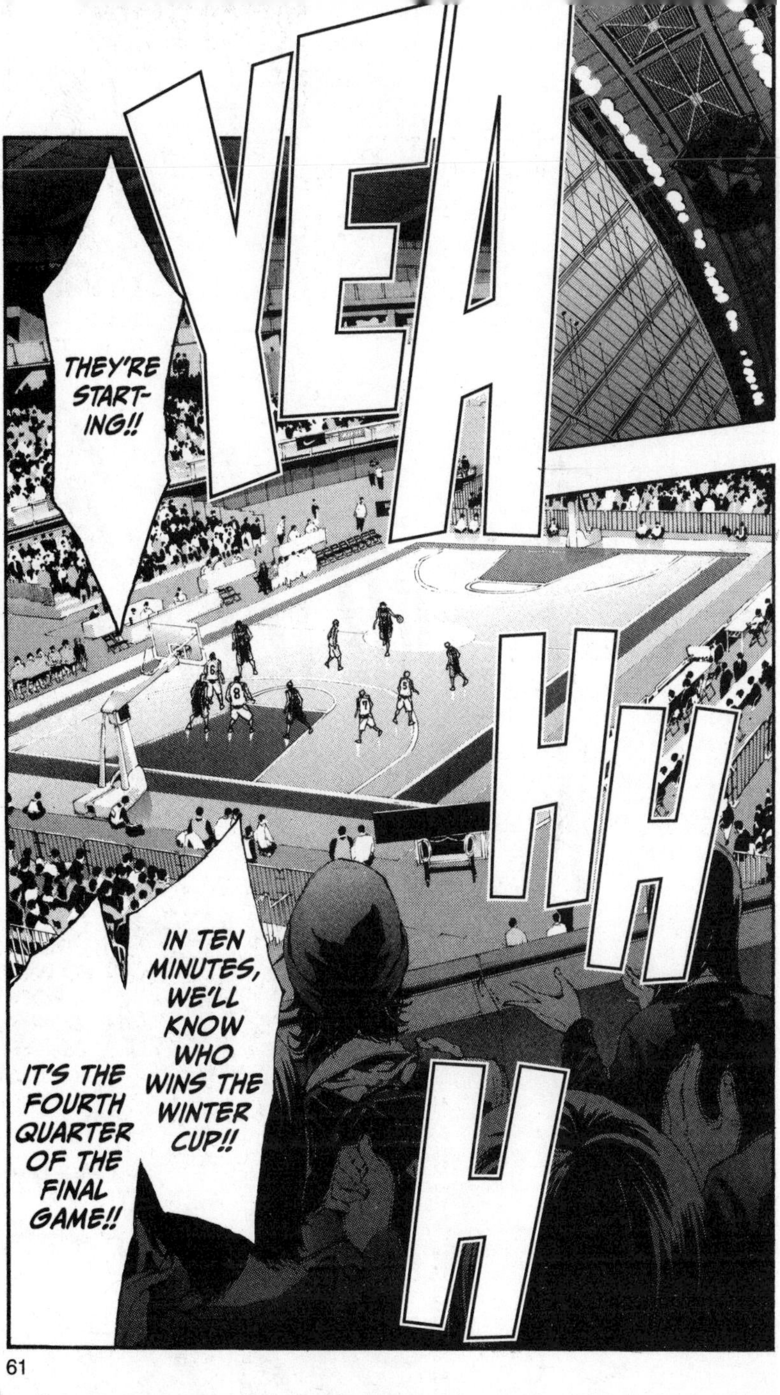
YEAHHH
THEY'RE START-ING!!
IN TEN MINUTES, WE'LL KNOW WHO WINS THE WINTER CUP!!
IT'S THE FOURTH QUARTER OF THE FINAL GAME!!

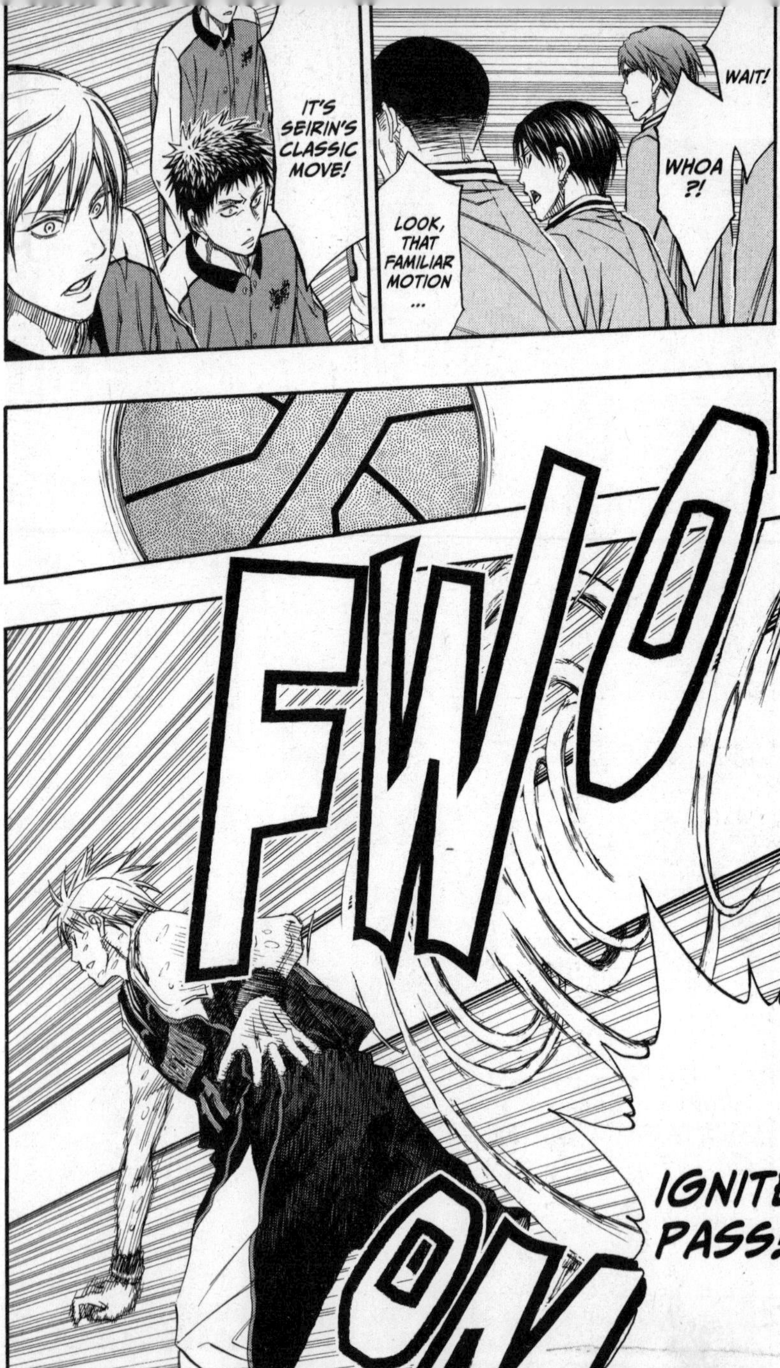
WAIT!
WHOA ?!
LOOK, THAT FAMILIAR MOTION ...
IT'S SEIRIN'S CLASSIC MOVE!
FWOOM
IGNITE PASS!!

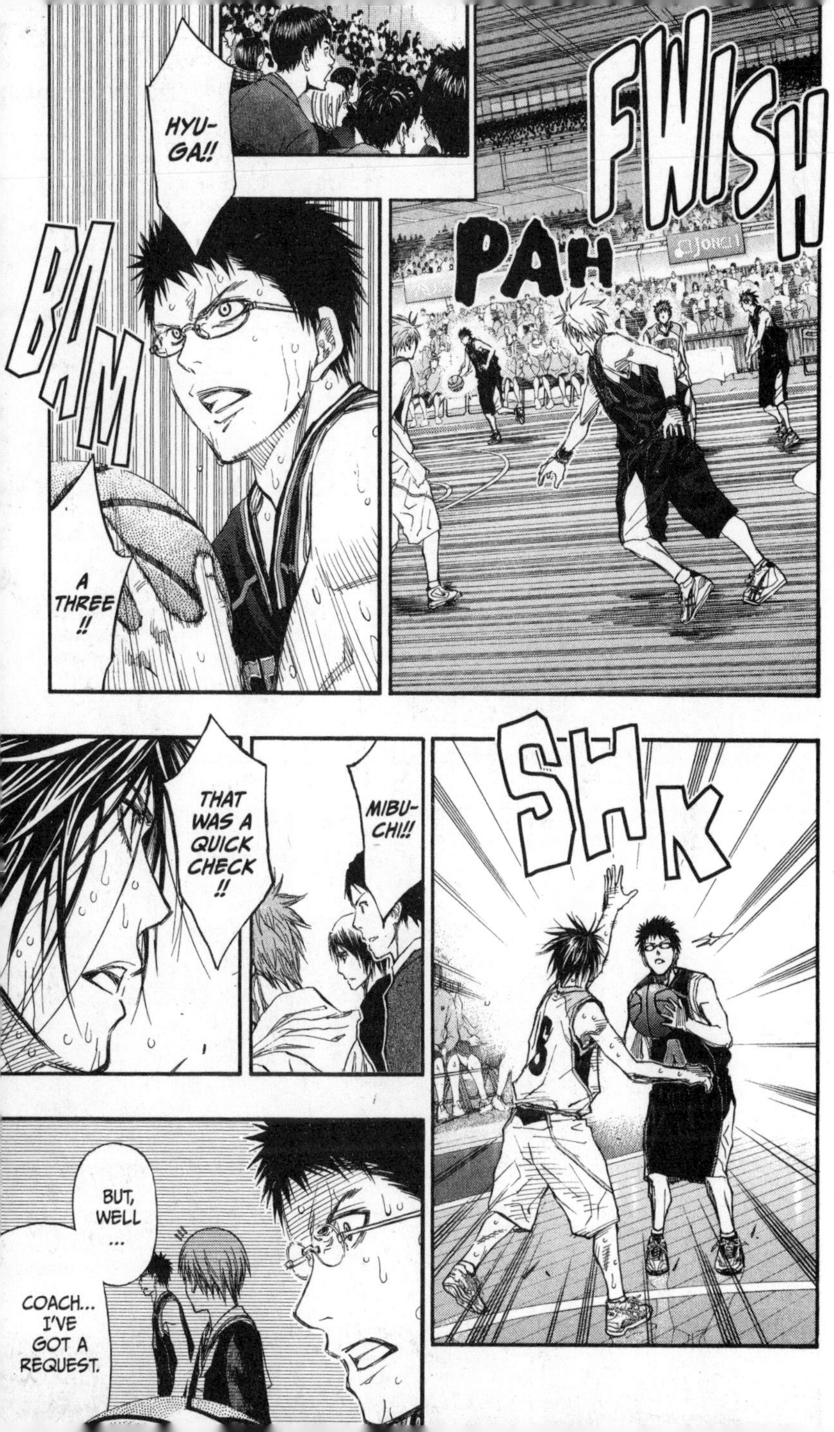
FWISH
PAH
HYU-GA!!
BAM
A THREE!!
SHK
MIBU-CHI!!
THAT WAS A QUICK CHECK!!
BUT, WELL...
COACH... I'VE GOT A REQUEST.

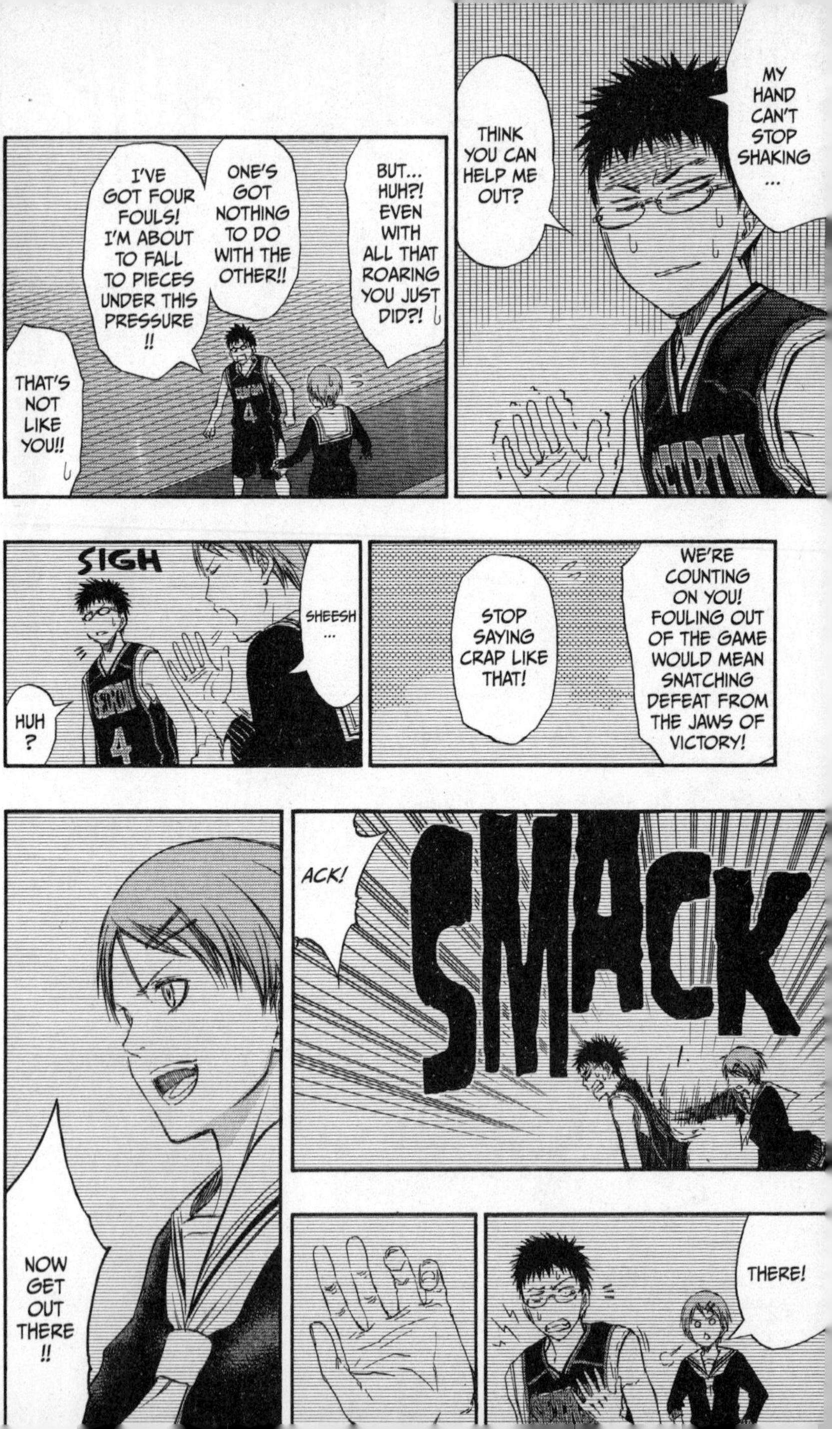
MY HAND CAN'T STOP SHAKING...
THINK YOU CAN HELP ME OUT?
BUT... HUH?! EVEN WITH ALL THAT ROARING YOU JUST DID?!
ONE'S GOT NOTHING TO DO WITH THE OTHER!!
I'VE GOT FOUR FOULS! I'M ABOUT TO FALL TO PIECES UNDER THIS PRESSURE!!
THAT'S NOT LIKE YOU!!
WE'RE COUNTING ON YOU! FOULING OUT OF THE GAME WOULD MEAN SNATCHING DEFEAT FROM THE JAWS OF VICTORY!
STOP SAYING CRAP LIKE THAT!
SHEESH...
SIGH
HUH?
ACK!
SMACK
THERE!
NOW GET OUT THERE!!

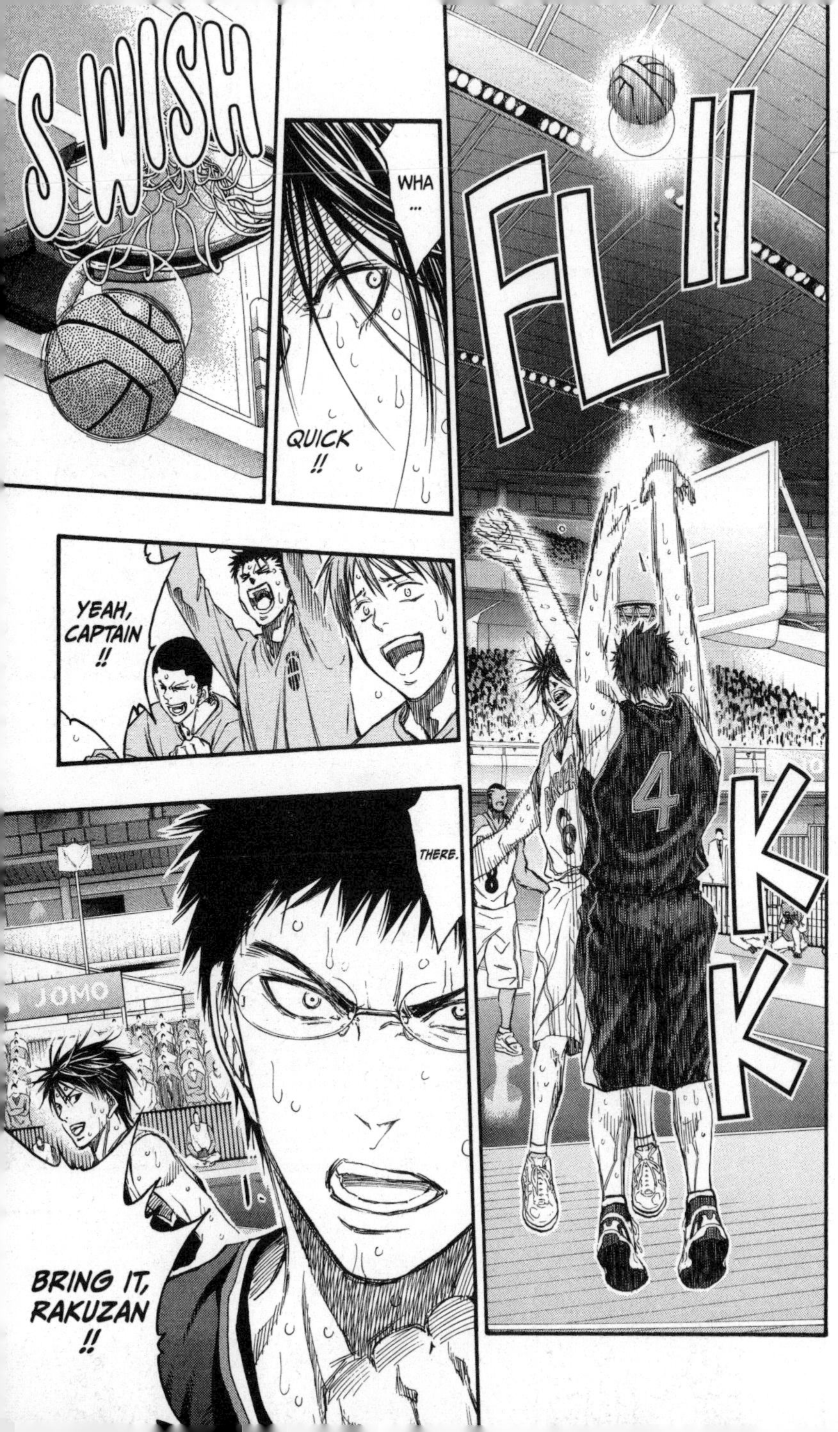
FLIIKK
WHA...
QUICK!!
SWISH
YEAH, CAPTAIN!!
THERE.
BRING IT, RAKUZAN!!

KUROKO'S BASKETBALL BLOOPERS
TAKE 3

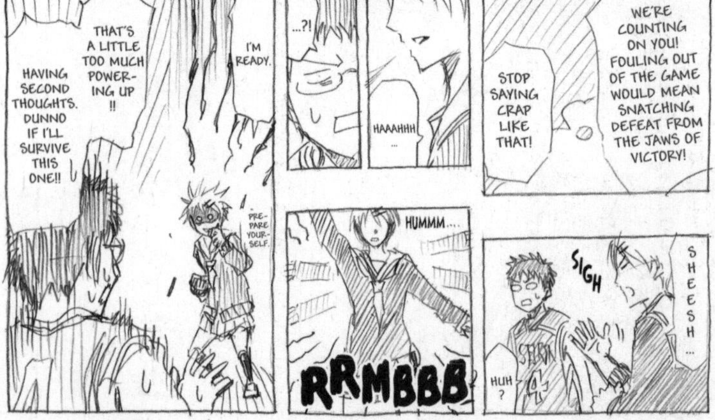
WE'RE COUNTING ON YOU! FOULING OUT OF THE GAME WOULD MEAN SNATCHING DEFEAT FROM THE JAWS OF VICTORY!
STOP SAYING CRAP LIKE THAT!
HAAAHHH...
...?!
SHEESH...
SIGH
HUH?
HUMMM....
RRMBBB
I'M READY.
THAT'S A LITTLE TOO MUCH POWERING UP!!
HAVING SECOND THOUGHTS. DUNNO IF I'LL SURVIVE THIS ONE!!
PREPARE YOURSELF.

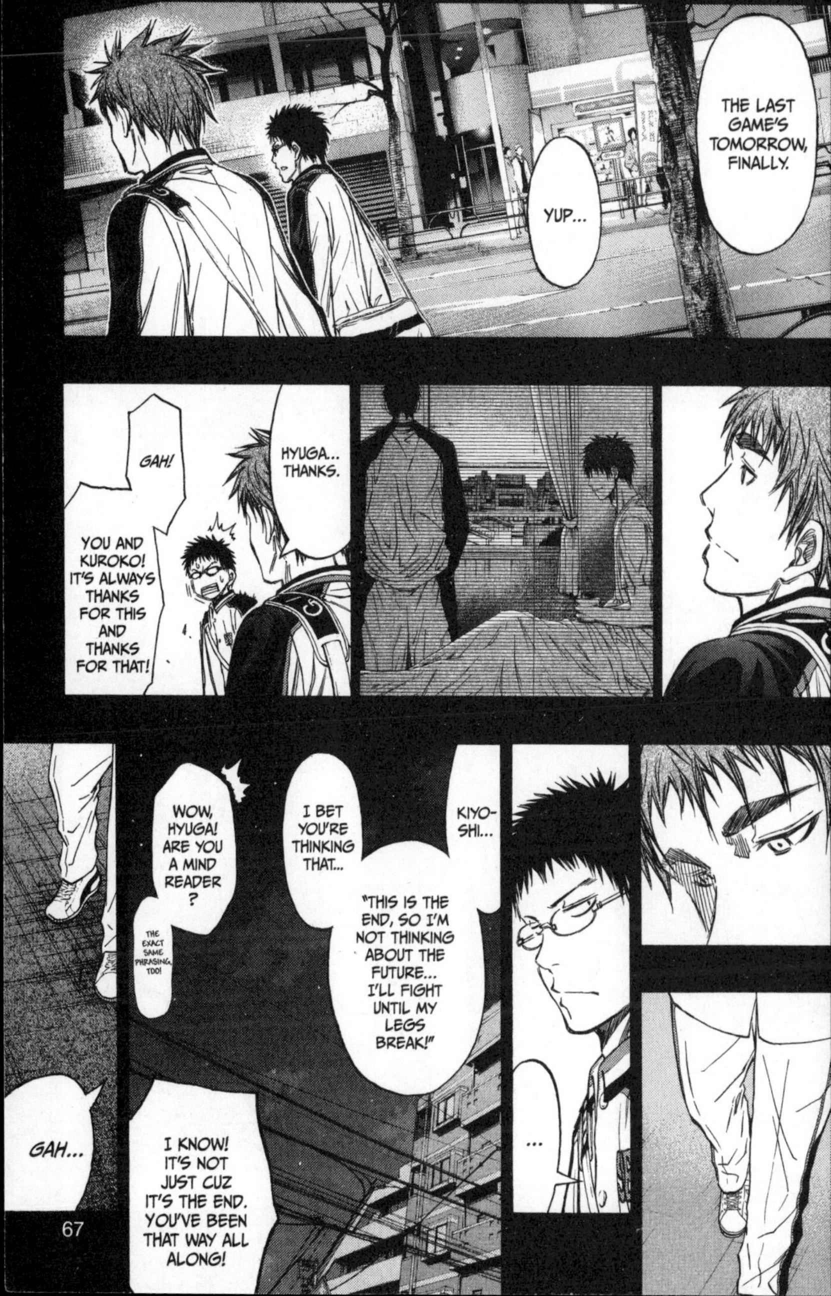
THE LAST GAME'S TOMORROW, FINALLY.
YUP...
HYUGA... THANKS.
GAH!
YOU AND KUROKO! IT'S ALWAYS THANKS FOR THIS AND THANKS FOR THAT!
KIYO-SHI...
...
I BET YOU'RE THINKING THAT...
"THIS IS THE END, SO I'M NOT THINKING ABOUT THE FUTURE... I'LL FIGHT UNTIL MY LEGS BREAK!"
WOW, HYUGA! ARE YOU A MIND READER?
THE EXACT SAME PHRASING, TOO!
I KNOW! IT'S NOT JUST CUZ IT'S THE END. YOU'VE BEEN THAT WAY ALL ALONG!
GAH...

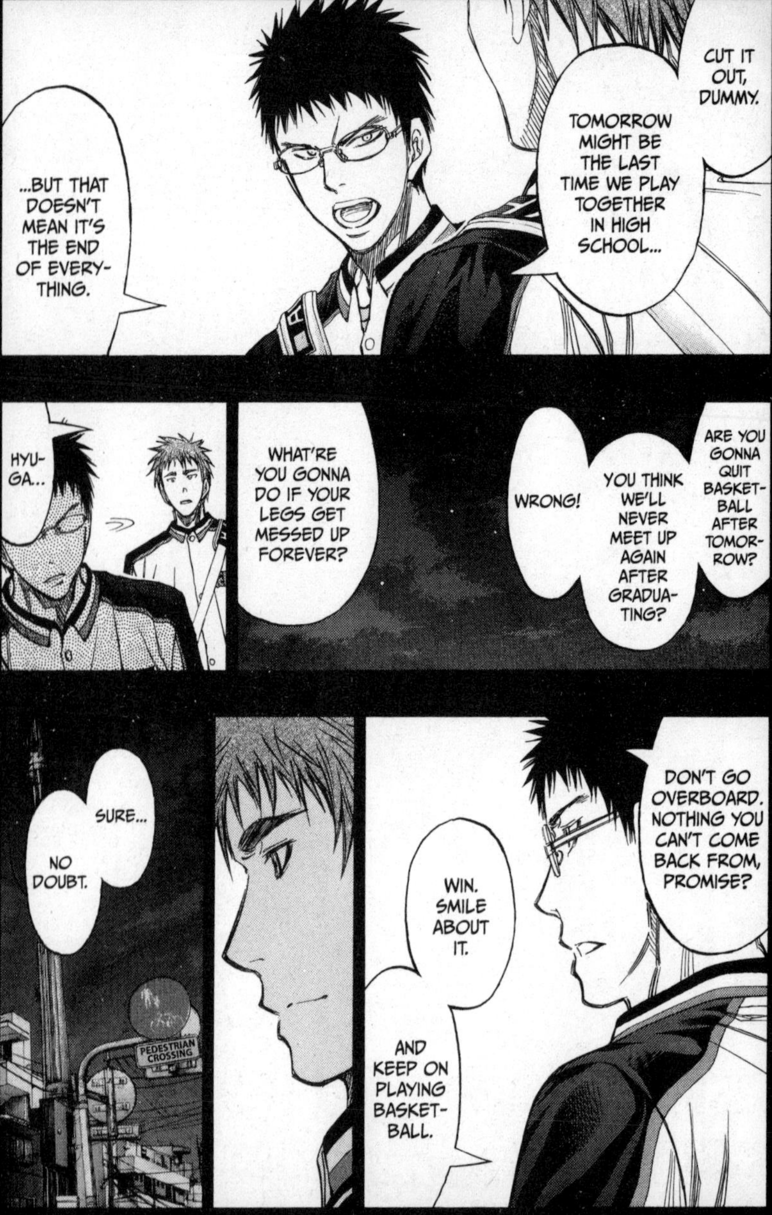
CUT IT OUT, DUMMY.
TOMORROW MIGHT BE THE LAST TIME WE PLAY TOGETHER IN HIGH SCHOOL...
...BUT THAT DOESN'T MEAN IT'S THE END OF EVERY-THING.
ARE YOU GONNA QUIT BASKET-BALL AFTER TOMOR-ROW?
YOU THINK WE'LL NEVER MEET UP AGAIN AFTER GRADUA-TING?
WRONG!
WHAT'RE YOU GONNA DO IF YOUR LEGS GET MESSED UP FOREVER?
HYU-GA...
DON'T GO OVERBOARD. NOTHING YOU CAN'T COME BACK FROM, PROMISE?
WIN. SMILE ABOUT IT.
AND KEEP ON PLAYING BASKET-BALL.
SURE...
NO DOUBT.
PEDESTRIAN CROSSING

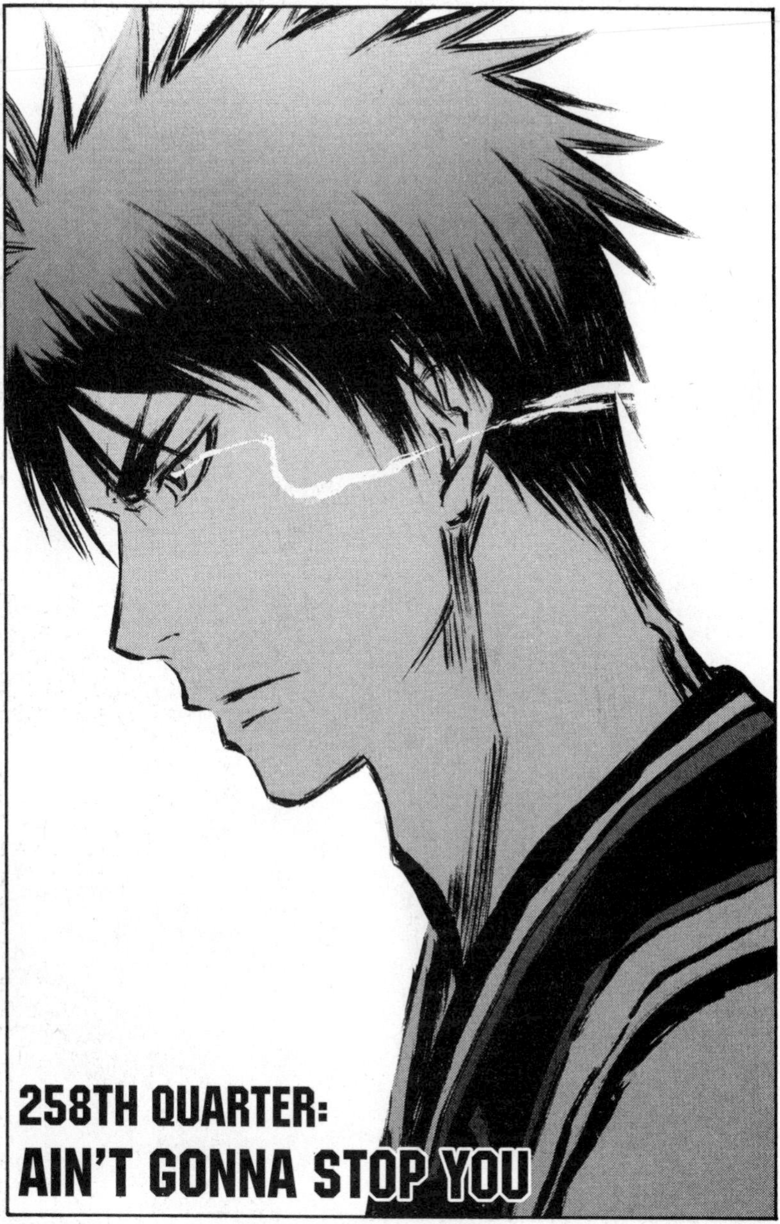
258TH QUARTER:
AIN'T GONNA STOP YOU

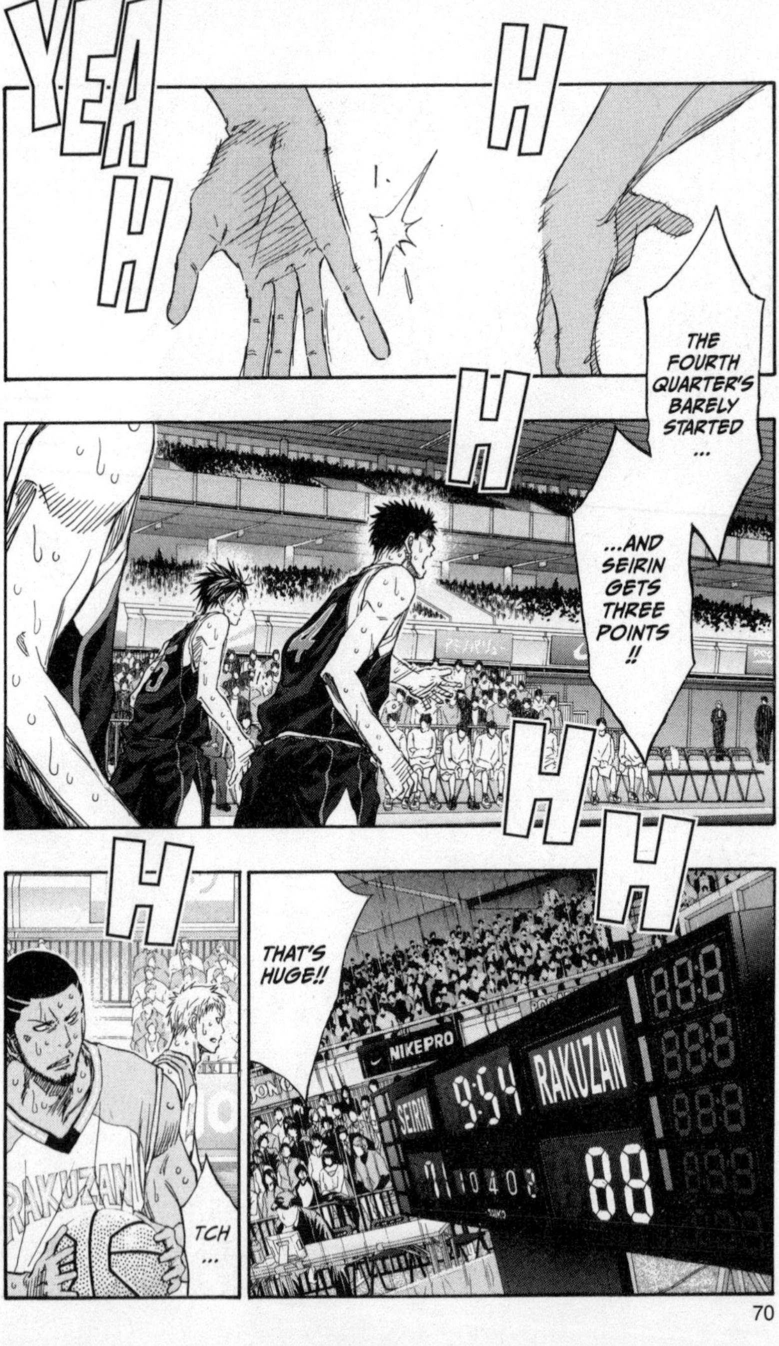
YEAHHHHHH
THE FOURTH QUARTER'S BARELY STARTED...
...AND SEIRIN GETS THREE POINTS!!
THAT'S HUGE!!
NIKEPRO
SEIRIN
9:54
RAKUZAN
TCH...

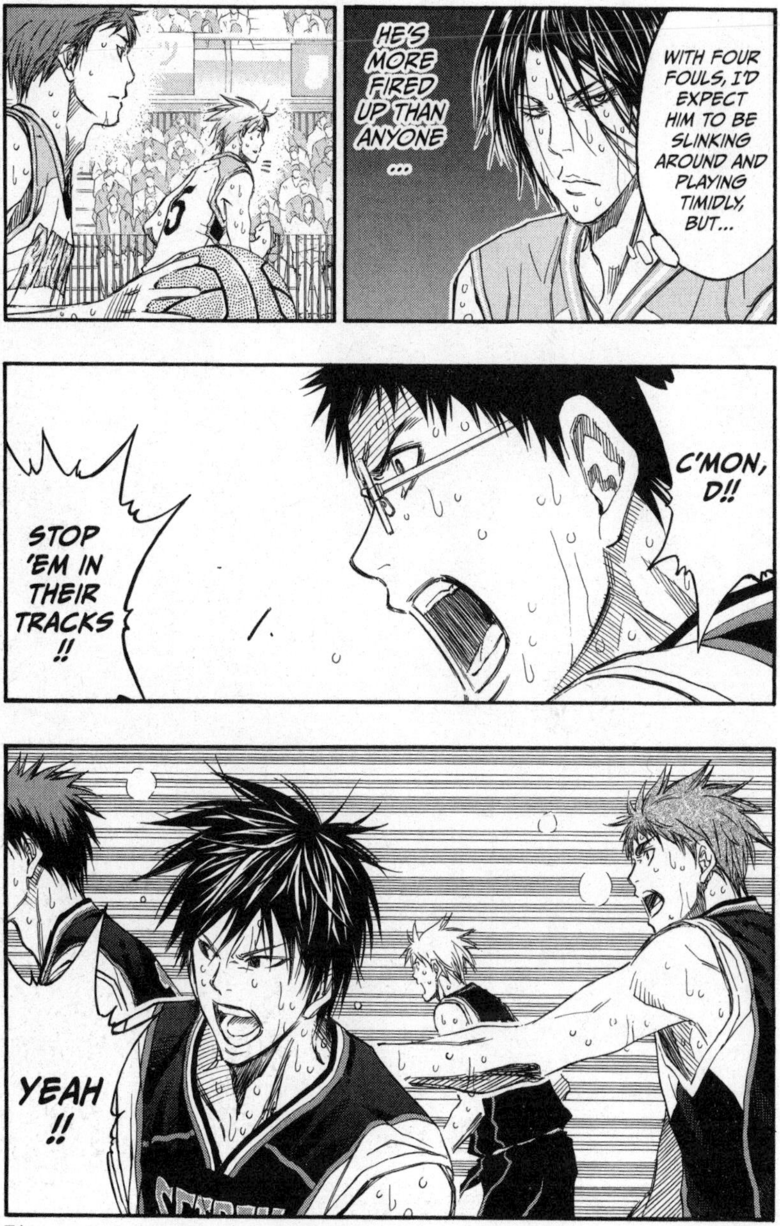
WITH FOUR FOULS, I'D EXPECT HIM TO BE SLINKING AROUND AND PLAYING TIMIDLY, BUT...
HE'S MORE FIRED UP THAN ANYONE ...
C'MON, D!!
STOP 'EM IN THEIR TRACKS!!
YEAH!!

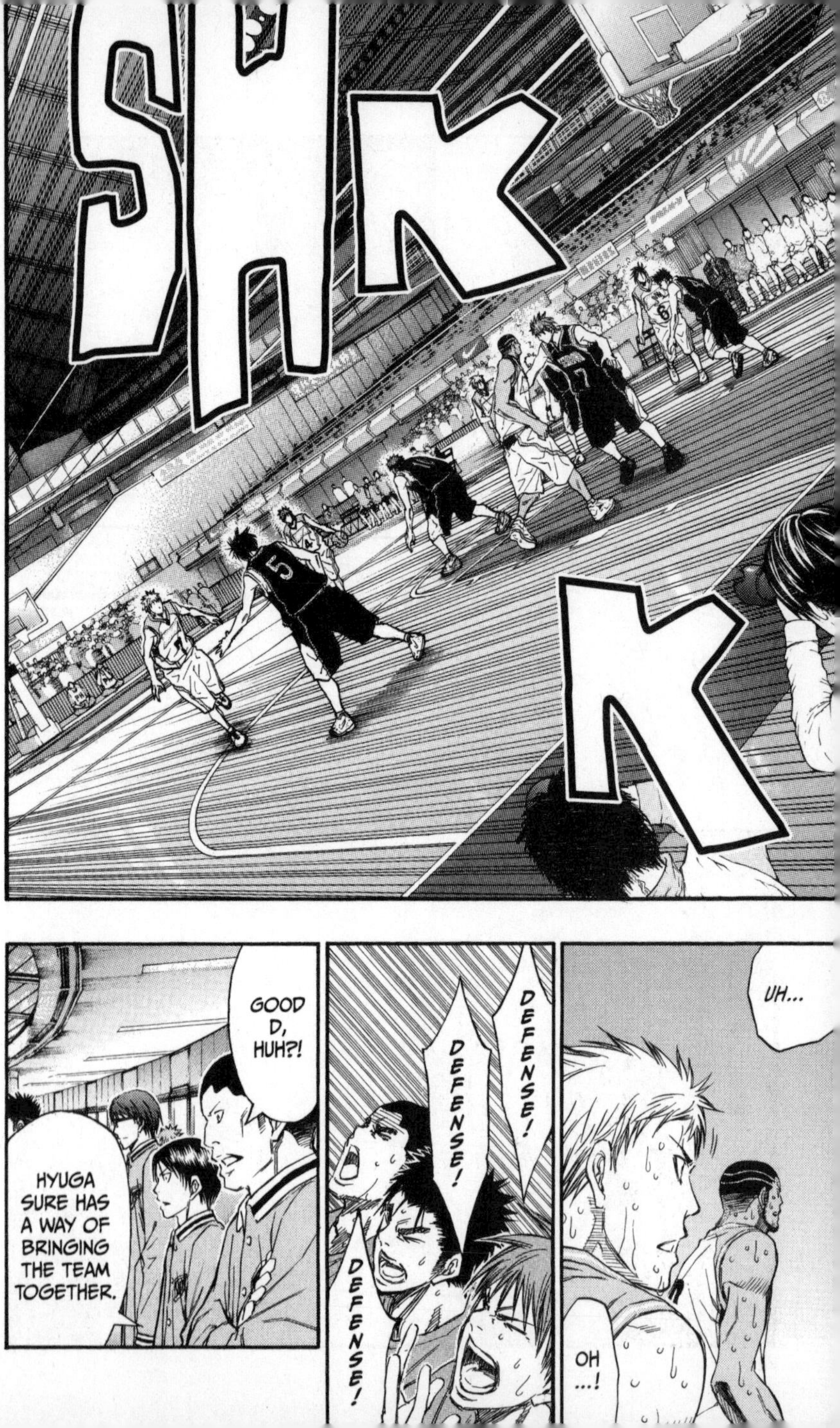
SHK
K
UH...
OH ...!
DEFENSE!
DEFENSE!
DEFENSE!
GOOD D, HUH?!
HYUGA SURE HAS A WAY OF BRINGING THE TEAM TOGETHER.

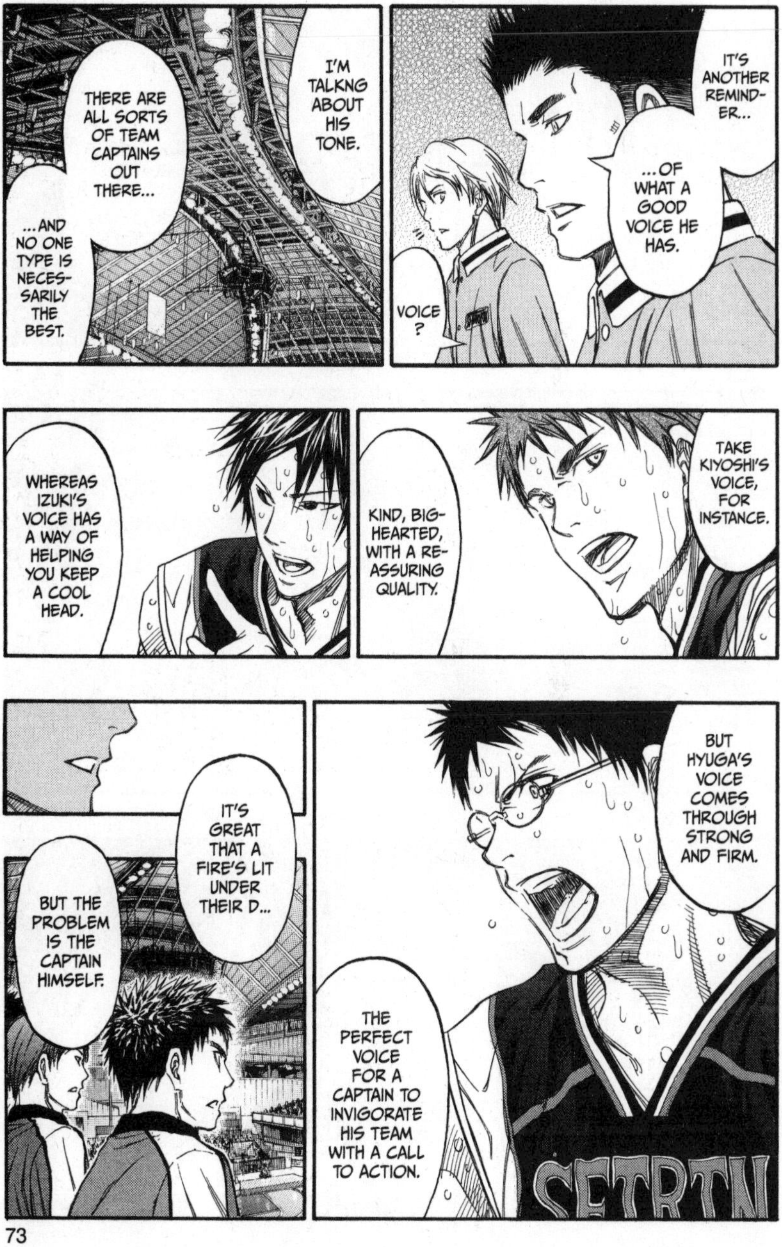
IT'S ANOTHER REMINDER...
...OF WHAT A GOOD VOICE HE HAS.
VOICE?
I'M TALKNG ABOUT HIS TONE.
THERE ARE ALL SORTS OF TEAM CAPTAINS OUT THERE...
...AND NO ONE TYPE IS NECESSARILY THE BEST.
TAKE KIYOSHI'S VOICE, FOR INSTANCE.
KIND, BIG-HEARTED, WITH A REASSURING QUALITY.
WHEREAS IZUKI'S VOICE HAS A WAY OF HELPING YOU KEEP A COOL HEAD.
BUT HYUGA'S VOICE COMES THROUGH STRONG AND FIRM.
THE PERFECT VOICE FOR A CAPTAIN TO INVIGORATE HIS TEAM WITH A CALL TO ACTION.
IT'S GREAT THAT A FIRE'S LIT UNDER THEIR D...
BUT THE PROBLEM IS THE CAPTAIN HIMSELF.

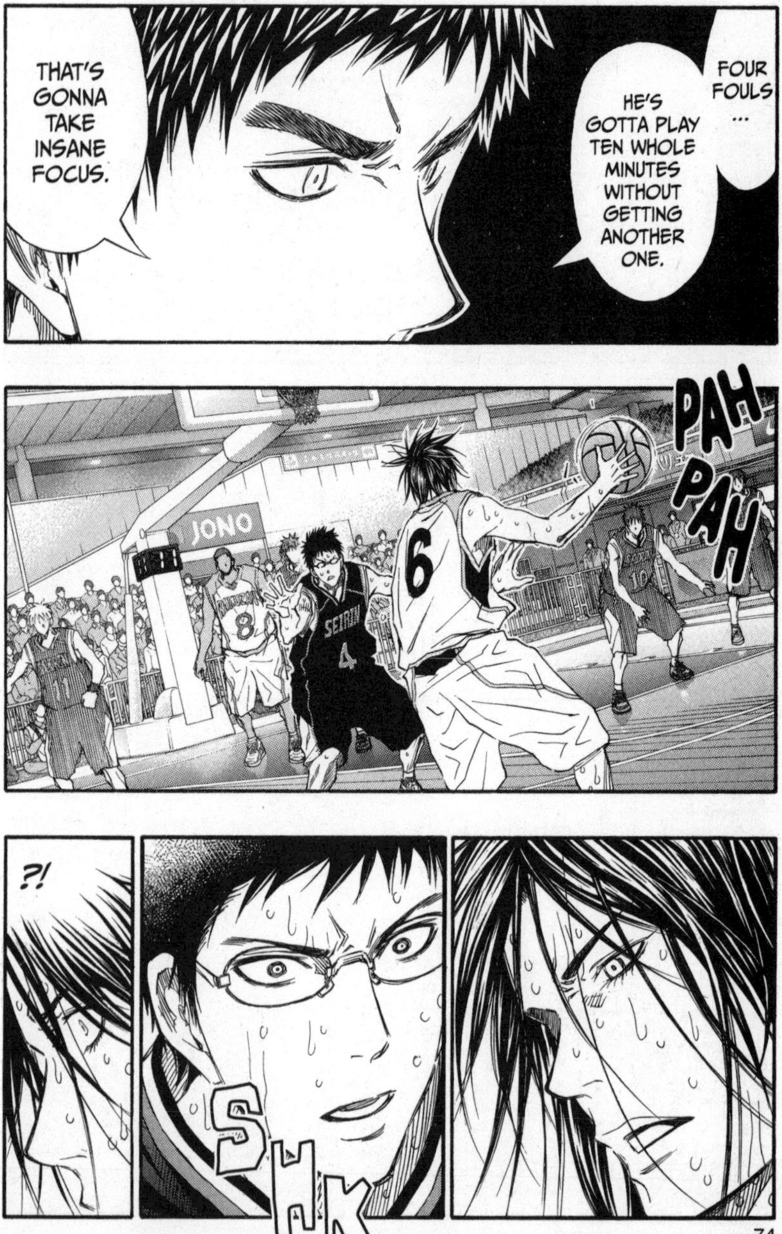
FOUR FOULS ...
HE'S GOTTA PLAY TEN WHOLE MINUTES WITHOUT GETTING ANOTHER ONE.
THAT'S GONNA TAKE INSANE FOCUS.
PAH PAH
JONO
?!
SHK

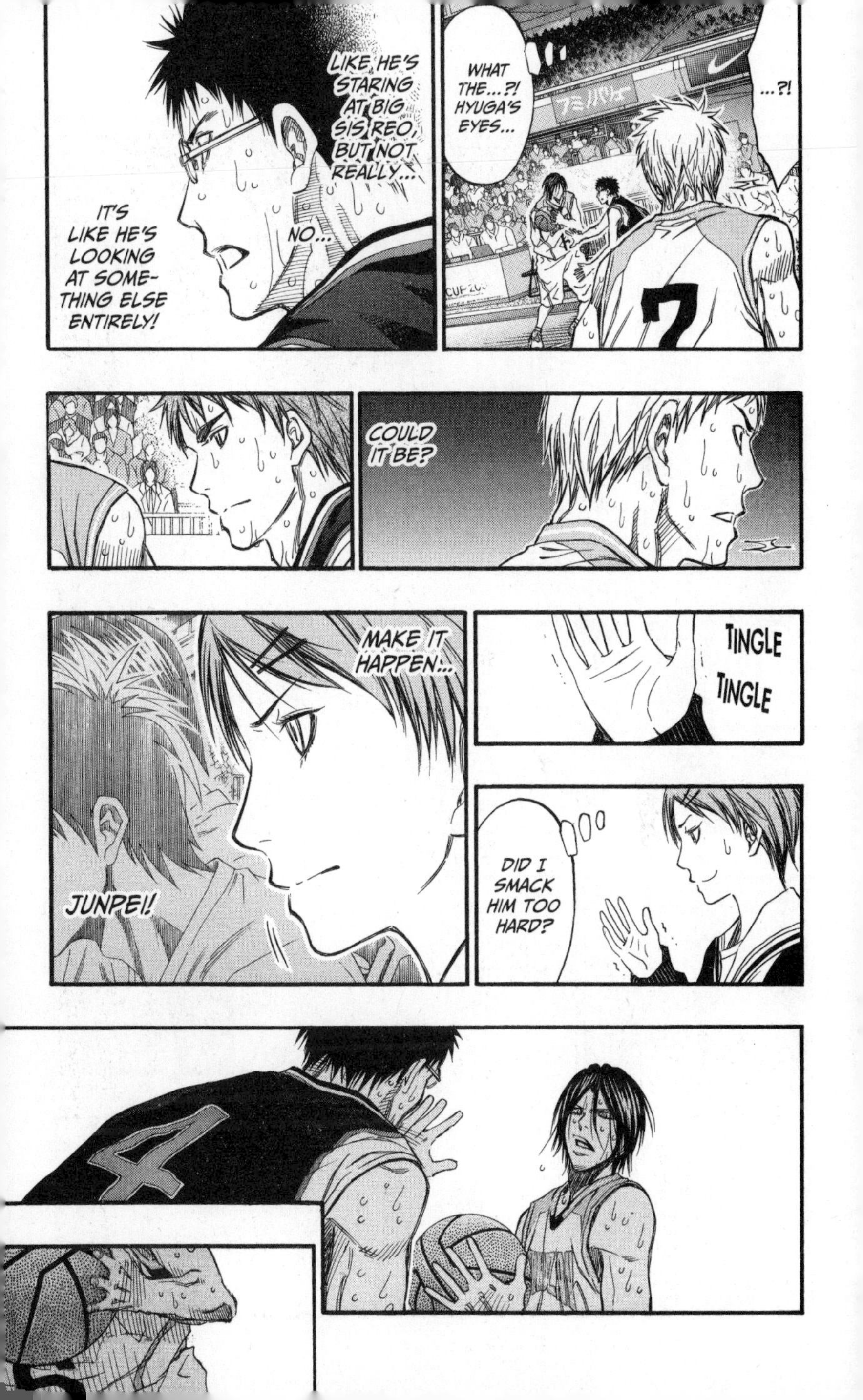
...?!
WHAT THE...?! HYUGA'S EYES...
LIKE HE'S STARING AT BIG SIS REO, BUT NOT REALLY...
NO...
IT'S LIKE HE'S LOOKING AT SOMETHING ELSE ENTIRELY!
COULD IT BE?
TINGLE
TINGLE
DID I SMACK HIM TOO HARD?
MAKE IT HAPPEN...
JUNPEI!

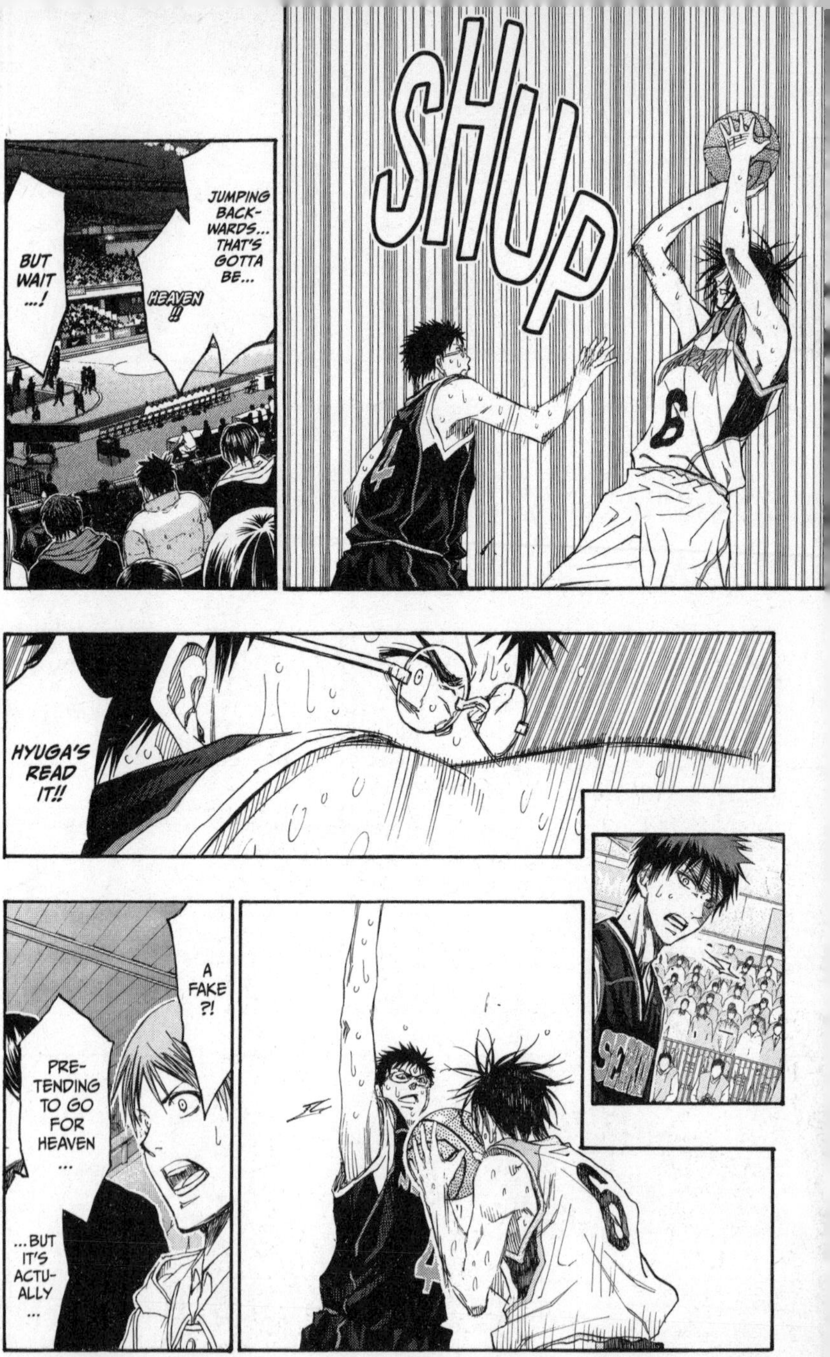
SHUP
JUMPING BACKWARDS... THAT'S GOTTA BE...
HEAVEN!!
BUT WAIT...!
HYUGA'S READ IT!!
A FAKE?!
PRETENDING TO GO FOR HEAVEN...
...BUT IT'S ACTUALLY...

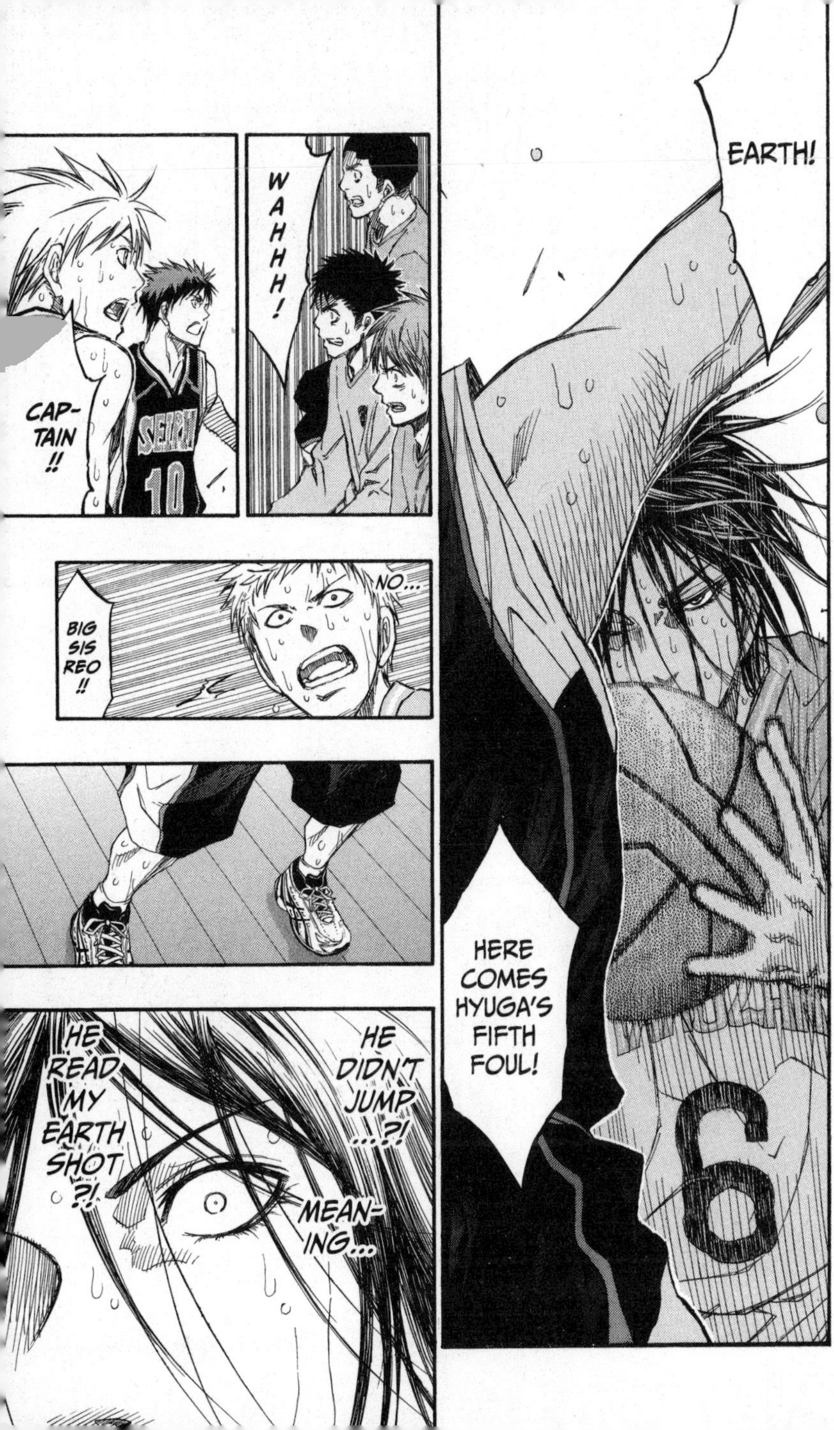
EARTH!
HERE COMES HYUGA'S FIFTH FOUL!
WAHHHH!
CAP-TAIN!!
NO...
BIG SIS REO!!
HE DIDN'T JUMP...?!
MEANING...
HE READ MY EARTH SHOT?!

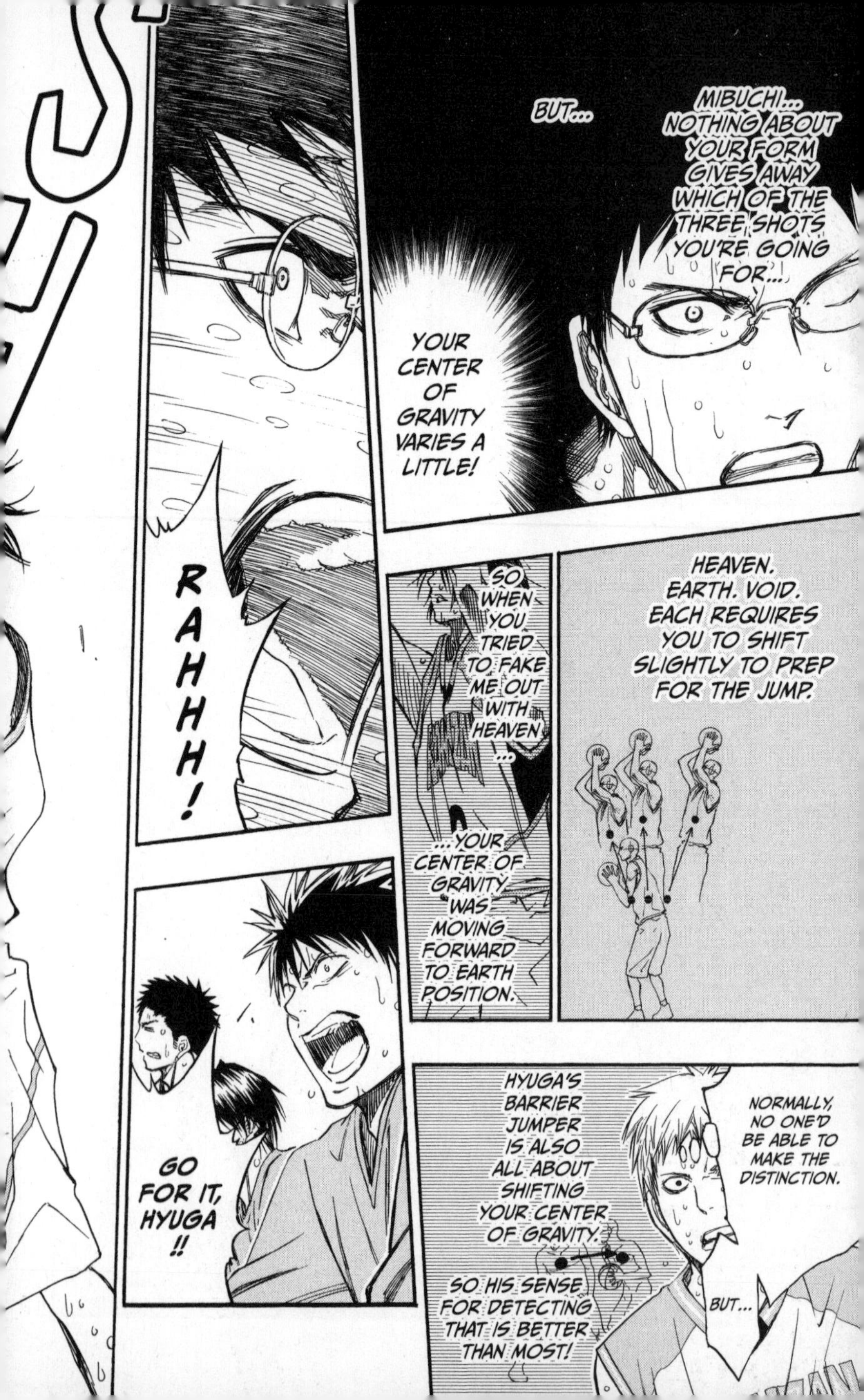
MIBUCHI... NOTHING ABOUT YOUR FORM GIVES AWAY WHICH OF THE THREE SHOTS YOU'RE GOING FOR...
BUT...
YOUR CENTER OF GRAVITY VARIES A LITTLE!
HEAVEN. EARTH. VOID. EACH REQUIRES YOU TO SHIFT SLIGHTLY TO PREP FOR THE JUMP.
SO WHEN YOU TRIED TO FAKE ME OUT WITH HEAVEN...
...YOUR CENTER OF GRAVITY WAS MOVING FORWARD TO EARTH POSITION.
RAHHHH!
NORMALLY, NO ONE'D BE ABLE TO MAKE THE DISTINCTION.
BUT...
HYUGA'S BARRIER JUMPER IS ALSO ALL ABOUT SHIFTING YOUR CENTER OF GRAVITY.
SO HIS SENSE FOR DETECTING THAT IS BETTER THAN MOST!
GO FOR IT, HYUGA!!

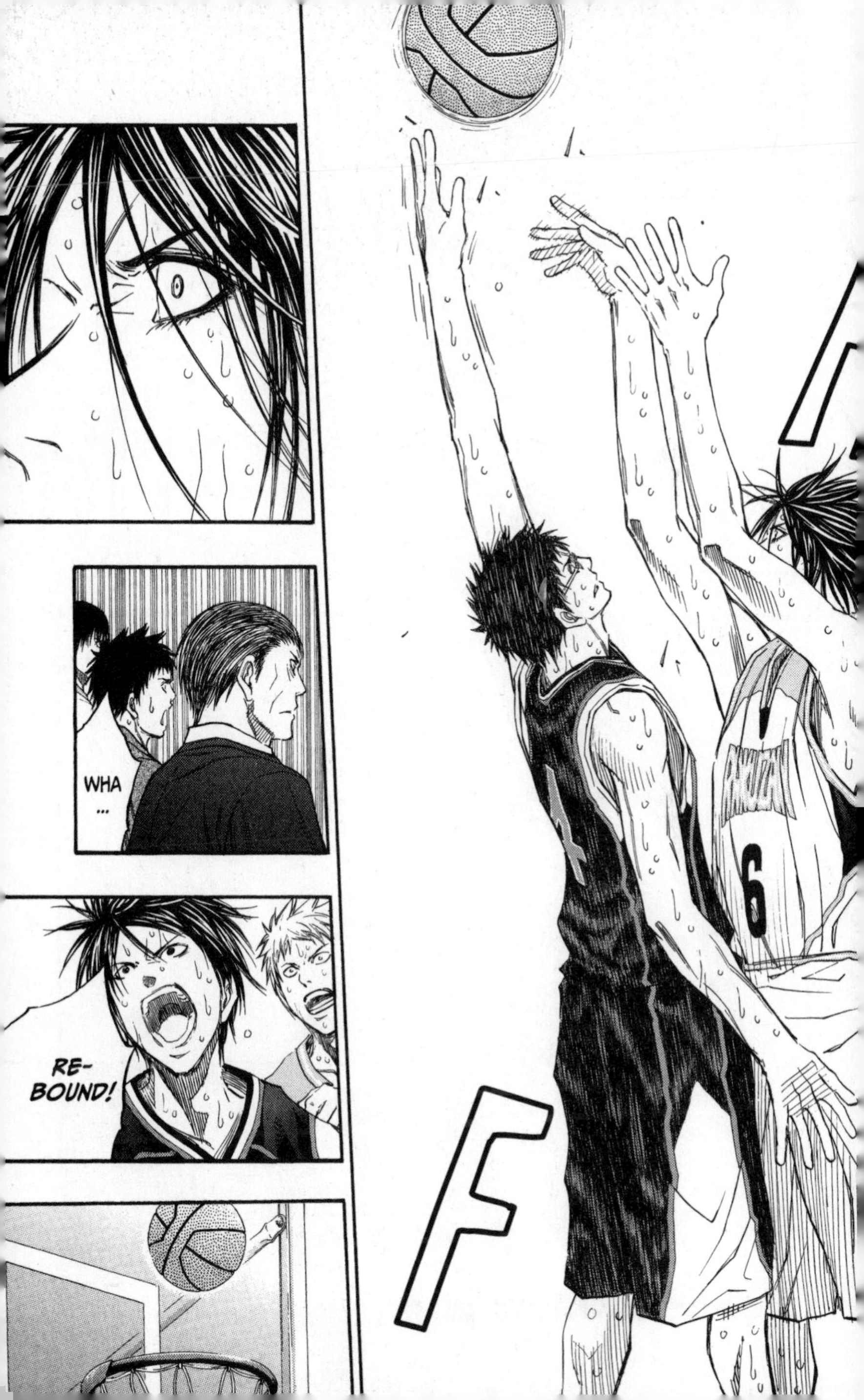
F
WHA
...
RE-
BOUND!

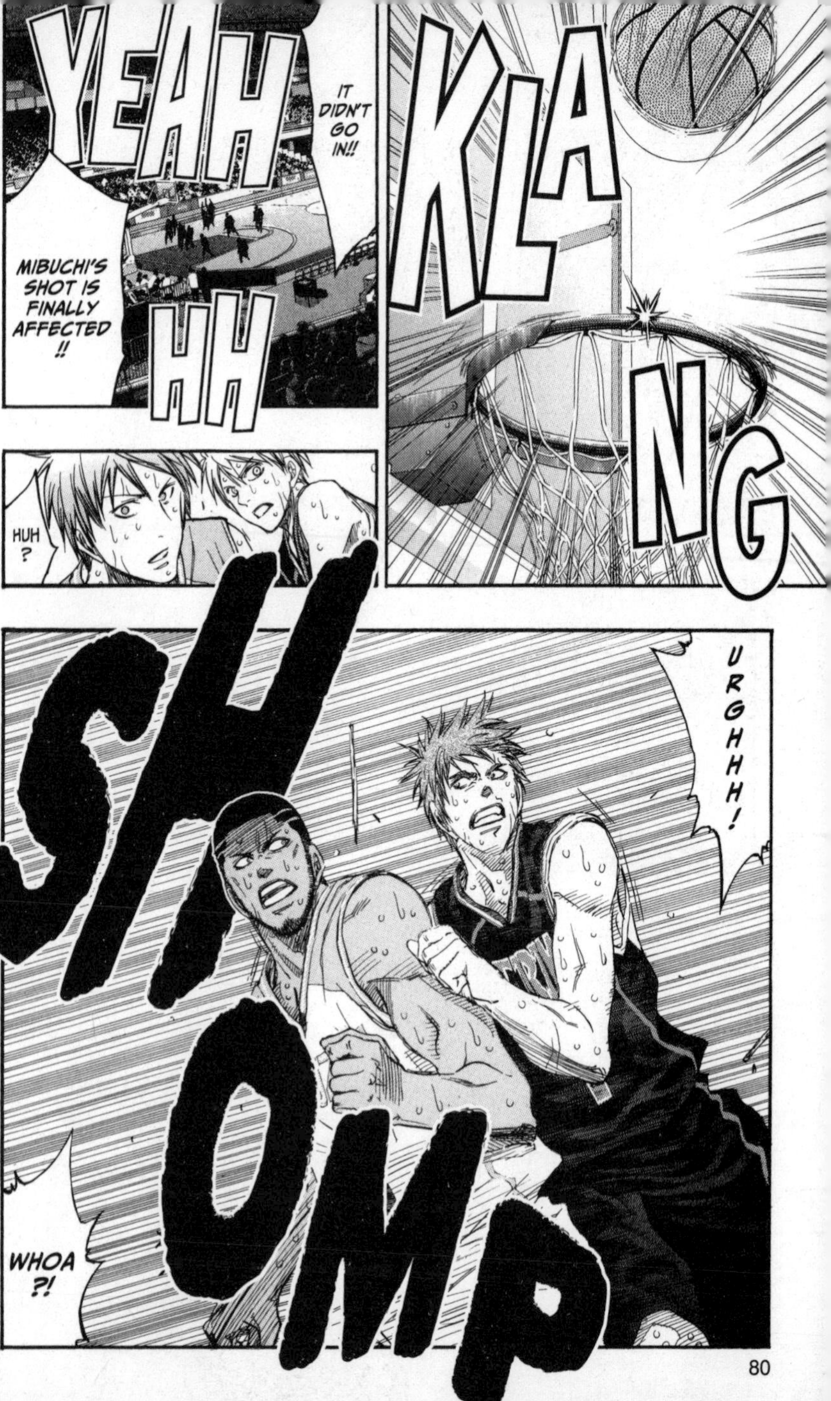
KLANG
YEAHHH
IT DIDN'T GO IN!!
MIBUCHI'S SHOT IS FINALLY AFFECTED!!
HUH?
URGHHH!
SHOMP
WHOA?!

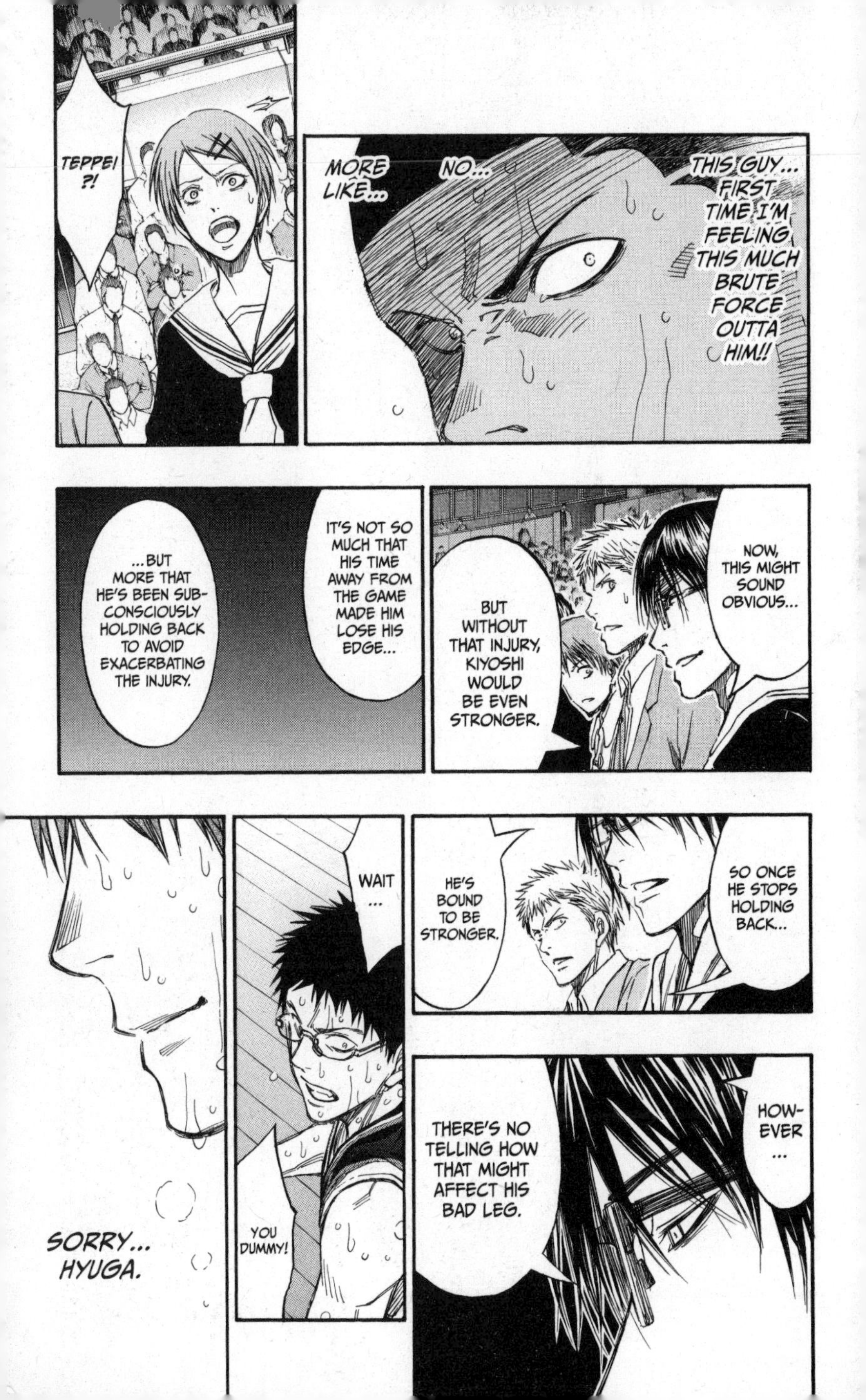
THIS GUY... FIRST TIME I'M FEELING THIS MUCH BRUTE FORCE OUTTA HIM!!
NO...
MORE LIKE...
TEPPEI ?!
NOW, THIS MIGHT SOUND OBVIOUS...
BUT WITHOUT THAT INJURY, KIYOSHI WOULD BE EVEN STRONGER.
IT'S NOT SO MUCH THAT HIS TIME AWAY FROM THE GAME MADE HIM LOSE HIS EDGE...
...BUT MORE THAT HE'S BEEN SUB-CONSCIOUSLY HOLDING BACK TO AVOID EXACERBATING THE INJURY.
SO ONCE HE STOPS HOLDING BACK...
HE'S BOUND TO BE STRONGER.
HOW-EVER...
THERE'S NO TELLING HOW THAT MIGHT AFFECT HIS BAD LEG.
WAIT...
YOU DUMMY!
SORRY... HYUGA.

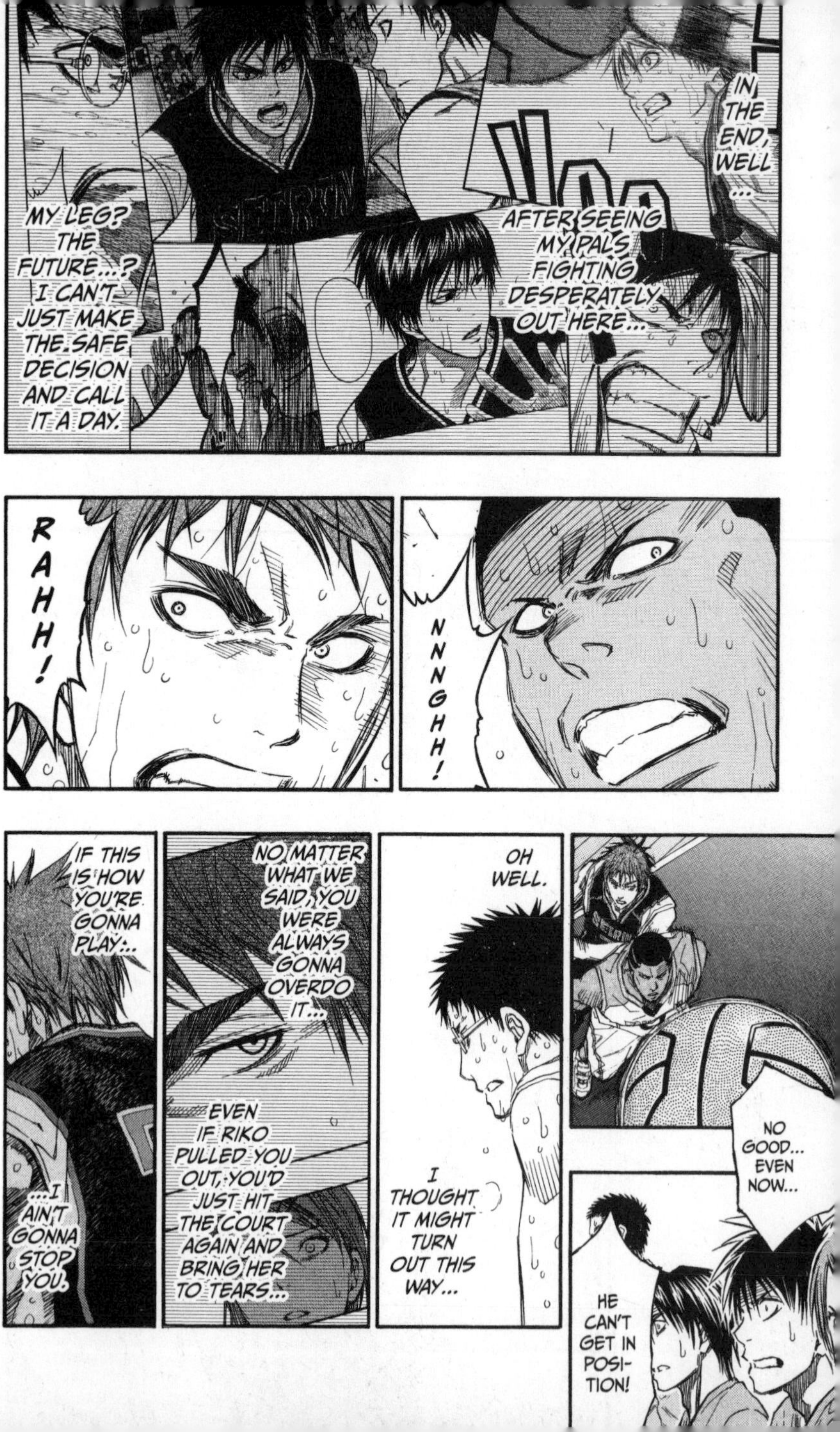

IN THE END, WELL...
AFTER SEEING MY PAL'S FIGHTING DESPERATELY OUT HERE...
MY LEG? THE FUTURE...? I CAN'T JUST MAKE THE SAFE DECISION AND CALL IT A DAY.
NNNGHH!
RAHHH!
NO GOOD... EVEN NOW...
HE CAN'T GET IN POSI-TION!
OH WELL.
I THOUGHT IT MIGHT TURN OUT THIS WAY...
NO MATTER WHAT WE SAID, YOU WERE ALWAYS GONNA OVERDO IT...
EVEN IF RIKO PULLED YOU OUT, YOU'D JUST HIT THE COURT AGAIN AND BRING HER TO TEARS...
IF THIS IS HOW YOU'RE GONNA PLAY...
...I AIN'T GONNA STOP YOU.

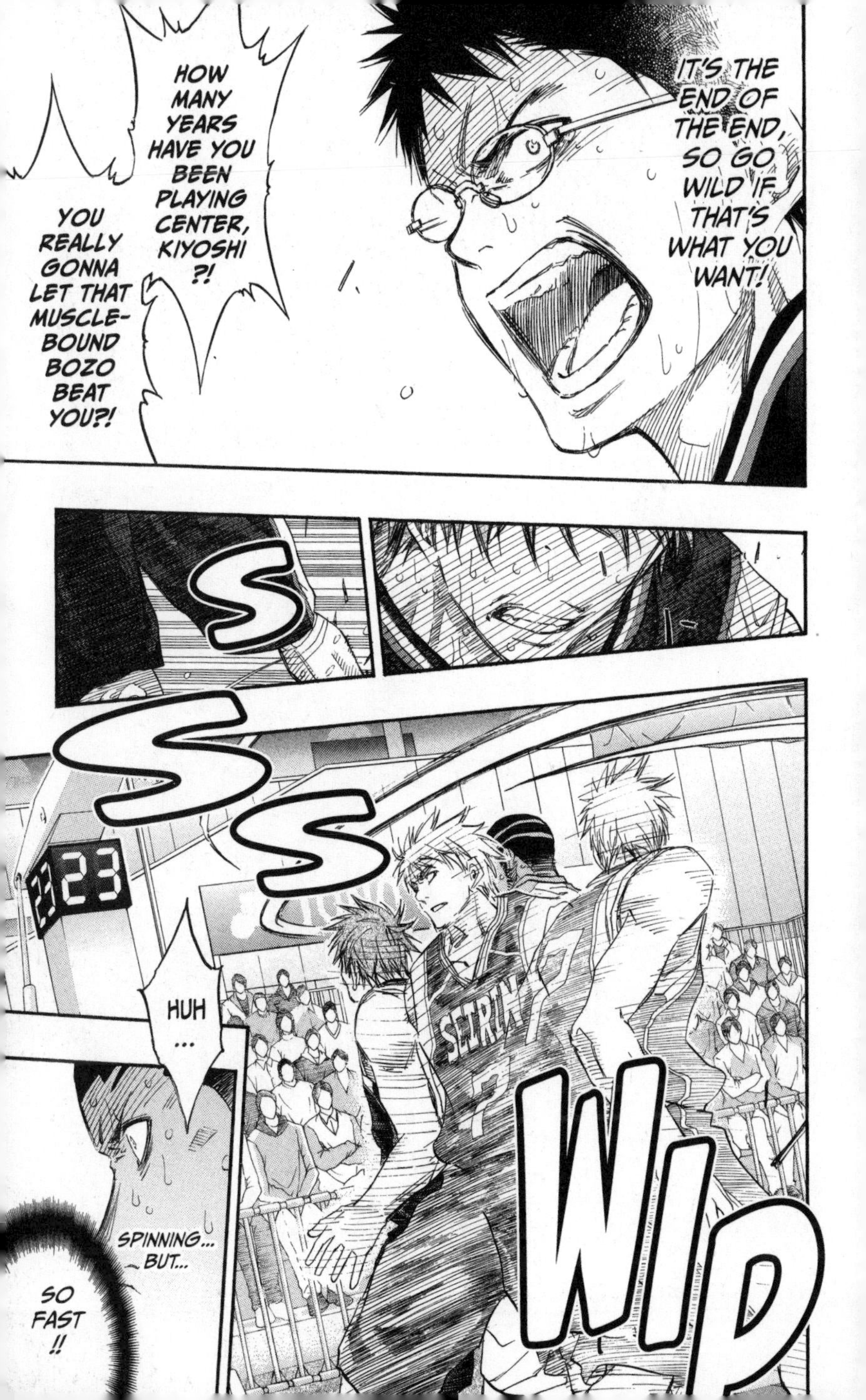
IT'S THE END OF THE END, SO GO WILD IF THAT'S WHAT YOU WANT!
HOW MANY YEARS HAVE YOU BEEN PLAYING CENTER, KIYOSHI ?!
YOU REALLY GONNA LET THAT MUSCLE-BOUND BOZO BEAT YOU?!
S
S
S
HUH ...
WIP
SPINNING... BUT...
SO FAST !!

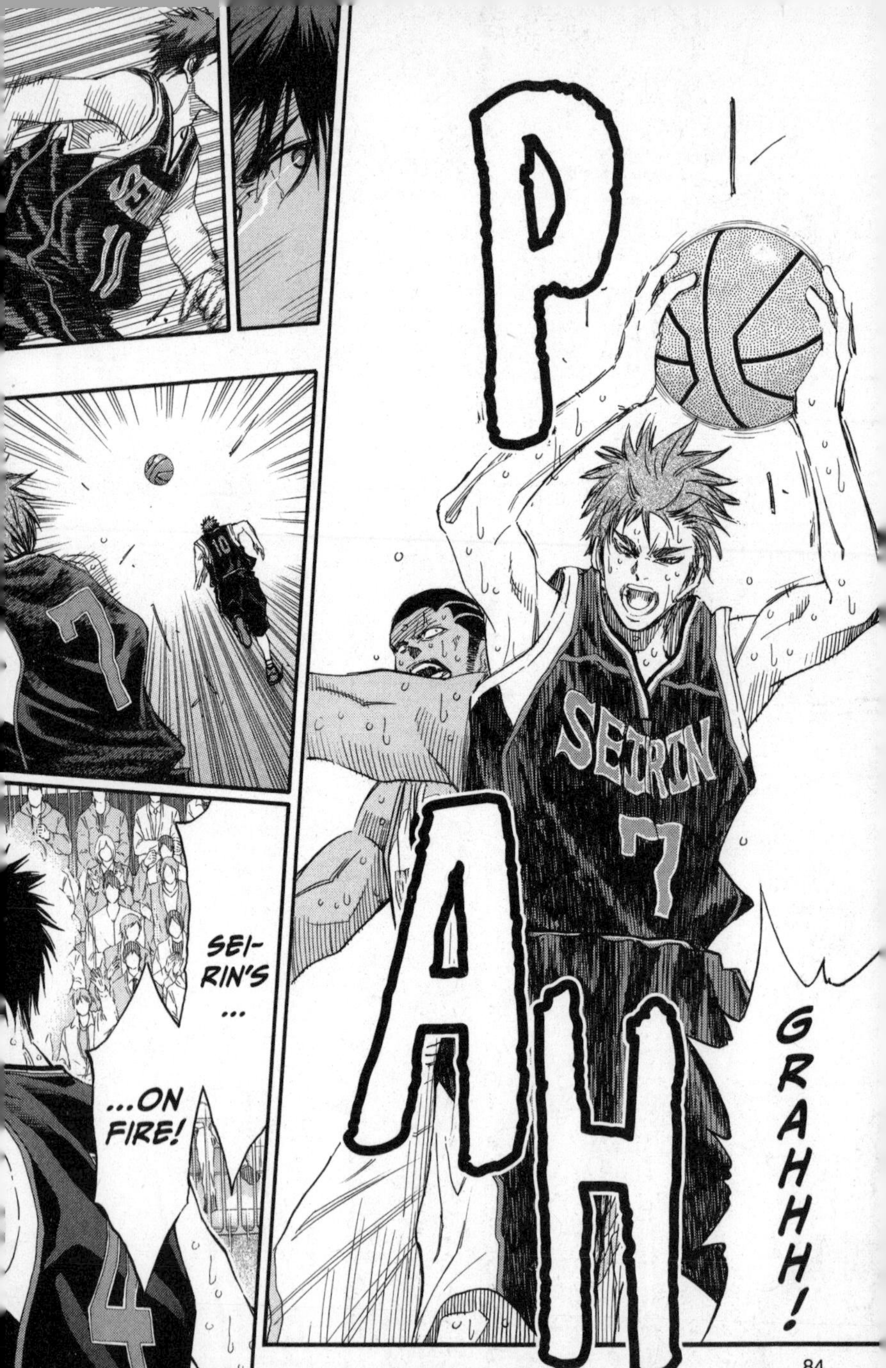
PAH
GRAHHH!
SEI-RIN'S...
...ON FIRE!

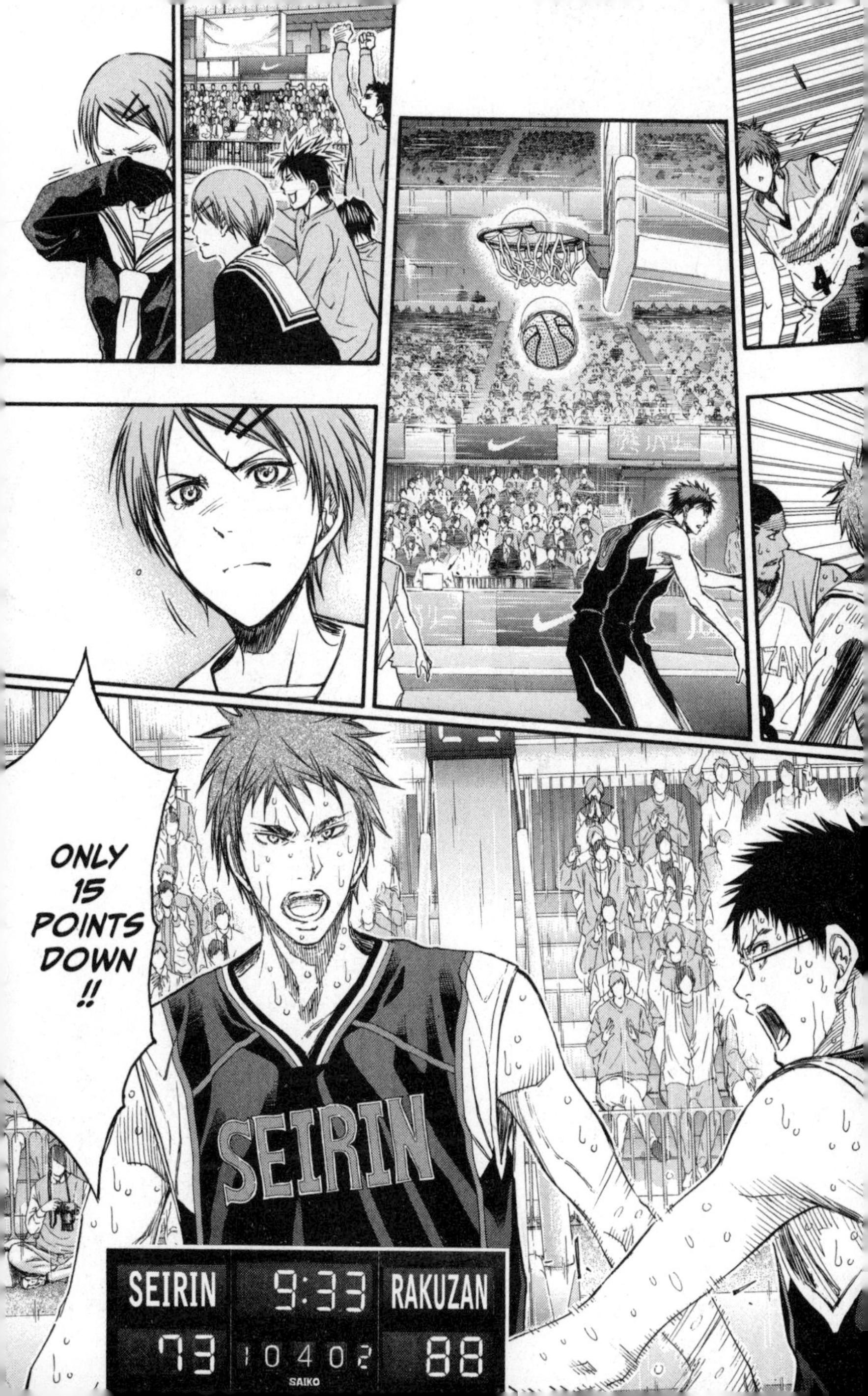
ONLY 15 POINTS DOWN !!
SEIRIN
SEIRIN 9:33 RAKUZAN
73 10402 88
SAIKO

KUROKO'S BASKETBALL
Q&A
W/ HALFWAY-DECENT ANSWERS

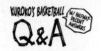

Q. WHEN KAGETORA CALLS SHUTOKU'S COACH "LITTLE MA" IN THE 115TH QUARTER, TAKAO SUGGESTS THAT THE BOYS TRY CALLING HIM THAT ONCE IN A WHILE. DID TAKAO EVER END UP DOING THAT?

(HEAD SCHOOL LUNCH OFFICIAL from FUKUOKA PREFECTURE)

A. HE DID. THE COACH CAUGHT HIM IN THE ACT AND TAKAO HAD TO RUN LAPS UNTIL HE PRACTICALLY DIED.

KUROKO'S BASKETBALL BLOOPERS
TAKE 1

IT'S ANOTHER REMINDER...
...OF WHAT A GOOD VOICE HE HAS.
VOICE?
I'M TALKNG ABOUT HIS TONE.
THERE ARE ALL SORTS OF TEAM CAPTAINS OUT THERE...
...AND NO ONE TYPE IS NECESSARILY THE BEST.
OTSUBO...
THAT'S A WEIRD THING TO FOCUS ON.
PRAISING A DUDE'S VOICE...
...

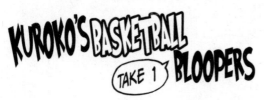

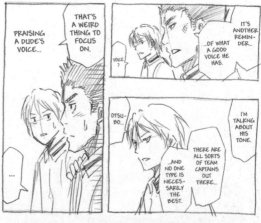

259TH QUARTER: THE ONE THING I'LL STOP!!

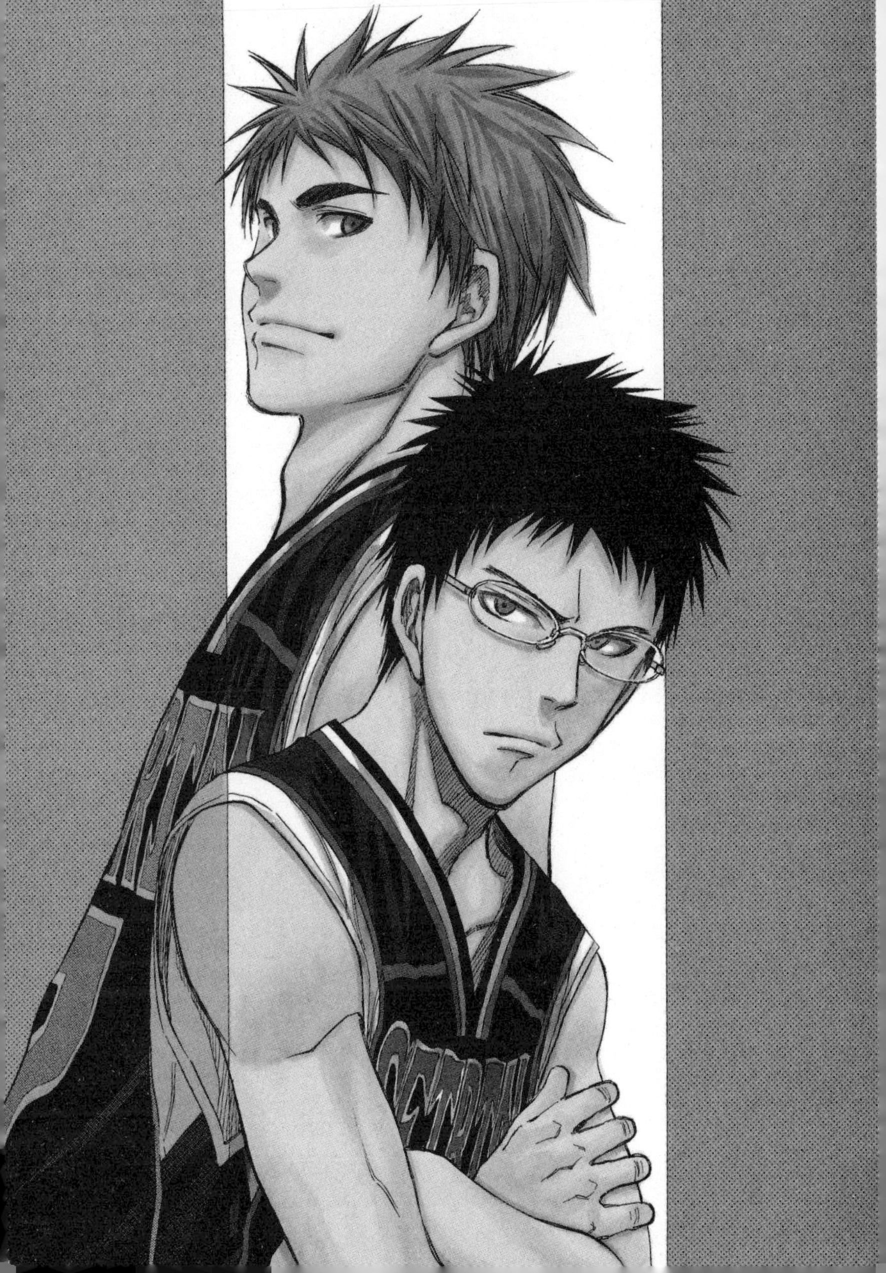

Kuroko's
BASKETBALL

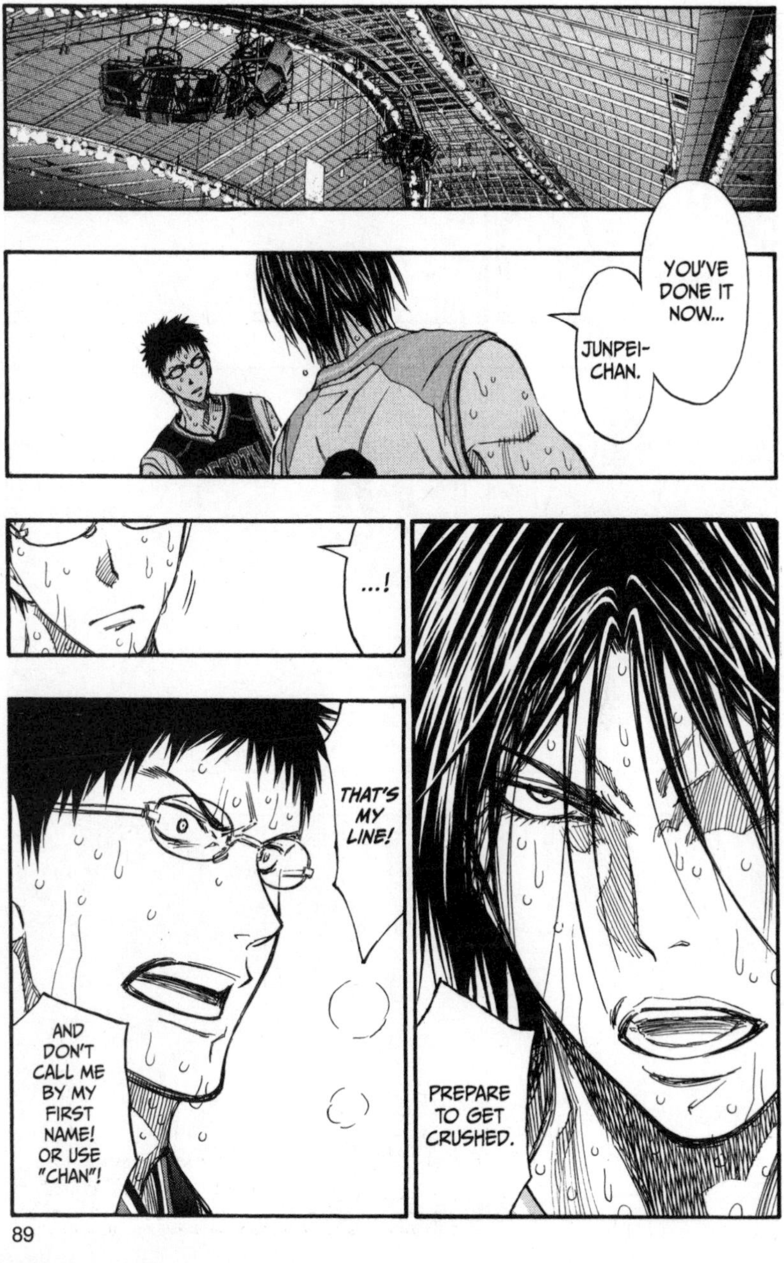
YOU'VE DONE IT NOW... JUNPEI-CHAN.
PREPARE TO GET CRUSHED.
...!
THAT'S MY LINE!
AND DON'T CALL ME BY MY FIRST NAME! OR USE "CHAN"!

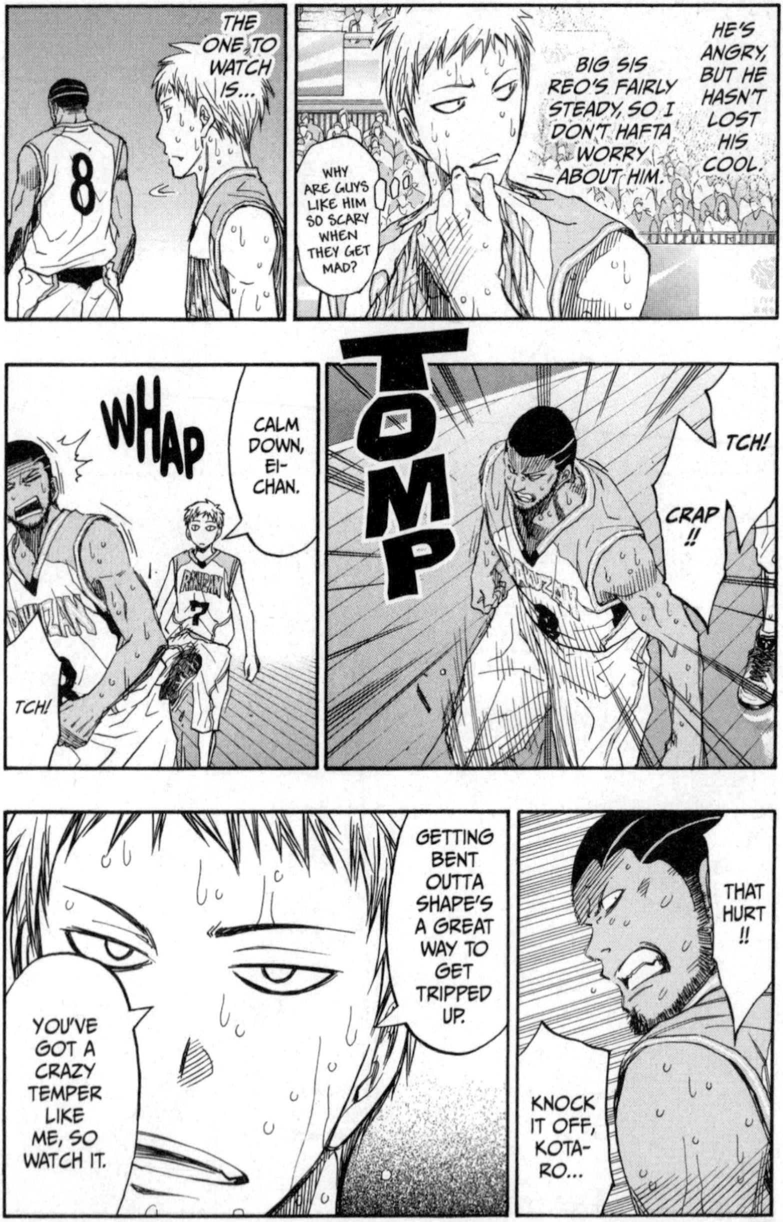
HE'S ANGRY, BUT HE HASN'T LOST HIS COOL.
BIG SIS REO'S FAIRLY STEADY, SO I DON'T HAFTA WORRY ABOUT HIM.
WHY ARE GUYS LIKE HIM SO SCARY WHEN THEY GET MAD?
THE ONE TO WATCH IS...
TOMP
TCH!
CRAP!!
CALM DOWN, EI-CHAN.
WHAP
TCH!
THAT HURT!!
KNOCK IT OFF, KOTARO...
GETTING BENT OUTTA SHAPE'S A GREAT WAY TO GET TRIPPED UP.
YOU'VE GOT A CRAZY TEMPER LIKE ME, SO WATCH IT.

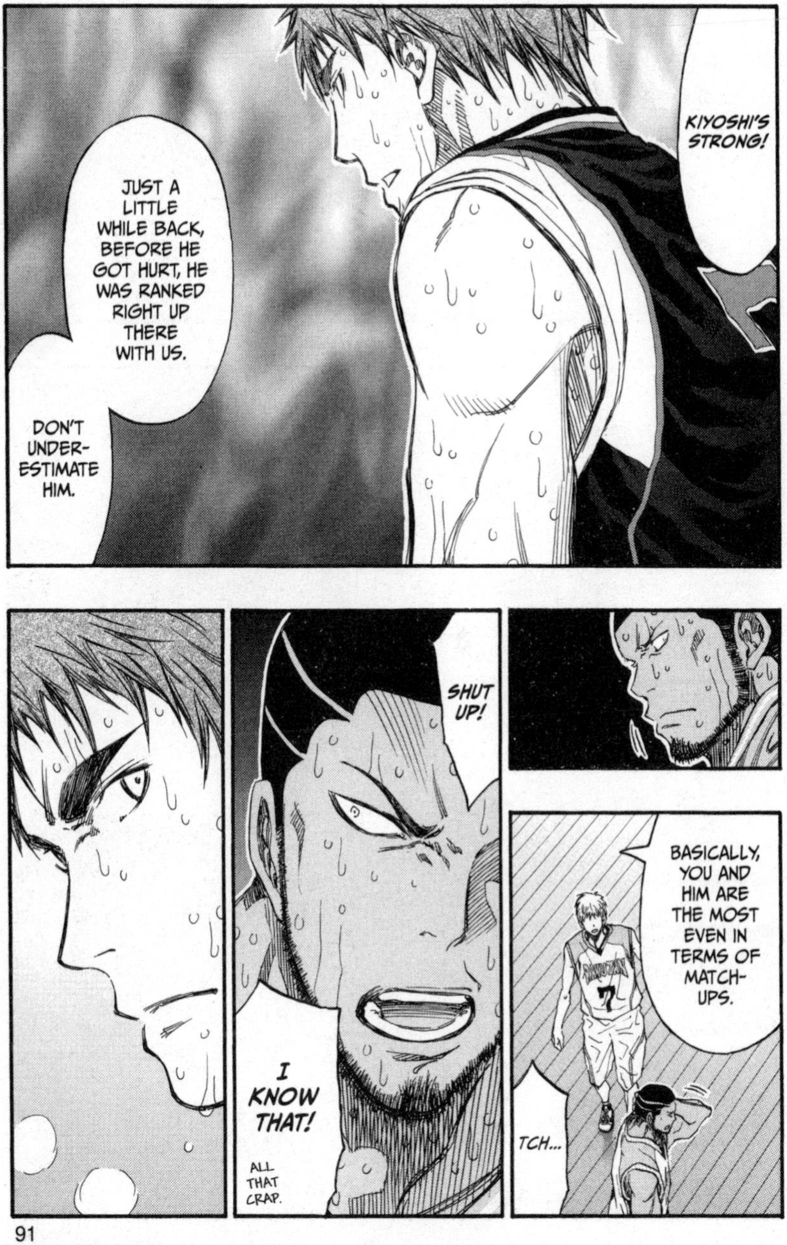
KIYOSHI'S STRONG!
JUST A LITTLE WHILE BACK, BEFORE HE GOT HURT, HE WAS RANKED RIGHT UP THERE WITH US.
DON'T UNDER-ESTIMATE HIM.
BASICALLY, YOU AND HIM ARE THE MOST EVEN IN TERMS OF MATCH-UPS.
TCH...
SHUT UP!
I KNOW THAT!
ALL THAT CRAP.

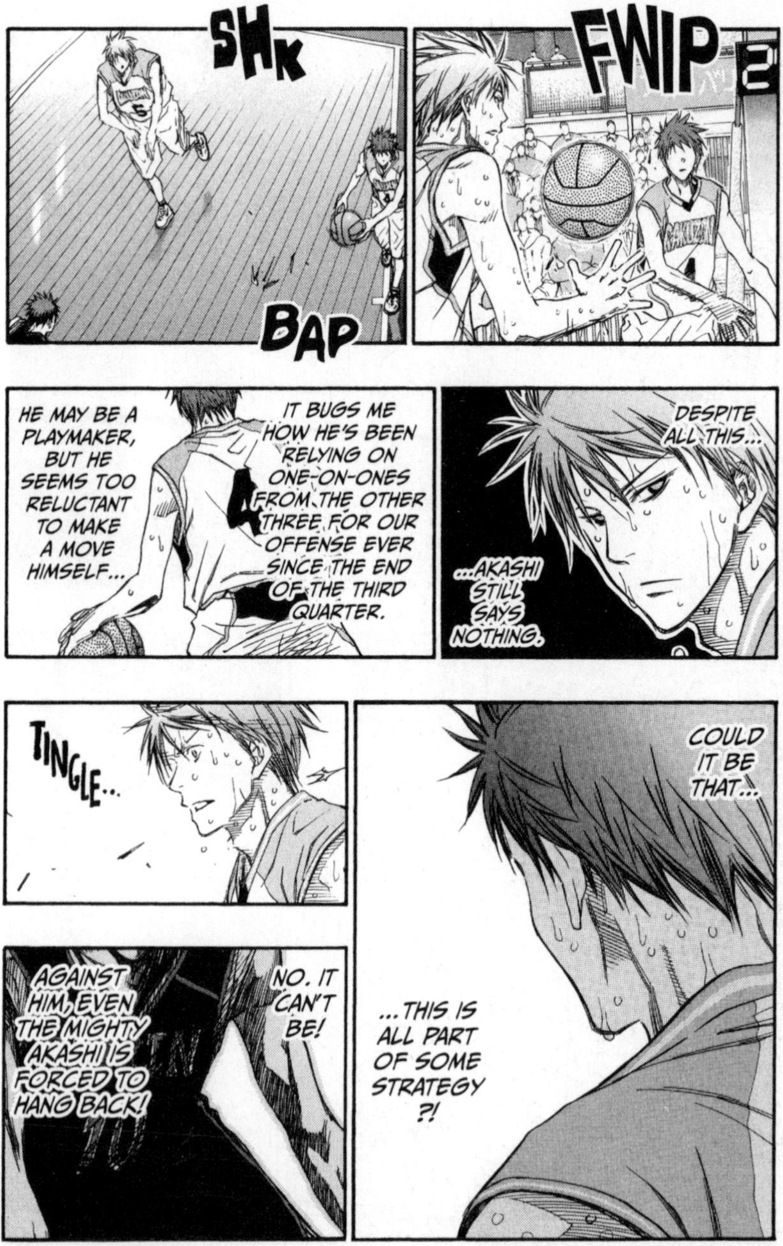
FWIP
SHK
BAP
DESPITE ALL THIS...
...AKASHI STILL SAYS NOTHING.
IT BUGS ME HOW HE'S BEEN RELYING ON ONE-ON-ONES FROM THE OTHER THREE FOR OUR OFFENSE EVER SINCE THE END OF THE THIRD QUARTER.
HE MAY BE A PLAYMAKER, BUT HE SEEMS TOO RELUCTANT TO MAKE A MOVE HIMSELF...
COULD IT BE THAT...
...THIS IS ALL PART OF SOME STRATEGY?!
TINGLE...
NO. IT CAN'T BE!
AGAINST HIM, EVEN THE MIGHTY AKASHI IS FORCED TO HANG BACK!

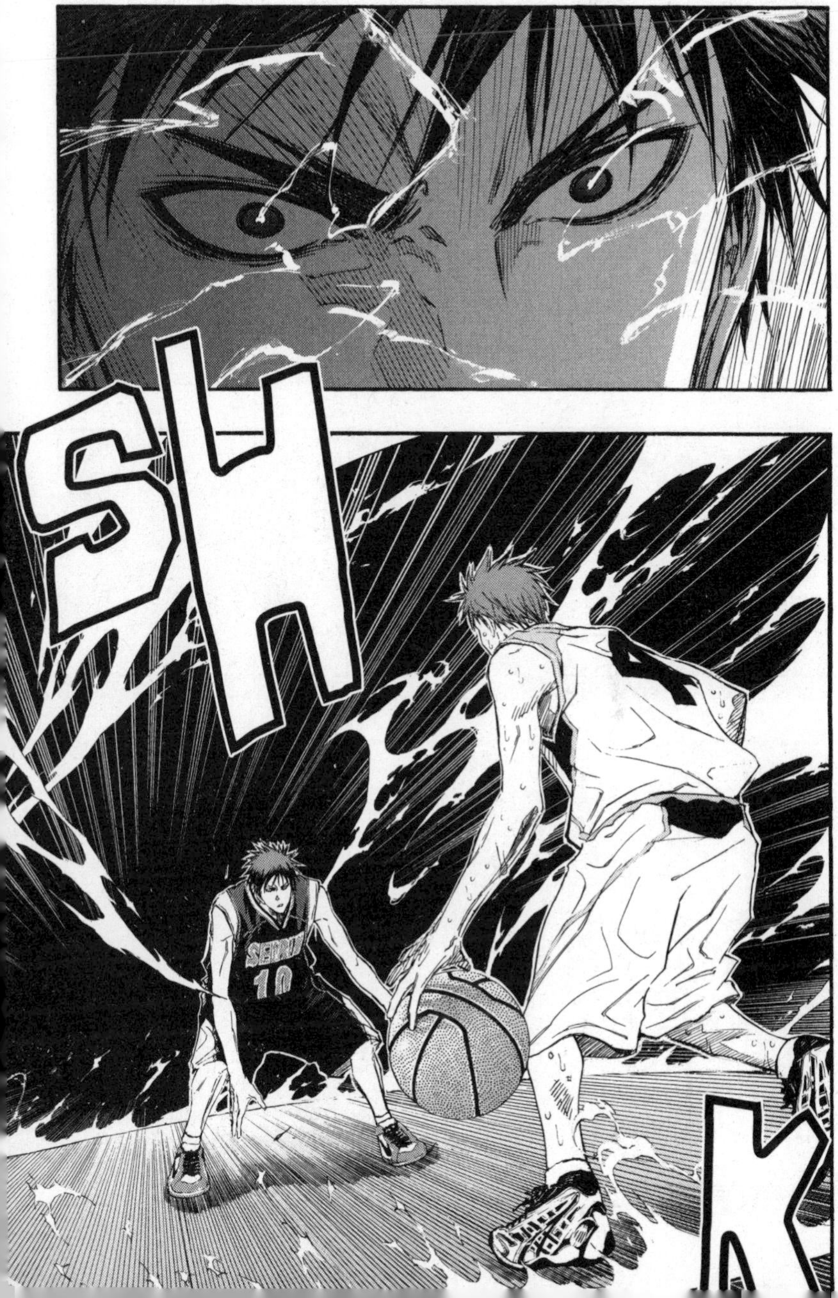
SHK

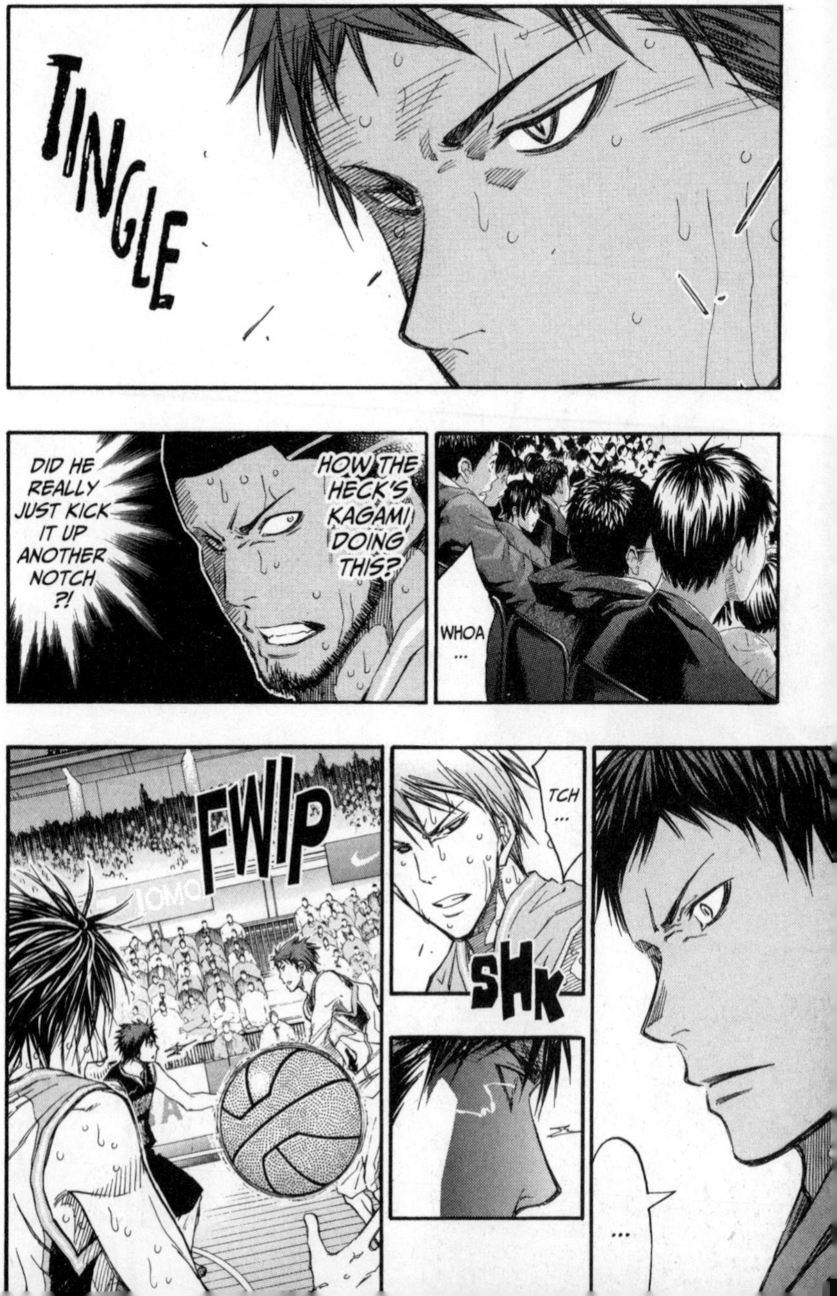
TINGLE
WHOA ...
HOW THE HECK'S KAGAMI DOING THIS?
DID HE REALLY JUST KICK IT UP ANOTHER NOTCH ?!
...
TCH ...
SHK
FWIP

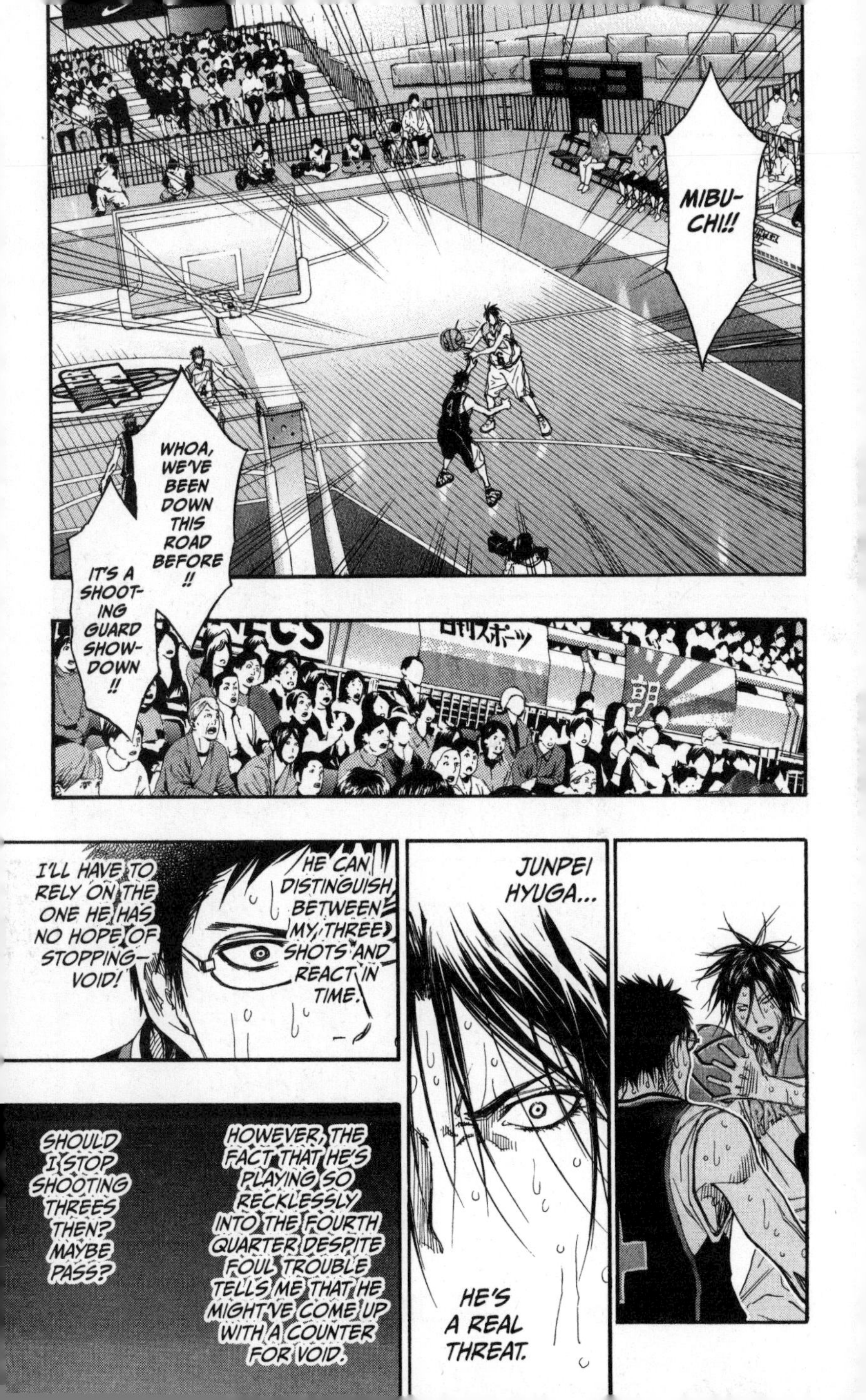
MIBU-CHI!!
WHOA, WE'VE BEEN DOWN THIS ROAD BEFORE!!
IT'S A SHOOTING GUARD SHOWDOWN!!
日刊スポーツ
JUNPEI HYUGA...
HE'S A REAL THREAT.
HE CAN DISTINGUISH BETWEEN MY THREE SHOTS AND REACT IN TIME.
I'LL HAVE TO RELY ON THE ONE HE HAS NO HOPE OF STOPPING—VOID!
HOWEVER, THE FACT THAT HE'S PLAYING SO RECKLESSLY INTO THE FOURTH QUARTER DESPITE FOUL TROUBLE TELLS ME THAT HE MIGHT'VE COME UP WITH A COUNTER FOR VOID.
SHOULD I STOP SHOOTING THREES THEN? MAYBE PASS?

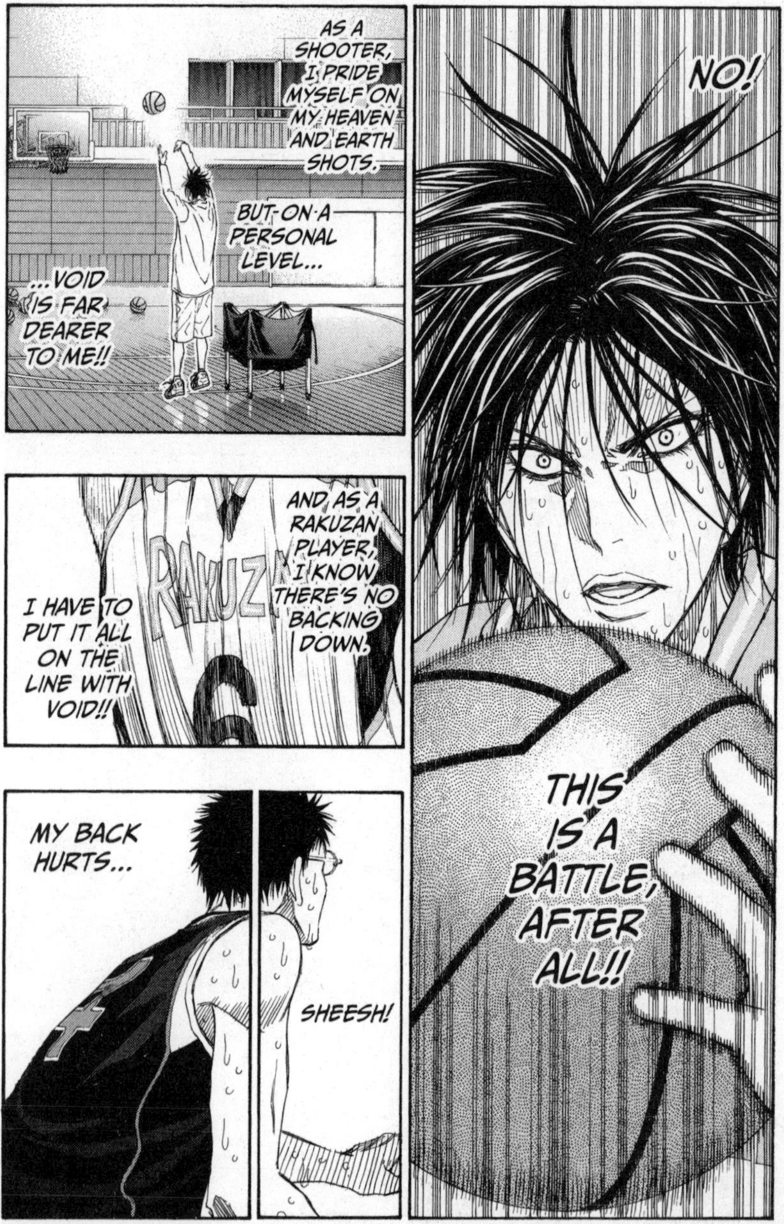
NO!
THIS IS A BATTLE, AFTER ALL!!
AS A SHOOTER, I PRIDE MYSELF ON MY HEAVEN AND EARTH SHOTS.
BUT ON A PERSONAL LEVEL...
...VOID IS FAR DEARER TO ME!!
AND AS A RAKUZAN PLAYER, I KNOW THERE'S NO BACKING DOWN.
I HAVE TO PUT IT ALL ON THE LINE WITH VOID!!
SHEESH!
MY BACK HURTS...

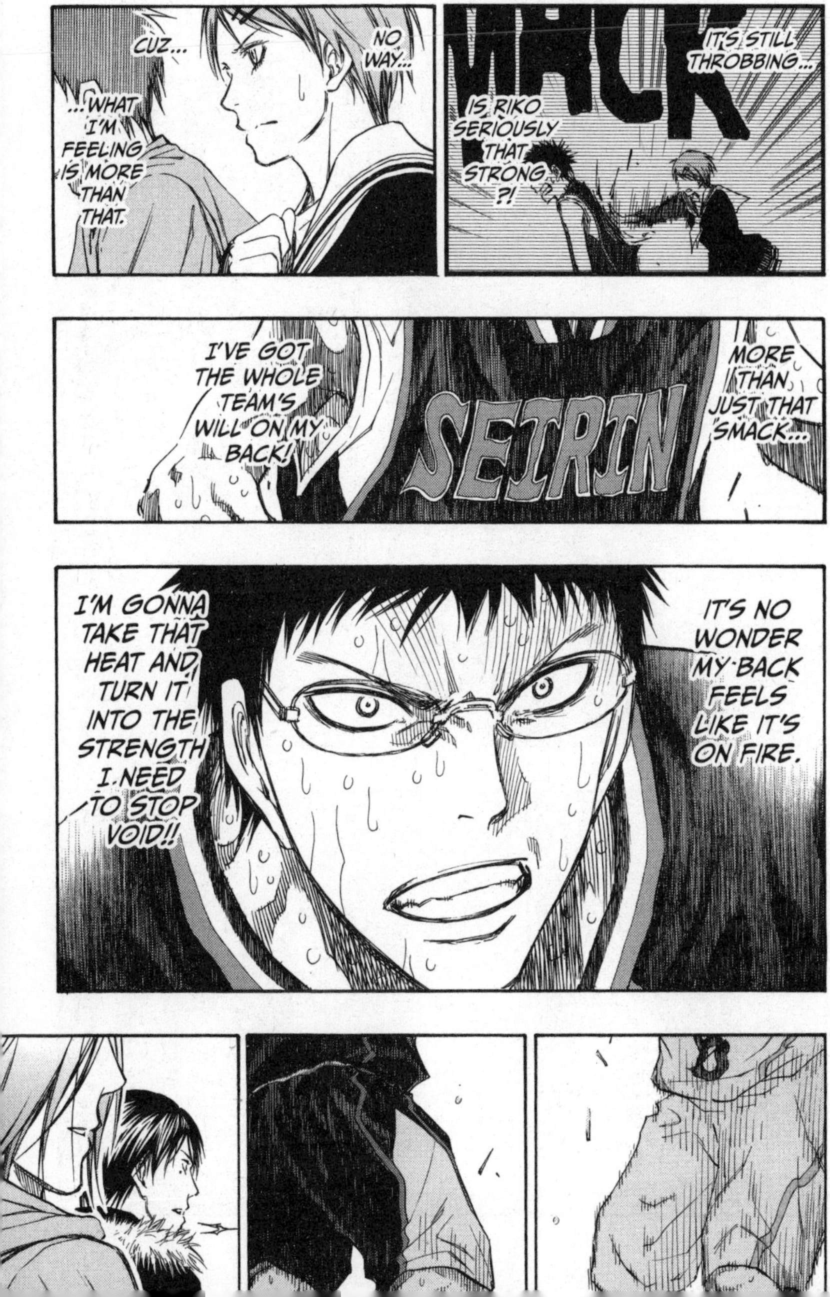
IT'S STILL THROBBING...
IS RIKO SERIOUSLY THAT STRONG?!
NO WAY...
CUZ...
...WHAT I'M FEELING IS MORE THAN THAT.
MORE THAN JUST THAT SMACK...
SEIRIN
I'VE GOT THE WHOLE TEAM'S WILL ON MY BACK!
IT'S NO WONDER MY BACK FEELS LIKE IT'S ON FIRE.
I'M GONNA TAKE THAT HEAT AND TURN IT INTO THE STRENGTH I NEED TO STOP VOID!!

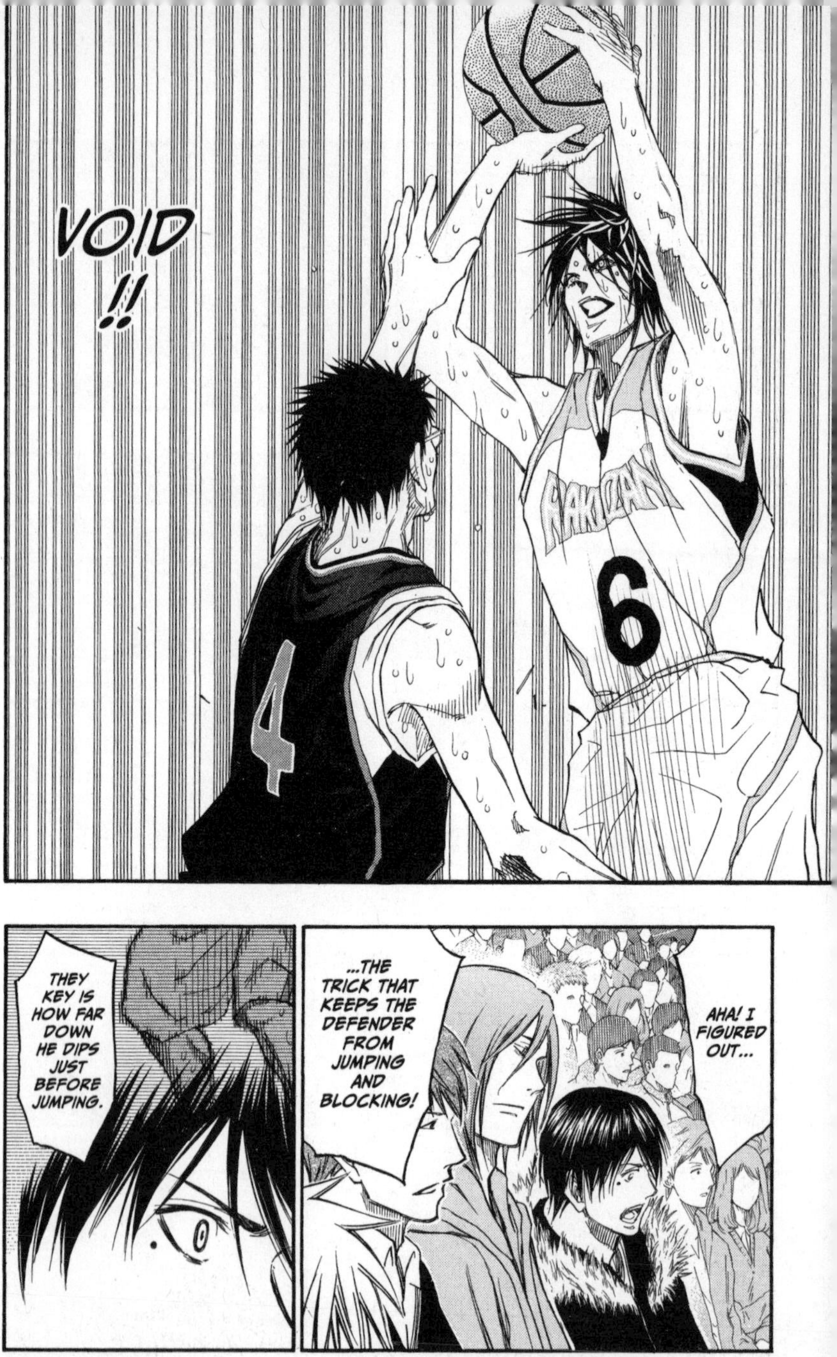
VOID!!
AHA! I FIGURED OUT...
...THE TRICK THAT KEEPS THE DEFENDER FROM JUMPING AND BLOCKING!
THEY KEY IS HOW FAR DOWN HE DIPS JUST BEFORE JUMPING.

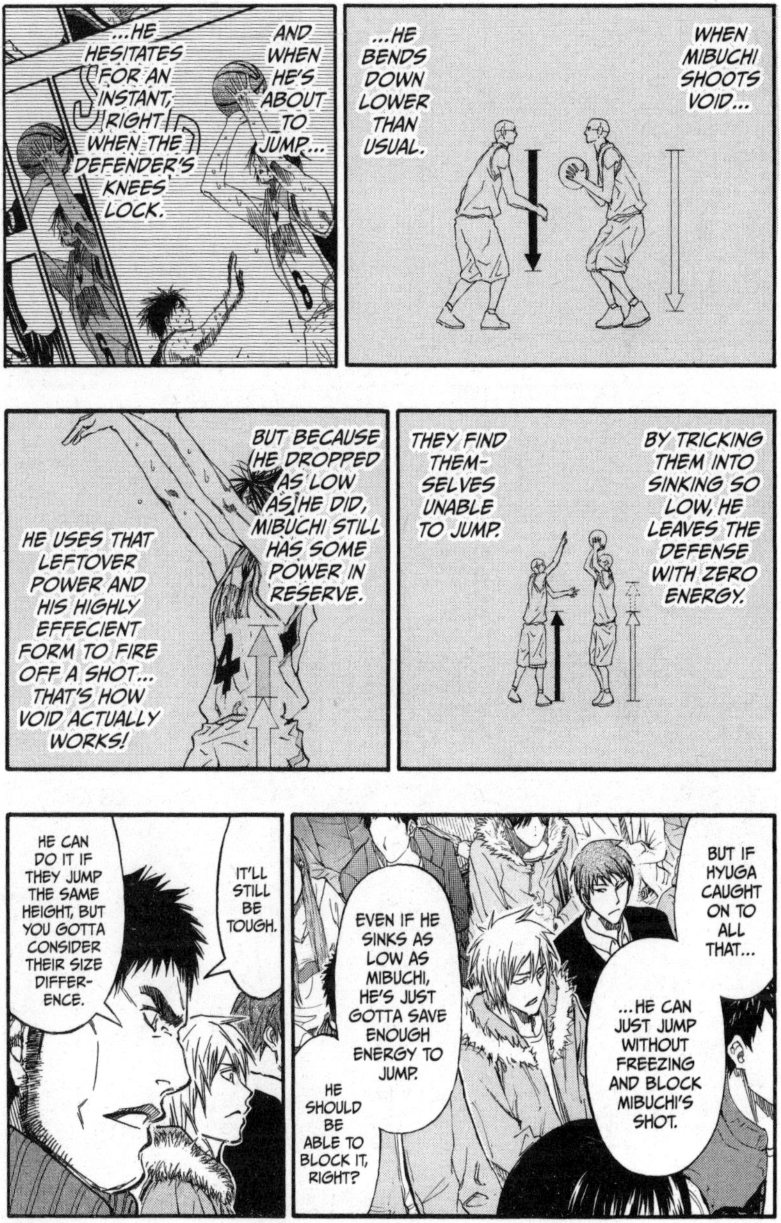
WHEN MIBUCHI SHOOTS VOID...
...HE BENDS DOWN LOWER THAN USUAL.
AND WHEN HE'S ABOUT TO JUMP...
...HE HESITATES FOR AN INSTANT, RIGHT WHEN THE DEFENDER'S KNEES LOCK.
BY TRICKING THEM INTO SINKING SO LOW, HE LEAVES THE DEFENSE WITH ZERO ENERGY.
THEY FIND THEM-SELVES UNABLE TO JUMP.
BUT BECAUSE HE DROPPED AS LOW AS HE DID, MIBUCHI STILL HAS SOME POWER IN RESERVE.
HE USES THAT LEFTOVER POWER AND HIS HIGHLY EFFECIENT FORM TO FIRE OFF A SHOT... THAT'S HOW VOID ACTUALLY WORKS!
BUT IF HYUGA CAUGHT ON TO ALL THAT...
...HE CAN JUST JUMP WITHOUT FREEZING AND BLOCK MIBUCHI'S SHOT.
EVEN IF HE SINKS AS LOW AS MIBUCHI, HE'S JUST GOTTA SAVE ENOUGH ENERGY TO JUMP.
HE SHOULD BE ABLE TO BLOCK IT, RIGHT?
IT'LL STILL BE TOUGH.
HE CAN DO IT IF THEY JUMP THE SAME HEIGHT, BUT YOU GOTTA CONSIDER THEIR SIZE DIFFER-ENCE.

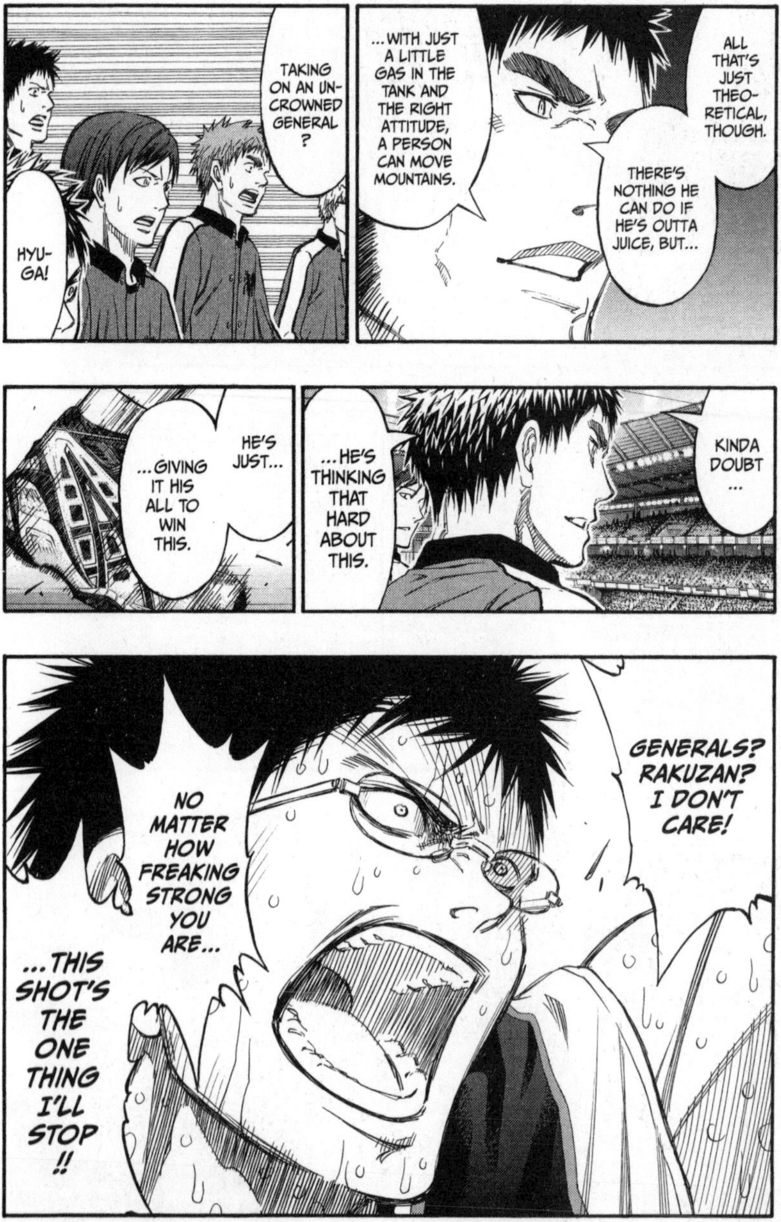
ALL THAT'S JUST THEORETICAL, THOUGH.
THERE'S NOTHING HE CAN DO IF HE'S OUTTA JUICE, BUT...
...WITH JUST A LITTLE GAS IN THE TANK AND THE RIGHT ATTITUDE, A PERSON CAN MOVE MOUNTAINS.
TAKING ON AN UNCROWNED GENERAL?
HYUGA!
KINDA DOUBT...
...HE'S THINKING THAT HARD ABOUT THIS.
HE'S JUST...
...GIVING IT HIS ALL TO WIN THIS.
GENERALS? RAKUZAN? I DON'T CARE!
NO MATTER HOW FREAKING STRONG YOU ARE...
...THIS SHOT'S THE ONE THING I'LL STOP!!

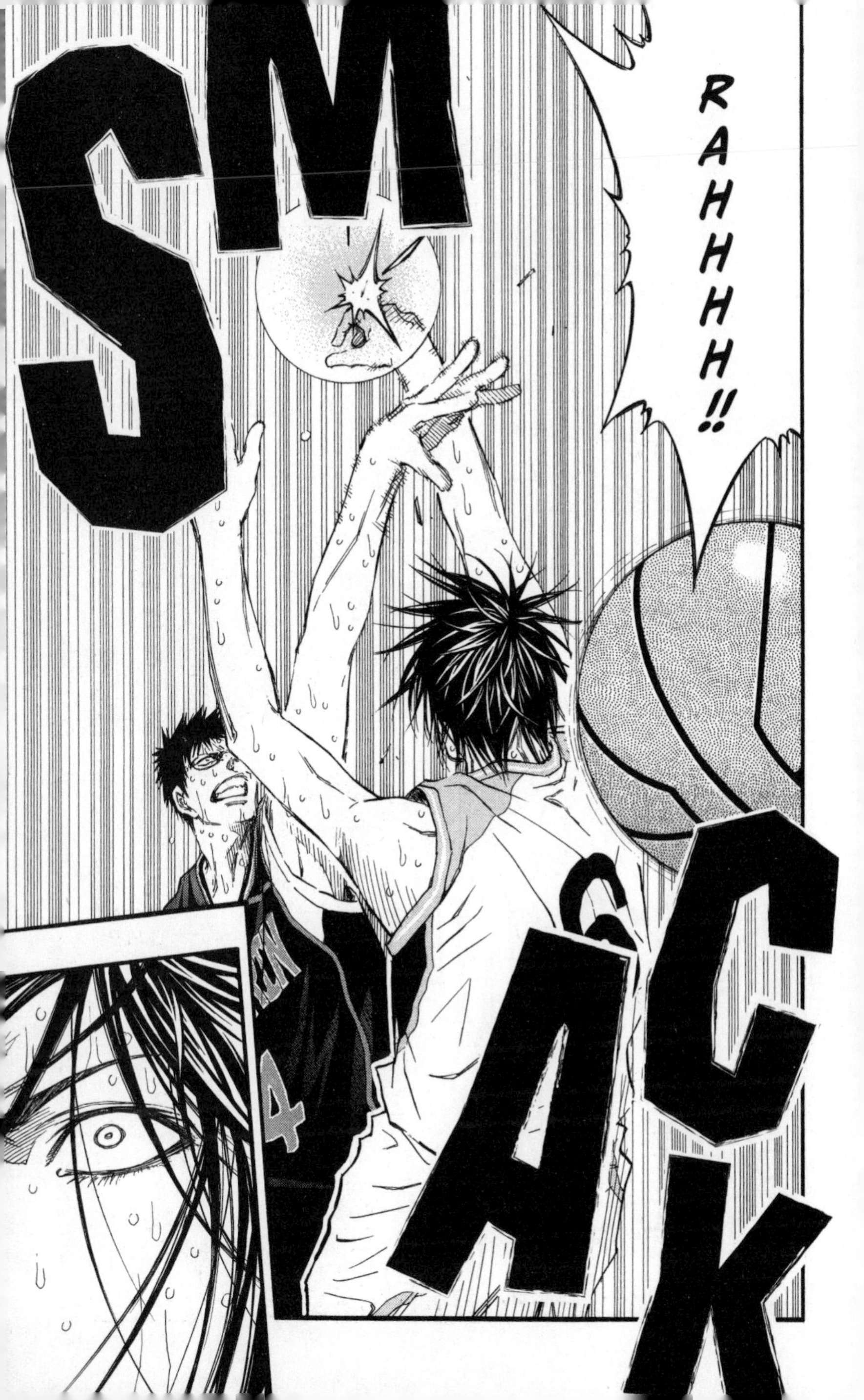
RAHHHHH!!
SMACK

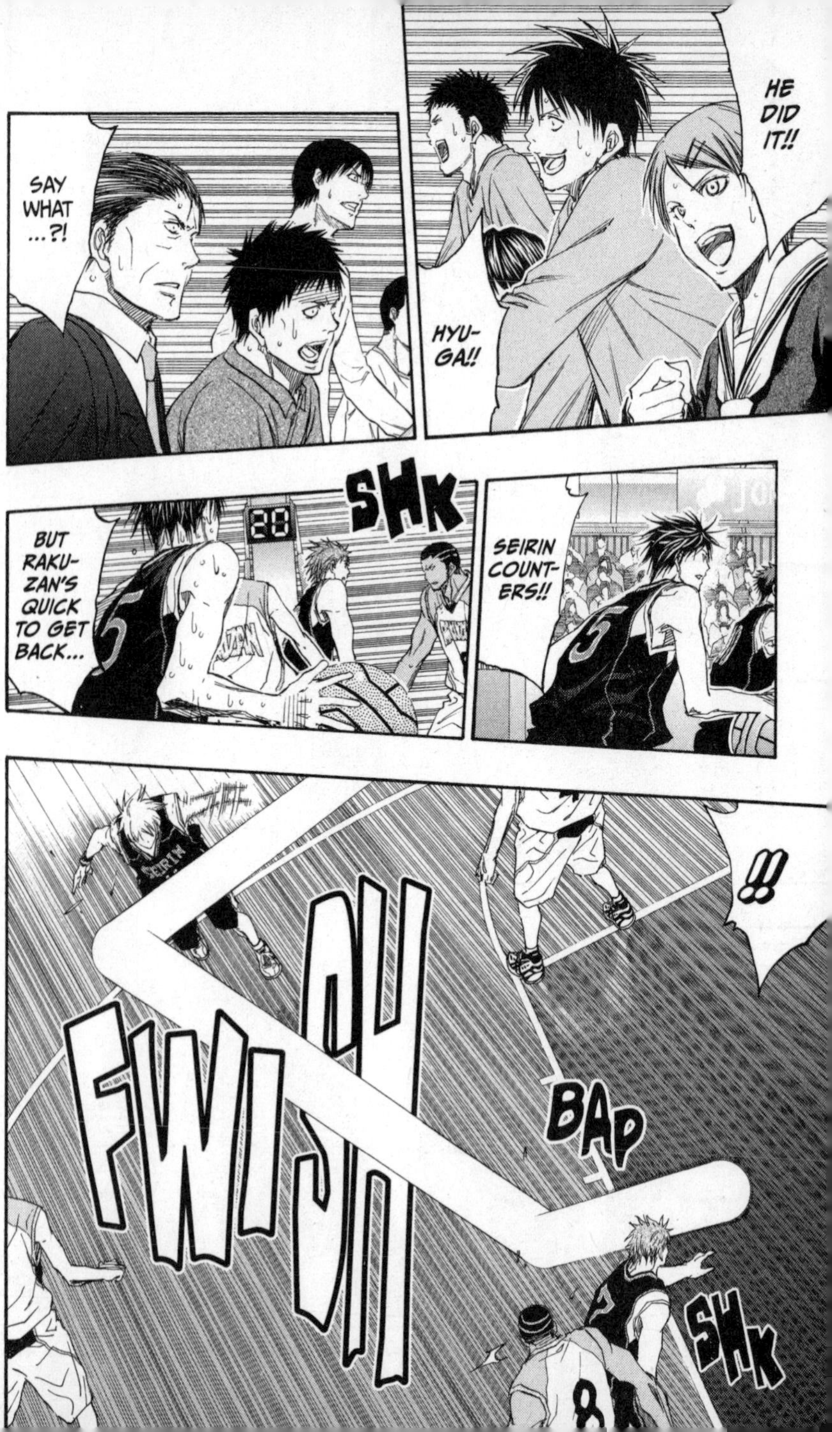
HE DID IT!!
HYU-GA!!
SAY WHAT ...?!
SEIRIN COUNT-ERS!!
SHK
BUT RAKU-ZAN'S QUICK TO GET BACK...
!!
FWISH
BAD
SHK

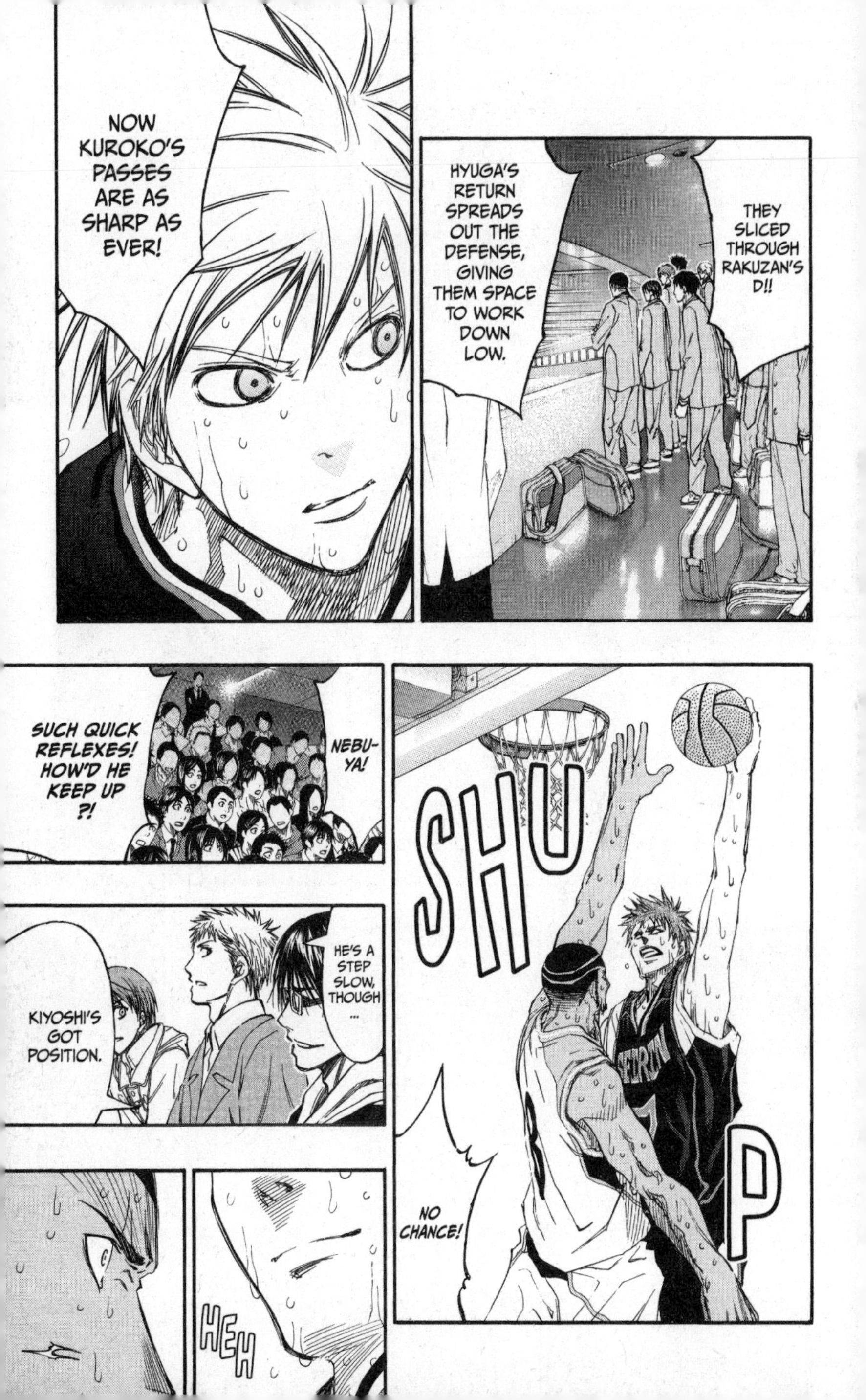

THEY SLICED THROUGH RAKUZAN'S D!!
HYUGA'S RETURN SPREADS OUT THE DEFENSE, GIVING THEM SPACE TO WORK DOWN LOW.
NOW KUROKO'S PASSES ARE AS SHARP AS EVER!
SHU
P
NO CHANCE!
NEBU-YA!
SUCH QUICK REFLEXES! HOW'D HE KEEP UP ?!
HE'S A STEP SLOW, THOUGH ...
KIYOSHI'S GOT POSITION.
HEH

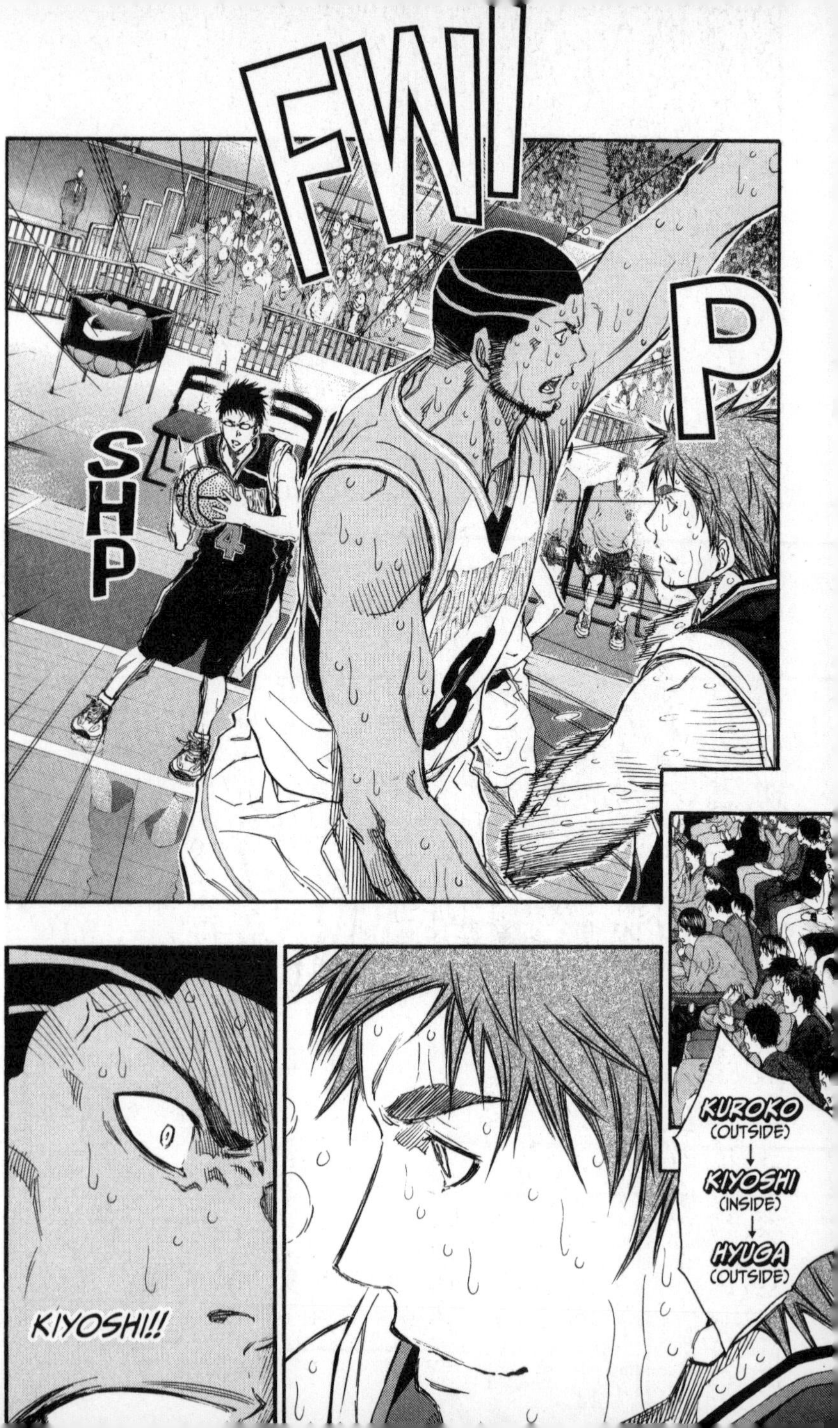
FWIP
SHP
KUROKO (OUTSIDE)
↓
KIYOSHI (INSIDE)
↓
HYUGA (OUTSIDE)
KIYOSHI!!

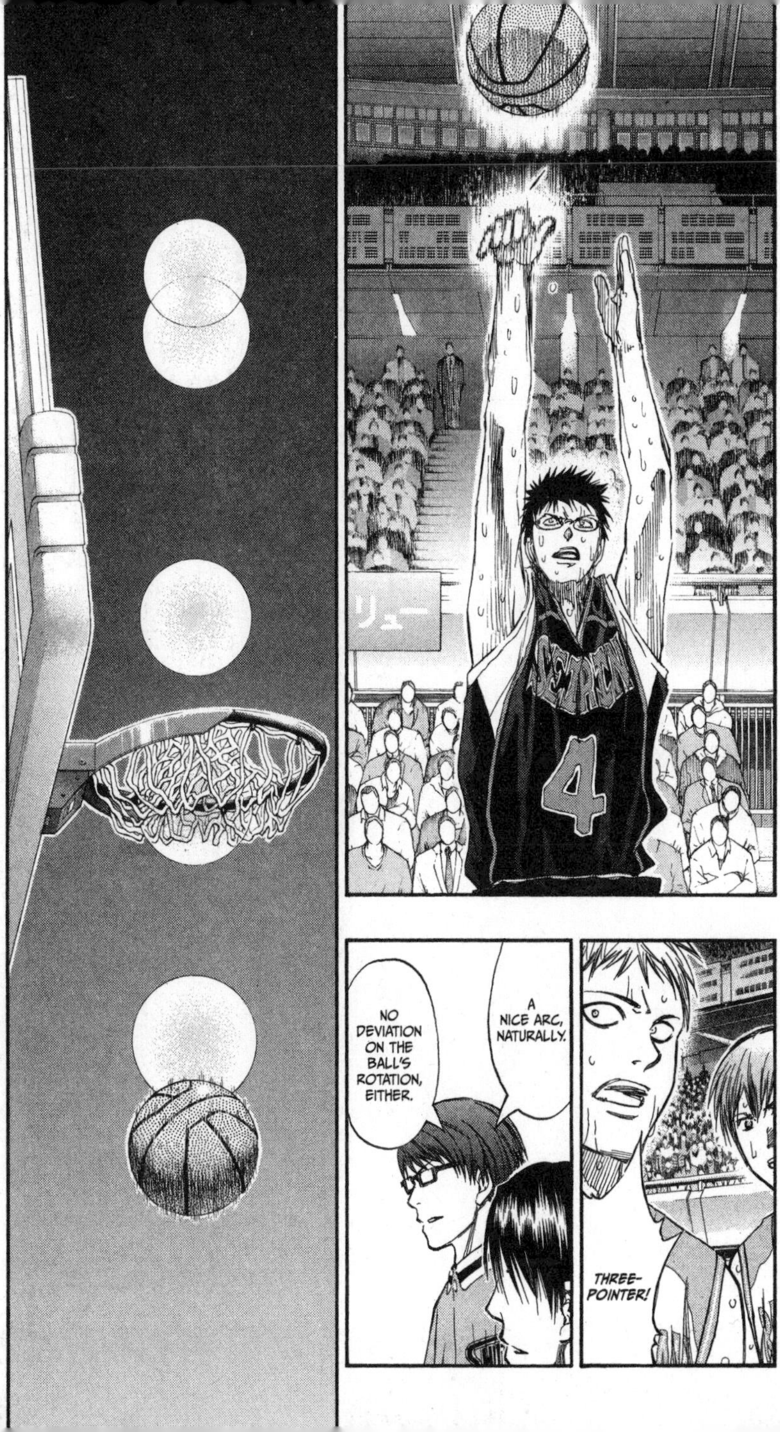
THREE-POINTER!
A NICE ARC, NATURALLY.
NO DEVIATION ON THE BALL'S ROTATION, EITHER.

KUROKO'S BASKETBALL BLOOPERS

TAKE 6

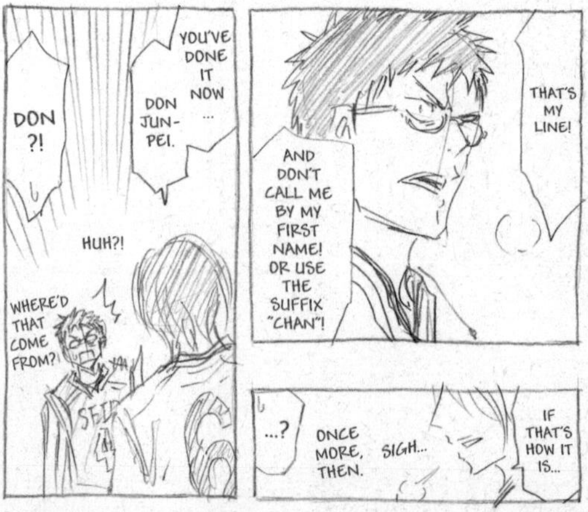
THAT'S MY LINE!
AND DON'T CALL ME BY MY FIRST NAME! OR USE THE SUFFIX "CHAN"!
IF THAT'S HOW IT IS...
SIGH...
ONCE MORE, THEN.
...?
YOU'VE DONE IT NOW ...
DON JUN-PEI.
DON ?!
HUH?!
WHERE'D THAT COME FROM?!

260TH QUARTER: A WARNING

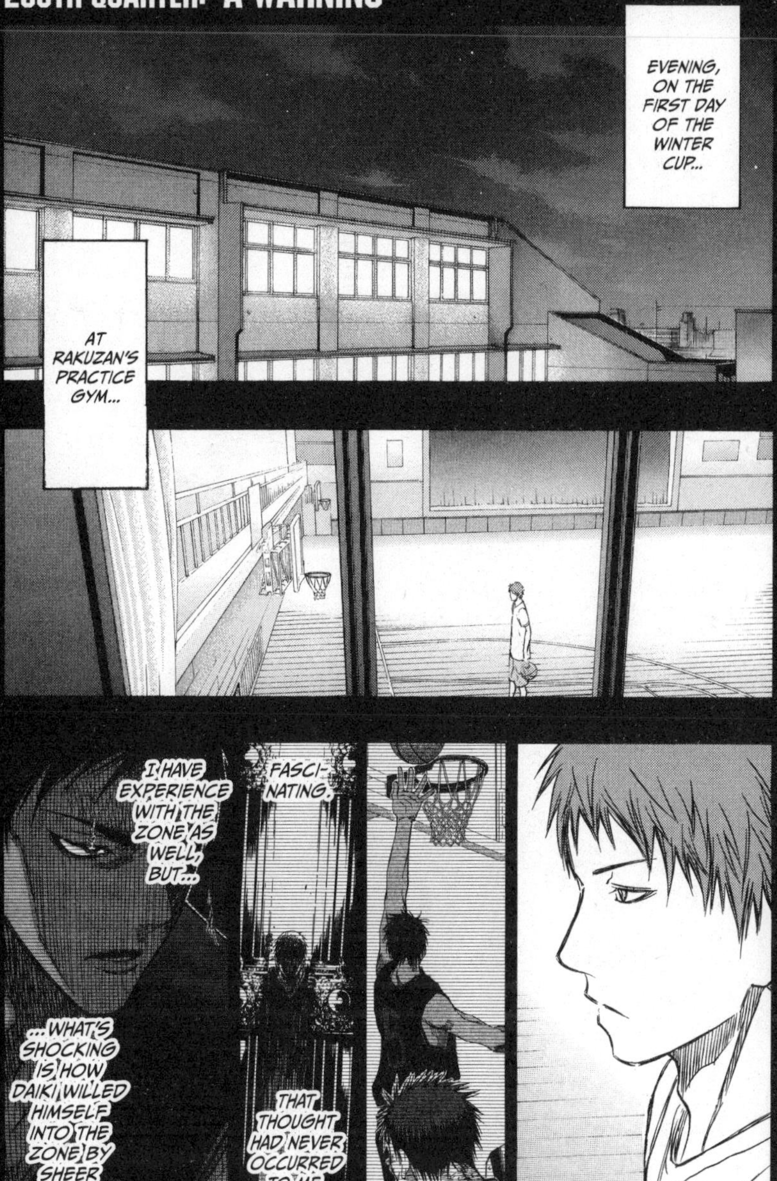
EVENING, ON THE FIRST DAY OF THE WINTER CUP...
AT RAKUZAN'S PRACTICE GYM...
FASCINATING.
THAT THOUGHT HAD NEVER OCCURRED TO ME.
I HAVE EXPERIENCE WITH THE ZONE AS WELL, BUT...
...WHAT'S SHOCKING IS HOW DAIKI WILLED HIMSELF INTO THE ZONE BY SHEER FORCE.

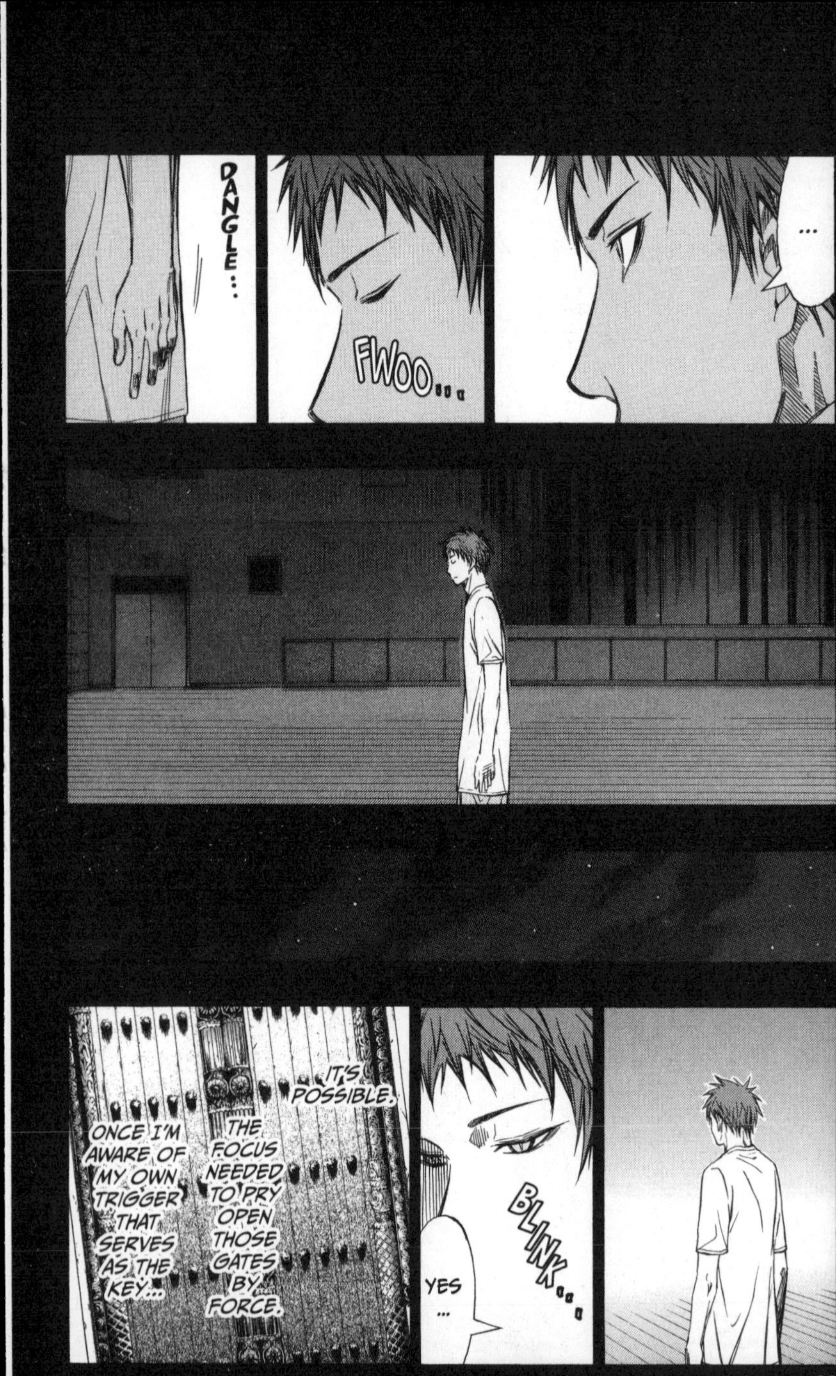
...
FWOO...
DANGLE...
BLINK...
YES ...
IT'S POSSIBLE.
THE FOCUS NEEDED TO PRY OPEN THOSE GATES BY FORCE.
ONCE I'M AWARE OF MY OWN TRIGGER THAT SERVES AS THE KEY...

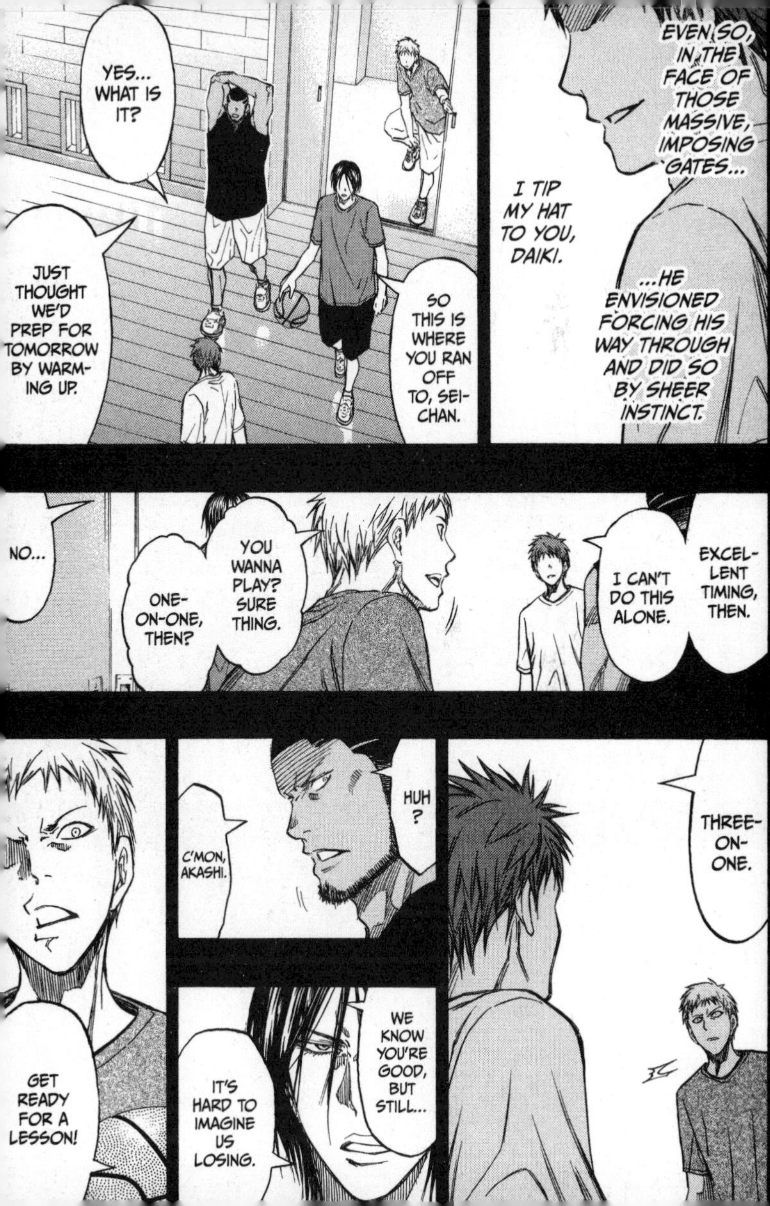
EVEN SO, IN THE FACE OF THOSE MASSIVE, IMPOSING GATES...
...HE ENVISIONED FORCING HIS WAY THROUGH AND DID SO BY SHEER INSTINCT.
I TIP MY HAT TO YOU, DAIKI.
SO THIS IS WHERE YOU RAN OFF TO, SEI-CHAN.
YES... WHAT IS IT?
JUST THOUGHT WE'D PREP FOR TOMORROW BY WARMING UP.
EXCELLENT TIMING, THEN.
I CAN'T DO THIS ALONE.
YOU WANNA PLAY? SURE THING.
ONE-ON-ONE, THEN?
NO...
THREE-ON-ONE.
HUH?
C'MON, AKASHI.
WE KNOW YOU'RE GOOD, BUT STILL...
IT'S HARD TO IMAGINE US LOSING.
GET READY FOR A LESSON!

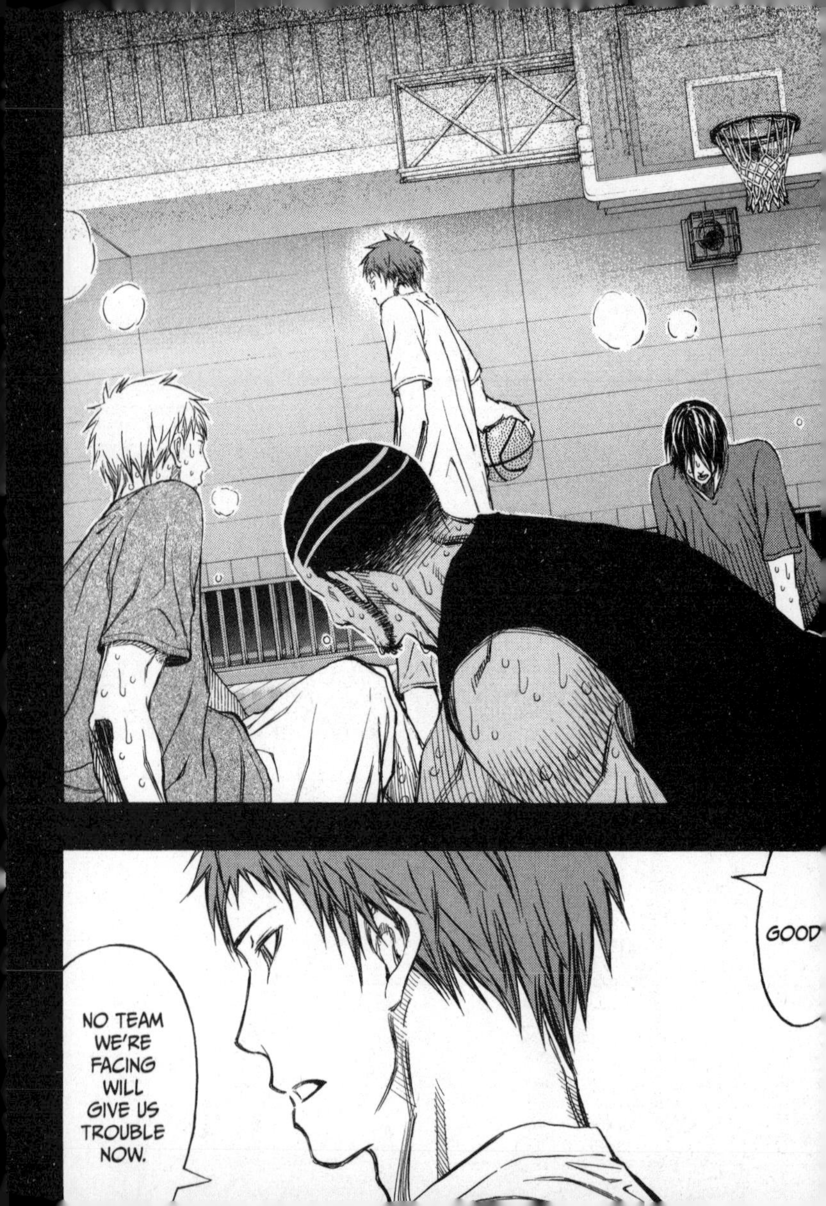
GOOD
NO TEAM WE'RE FACING WILL GIVE US TROUBLE NOW.

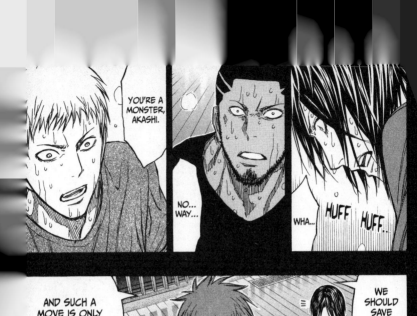

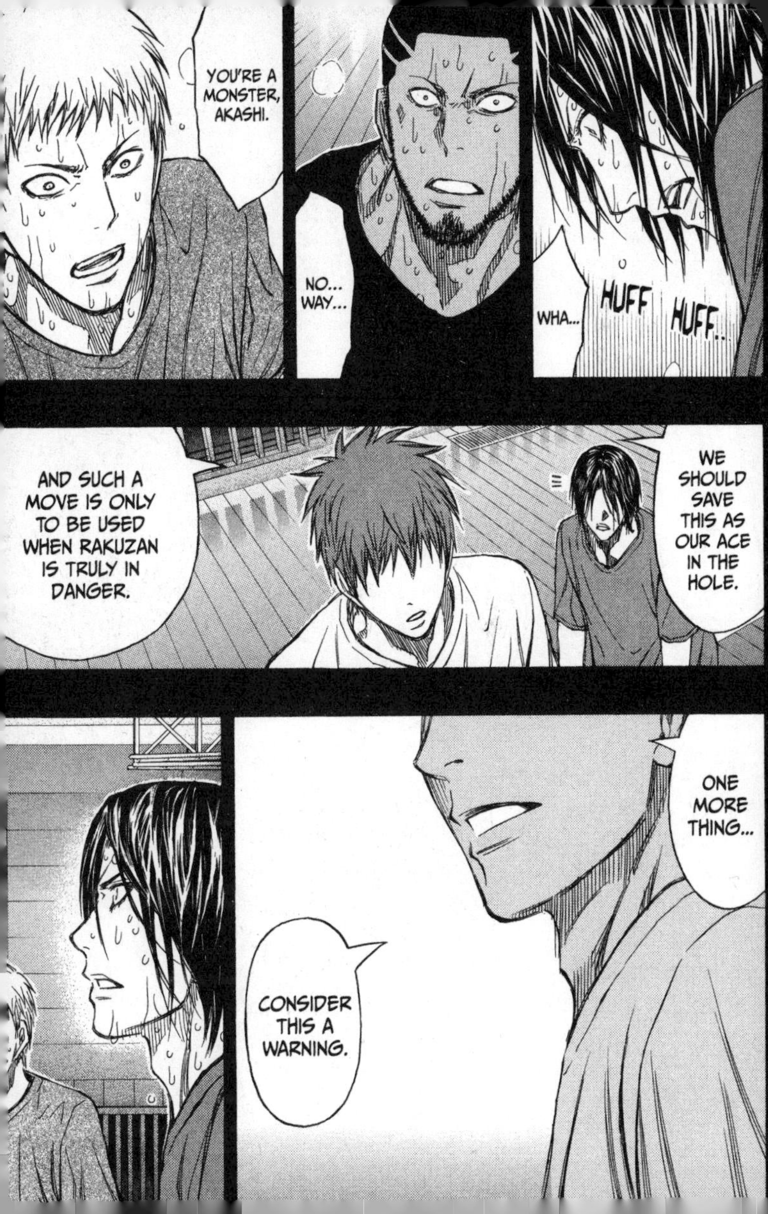
WHA...
HUFF HUFF...
NO... WAY...
YOU'RE A MONSTER, AKASHI.
WE SHOULD SAVE THIS AS OUR ACE IN THE HOLE.
AND SUCH A MOVE IS ONLY TO BE USED WHEN RAKUZAN IS TRULY IN DANGER.
ONE MORE THING...
CONSIDER THIS A WARNING.

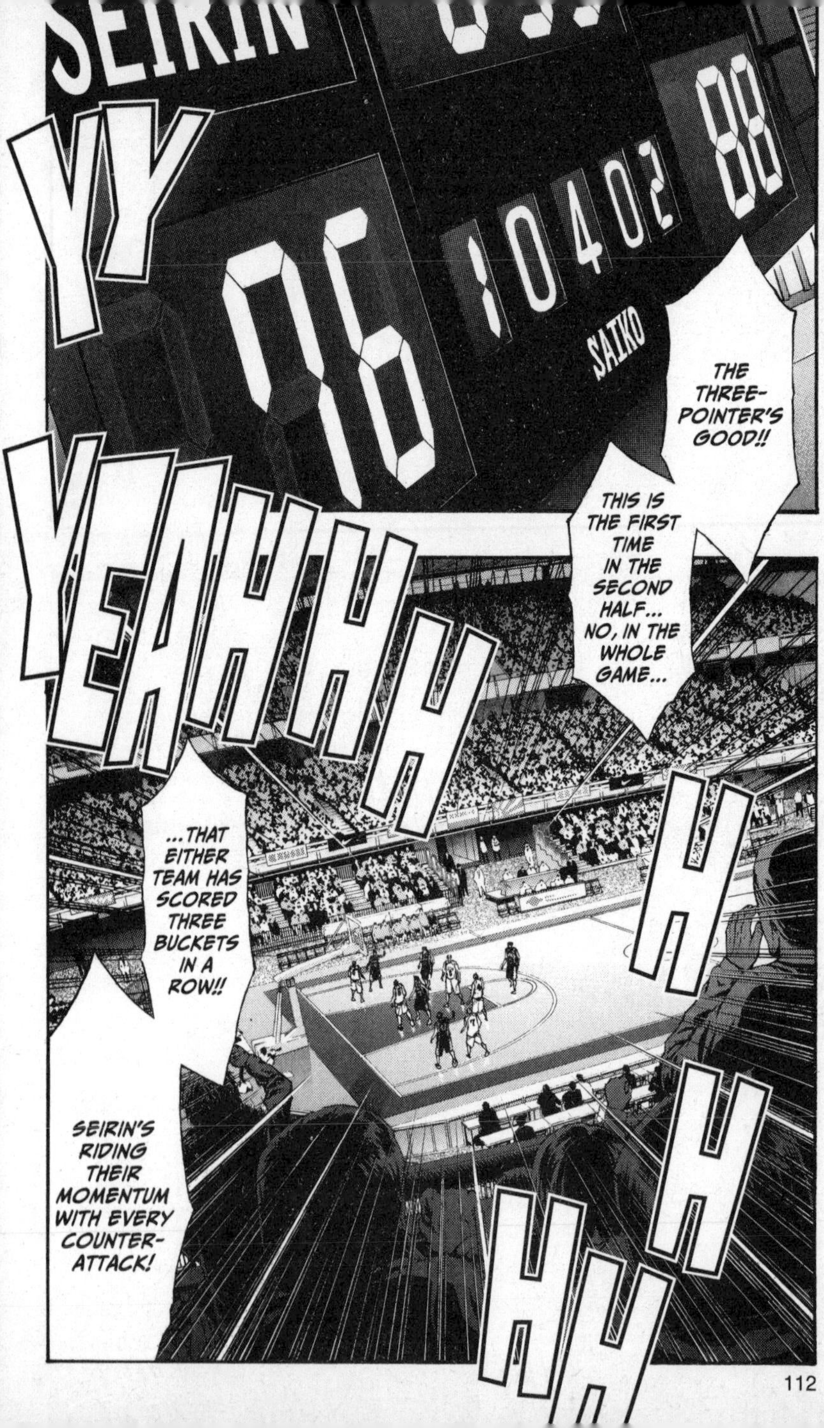
SEIRIN
96
88
SAIKO
THE THREE-POINTER'S GOOD!!
YYYEAHHHHHHHH
THIS IS THE FIRST TIME IN THE SECOND HALF... NO, IN THE WHOLE GAME...
...THAT EITHER TEAM HAS SCORED THREE BUCKETS IN A ROW!!
SEIRIN'S RIDING THEIR MOMENTUM WITH EVERY COUNTER-ATTACK!

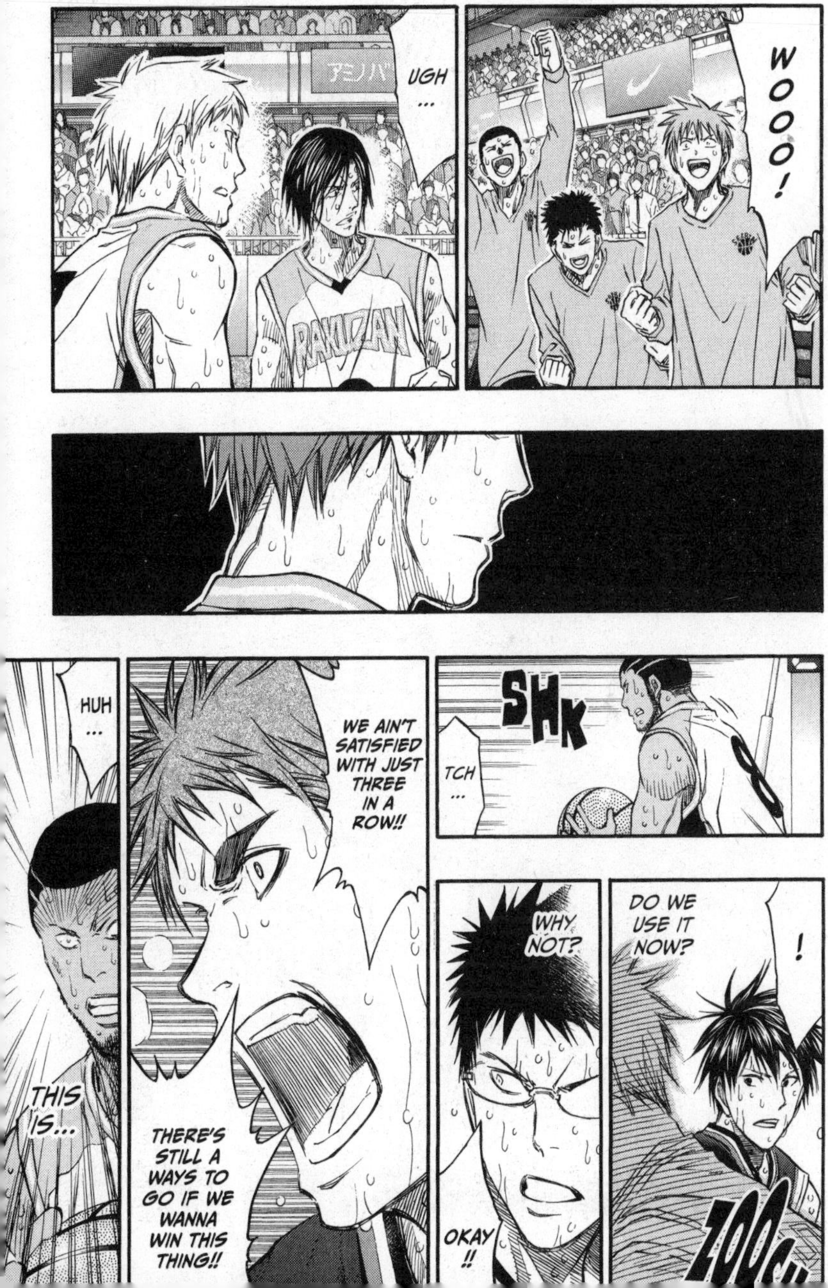
WOOOO!
UGH ...
SHK
TCH ...
DO WE USE IT NOW?
!
WHY NOT?
OKAY !!
WE AIN'T SATISFIED WITH JUST THREE IN A ROW!!
THERE'S STILL A WAYS TO GO IF WE WANNA WIN THIS THING!!
HUH ...
THIS IS...

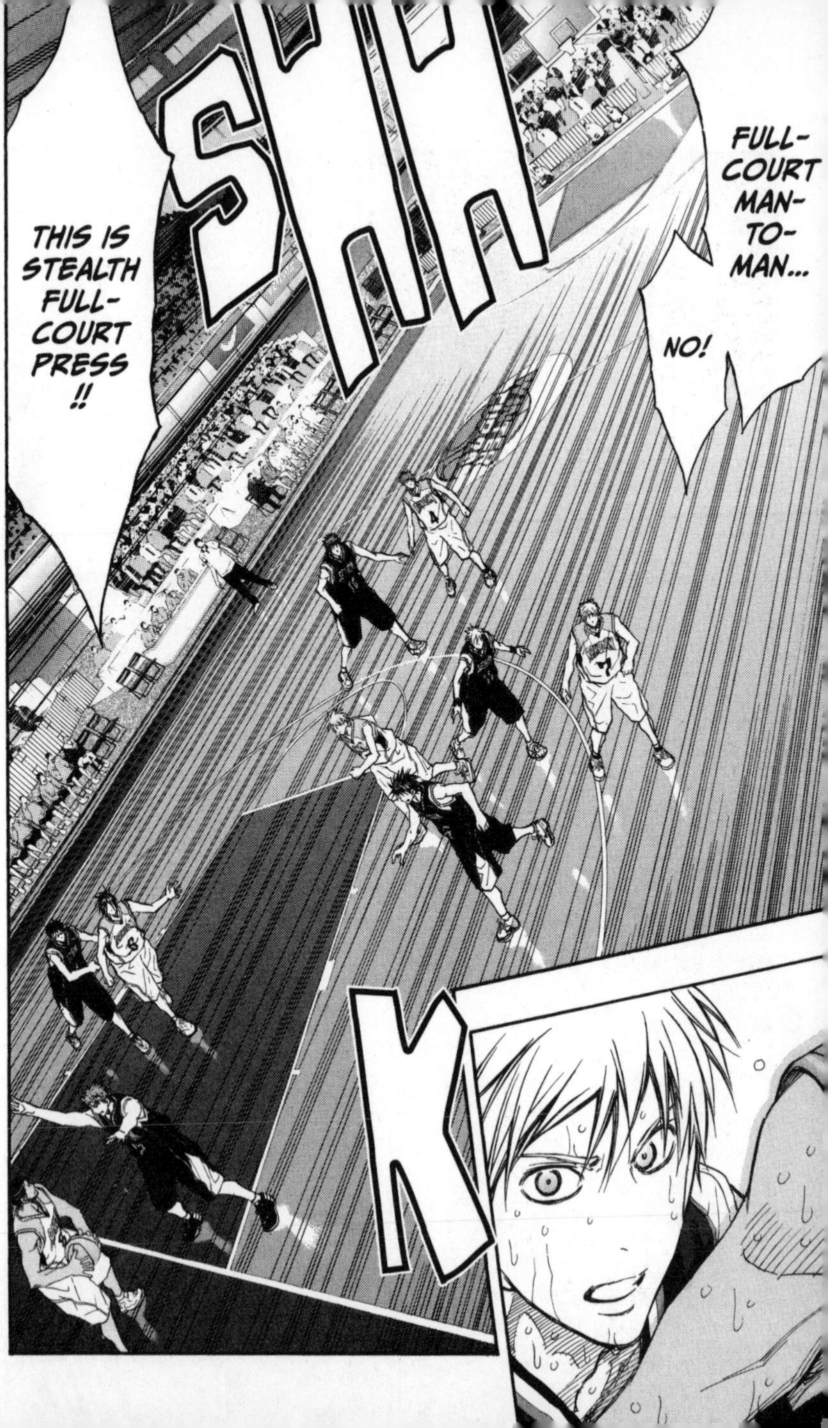
FULL-COURT MAN-TO-MAN...
NO!
THIS IS STEALTH FULL-COURT PRESS!!

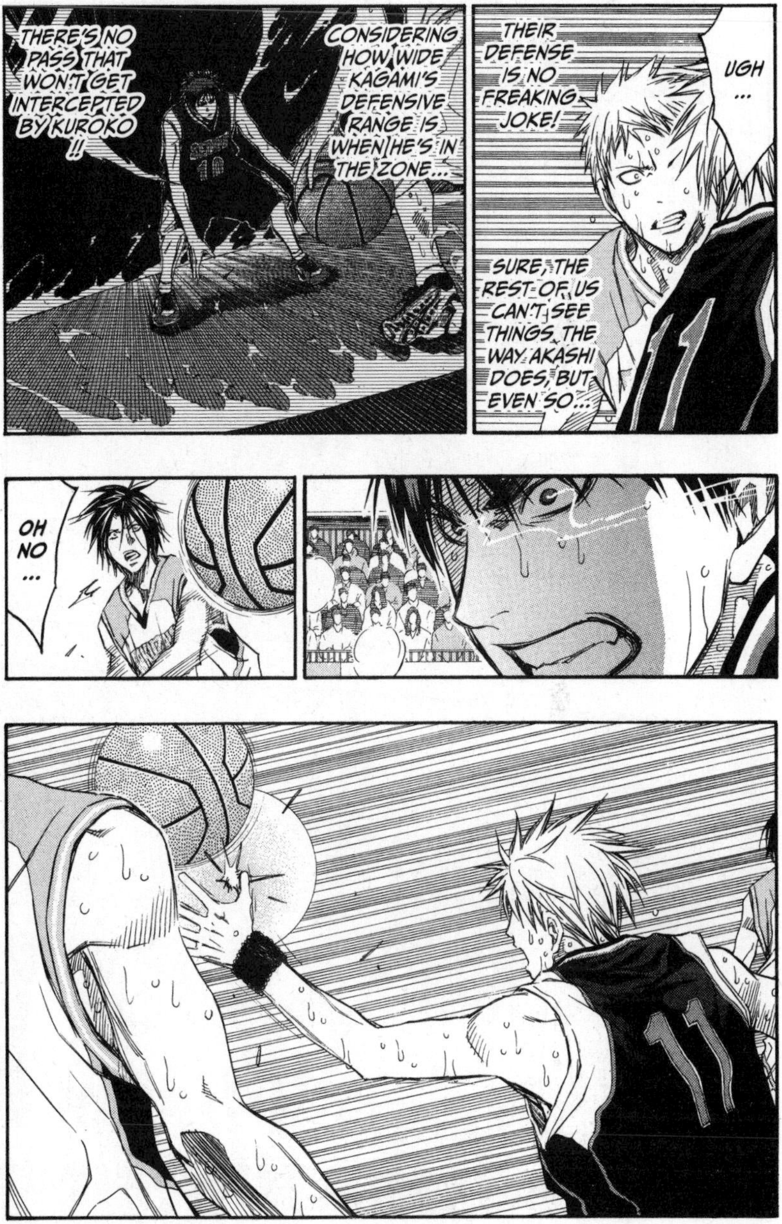
UGH ...
THEIR DEFENSE IS NO FREAKING JOKE!
SURE, THE REST OF US CAN'T SEE THINGS THE WAY AKASHI DOES, BUT EVEN SO...
CONSIDERING HOW WIDE KAGAMI'S DEFENSIVE RANGE IS WHEN HE'S IN THE ZONE...
THERE'S NO PASS THAT WON'T GET INTERCEPTED BY KUROKO !!
OH NO ...

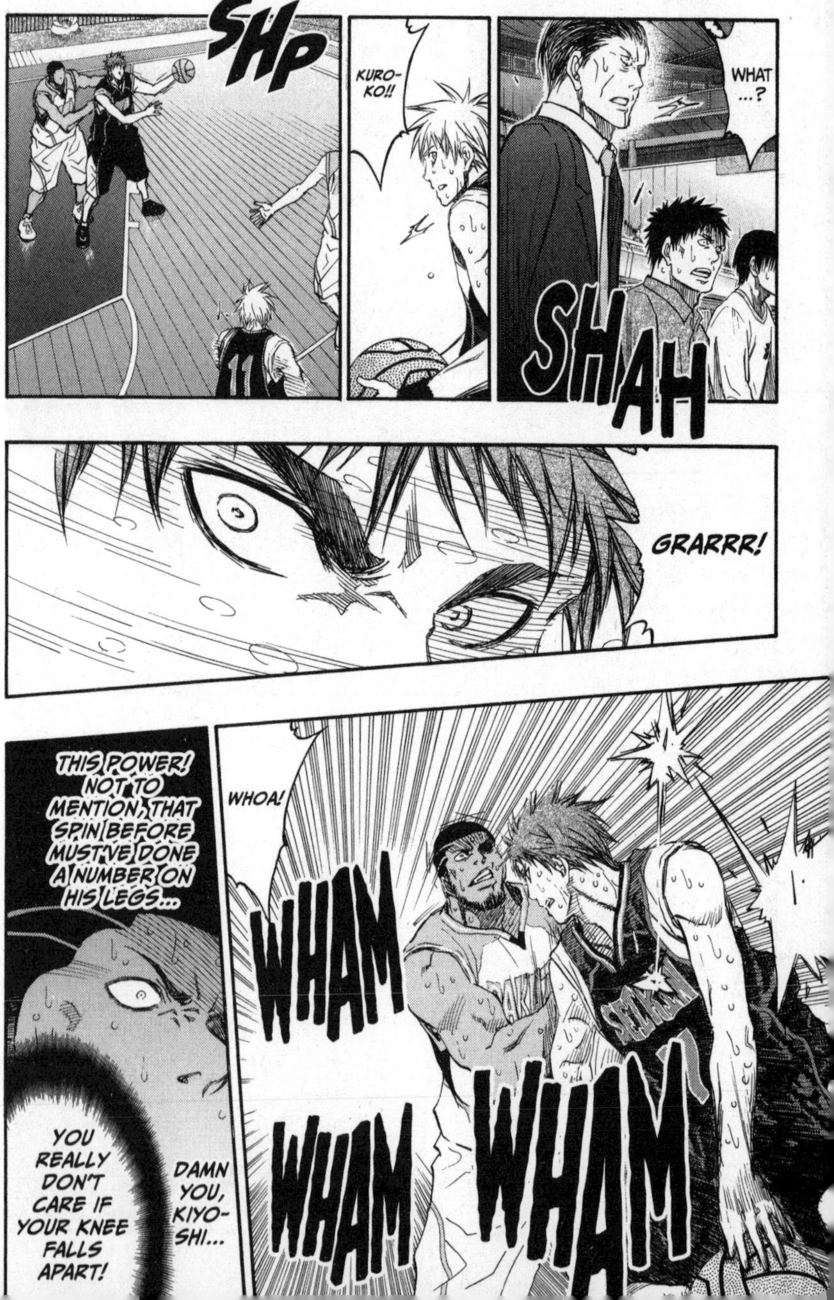
WHAT ...?
SHAH
KURO-KO!!
SHP
GRARRR!
WHOA!
WHAM
WHAM
WHAM
THIS POWER! NOT TO MENTION THAT SPIN BEFORE MUST'VE DONE A NUMBER ON HIS LEGS...
DAMN YOU, KIYO-SHI...
YOU REALLY DON'T CARE IF YOUR KNEE FALLS APART!

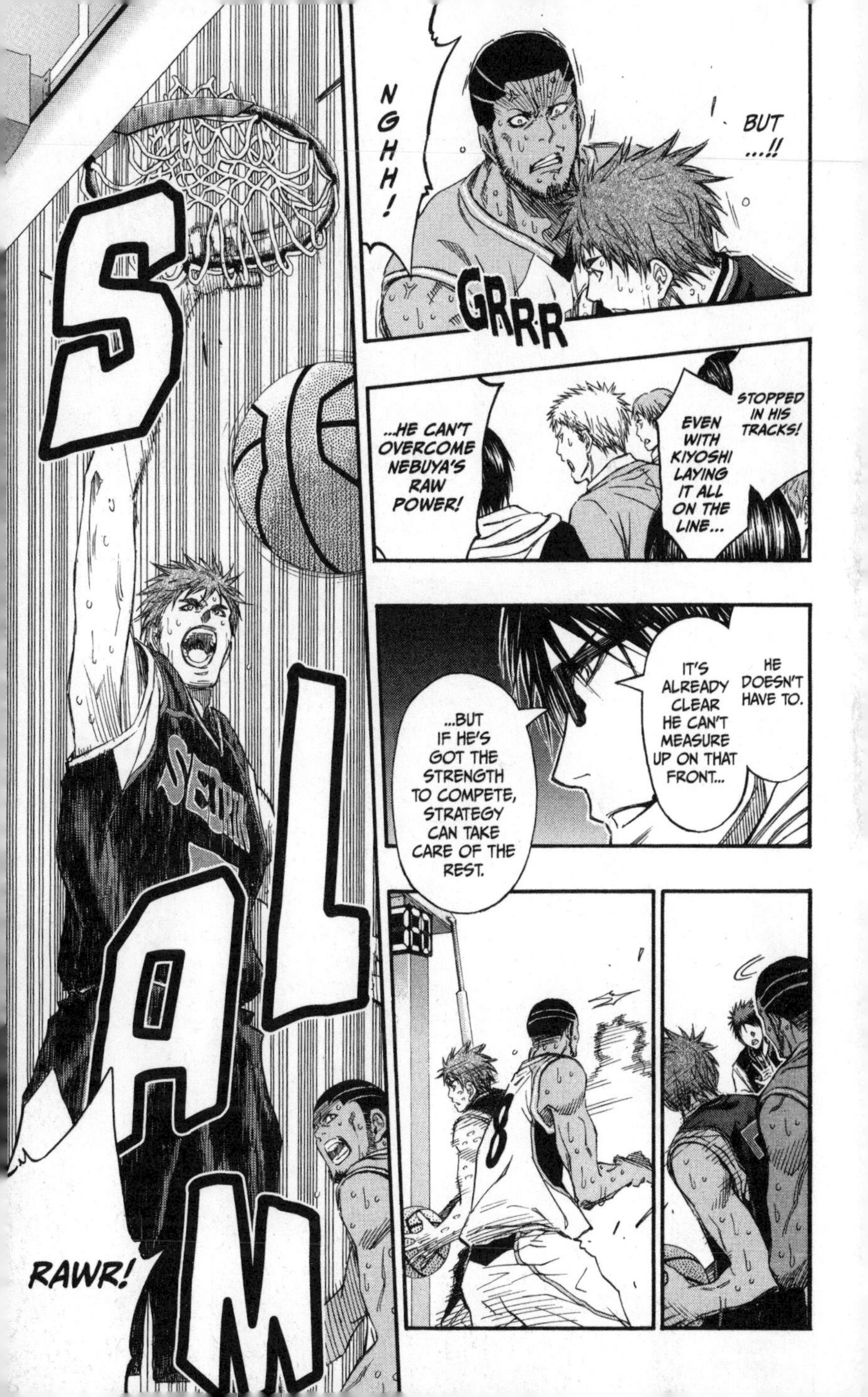
BUT ...!!
NGHH!
GRRR
STOPPED IN HIS TRACKS!
EVEN WITH KIYOSHI LAYING IT ALL ON THE LINE...
...HE CAN'T OVERCOME NEBUYA'S RAW POWER!
HE DOESN'T HAVE TO.
IT'S ALREADY CLEAR HE CAN'T MEASURE UP ON THAT FRONT...
...BUT IF HE'S GOT THE STRENGTH TO COMPETE, STRATEGY CAN TAKE CARE OF THE REST.
SLAM
RAWR!

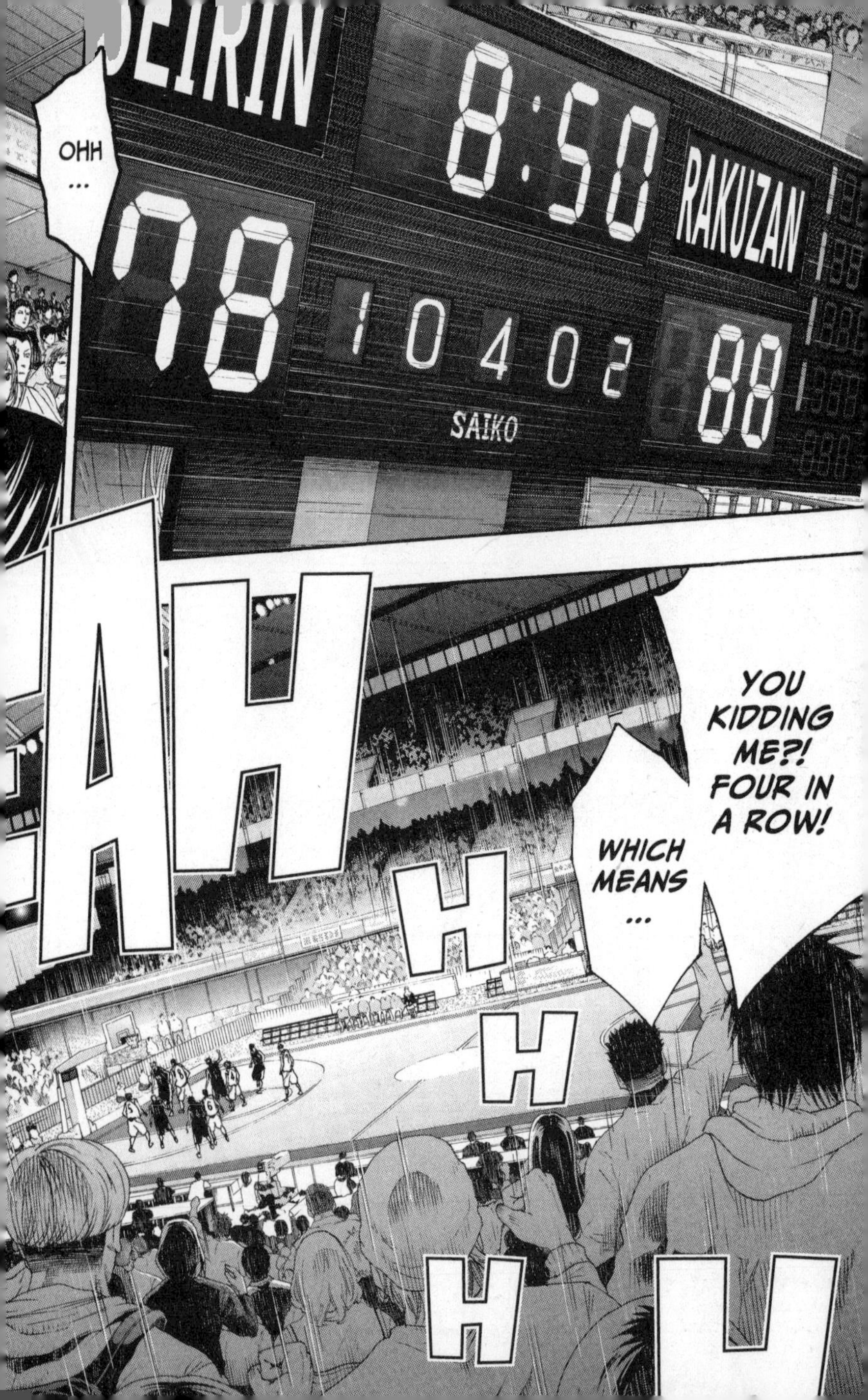

EIRIN
8:50
RAKUZAN
78
88
SAIKO
OHH ...
YOU KIDDING ME?! FOUR IN A ROW!
WHICH MEANS ...
AHHHH

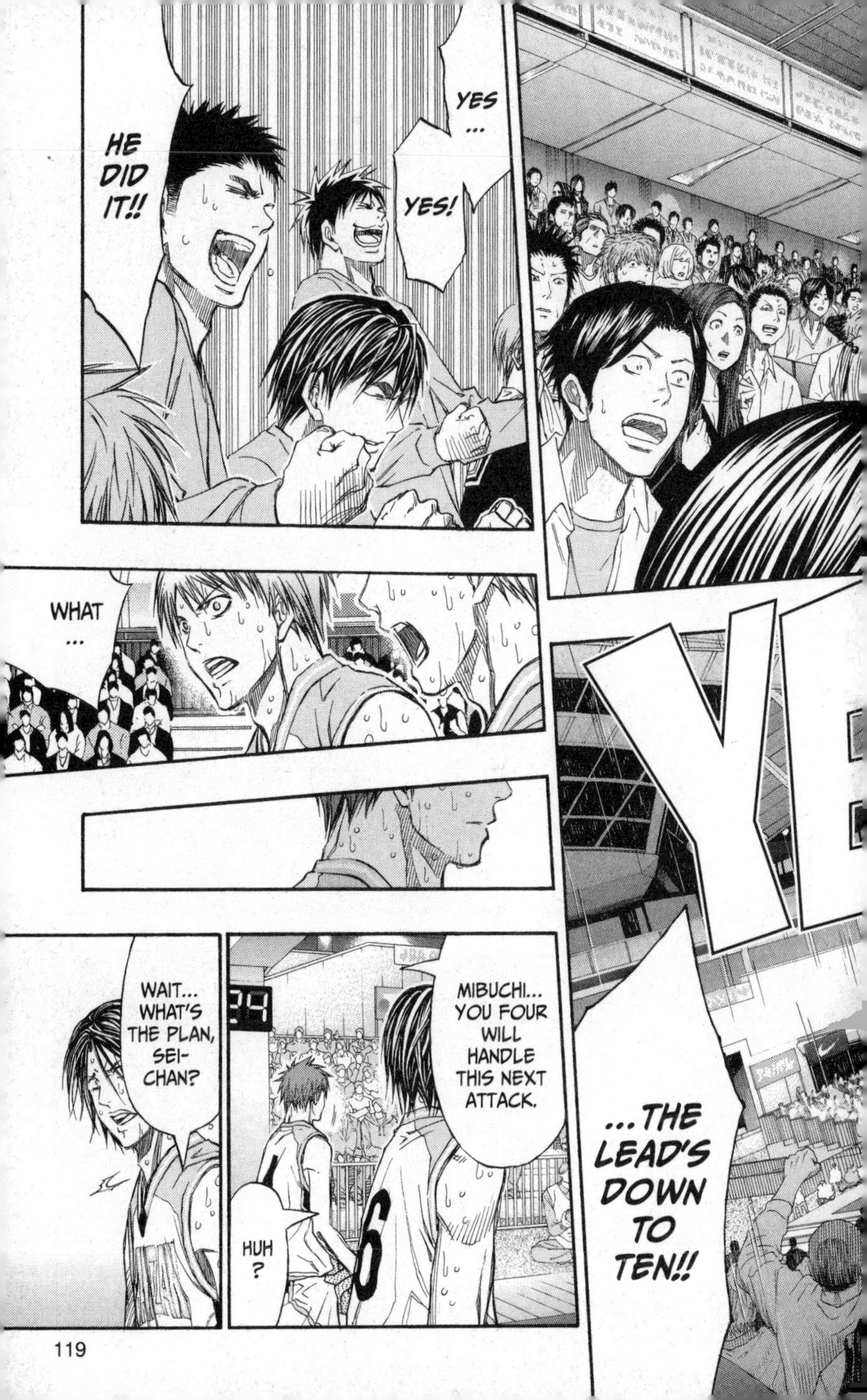
YES ... YES!
HE DID IT!!
YE
...THE LEAD'S DOWN TO TEN!!
WHAT ...
MIBUCHI... YOU FOUR WILL HANDLE THIS NEXT ATTACK.
HUH ?
WAIT... WHAT'S THE PLAN, SEI-CHAN?

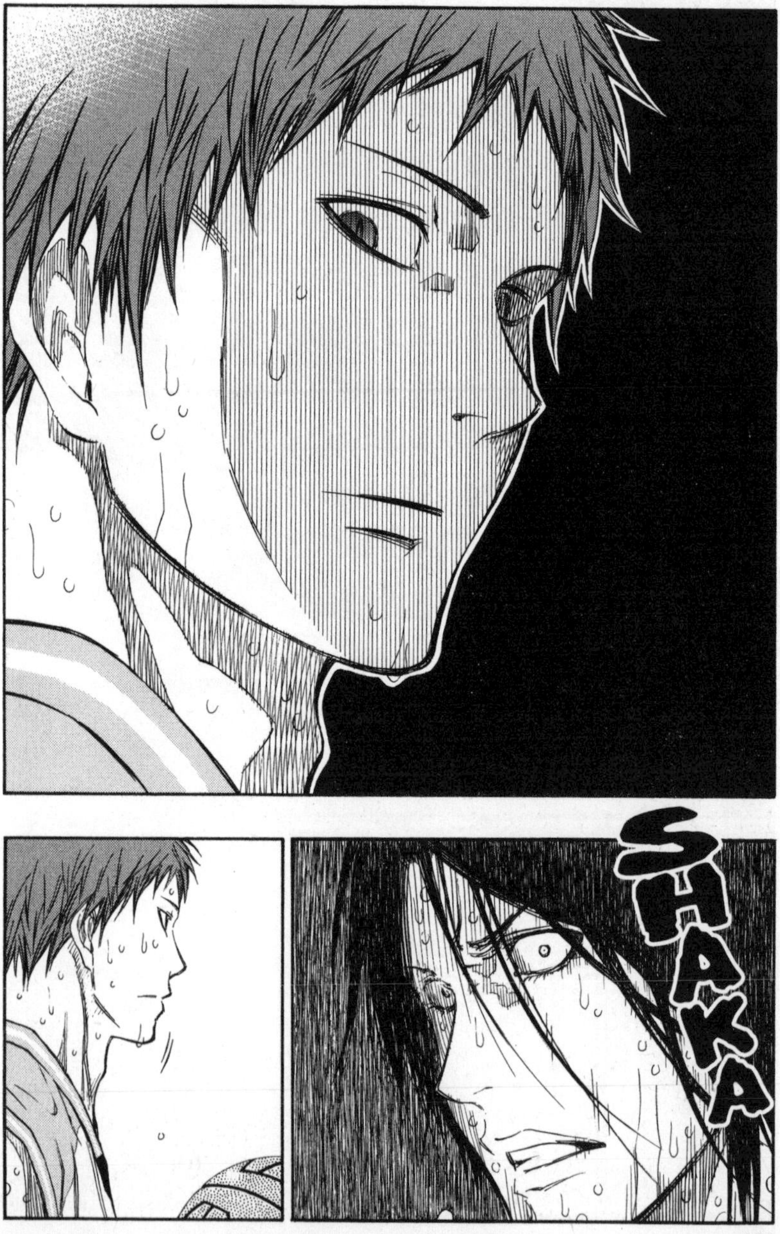
SHAKA

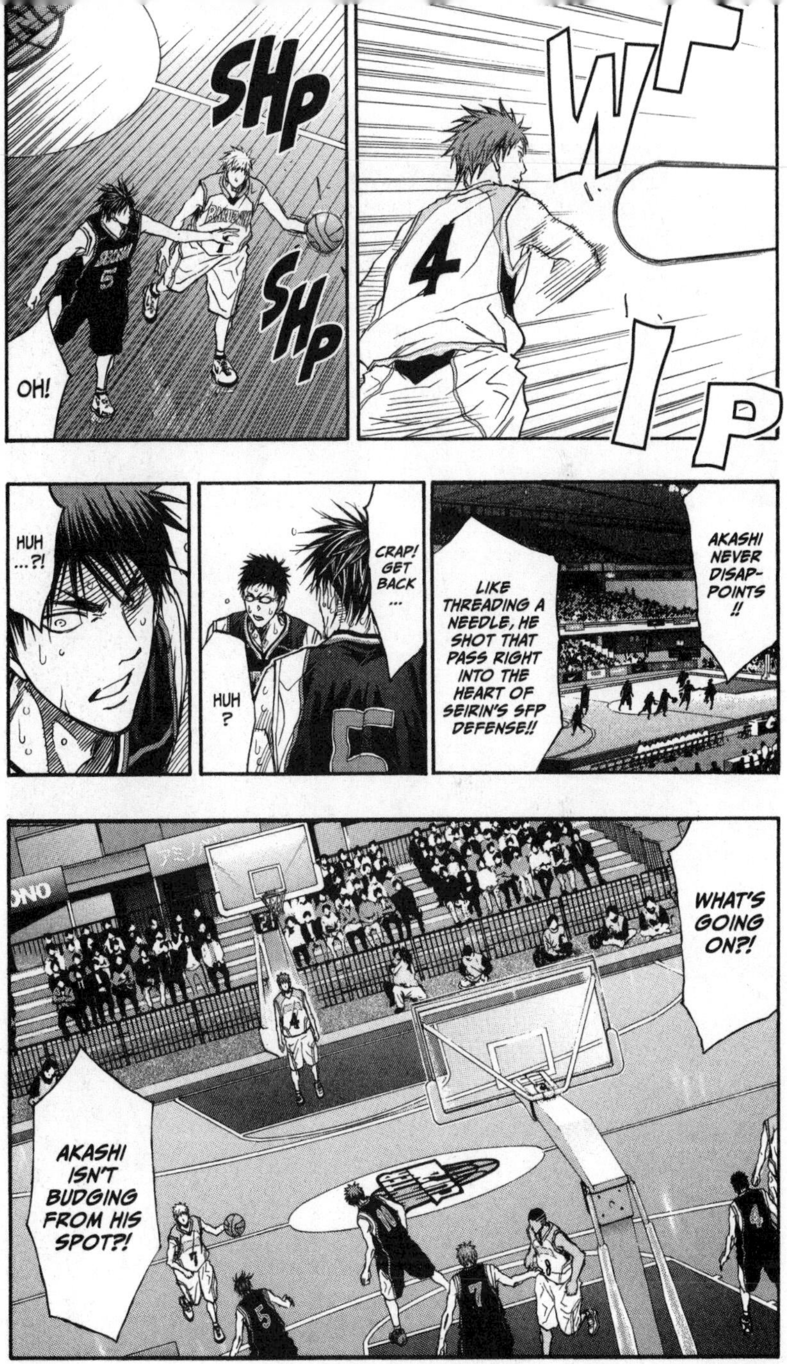
WHIP
SHP
SHP
OH!
AKASHI NEVER DISAPPOINTS!!
LIKE THREADING A NEEDLE, HE SHOT THAT PASS RIGHT INTO THE HEART OF SEIRIN'S SFP DEFENSE!!
CRAP! GET BACK...
HUH?
HUH...?!
WHAT'S GOING ON?!
AKASHI ISN'T BUDGING FROM HIS SPOT?!

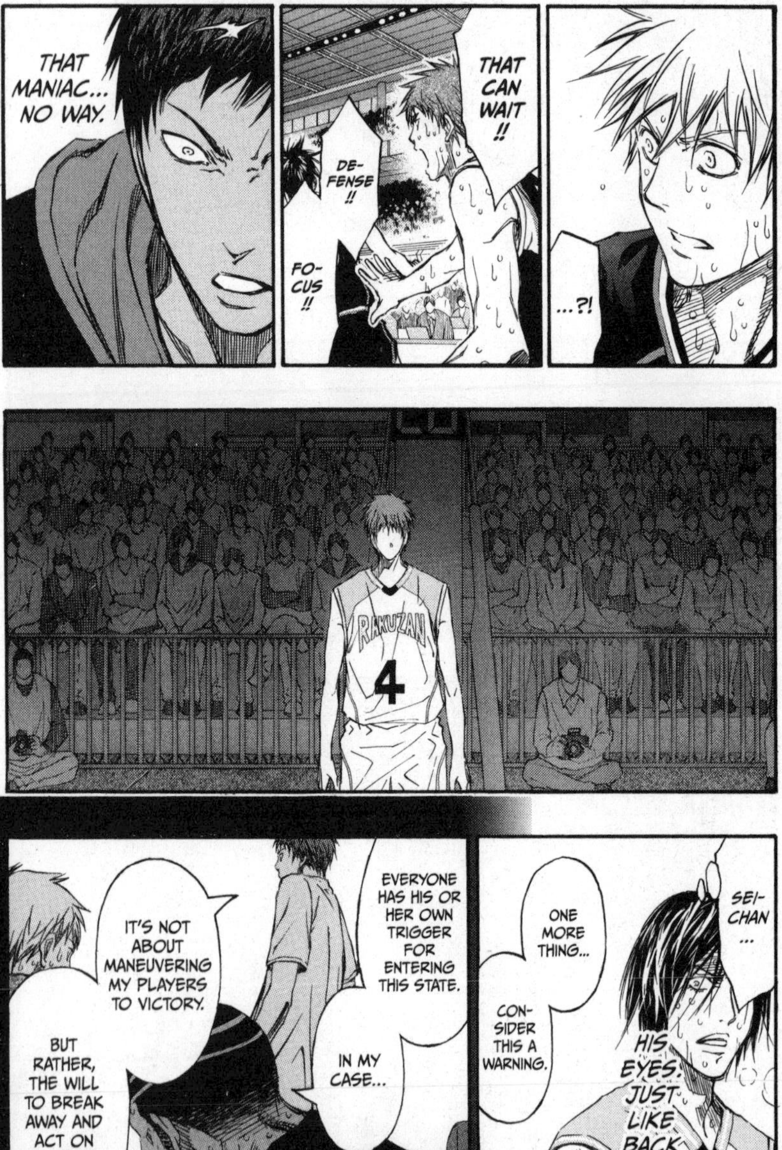
...?!
THAT CAN WAIT !!
DE-FENSE !!
FO-CUS !!
THAT MANIAC... NO WAY.
SEI-CHAN ...
ONE MORE THING...
CON-SIDER THIS A WARNING.
HIS EYES. JUST LIKE BACK THEN...
EVERYONE HAS HIS OR HER OWN TRIGGER FOR ENTERING THIS STATE.
IN MY CASE...
IT'S NOT ABOUT MANEUVERING MY PLAYERS TO VICTORY.
BUT RATHER, THE WILL TO BREAK AWAY AND ACT ON MY OWN.

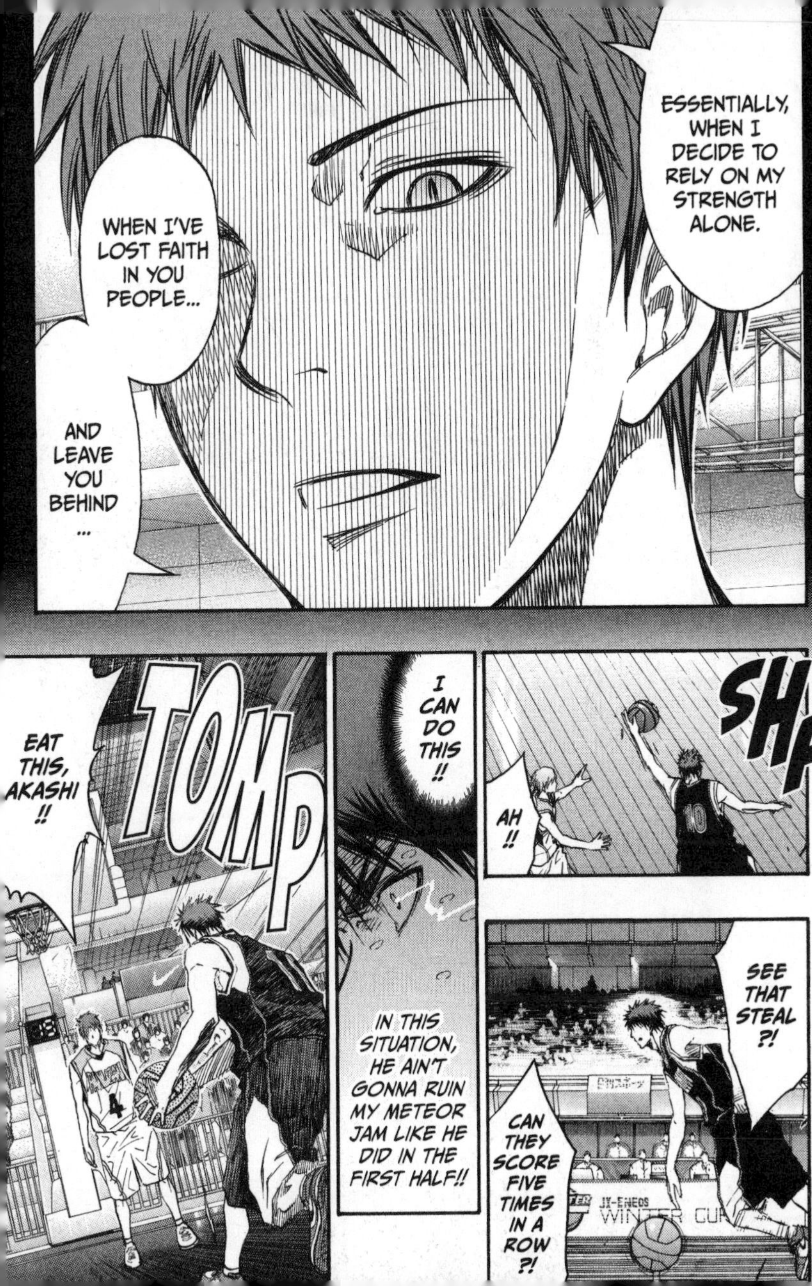
ESSENTIALLY, WHEN I DECIDE TO RELY ON MY STRENGTH ALONE.
WHEN I'VE LOST FAITH IN YOU PEOPLE...
AND LEAVE YOU BEHIND ...
SHP
AH!!
SEE THAT STEAL?!
CAN THEY SCORE FIVE TIMES IN A ROW?!
JX-ENEOS
I CAN DO THIS!!
IN THIS SITUATION, HE AIN'T GONNA RUIN MY METEOR JAM LIKE HE DID IN THE FIRST HALF!!
TOMP
EAT THIS, AKASHI!!

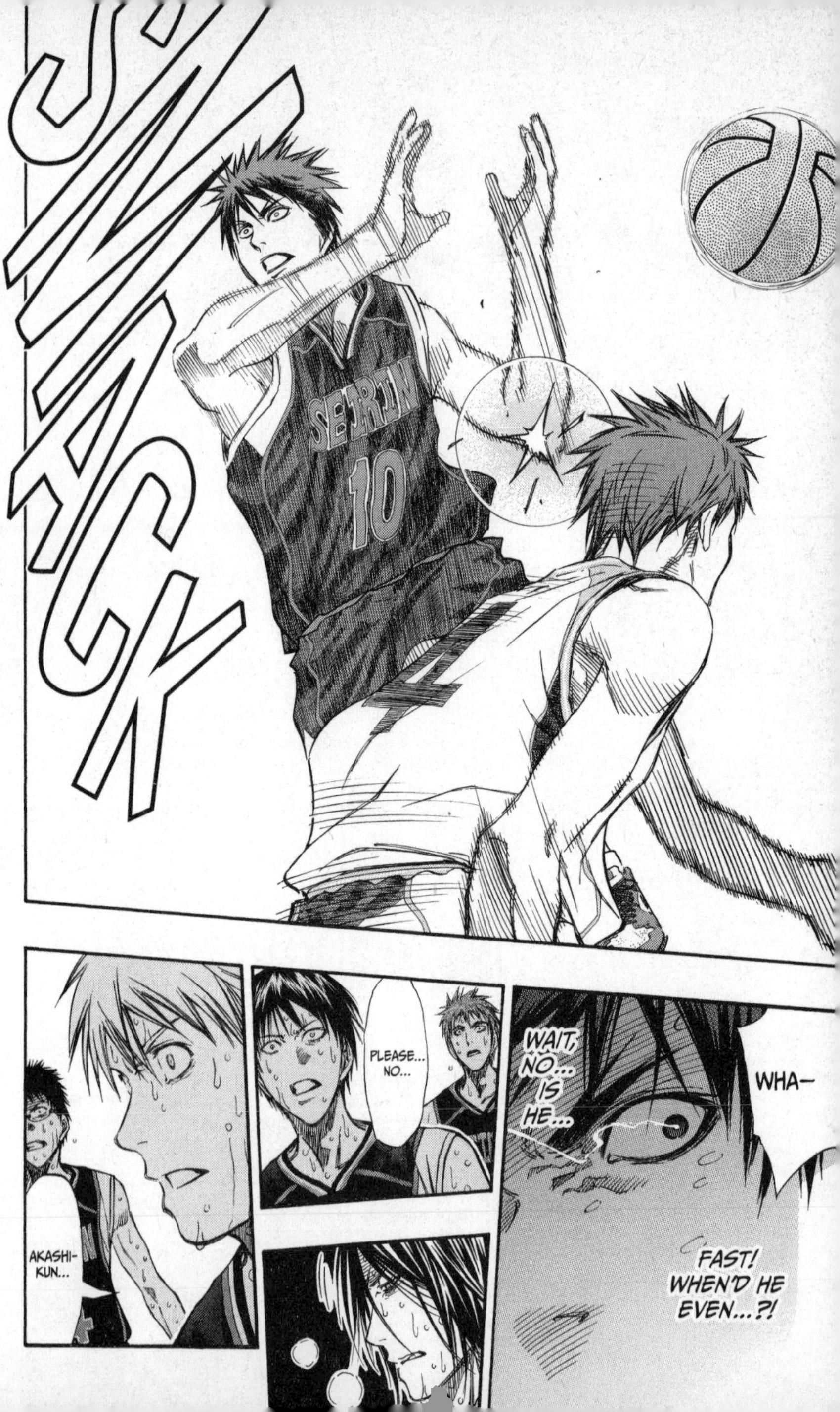
SMACK
SEIRIN 10
WHA—
WAIT, NO... IS HE...
FAST! WHEN'D HE EVEN...?!
PLEASE... NO...
AKASHI-KUN...

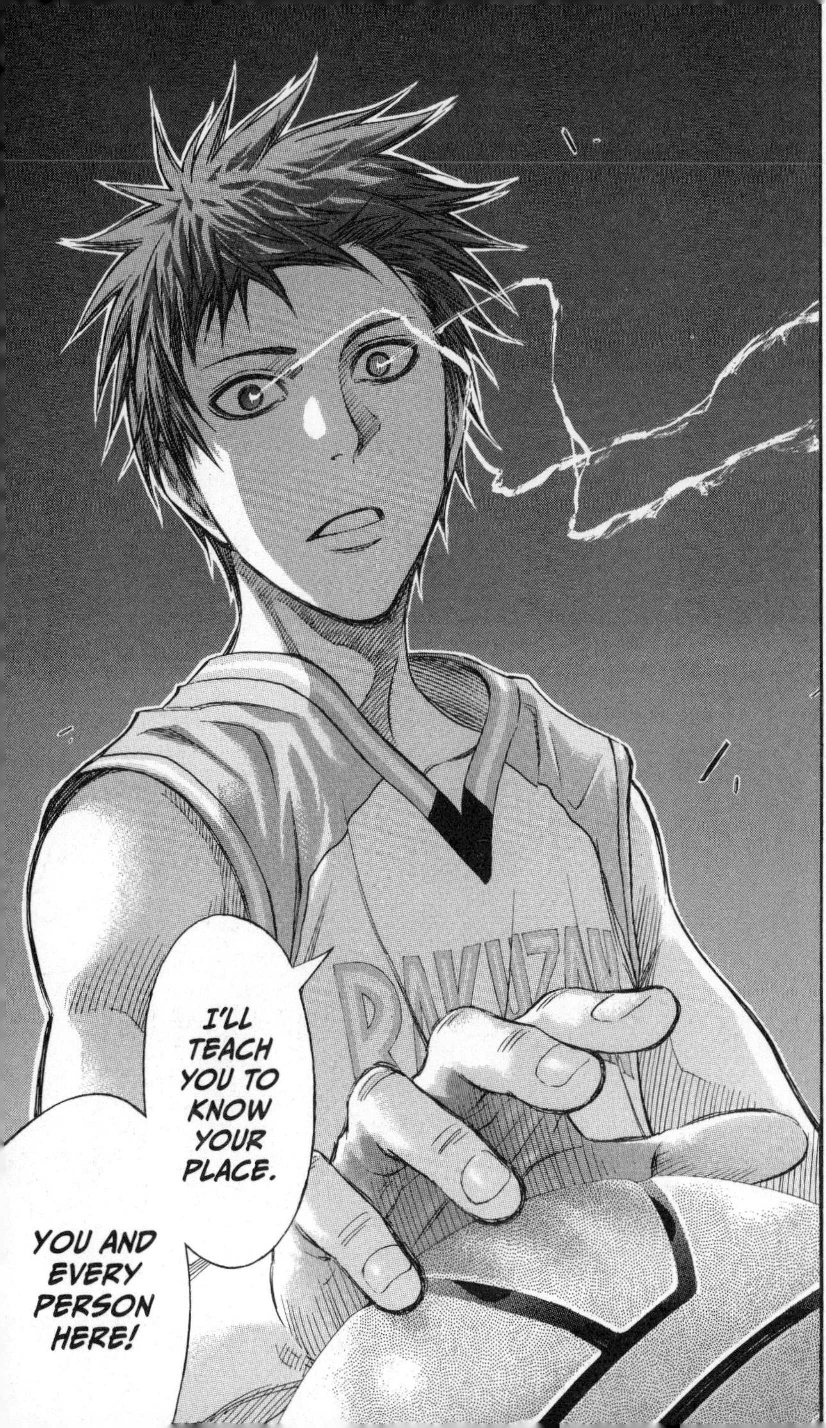
I'LL TEACH YOU TO KNOW YOUR PLACE.
YOU AND EVERY PERSON HERE!

KUROKO'S BASKETBALL Q&A (W/ HALFWAY-DECENT ANSWERS)

Q. IN 180TH QUARTER, TAKAO AND MIDORIMA PERFORM A MOVE THAT REMINDS PEOPLE OF KUROKO AND KAGAMI. DOES THAT MOVE HAVE A NAME? IF SO, I'D REALLY LIKE TO KNOW IT.
(OLD MAN T from NAGANO PRECECTURE)

A. "SKY DIRECT THREE-POINT SHOT."

KUROKO'S BASKETBALL BLOOPERS TAKE 2

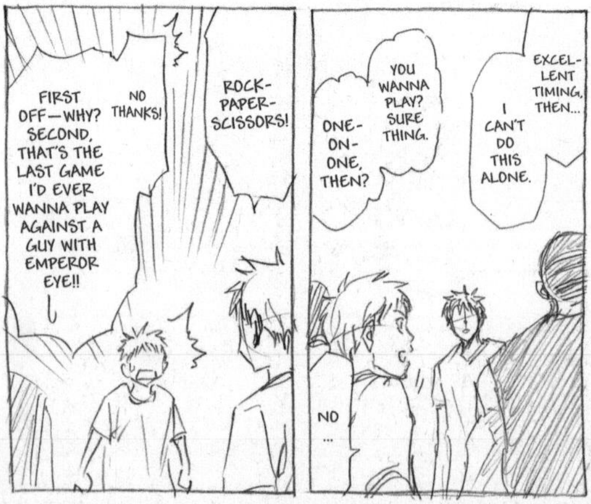
EXCEL-LENT TIMING, THEN...
I CAN'T DO THIS ALONE.
YOU WANNA PLAY? SURE THING.
ONE-ON-ONE, THEN?
NO ...
ROCK-PAPER-SCISSORS!
NO THANKS!
FIRST OFF—WHY? SECOND, THAT'S THE LAST GAME I'D EVER WANNA PLAY AGAINST A GUY WITH EMPEROR EYE!!

261ST QUARTER: AND THAT'S ENOUGH

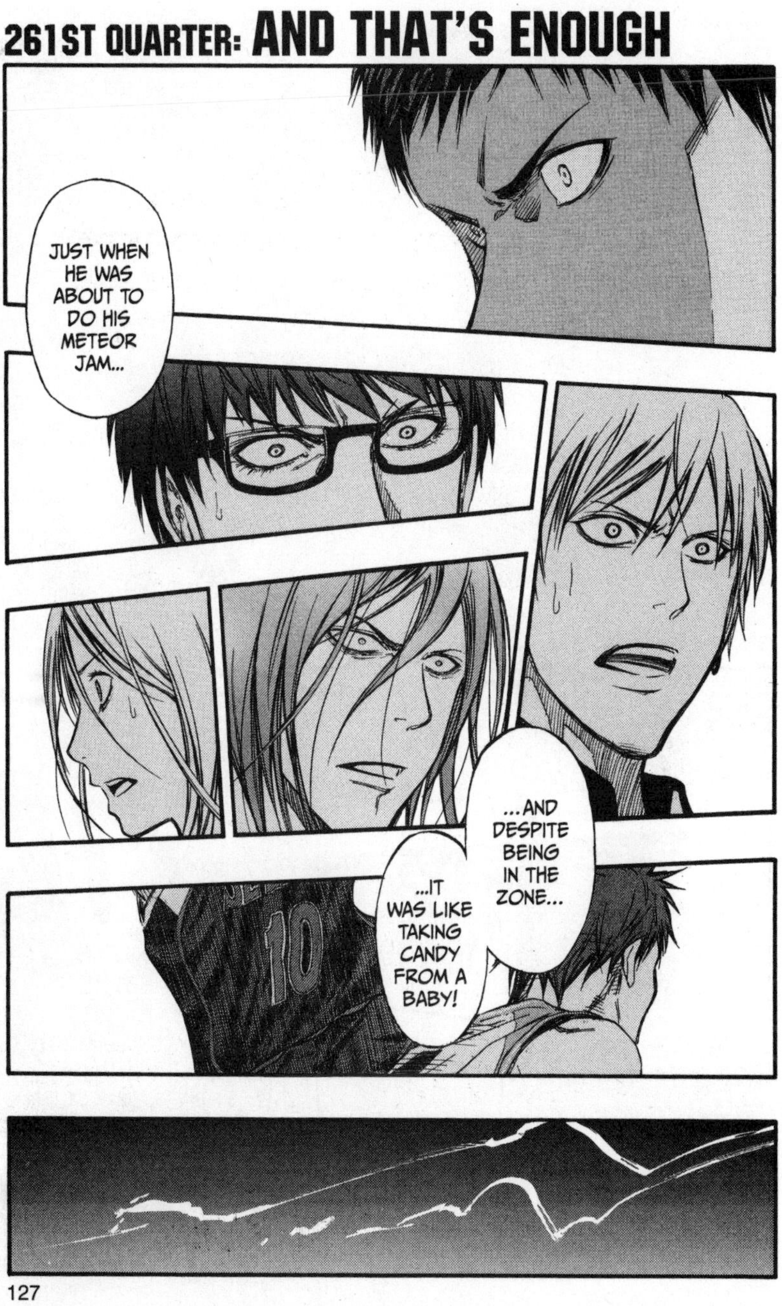
JUST WHEN HE WAS ABOUT TO DO HIS METEOR JAM...
...AND DESPITE BEING IN THE ZONE...
...IT WAS LIKE TAKING CANDY FROM A BABY!

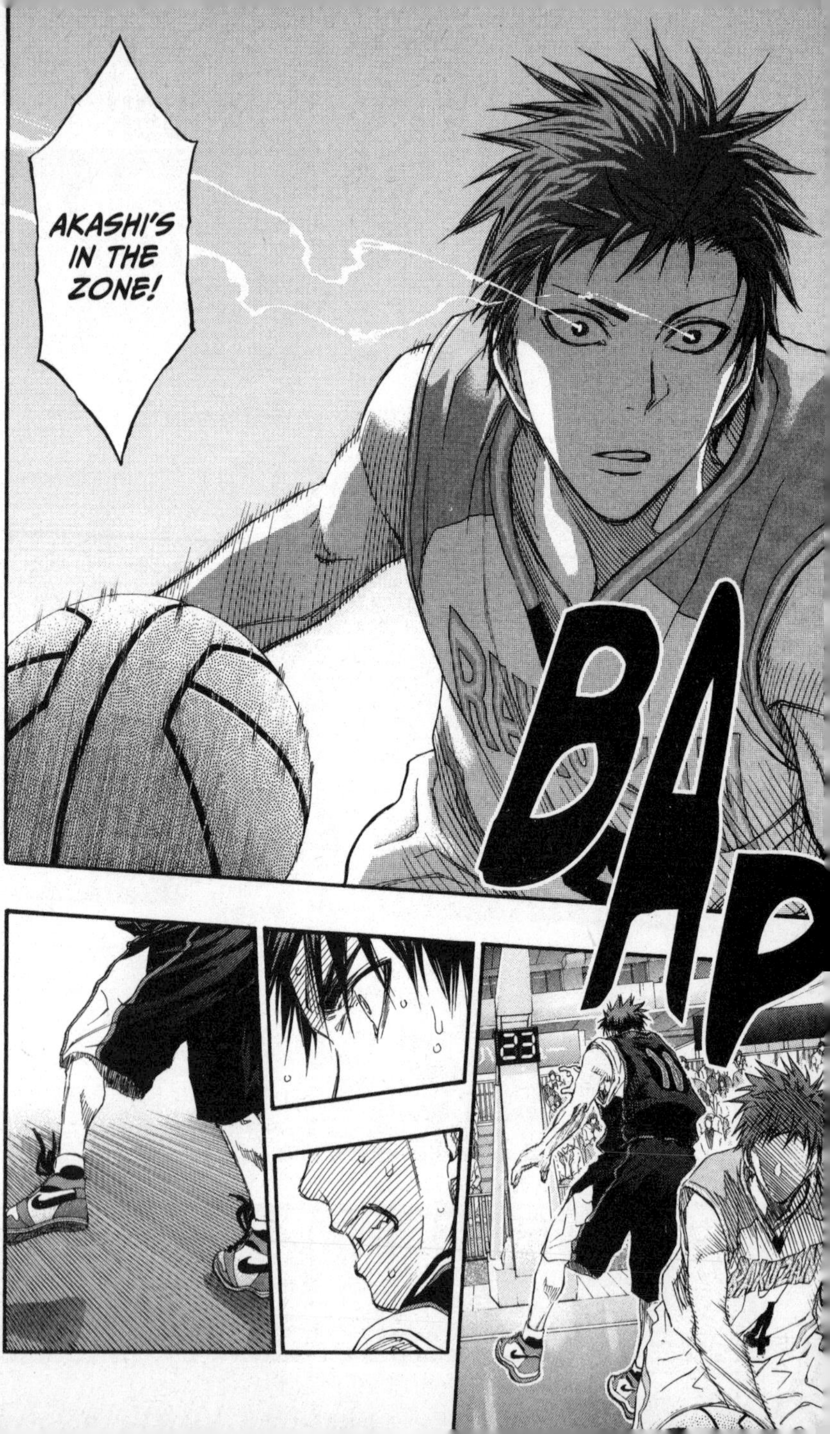
AKASHI'S IN THE ZONE!
BAP

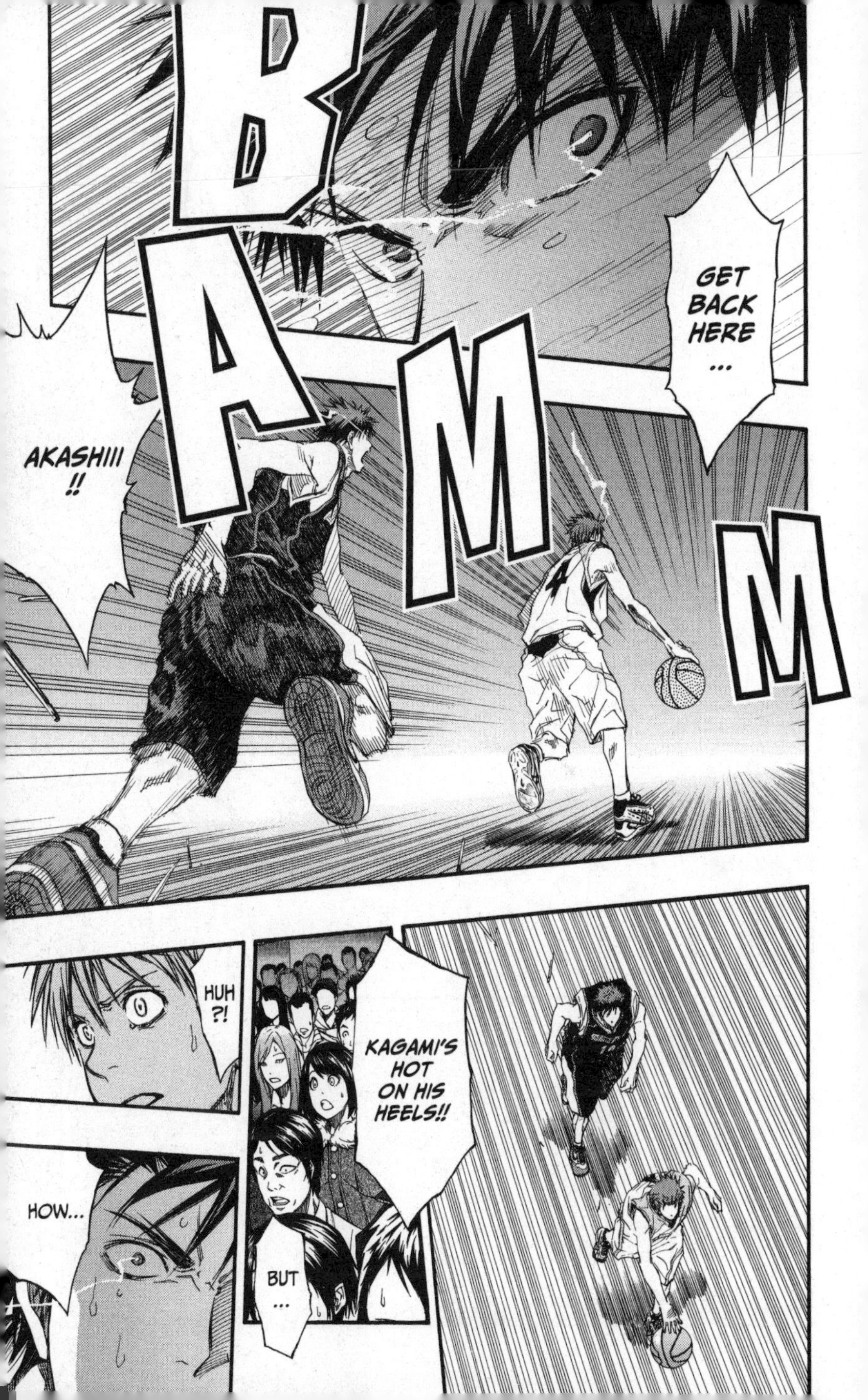
GET BACK HERE ...
BAMM
AKASHIII !!
KAGAMI'S HOT ON HIS HEELS!!
BUT ...
HUH ?!
HOW...

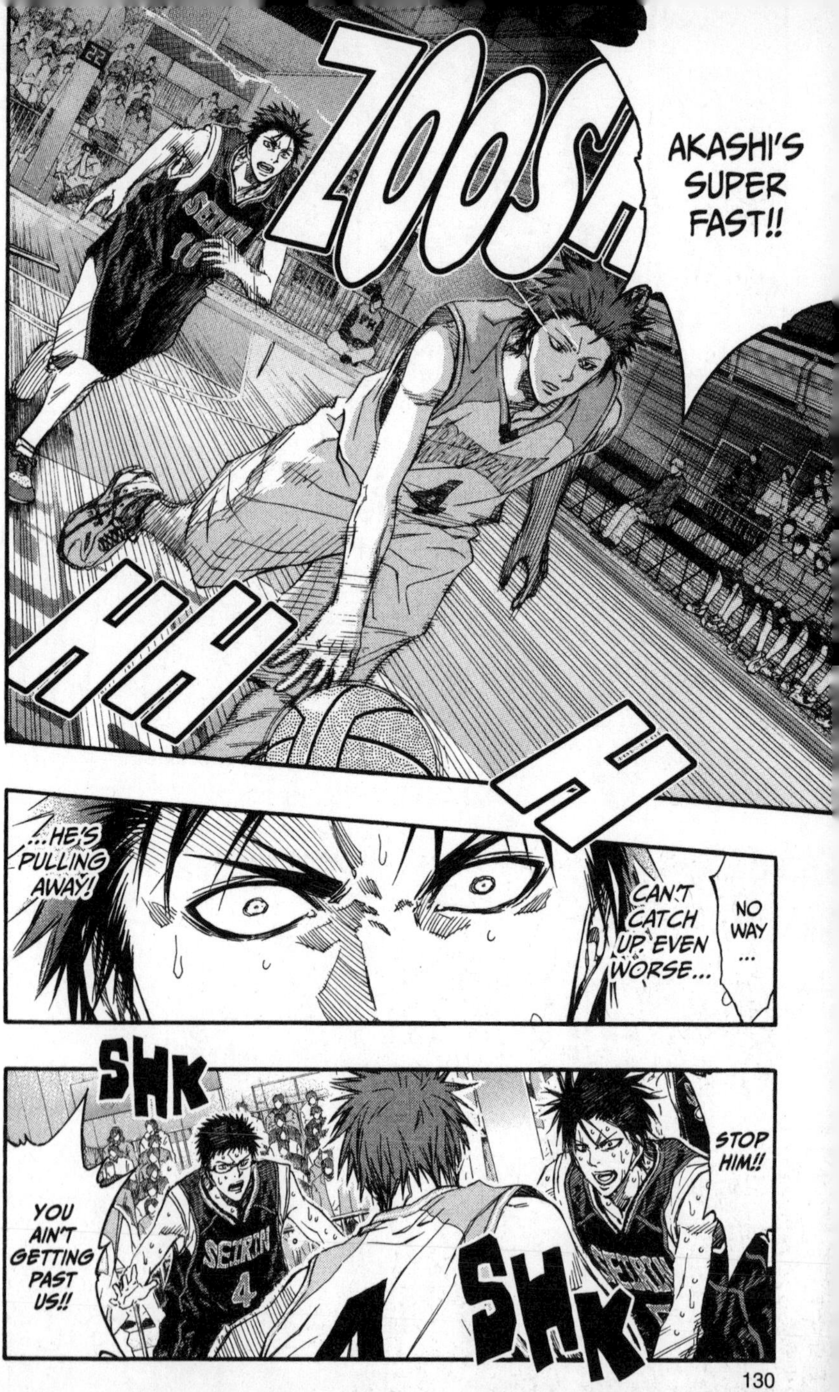
ZOOSH
AKASHI'S SUPER FAST!!
HH
H
NO WAY ...
CAN'T CATCH UP. EVEN WORSE...
...HE'S PULLING AWAY!
STOP HIM!!
SHK
YOU AIN'T GETTING PAST US!!
SHK

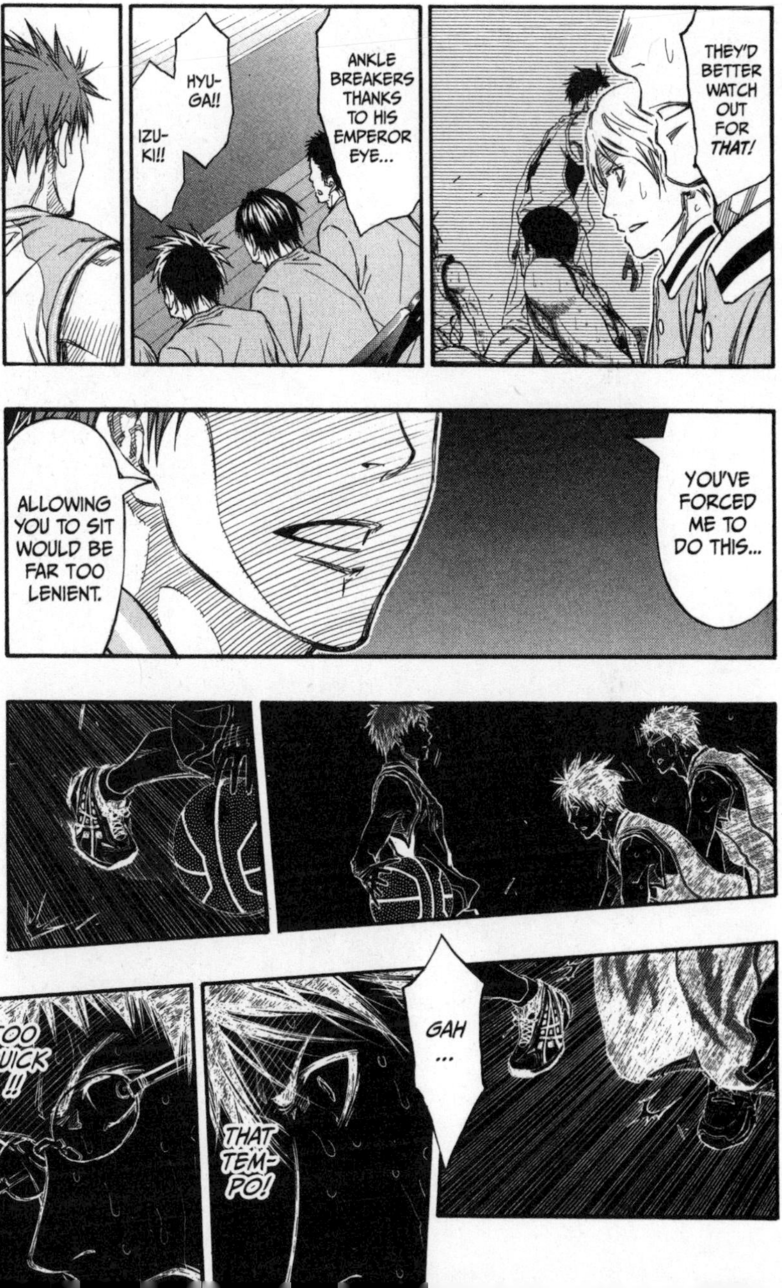
THEY'D BETTER WATCH OUT FOR *THAT!*
ANKLE BREAKERS THANKS TO HIS EMPEROR EYE...
HYU-GA!!
IZU-KI!!
YOU'VE FORCED ME TO DO THIS...
ALLOWING YOU TO SIT WOULD BE FAR TOO LENIENT.
GAH ...
THAT TEM-PO!
TOO QUICK!!

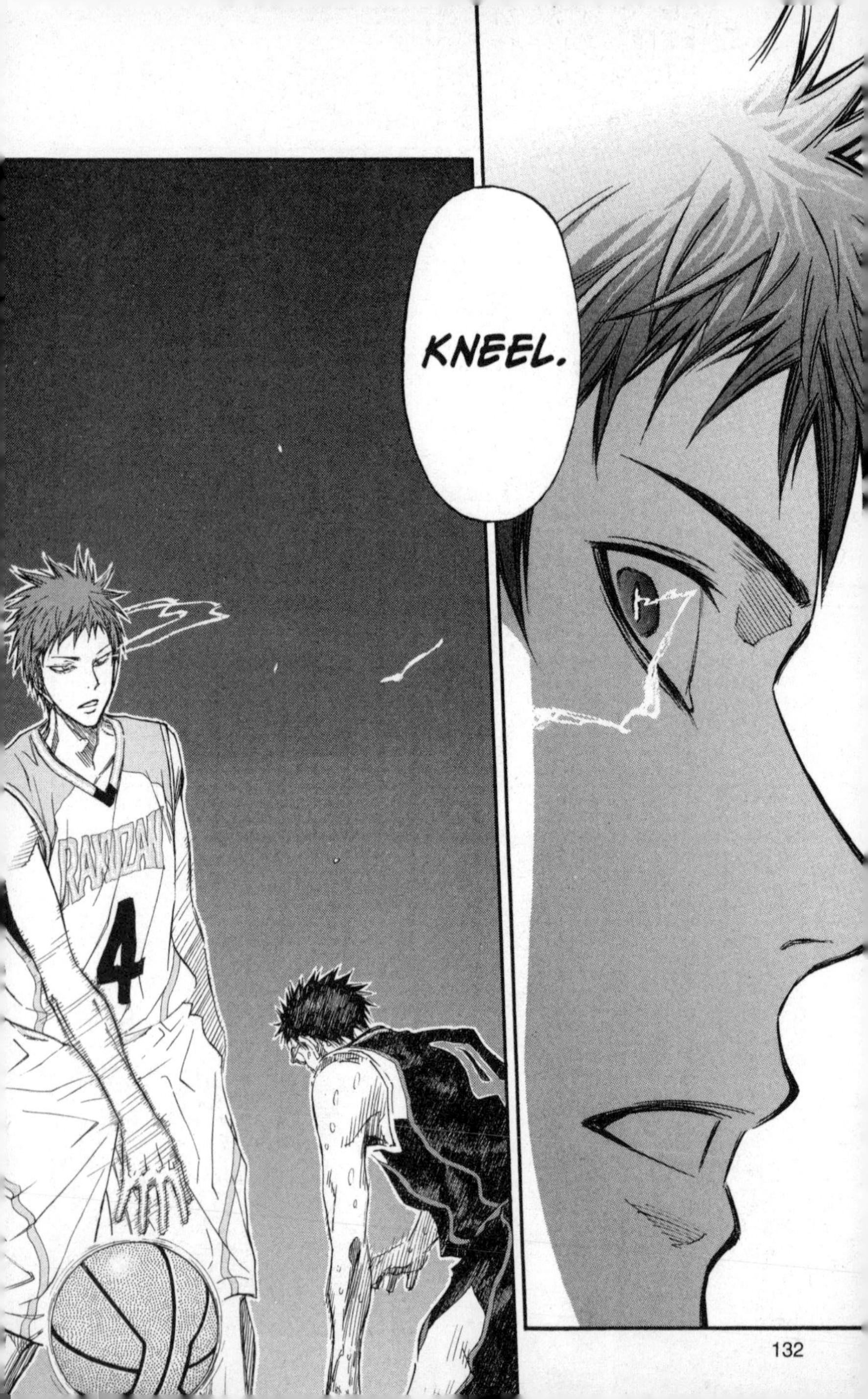
KNEEL.
RAKUZAN
4

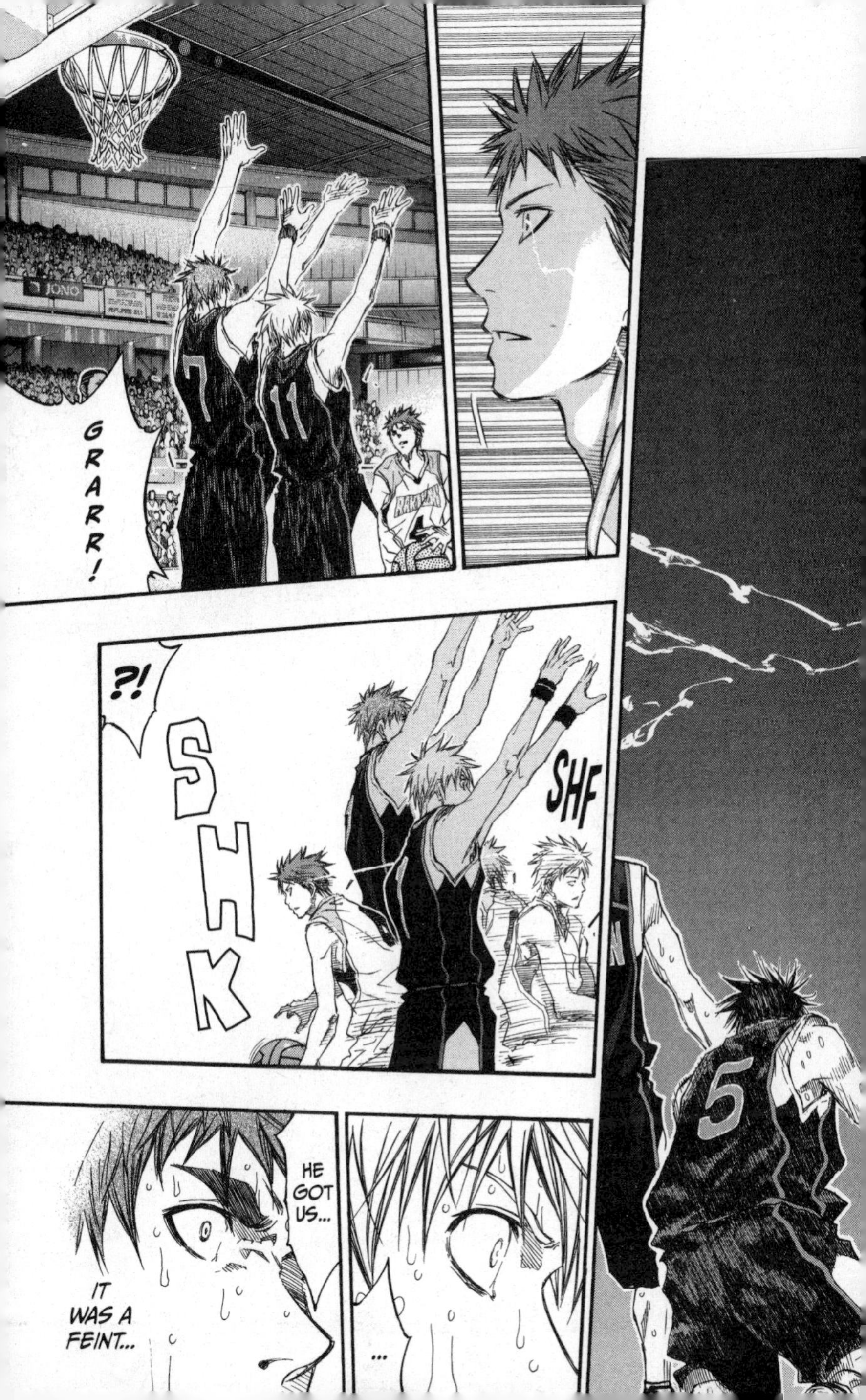
GRARR!
?!
SHF
SHK
...
HE GOT US...
IT WAS A FEINT...

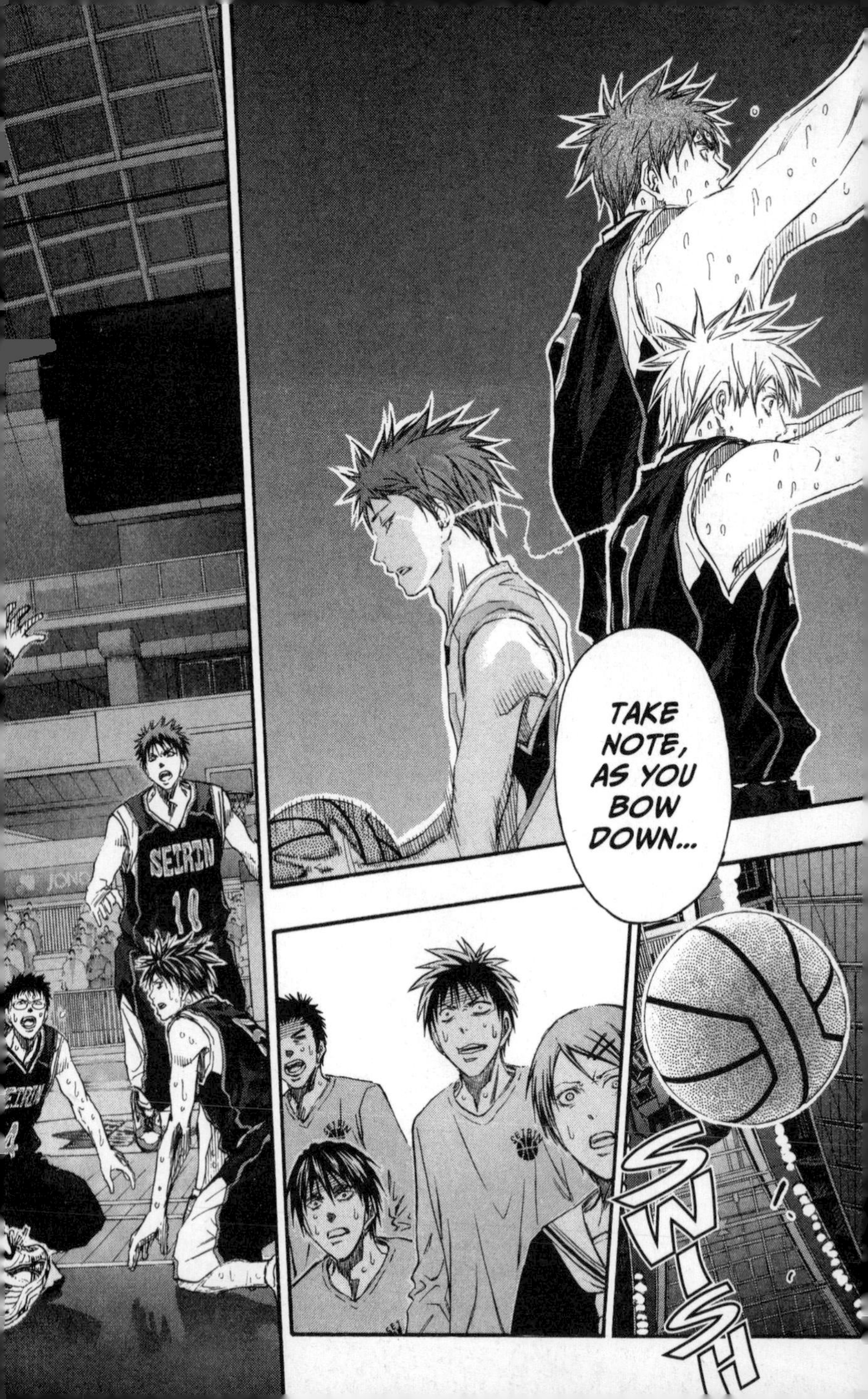
TAKE NOTE, AS YOU BOW DOWN...
SWISH
SEIRIN
SEIRIN

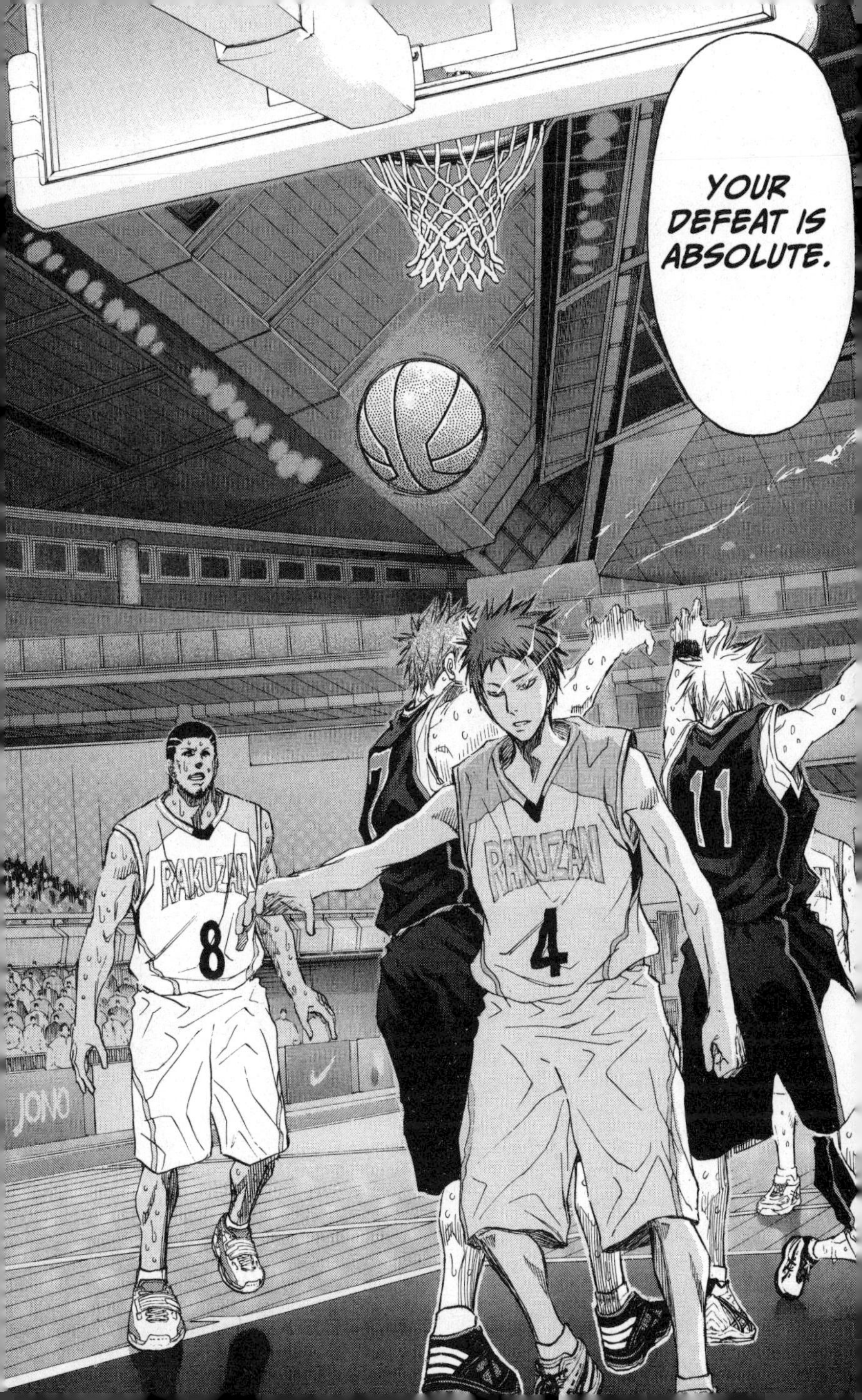
YOUR DEFEAT IS ABSOLUTE.
RAKUZAN
8
RAKUZAN
4
11
JONO

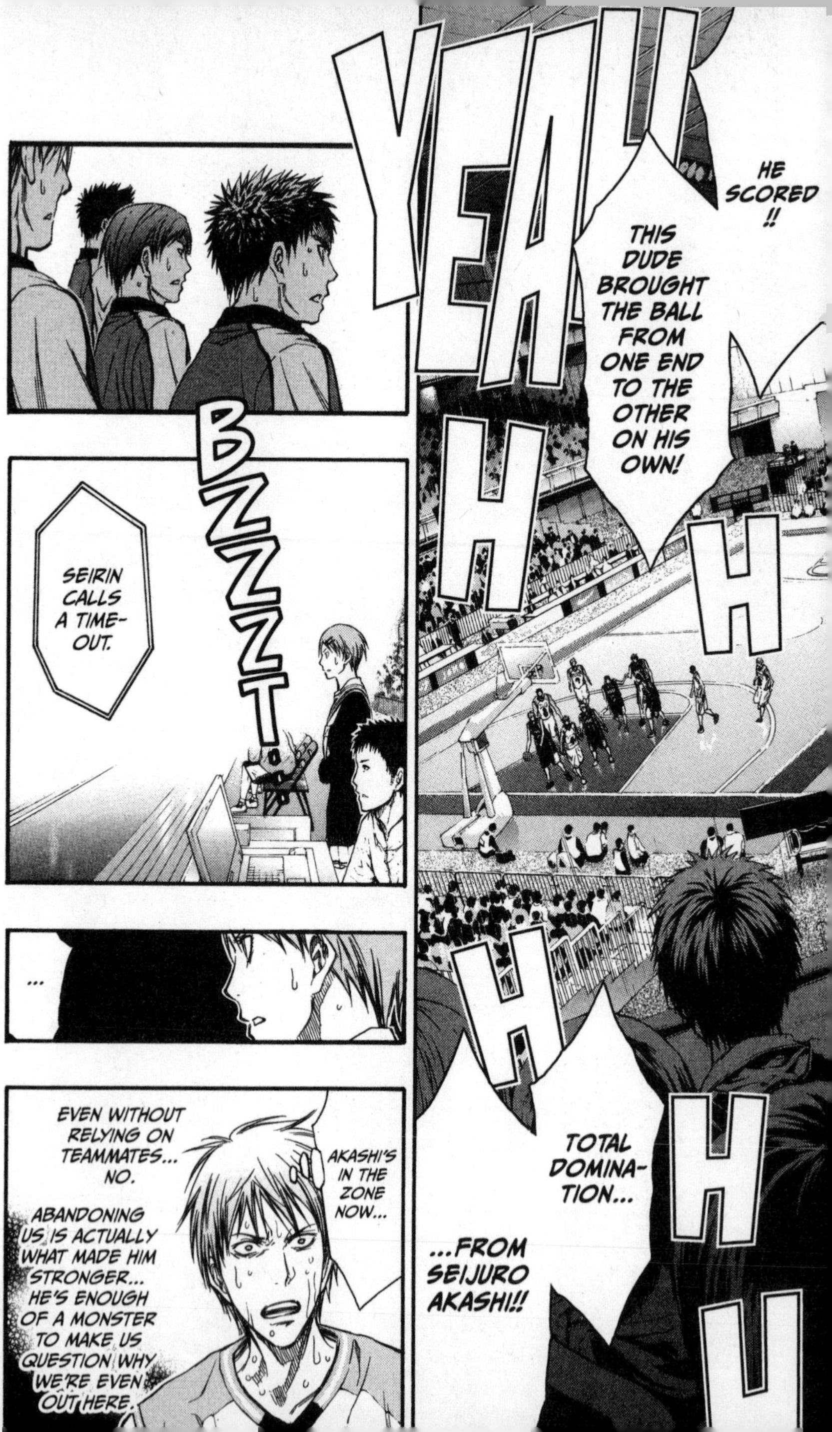
YEAHHHHH
HE SCORED !!
THIS DUDE BROUGHT THE BALL FROM ONE END TO THE OTHER ON HIS OWN!
TOTAL DOMINA-TION...
...FROM SEIJURO AKASHI!!
BZZZZT
SEIRIN CALLS A TIME-OUT.
...
AKASHI'S IN THE ZONE NOW...
EVEN WITHOUT RELYING ON TEAMMATES... NO.
ABANDONING US IS ACTUALLY WHAT MADE HIM STRONGER... HE'S ENOUGH OF A MONSTER TO MAKE US QUESTION WHY WE'RE EVEN OUT HERE.

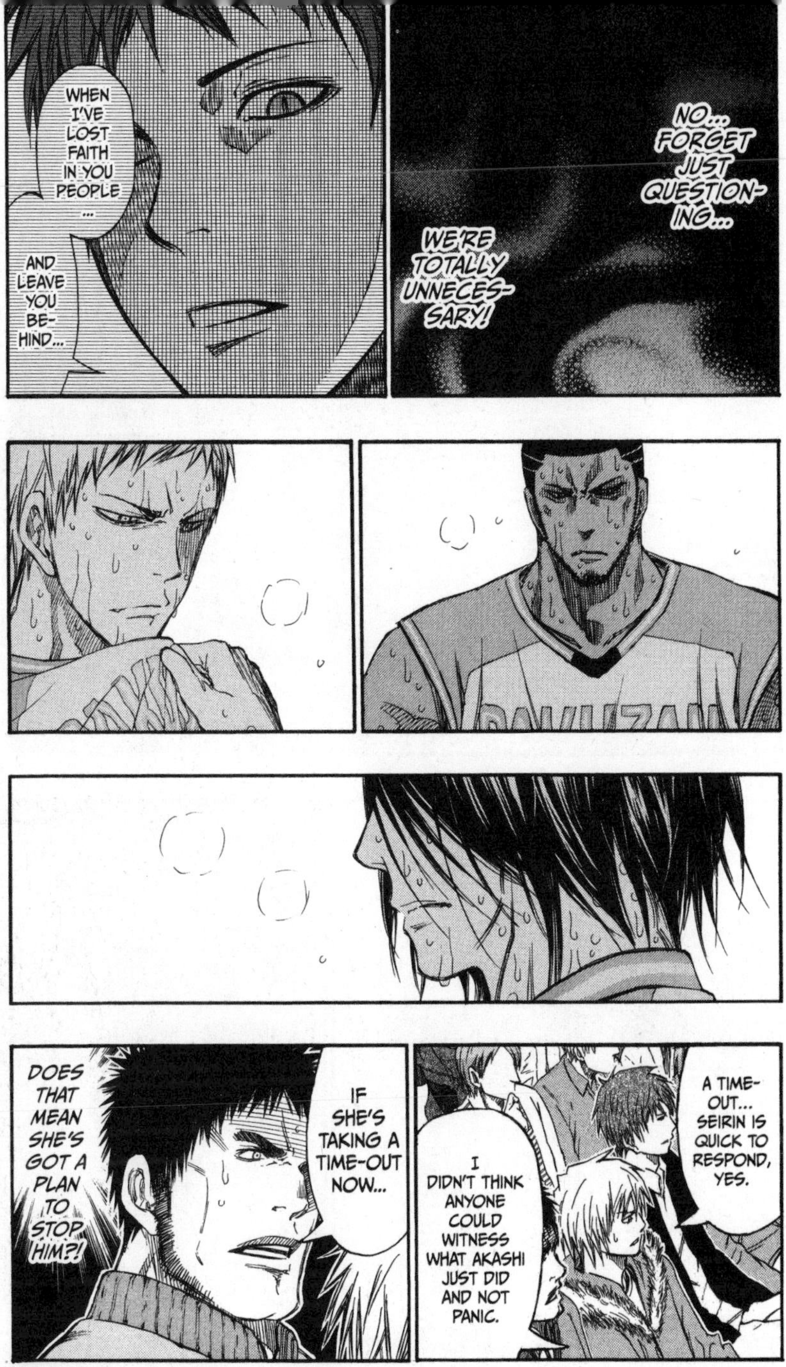
NO... FORGET JUST QUESTIONING...
WE'RE TOTALLY UNNECESSARY!
WHEN I'VE LOST FAITH IN YOU PEOPLE ...
AND LEAVE YOU BEHIND...
A TIME-OUT... SEIRIN IS QUICK TO RESPOND, YES.
I DIDN'T THINK ANYONE COULD WITNESS WHAT AKASHI JUST DID AND NOT PANIC.
IF SHE'S TAKING A TIME-OUT NOW...
DOES THAT MEAN SHE'S GOT A PLAN TO STOP HIM?!

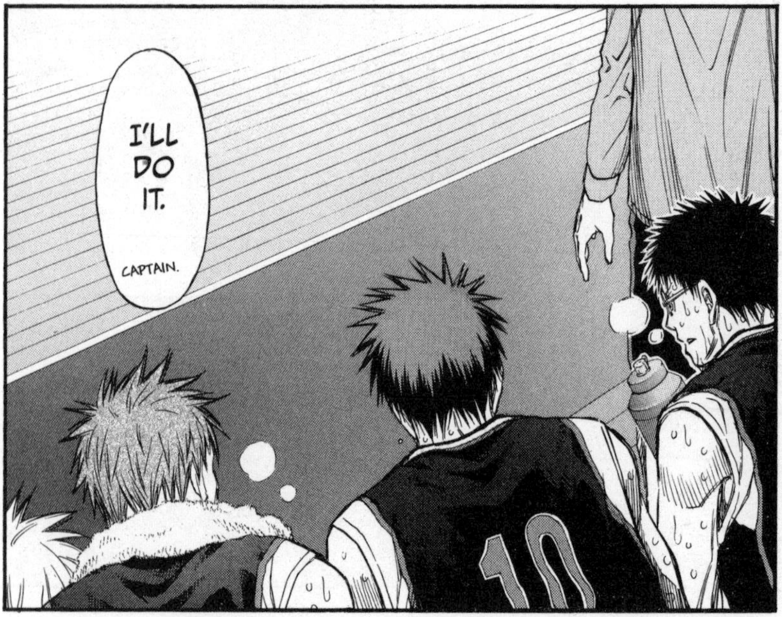

I'LL DO IT.
CAPTAIN.

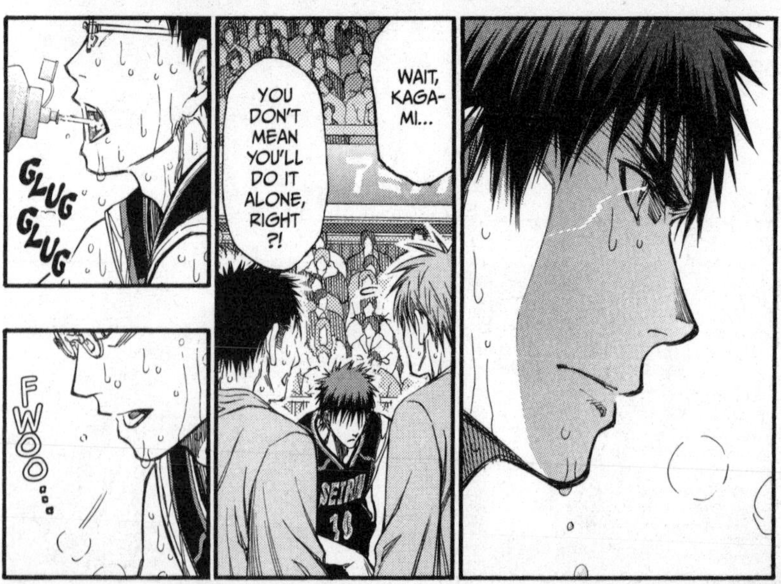

WAIT, KAGA-MI...
YOU DON'T MEAN YOU'LL DO IT ALONE, RIGHT ?!
GLUG GLUG
FWOO...

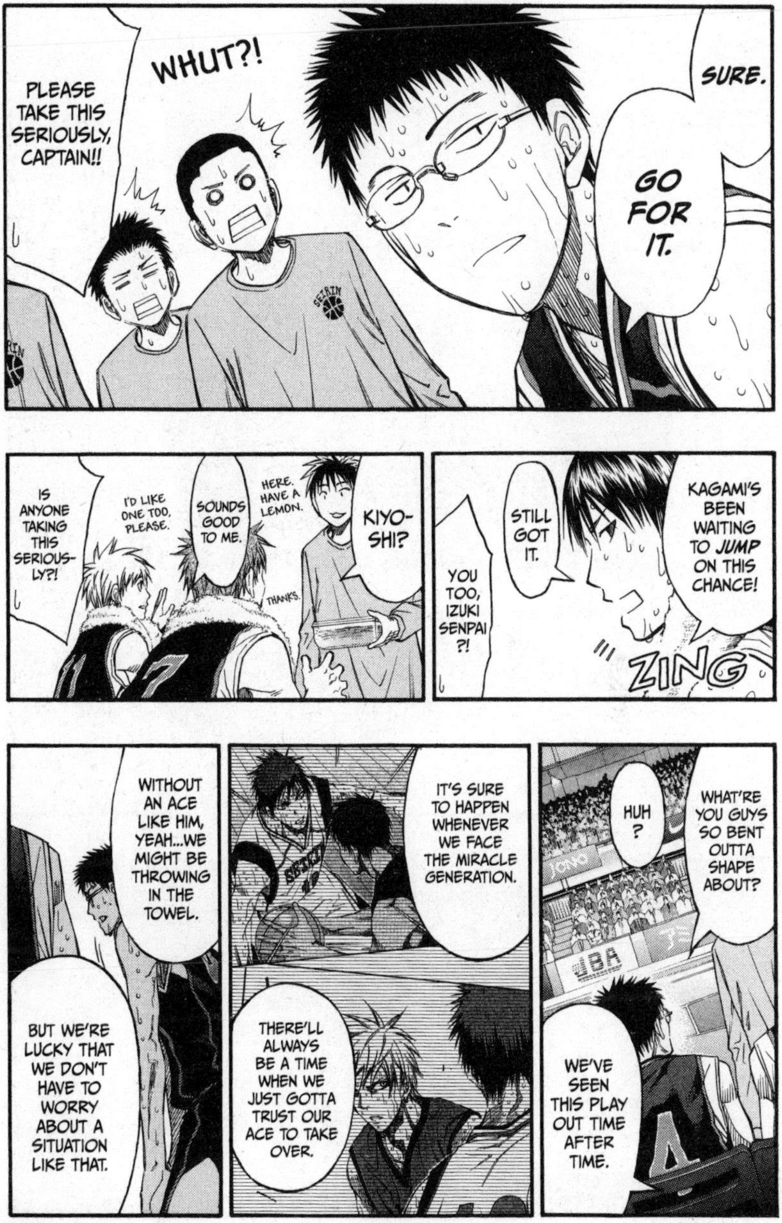
SURE.
GO FOR IT.
WHUT?!
PLEASE TAKE THIS SERIOUSLY, CAPTAIN!!
KAGAMI'S BEEN WAITING TO *JUMP* ON THIS CHANCE!
ZING
STILL GOT IT.
YOU TOO, IZUKI SENPAI?!
KIYO-SHI?
HERE. HAVE A LEMON.
SOUNDS GOOD TO ME.
THANKS.
I'D LIKE ONE TOO, PLEASE.
IS ANYONE TAKING THIS SERIOUS-LY?!
WHAT'RE YOU GUYS SO BENT OUTTA SHAPE ABOUT?
HUH?
WE'VE SEEN THIS PLAY OUT TIME AFTER TIME.
IT'S SURE TO HAPPEN WHENEVER WE FACE THE MIRACLE GENERATION.
THERE'LL ALWAYS BE A TIME WHEN WE JUST GOTTA TRUST OUR ACE TO TAKE OVER.
WITHOUT AN ACE LIKE HIM, YEAH...WE MIGHT BE THROWING IN THE TOWEL.
BUT WE'RE LUCKY THAT WE DON'T HAVE TO WORRY ABOUT A SITUATION LIKE THAT.

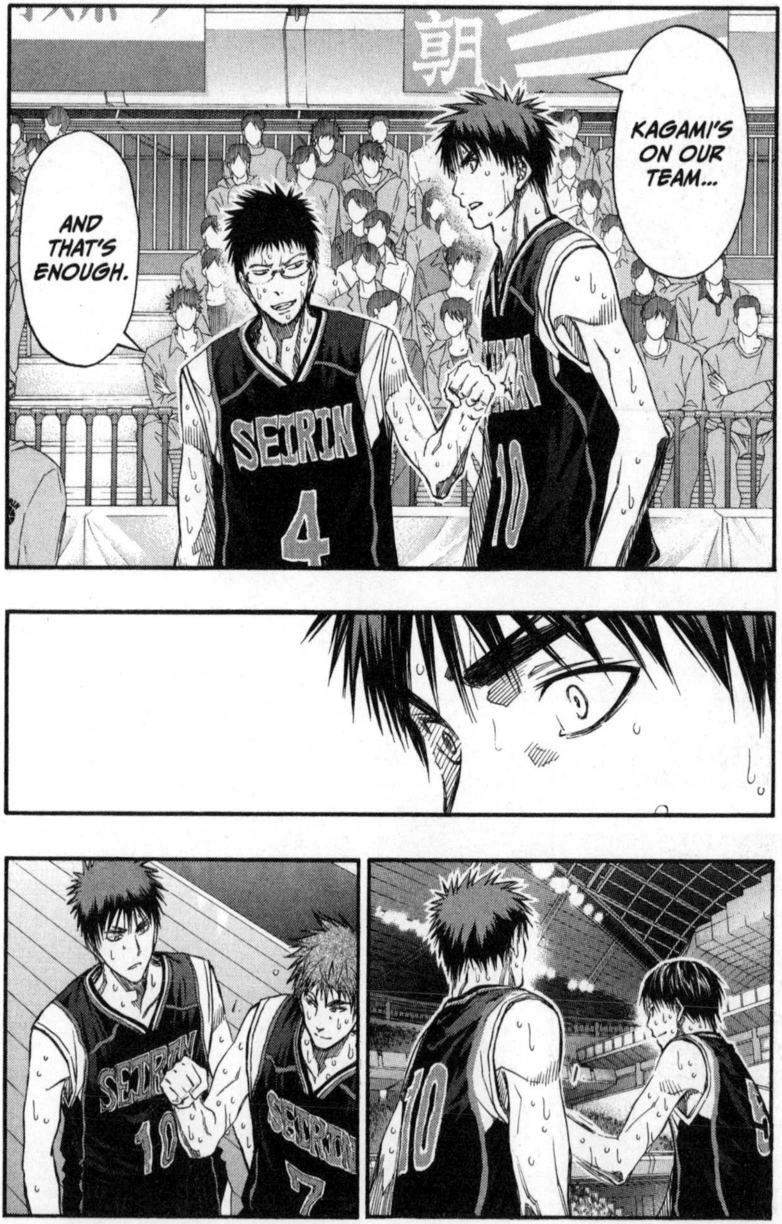
KAGAMI'S ON OUR TEAM...
AND THAT'S ENOUGH.

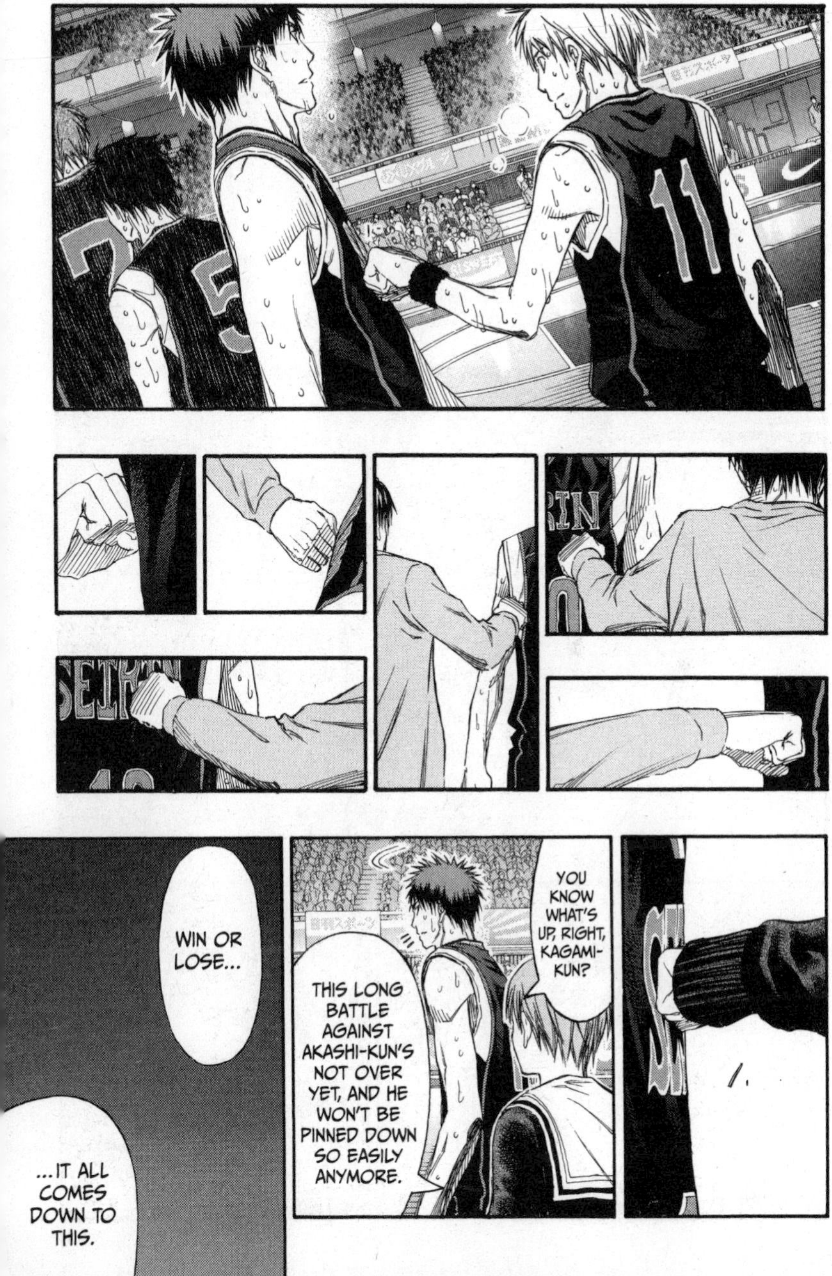
YOU KNOW WHAT'S UP, RIGHT, KAGAMI-KUN?
THIS LONG BATTLE AGAINST AKASHI-KUN'S NOT OVER YET, AND HE WON'T BE PINNED DOWN SO EASILY ANYMORE.
WIN OR LOSE...
...IT ALL COMES DOWN TO THIS.

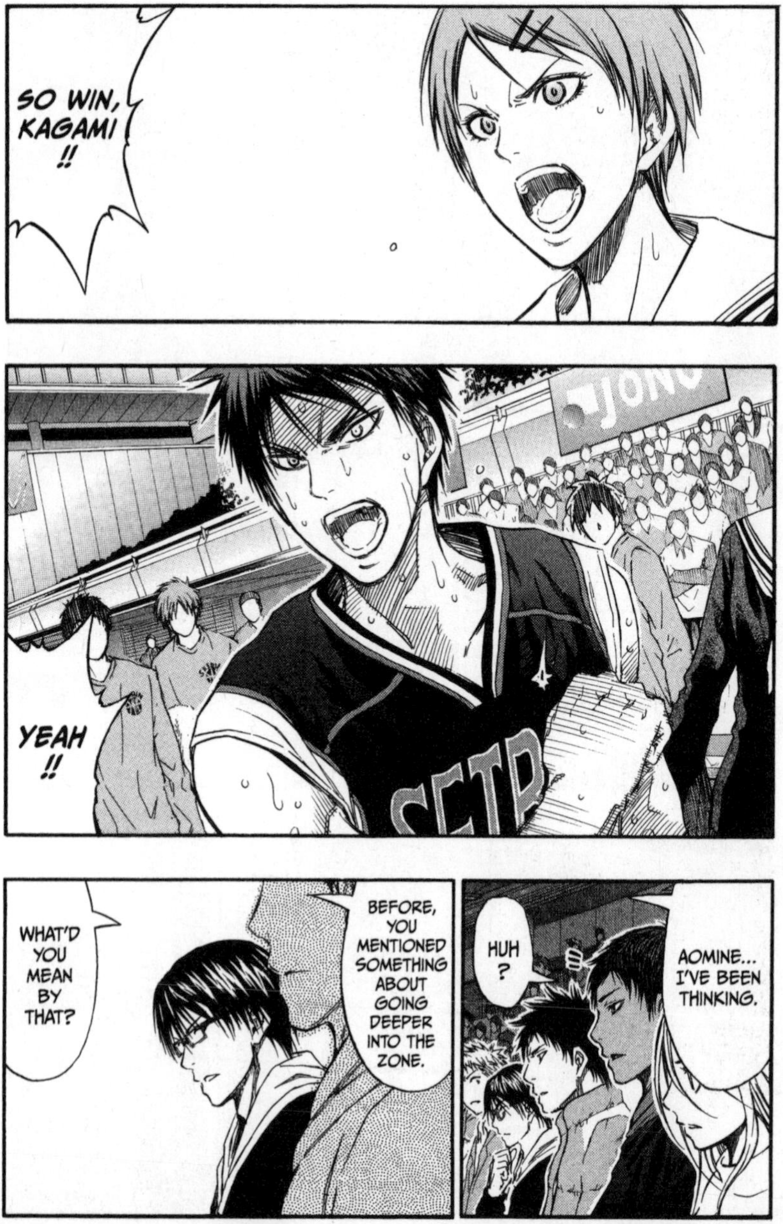
SO WIN, KAGAMI!!
YEAH!!
AOMINE... I'VE BEEN THINKING.
HUH?
BEFORE, YOU MENTIONED SOMETHING ABOUT GOING DEEPER INTO THE ZONE.
WHAT'D YOU MEAN BY THAT?

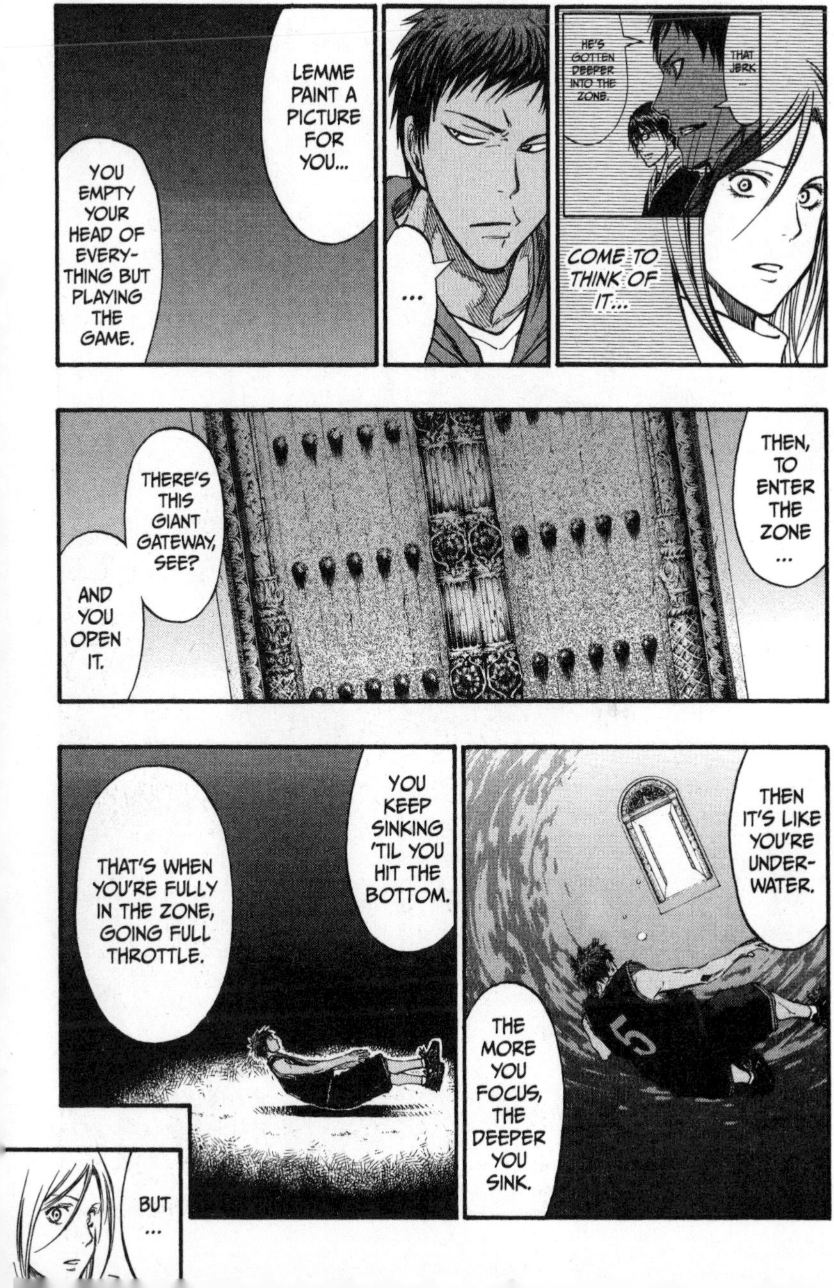
THAT JERK...
HE'S GOTTEN DEEPER INTO THE ZONE.
COME TO THINK OF IT...
...
LEMME PAINT A PICTURE FOR YOU...
YOU EMPTY YOUR HEAD OF EVERYTHING BUT PLAYING THE GAME.
THEN, TO ENTER THE ZONE...
THERE'S THIS GIANT GATEWAY, SEE?
AND YOU OPEN IT.
THEN IT'S LIKE YOU'RE UNDERWATER.
THE MORE YOU FOCUS, THE DEEPER YOU SINK.
YOU KEEP SINKING 'TIL YOU HIT THE BOTTOM.
THAT'S WHEN YOU'RE FULLY IN THE ZONE, GOING FULL THROTTLE.
BUT...

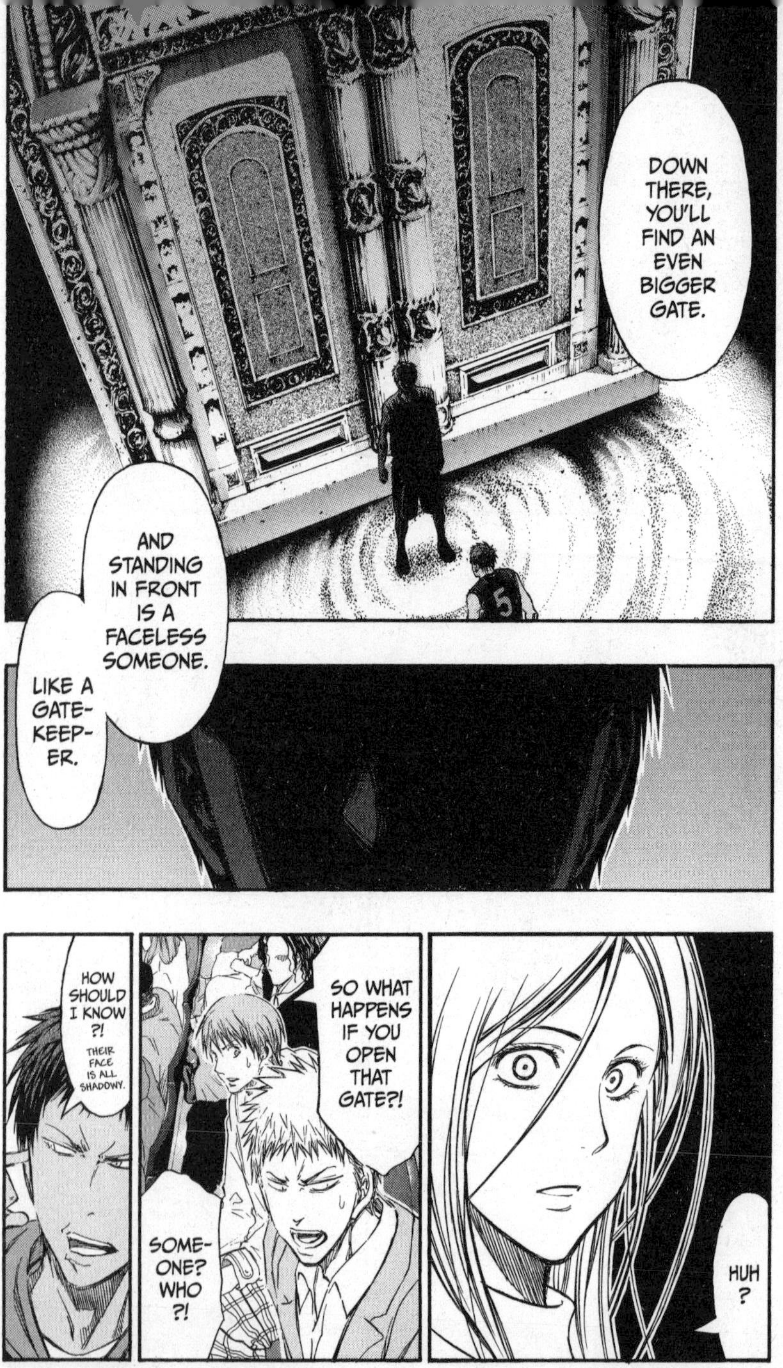
DOWN THERE, YOU'LL FIND AN EVEN BIGGER GATE.
AND STANDING IN FRONT IS A FACELESS SOMEONE.
LIKE A GATE-KEEP-ER.
HUH?
SO WHAT HAPPENS IF YOU OPEN THAT GATE?!
SOME-ONE? WHO?!
HOW SHOULD I KNOW?!
THEIR FACE IS ALL SHADOWY.

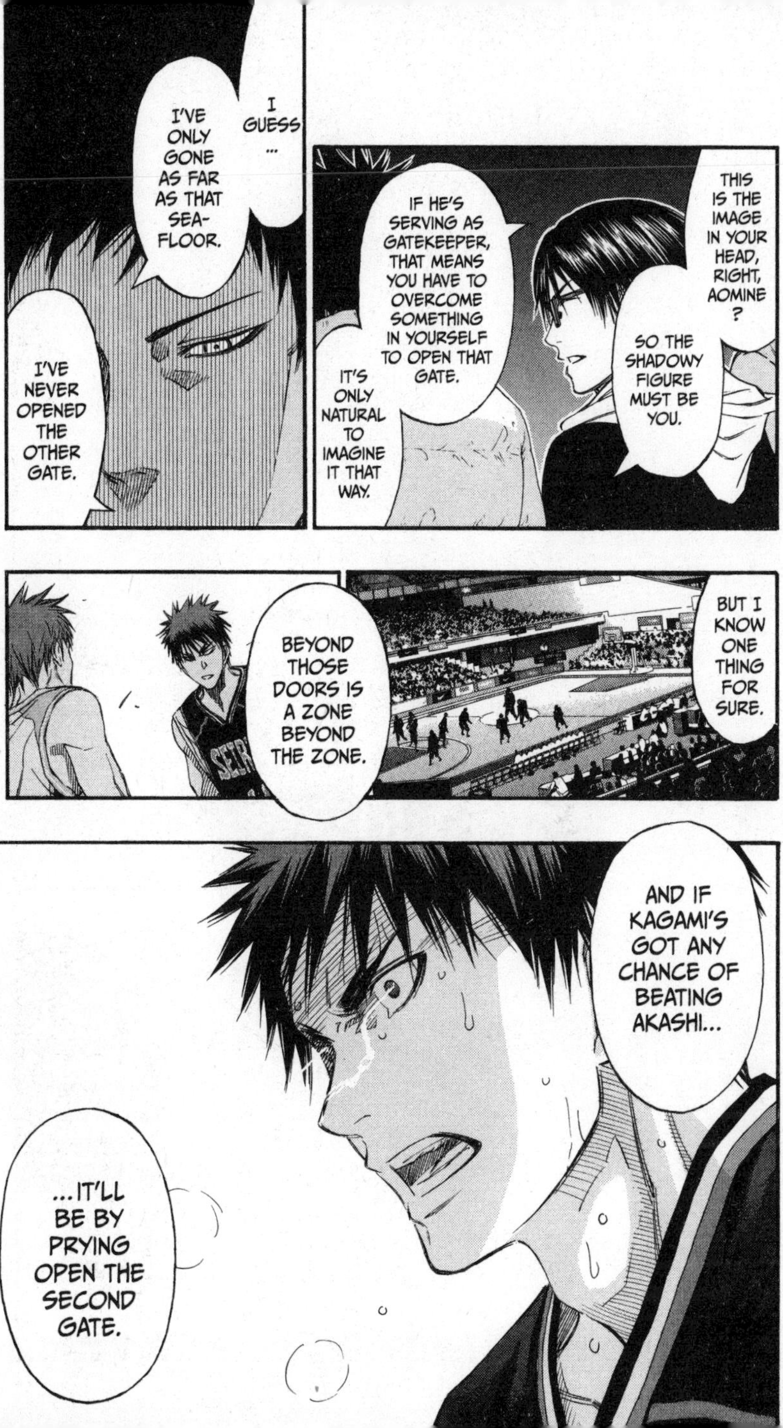
THIS IS THE IMAGE IN YOUR HEAD, RIGHT, AOMINE?
SO THE SHADOWY FIGURE MUST BE YOU.
IF HE'S SERVING AS GATEKEEPER, THAT MEANS YOU HAVE TO OVERCOME SOMETHING IN YOURSELF TO OPEN THAT GATE.
IT'S ONLY NATURAL TO IMAGINE IT THAT WAY.
I GUESS...
I'VE ONLY GONE AS FAR AS THAT SEA-FLOOR.
I'VE NEVER OPENED THE OTHER GATE.
BUT I KNOW ONE THING FOR SURE.
BEYOND THOSE DOORS IS A ZONE BEYOND THE ZONE.
AND IF KAGAMI'S GOT ANY CHANCE OF BEATING AKASHI...
...IT'LL BE BY PRYING OPEN THE SECOND GATE.

KUROKO'S BASKETBALL BLOOPERS
TAKE 4

THEN, TO ENTER THE ZONE...

THERE'S THIS GIANT GATEWAY, SEE?

AND YOU OPEN IT.

H-HANG ON!! THAT DESIGN'S A LITTLE UNDER-WHELMING, DON'TCHA THINK?!

YOU COULD JUST SMASH THE KNOB OFF AND STROLL ON THROUGH!

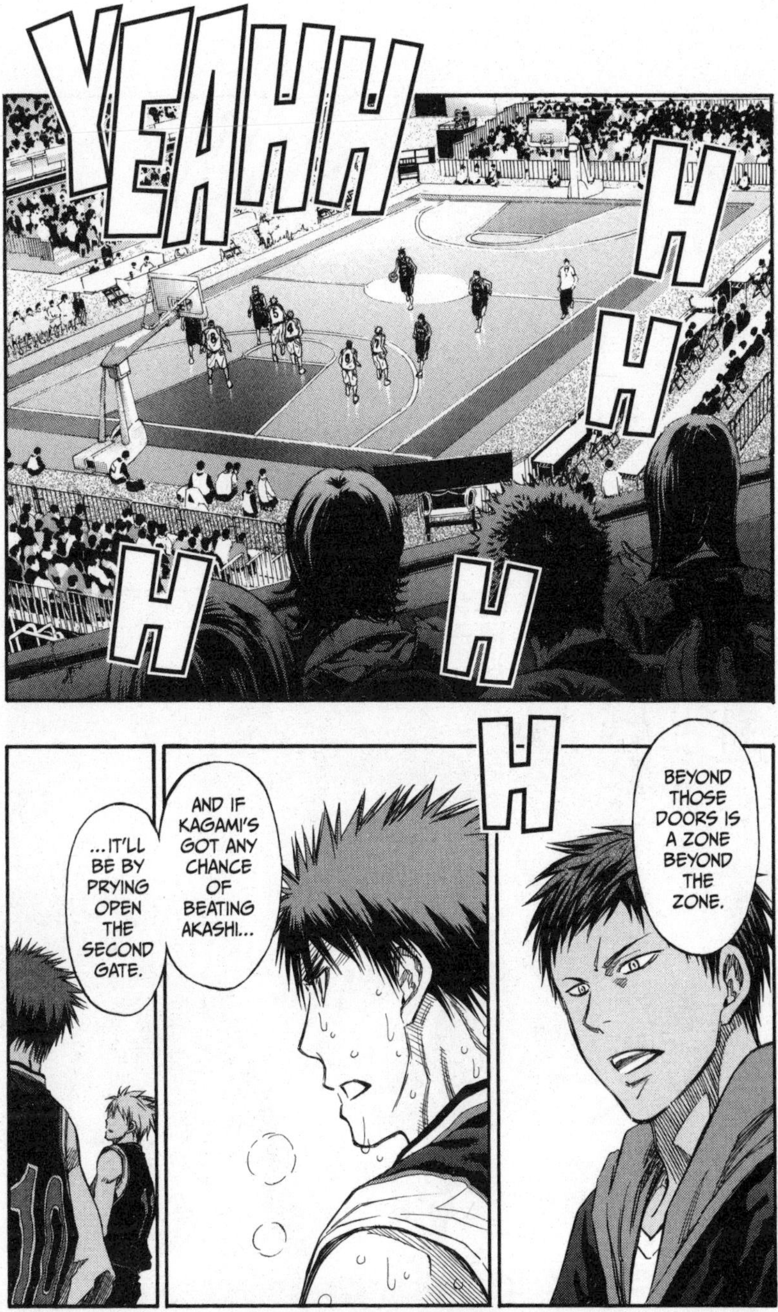
YEAHHHHHHHH
H
BEYOND THOSE DOORS IS A ZONE BEYOND THE ZONE.
AND IF KAGAMI'S GOT ANY CHANCE OF BEATING AKASHI...
...IT'LL BE BY PRYING OPEN THE SECOND GATE.

262ND QUARTER: HOW ABOUT GIVING UP?

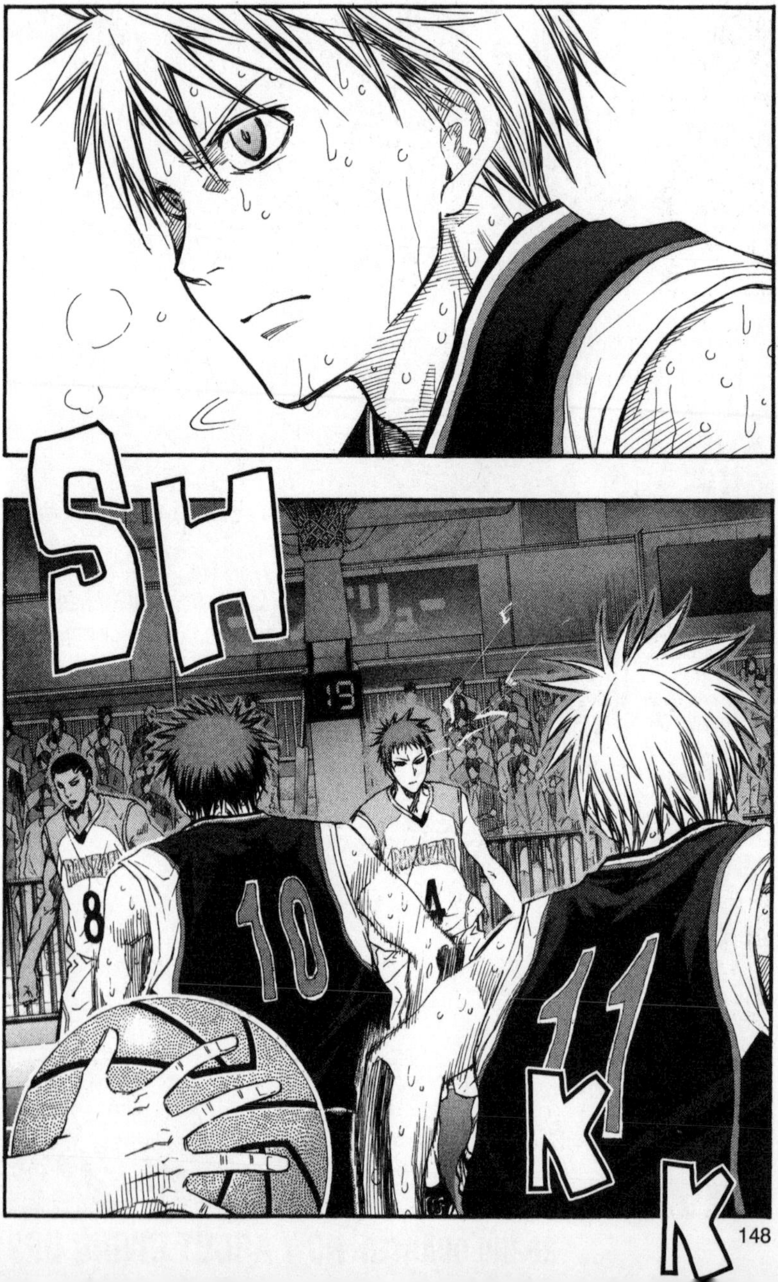
SH
KK

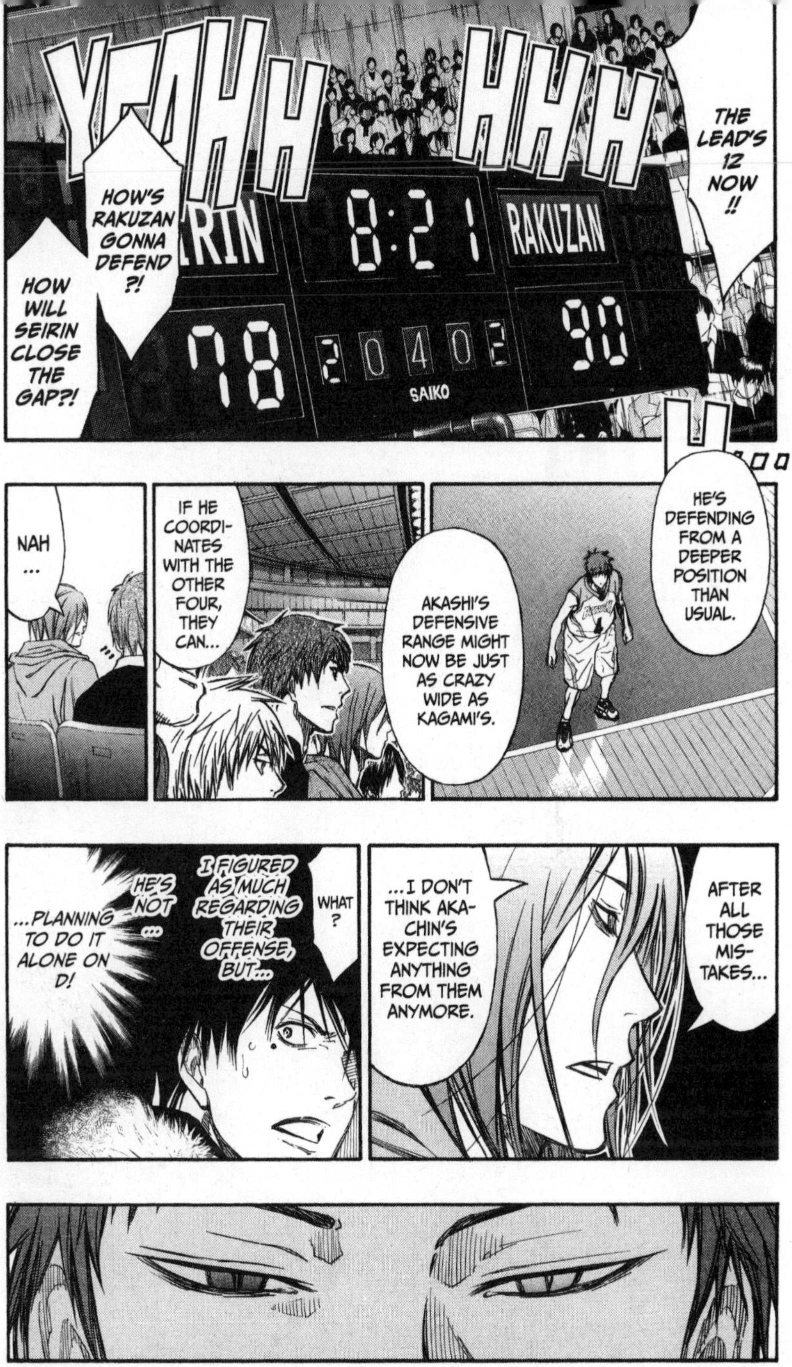
YEAHH
HHHH
THE LEAD'S 12 NOW!!
HOW'S RAKUZAN GONNA DEFEND?!
HOW WILL SEIRIN CLOSE THE GAP?!
IRIN
8:21
RAKUZAN
78
90
SAIKO
H...
HE'S DEFENDING FROM A DEEPER POSITION THAN USUAL.
AKASHI'S DEFENSIVE RANGE MIGHT NOW BE JUST AS CRAZY WIDE AS KAGAMI'S.
IF HE COORDINATES WITH THE OTHER FOUR, THEY CAN...
NAH...
AFTER ALL THOSE MISTAKES...
...I DON'T THINK AKA-CHIN'S EXPECTING ANYTHING FROM THEM ANYMORE.
WHAT?
I FIGURED AS MUCH REGARDING THEIR OFFENSE, BUT...
HE'S NOT...
...PLANNING TO DO IT ALONE ON D!

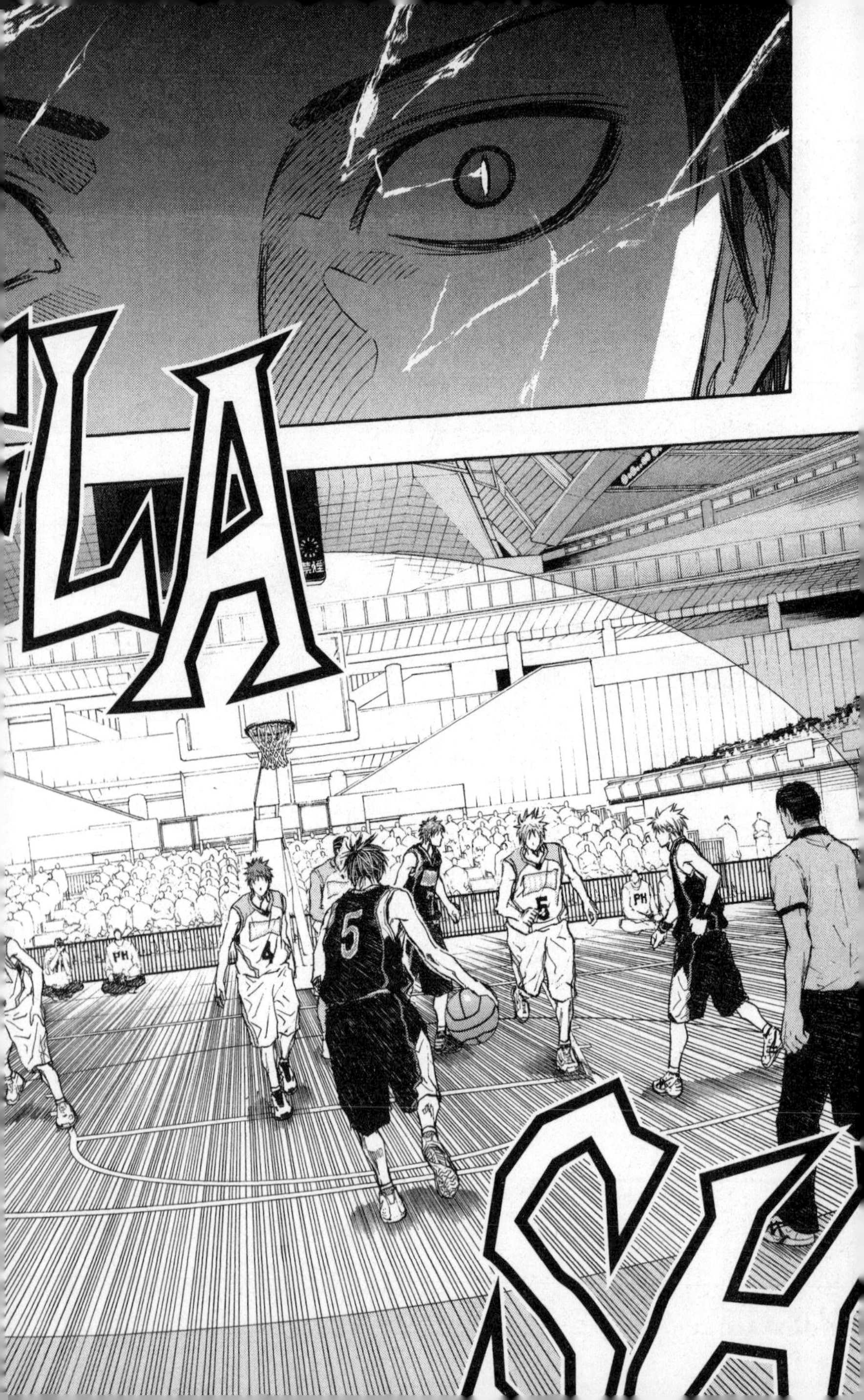
LA
SH

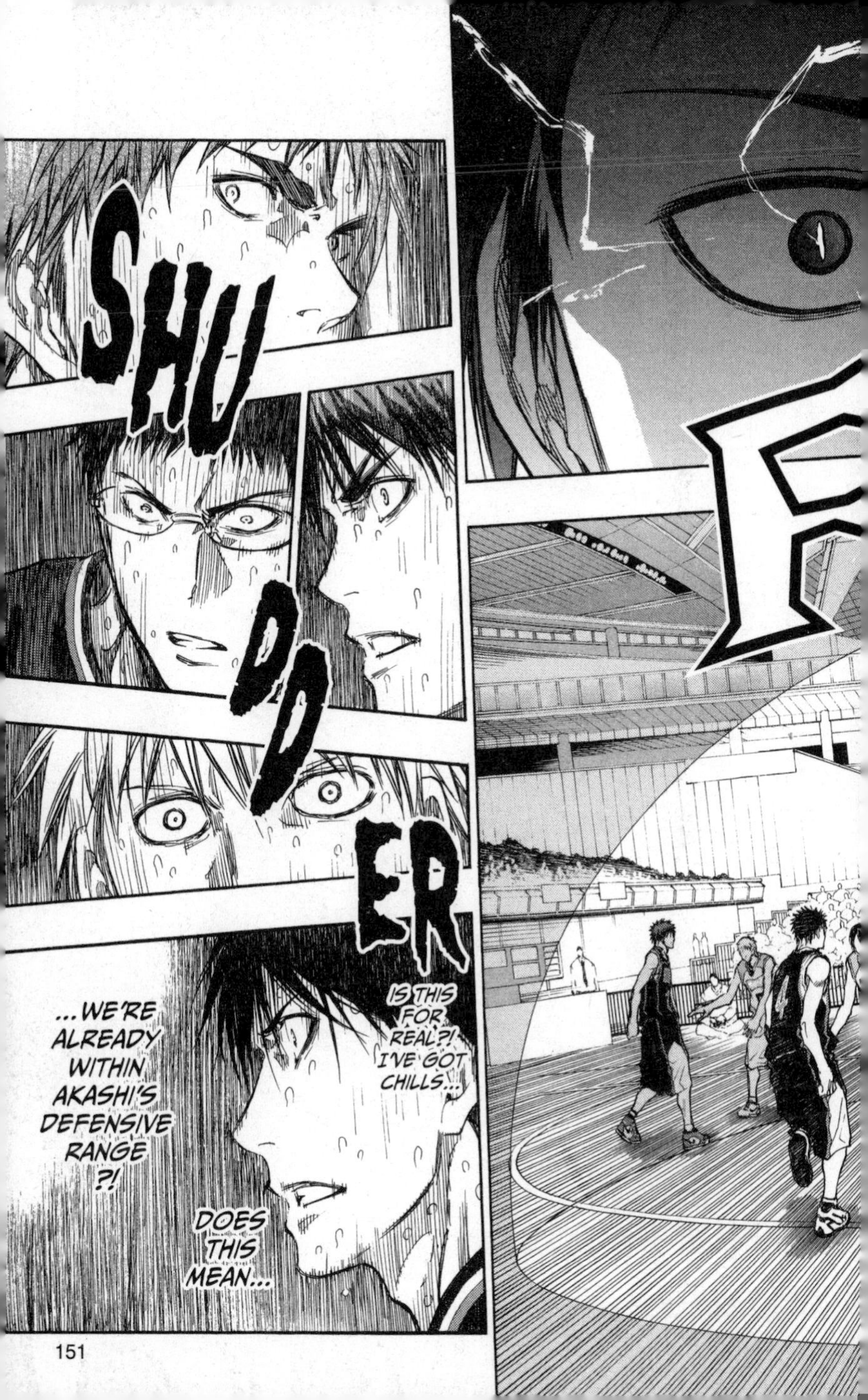

F
SHUDDER
IS THIS FOR REAL?! I'VE GOT CHILLS...
...WE'RE ALREADY WITHIN AKASHI'S DEFENSIVE RANGE?!
DOES THIS MEAN...

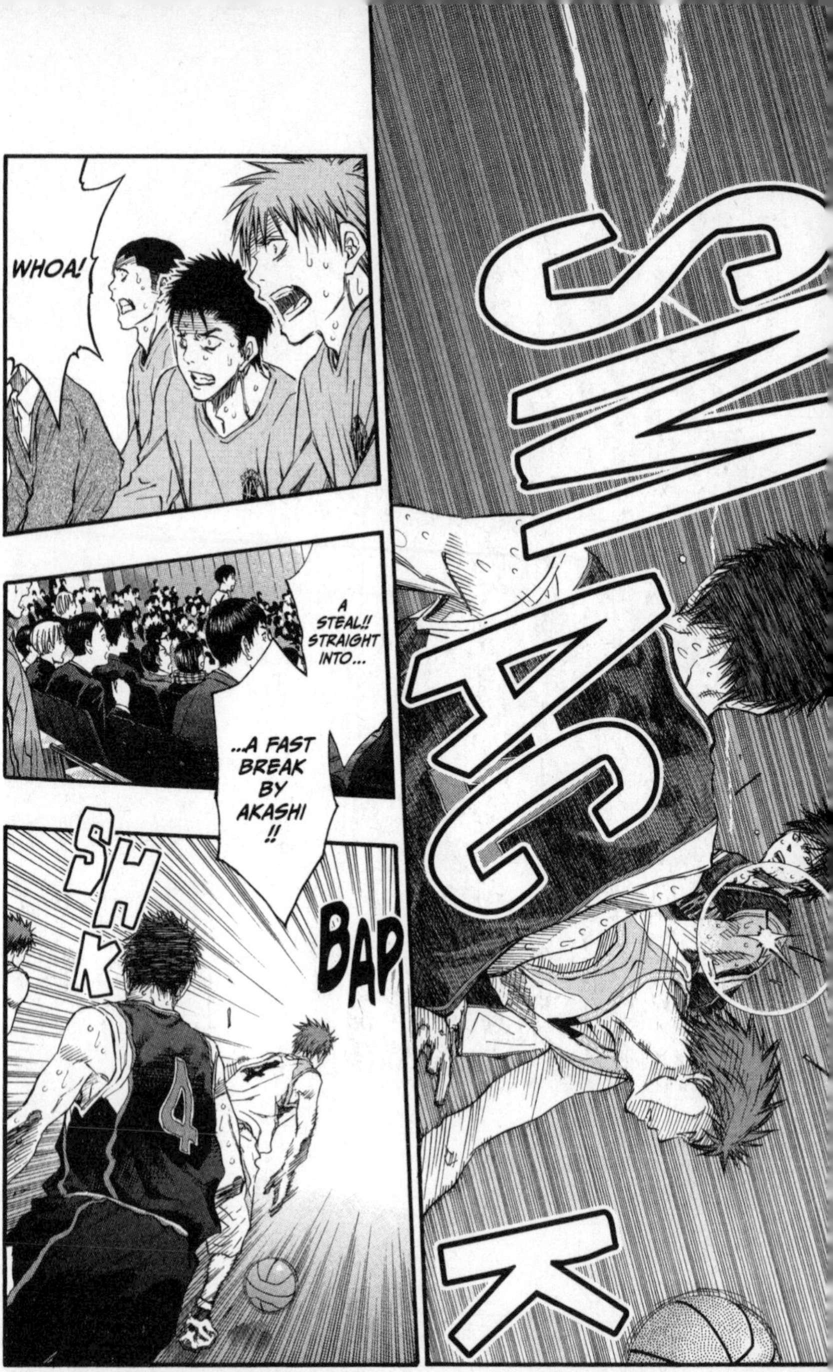
SWACK
WHOA!
A STEAL!! STRAIGHT INTO...
...A FAST BREAK BY AKASHI!!
BAP
SHK

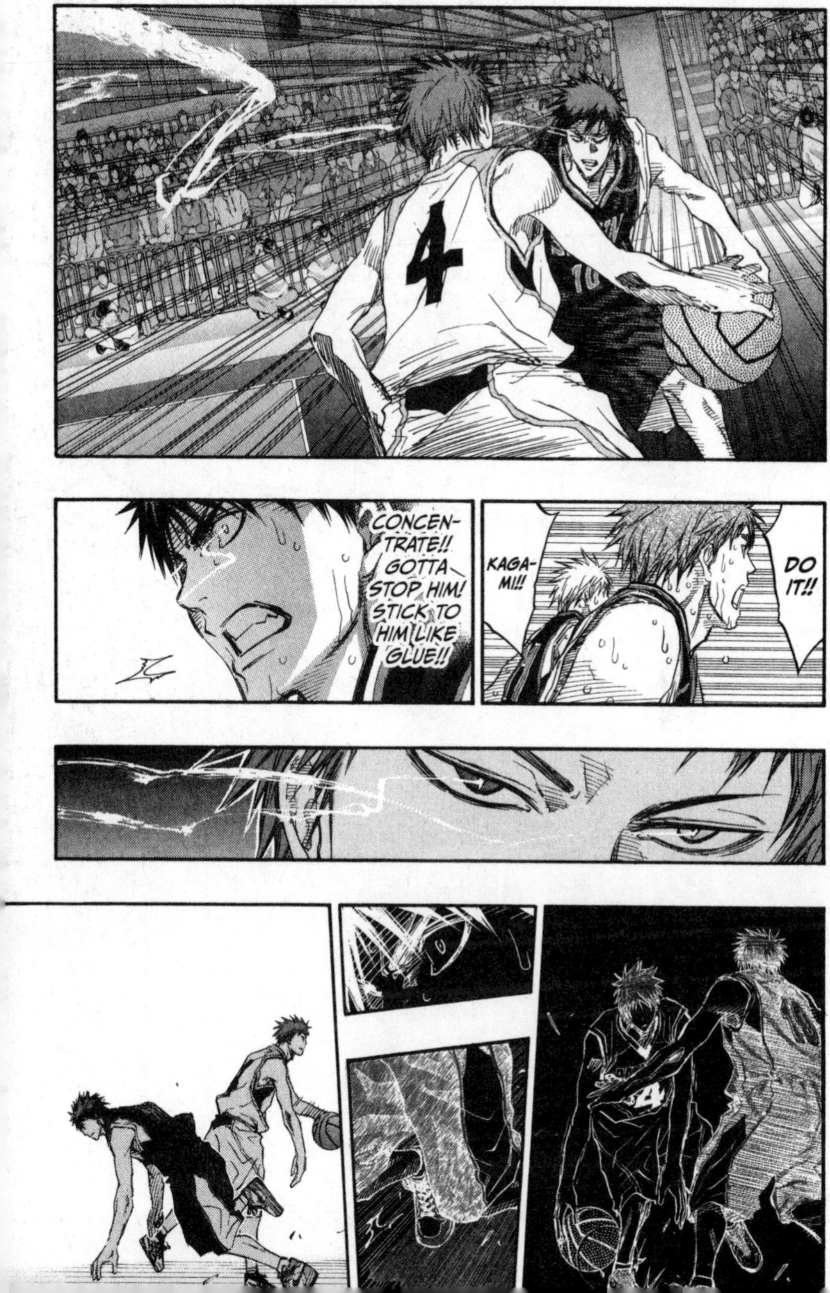
DO IT!!
KAGA-MI!!
CONCEN-TRATE!! GOTTA STOP HIM! STICK TO HIM LIKE GLUE!!

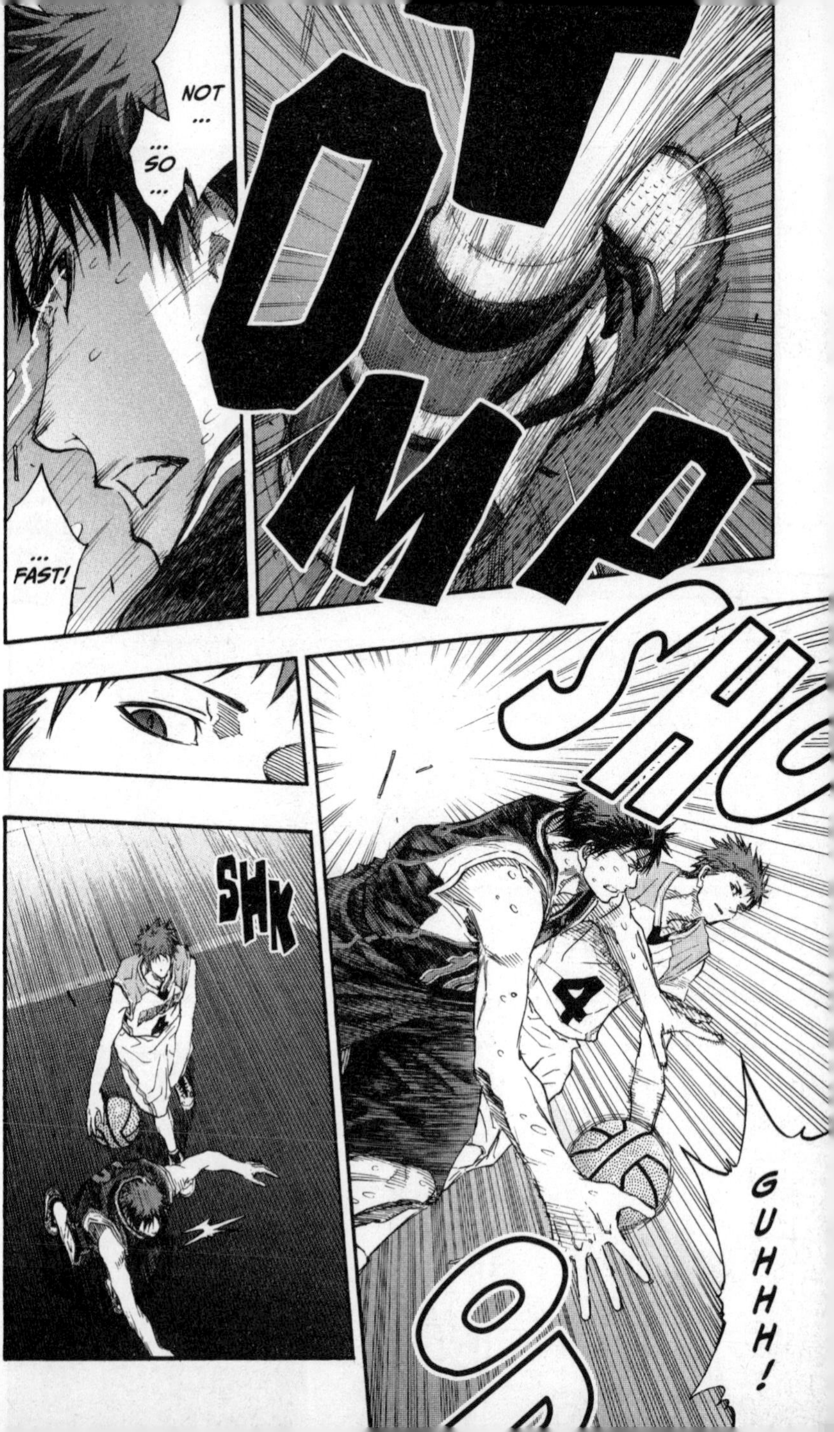
NOT...
...SO...
...FAST!
GUHHH!
SHK

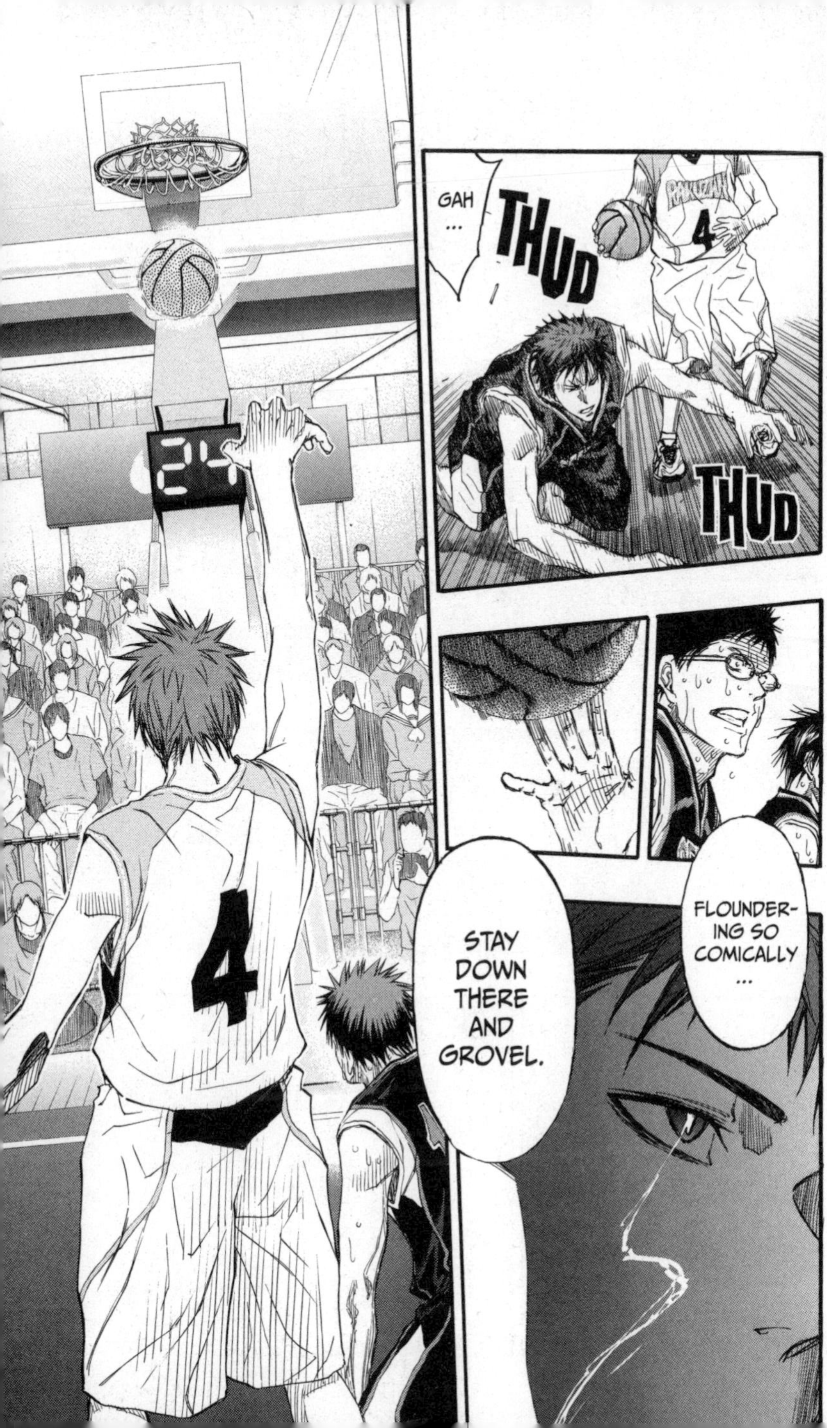
GAH ...
THUD
THUD
FLOUNDER-ING SO COMICALLY ...
STAY DOWN THERE AND GROVEL.

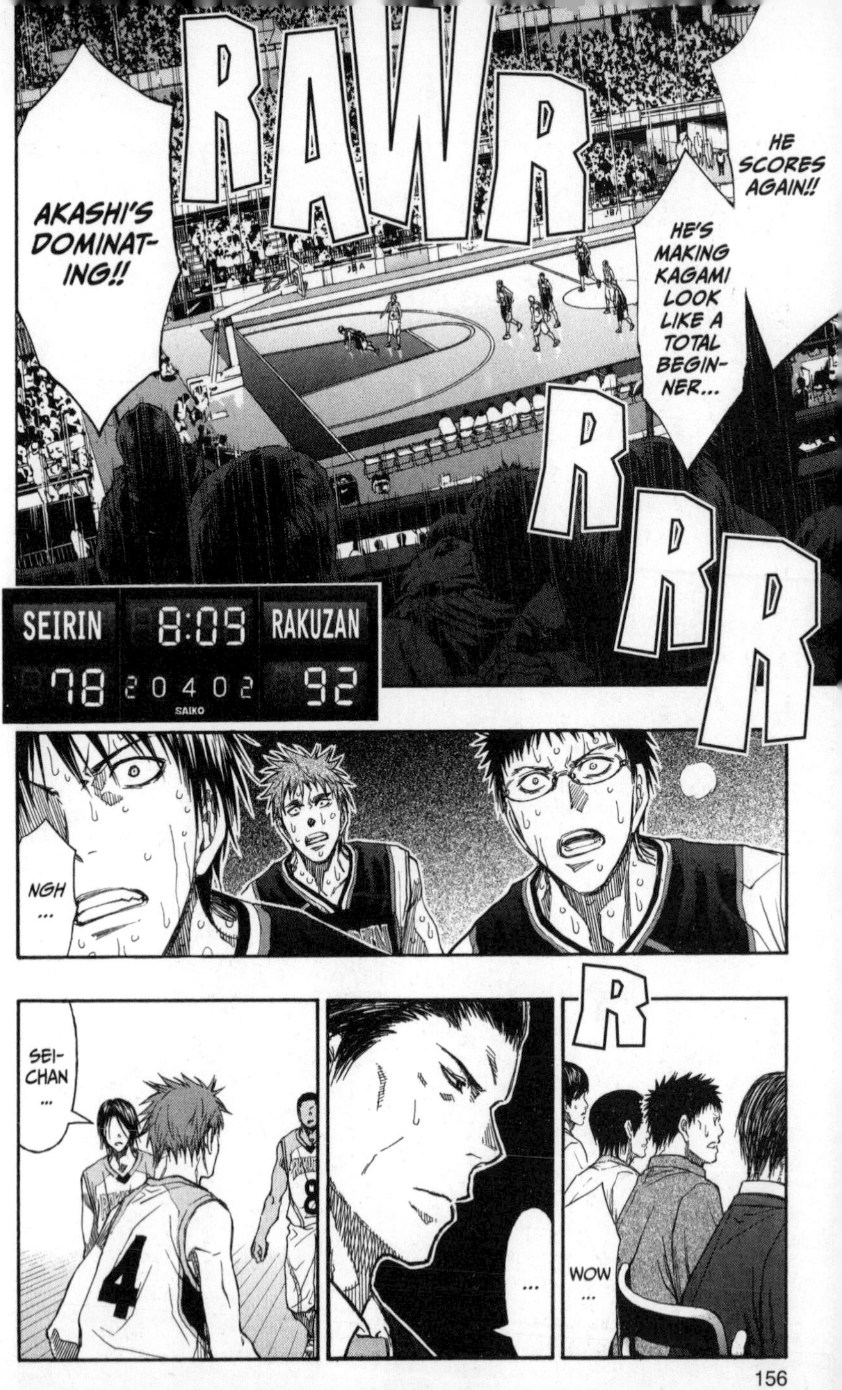

HE SCORES AGAIN!!
HE'S MAKING KAGAMI LOOK LIKE A TOTAL BEGINNER...
AKASHI'S DOMINATING!!
RAWR
RRRR
SEIRIN 8:05 RAKUZAN
78 2 0 4 0 2 92
SAIKO
NGH...
R
WOW...
...
SEI-CHAN...

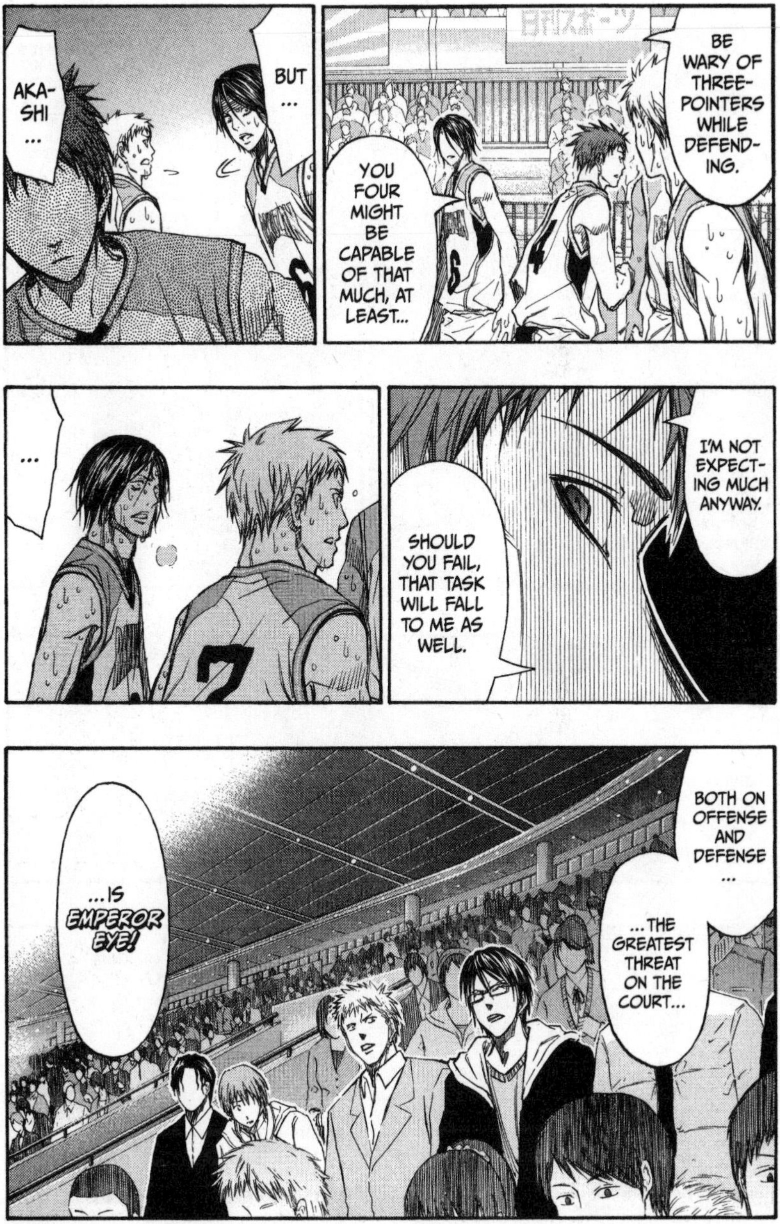
日刊スポーツ
BE WARY OF THREE-POINTERS WHILE DEFENDING.
YOU FOUR MIGHT BE CAPABLE OF THAT MUCH, AT LEAST...
BUT ...
AKA-SHI ...
I'M NOT EXPECTING MUCH ANYWAY.
SHOULD YOU FAIL, THAT TASK WILL FALL TO ME AS WELL.
...
BOTH ON OFFENSE AND DEFENSE ...
...THE GREATEST THREAT ON THE COURT...
...IS *EMPEROR EYE!*

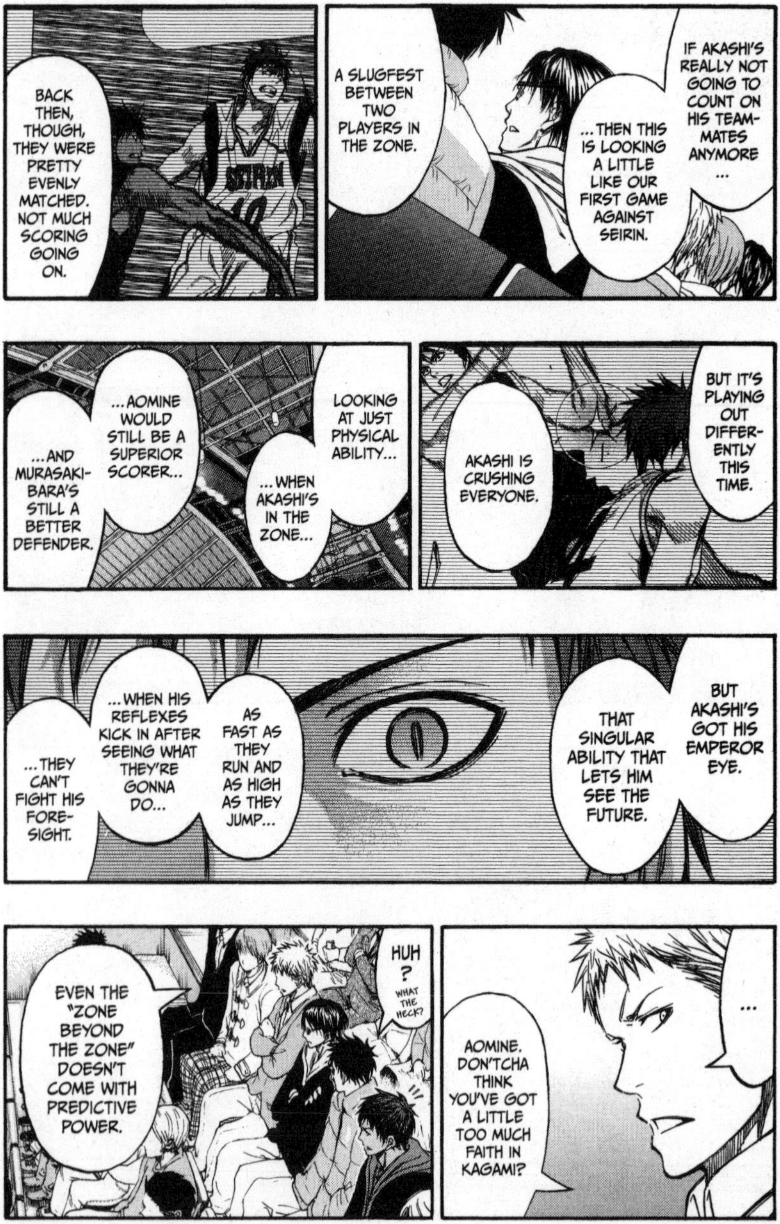
IF AKASHI'S REALLY NOT GOING TO COUNT ON HIS TEAMMATES ANYMORE...
...THEN THIS IS LOOKING A LITTLE LIKE OUR FIRST GAME AGAINST SEIRIN.
A SLUGFEST BETWEEN TWO PLAYERS IN THE ZONE.
BACK THEN, THOUGH, THEY WERE PRETTY EVENLY MATCHED. NOT MUCH SCORING GOING ON.
BUT IT'S PLAYING OUT DIFFERENTLY THIS TIME.
AKASHI IS CRUSHING EVERYONE.
LOOKING AT JUST PHYSICAL ABILITY...
...WHEN AKASHI'S IN THE ZONE...
...AOMINE WOULD STILL BE A SUPERIOR SCORER...
...AND MURASAKIBARA'S STILL A BETTER DEFENDER.
BUT AKASHI'S GOT HIS EMPEROR EYE.
THAT SINGULAR ABILITY THAT LETS HIM SEE THE FUTURE.
AS FAST AS THEY RUN AND AS HIGH AS THEY JUMP...
...WHEN HIS REFLEXES KICK IN AFTER SEEING WHAT THEY'RE GONNA DO...
...THEY CAN'T FIGHT HIS FORESIGHT.
...
AOMINE. DON'TCHA THINK YOU'VE GOT A LITTLE TOO MUCH FAITH IN KAGAMI?
HUH? WHAT THE HECK?
EVEN THE "ZONE BEYOND THE ZONE" DOESN'T COME WITH PREDICTIVE POWER.

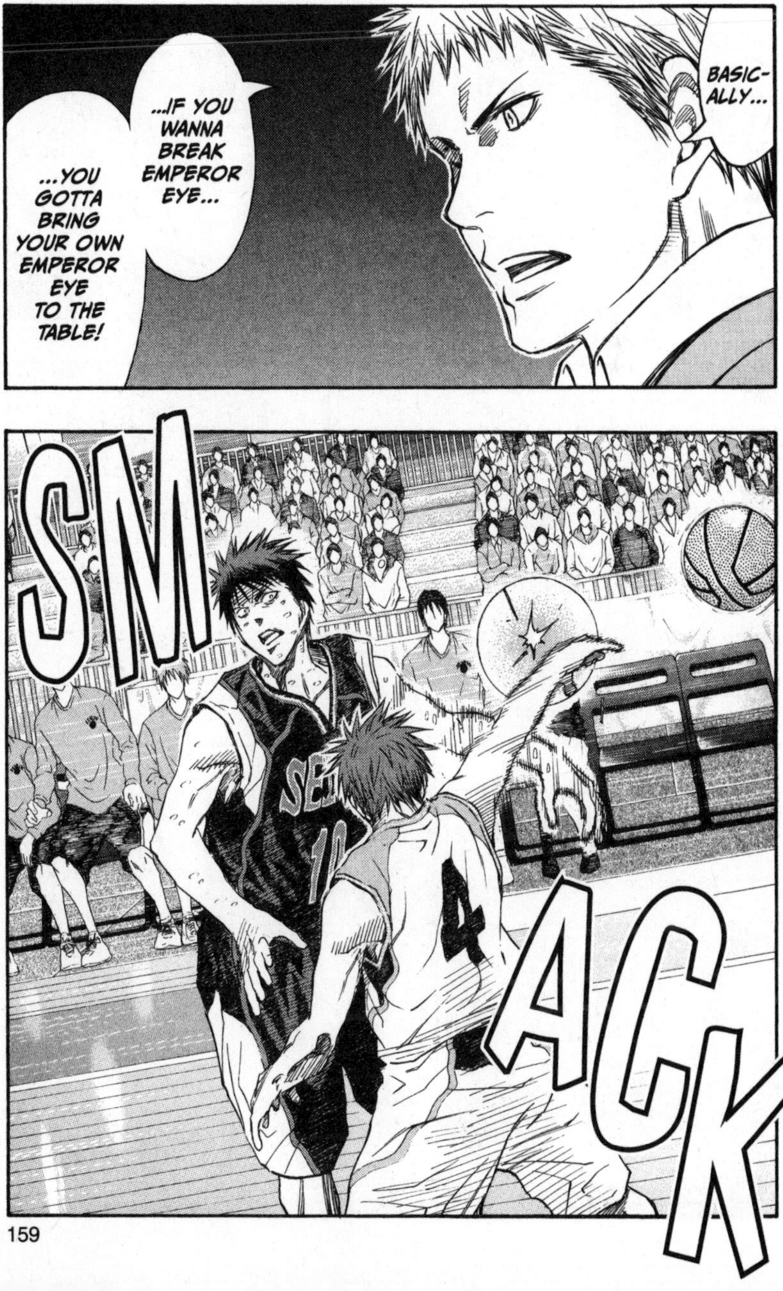
BASIC-ALLY...
...IF YOU WANNA BREAK EMPEROR EYE...
...YOU GOTTA BRING YOUR OWN EMPEROR EYE TO THE TABLE!
SMACK

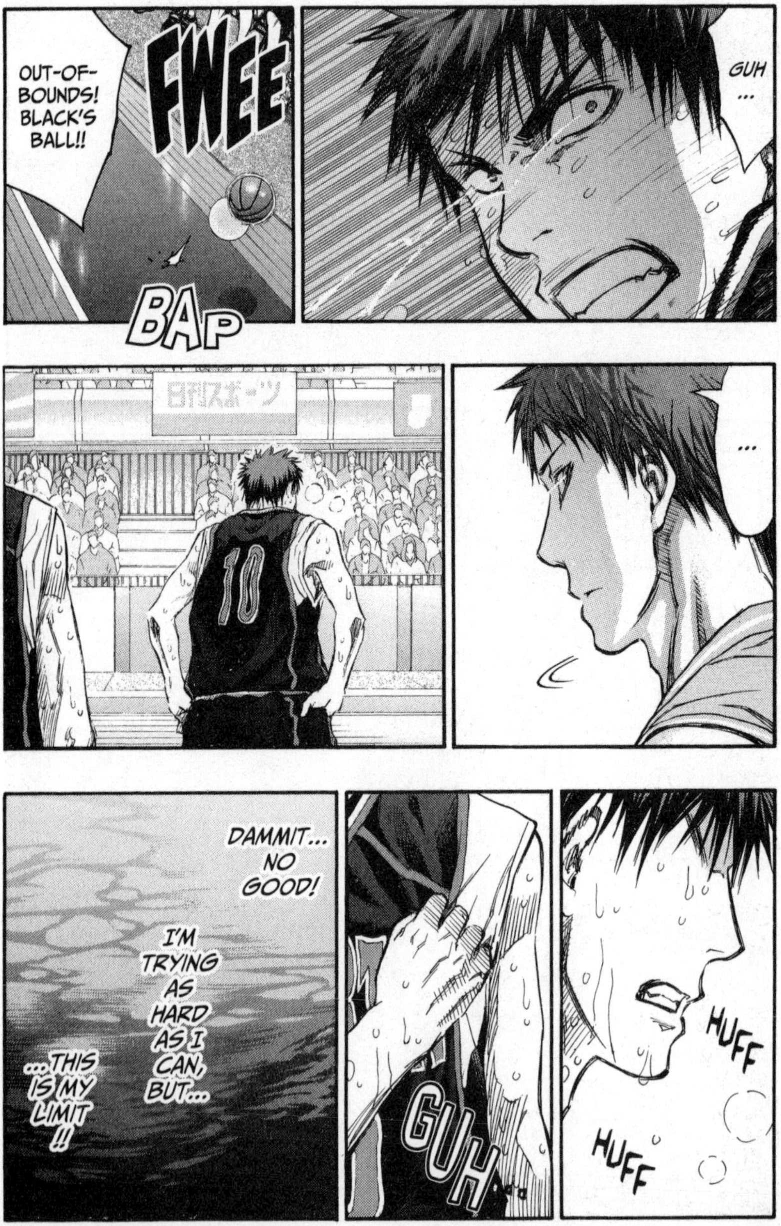
GUH ...
OUT-OF-BOUNDS! BLACK'S BALL!!
FWEE
BAP
...
日刊スポーツ
HUFF
HUFF
GUH
DAMMIT... NO GOOD!
I'M TRYING AS HARD AS I CAN, BUT...
...THIS IS MY LIMIT!!

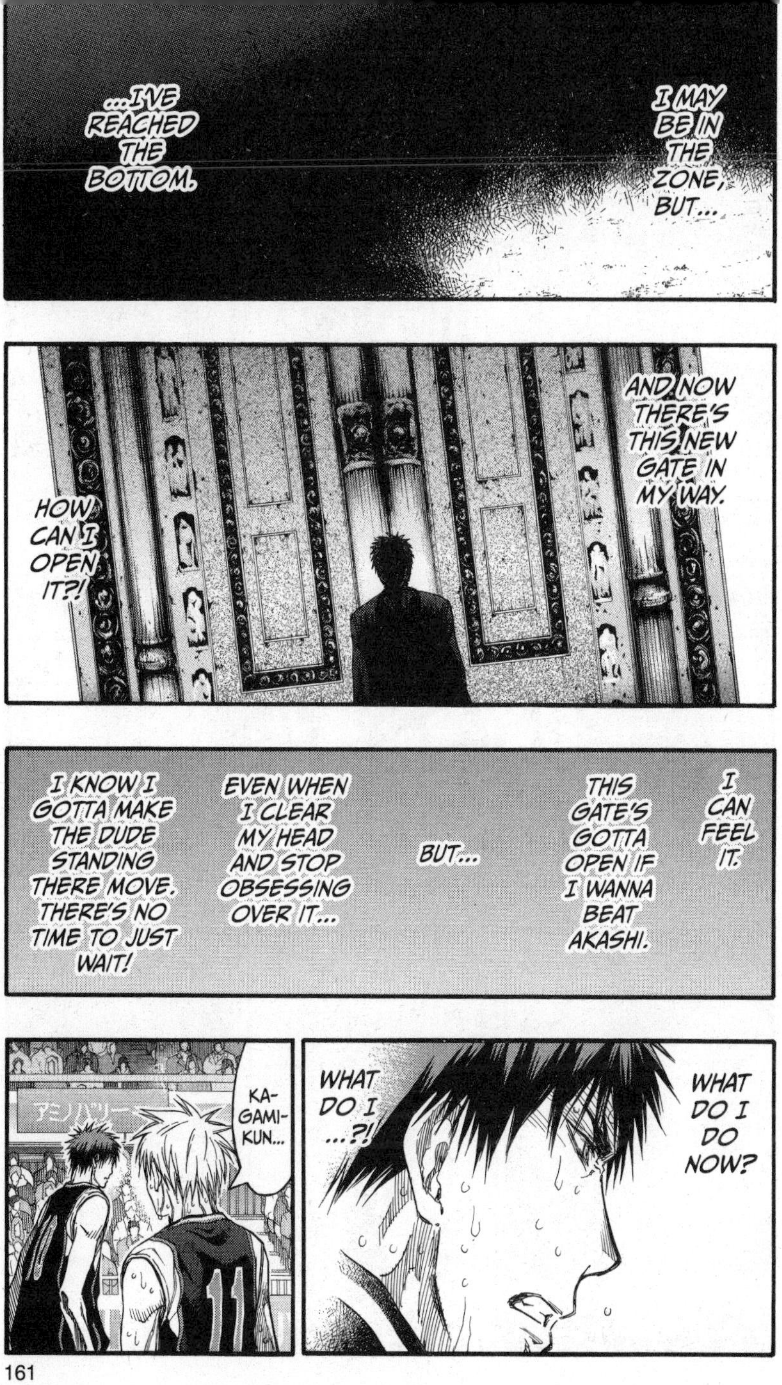
I MAY BE IN THE ZONE, BUT...
...I'VE REACHED THE BOTTOM.
AND NOW THERE'S THIS NEW GATE IN MY WAY.
HOW CAN I OPEN IT?!
I CAN FEEL IT.
THIS GATE'S GOTTA OPEN IF I WANNA BEAT AKASHI.
BUT...
EVEN WHEN I CLEAR MY HEAD AND STOP OBSESSING OVER IT...
I KNOW I GOTTA MAKE THE DUDE STANDING THERE MOVE. THERE'S NO TIME TO JUST WAIT!
WHAT DO I DO NOW?
WHAT DO I ...?!
KA-GAMI-KUN...

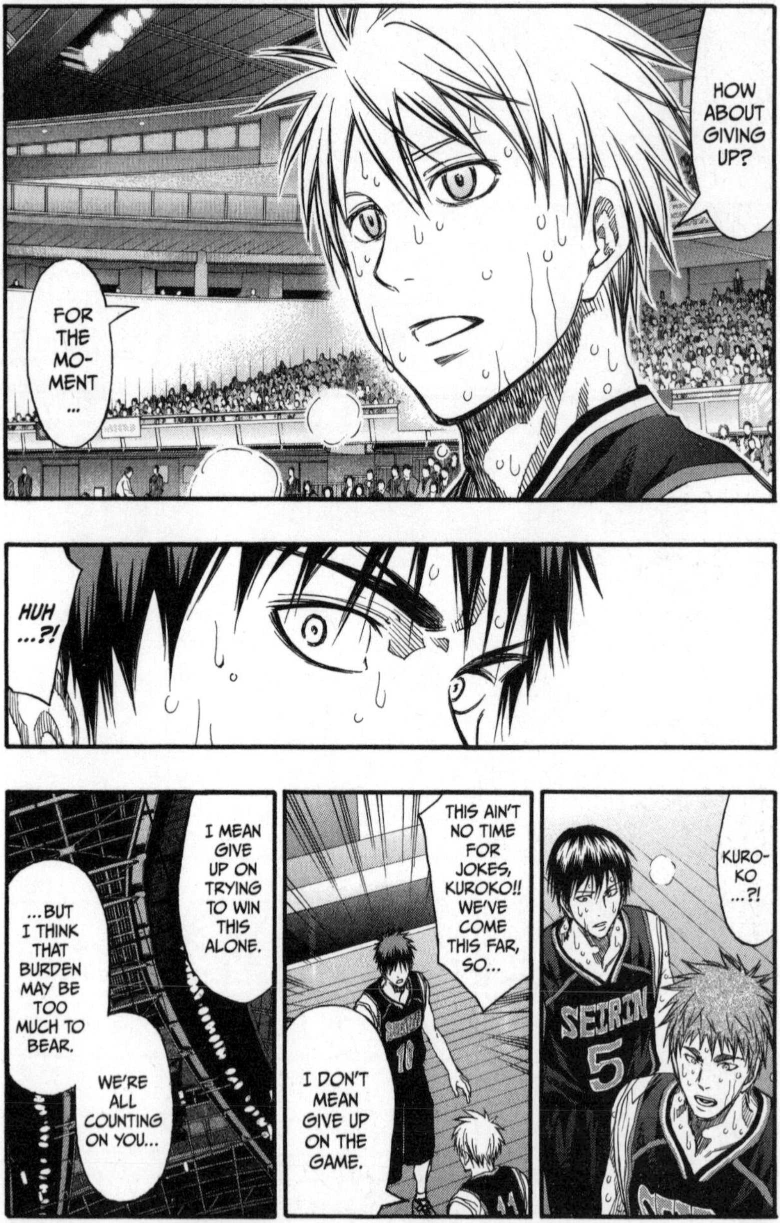
HOW ABOUT GIVING UP?
FOR THE MO-MENT ...
HUH ...?!
KURO-KO ...?!
THIS AIN'T NO TIME FOR JOKES, KUROKO!! WE'VE COME THIS FAR, SO...
I DON'T MEAN GIVE UP ON THE GAME.
I MEAN GIVE UP ON TRYING TO WIN THIS ALONE.
...BUT I THINK THAT BURDEN MAY BE TOO MUCH TO BEAR.
WE'RE ALL COUNTING ON YOU...

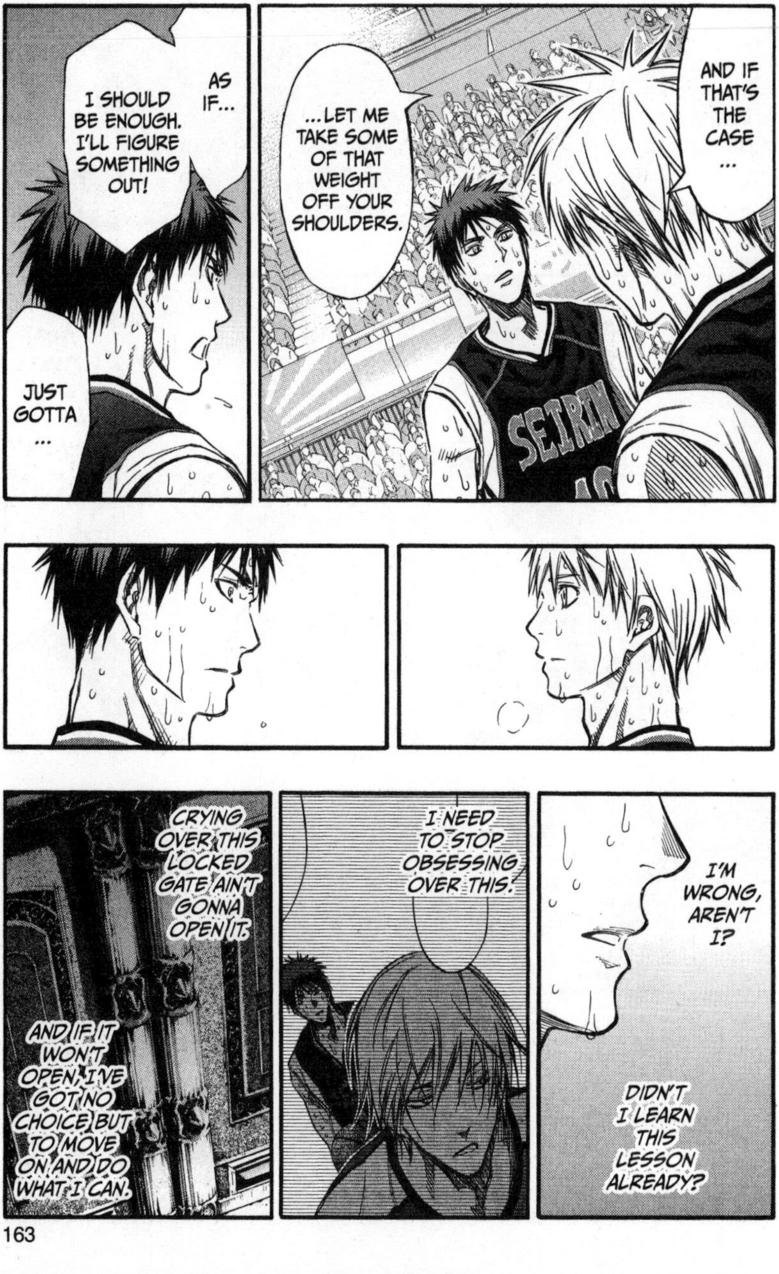

AND IF THAT'S THE CASE ...
...LET ME TAKE SOME OF THAT WEIGHT OFF YOUR SHOULDERS.
SEIRIN
AS IF...
I SHOULD BE ENOUGH. I'LL FIGURE SOMETHING OUT!
JUST GOTTA ...
I'M WRONG, AREN'T I?
DIDN'T I LEARN THIS LESSON ALREADY?
I NEED TO STOP OBSESSING OVER THIS.
CRYING OVER THIS LOCKED GATE AIN'T GONNA OPEN IT.
AND IF IT WON'T OPEN, I'VE GOT NO CHOICE BUT TO MOVE ON AND DO WHAT I CAN.

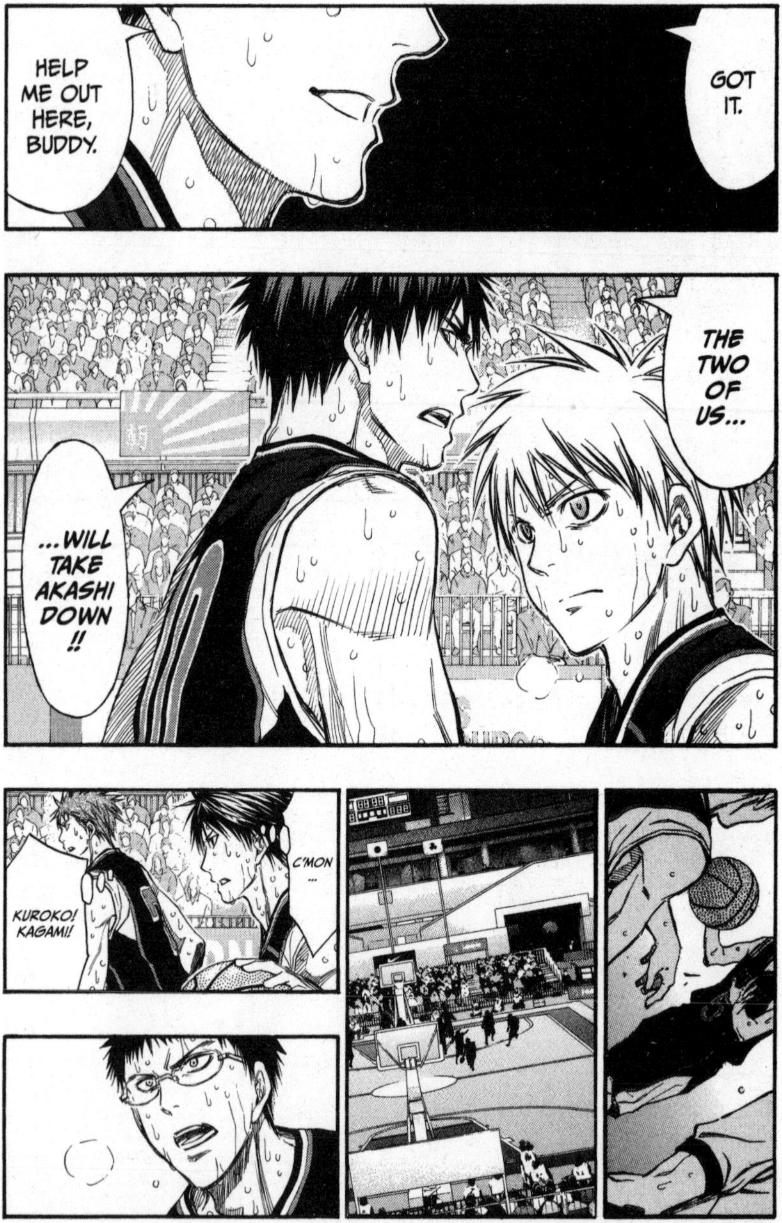
HELP ME OUT HERE, BUDDY.
GOT IT.
THE TWO OF US...
...WILL TAKE AKASHI DOWN!!
C'MON ...
KUROKO! KAGAMI!

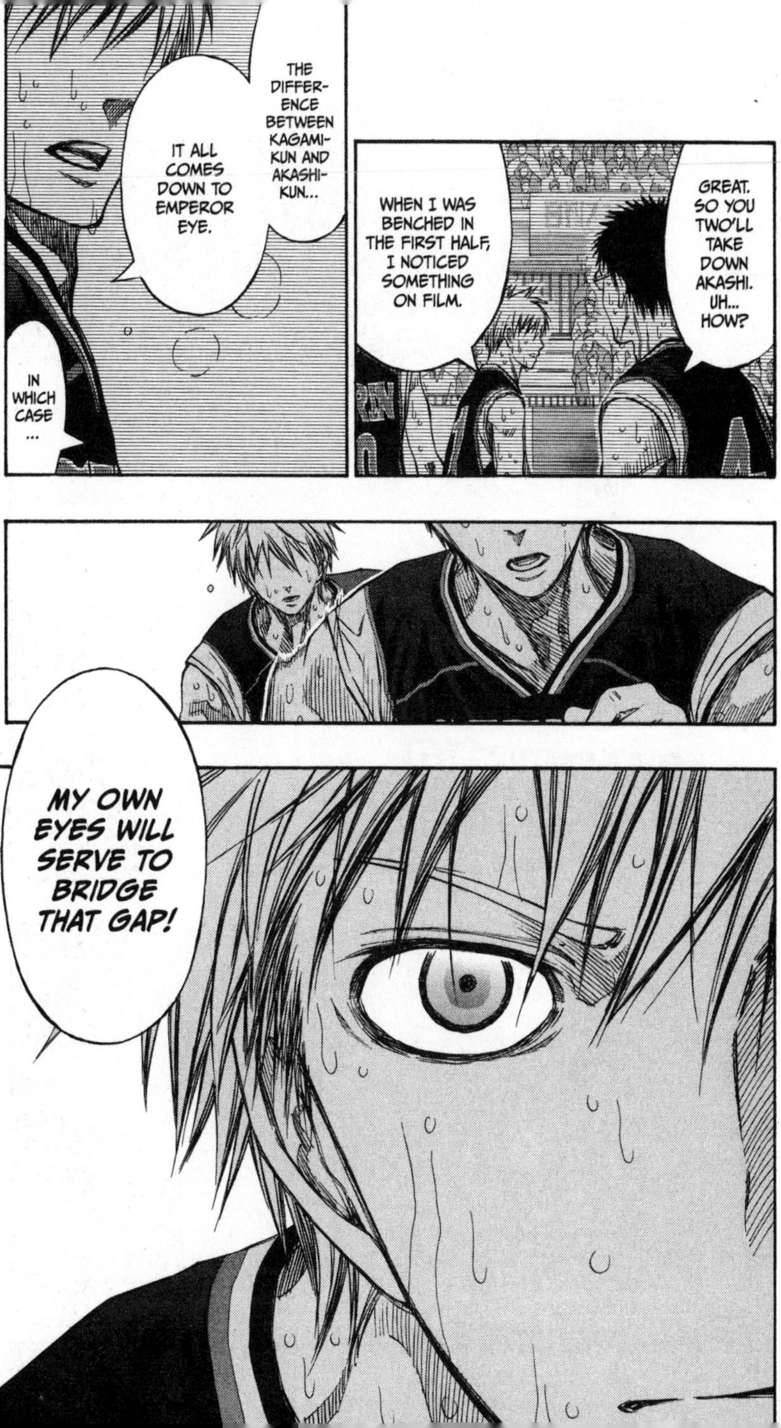
GREAT. SO YOU TWO'LL TAKE DOWN AKASHI. UH... HOW?
WHEN I WAS BENCHED IN THE FIRST HALF, I NOTICED SOMETHING ON FILM.
THE DIFFERENCE BETWEEN KAGAMI-KUN AND AKASHI-KUN...
IT ALL COMES DOWN TO EMPEROR EYE.
IN WHICH CASE...
MY OWN EYES WILL SERVE TO BRIDGE THAT GAP!

KUROKO'S BASKETBALL Q&A (W/ HALFWAY-DECENT ANSWERS)

Q. **WHEN MOMOI, ALEX, COACH ARAKI, RIKO, AND BIG SIS REO WEAR LUCKY UNDERWEAR, WHAT COLOR DO THEY EACH CHOOSE, RESPECTIVELY?**
(BAD YEAR BEAVER from AICHI PREFECURE)

A. WHY IS BIG SIS REO ON THAT LIST?

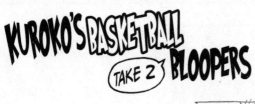

KUROKO'S BASKETBALL BLOOPERS (TAKE 2)

AND NOW THERE'S THIS NEW GATE IN MY WAY.
AND WHAT'S WITH THE DESIGN?!
IMA
HOW DO I OPEN IT?!

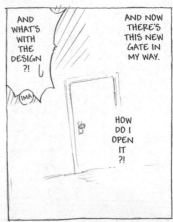

263RD QUARTER: STOP AKASHI!!

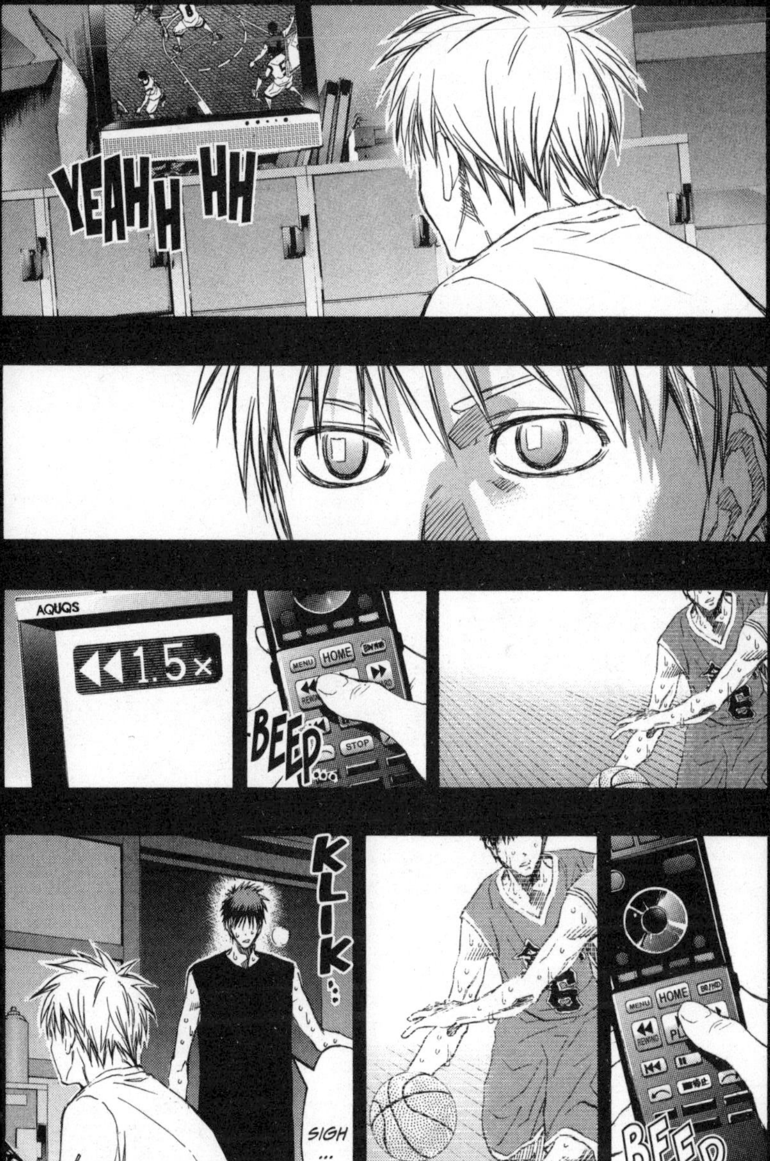
YEAHHHH
MENU
HOME
REWIND
STOP
BEEP...
AQUQS
1.5x
MENU
HOME
REWIND
BEEP...
KLIK..
SIGH...

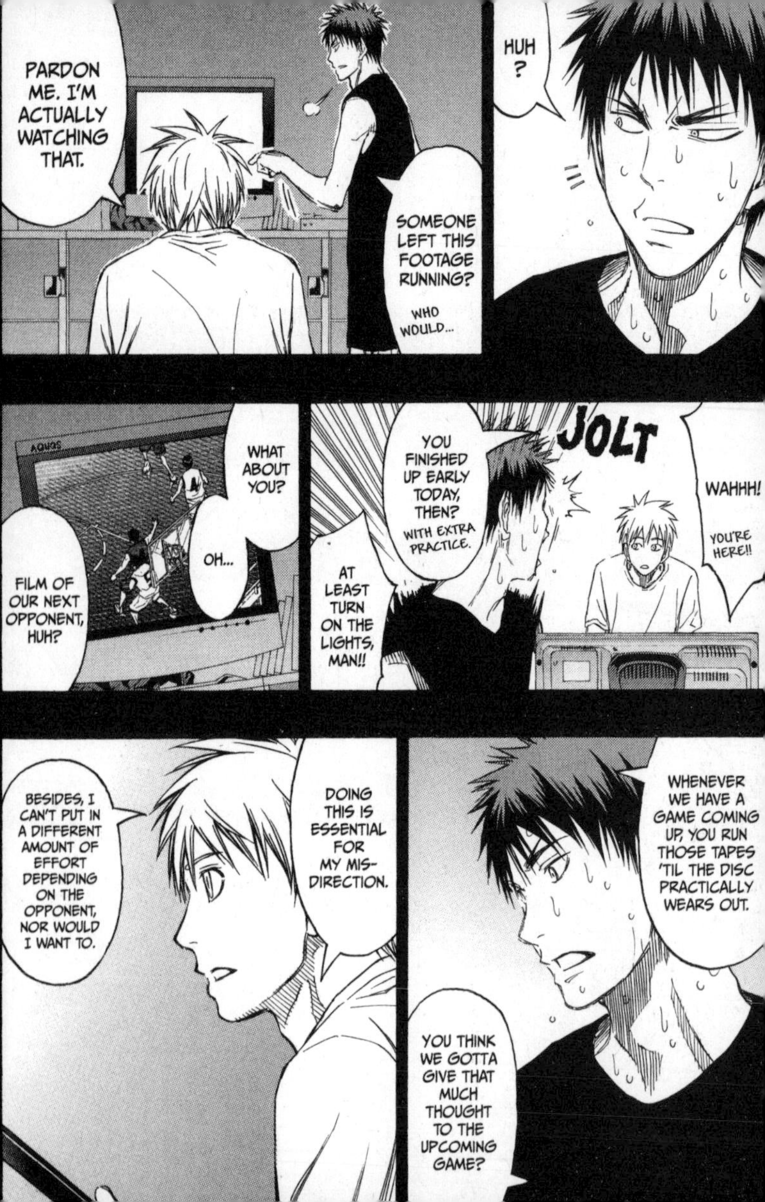
HUH ?
SOMEONE LEFT THIS FOOTAGE RUNNING?
WHO WOULD...
PARDON ME. I'M ACTUALLY WATCHING THAT.
JOLT
WAHHH!
YOU'RE HERE!!
YOU FINISHED UP EARLY TODAY, THEN? WITH EXTRA PRACTICE.
AT LEAST TURN ON THE LIGHTS, MAN!!
WHAT ABOUT YOU?
OH...
FILM OF OUR NEXT OPPONENT, HUH?
WHENEVER WE HAVE A GAME COMING UP, YOU RUN THOSE TAPES 'TIL THE DISC PRACTICALLY WEARS OUT.
YOU THINK WE GOTTA GIVE THAT MUCH THOUGHT TO THE UPCOMING GAME?
DOING THIS IS ESSENTIAL FOR MY MIS-DIRECTION.
BESIDES, I CAN'T PUT IN A DIFFERENT AMOUNT OF EFFORT DEPENDING ON THE OPPONENT, NOR WOULD I WANT TO.

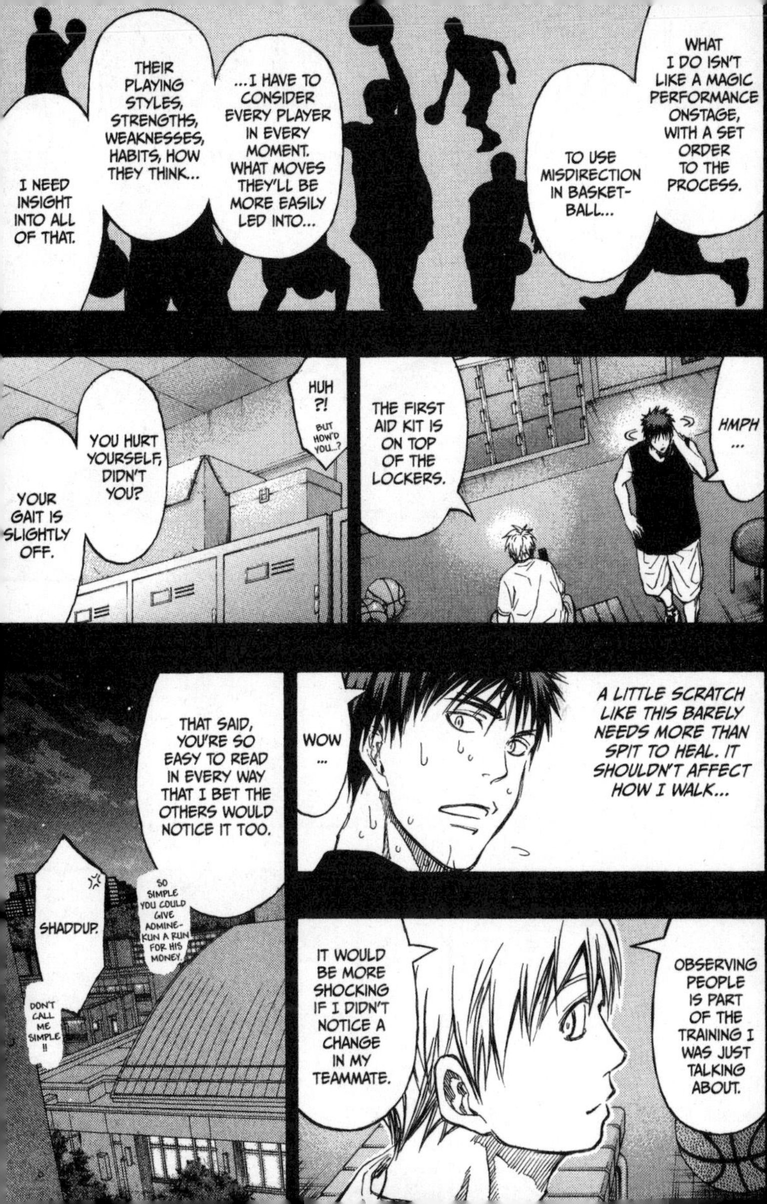
WHAT I DO ISN'T LIKE A MAGIC PERFORMANCE ONSTAGE, WITH A SET ORDER TO THE PROCESS.
TO USE MISDIRECTION IN BASKET-BALL...
...I HAVE TO CONSIDER EVERY PLAYER IN EVERY MOMENT. WHAT MOVES THEY'LL BE MORE EASILY LED INTO...
THEIR PLAYING STYLES, STRENGTHS, WEAKNESSES, HABITS, HOW THEY THINK...
I NEED INSIGHT INTO ALL OF THAT.
HMPH ...
THE FIRST AID KIT IS ON TOP OF THE LOCKERS.
HUH ?!
BUT HOW'D YOU...?
YOU HURT YOURSELF, DIDN'T YOU?
YOUR GAIT IS SLIGHTLY OFF.
A LITTLE SCRATCH LIKE THIS BARELY NEEDS MORE THAN SPIT TO HEAL. IT SHOULDN'T AFFECT HOW I WALK...
WOW ...
OBSERVING PEOPLE IS PART OF THE TRAINING I WAS JUST TALKING ABOUT.
IT WOULD BE MORE SHOCKING IF I DIDN'T NOTICE A CHANGE IN MY TEAMMATE.
THAT SAID, YOU'RE SO EASY TO READ IN EVERY WAY THAT I BET THE OTHERS WOULD NOTICE IT TOO.
SO SIMPLE YOU COULD GIVE ADMINE-KUN A RUN FOR HIS MONEY.
SHADDUP.
DON'T CALL ME SIMPLE !!

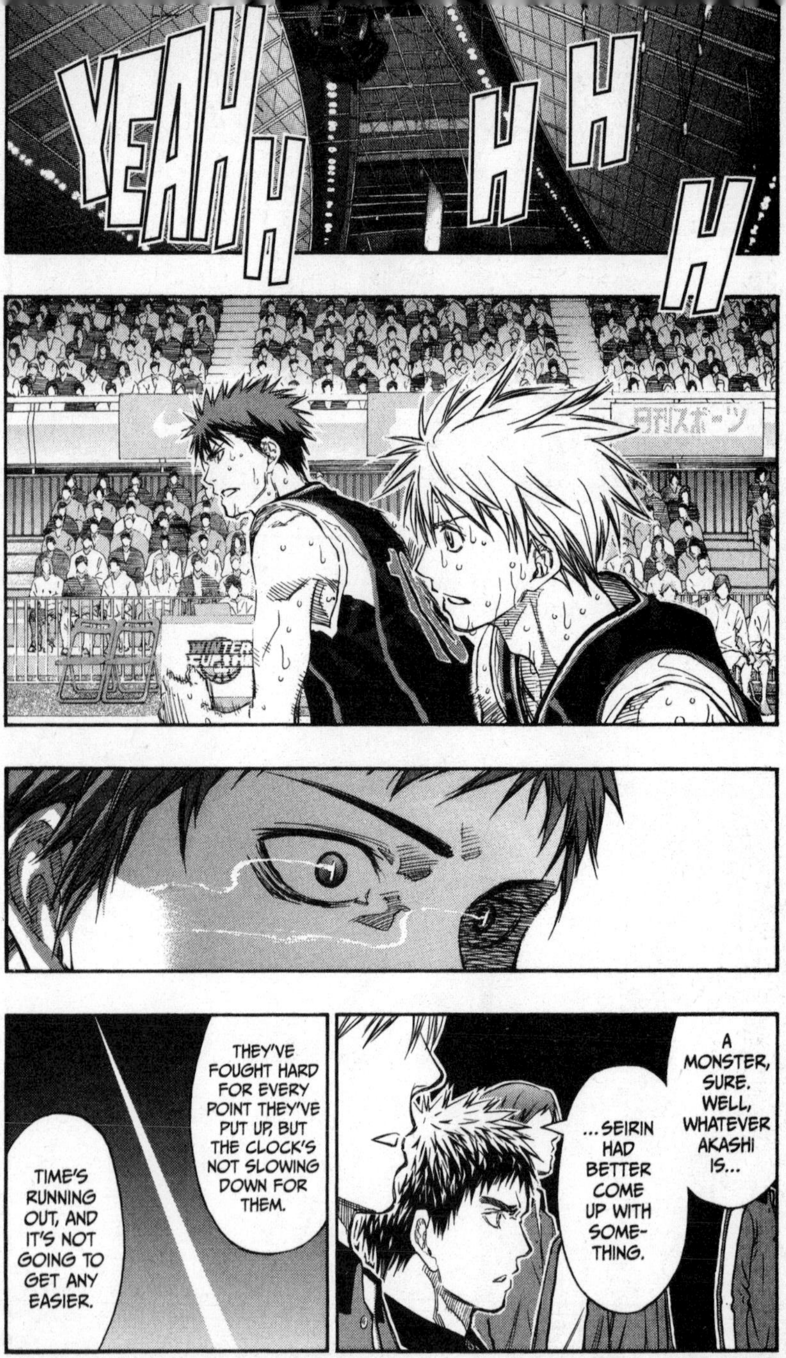
YEAHHHHHH
月刊スポーツ
A MONSTER, SURE. WELL, WHATEVER AKASHI IS...
...SEIRIN HAD BETTER COME UP WITH SOME-THING.
THEY'VE FOUGHT HARD FOR EVERY POINT THEY'VE PUT UP, BUT THE CLOCK'S NOT SLOWING DOWN FOR THEM.
TIME'S RUNNING OUT, AND IT'S NOT GOING TO GET ANY EASIER.

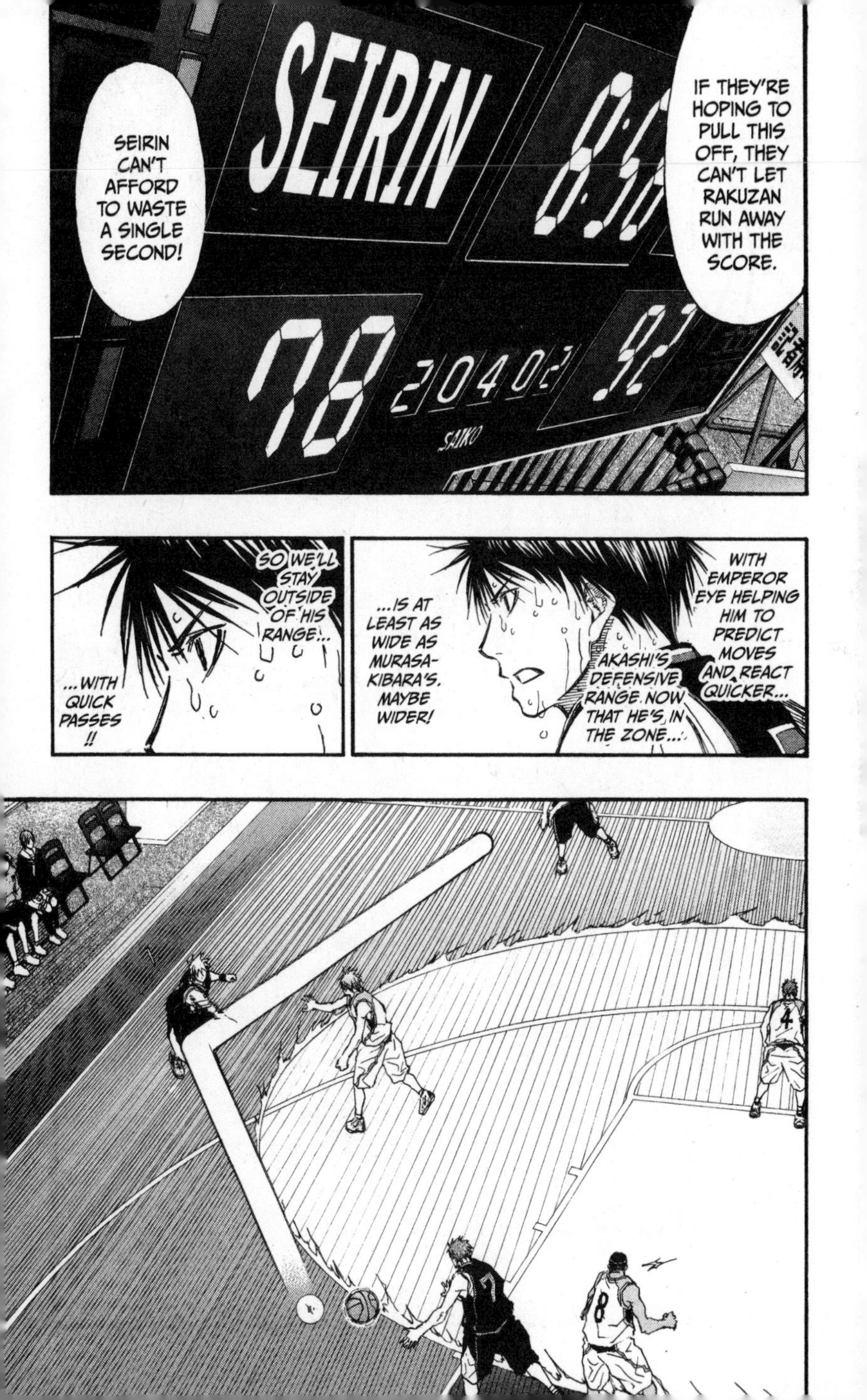
SEIRIN
IF THEY'RE HOPING TO PULL THIS OFF, THEY CAN'T LET RAKUZAN RUN AWAY WITH THE SCORE.
SEIRIN CAN'T AFFORD TO WASTE A SINGLE SECOND!
WITH EMPEROR EYE HELPING HIM TO PREDICT MOVES AND REACT QUICKER...
AKASHI'S DEFENSIVE RANGE NOW THAT HE'S IN THE ZONE...
...IS AT LEAST AS WIDE AS MURASA-KIBARA'S. MAYBE WIDER!
SO WE'LL STAY OUTSIDE OF HIS RANGE...
...WITH QUICK PASSES!!

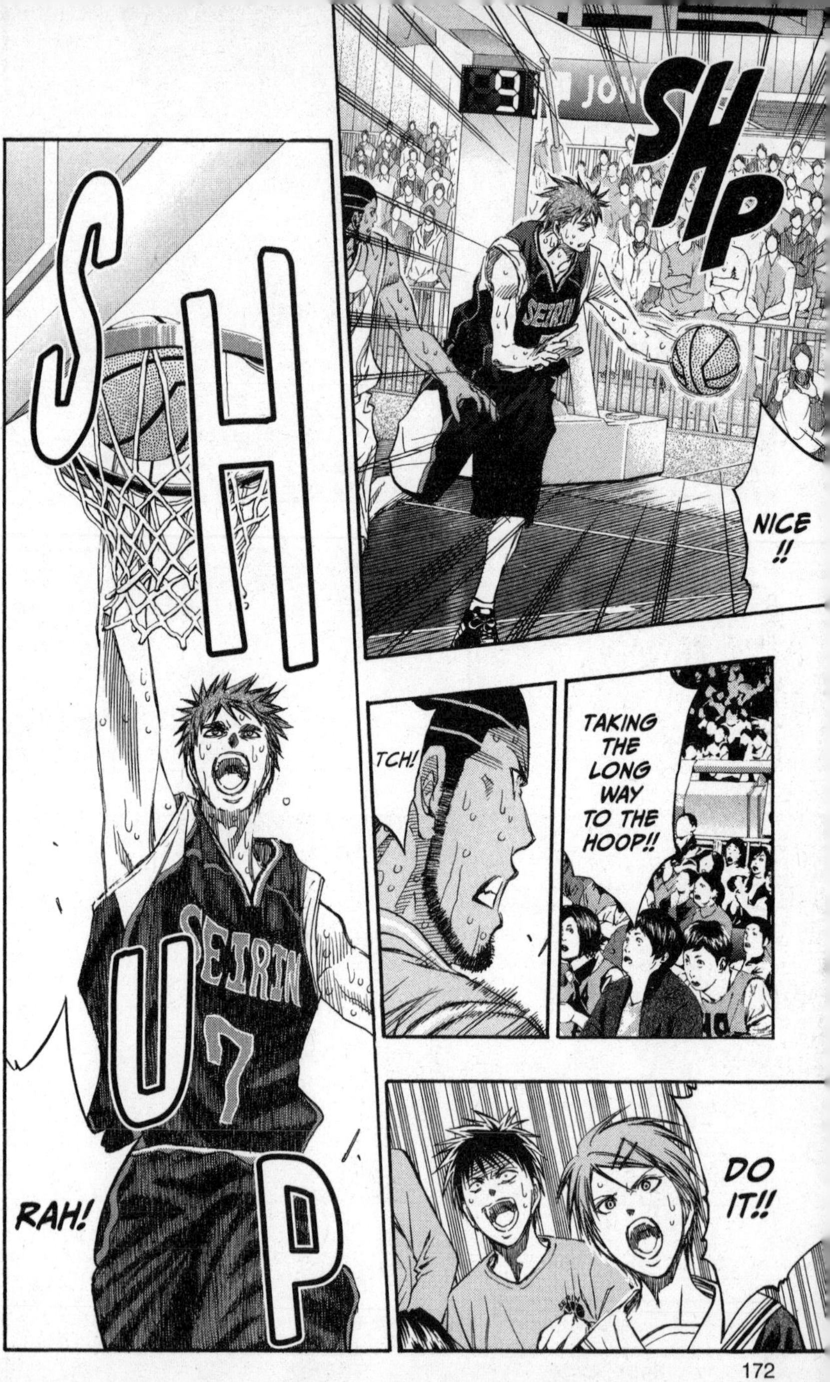
SHP
NICE!!
TAKING THE LONG WAY TO THE HOOP!!
TCH!
DO IT!!
SHUP
RAH!

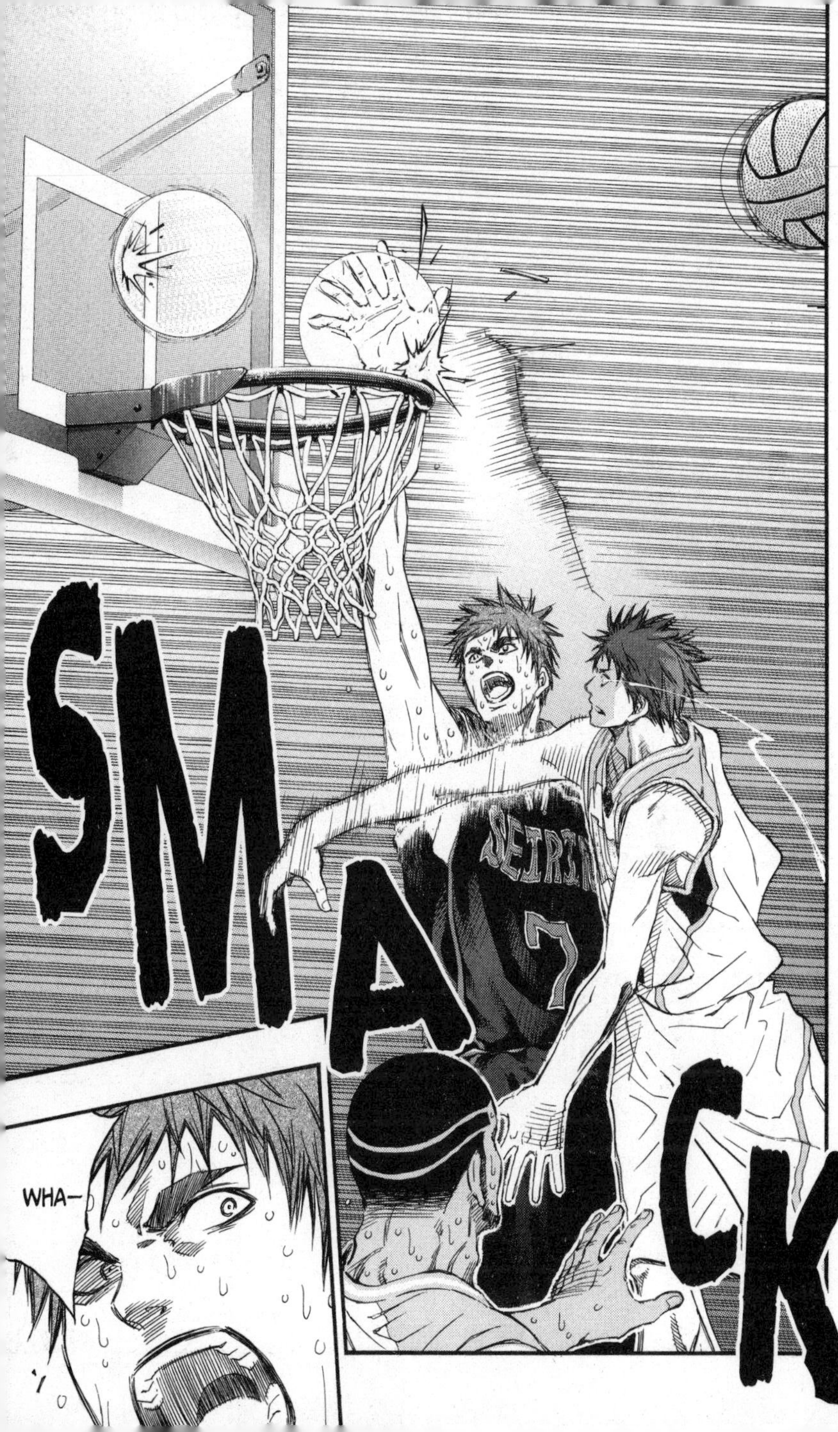
SMACK
WHA-

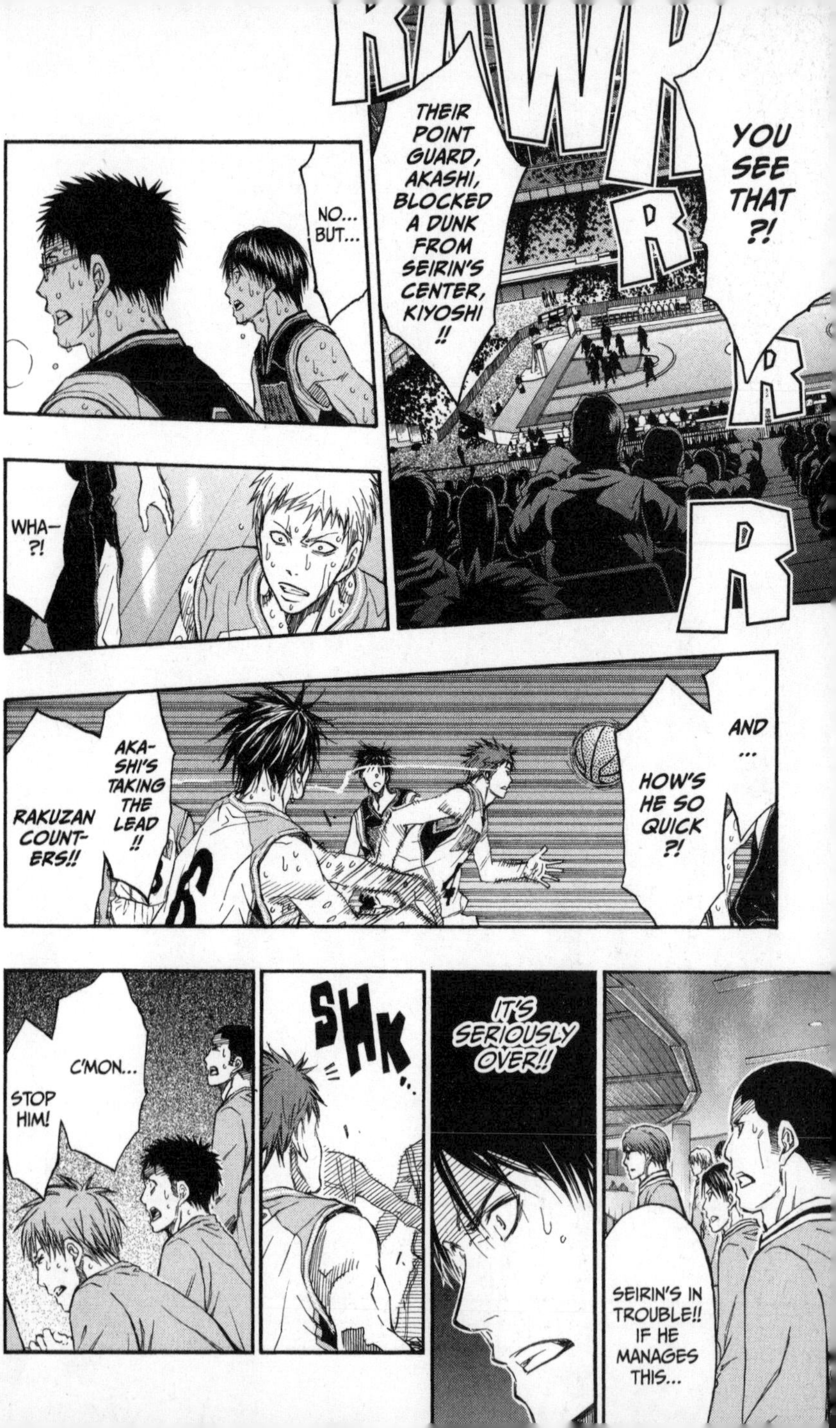
RAWRRRR
YOU SEE THAT?!
THEIR POINT GUARD, AKASHI, BLOCKED A DUNK FROM SEIRIN'S CENTER, KIYOSHI!!
NO... BUT...
WHA-?!
AND ... HOW'S HE SO QUICK?!
AKA-SHI'S TAKING THE LEAD!!
RAKUZAN COUNT-ERS!!
SEIRIN'S IN TROUBLE!! IF HE MANAGES THIS...
IT'S SERIOUSLY OVER!!
SHK
C'MON...
STOP HIM!

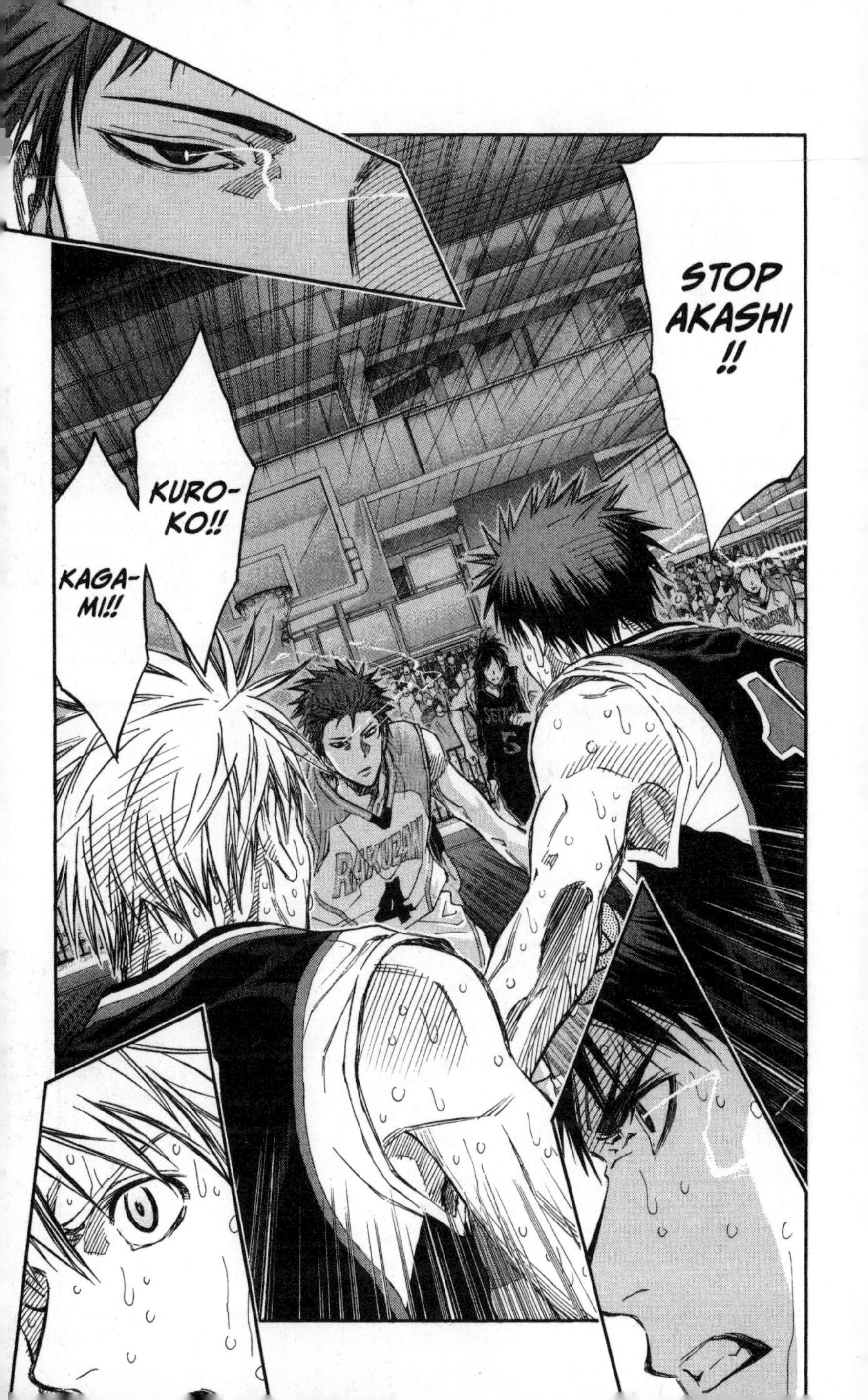
STOP AKASHI!!
KURO-KO!!
KAGA-MI!!

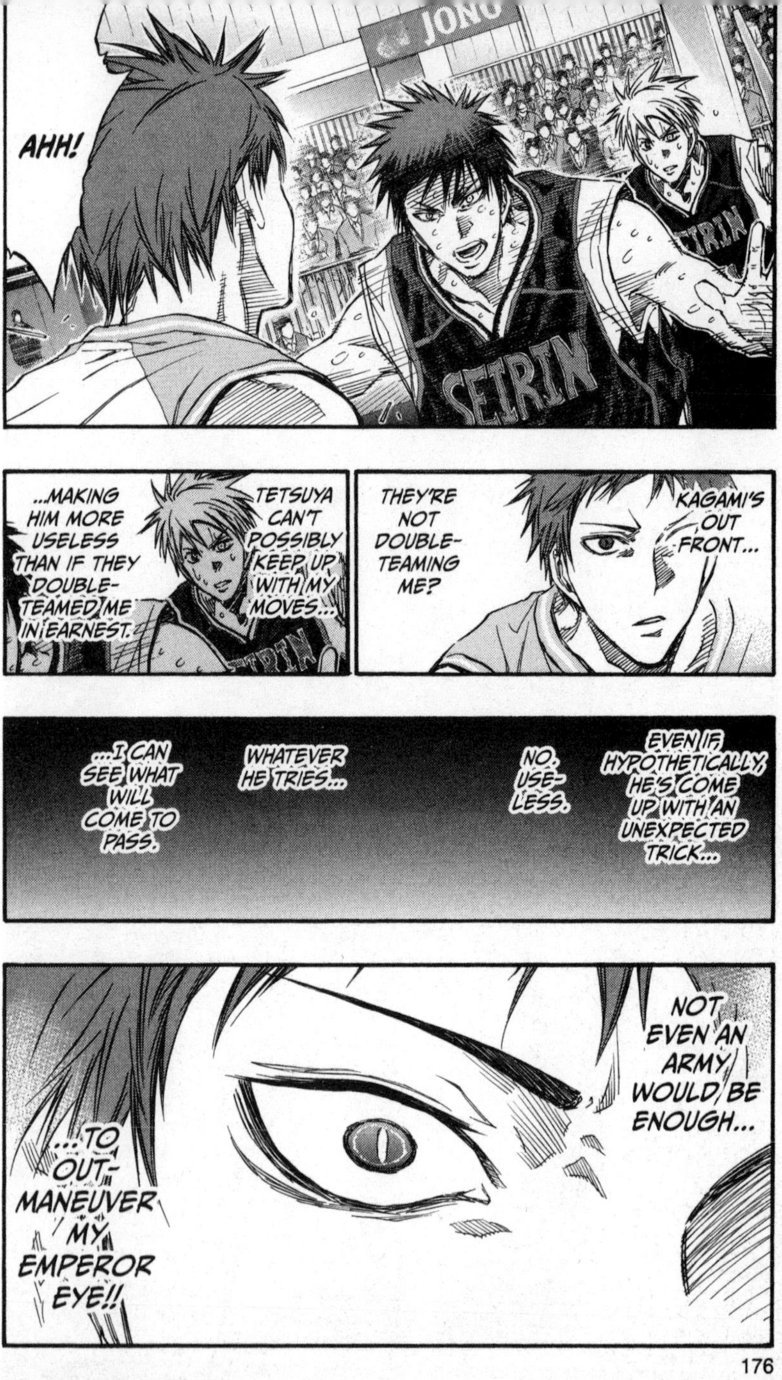
AHH!
KAGAMI'S OUT FRONT...
THEY'RE NOT DOUBLE-TEAMING ME?
TETSUYA CAN'T POSSIBLY KEEP UP WITH MY MOVES...
...MAKING HIM MORE USELESS THAN IF THEY DOUBLE-TEAMED ME IN EARNEST.
EVEN IF, HYPOTHETICALLY, HE'S COME UP WITH AN UNEXPECTED TRICK...
NO. USE-LESS.
WHATEVER HE TRIES...
...I CAN SEE WHAT WILL COME TO PASS.
NOT EVEN AN ARMY WOULD BE ENOUGH...
...TO OUT-MANEUVER MY EMPEROR EYE!!

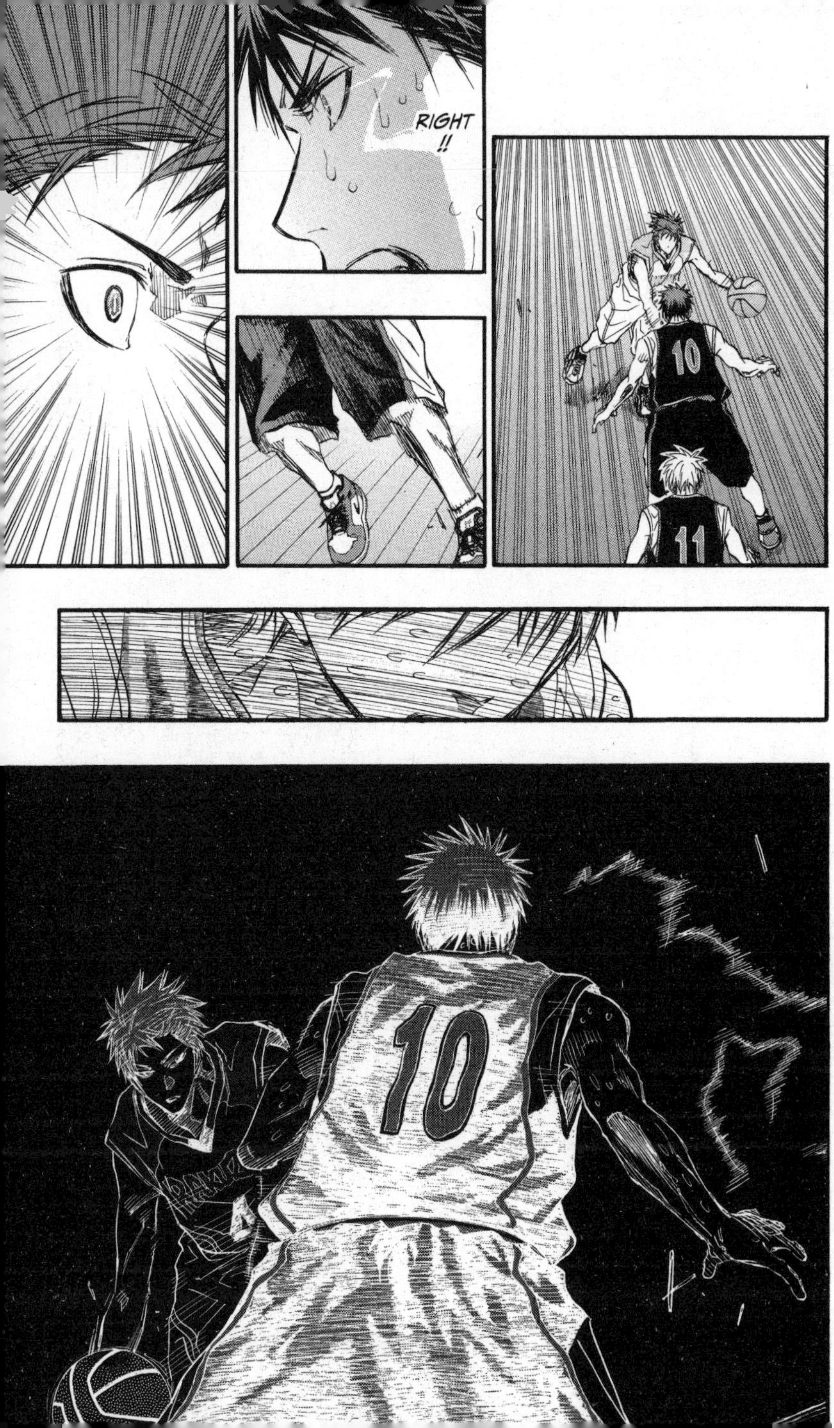
RIGHT !!

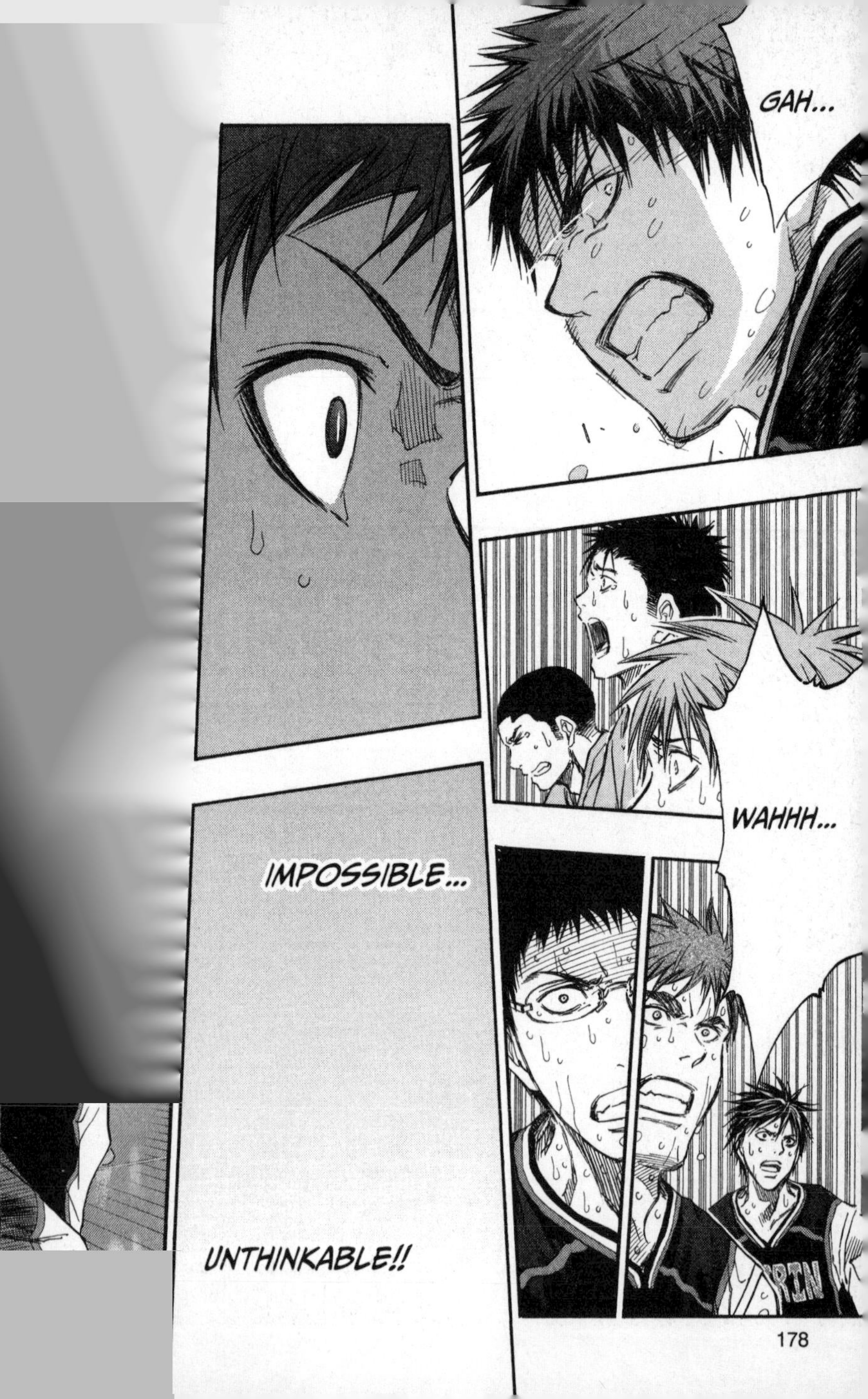
GAH...
WAHHH...
IMPOSSIBLE...
UNTHINKABLE!!

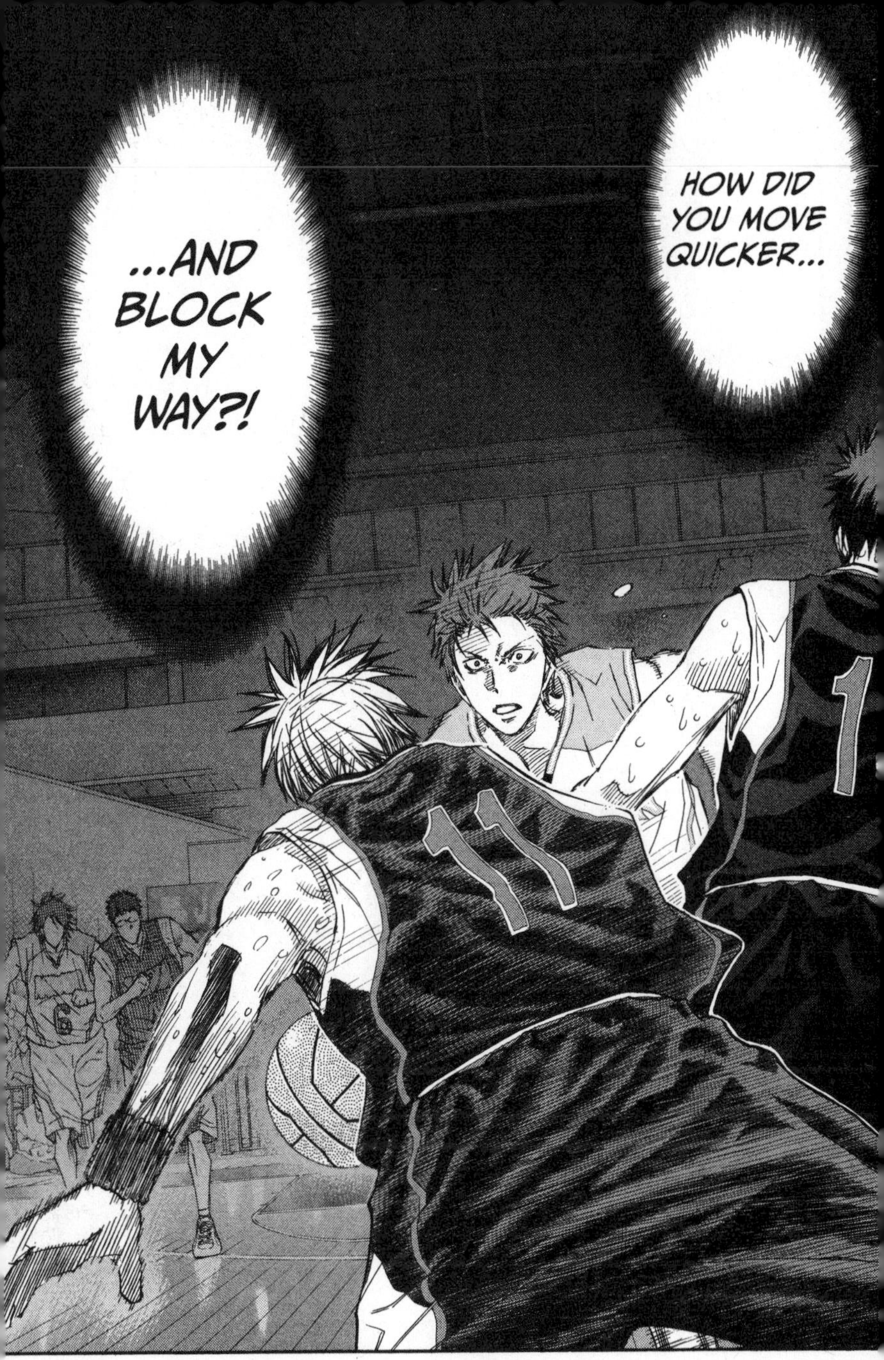
HOW DID YOU MOVE QUICKER...
...AND BLOCK MY WAY?!

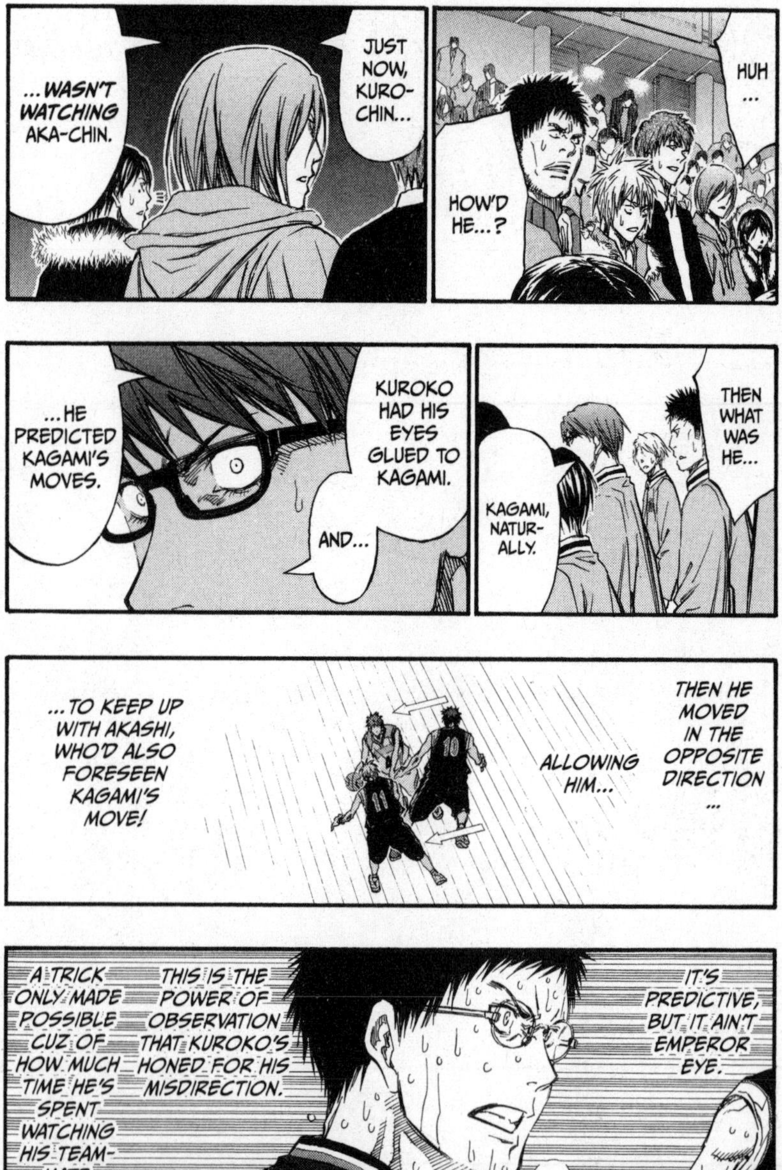
HUH ...
HOW'D HE...?
JUST NOW, KURO-CHIN...
...WASN'T WATCHING AKA-CHIN.
THEN WHAT WAS HE...
KAGAMI, NATUR-ALLY.
KUROKO HAD HIS EYES GLUED TO KAGAMI.
AND...
...HE PREDICTED KAGAMI'S MOVES.
THEN HE MOVED IN THE OPPOSITE DIRECTION ...
ALLOWING HIM...
...TO KEEP UP WITH AKASHI, WHO'D ALSO FORESEEN KAGAMI'S MOVE!
IT'S PREDICTIVE, BUT IT AIN'T EMPEROR EYE.
THIS IS THE POWER OF OBSERVATION THAT KUROKO'S HONED FOR HIS MISDIRECTION.
A TRICK ONLY MADE POSSIBLE CUZ OF HOW MUCH TIME HE'S SPENT WATCHING HIS TEAM-MATE.

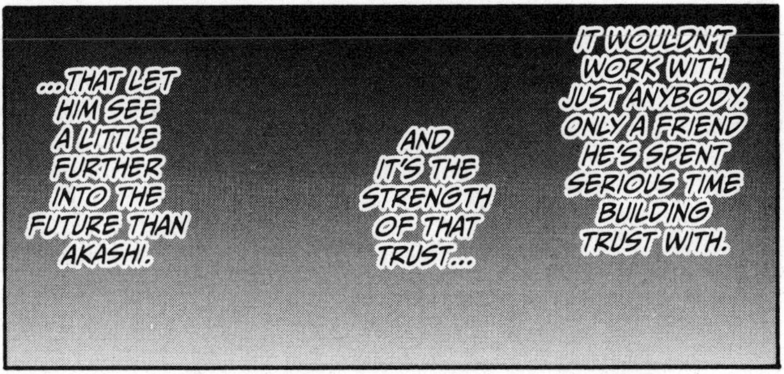
IT WOULDN'T WORK WITH JUST ANYBODY. ONLY A FRIEND HE'S SPENT SERIOUS TIME BUILDING TRUST WITH.
AND IT'S THE STRENGTH OF THAT TRUST...
...THAT LET HIM SEE A LITTLE FURTHER INTO THE FUTURE THAN AKASHI.

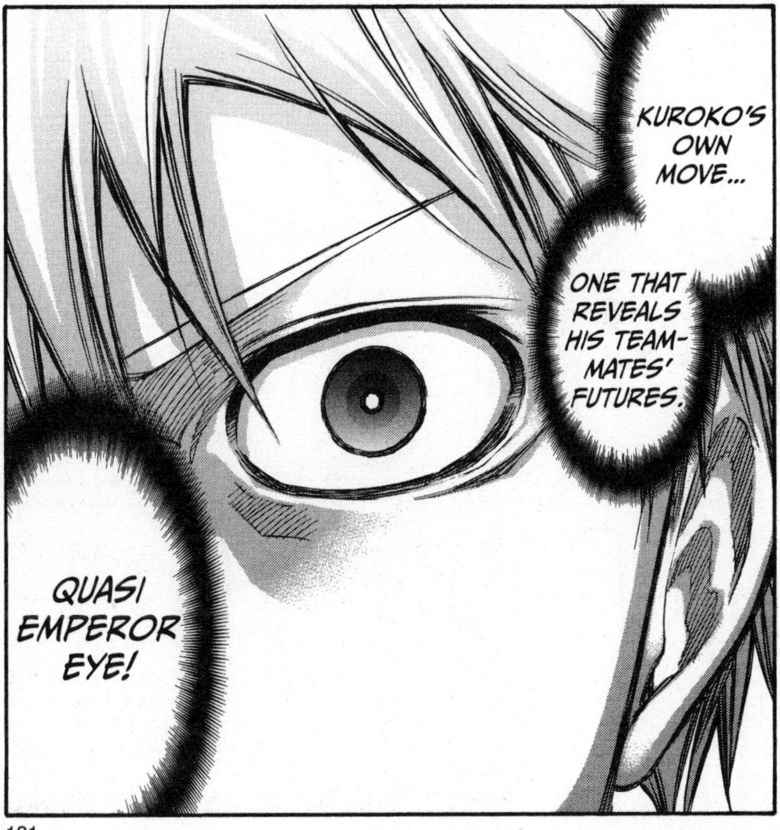
KUROKO'S OWN MOVE...
ONE THAT REVEALS HIS TEAM-MATES' FUTURES.
QUASI EMPEROR EYE!

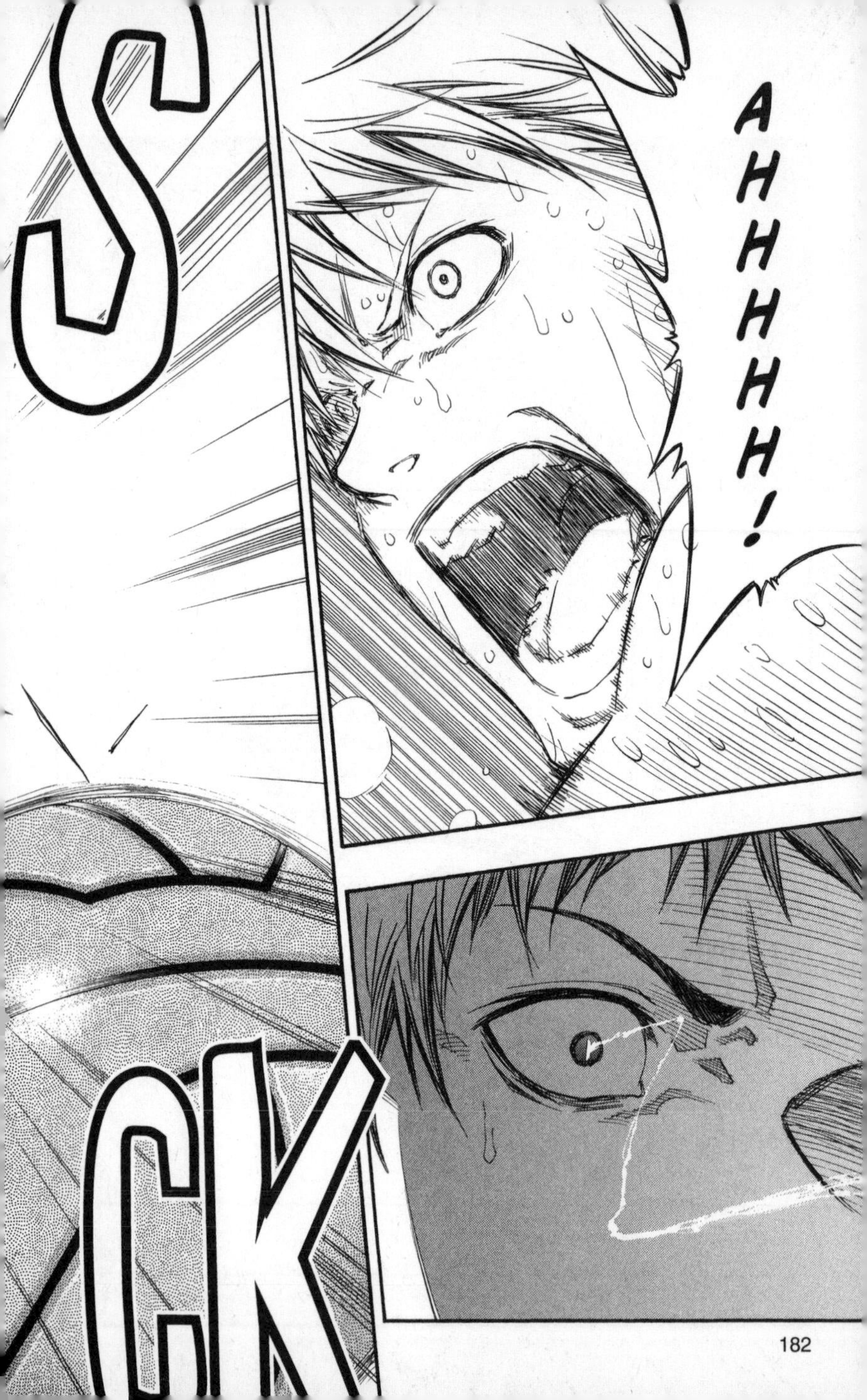
AHHHHH!
S
CK

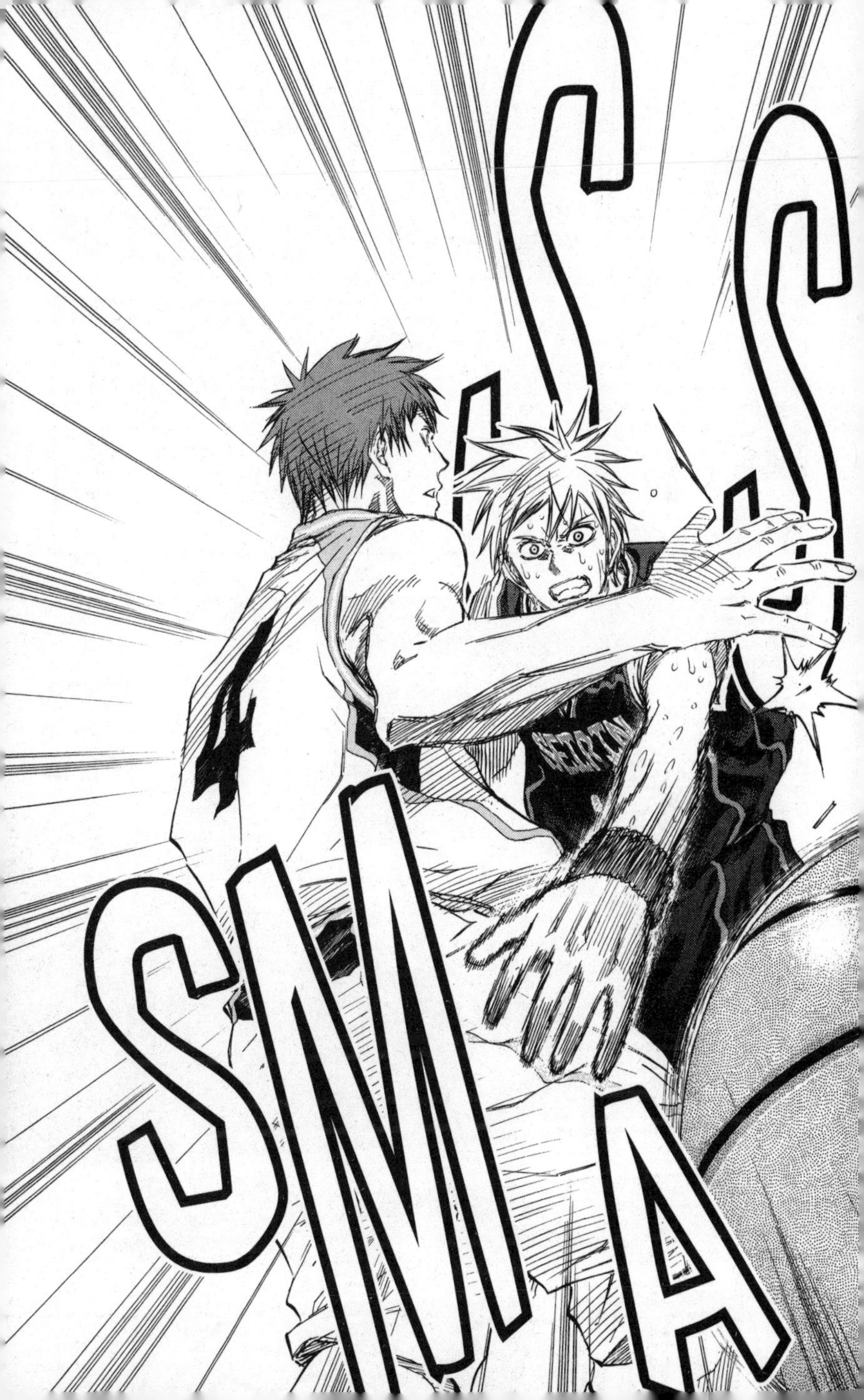

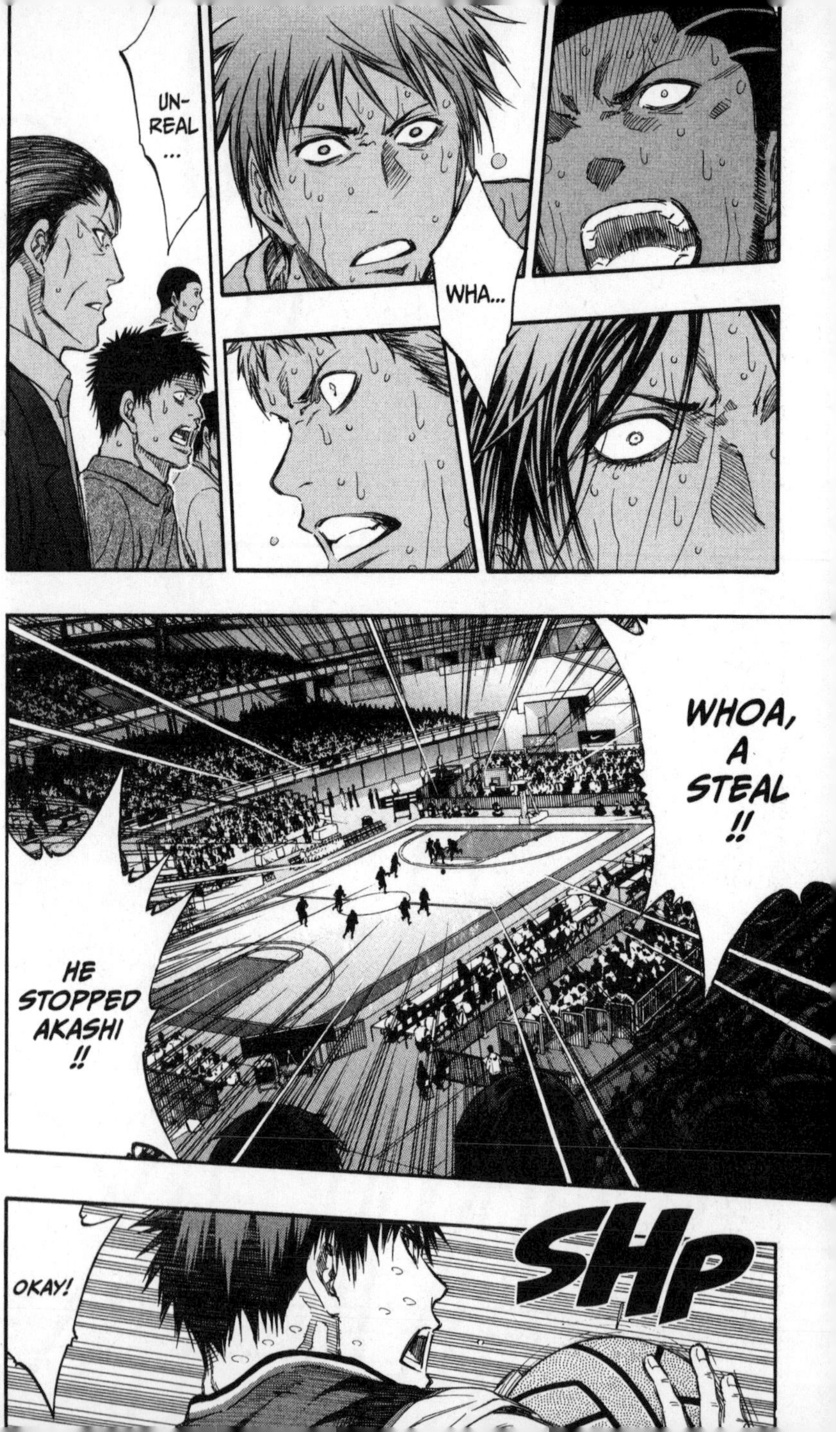
WHA...
UN-REAL...
WHOA, A STEAL!!
HE STOPPED AKASHI!!
SHP
OKAY!

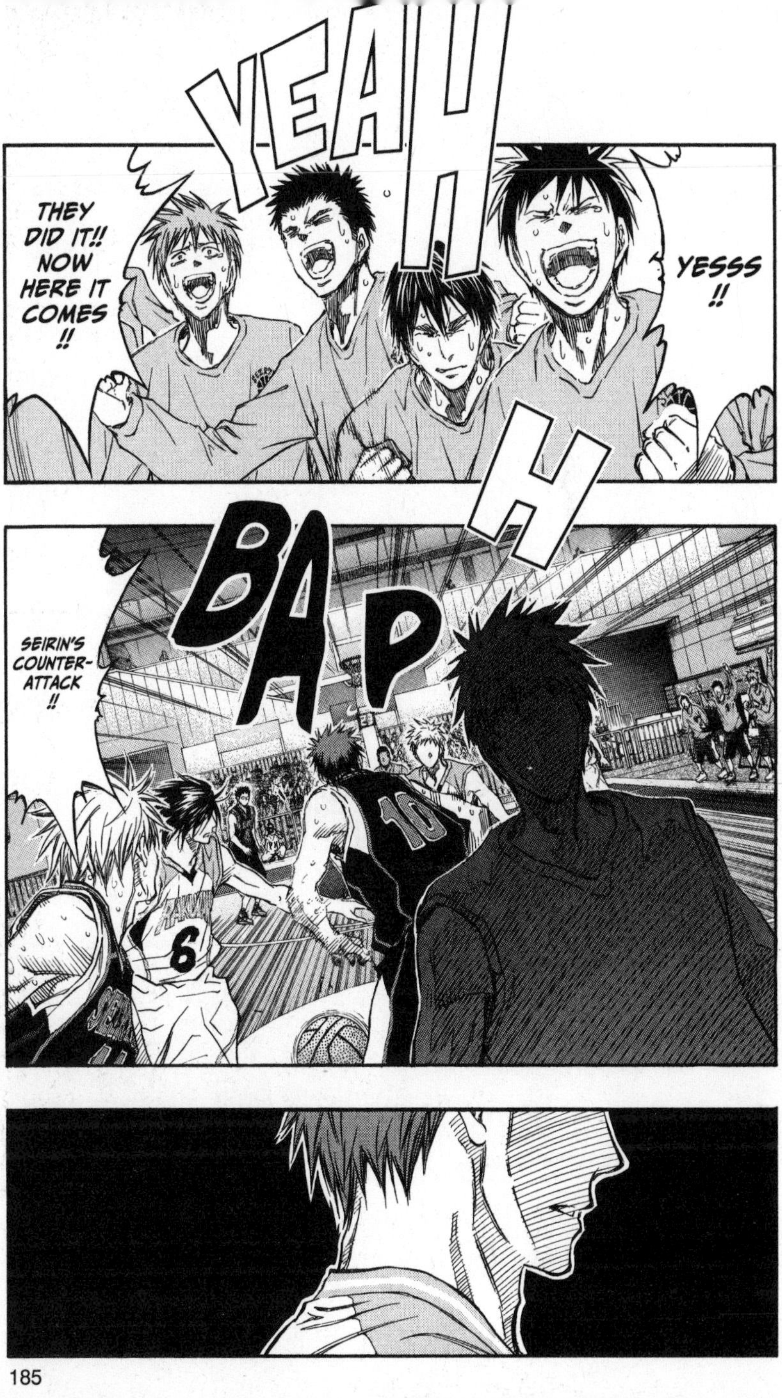
YEAHH
YESSS!!
THEY DID IT!! NOW HERE IT COMES!!
BAP
SEIRIN'S COUNTER-ATTACK!!

KUROKO'S BASKETBALL BLOOPERS

TAKE 7

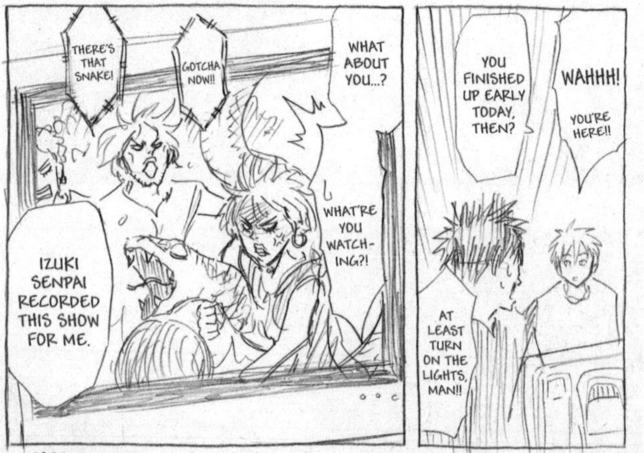
YOU FINISHED UP EARLY TODAY, THEN?
WAHHH!
YOU'RE HERE!!
AT LEAST TURN ON THE LIGHTS, MAN!!
WHAT ABOUT YOU...?
GOTCHA NOW!!
THERE'S THAT SNAKE!
WHAT'RE YOU WATCHING?!
IZUKI SENPAI RECORDED THIS SHOW FOR ME.

*SEE VOLUME 14

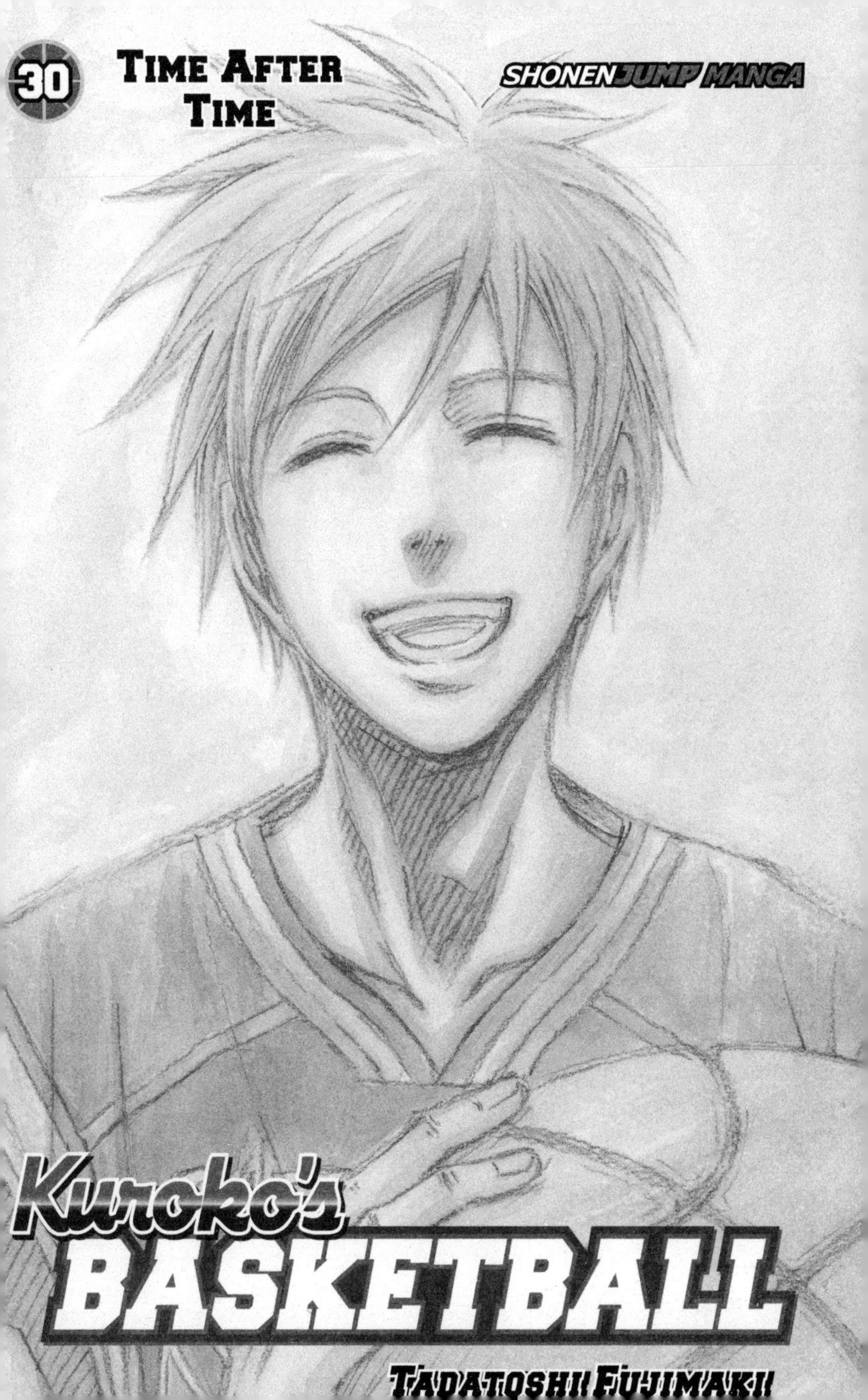
30
TIME AFTER TIME
SHONEN JUMP MANGA
Kuroko's
BASKETBALL
TADATOSHI FUJIMAKI

TADATOSHI FUJIMAKI

And before I knew it, it was over. There are lots of memories, but I can't remember most of them very well off the top of my head. That's how frantic I've been. But also satisfied.

The entire story only covers a single year of high school, but Kuroko and friends would pretty much still be the same come graduation.

—2014

264TH QUARTER: FIRST TIME EVER

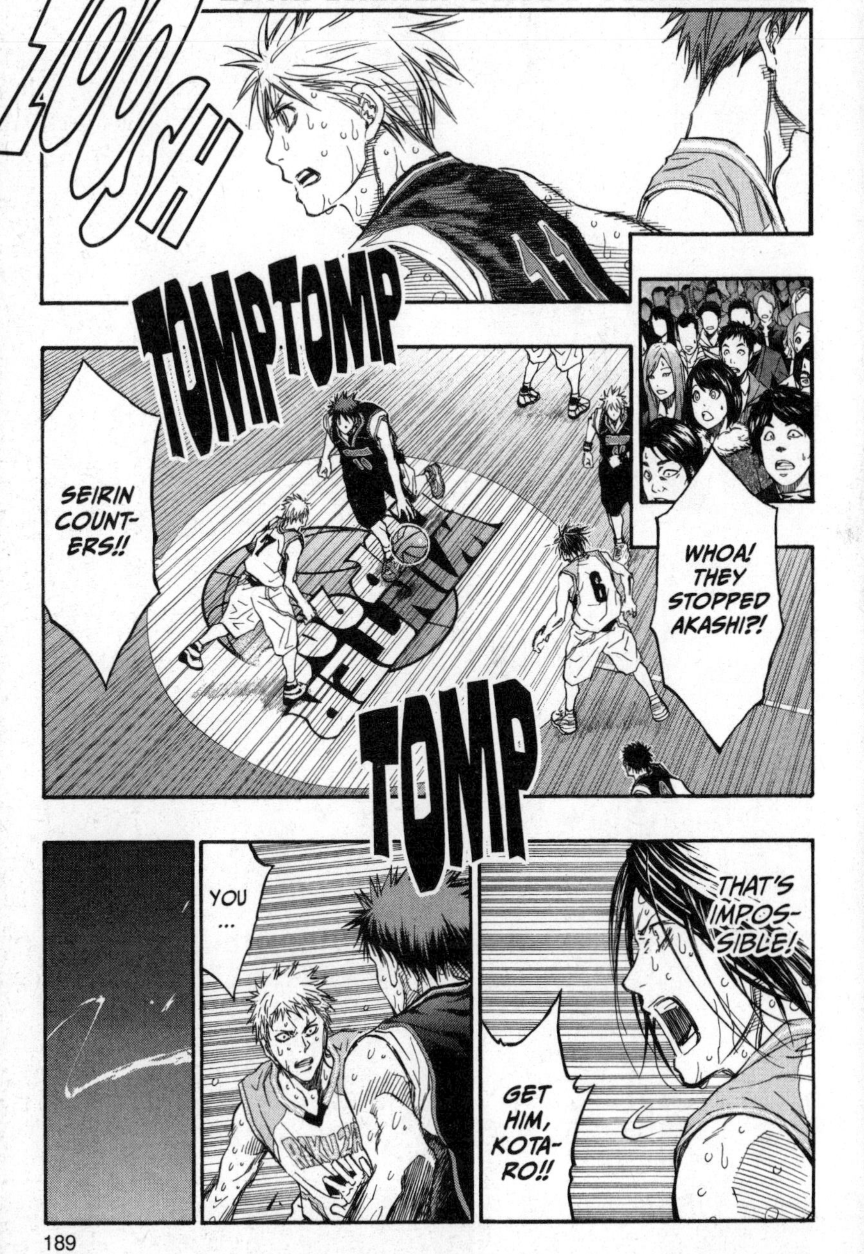
ZOOSH
WHOA! THEY STOPPED AKASHI?!
TOMP TOMP
SEIRIN COUNTERS!!
TOMP
THAT'S IMPOSSIBLE!
GET HIM, KOTARO!!
YOU ...

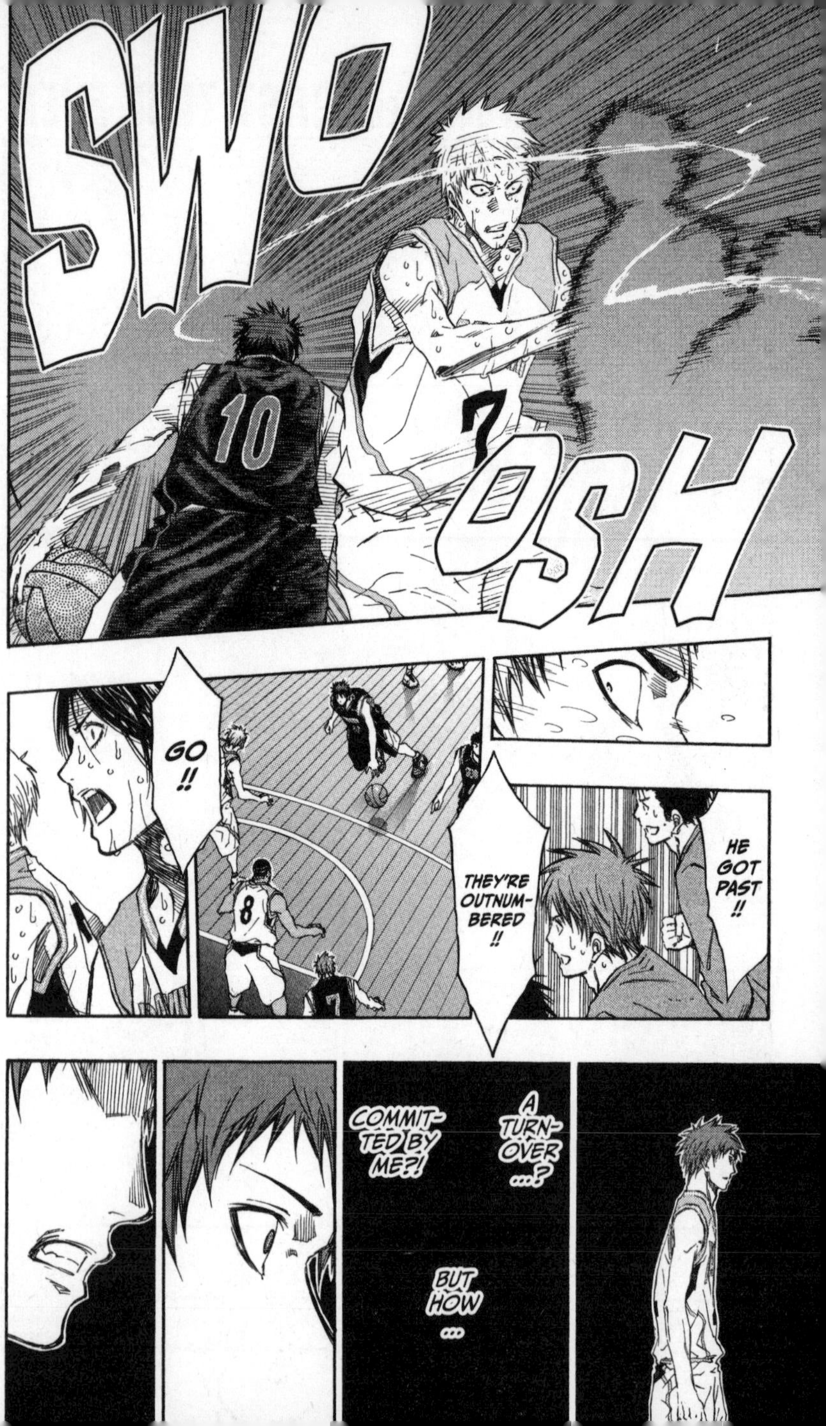
SWO
OSH
HE GOT PAST!!
THEY'RE OUTNUMBERED!!
GO!!
A TURNOVER...?
COMMITTED BY ME?!
BUT HOW...

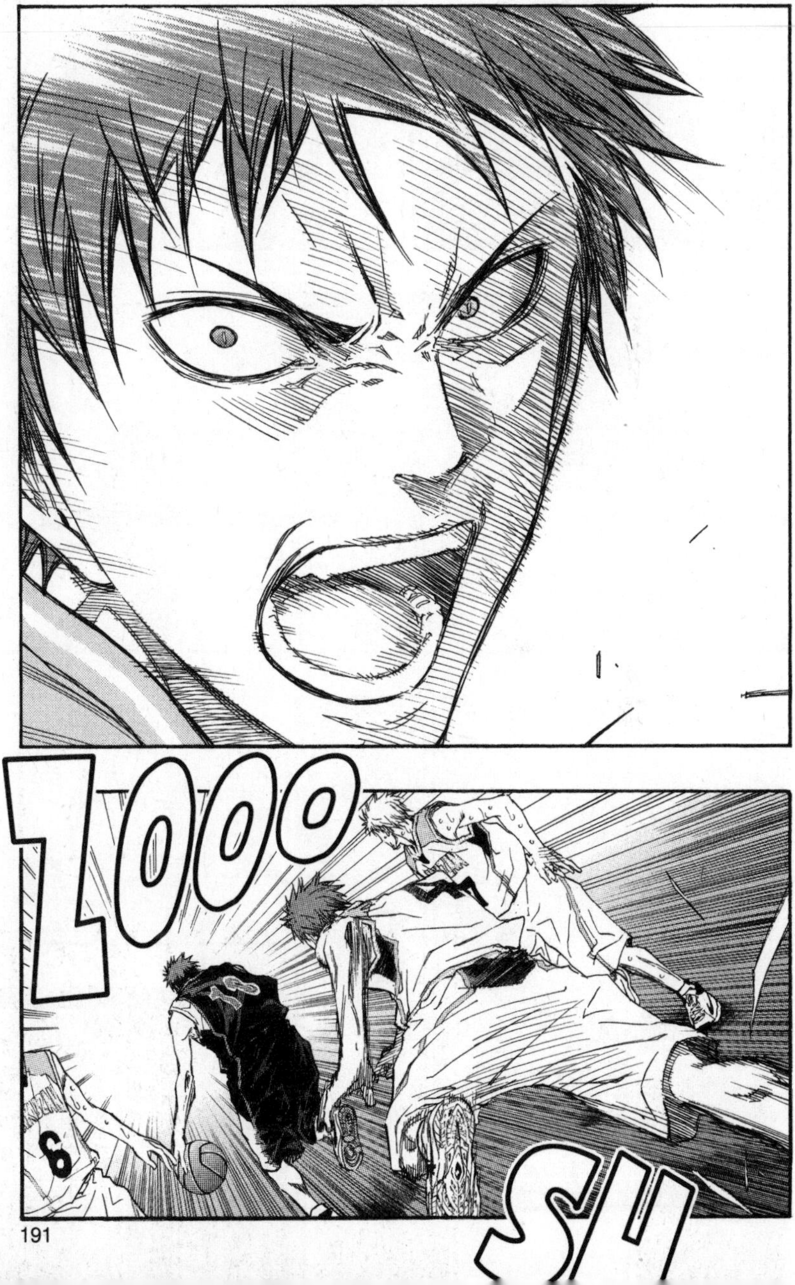
ZOOO
SH

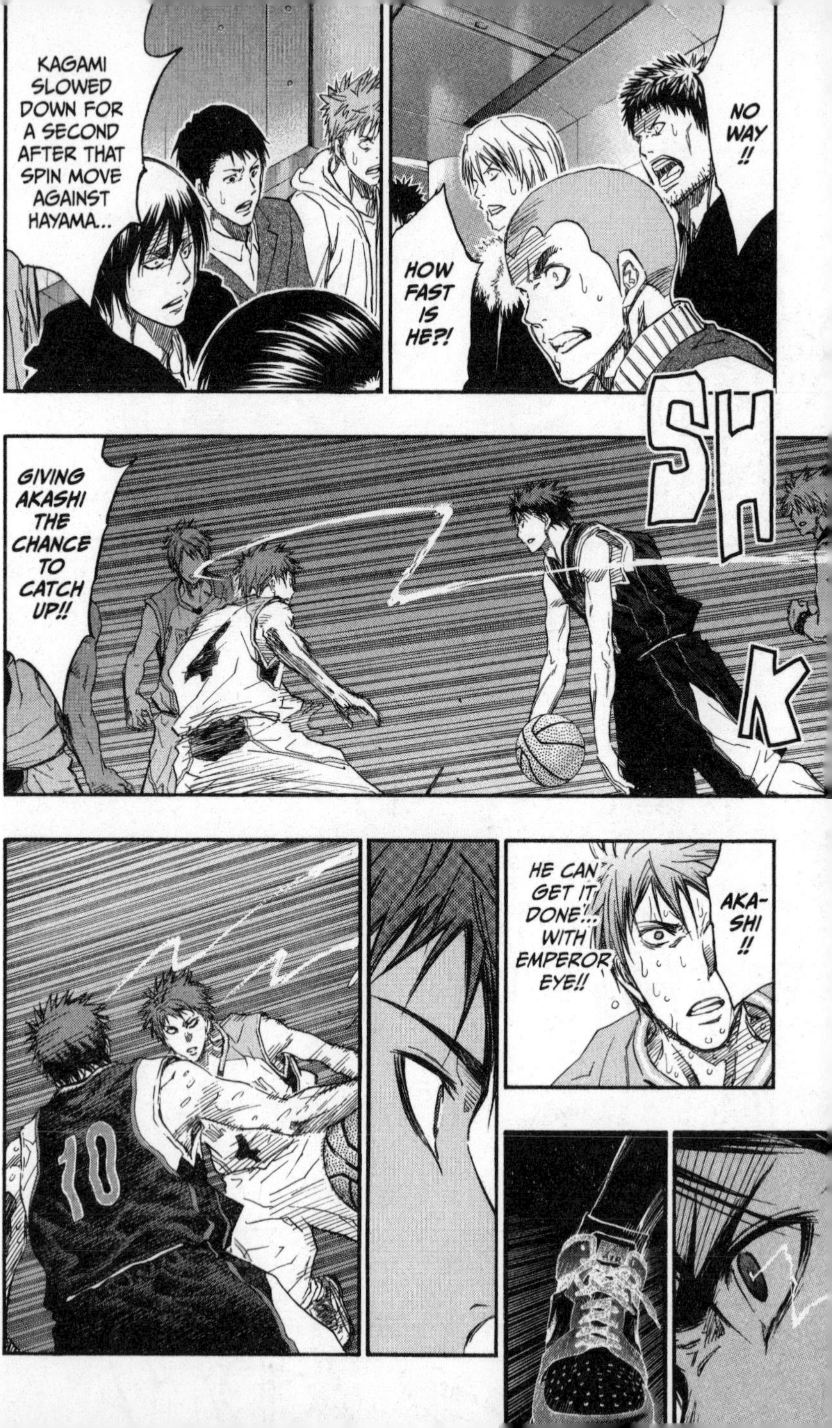
NO WAY!!
HOW FAST IS HE?!
KAGAMI SLOWED DOWN FOR A SECOND AFTER THAT SPIN MOVE AGAINST HAYAMA...
SHK
GIVING AKASHI THE CHANCE TO CATCH UP!!
AKA-SHI!!
HE CAN GET IT DONE... WITH EMPEROR EYE!!

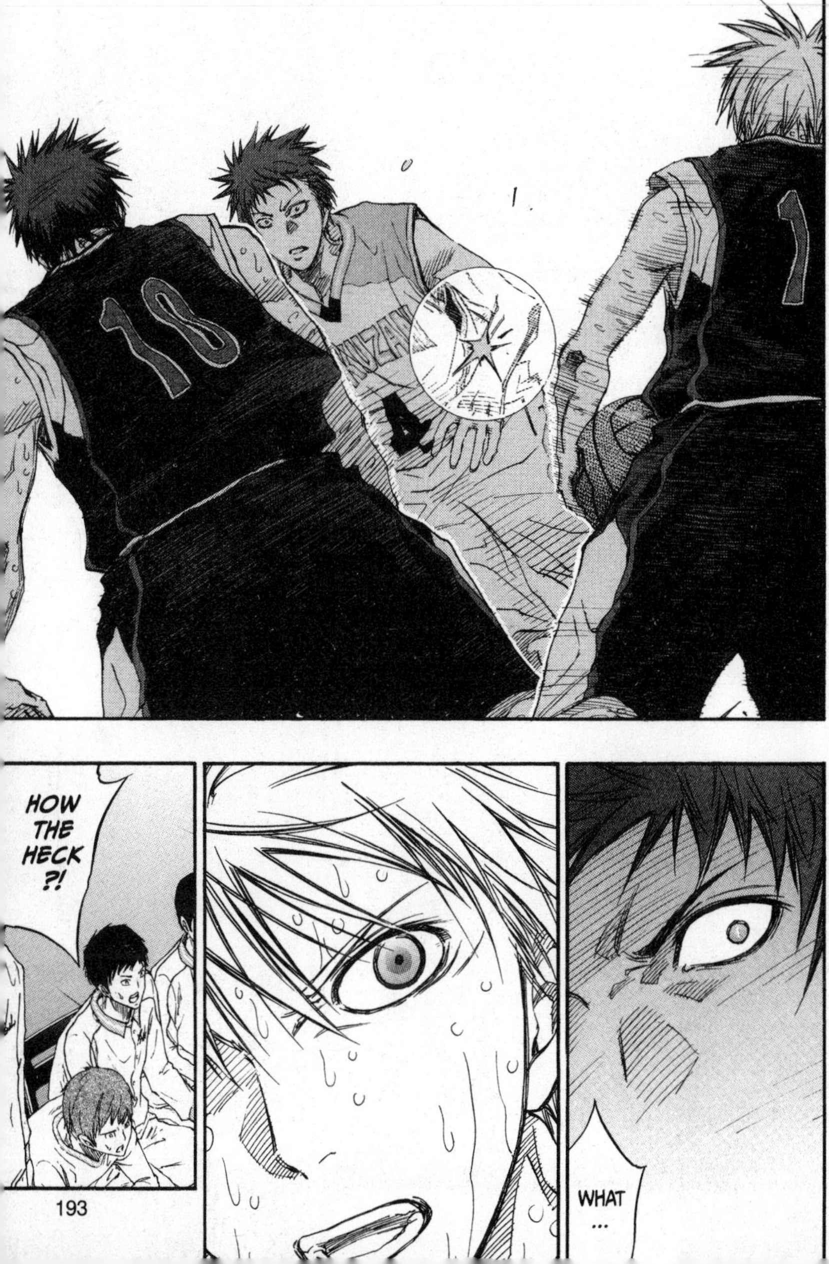
WHAT ...
HOW THE HECK ?!

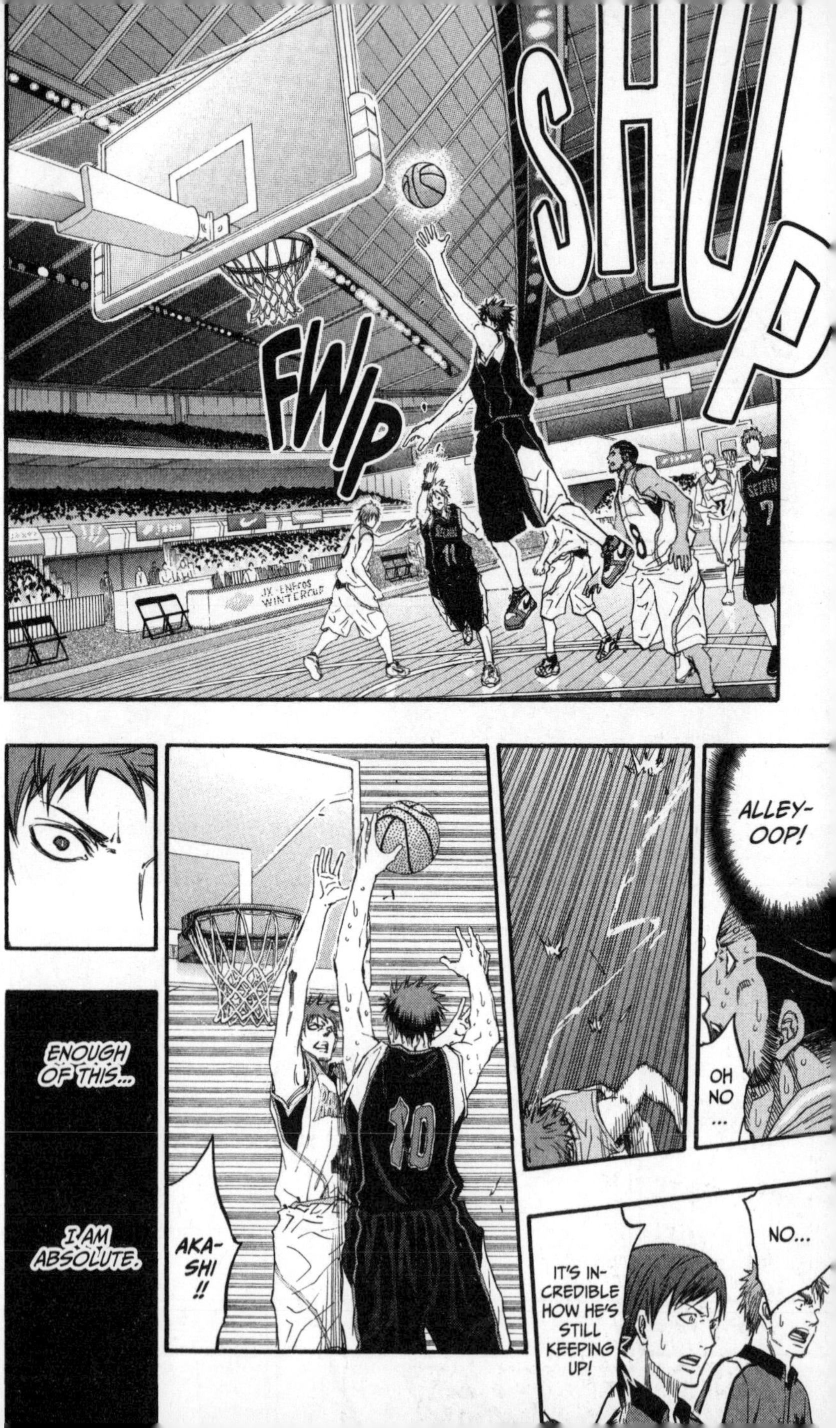
SHUP
FWIP
JX-ENEOS WINTERCUP
ALLEY-OOP!
OH NO ...
NO...
IT'S INCREDIBLE HOW HE'S STILL KEEPING UP!
AKA-SHI!!
ENOUGH OF THIS...
I AM ABSOLUTE.

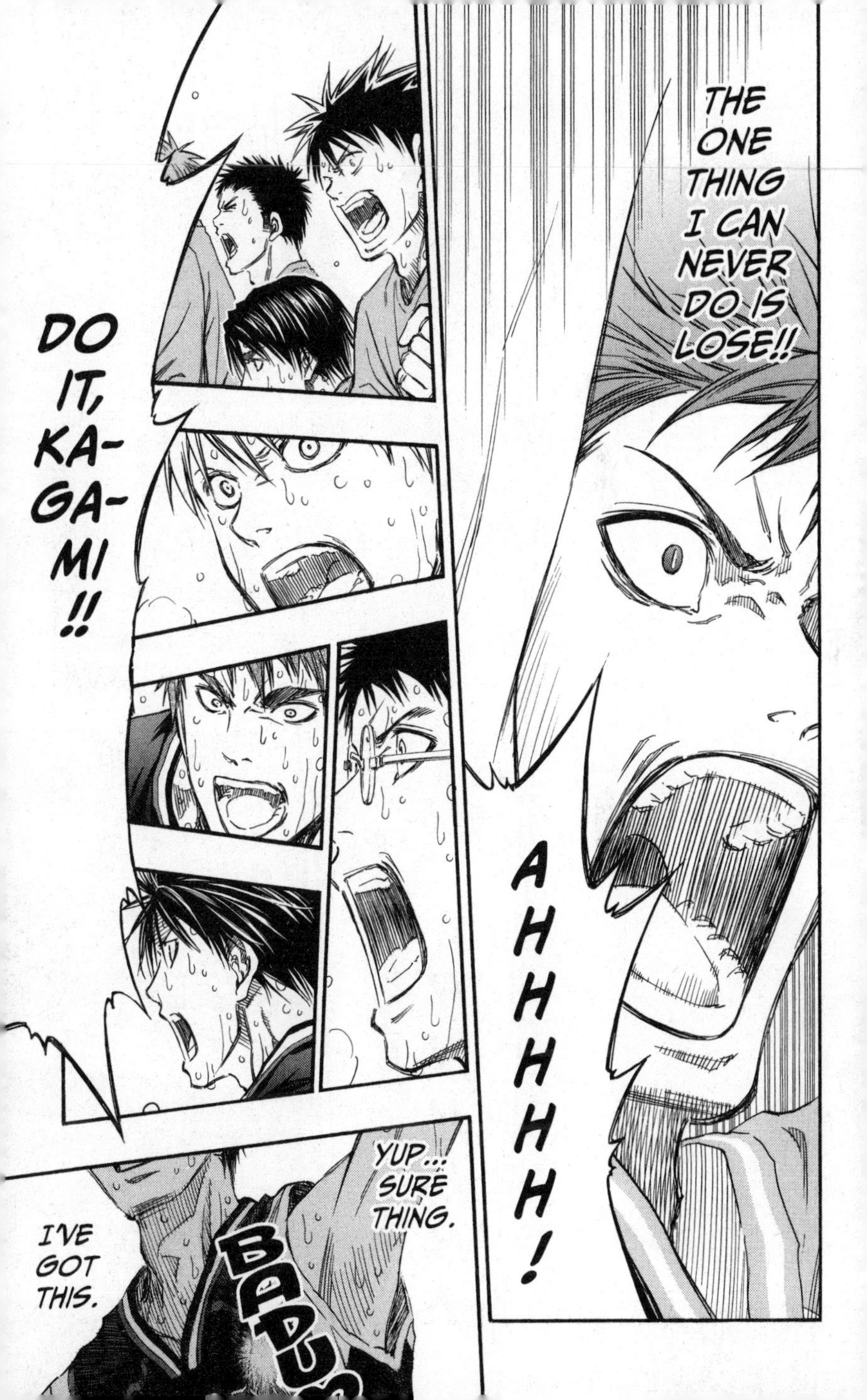
THE ONE THING I CAN NEVER DO IS LOSE!!
AHHHHHH!
DO IT, KA-GA-MI!!
YUP... SURE THING.
I'VE GOT THIS.
BADUS

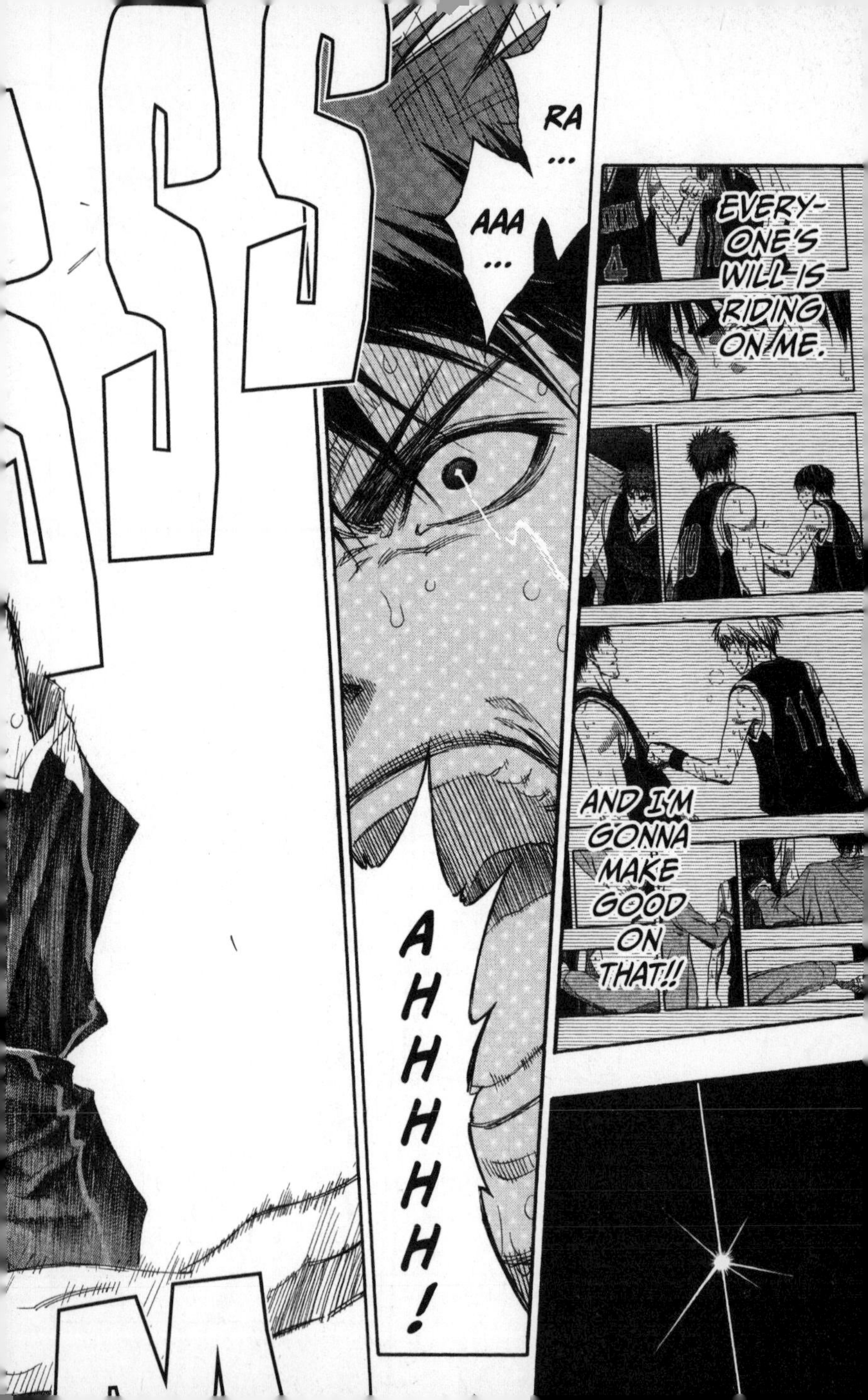
EVERY-ONE'S WILL IS RIDING ON ME.
AND I'M GONNA MAKE GOOD ON THAT!!
RA...
AAA...
AHHHHHH!

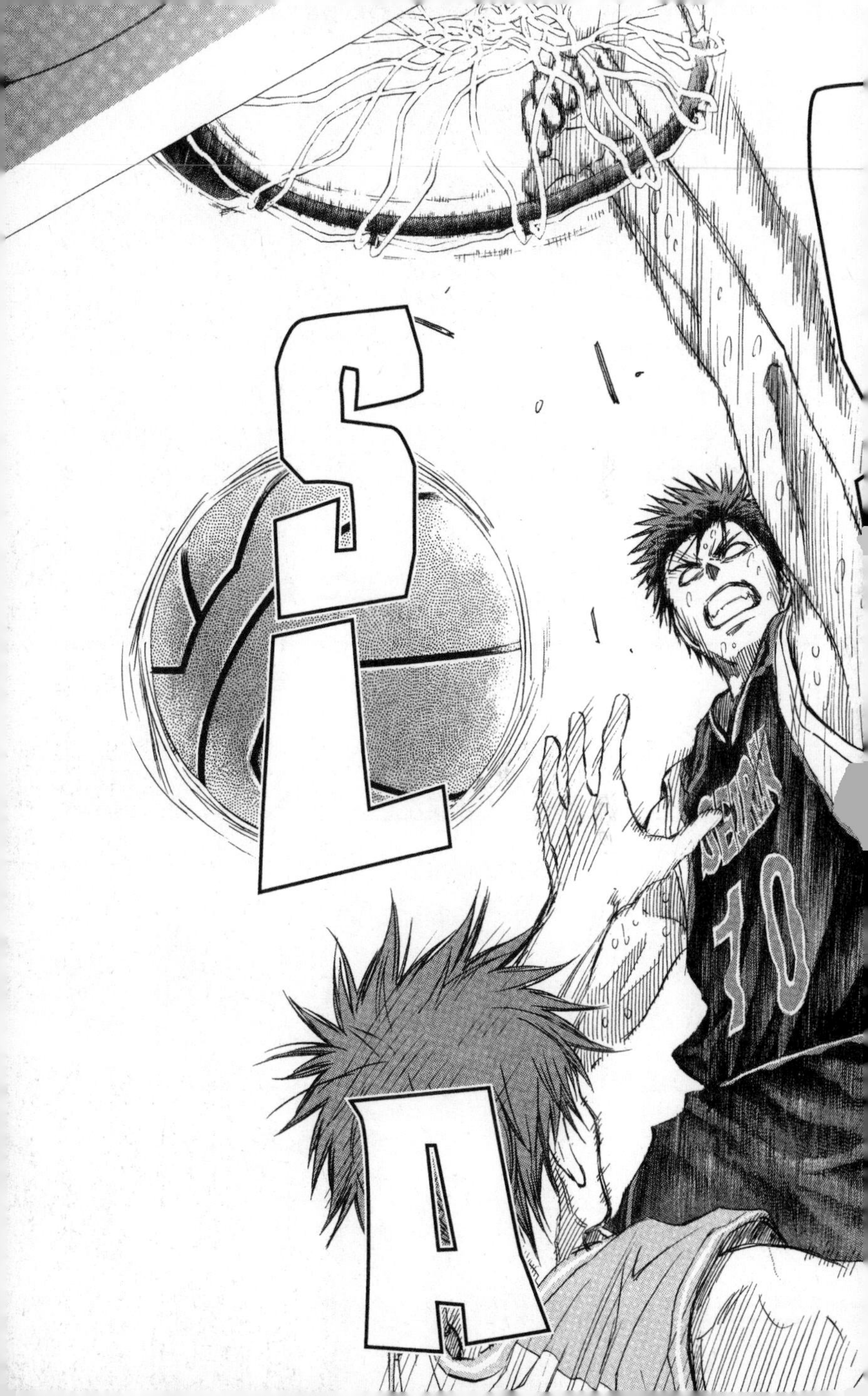
SLA

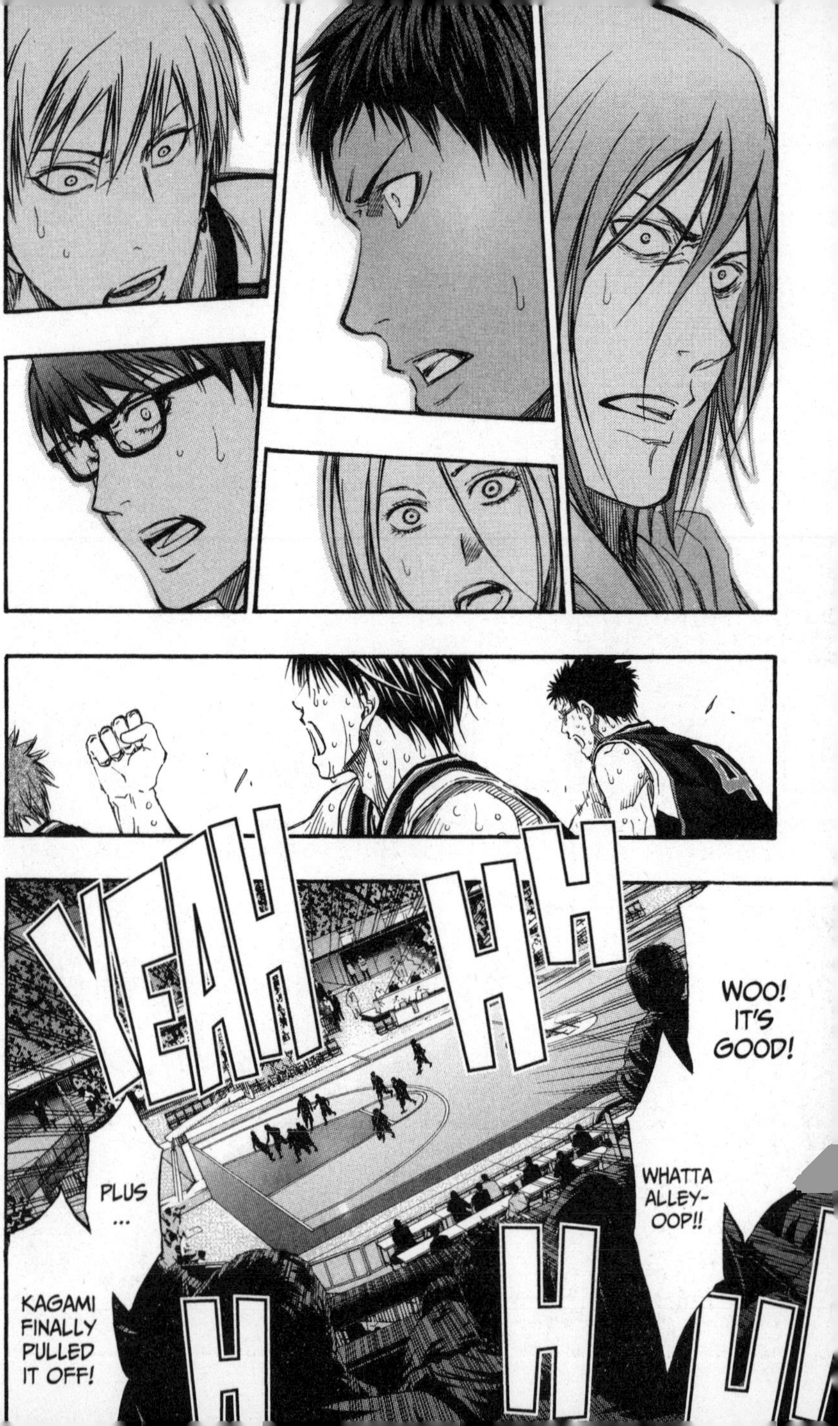
YEAHHHH
WOO! IT'S GOOD!
WHATTA ALLEY-OOP!!
PLUS...
KAGAMI FINALLY PULLED IT OFF!

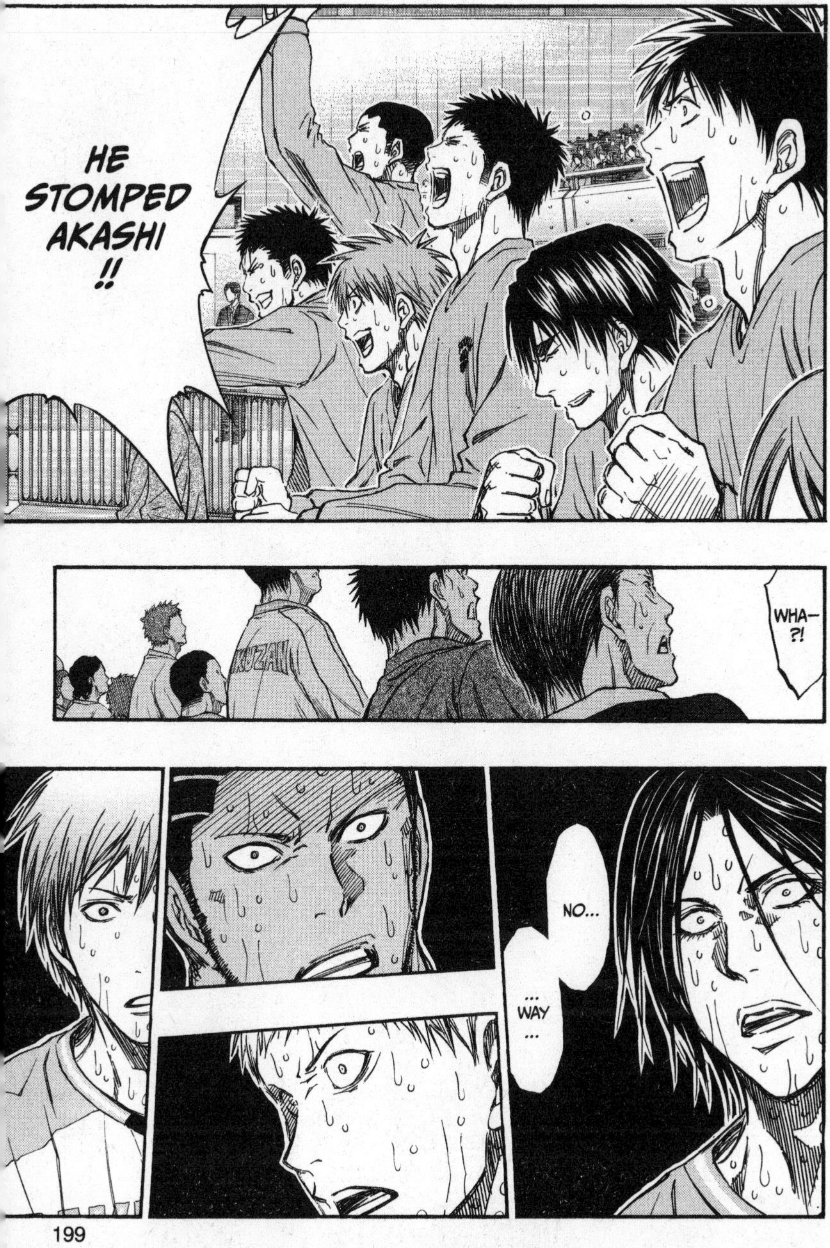
HE STOMPED AKASHI !!
WHA— ?!
NO...
... WAY ...

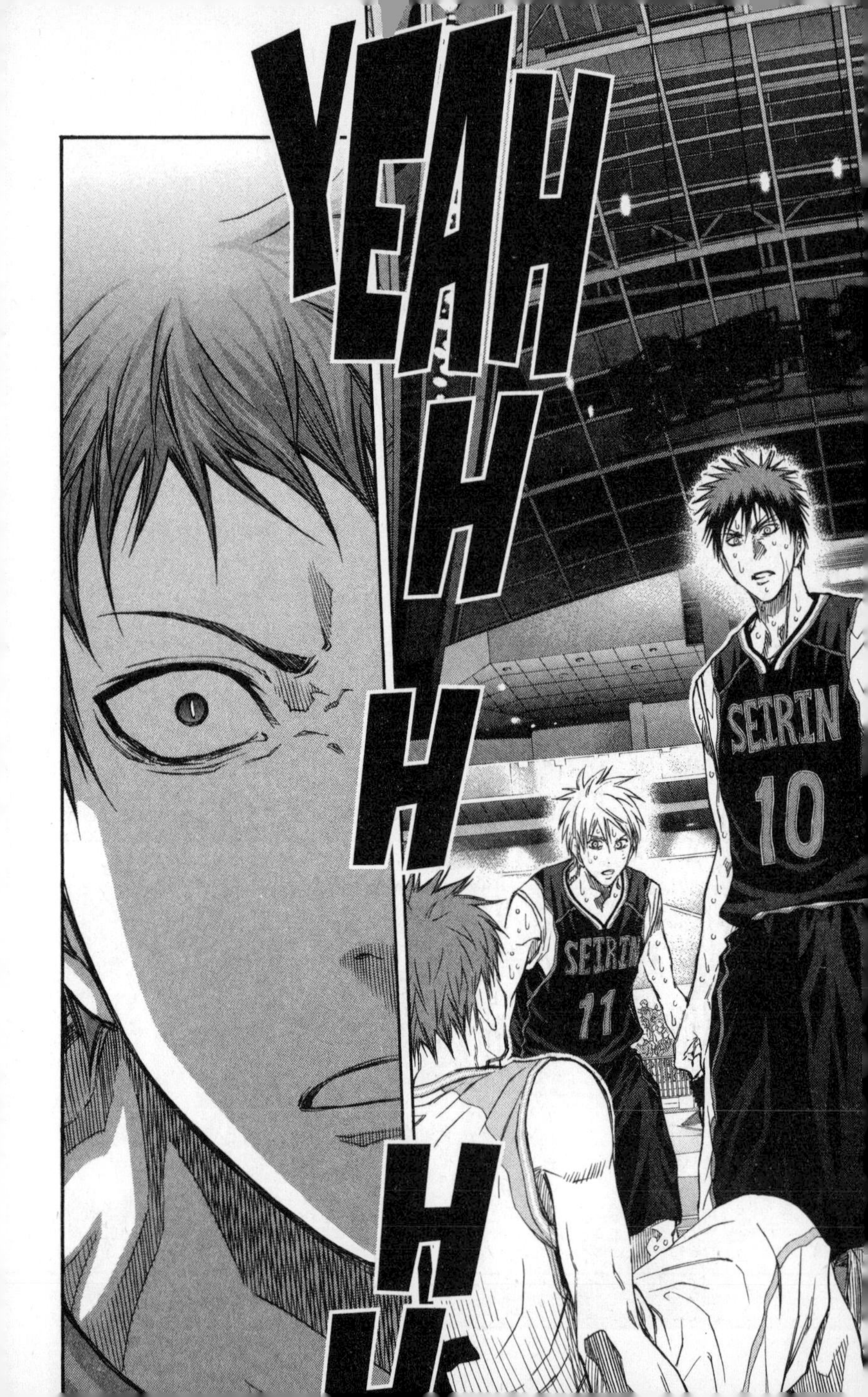
YEAHHHH!!
SEIRIN
10
SEIRIN
11

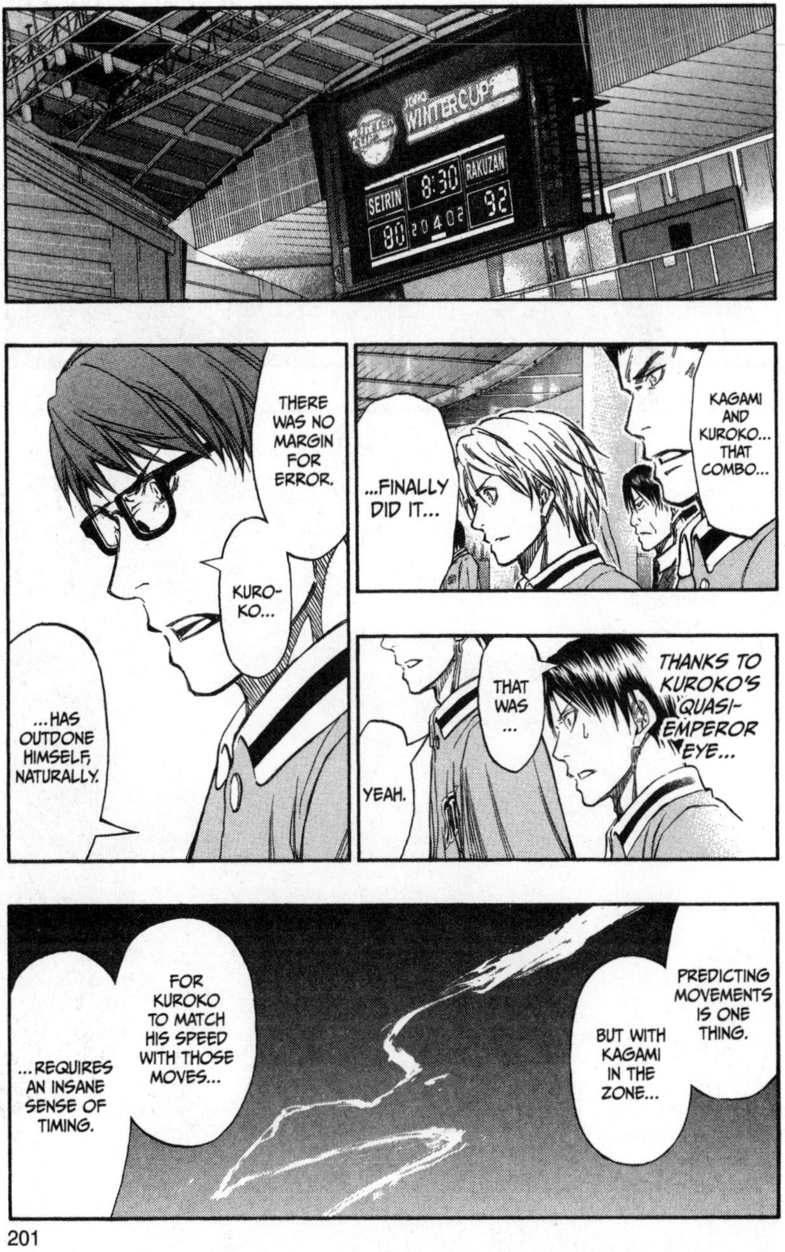
WINTERCUP
SEIRIN
8:30
RAKUZAN
80
92
KAGAMI AND KUROKO... THAT COMBO...
...FINALLY DID IT...
THANKS TO KUROKO'S QUASI-EMPEROR EYE...
THAT WAS ...
YEAH.
THERE WAS NO MARGIN FOR ERROR.
KURO-KO...
...HAS OUTDONE HIMSELF, NATURALLY.
PREDICTING MOVEMENTS IS ONE THING.
BUT WITH KAGAMI IN THE ZONE...
FOR KUROKO TO MATCH HIS SPEED WITH THOSE MOVES...
...REQUIRES AN INSANE SENSE OF TIMING.

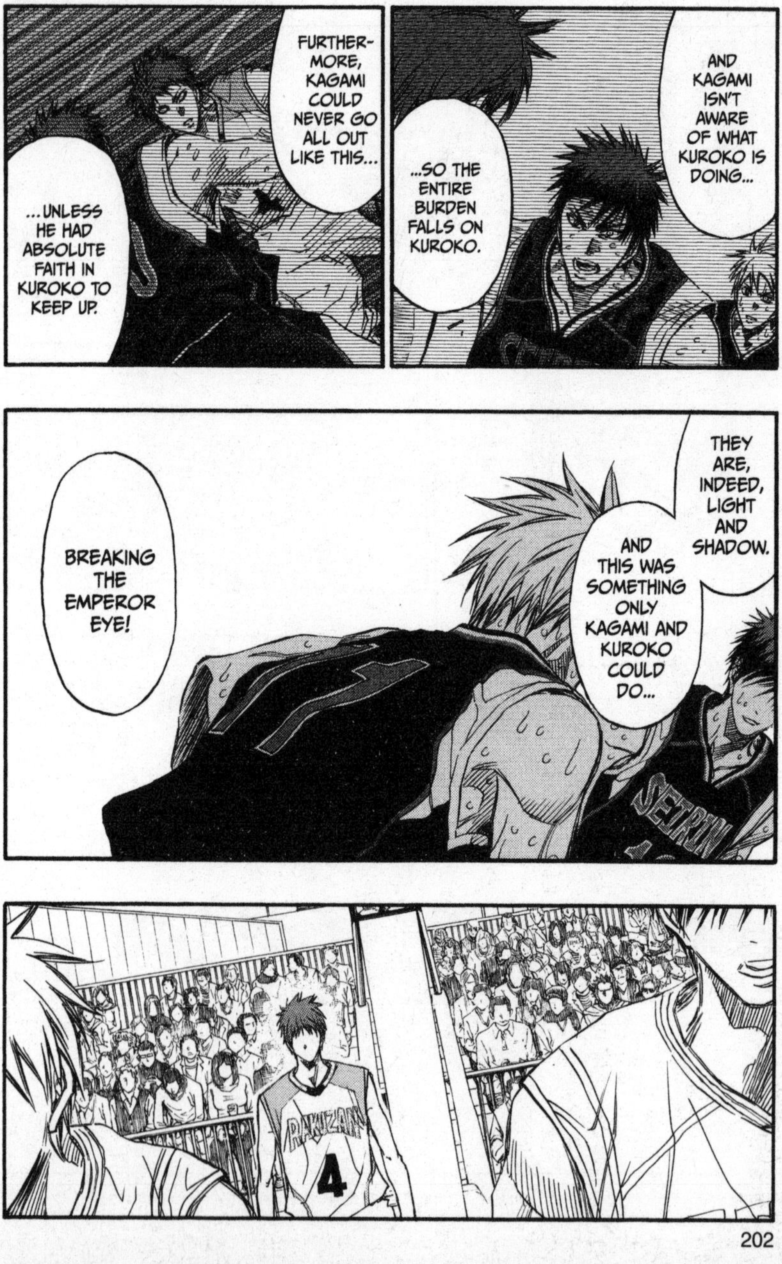
AND KAGAMI ISN'T AWARE OF WHAT KUROKO IS DOING...
...SO THE ENTIRE BURDEN FALLS ON KUROKO.
FURTHER-MORE, KAGAMI COULD NEVER GO ALL OUT LIKE THIS...
...UNLESS HE HAD ABSOLUTE FAITH IN KUROKO TO KEEP UP.
THEY ARE, INDEED, LIGHT AND SHADOW.
AND THIS WAS SOMETHING ONLY KAGAMI AND KUROKO COULD DO...
BREAKING THE EMPEROR EYE!
SEIRIN
RAKUZAN
4

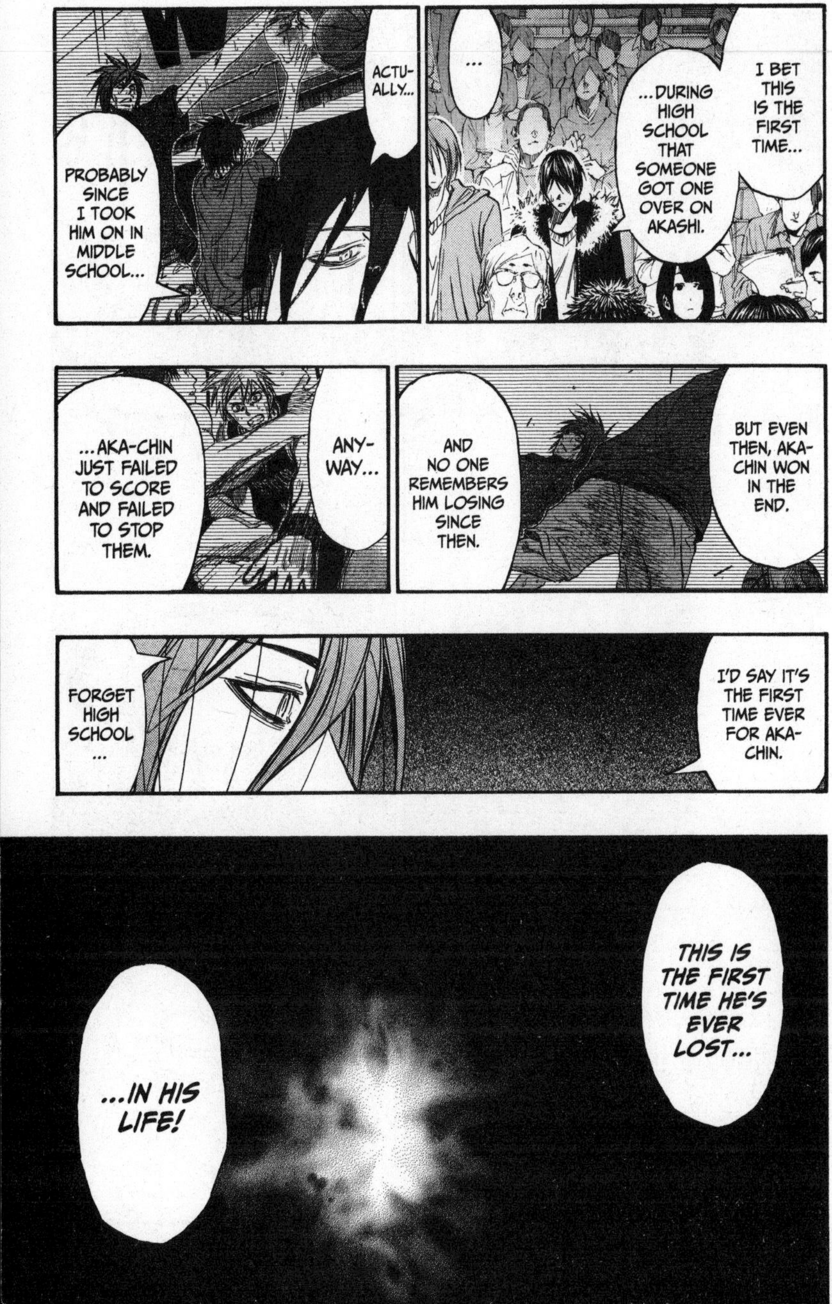
I BET THIS IS THE FIRST TIME...
...DURING HIGH SCHOOL THAT SOMEONE GOT ONE OVER ON AKASHI.
...
ACTU-ALLY...
PROBABLY SINCE I TOOK HIM ON IN MIDDLE SCHOOL...
BUT EVEN THEN, AKA-CHIN WON IN THE END.
AND NO ONE REMEMBERS HIM LOSING SINCE THEN.
ANY-WAY...
...AKA-CHIN JUST FAILED TO SCORE AND FAILED TO STOP THEM.
I'D SAY IT'S THE FIRST TIME EVER FOR AKA-CHIN.
FORGET HIGH SCHOOL...
THIS IS THE FIRST TIME HE'S EVER LOST...
...IN HIS LIFE!

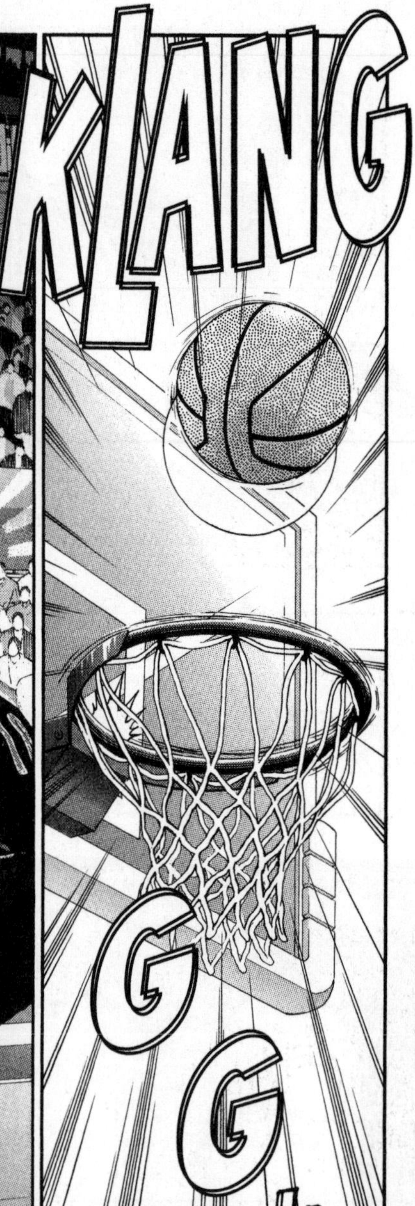
KLANG
GG..
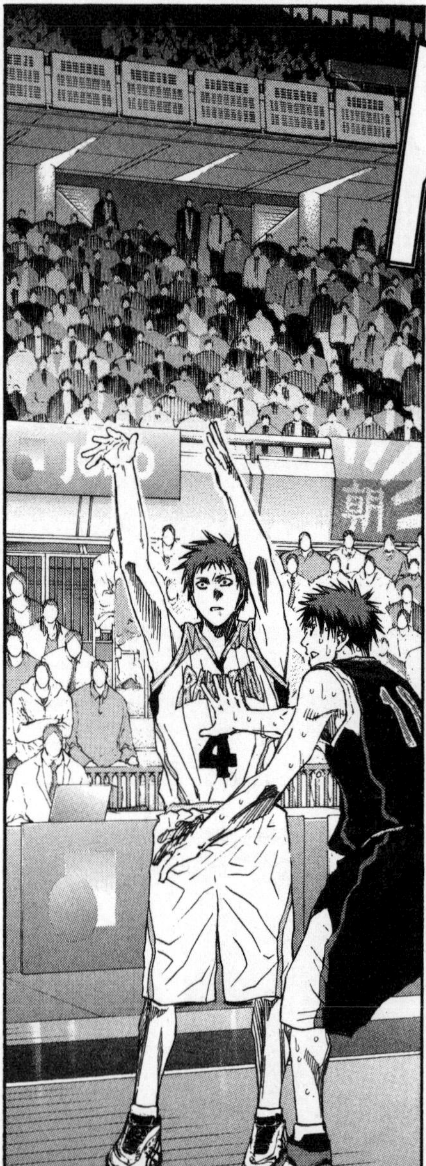

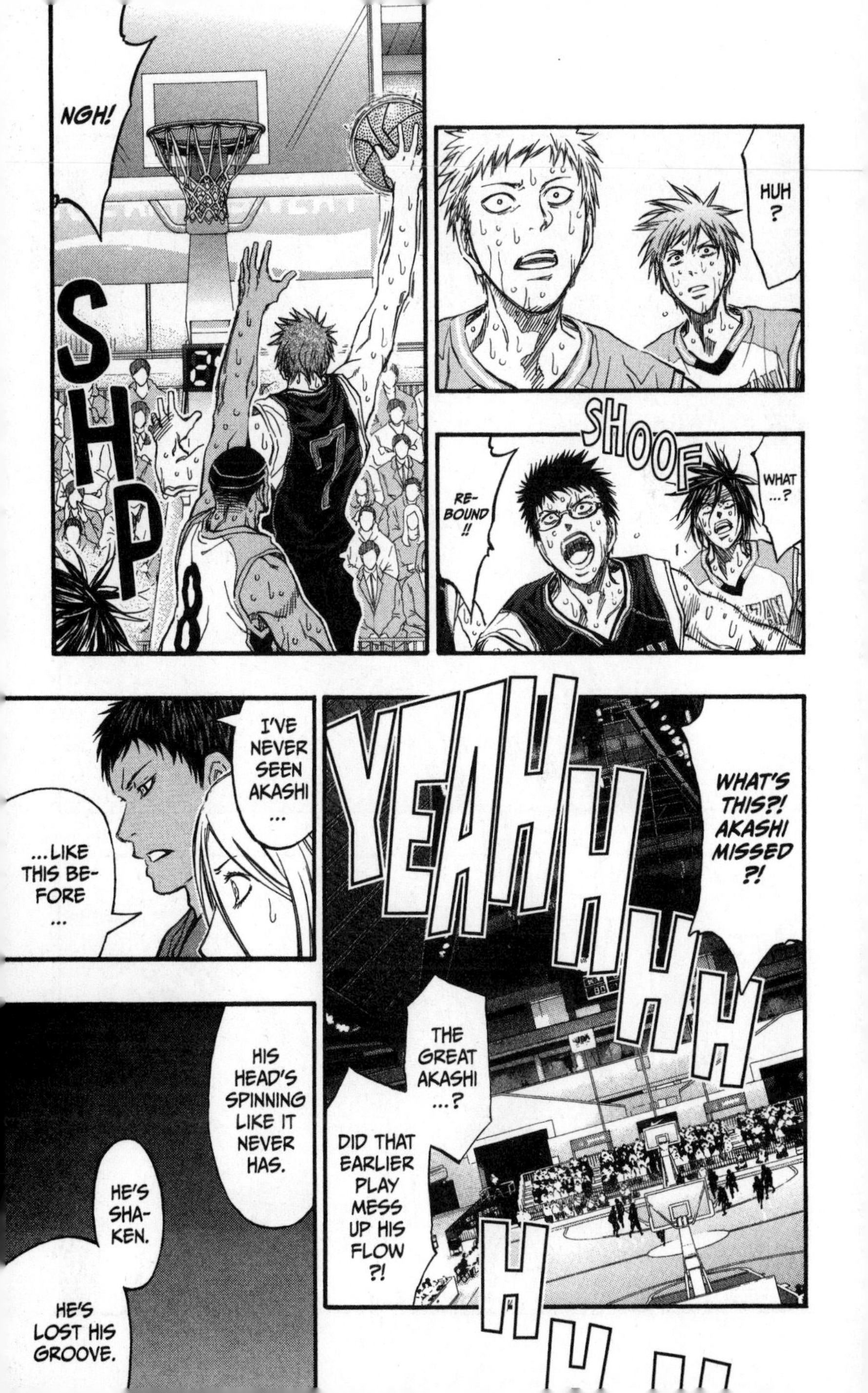
HUH?
WHAT...?
SHOOF
RE-BOUND!!
NGH!
SHP
YEAHHHHHH
WHAT'S THIS?! AKASHI MISSED?!
THE GREAT AKASHI...?
DID THAT EARLIER PLAY MESS UP HIS FLOW?!
I'VE NEVER SEEN AKASHI...
...LIKE THIS BE-FORE...
HIS HEAD'S SPINNING LIKE IT NEVER HAS.
HE'S SHA-KEN.
HE'S LOST HIS GROOVE.

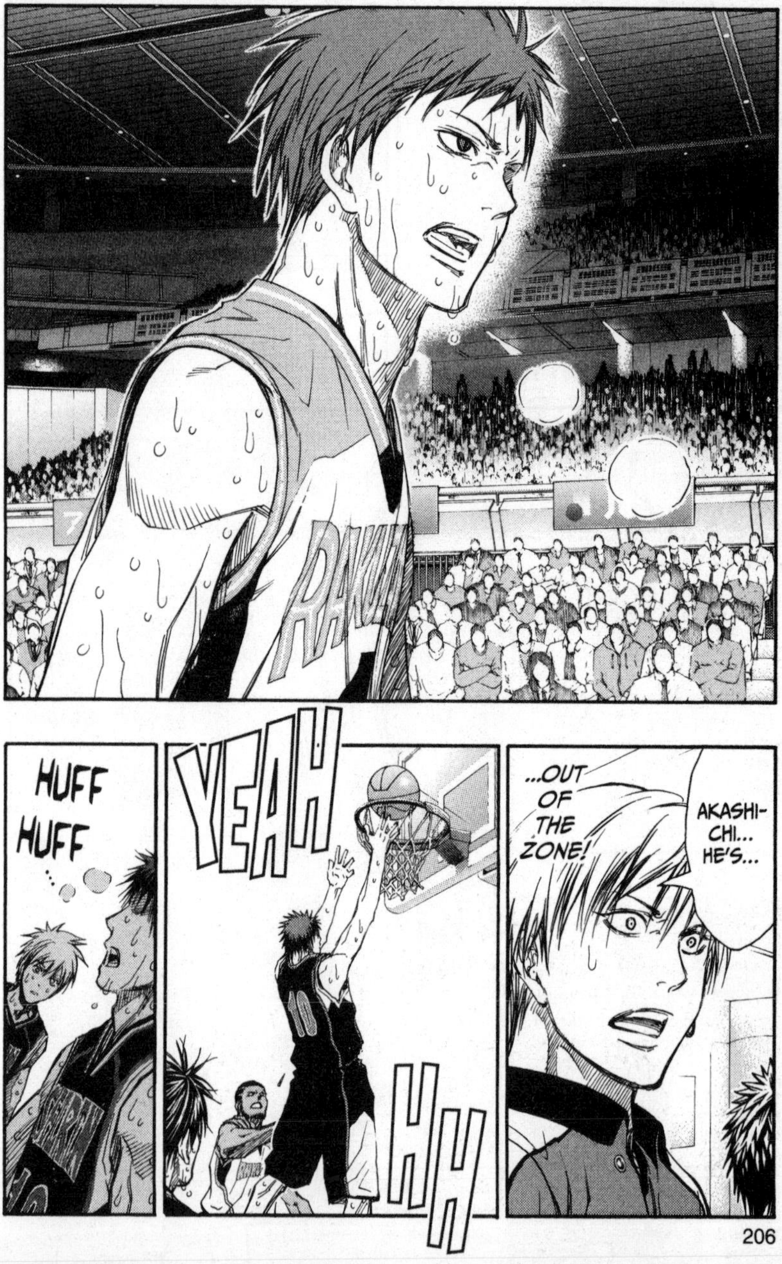
AKASHI-CHI... HE'S...
...OUT OF THE ZONE!
YEAH
HHH
HUFF HUFF
...

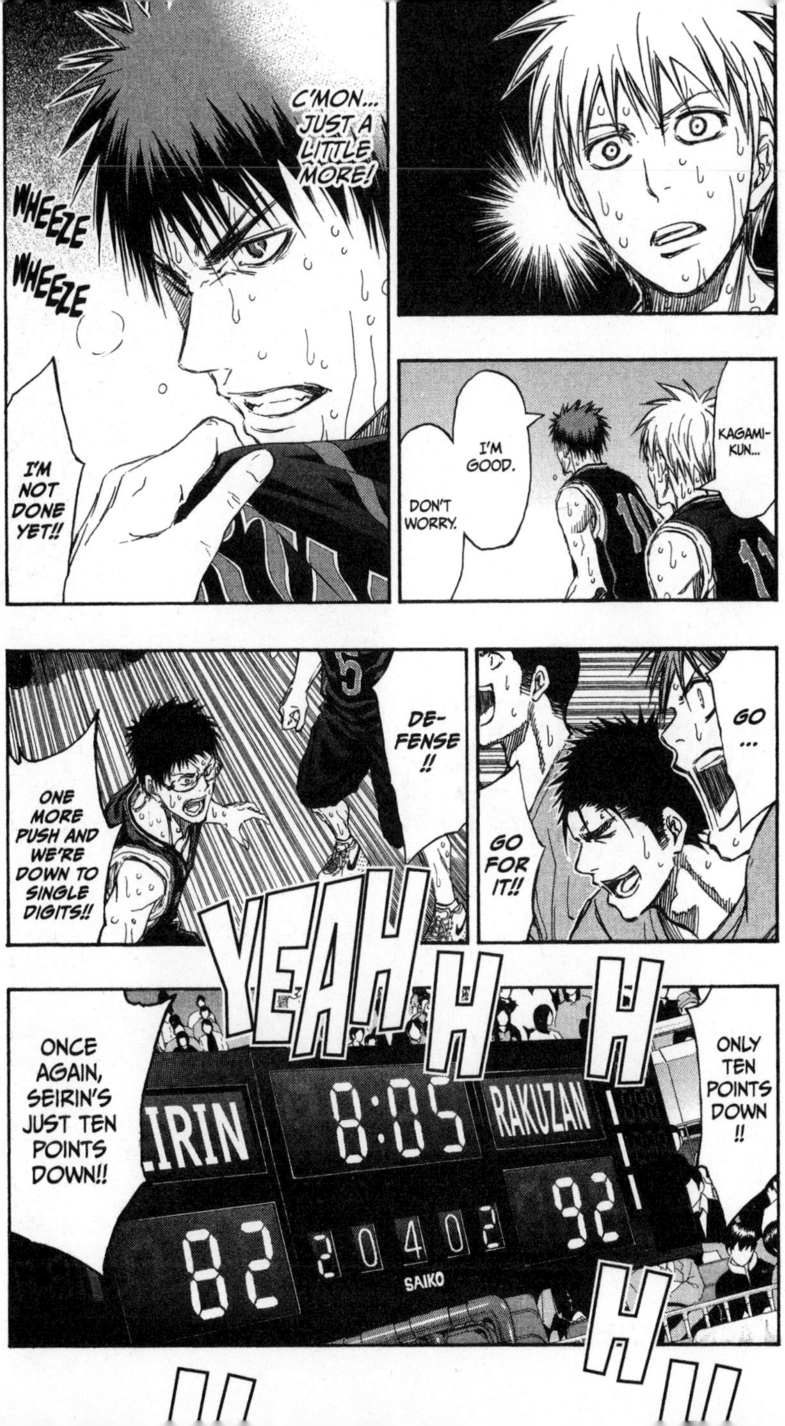
KAGAMI-KUN...
I'M GOOD.
DON'T WORRY.
C'MON... JUST A LITTLE MORE!
WHEEZE
WHEEZE
I'M NOT DONE YET!!
GO...
GO FOR IT!!
DE-FENSE!!
ONE MORE PUSH AND WE'RE DOWN TO SINGLE DIGITS!!
YEAHHHH!!
ONLY TEN POINTS DOWN!!
IRIN
8:05
RAKUZAN
82
92
SAIKO
ONCE AGAIN, SEIRIN'S JUST TEN POINTS DOWN!!

KUROKO'S BASKETBALL BLOOPERS

TAKE 2

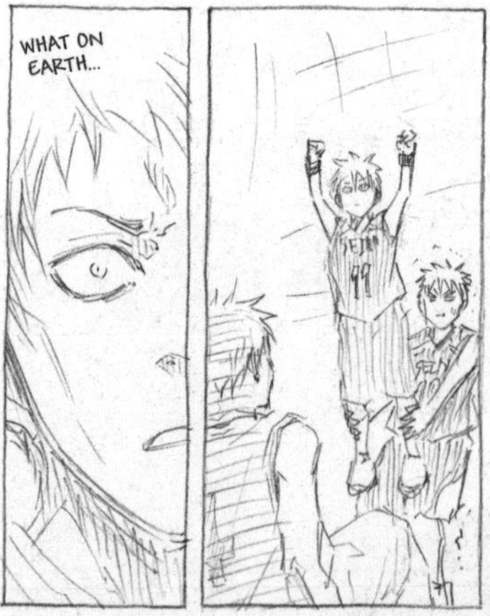
WHAT ON EARTH...

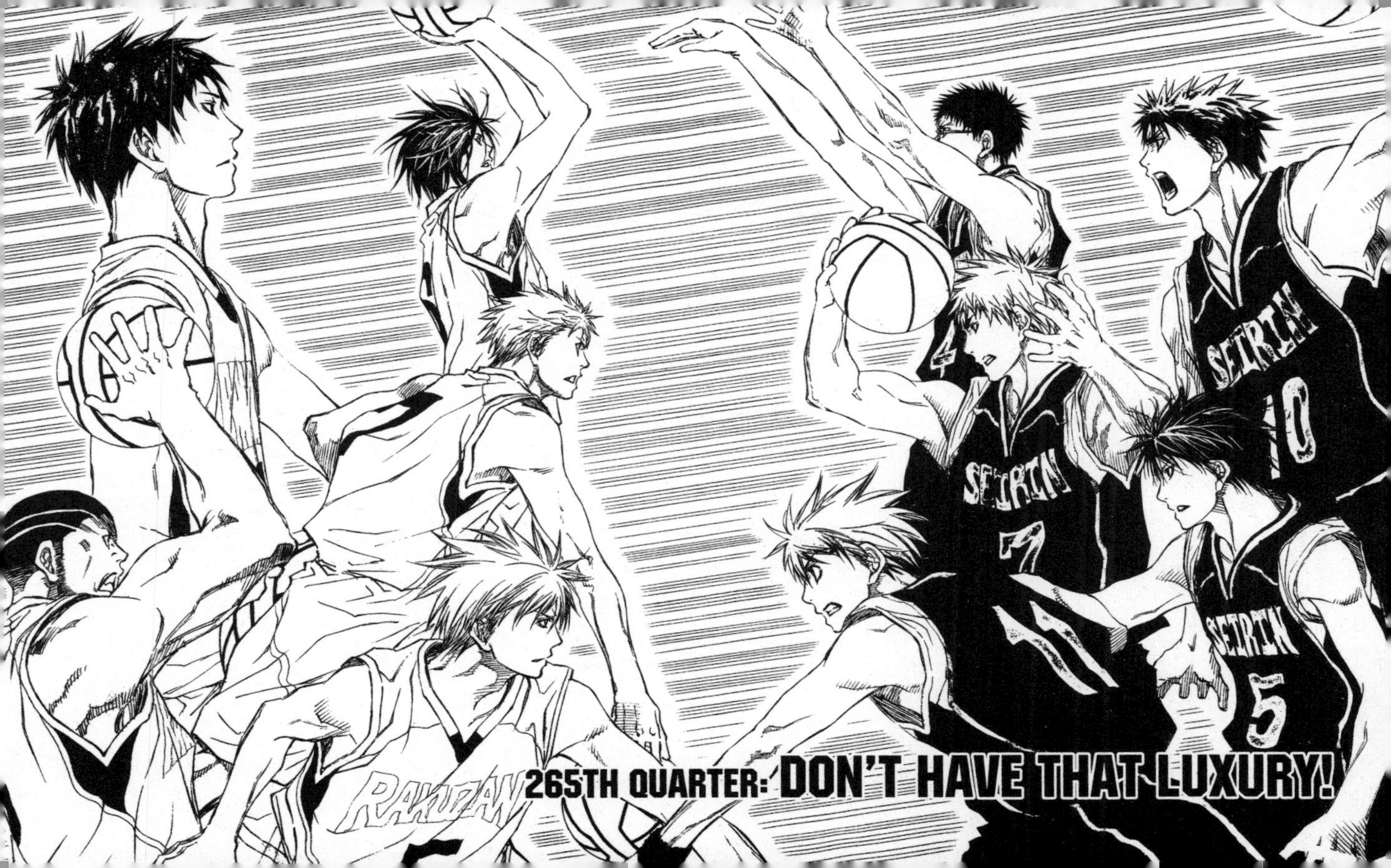
265TH QUARTER: DON'T HAVE THAT LUXURY!
RAKUZAN
SEIRIN
SEIRIN
SEIRIN

Kuroko's
BASKETBALL

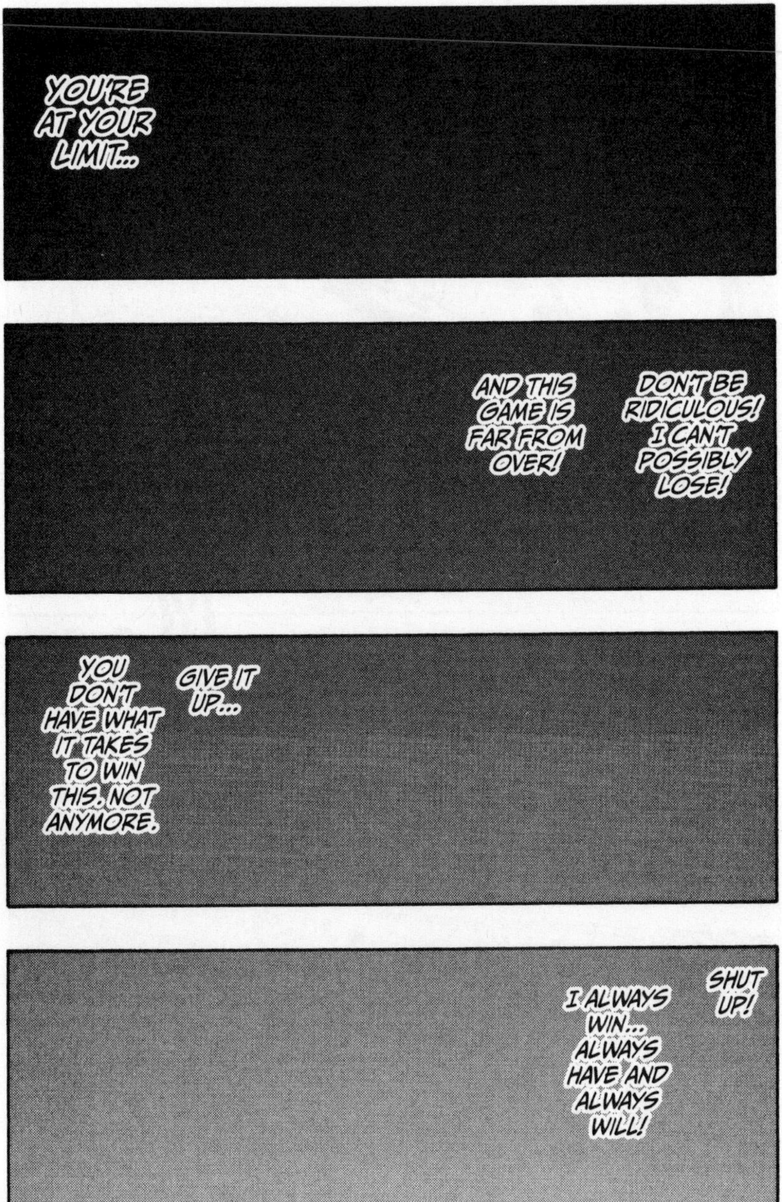
YOU'RE AT YOUR LIMIT...
DON'T BE RIDICULOUS! I CAN'T POSSIBLY LOSE!
AND THIS GAME IS FAR FROM OVER!
GIVE IT UP...
YOU DON'T HAVE WHAT IT TAKES TO WIN THIS. NOT ANYMORE.
SHUT UP!
I ALWAYS WIN... ALWAYS HAVE AND ALWAYS WILL!

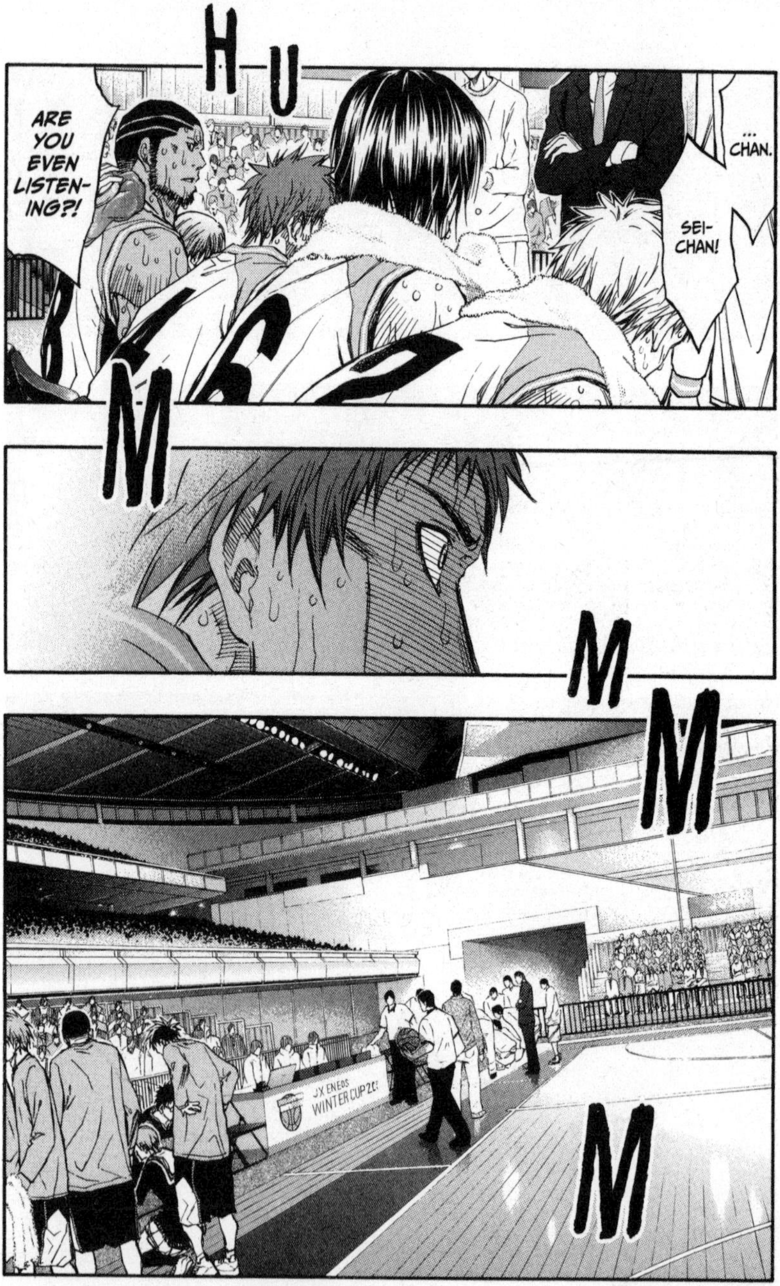
...CHAN.
SEI-CHAN!
ARE YOU EVEN LISTEN-ING?!
HUMMMM
JX ENEOS WINTER CUP

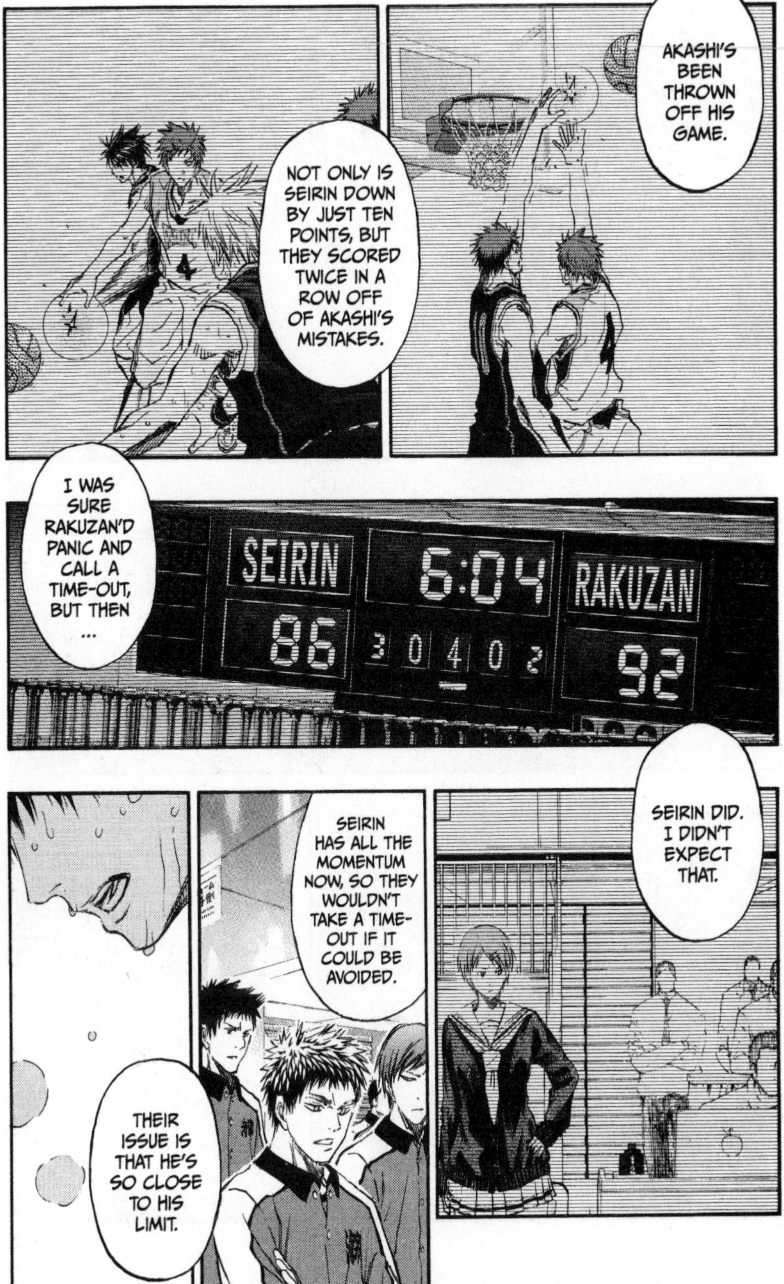
AKASHI'S BEEN THROWN OFF HIS GAME.
NOT ONLY IS SEIRIN DOWN BY JUST TEN POINTS, BUT THEY SCORED TWICE IN A ROW OFF OF AKASHI'S MISTAKES.
I WAS SURE RAKUZAN'D PANIC AND CALL A TIME-OUT, BUT THEN ...
SEIRIN
6:04
RAKUZAN
86
3 0 4 0 2
92
SEIRIN DID. I DIDN'T EXPECT THAT.
SEIRIN HAS ALL THE MOMENTUM NOW, SO THEY WOULDN'T TAKE A TIME-OUT IF IT COULD BE AVOIDED.
THEIR ISSUE IS THAT HE'S SO CLOSE TO HIS LIMIT.

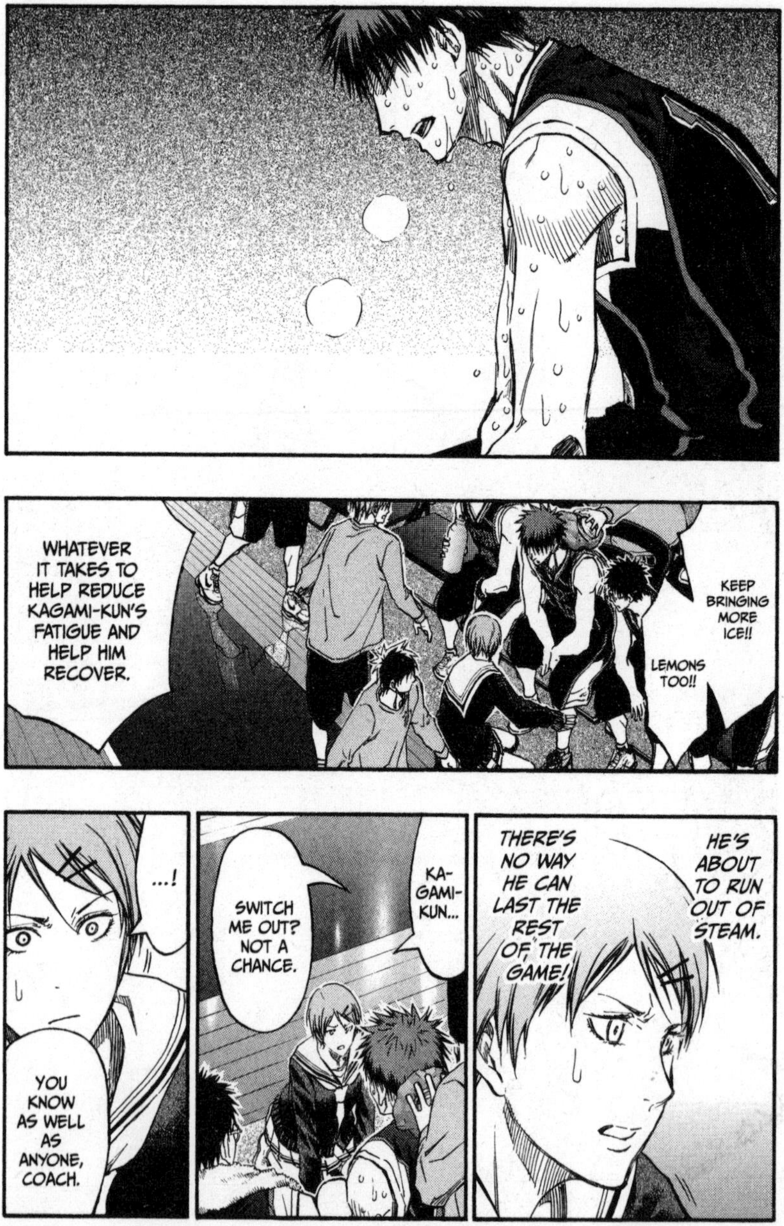
KEEP BRINGING MORE ICE!!
LEMONS TOO!!
WHATEVER IT TAKES TO HELP REDUCE KAGAMI-KUN'S FATIGUE AND HELP HIM RECOVER.
HE'S ABOUT TO RUN OUT OF STEAM.
THERE'S NO WAY HE CAN LAST THE REST OF THE GAME!
KA-GAMI-KUN...
SWITCH ME OUT? NOT A CHANCE.
...!
YOU KNOW AS WELL AS ANYONE, COACH.

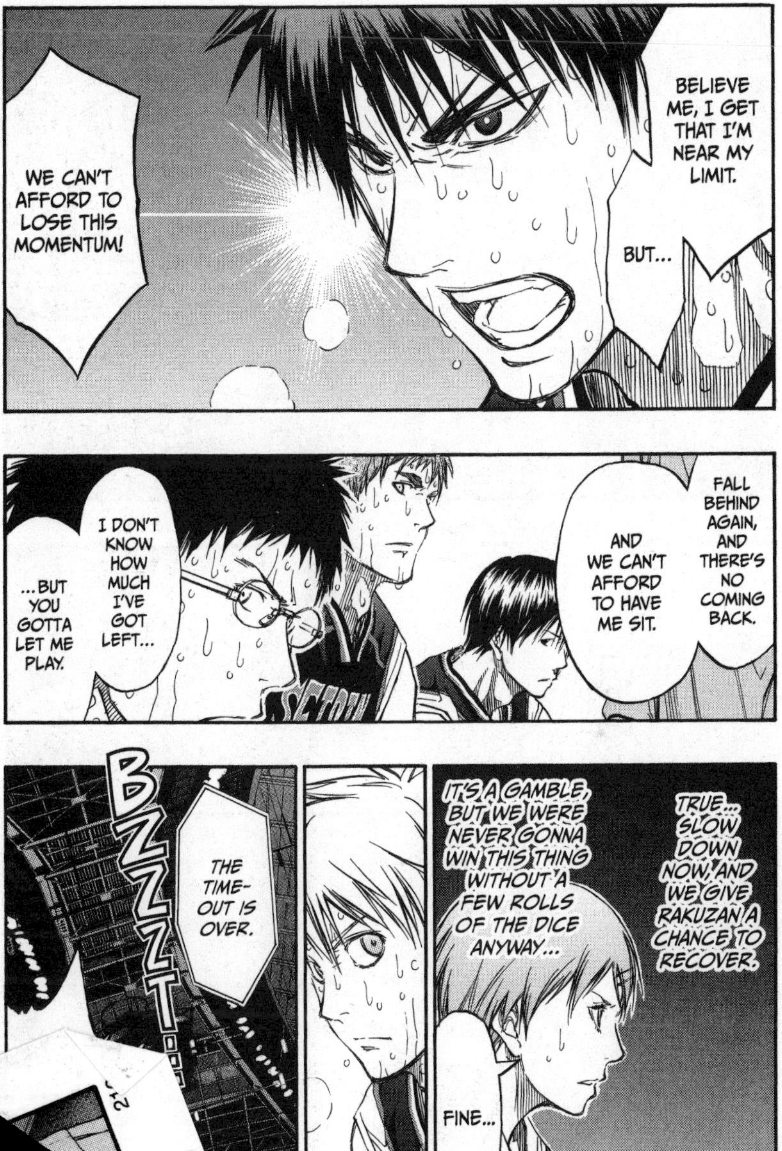
BELIEVE ME, I GET THAT I'M NEAR MY LIMIT.
BUT...
WE CAN'T AFFORD TO LOSE THIS MOMENTUM!
FALL BEHIND AGAIN, AND THERE'S NO COMING BACK.
AND WE CAN'T AFFORD TO HAVE ME SIT.
I DON'T KNOW HOW MUCH I'VE GOT LEFT...
...BUT YOU GOTTA LET ME PLAY.
TRUE... SLOW DOWN NOW, AND WE GIVE RAKUZAN A CHANCE TO RECOVER.
IT'S A GAMBLE, BUT WE WERE NEVER GONNA WIN THIS THING WITHOUT A FEW ROLLS OF THE DICE ANYWAY...
FINE...
BZZZT
THE TIME-OUT IS OVER.

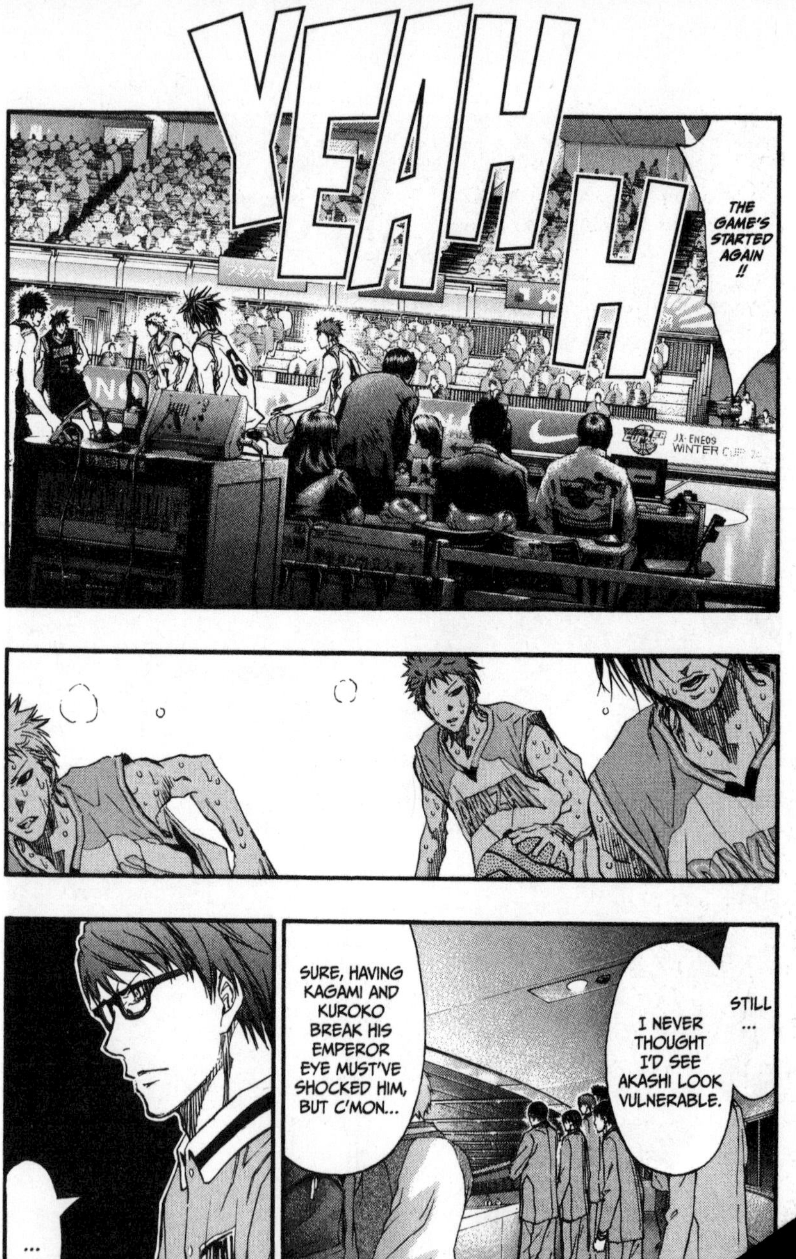
YEAHH
THE GAME'S STARTED AGAIN!!
JX-ENEOS WINTER CUP
STILL...
I NEVER THOUGHT I'D SEE AKASHI LOOK VULNERABLE.
SURE, HAVING KAGAMI AND KUROKO BREAK HIS EMPEROR EYE MUST'VE SHOCKED HIM, BUT C'MON...
...

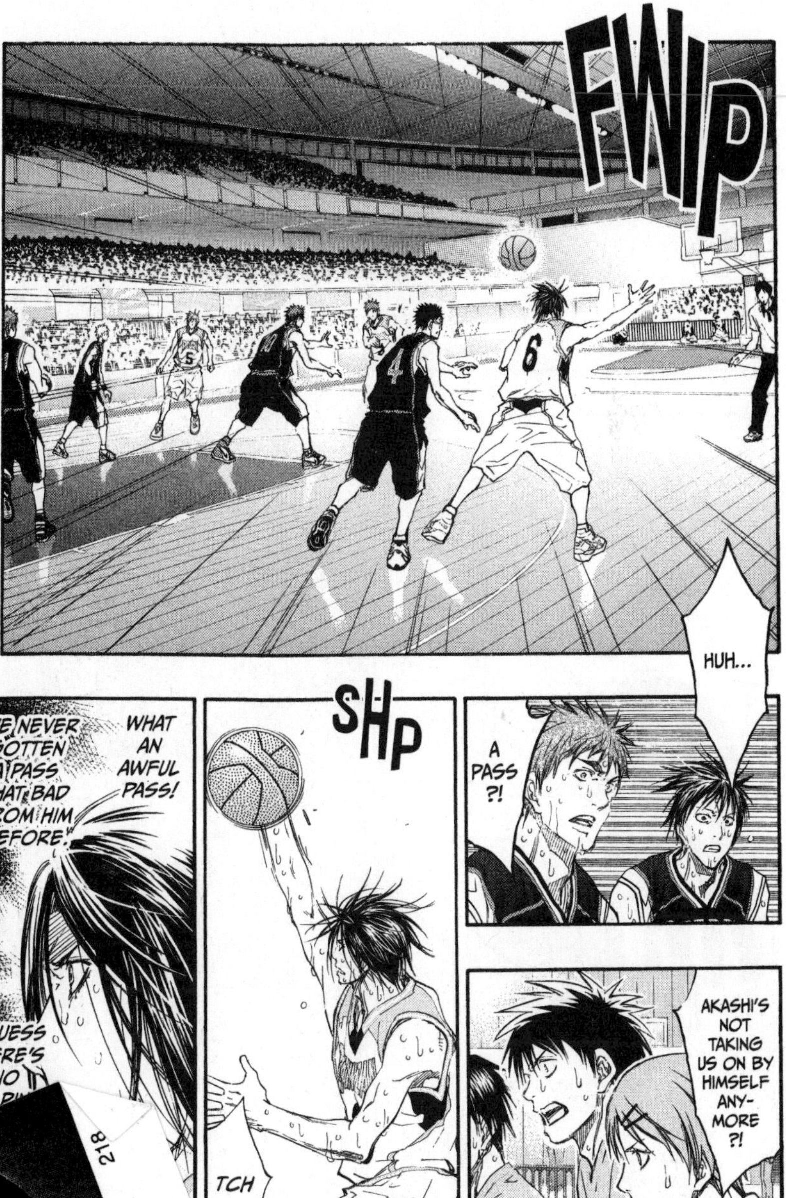
FWIP
HUH...
A PASS ?!
AKASHI'S NOT TAKING US ON BY HIMSELF ANY-MORE ?!
SHP
TCH ...
WHAT AN AWFUL PASS!
I'VE NEVER GOTTEN A PASS THAT BAD FROM HIM BEFORE!
I GUESS THERE'S NO HELP

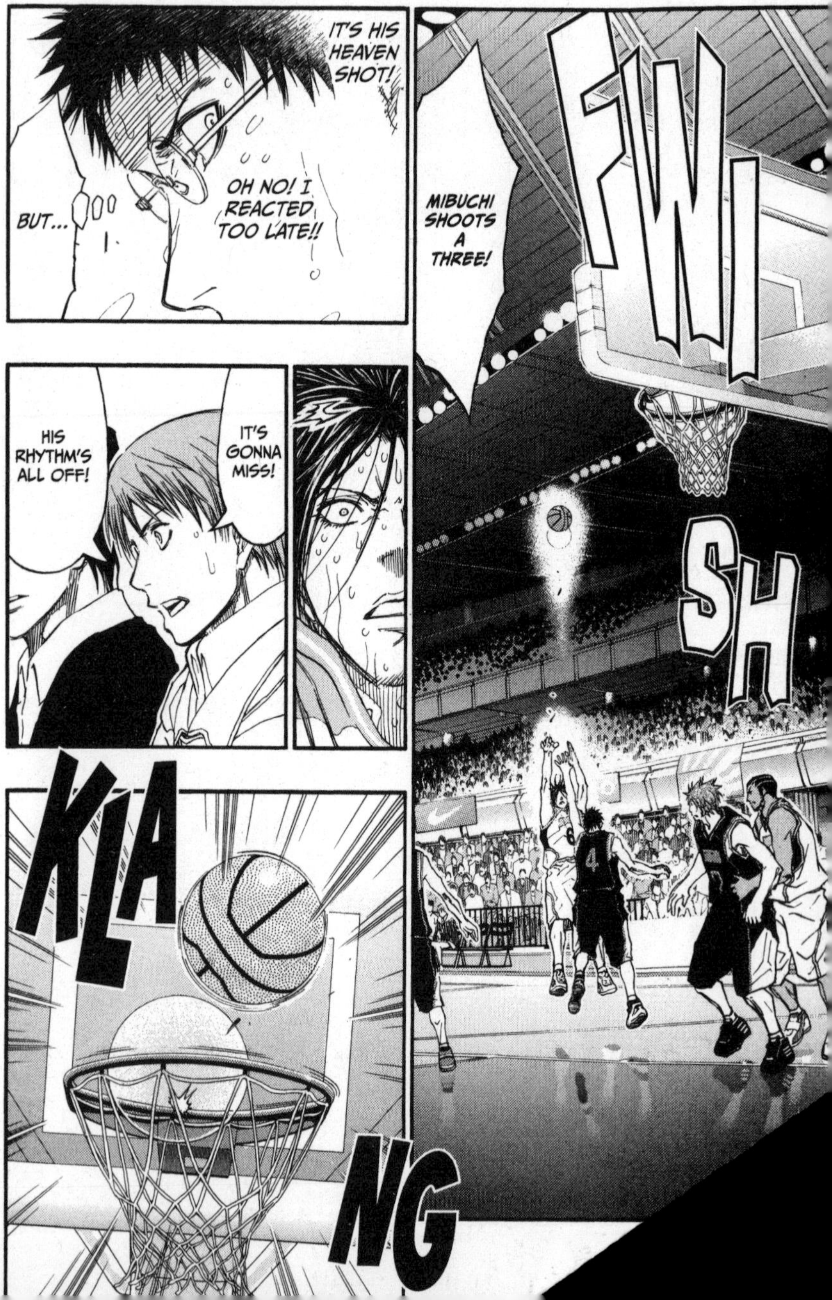
MIBUCHI SHOOTS A THREE!
FWI
SH
IT'S HIS HEAVEN SHOT!
OH NO! I REACTED TOO LATE!!
BUT...
IT'S GONNA MISS!
HIS RHYTHM'S ALL OFF!
KLA
NG

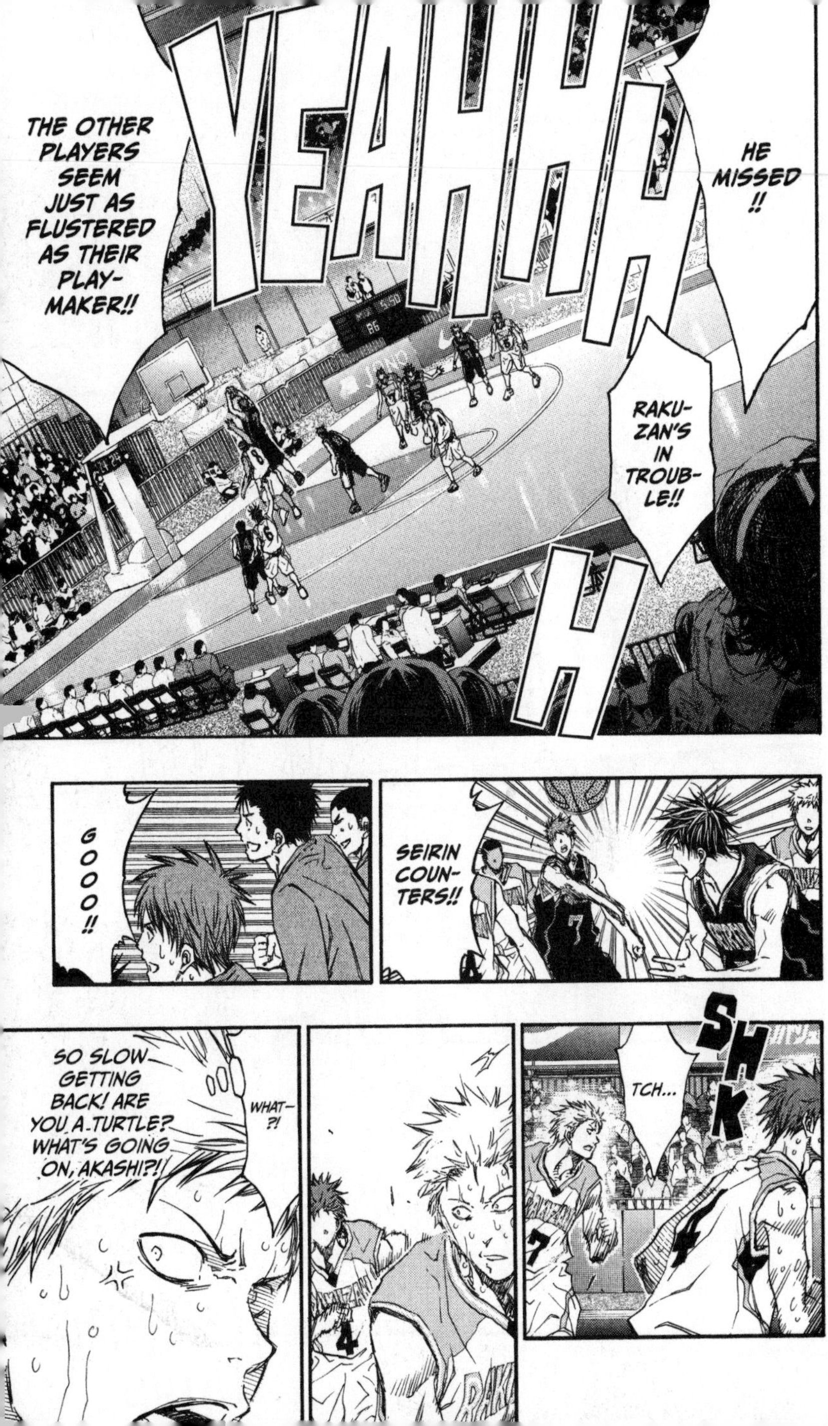
HE MISSED!!
YEAHHHH
RAKUZAN'S IN TROUBLE!!
THE OTHER PLAYERS SEEM JUST AS FLUSTERED AS THEIR PLAYMAKER!!
SEIRIN COUNTERS!!
GOOOO!!
SHK
TCH...
WHAT—?!
SO SLOW GETTING BACK! ARE YOU A TURTLE? WHAT'S GOING ON, AKASHI?!

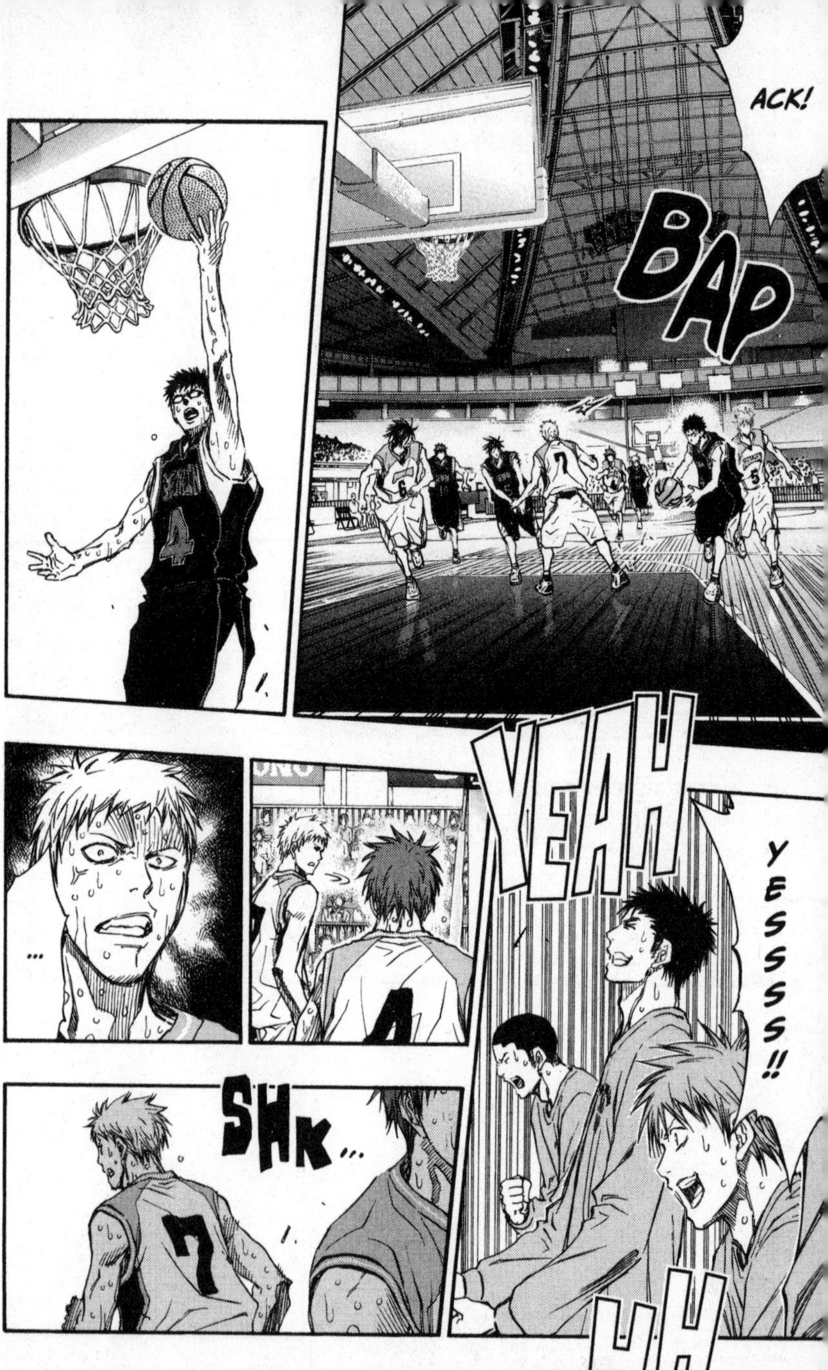
ACK!
BAP
YEAH
YESSSSS!!
HH
...
SHK...

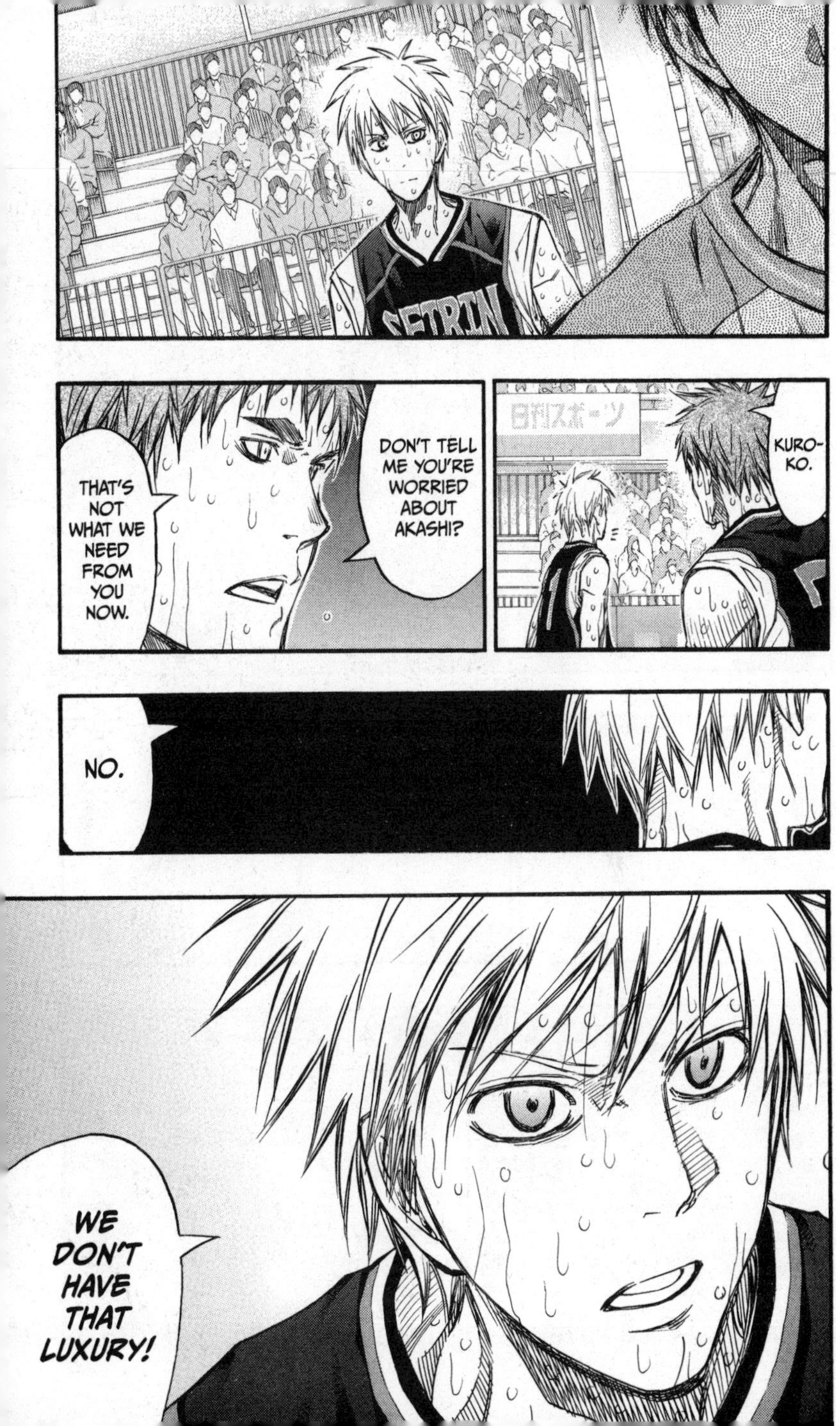

KURO-KO.
日刊スポーツ
DON'T TELL ME YOU'RE WORRIED ABOUT AKASHI?
THAT'S NOT WHAT WE NEED FROM YOU NOW.
NO.
WE DON'T HAVE THAT LUXURY!

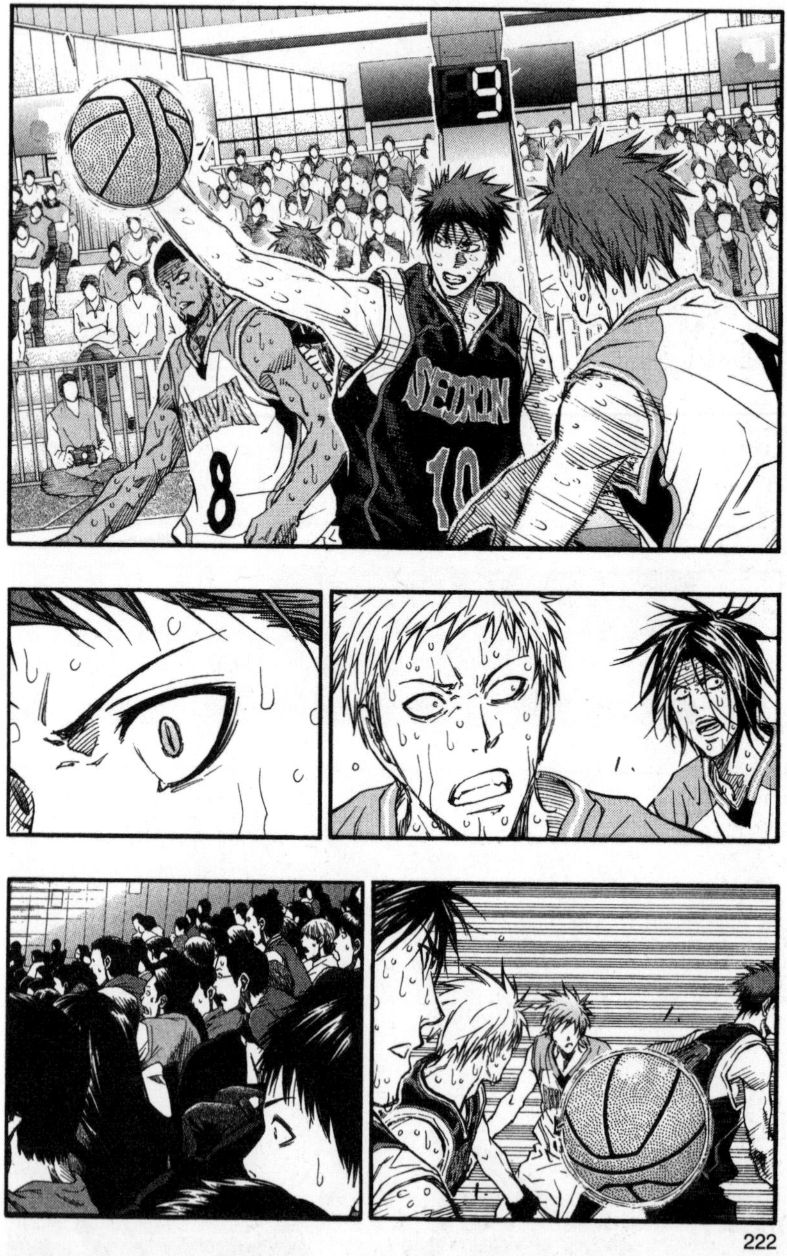
SEIRIN

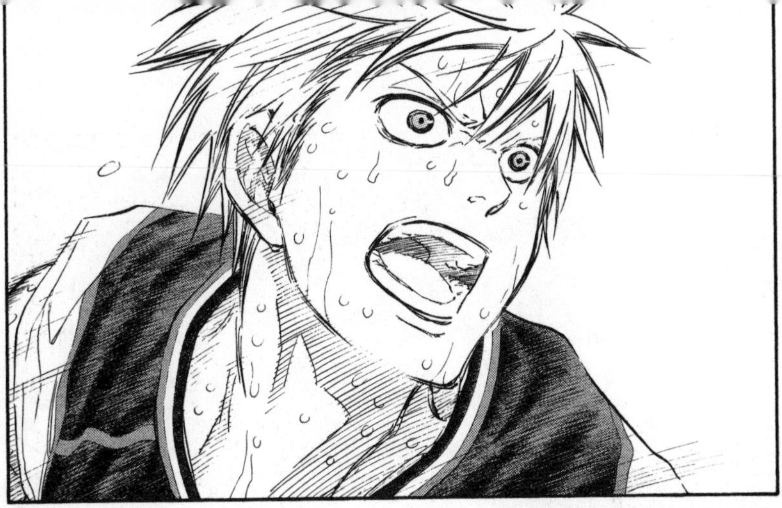

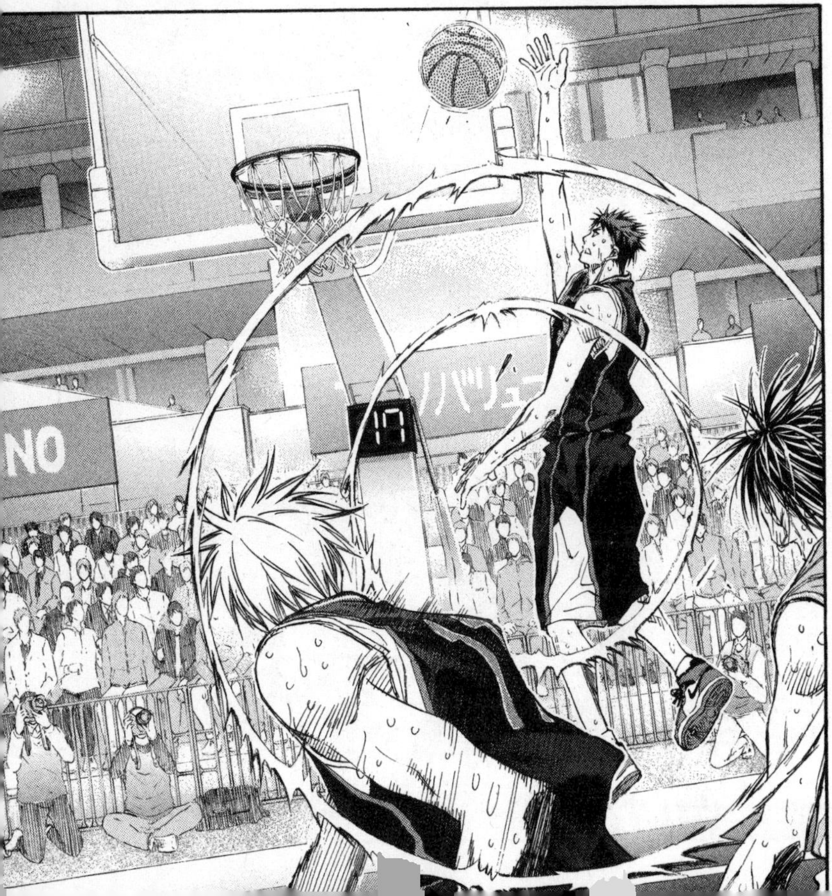
NO
17

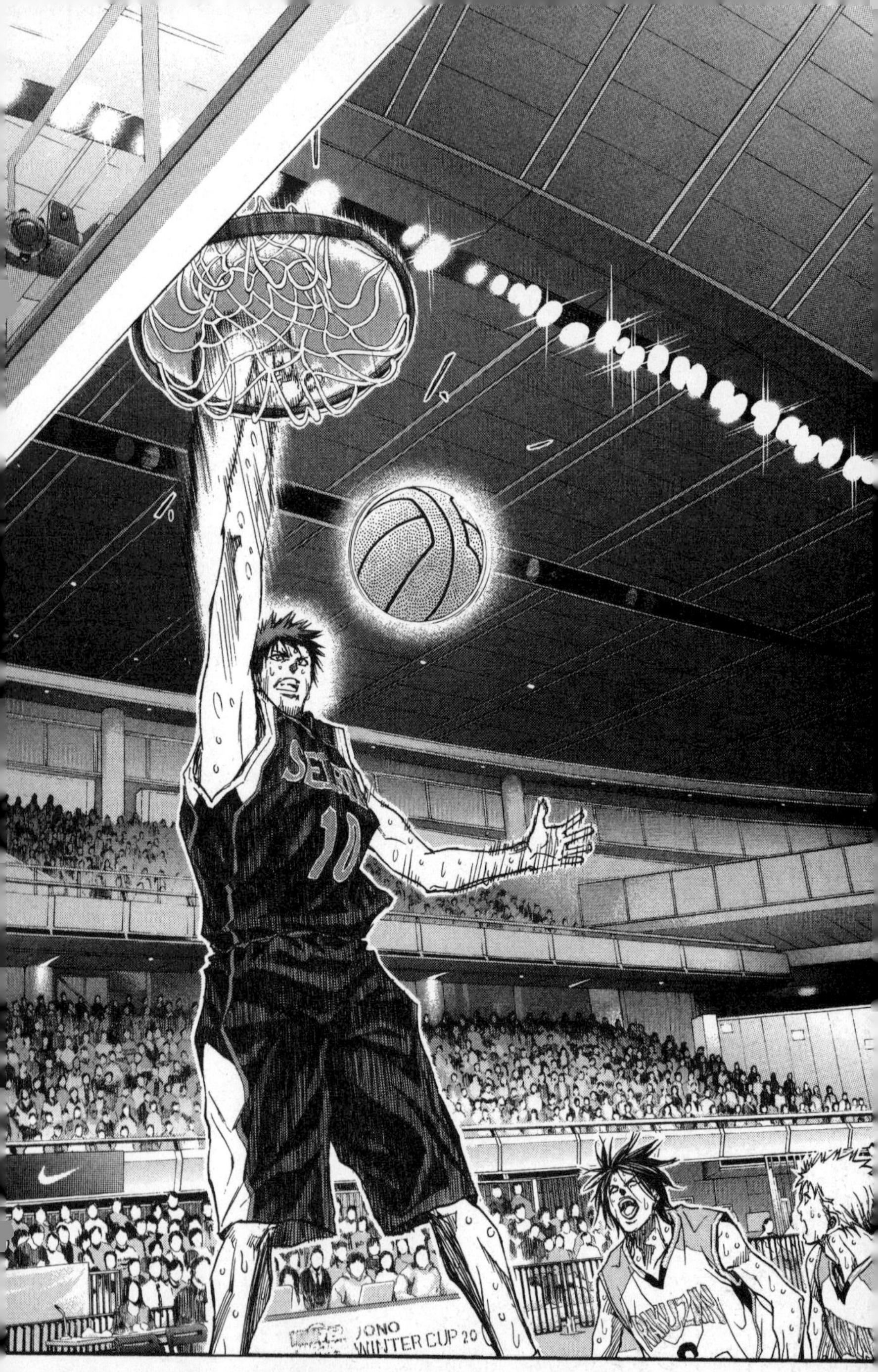
JONO
WINTER CUP 20

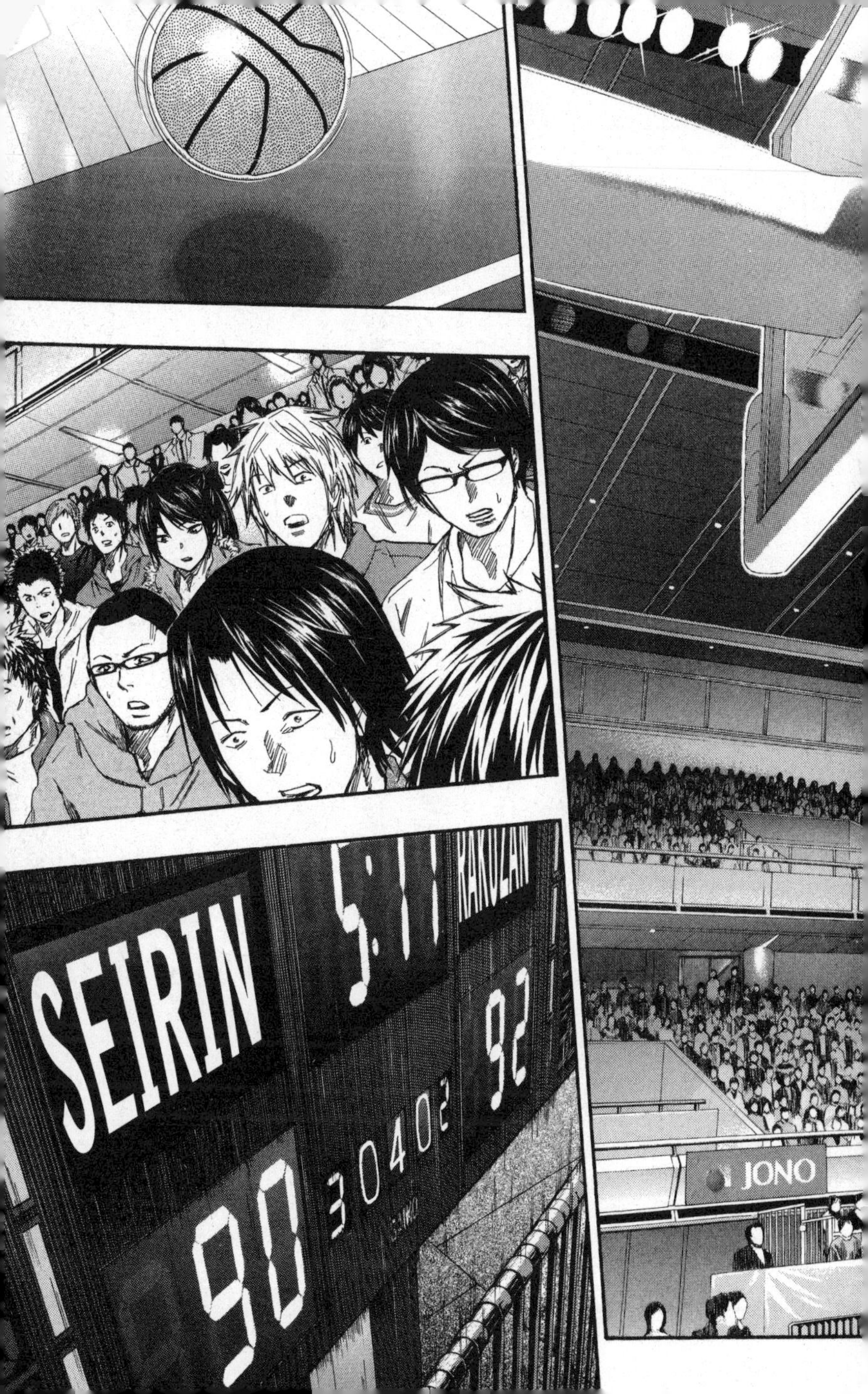
JONO
SEIRIN
92
90

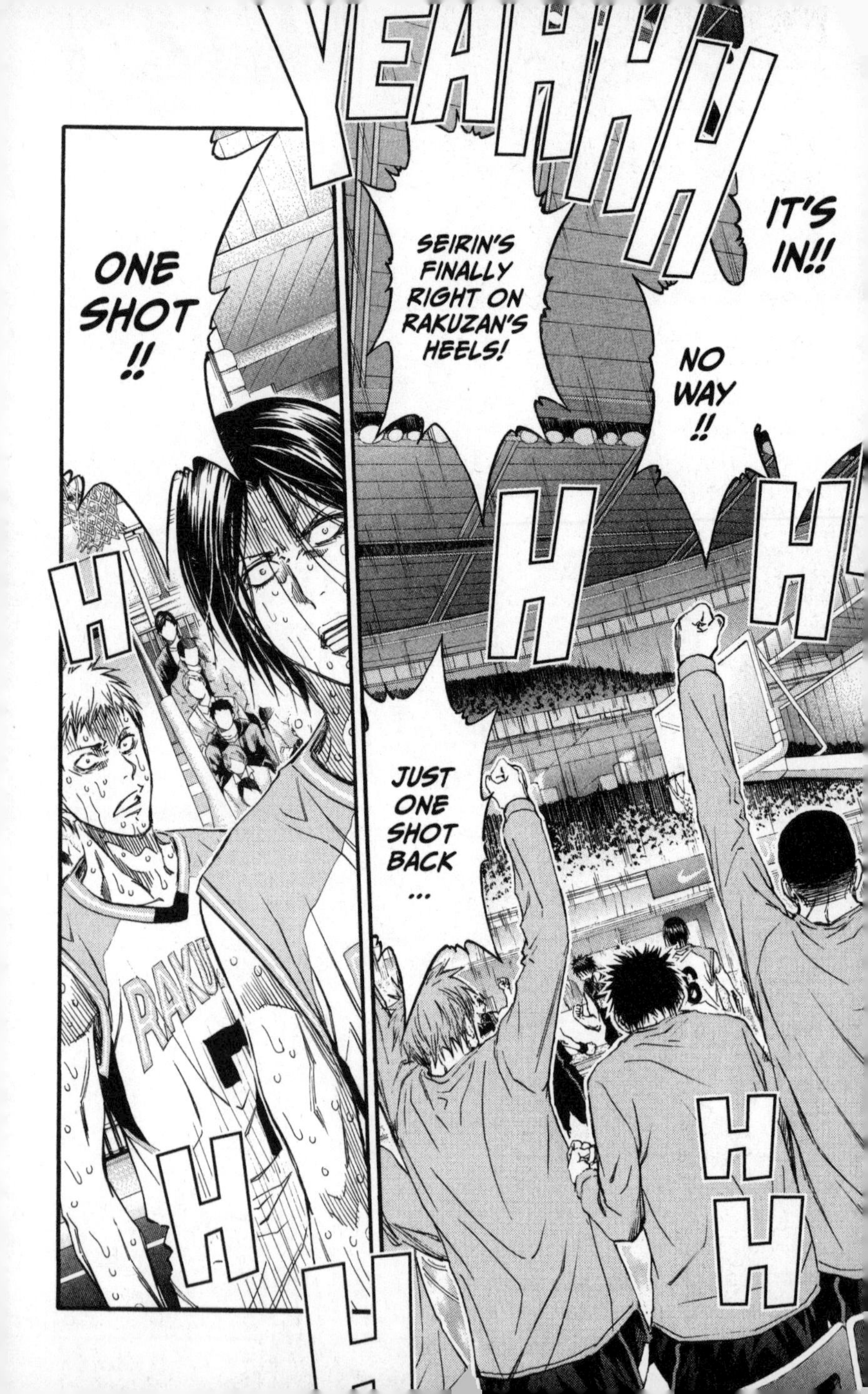
YEAHHH
IT'S IN!!
SEIRIN'S FINALLY RIGHT ON RAKUZAN'S HEELS!
NO WAY!!
JUST ONE SHOT BACK...
HHHH
ONE SHOT!!

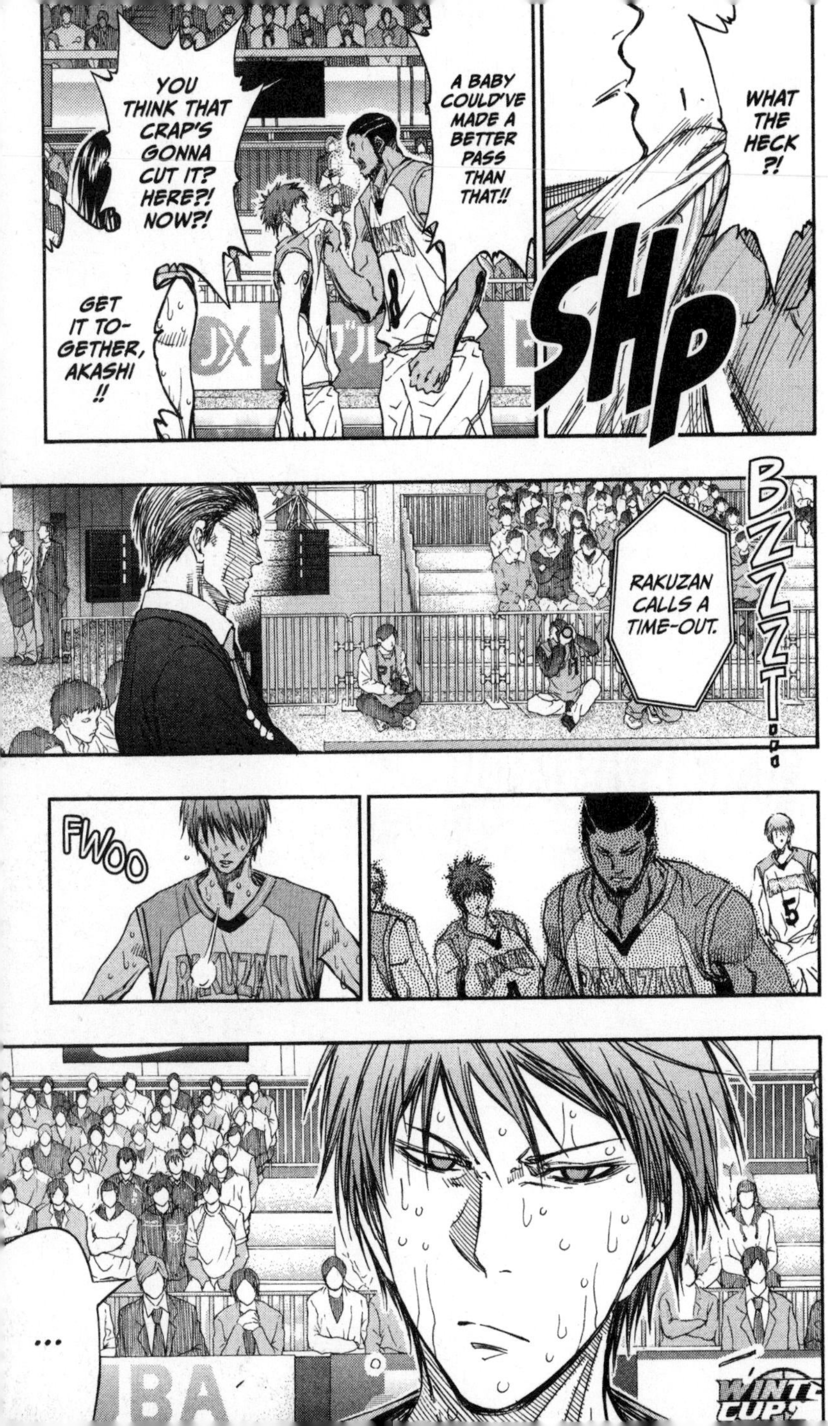
WHAT THE HECK?!
SHP
A BABY COULD'VE MADE A BETTER PASS THAN THAT!!
YOU THINK THAT CRAP'S GONNA CUT IT? HERE?! NOW?!
GET IT TO-GETHER, AKASHI!!
BZZZT
RAKUZAN CALLS A TIME-OUT.
FWOO
...

KUROKO'S BASKETBALL

Q&A

(W/ HALFWAY-DECENT ANSWERS)

Q. HOW DID HANAMIYA-KUN COME TO BE THE WAY HE IS?
(SAKI FURO from HYOGO PREFECTURE)

A. I WONDER...

KUROKO'S BASKETBALL BLOOPERS

TAKE 3

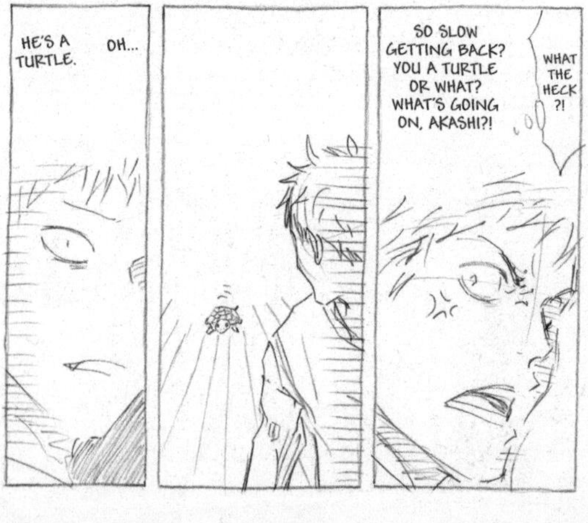
SO SLOW GETTING BACK? YOU A TURTLE OR WHAT? WHAT'S GOING ON, AKASHI?!
WHAT THE HECK ?!
OH...
HE'S A TURTLE.

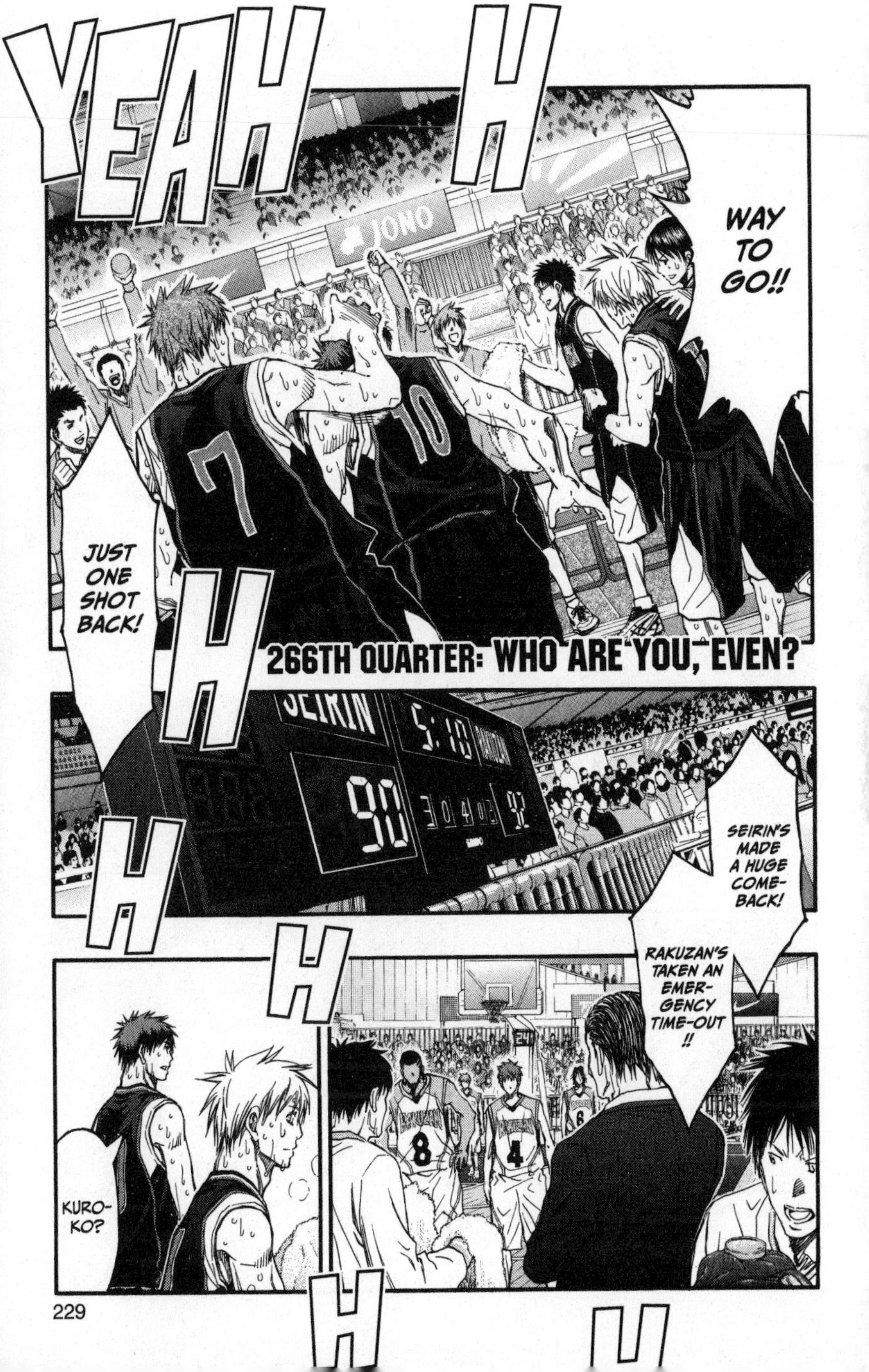
YEAHHHHHHHH
WAY TO GO!!
JUST ONE SHOT BACK!
266TH QUARTER: WHO ARE YOU, EVEN?
SEIRIN
98
SEIRIN'S MADE A HUGE COME-BACK!
RAKUZAN'S TAKEN AN EMER-GENCY TIME-OUT!!
KURO-KO?

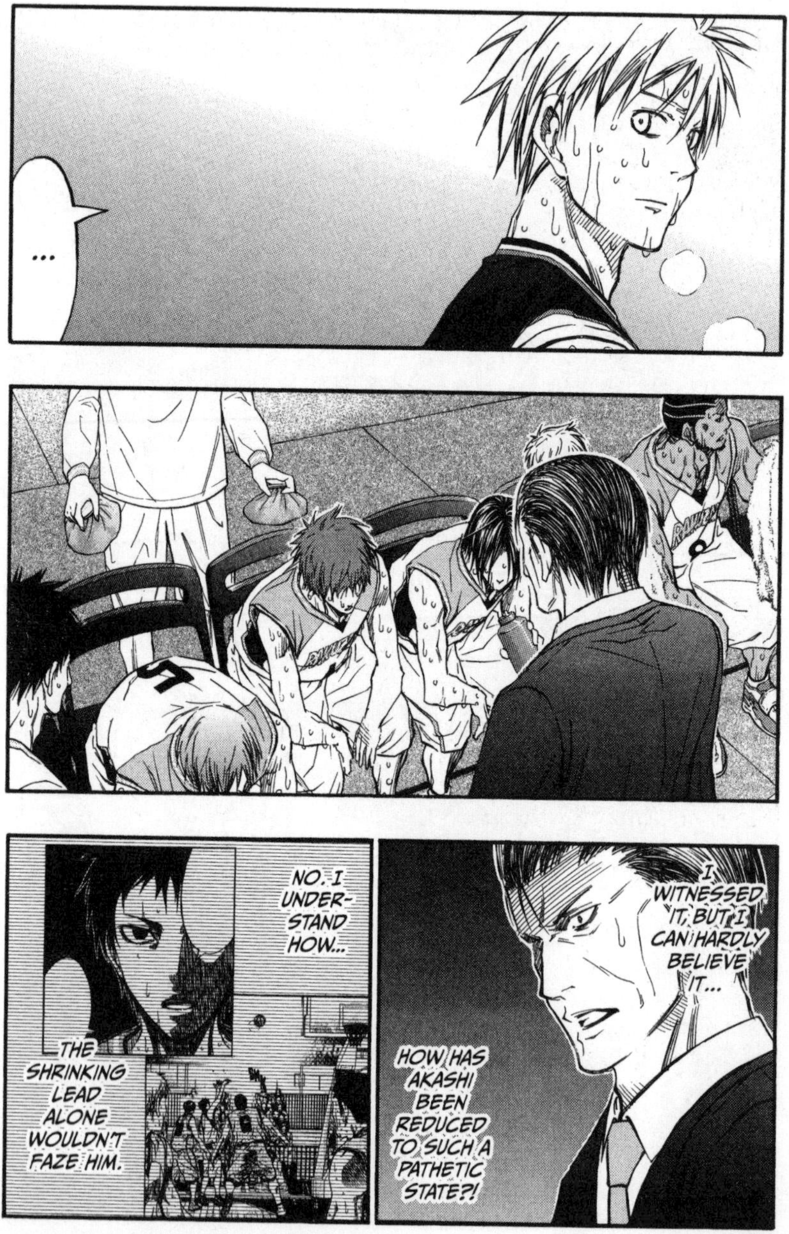
...
I WITNESSED IT, BUT I CAN HARDLY BELIEVE IT...
HOW HAS AKASHI BEEN REDUCED TO SUCH A PATHETIC STATE?!
NO. I UNDER-STAND HOW...
THE SHRINKING LEAD ALONE WOULDN'T FAZE HIM.

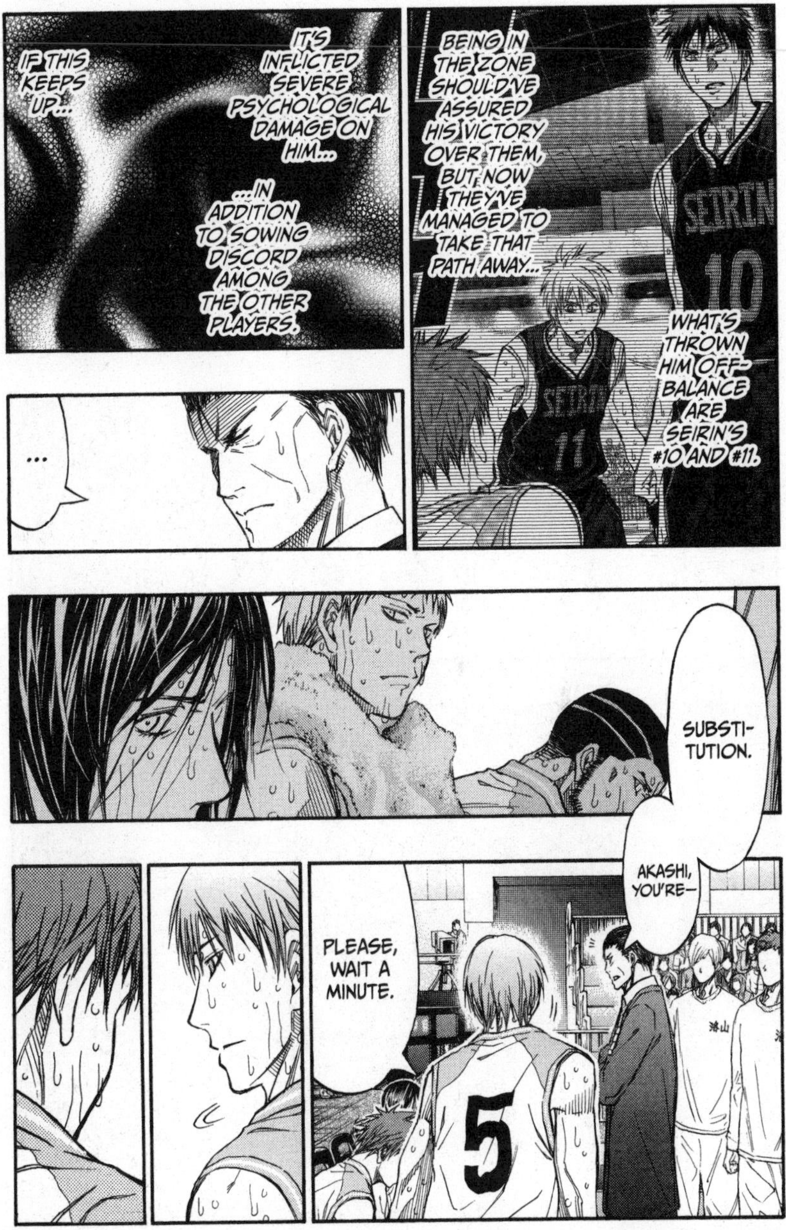
BEING IN THE ZONE SHOULD'VE ASSURED HIS VICTORY OVER THEM, BUT NOW THEY'VE MANAGED TO TAKE THAT PATH AWAY...
WHAT'S THROWN HIM OFF-BALANCE ARE SEIRIN'S #10 AND #11.
IT'S INFLICTED SEVERE PSYCHOLOGICAL DAMAGE ON HIM...
...IN ADDITION TO SOWING DISCORD AMONG THE OTHER PLAYERS.
IF THIS KEEPS UP...
...
SUBSTI-TUTION.
AKASHI, YOU'RE—
PLEASE, WAIT A MINUTE.

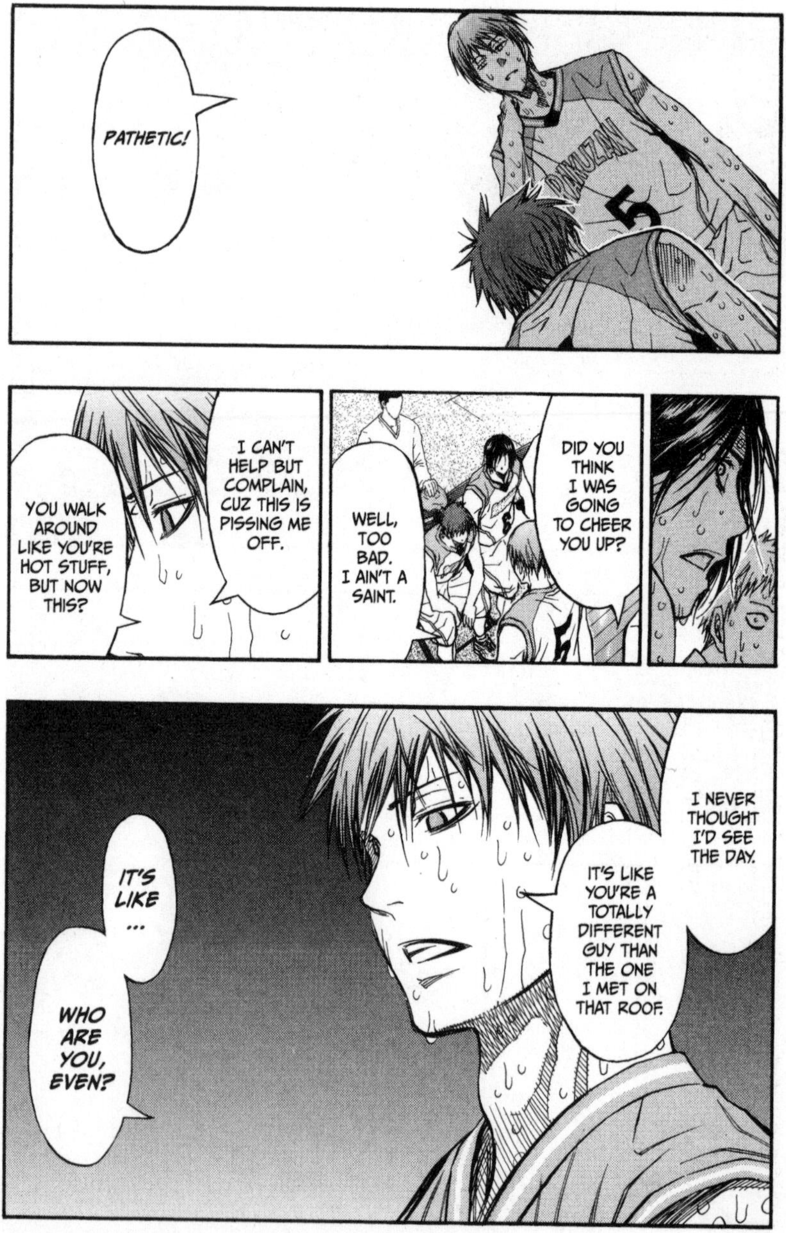
PATHETIC!
DID YOU THINK I WAS GOING TO CHEER YOU UP?
WELL, TOO BAD. I AIN'T A SAINT.
I CAN'T HELP BUT COMPLAIN, CUZ THIS IS PISSING ME OFF.
YOU WALK AROUND LIKE YOU'RE HOT STUFF, BUT NOW THIS?
I NEVER THOUGHT I'D SEE THE DAY.
IT'S LIKE YOU'RE A TOTALLY DIFFERENT GUY THAN THE ONE I MET ON THAT ROOF.
IT'S LIKE...
WHO ARE YOU, EVEN?

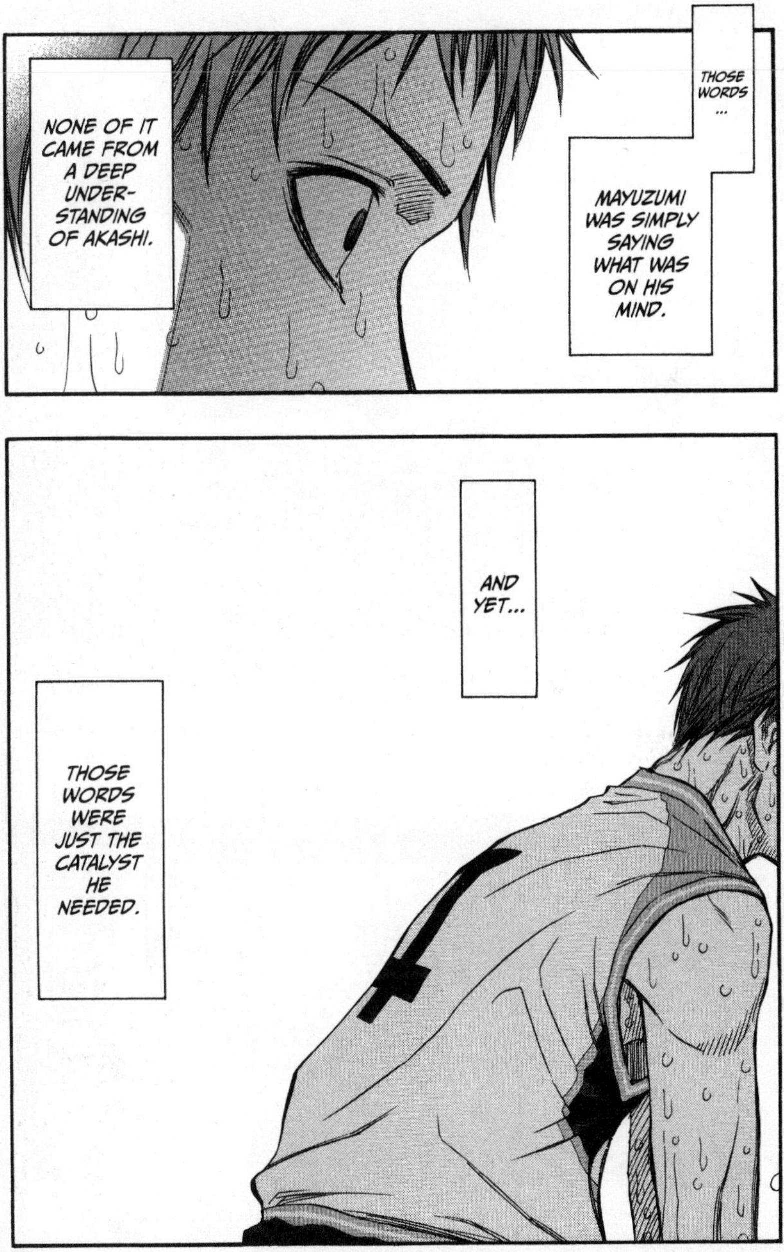
THOSE WORDS ...
MAYUZUMI WAS SIMPLY SAYING WHAT WAS ON HIS MIND.
NONE OF IT CAME FROM A DEEP UNDER-STANDING OF AKASHI.
AND YET...
THOSE WORDS WERE JUST THE CATALYST HE NEEDED.

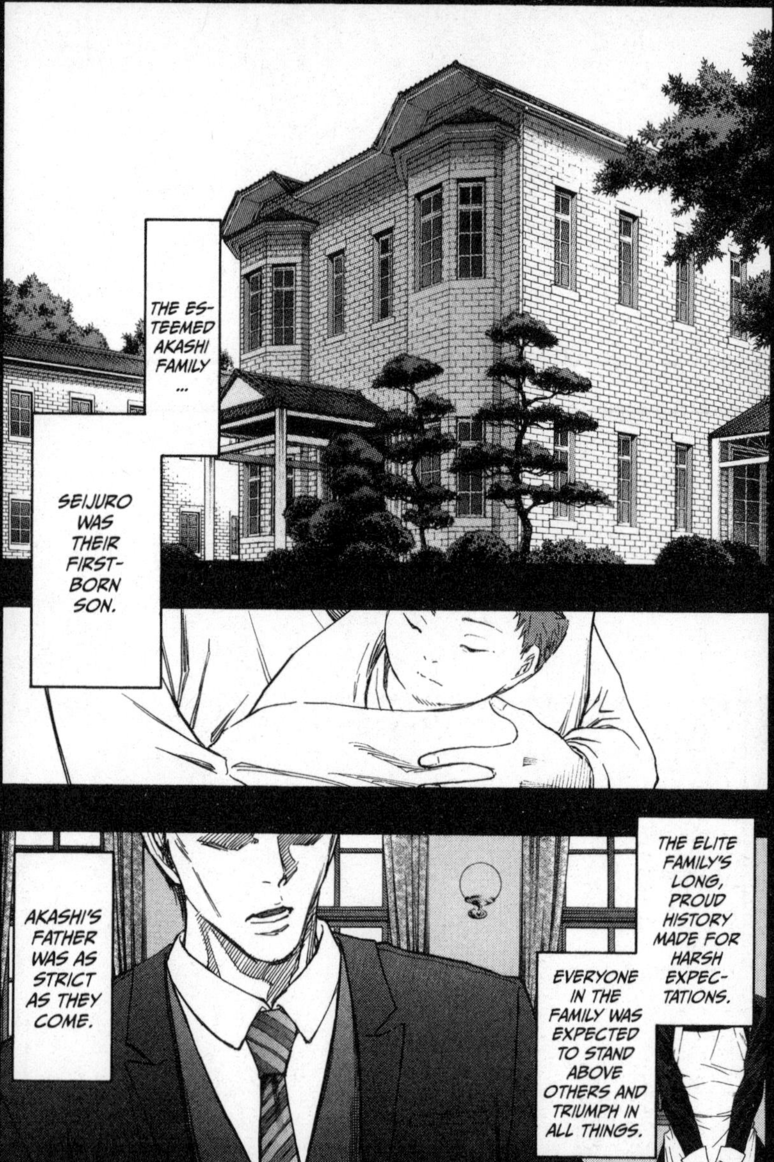
THE ESTEEMED AKASHI FAMILY ...
SEIJURO WAS THEIR FIRSTBORN SON.
THE ELITE FAMILY'S LONG, PROUD HISTORY MADE FOR HARSH EXPECTATIONS.
EVERYONE IN THE FAMILY WAS EXPECTED TO STAND ABOVE OTHERS AND TRIUMPH IN ALL THINGS.
AKASHI'S FATHER WAS AS STRICT AS THEY COME.

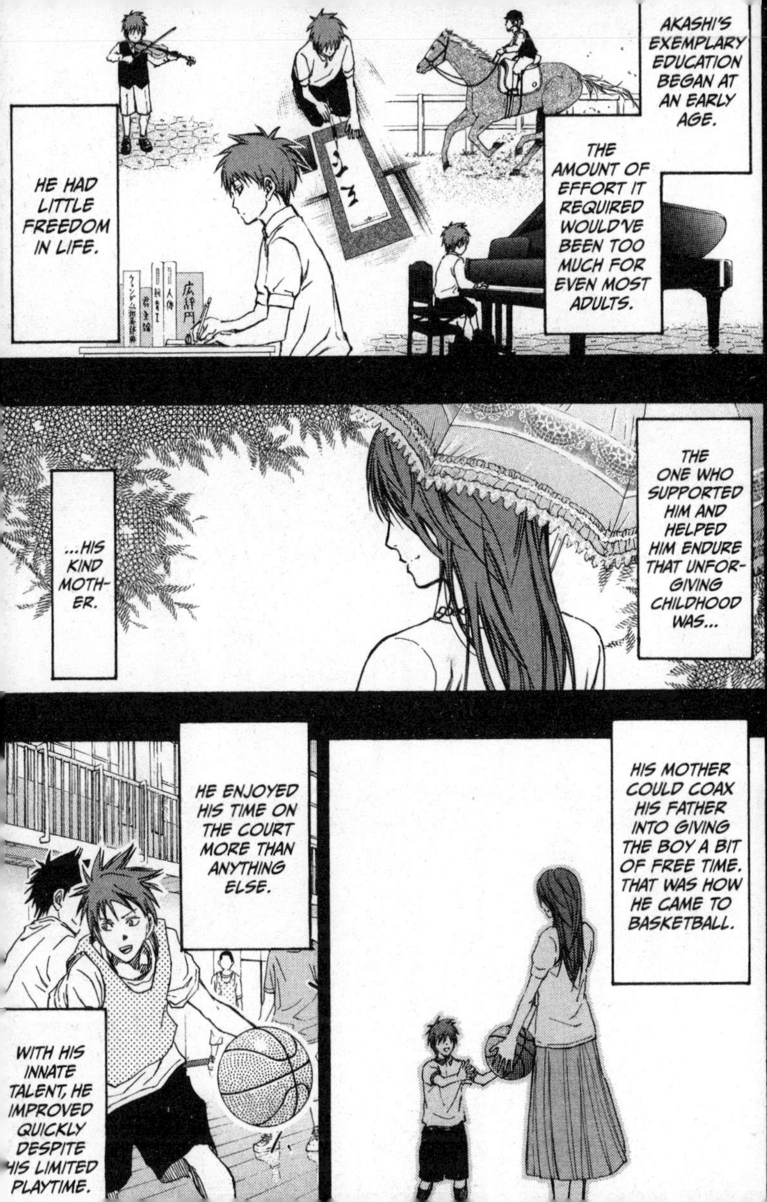
AKASHI'S EXEMPLARY EDUCATION BEGAN AT AN EARLY AGE.
THE AMOUNT OF EFFORT IT REQUIRED WOULD'VE BEEN TOO MUCH FOR EVEN MOST ADULTS.
HE HAD LITTLE FREEDOM IN LIFE.
THE ONE WHO SUPPORTED HIM AND HELPED HIM ENDURE THAT UNFOR-GIVING CHILDHOOD WAS...
...HIS KIND MOTH-ER.
HIS MOTHER COULD COAX HIS FATHER INTO GIVING THE BOY A BIT OF FREE TIME. THAT WAS HOW HE CAME TO BASKETBALL.
HE ENJOYED HIS TIME ON THE COURT MORE THAN ANYTHING ELSE.
WITH HIS INNATE TALENT, HE IMPROVED QUICKLY DESPITE HIS LIMITED PLAYTIME.

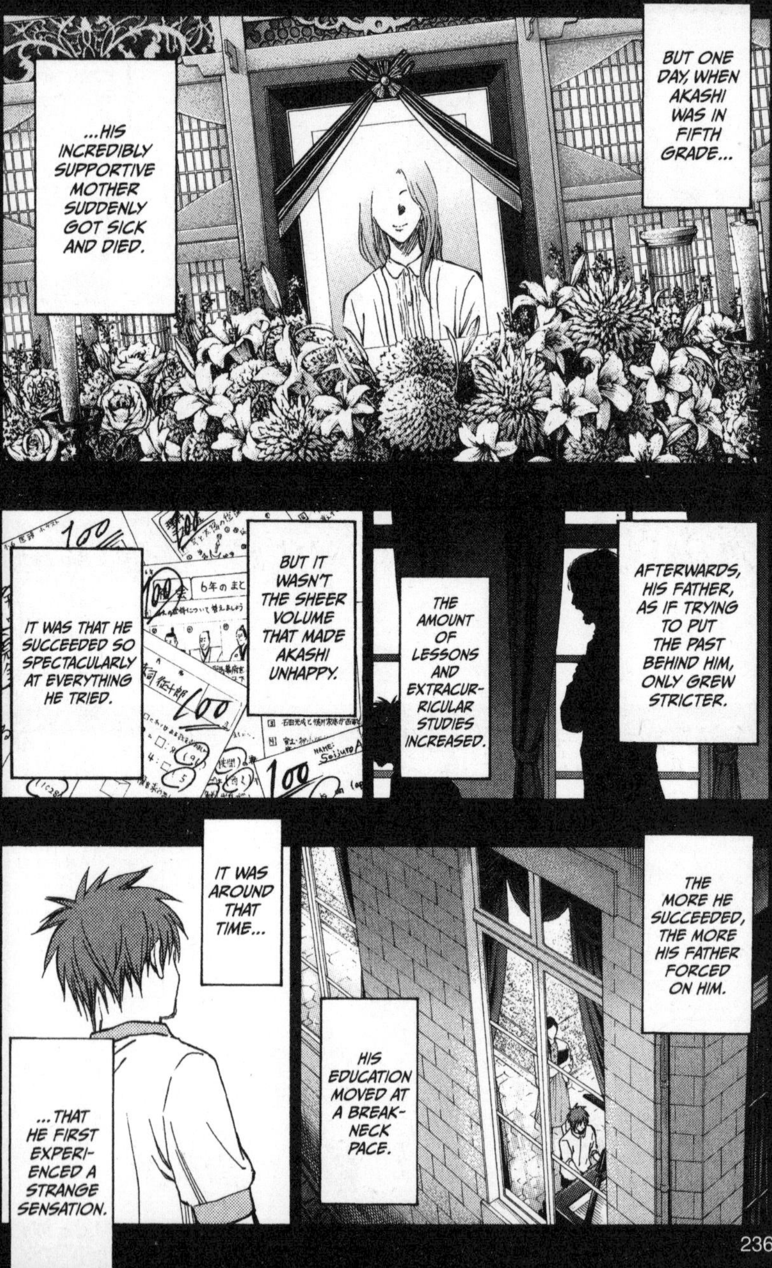

BUT ONE DAY, WHEN AKASHI WAS IN FIFTH GRADE...
...HIS INCREDIBLY SUPPORTIVE MOTHER SUDDENLY GOT SICK AND DIED.
AFTERWARDS, HIS FATHER, AS IF TRYING TO PUT THE PAST BEHIND HIM, ONLY GREW STRICTER.
THE AMOUNT OF LESSONS AND EXTRACURRICULAR STUDIES INCREASED.
BUT IT WASN'T THE SHEER VOLUME THAT MADE AKASHI UNHAPPY.
IT WAS THAT HE SUCCEEDED SO SPECTACULARLY AT EVERYTHING HE TRIED.
THE MORE HE SUCCEEDED, THE MORE HIS FATHER FORCED ON HIM.
HIS EDUCATION MOVED AT A BREAKNECK PACE.
IT WAS AROUND THAT TIME...
...THAT HE FIRST EXPERIENCED A STRANGE SENSATION.

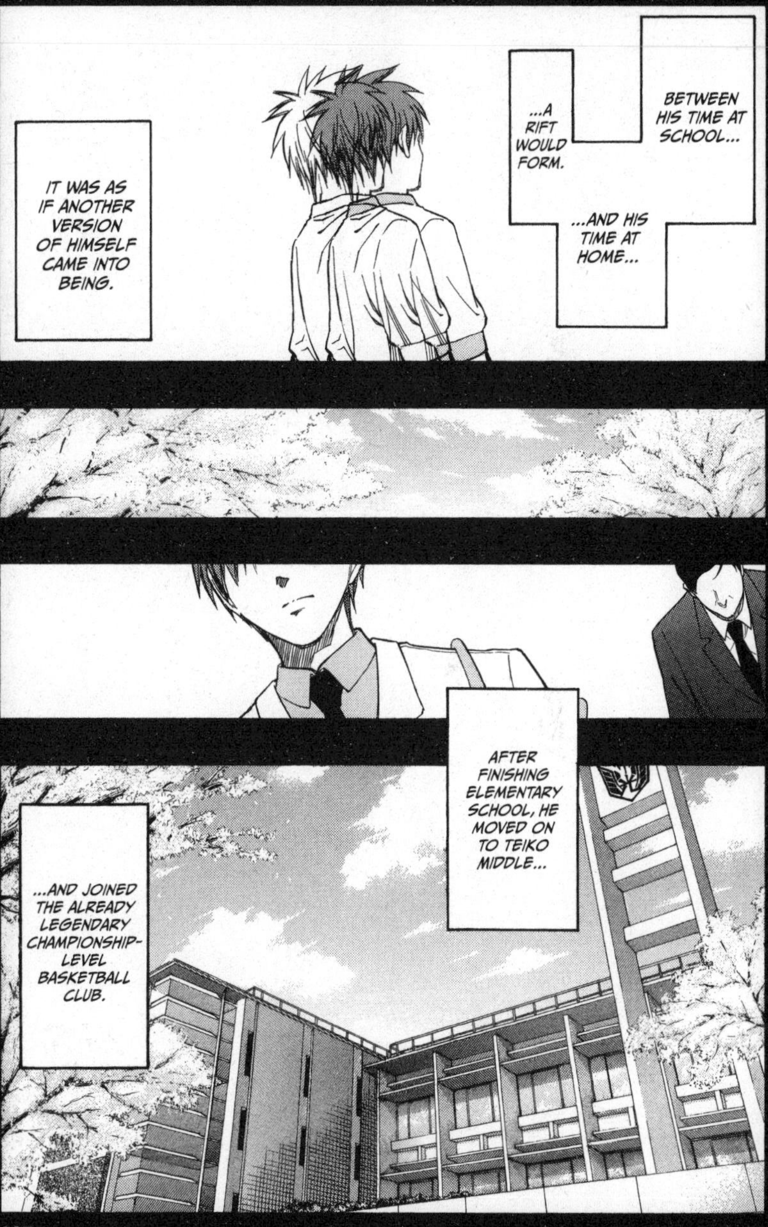
BETWEEN HIS TIME AT SCHOOL...
...AND HIS TIME AT HOME...
...A RIFT WOULD FORM.
IT WAS AS IF ANOTHER VERSION OF HIMSELF CAME INTO BEING.
AFTER FINISHING ELEMENTARY SCHOOL, HE MOVED ON TO TEIKO MIDDLE...
...AND JOINED THE ALREADY LEGENDARY CHAMPIONSHIP-LEVEL BASKETBALL CLUB.

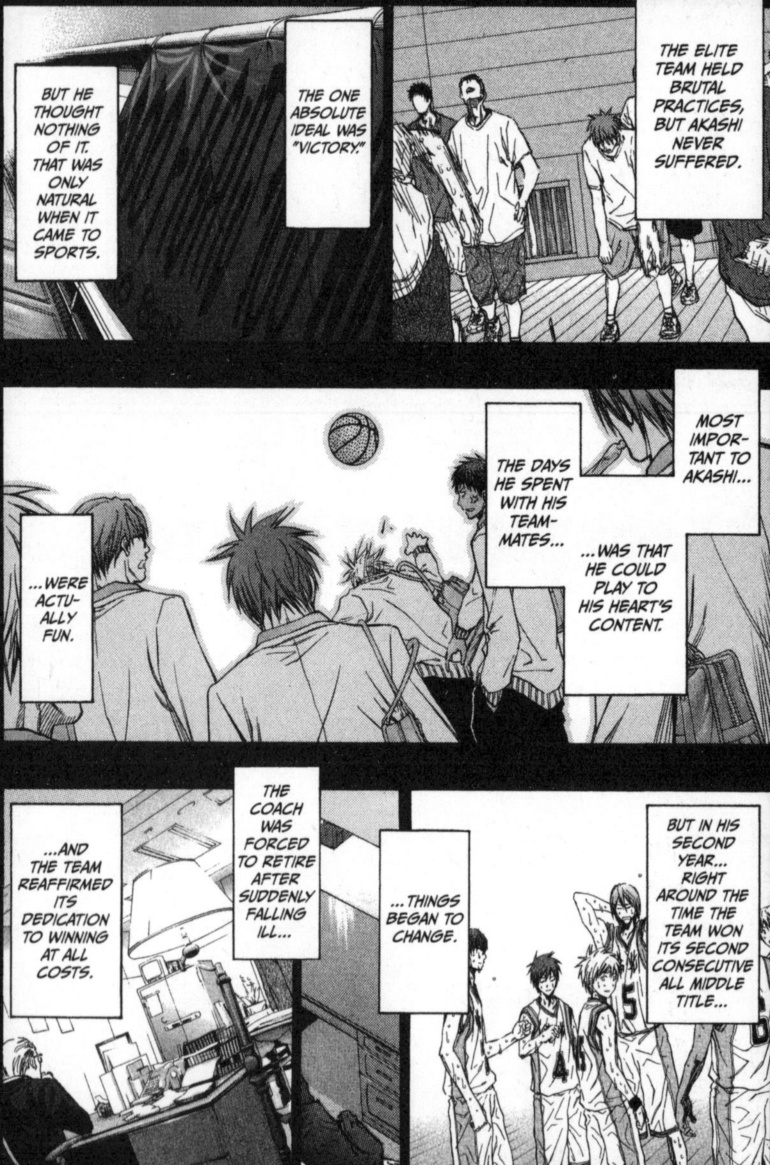
THE ELITE TEAM HELD BRUTAL PRACTICES, BUT AKASHI NEVER SUFFERED.
THE ONE ABSOLUTE IDEAL WAS "VICTORY."
BUT HE THOUGHT NOTHING OF IT. THAT WAS ONLY NATURAL WHEN IT CAME TO SPORTS.
MOST IMPOR-TANT TO AKASHI...
...WAS THAT HE COULD PLAY TO HIS HEART'S CONTENT.
THE DAYS HE SPENT WITH HIS TEAM-MATES...
...WERE ACTU-ALLY FUN.
BUT IN HIS SECOND YEAR... RIGHT AROUND THE TIME THE TEAM WON ITS SECOND CONSECUTIVE ALL MIDDLE TITLE...
...THINGS BEGAN TO CHANGE.
THE COACH WAS FORCED TO RETIRE AFTER SUDDENLY FALLING ILL...
...AND THE TEAM REAFFIRMED ITS DEDICATION TO WINNING AT ALL COSTS.

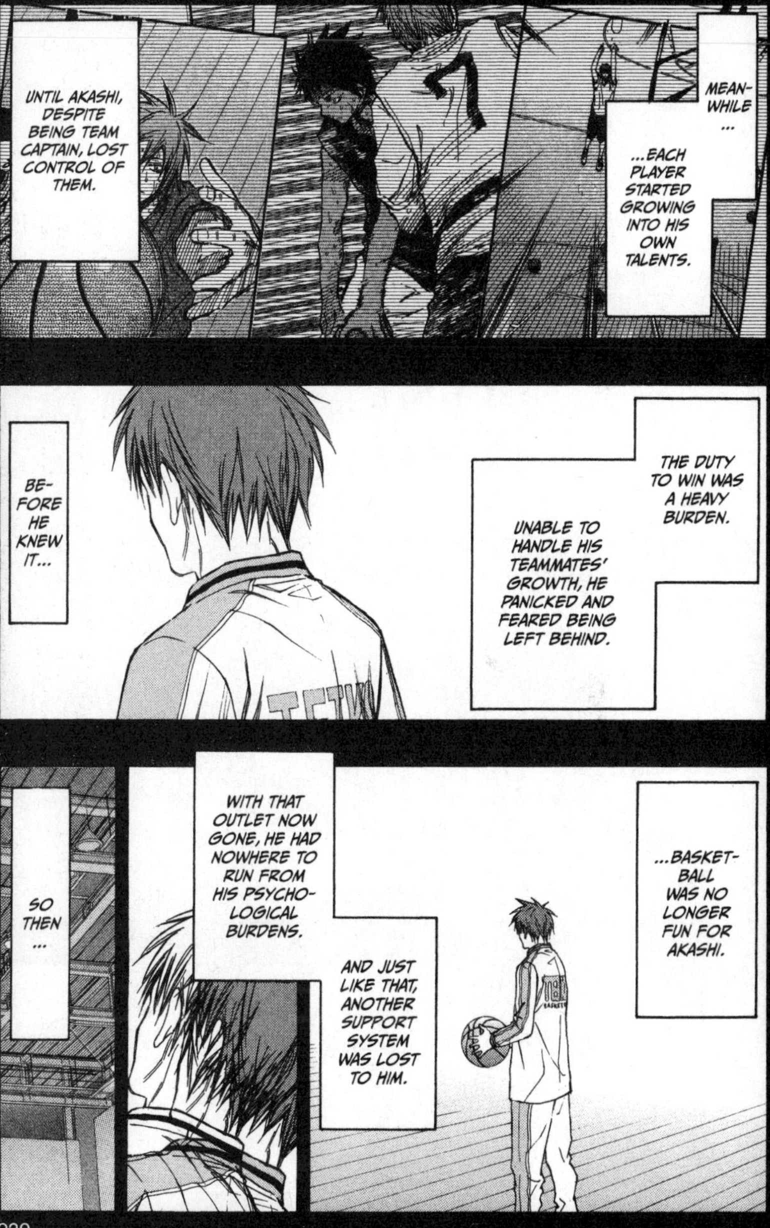
MEAN-WHILE ...
...EACH PLAYER STARTED GROWING INTO HIS OWN TALENTS.
UNTIL AKASHI, DESPITE BEING TEAM CAPTAIN, LOST CONTROL OF THEM.
THE DUTY TO WIN WAS A HEAVY BURDEN.
UNABLE TO HANDLE HIS TEAMMATES' GROWTH, HE PANICKED AND FEARED BEING LEFT BEHIND.
BE-FORE HE KNEW IT...
...BASKET-BALL WAS NO LONGER FUN FOR AKASHI.
WITH THAT OUTLET NOW GONE, HE HAD NOWHERE TO RUN FROM HIS PSYCHO-LOGICAL BURDENS.
AND JUST LIKE THAT, ANOTHER SUPPORT SYSTEM WAS LOST TO HIM.
SO THEN ...

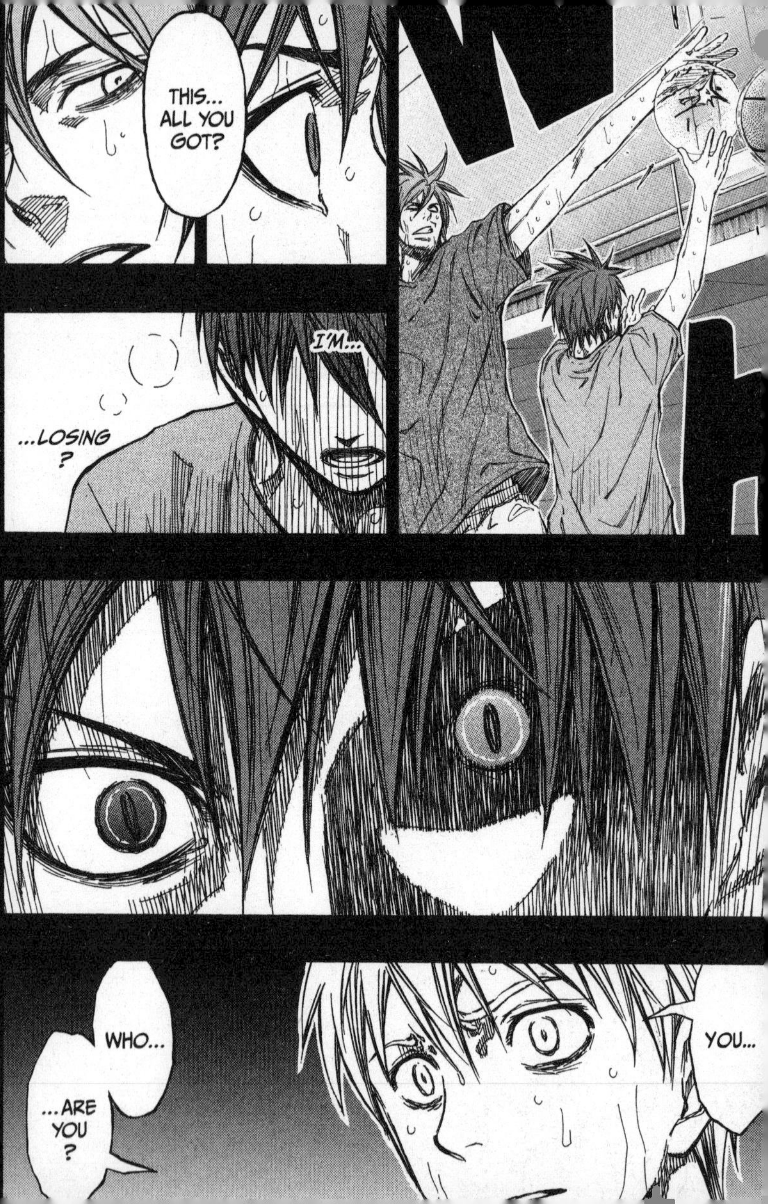
THIS... ALL YOU GOT?
I'M...
...LOSING ?
YOU...
WHO...
...ARE YOU ?

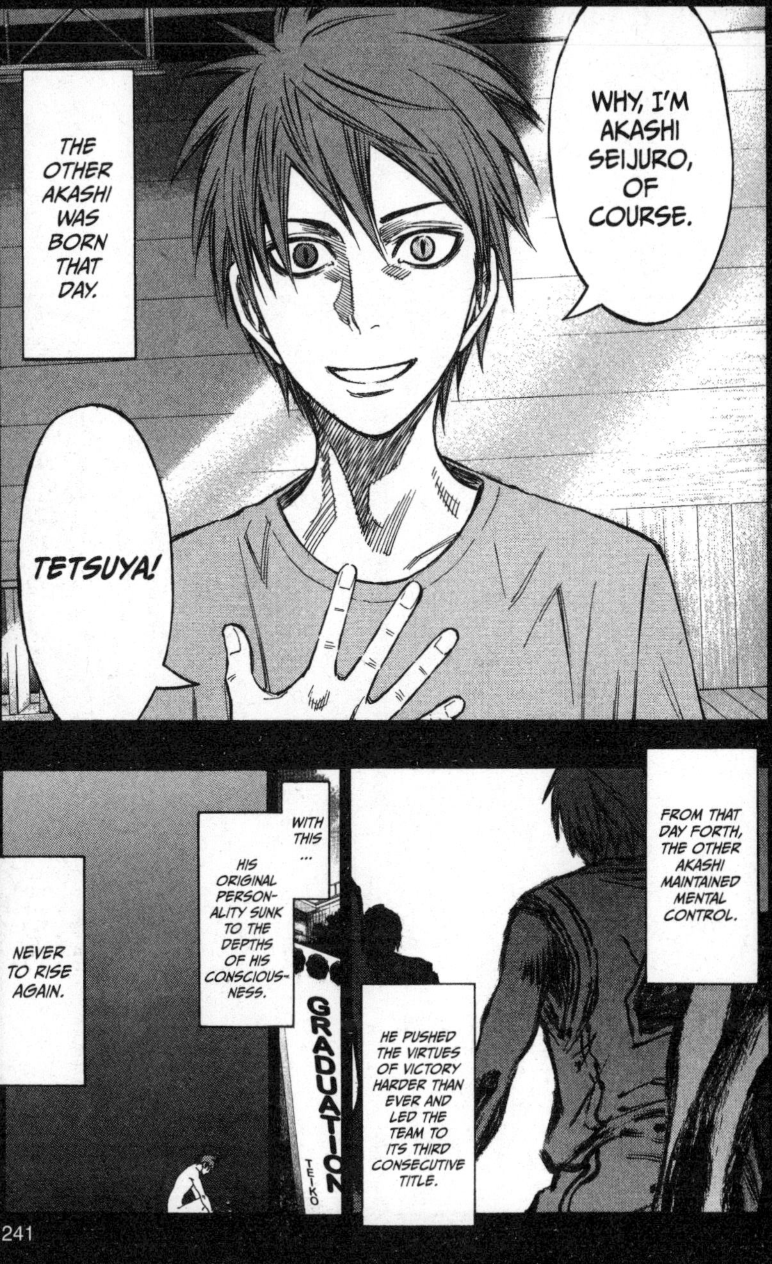
WHY, I'M AKASHI SEIJURO, OF COURSE.
THE OTHER AKASHI WAS BORN THAT DAY.
TETSUYA!
FROM THAT DAY FORTH, THE OTHER AKASHI MAINTAINED MENTAL CONTROL.
HE PUSHED THE VIRTUES OF VICTORY HARDER THAN EVER AND LED THE TEAM TO ITS THIRD CONSECUTIVE TITLE.
GRADUATION
TEIKO
WITH THIS ...
HIS ORIGINAL PERSONALITY SUNK TO THE DEPTHS OF HIS CONSCIOUSNESS.
NEVER TO RISE AGAIN.

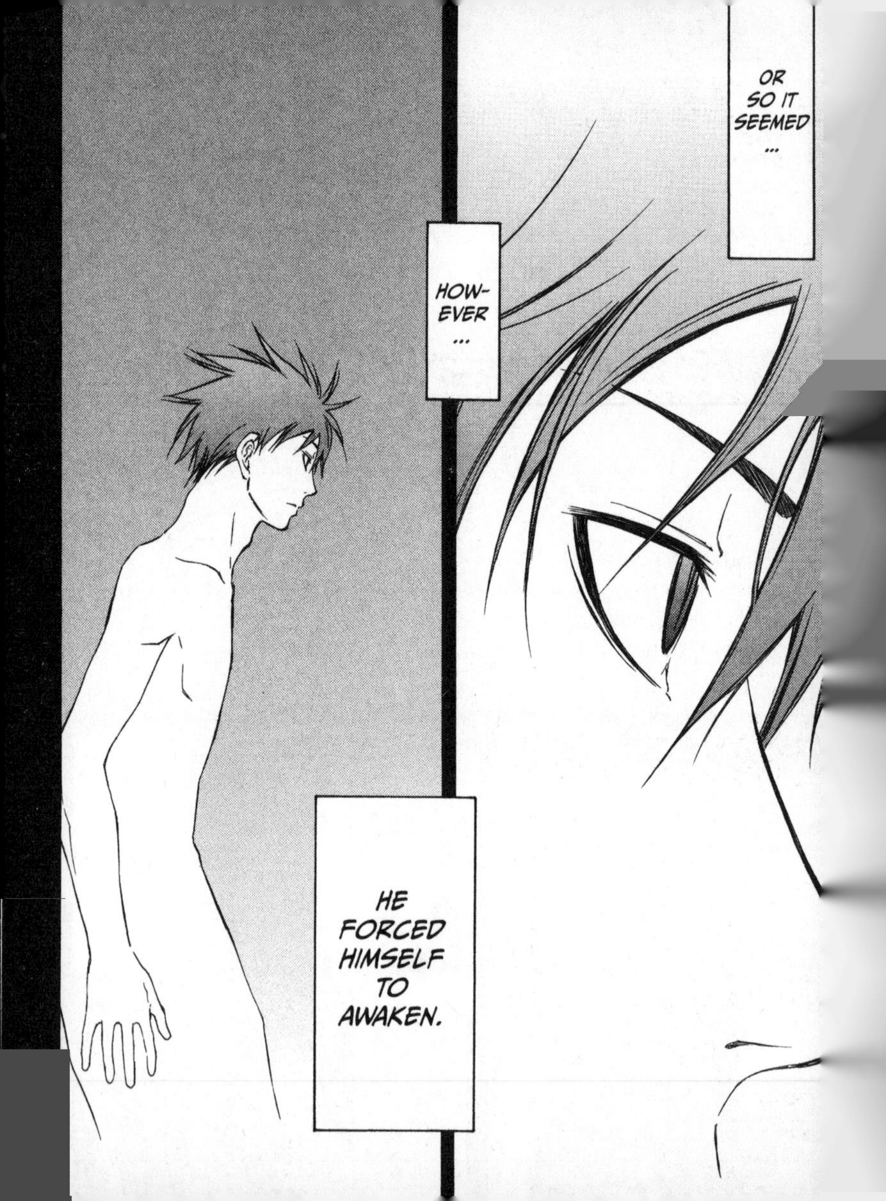
OR SO IT SEEMED ...
HOW-EVER ...
HE FORCED HIMSELF TO AWAKEN.

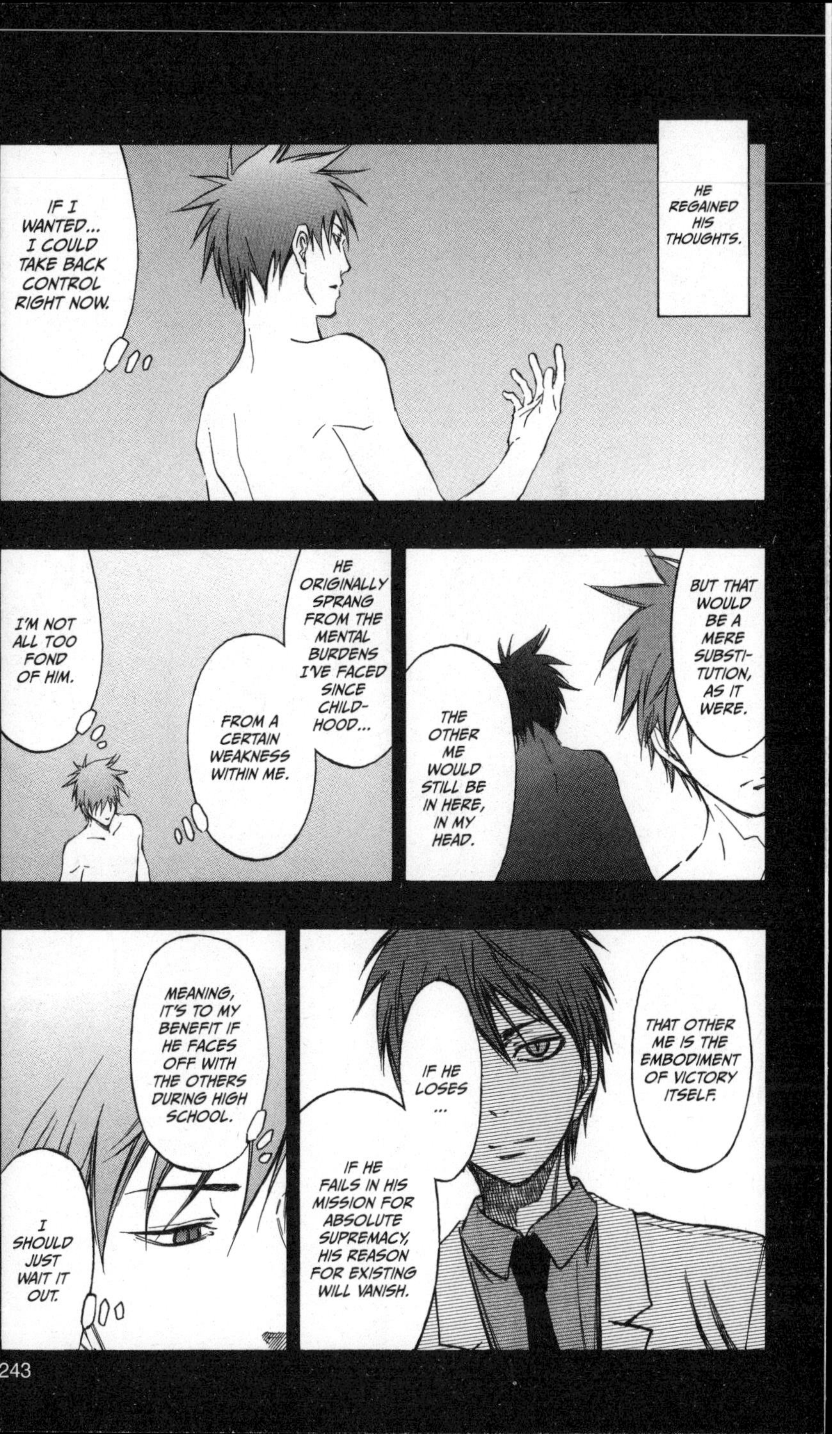
HE REGAINED HIS THOUGHTS.
IF I WANTED... I COULD TAKE BACK CONTROL RIGHT NOW.
BUT THAT WOULD BE A MERE SUBSTITUTION, AS IT WERE.
THE OTHER ME WOULD STILL BE IN HERE, IN MY HEAD.
HE ORIGINALLY SPRANG FROM THE MENTAL BURDENS I'VE FACED SINCE CHILDHOOD...
FROM A CERTAIN WEAKNESS WITHIN ME.
I'M NOT ALL TOO FOND OF HIM.
THAT OTHER ME IS THE EMBODIMENT OF VICTORY ITSELF.
IF HE LOSES...
IF HE FAILS IN HIS MISSION FOR ABSOLUTE SUPREMACY, HIS REASON FOR EXISTING WILL VANISH.
MEANING, IT'S TO MY BENEFIT IF HE FACES OFF WITH THE OTHERS DURING HIGH SCHOOL.
I SHOULD JUST WAIT IT OUT.

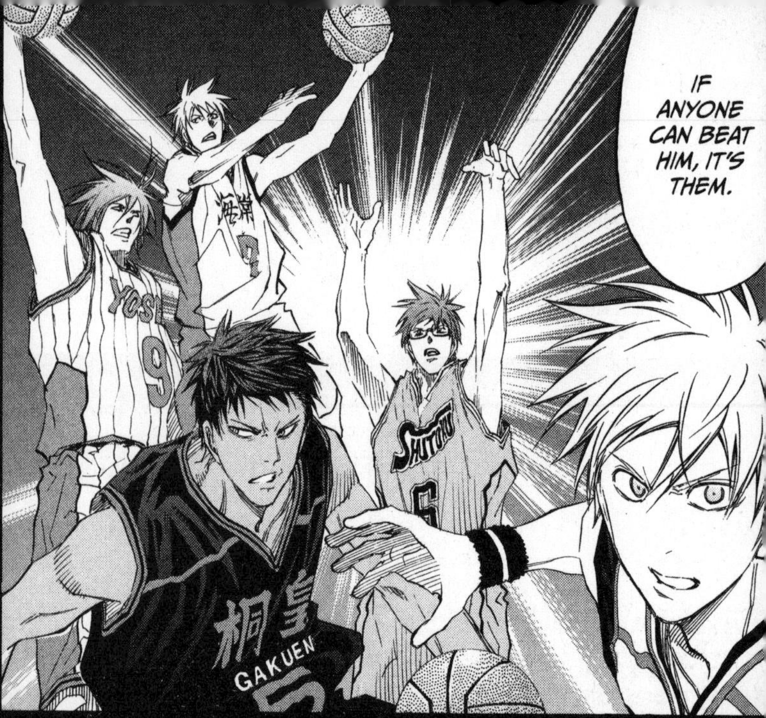
IF ANYONE CAN BEAT HIM, IT'S THEM.
SHUTOKU
桐皇
GAKUEN

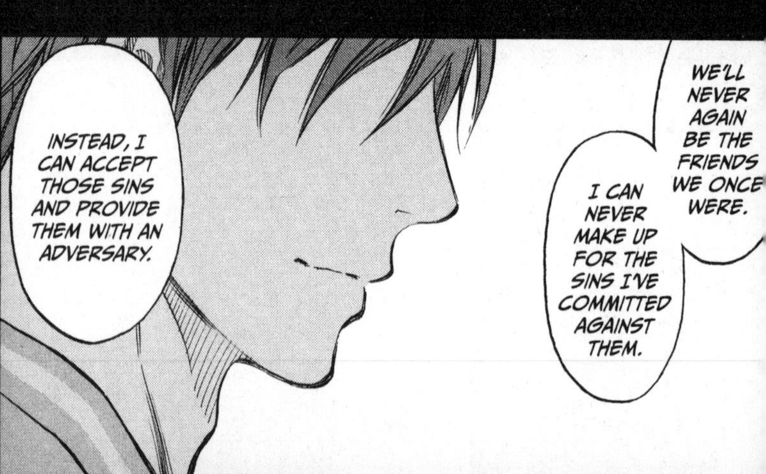
WE'LL NEVER AGAIN BE THE FRIENDS WE ONCE WERE.
I CAN NEVER MAKE UP FOR THE SINS I'VE COMMITTED AGAINST THEM.
INSTEAD, I CAN ACCEPT THOSE SINS AND PROVIDE THEM WITH AN ADVERSARY.

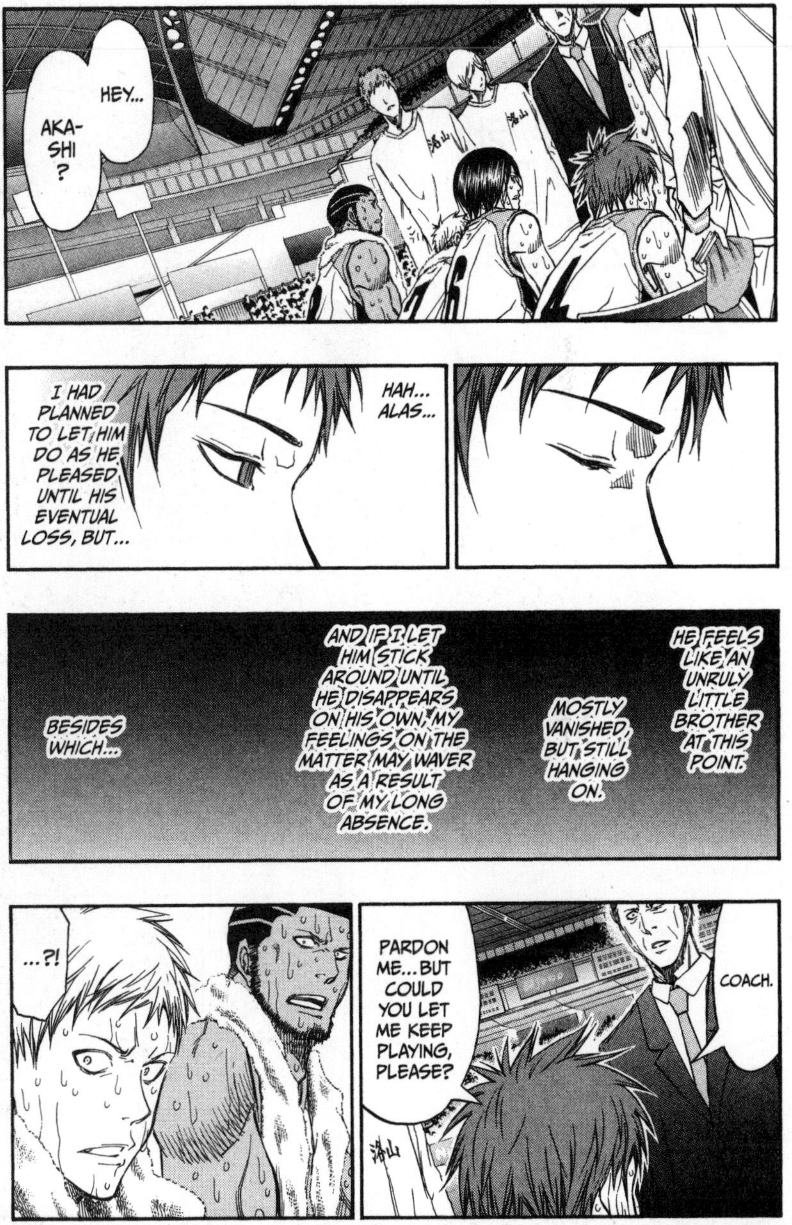
HEY...
AKA-SHI?
HAH... ALAS...
I HAD PLANNED TO LET HIM DO AS HE PLEASED UNTIL HIS EVENTUAL LOSS, BUT...
HE FEELS LIKE AN UNRULY LITTLE BROTHER AT THIS POINT.
MOSTLY VANISHED, BUT STILL HANGING ON.
AND IF I LET HIM STICK AROUND UNTIL HE DISAPPEARS ON HIS OWN, MY FEELINGS ON THE MATTER MAY WAVER AS A RESULT OF MY LONG ABSENCE.
BESIDES WHICH...
COACH.
PARDON ME... BUT COULD YOU LET ME KEEP PLAYING, PLEASE?
...?!

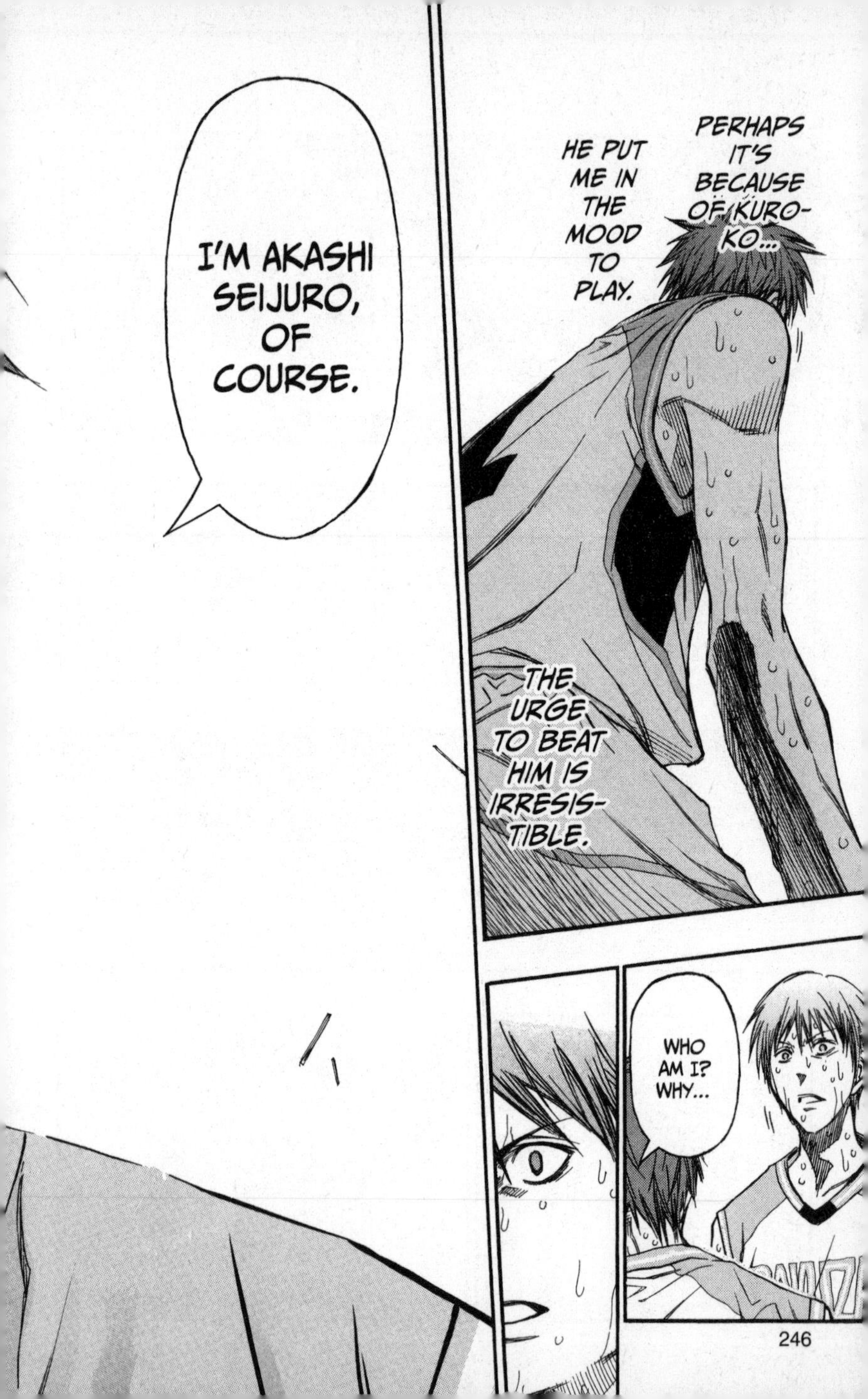
PERHAPS IT'S BECAUSE OF KURO-KO...
HE PUT ME IN THE MOOD TO PLAY.
THE URGE TO BEAT HIM IS IRRESIS-TIBLE.
WHO AM I? WHY...
I'M AKASHI SEIJURO, OF COURSE.

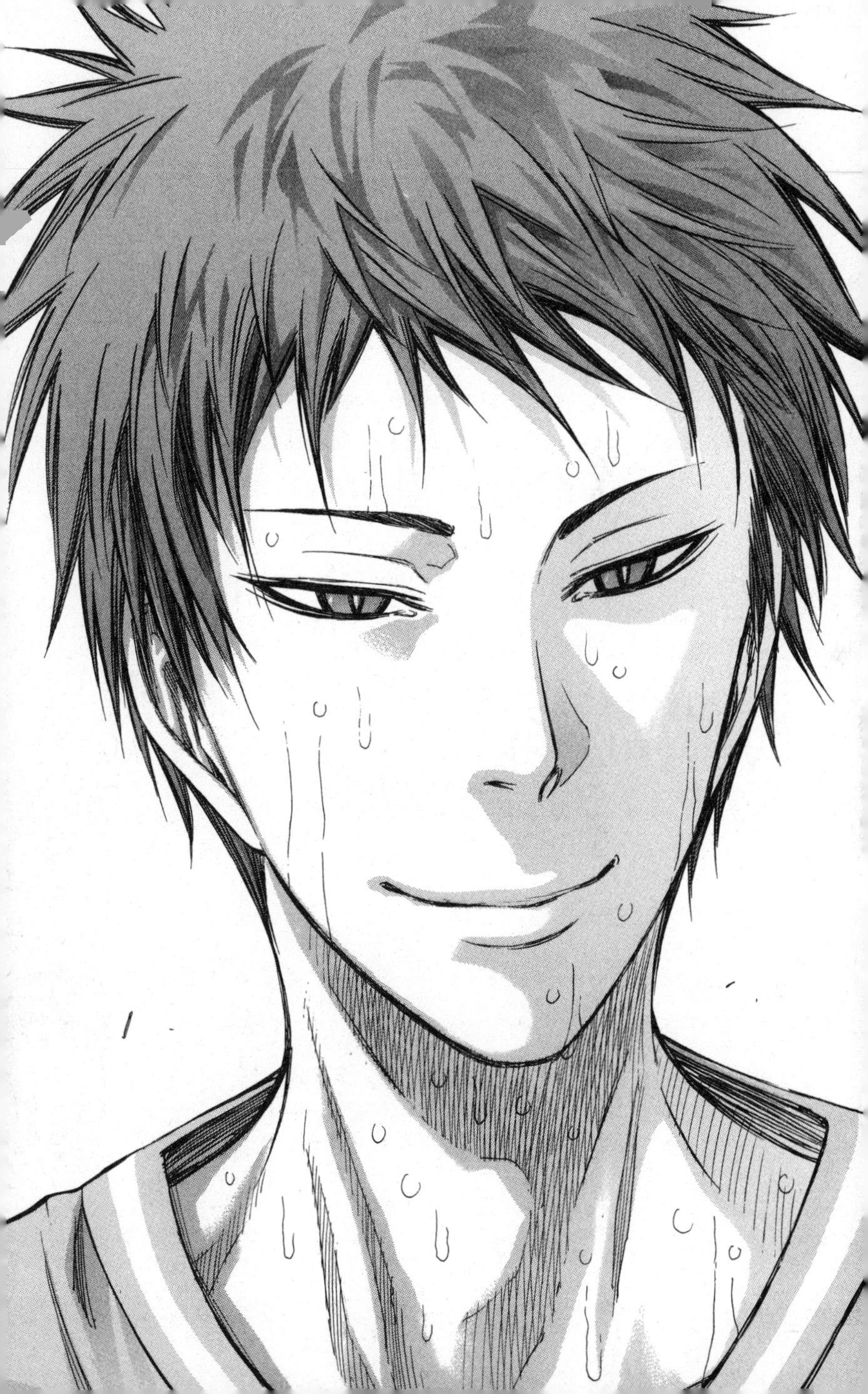

KUROKO'S BASKETBALL BLOOPERS

TAKE 5

I'M AKASHI SEIJURO, OF COURSE.

THE BIG BROTHER VERSION.

WHAT'S THAT SUPPOSED TO MEAN ?!

MAYU-ZUMI

267TH QUARTER: LONG TIME NO SEE

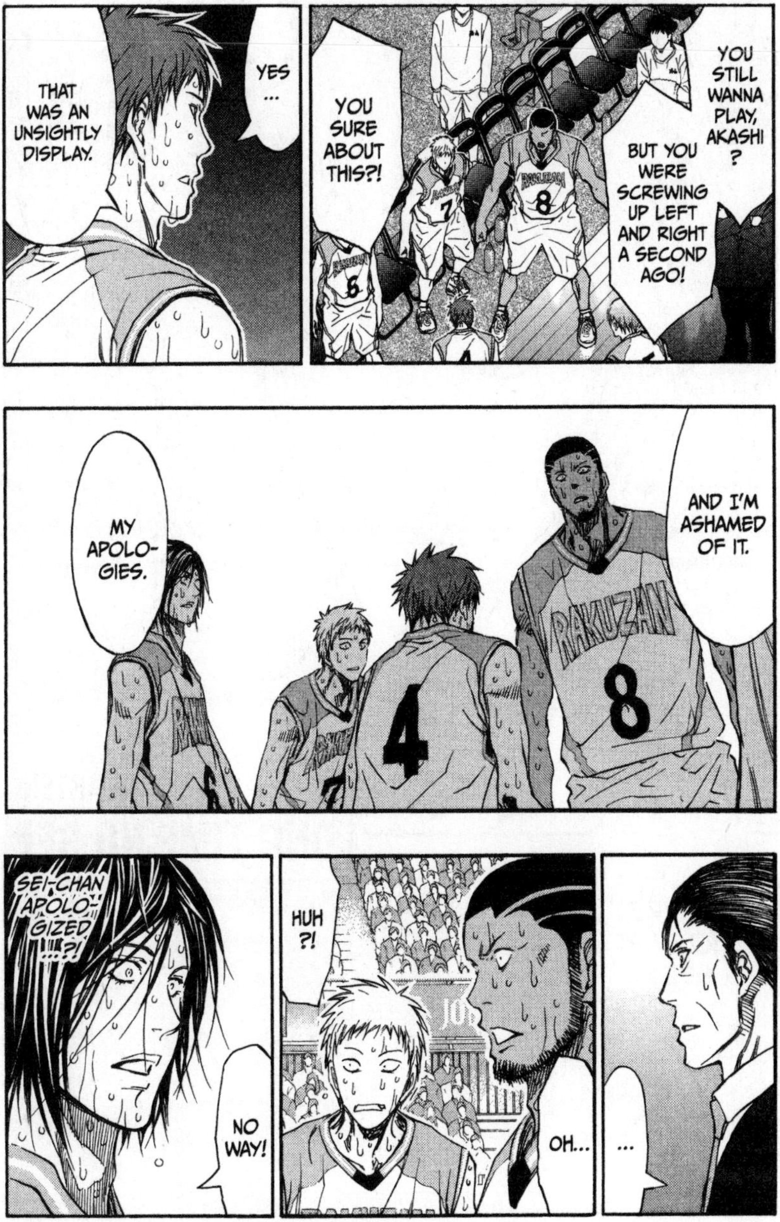
YOU STILL WANNA PLAY, AKASHI?
BUT YOU WERE SCREWING UP LEFT AND RIGHT A SECOND AGO!
YOU SURE ABOUT THIS?!
YES ...
THAT WAS AN UNSIGHTLY DISPLAY.
AND I'M ASHAMED OF IT.
MY APOLOGIES.
...
OH...
HUH?!
SEI-CHAN APOLOGIZED ...?!
NO WAY!

267TH QUARTER: LONG-TIME-NO-SEE

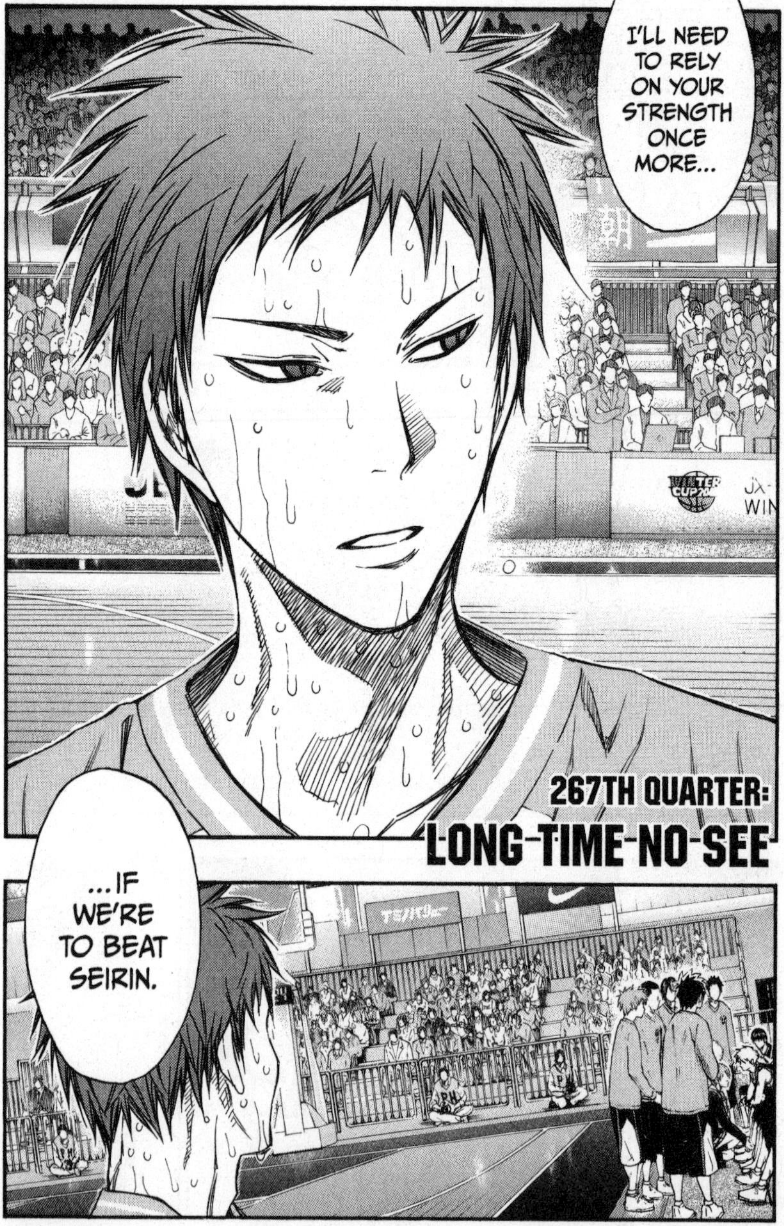
I'LL NEED TO RELY ON YOUR STRENGTH ONCE MORE...
...IF WE'RE TO BEAT SEIRIN.

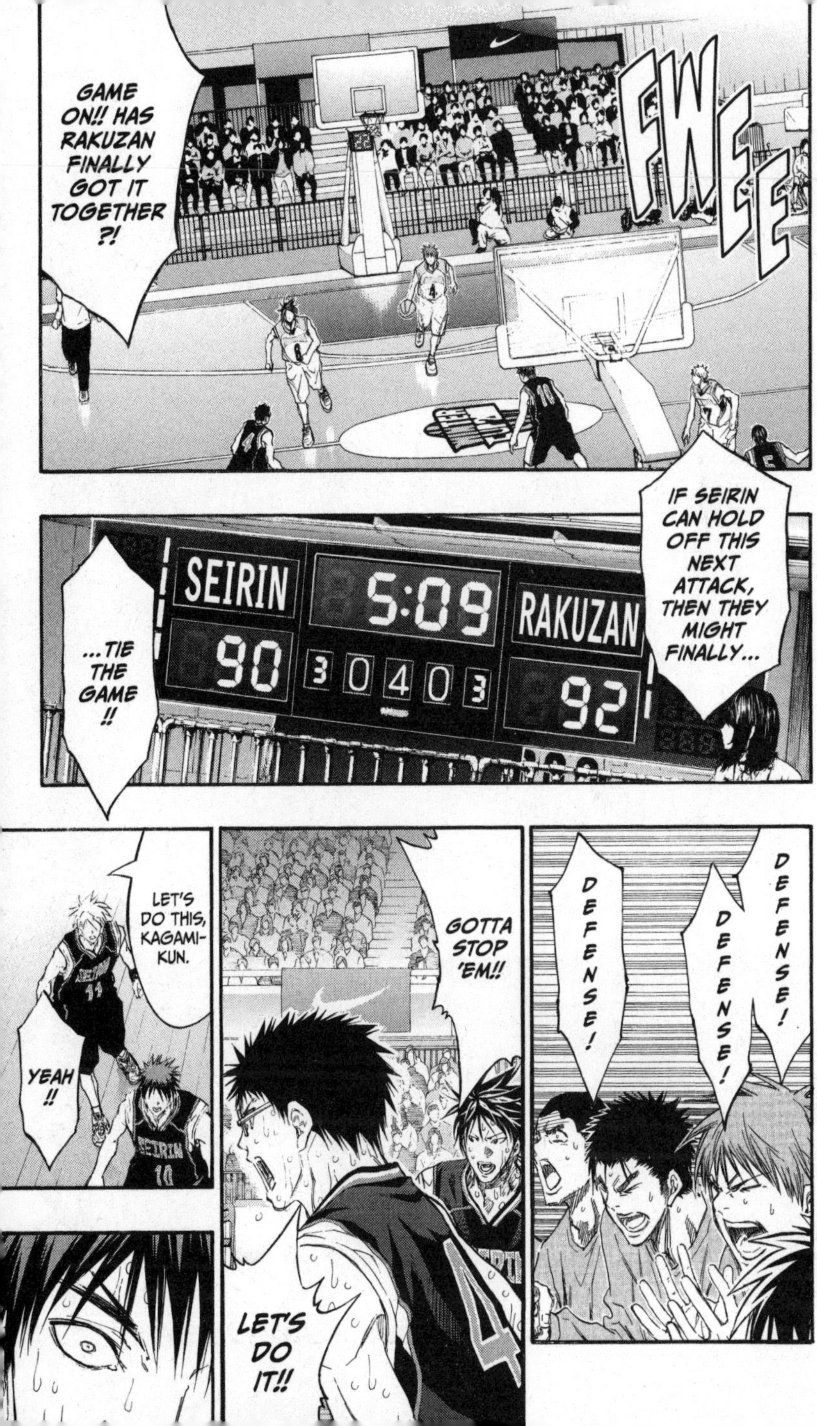

FWEE
GAME ON!! HAS RAKUZAN FINALLY GOT IT TOGETHER?!
IF SEIRIN CAN HOLD OFF THIS NEXT ATTACK, THEN THEY MIGHT FINALLY...
SEIRIN
5:09
RAKUZAN
90
92
...TIE THE GAME!!
DEFENSE!
DEFENSE!
DEFENSE!
GOTTA STOP 'EM!!
LET'S DO IT!!
LET'S DO THIS, KAGAMI-KUN.
YEAH!!

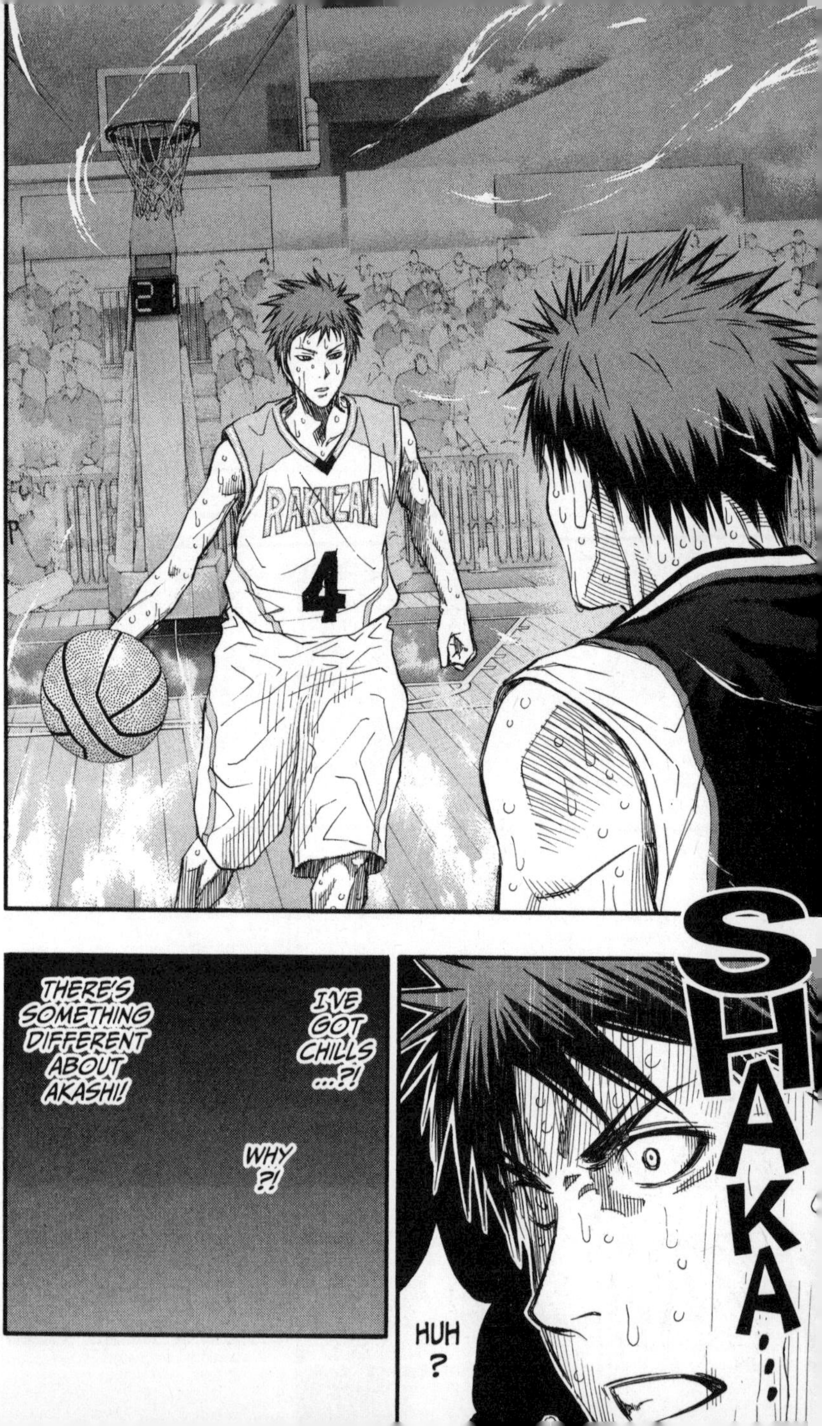
RAKUZAN
4
SHAKA...
HUH ?
I'VE GOT CHILLS ...?!
WHY ?!
THERE'S SOMETHING DIFFERENT ABOUT AKASHI!

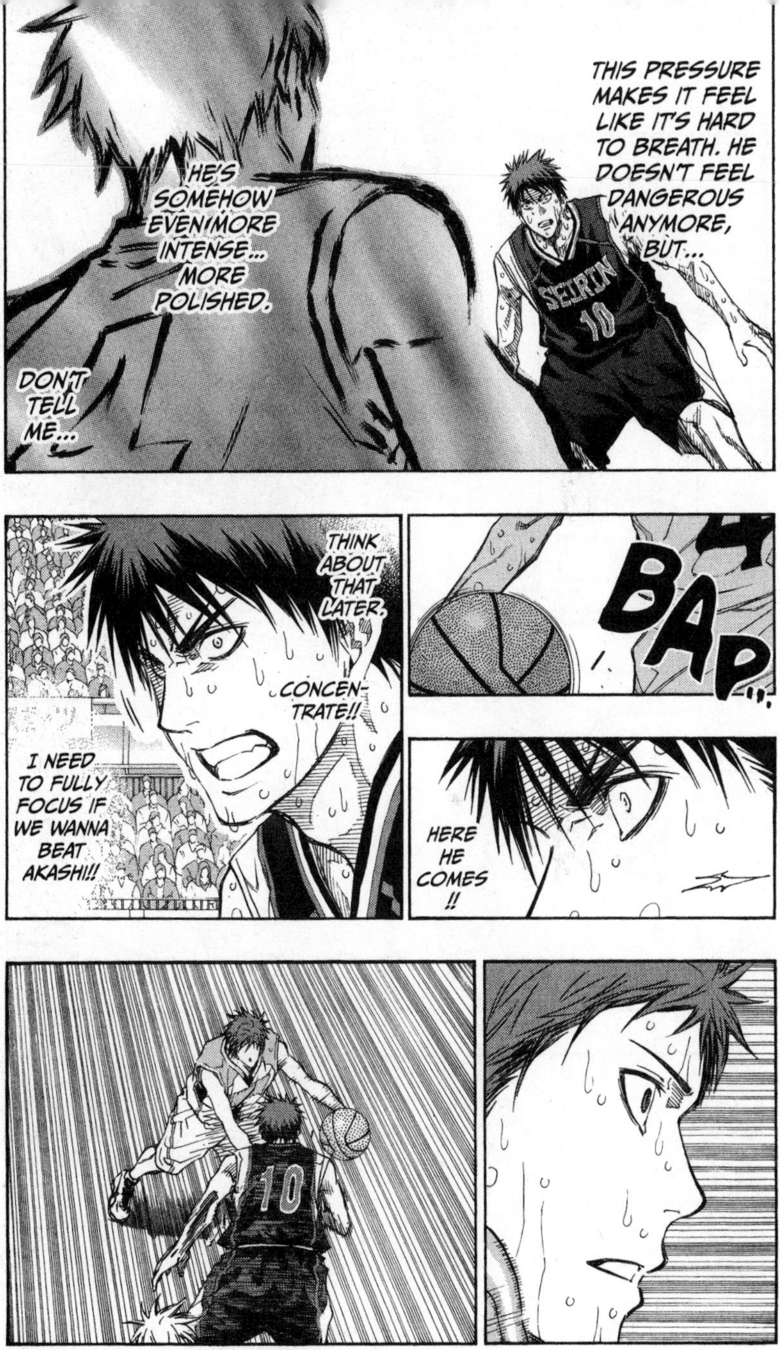
THIS PRESSURE MAKES IT FEEL LIKE IT'S HARD TO BREATH. HE DOESN'T FEEL DANGEROUS ANYMORE, BUT...
HE'S SOMEHOW EVEN MORE INTENSE... MORE POLISHED.
DON'T TELL ME...
BAP..
HERE HE COMES!!
THINK ABOUT THAT LATER.
CONCEN-TRATE!!
I NEED TO FULLY FOCUS IF WE WANNA BEAT AKASHI!!

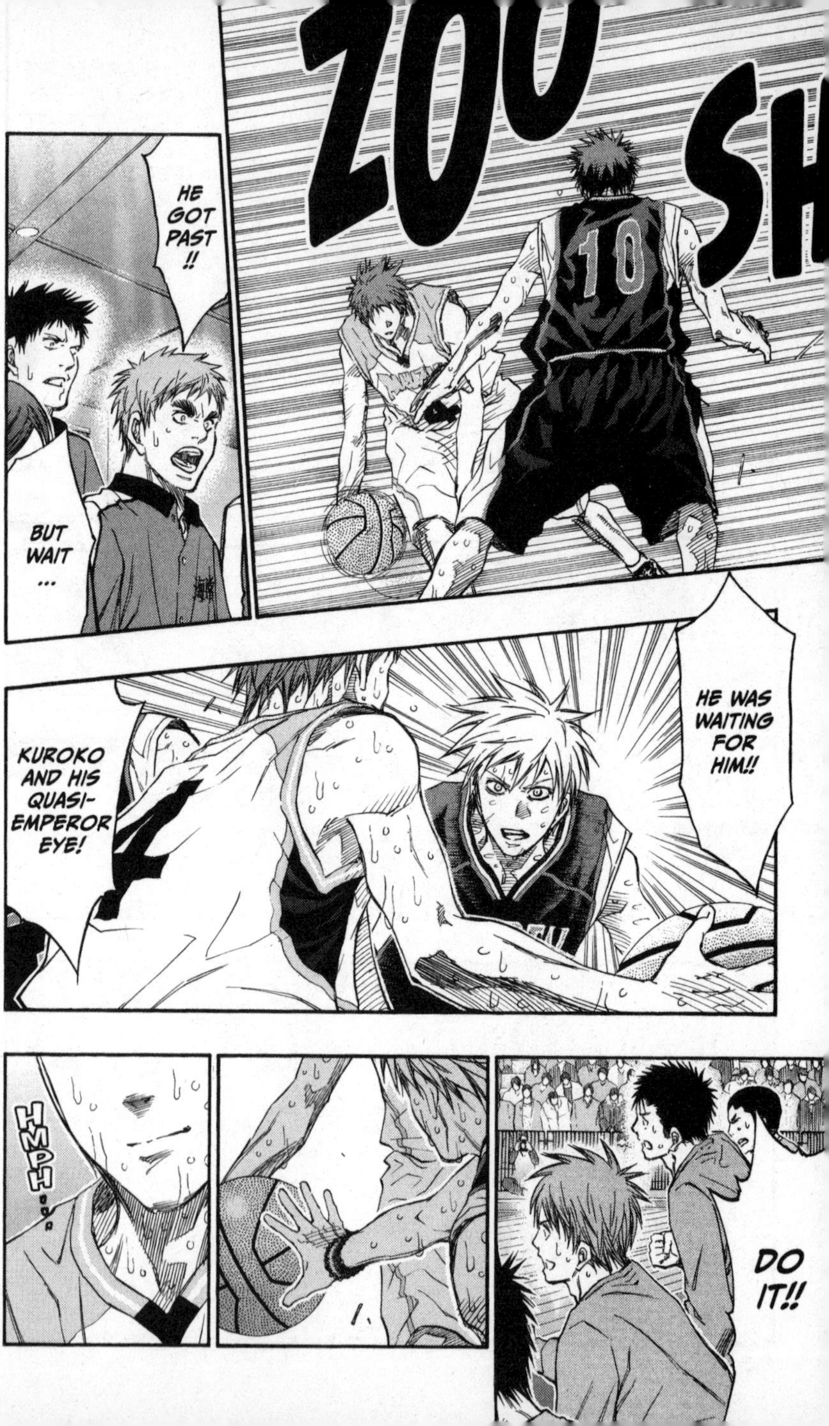

ZOU SH
HE GOT PAST !!
BUT WAIT ...
HE WAS WAITING FOR HIM!!
KUROKO AND HIS QUASI-EMPEROR EYE!
DO IT!!
HMPH...

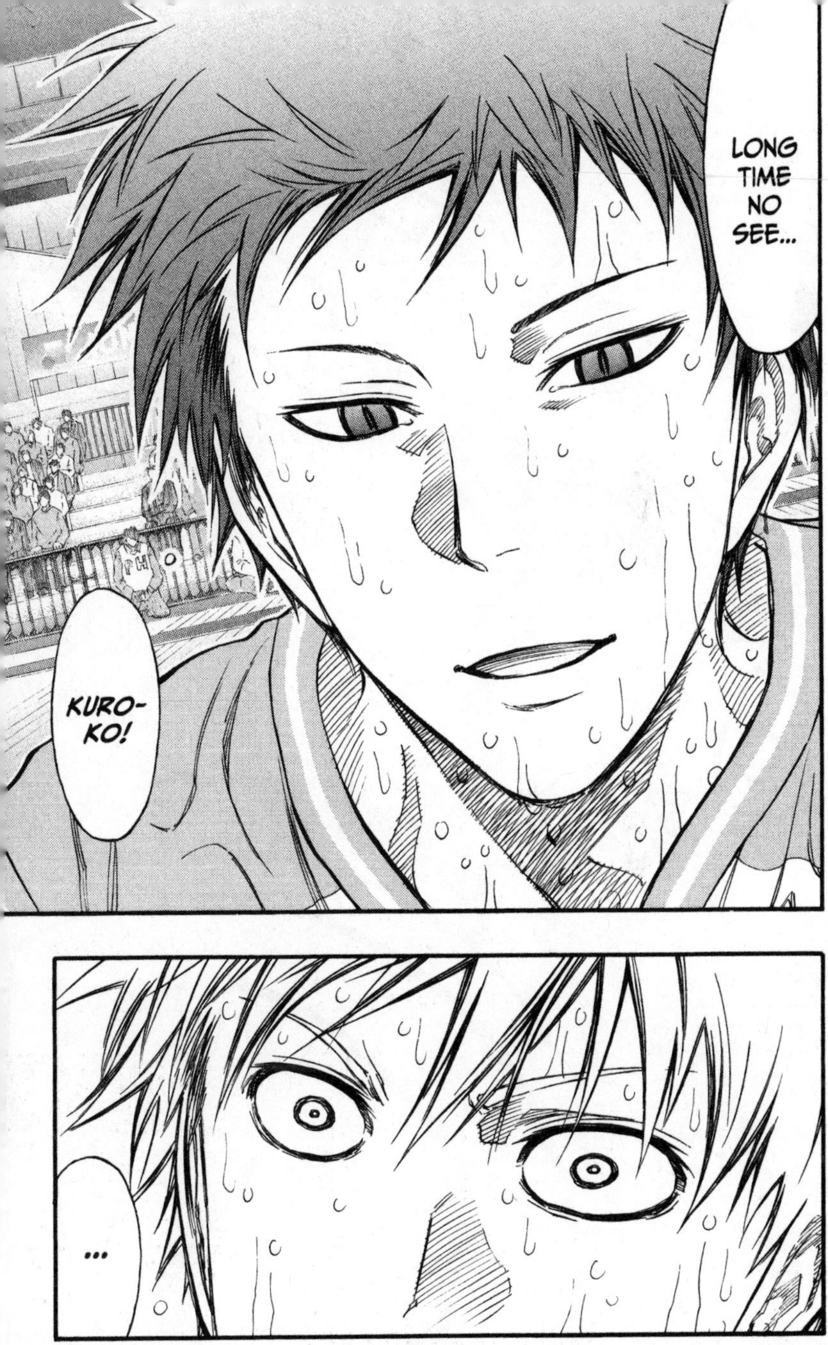
LONG TIME NO SEE...
KURO-KO!
...

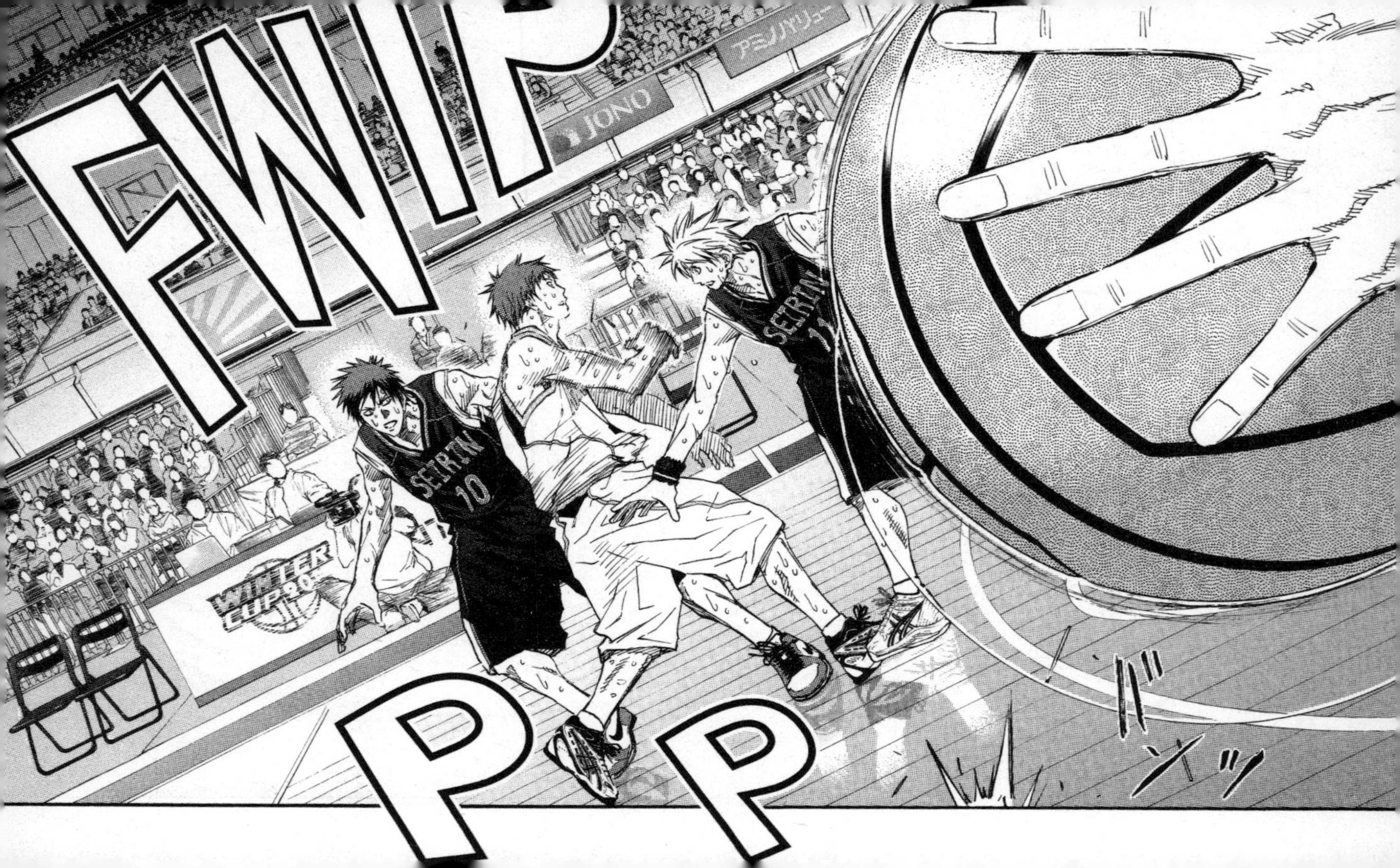
FWIP
PP
JONO
SEIRIN
10
SEIRIN
WINTER CUP

!!

AH...

SHP

SHK

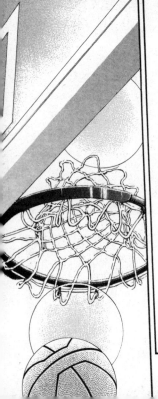

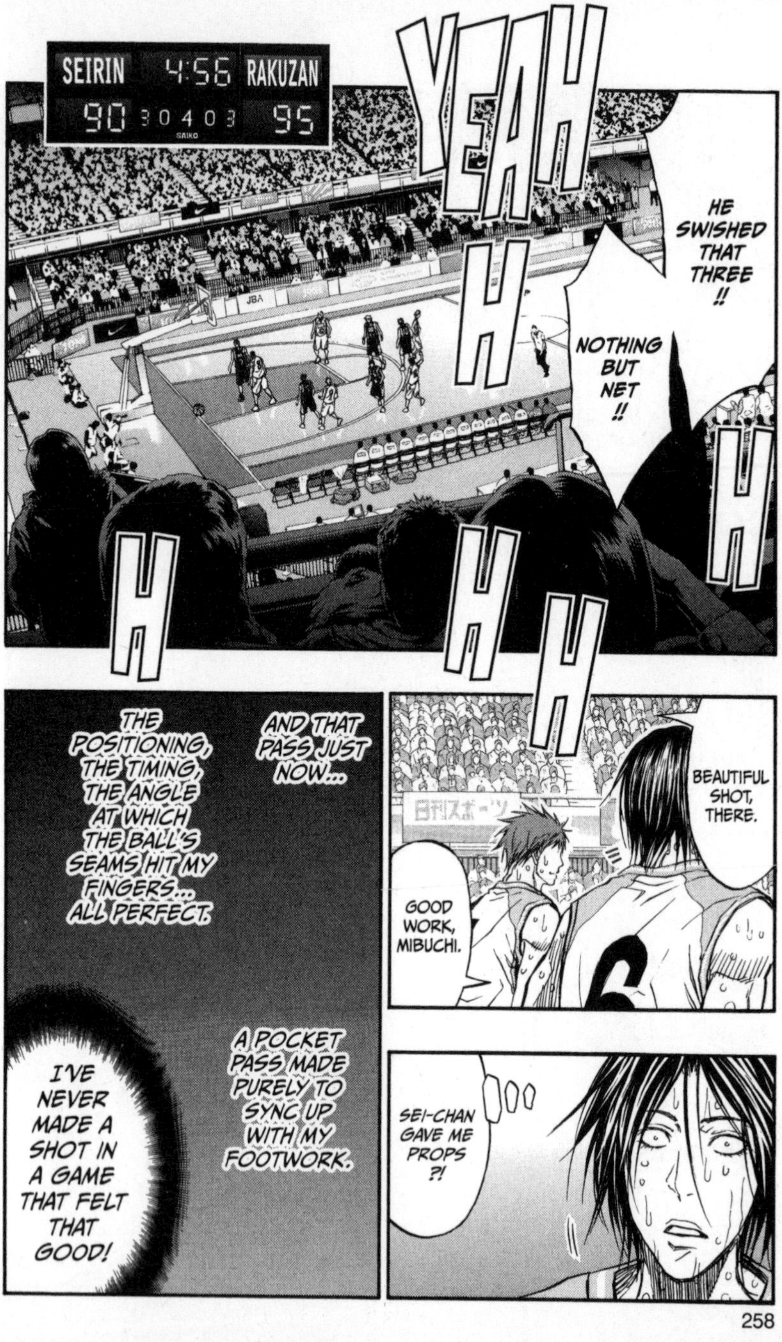
SEIRIN 4:56 RAKUZAN
90 3 0 4 0 3 95
SAIKO
JBA
YEAHHHHHHH
HE SWISHED THAT THREE!!
NOTHING BUT NET!!
BEAUTIFUL SHOT, THERE.
日刊スポーツ
GOOD WORK, MIBUCHI.
SEI-CHAN GAVE ME PROPS?!
THE POSITIONING, THE TIMING, THE ANGLE AT WHICH THE BALL'S SEAMS HIT MY FINGERS... ALL PERFECT.
AND THAT PASS JUST NOW...
A POCKET PASS MADE PURELY TO SYNC UP WITH MY FOOTWORK.
I'VE NEVER MADE A SHOT IN A GAME THAT FELT THAT GOOD!

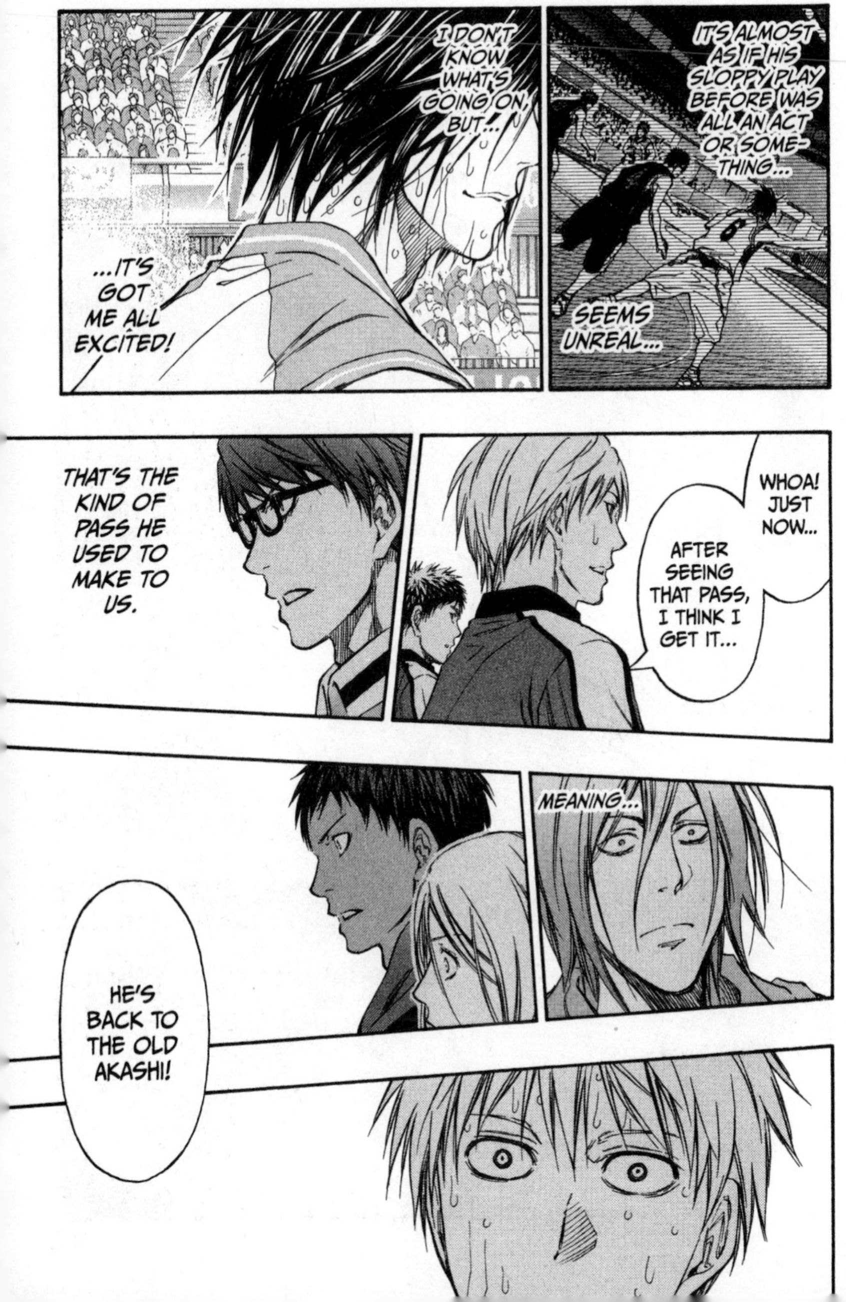
IT'S ALMOST AS IF HIS SLOPPY PLAY BEFORE WAS ALL AN ACT OR SOME-THING...
SEEMS UNREAL...
I DON'T KNOW WHAT'S GOING ON, BUT...
...IT'S GOT ME ALL EXCITED!
WHOA! JUST NOW...
AFTER SEEING THAT PASS, I THINK I GET IT...
THAT'S THE KIND OF PASS HE USED TO MAKE TO US.
MEANING...
HE'S BACK TO THE OLD AKASHI!

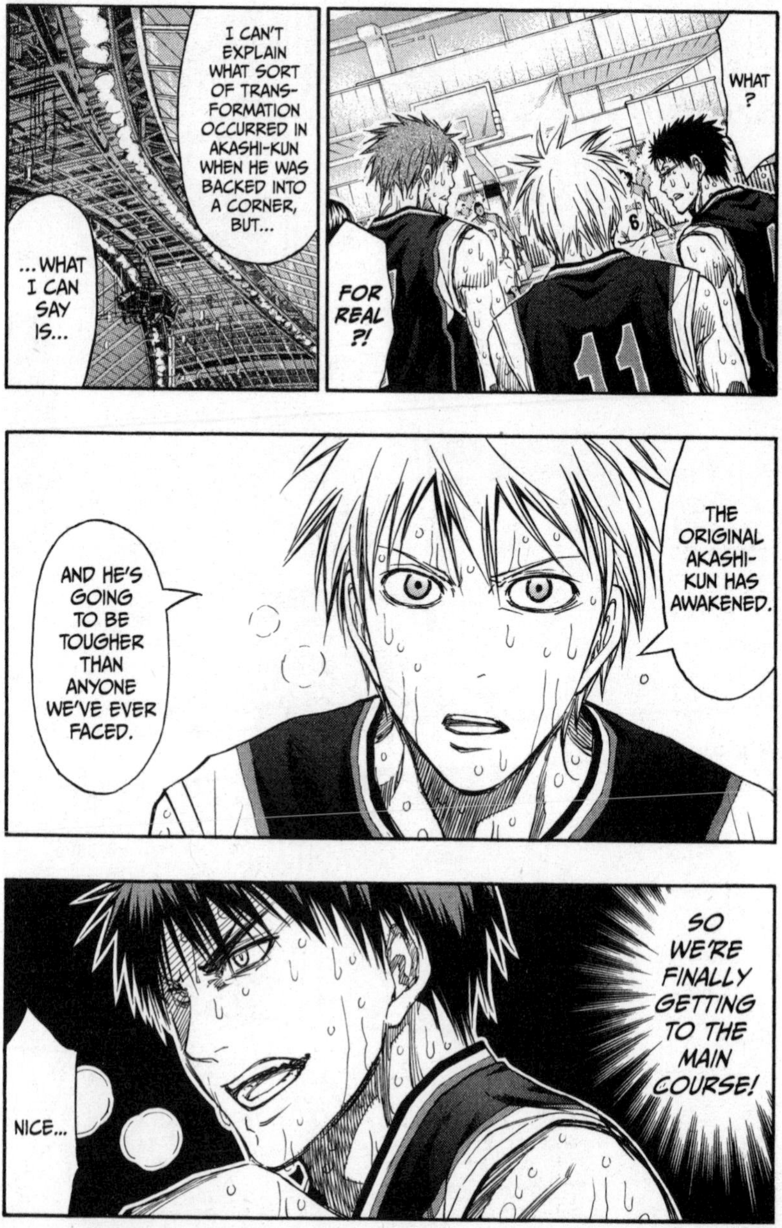
WHAT?
FOR REAL?!
I CAN'T EXPLAIN WHAT SORT OF TRANS-FORMATION OCCURRED IN AKASHI-KUN WHEN HE WAS BACKED INTO A CORNER, BUT...
...WHAT I CAN SAY IS...
THE ORIGINAL AKASHI-KUN HAS AWAKENED.
AND HE'S GOING TO BE TOUGHER THAN ANYONE WE'VE EVER FACED.
SO WE'RE FINALLY GETTING TO THE MAIN COURSE!
NICE...

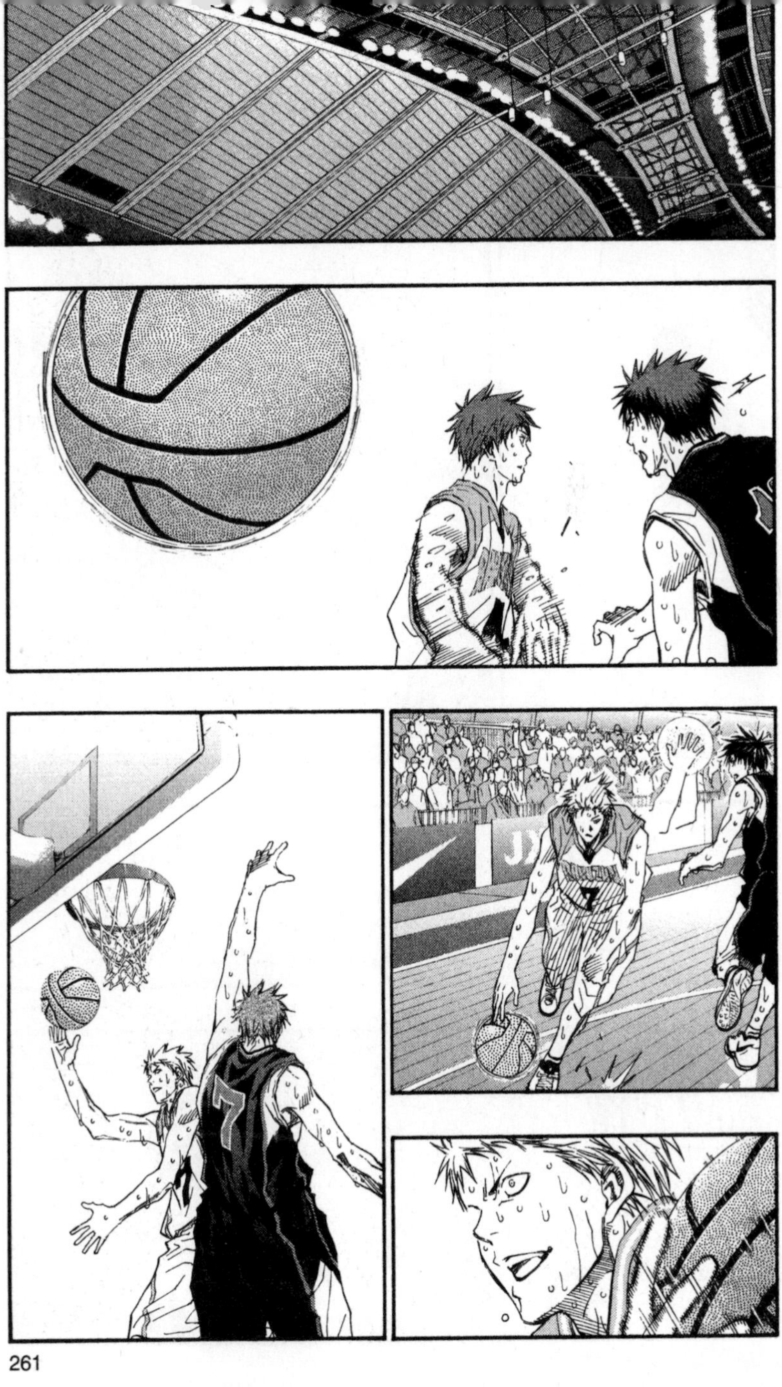
JX

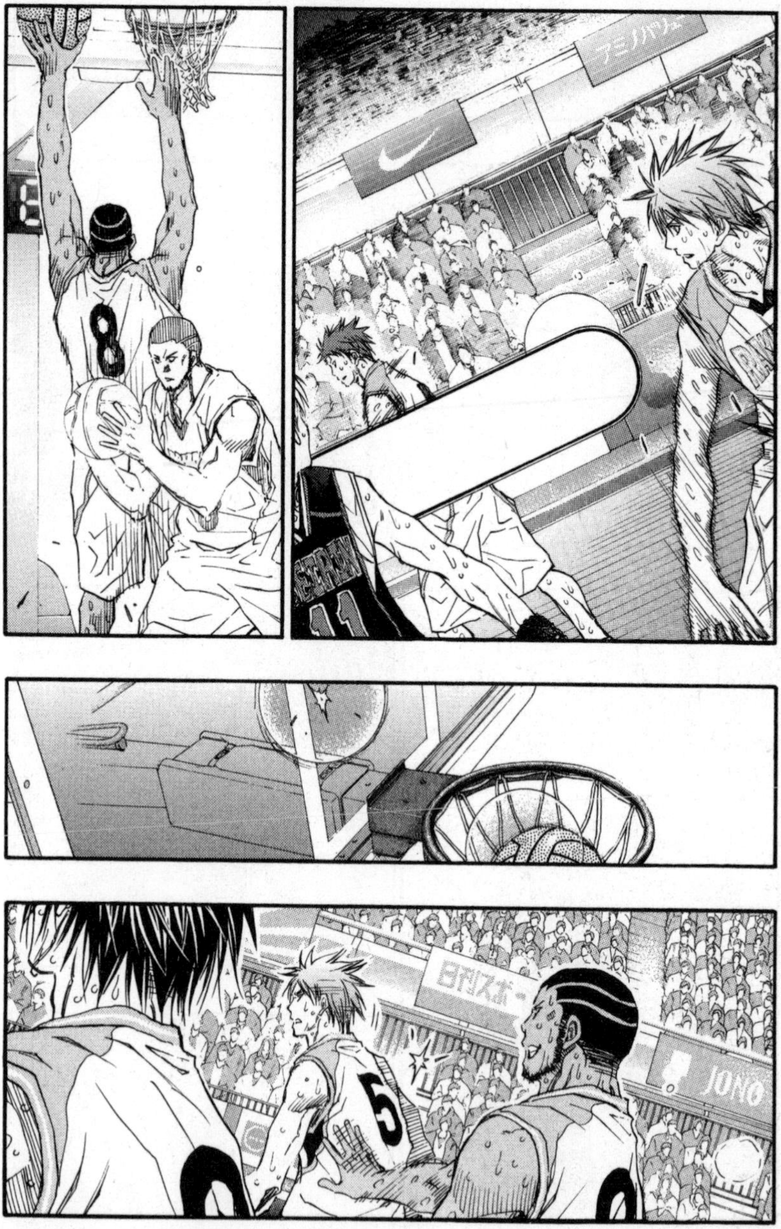
日刊スポー
JONO

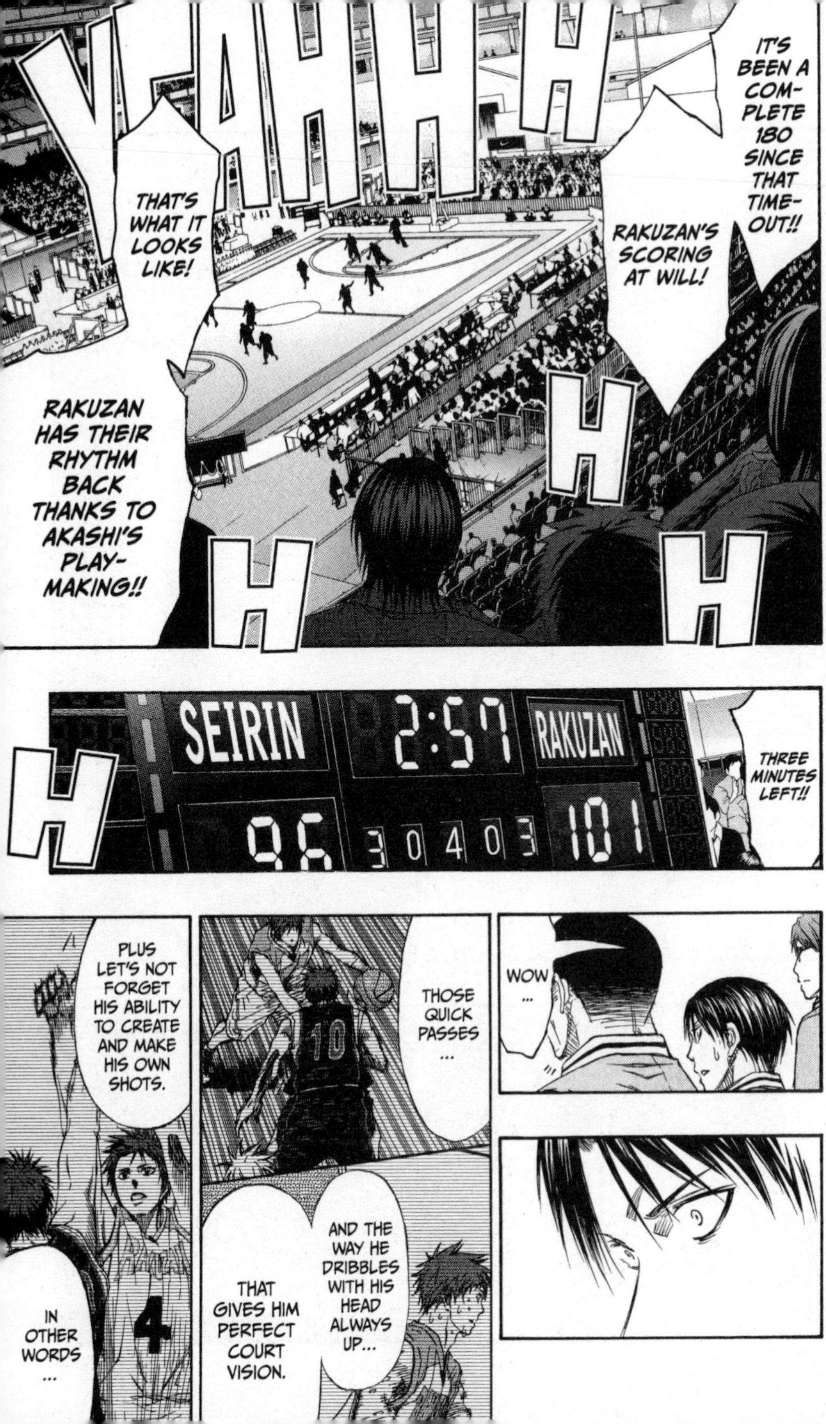
IT'S BEEN A COMPLETE 180 SINCE THAT TIME-OUT!!
RAKUZAN'S SCORING AT WILL!
THAT'S WHAT IT LOOKS LIKE!
RAKUZAN HAS THEIR RHYTHM BACK THANKS TO AKASHI'S PLAY-MAKING!!
THREE MINUTES LEFT!!
SEIRIN
2:57
RAKUZAN
96
3 0 4 0 3
101
WOW ...
THOSE QUICK PASSES ...
AND THE WAY HE DRIBBLES WITH HIS HEAD ALWAYS UP...
THAT GIVES HIM PERFECT COURT VISION.
PLUS LET'S NOT FORGET HIS ABILITY TO CREATE AND MAKE HIS OWN SHOTS.
IN OTHER WORDS ...

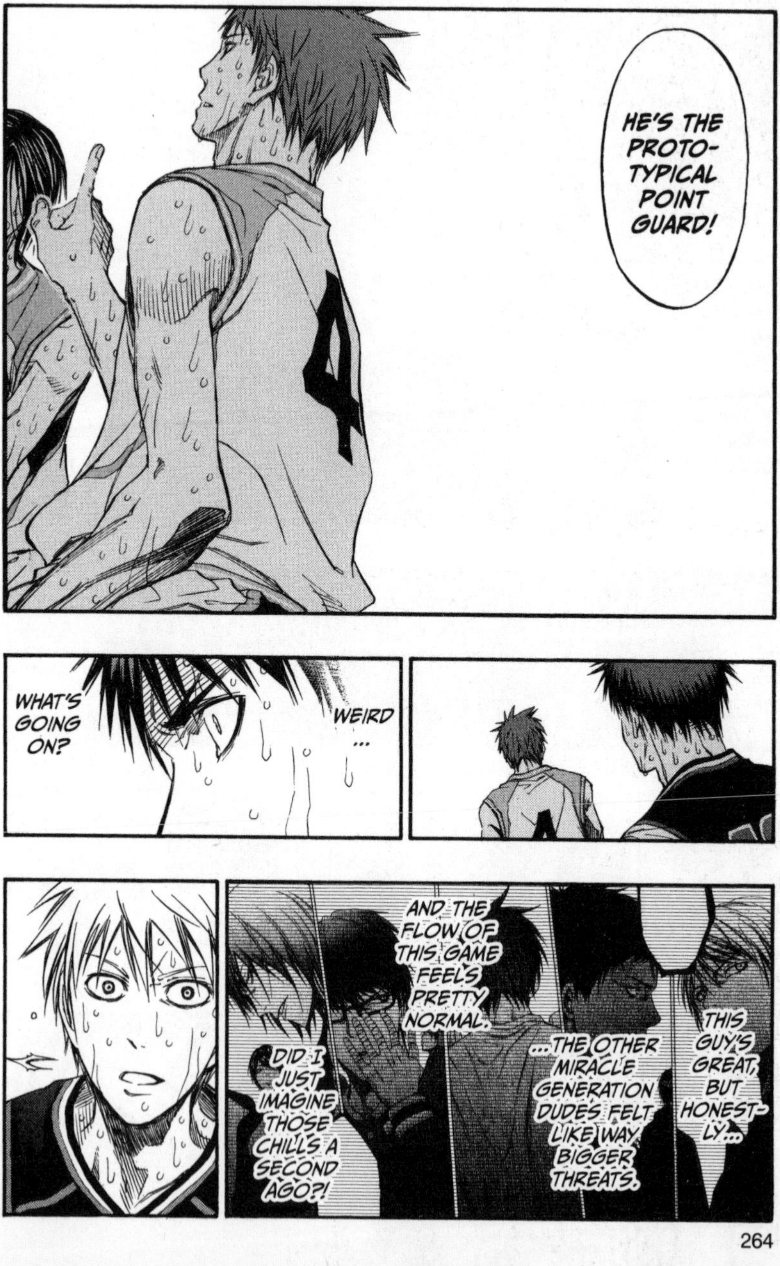
HE'S THE PROTO-TYPICAL POINT GUARD!
WEIRD ...
WHAT'S GOING ON?
THIS GUY'S GREAT, BUT HONEST-LY...
...THE OTHER MIRACLE GENERATION DUDES FELT LIKE WAY BIGGER THREATS.
AND THE FLOW OF THIS GAME FEELS PRETTY NORMAL.
DID I JUST IMAGINE THOSE CHILLS A SECOND AGO?!

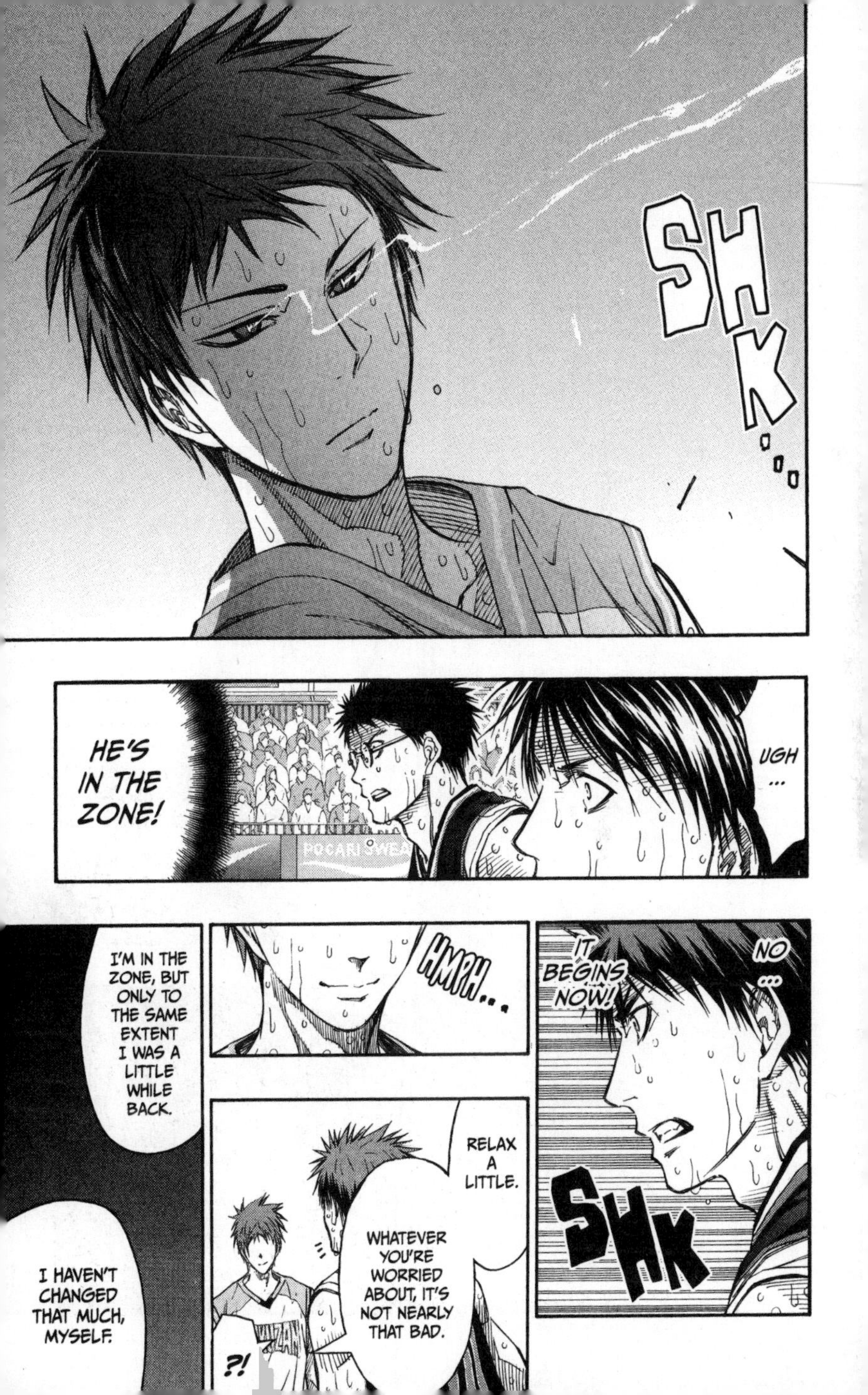
SHK...
UGH...
HE'S IN THE ZONE!
POCARI SWEA
NO...
IT BEGINS NOW!
SHK
HMPH...
RELAX A LITTLE.
WHATEVER YOU'RE WORRIED ABOUT, IT'S NOT NEARLY THAT BAD.
?!
I'M IN THE ZONE, BUT ONLY TO THE SAME EXTENT I WAS A LITTLE WHILE BACK.
I HAVEN'T CHANGED THAT MUCH, MYSELF.

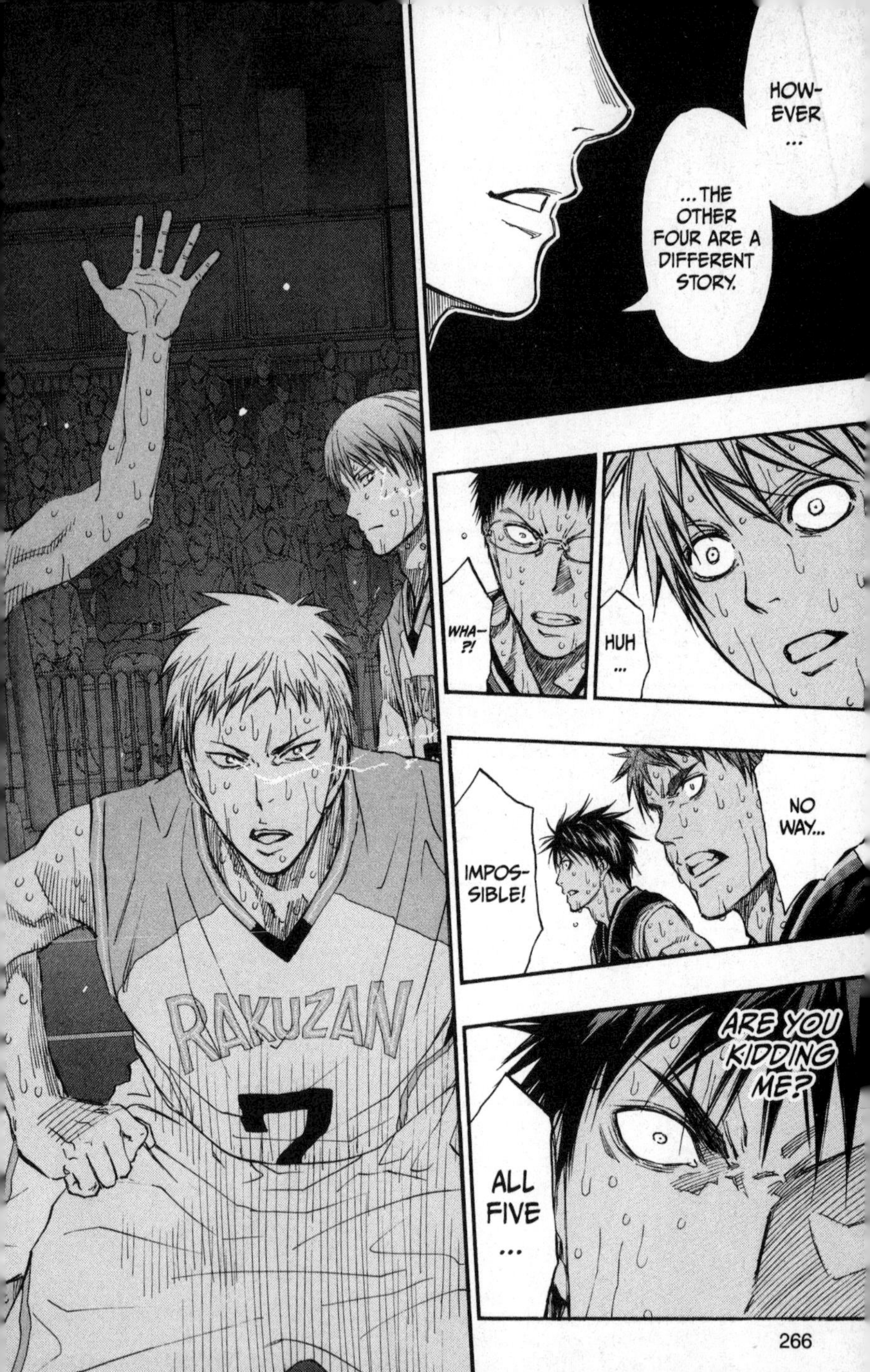
HOW-EVER...
...THE OTHER FOUR ARE A DIFFERENT STORY.
HUH...
WHA-?!
NO WAY...
IMPOSSIBLE!
ARE YOU KIDDING ME?
ALL FIVE...

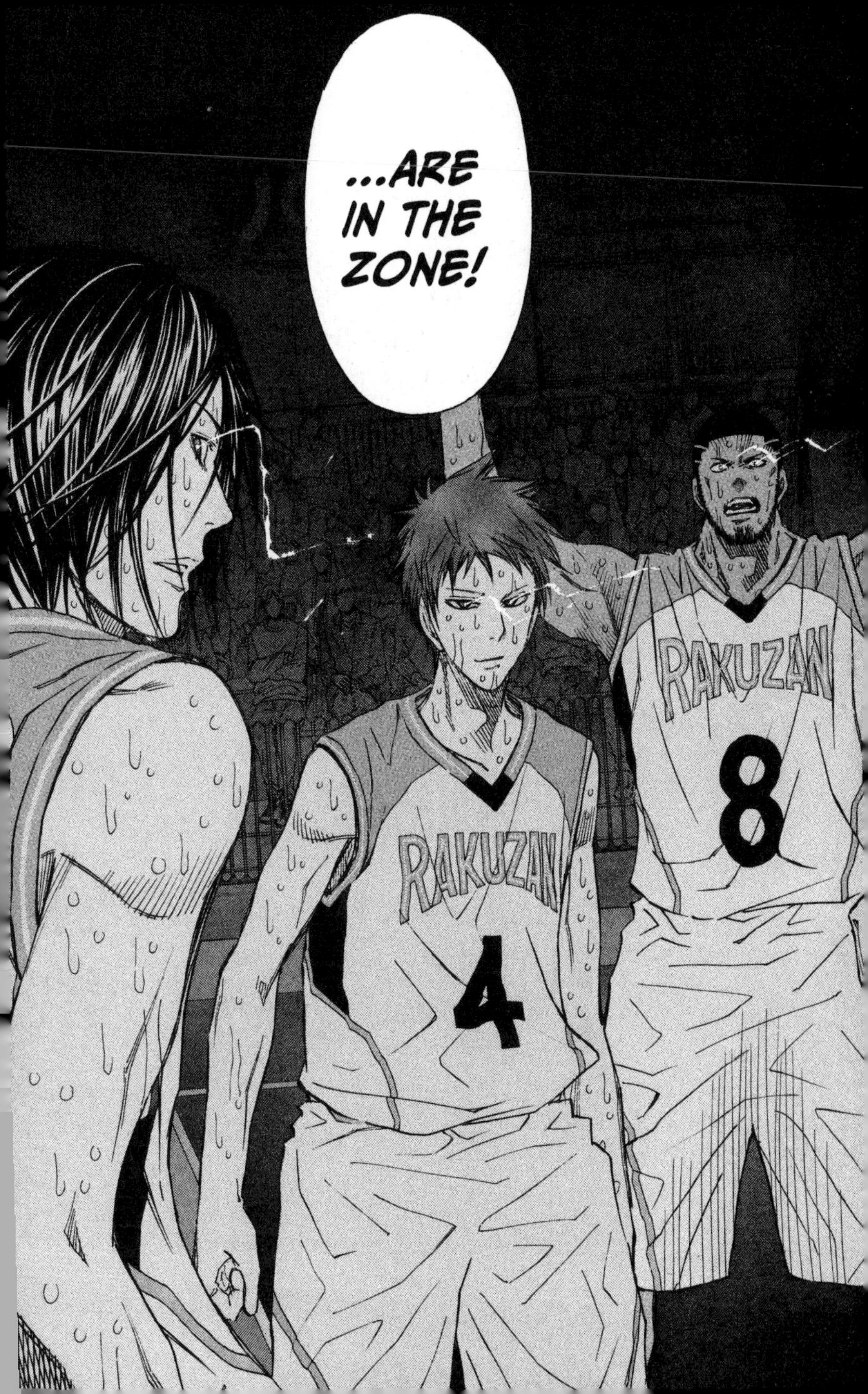
...ARE IN THE ZONE!
RAKUZAN
8
RAKUZAN
4

KUROKO'S BASKETBALL

Q&A

W/ HALFWAY-DECENT ANSWERS

Q. **THE MIRACLE GENERATION BOYS EACH HAVE THEIR OWN TALENTS IN BASKETBALL, BUT SPORTS ASIDE, WHAT ARE EACH OF THEM REALLY BAD AT?**
(LEGENDARY FOOT SOLDIER from SHIGA PREFECTURE)

A. KISE → SUCKS AT DRAWING
AOMINE → CAN'T CLEAN
AKASHI → CAN'T TELL A JOKE TO SAVE HIS LIFE
MIDORIMA → TERRIBLE AT COOKING
MURASAKIBARA → TONE-DEAF (EXCEPTION: CHARACTER THEME SONGS)

KUROKO'S BASKETBALL BLOOPERS

TAKE 1

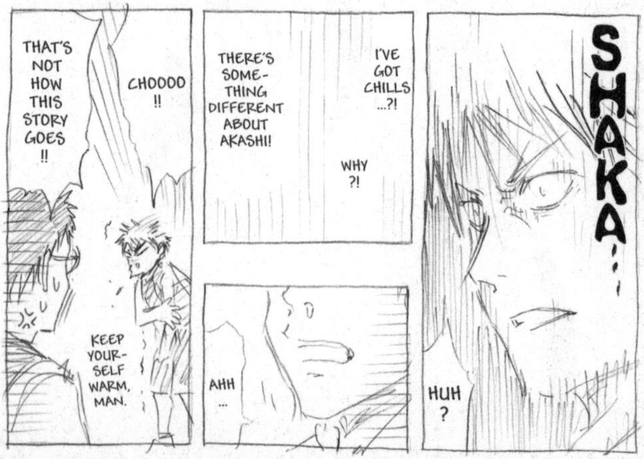
SHAKA...
HUH ?
I'VE GOT CHILLS ...?!
THERE'S SOME-THING DIFFERENT ABOUT AKASHI!
WHY ?!
AHH ...
CHOOOO !!
THAT'S NOT HOW THIS STORY GOES !!
KEEP YOUR-SELF WARM, MAN.

268TH QUARTER: WHAT'S SEIRIN'S MOVE?

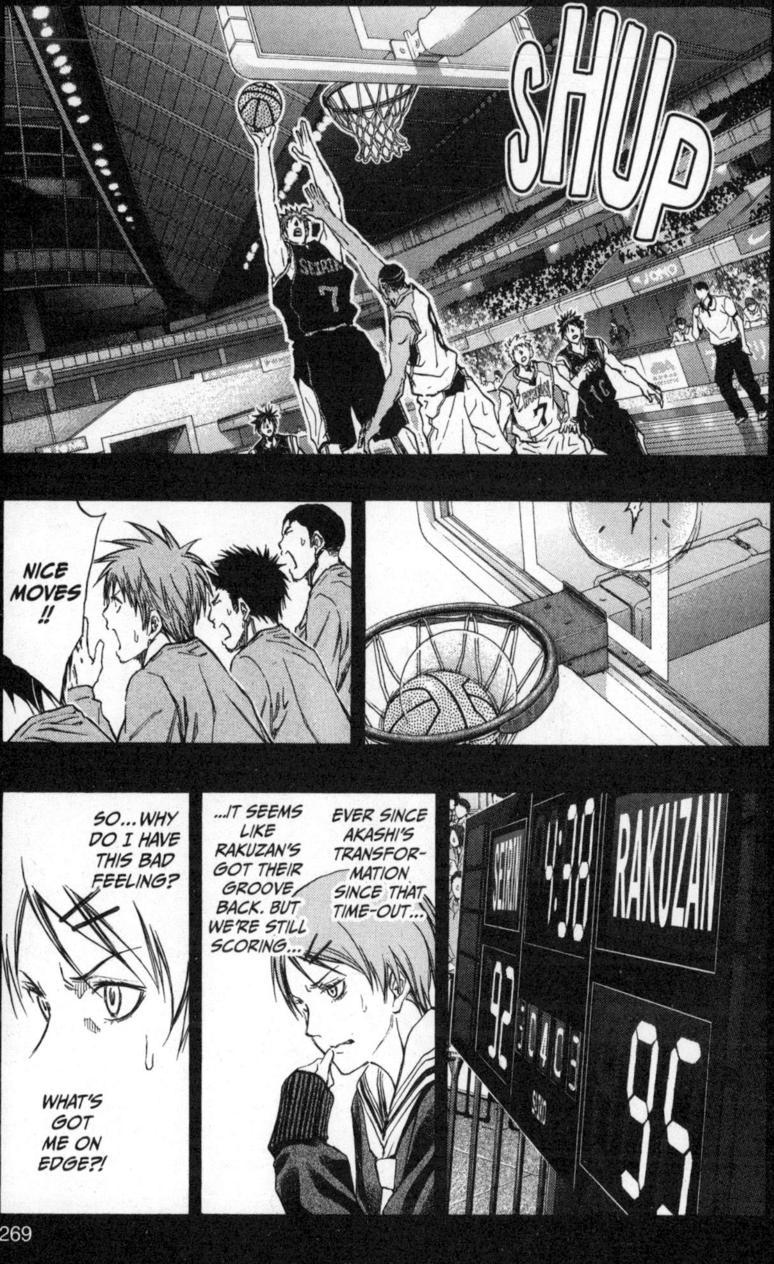
SHUP
NICE MOVES!!
SEIRIN
RAKUZAN
92
95
EVER SINCE AKASHI'S TRANSFORMATION SINCE THAT TIME-OUT...
...IT SEEMS LIKE RAKUZAN'S GOT THEIR GROOVE BACK. BUT WE'RE STILL SCORING...
SO... WHY DO I HAVE THIS BAD FEELING?
WHAT'S GOT ME ON EDGE?!

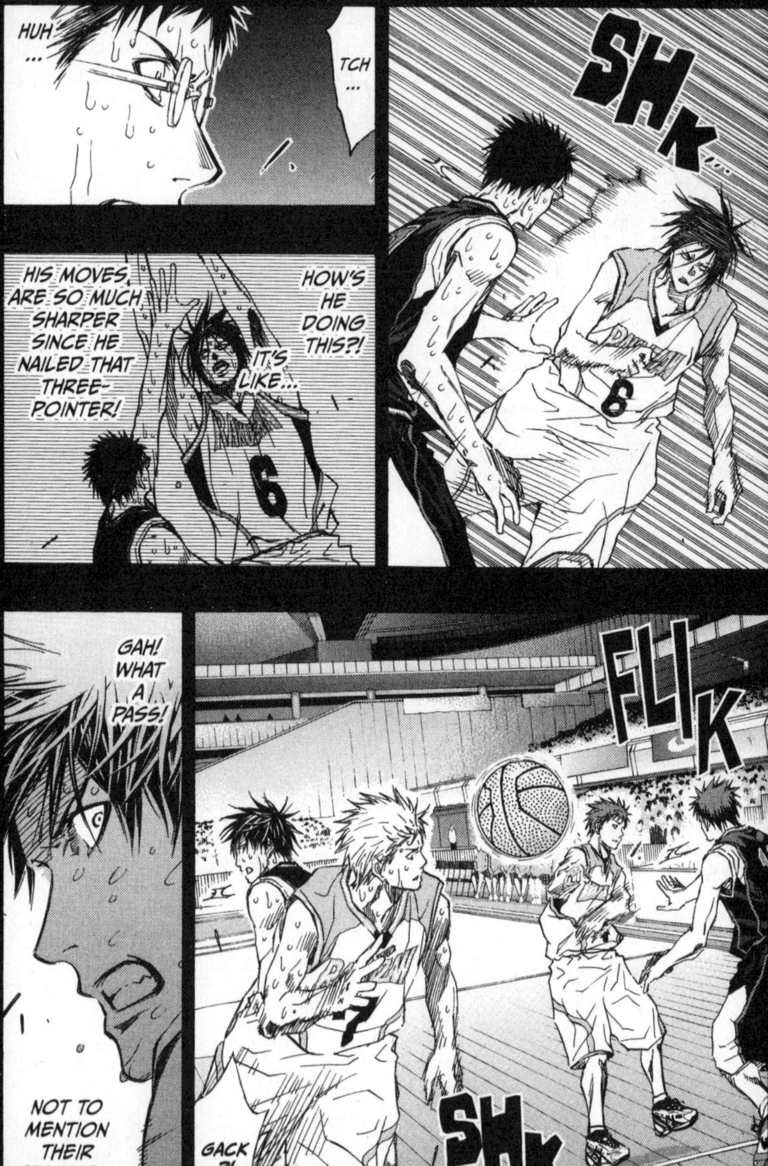
SHK...
TCH...
HUH...
HOW'S HE DOING THIS?!
IT'S LIKE...
HIS MOVES ARE SO MUCH SHARPER SINCE HE NAILED THAT THREE-POINTER!
FLIK
SHK
GACK?!
GAH! WHAT A PASS!
NOT TO MENTION THEIR SPACING...

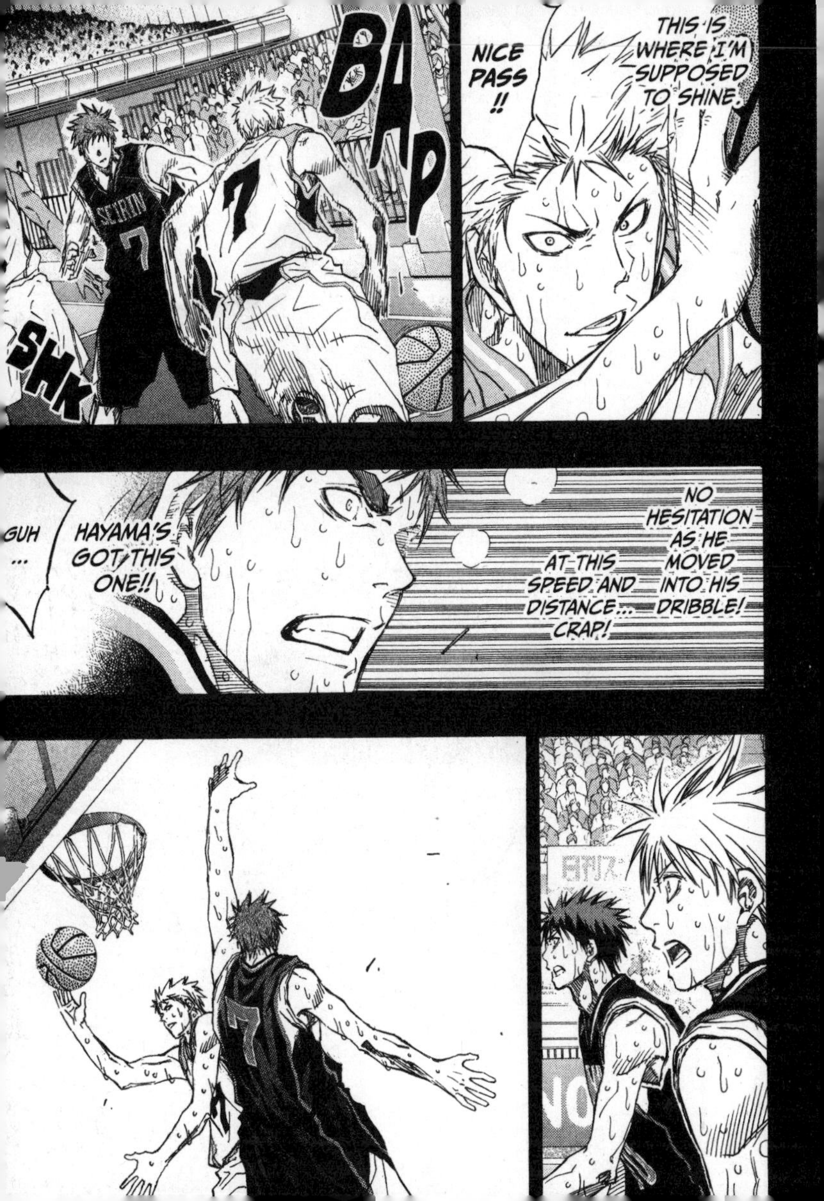
THIS IS WHERE I'M SUPPOSED TO SHINE.
NICE PASS!!
BAP
SHK
NO HESITATION AS HE MOVED INTO HIS DRIBBLE!
AT THIS SPEED AND DISTANCE... CRAP!
HAYAMA'S GOT THIS ONE!!
GUH ...

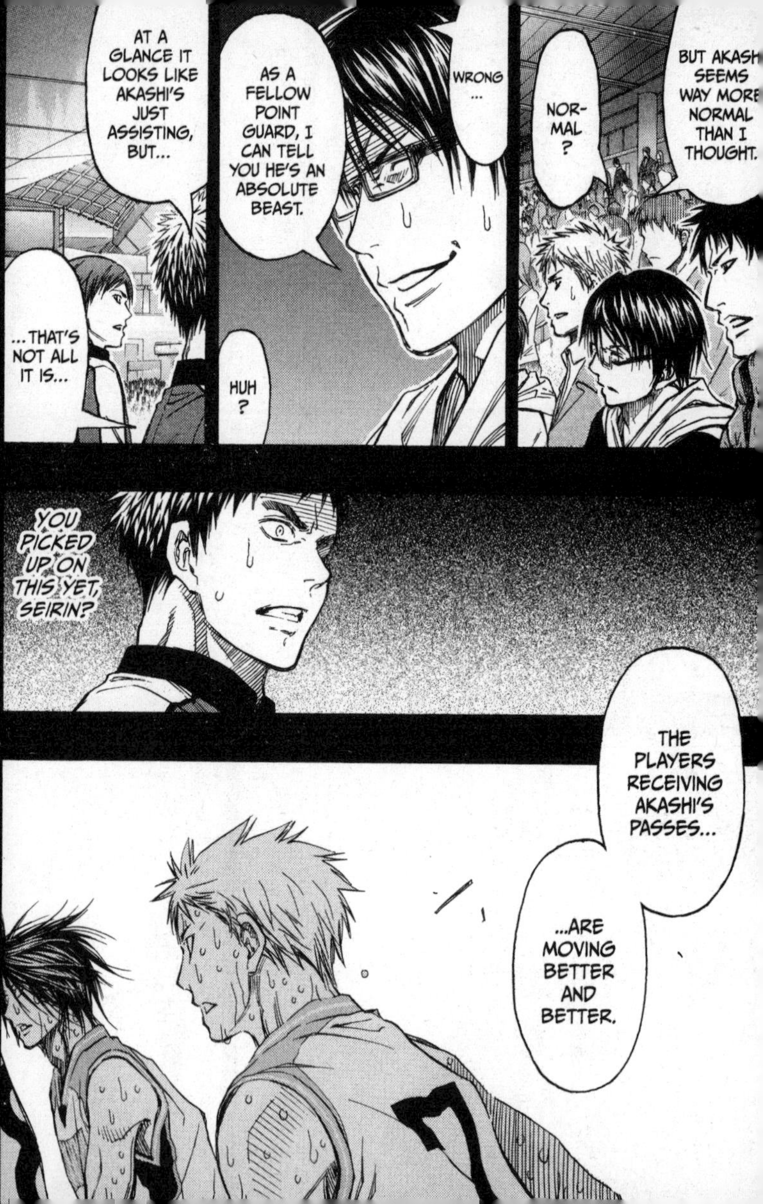
BUT AKASH SEEMS WAY MORE NORMAL THAN I THOUGHT.
NOR-MAL?
WRONG...
AS A FELLOW POINT GUARD, I CAN TELL YOU HE'S AN ABSOLUTE BEAST.
HUH?
AT A GLANCE IT LOOKS LIKE AKASHI'S JUST ASSISTING, BUT...
...THAT'S NOT ALL IT IS...
YOU PICKED UP ON THIS YET, SEIRIN?
THE PLAYERS RECEIVING AKASHI'S PASSES...
...ARE MOVING BETTER AND BETTER.

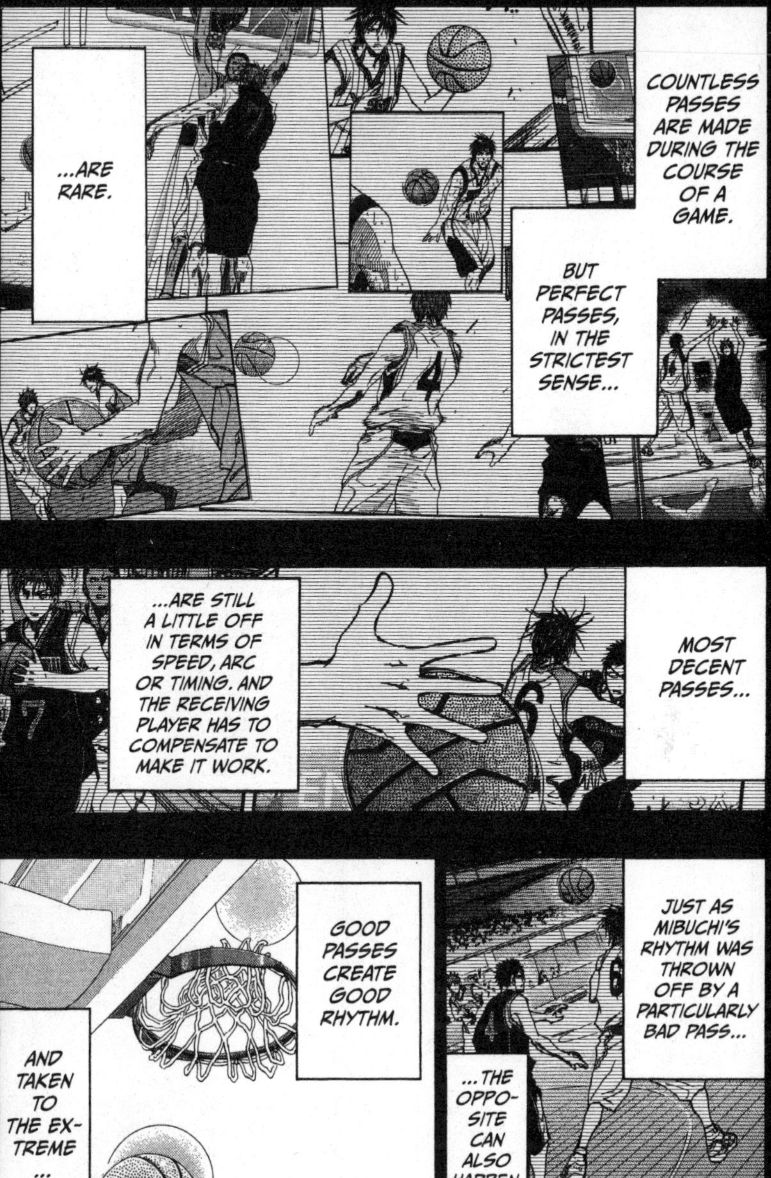
COUNTLESS PASSES ARE MADE DURING THE COURSE OF A GAME.
BUT PERFECT PASSES, IN THE STRICTEST SENSE...
...ARE RARE.
MOST DECENT PASSES...
...ARE STILL A LITTLE OFF IN TERMS OF SPEED, ARC OR TIMING. AND THE RECEIVING PLAYER HAS TO COMPENSATE TO MAKE IT WORK.
JUST AS MIBUCHI'S RHYTHM WAS THROWN OFF BY A PARTICULARLY BAD PASS...
...THE OPPO-SITE CAN ALSO HAPPEN.
GOOD PASSES CREATE GOOD RHYTHM.
AND TAKEN TO THE EX-TREME ...

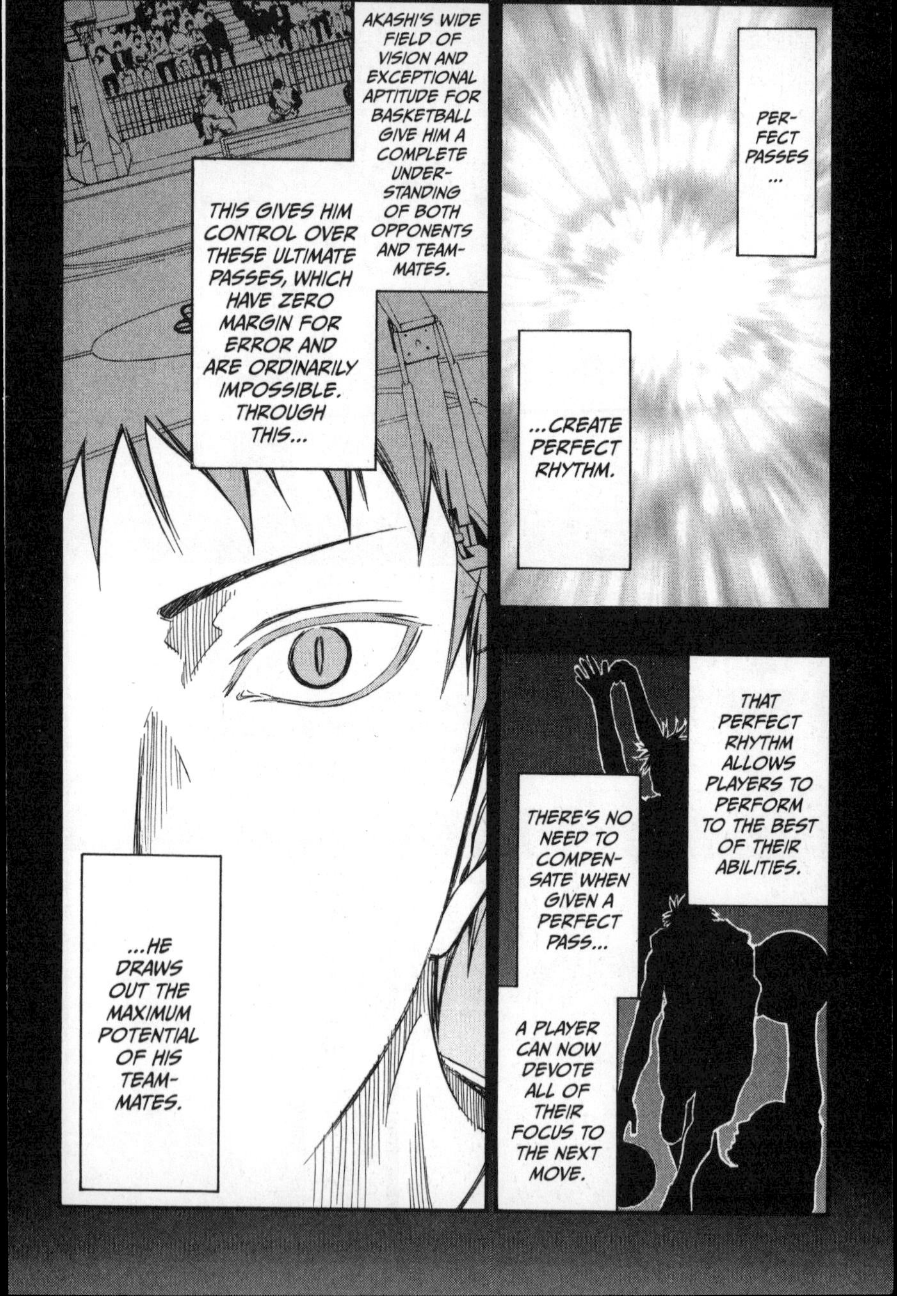
PER-FECT PASSES...
...CREATE PERFECT RHYTHM.
THAT PERFECT RHYTHM ALLOWS PLAYERS TO PERFORM TO THE BEST OF THEIR ABILITIES.
THERE'S NO NEED TO COMPEN-SATE WHEN GIVEN A PERFECT PASS...
A PLAYER CAN NOW DEVOTE ALL OF THEIR FOCUS TO THE NEXT MOVE.
AKASHI'S WIDE FIELD OF VISION AND EXCEPTIONAL APTITUDE FOR BASKETBALL GIVE HIM A COMPLETE UNDER-STANDING OF BOTH OPPONENTS AND TEAM-MATES.
THIS GIVES HIM CONTROL OVER THESE ULTIMATE PASSES, WHICH HAVE ZERO MARGIN FOR ERROR AND ARE ORDINARILY IMPOSSIBLE. THROUGH THIS...
...HE DRAWS OUT THE MAXIMUM POTENTIAL OF HIS TEAM-MATES.

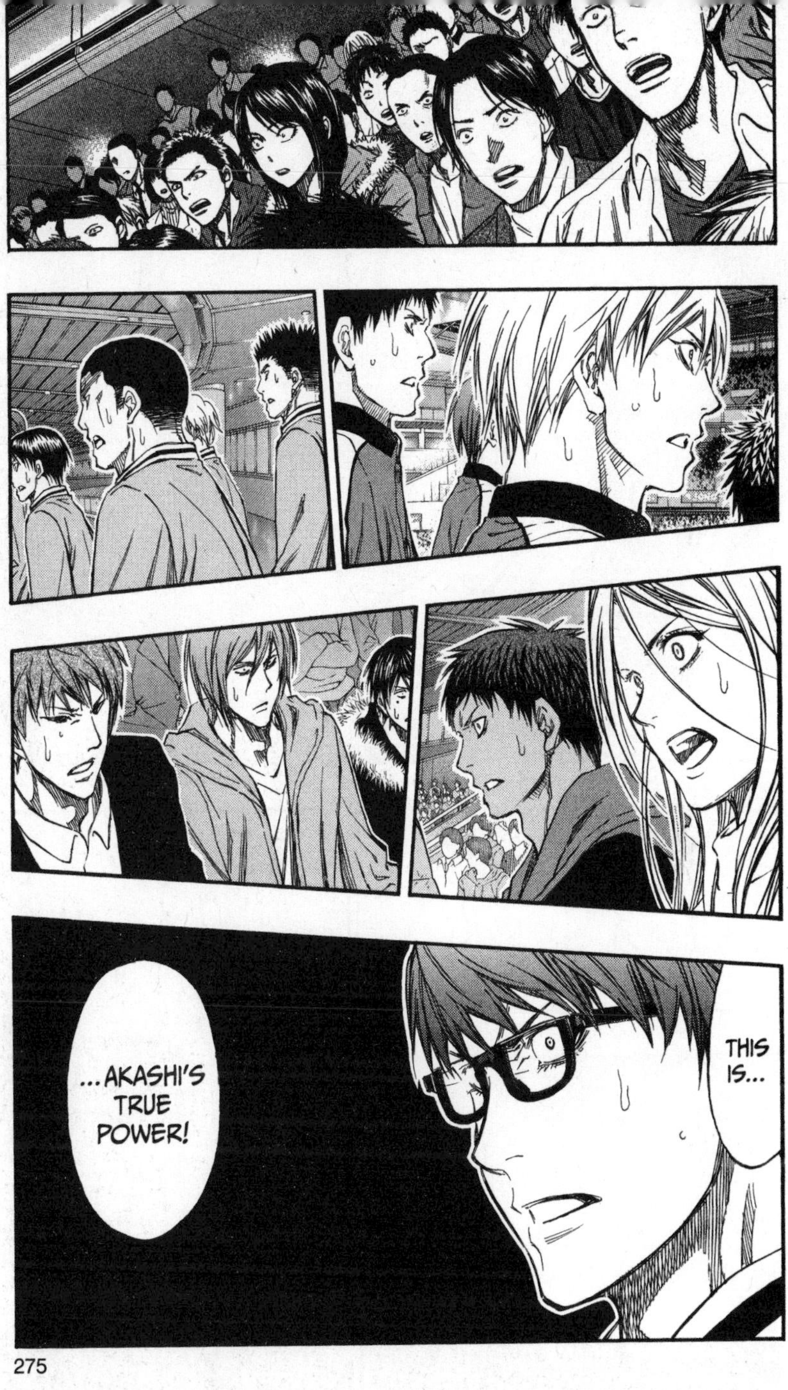
THIS IS...
...AKASHI'S TRUE POWER!

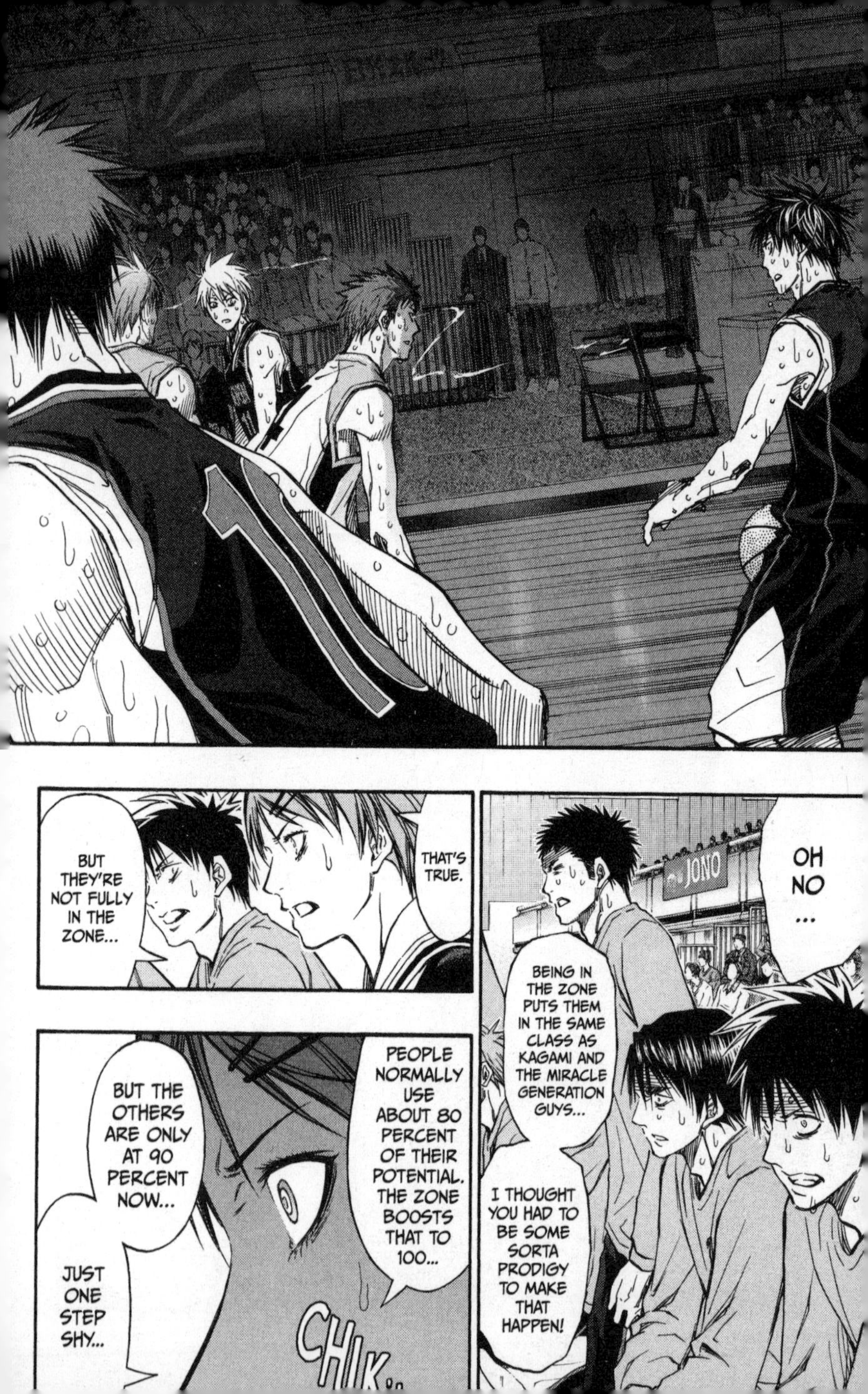

JONO
OH NO ...
BEING IN THE ZONE PUTS THEM IN THE SAME CLASS AS KAGAMI AND THE MIRACLE GENERATION GUYS...
I THOUGHT YOU HAD TO BE SOME SORTA PRODIGY TO MAKE THAT HAPPEN!
THAT'S TRUE.
BUT THEY'RE NOT FULLY IN THE ZONE...
PEOPLE NORMALLY USE ABOUT 80 PERCENT OF THEIR POTENTIAL. THE ZONE BOOSTS THAT TO 100...
BUT THE OTHERS ARE ONLY AT 90 PERCENT NOW...
JUST ONE STEP SHY...
CHIK..

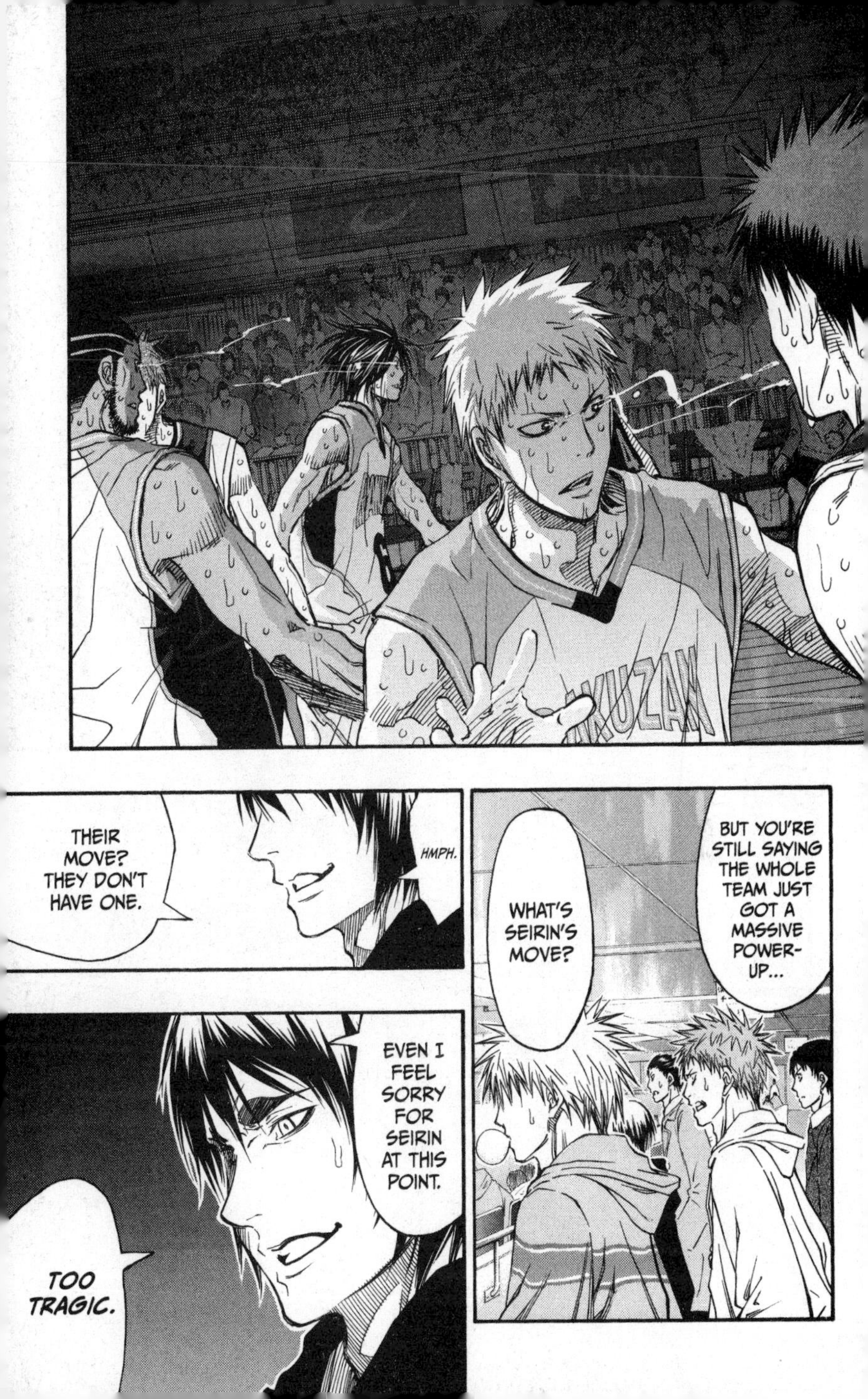
BUT YOU'RE STILL SAYING THE WHOLE TEAM JUST GOT A MASSIVE POWER-UP...
WHAT'S SEIRIN'S MOVE?
HMPH.
THEIR MOVE? THEY DON'T HAVE ONE.
EVEN I FEEL SORRY FOR SEIRIN AT THIS POINT.
TOO TRAGIC.

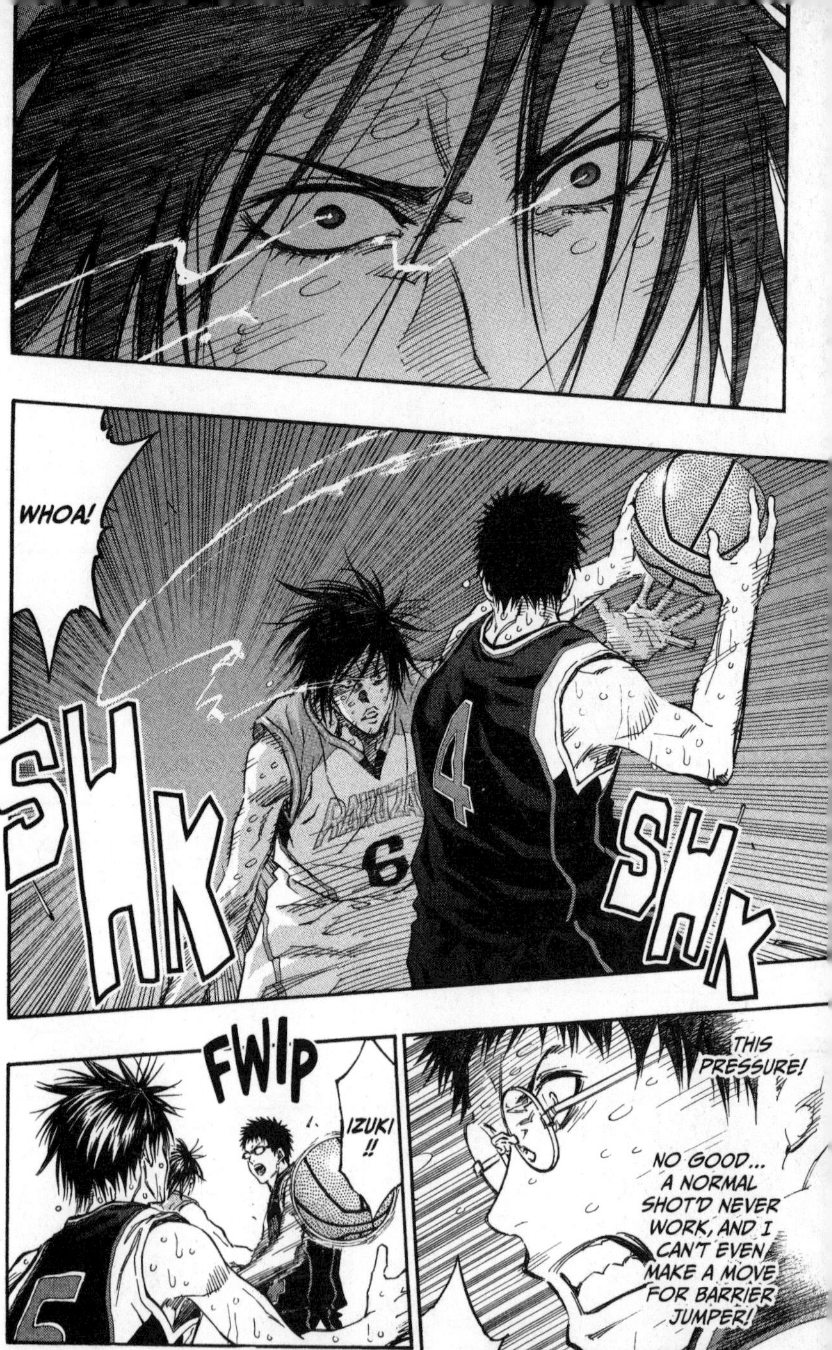
WHOA!
SHK
SHK
THIS PRESSURE!
NO GOOD... A NORMAL SHOT'D NEVER WORK, AND I CAN'T EVEN MAKE A MOVE FOR BARRIER JUMPER!
GUH...
FWIP
IZUKI!!

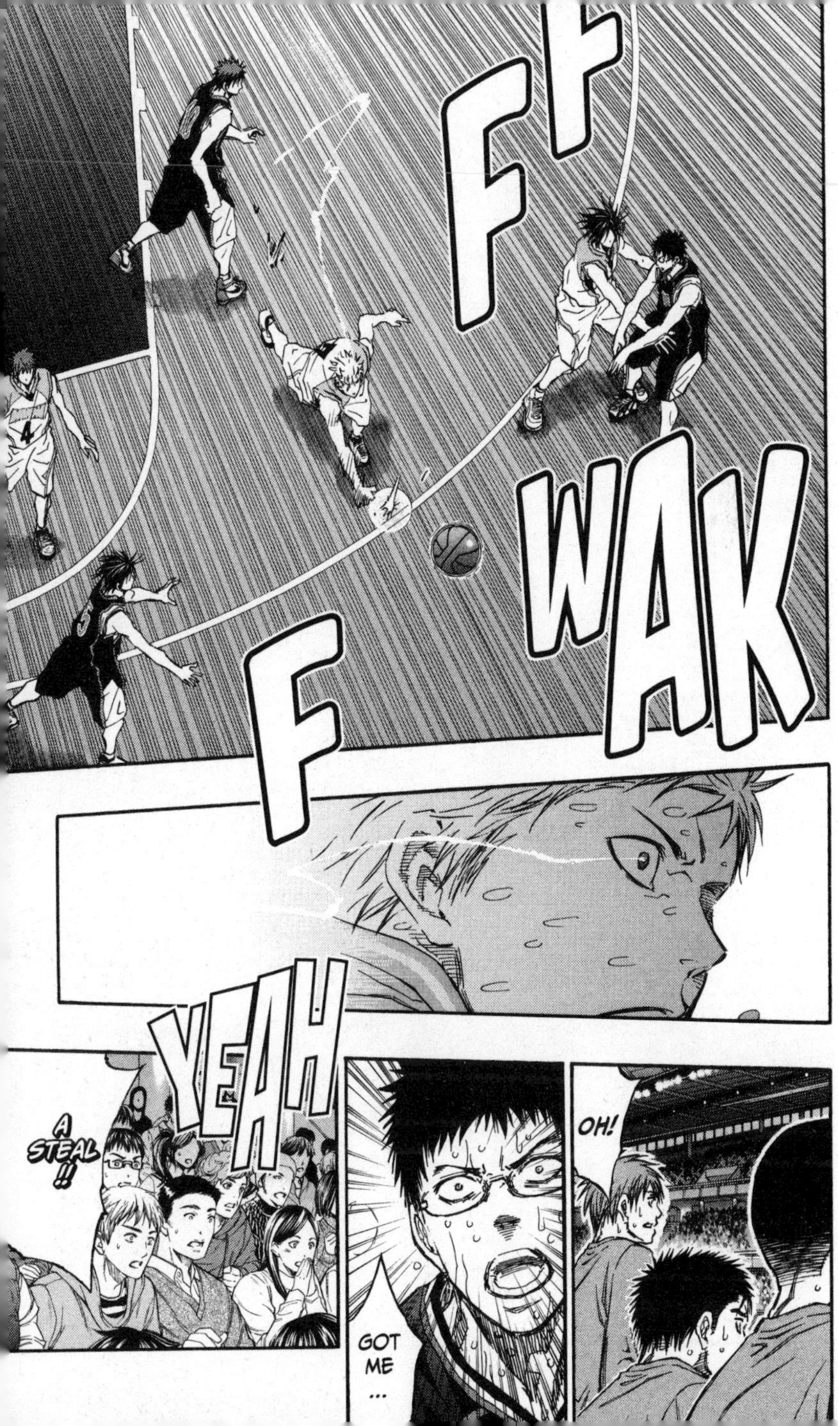
FF
FWAK
OH!
GOT ME ...
YEAH
A STEAL !!

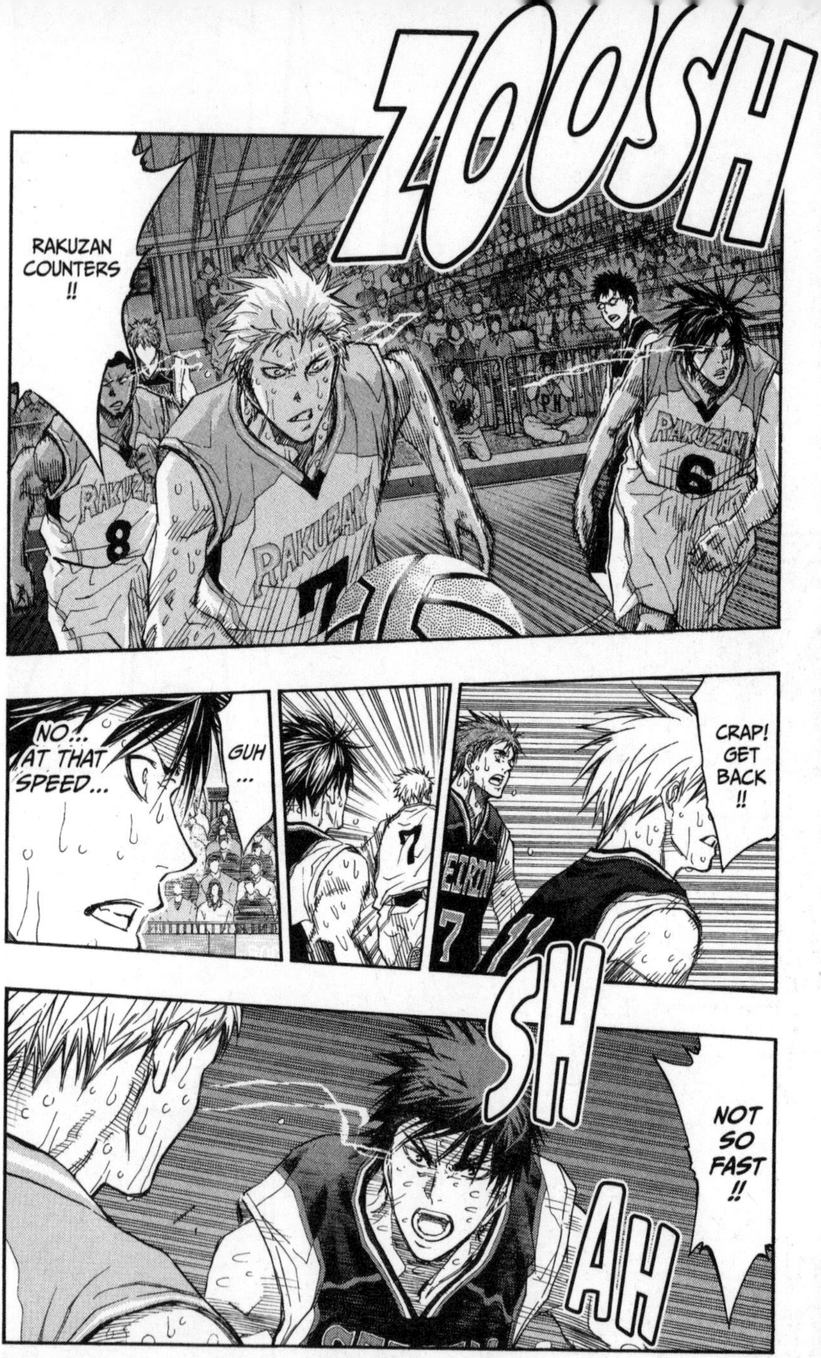
ZOOSH
RAKUZAN COUNTERS !!
CRAP! GET BACK !!
GUH ...
NO... AT THAT SPEED...
SH
NOT SO FAST !!
AH

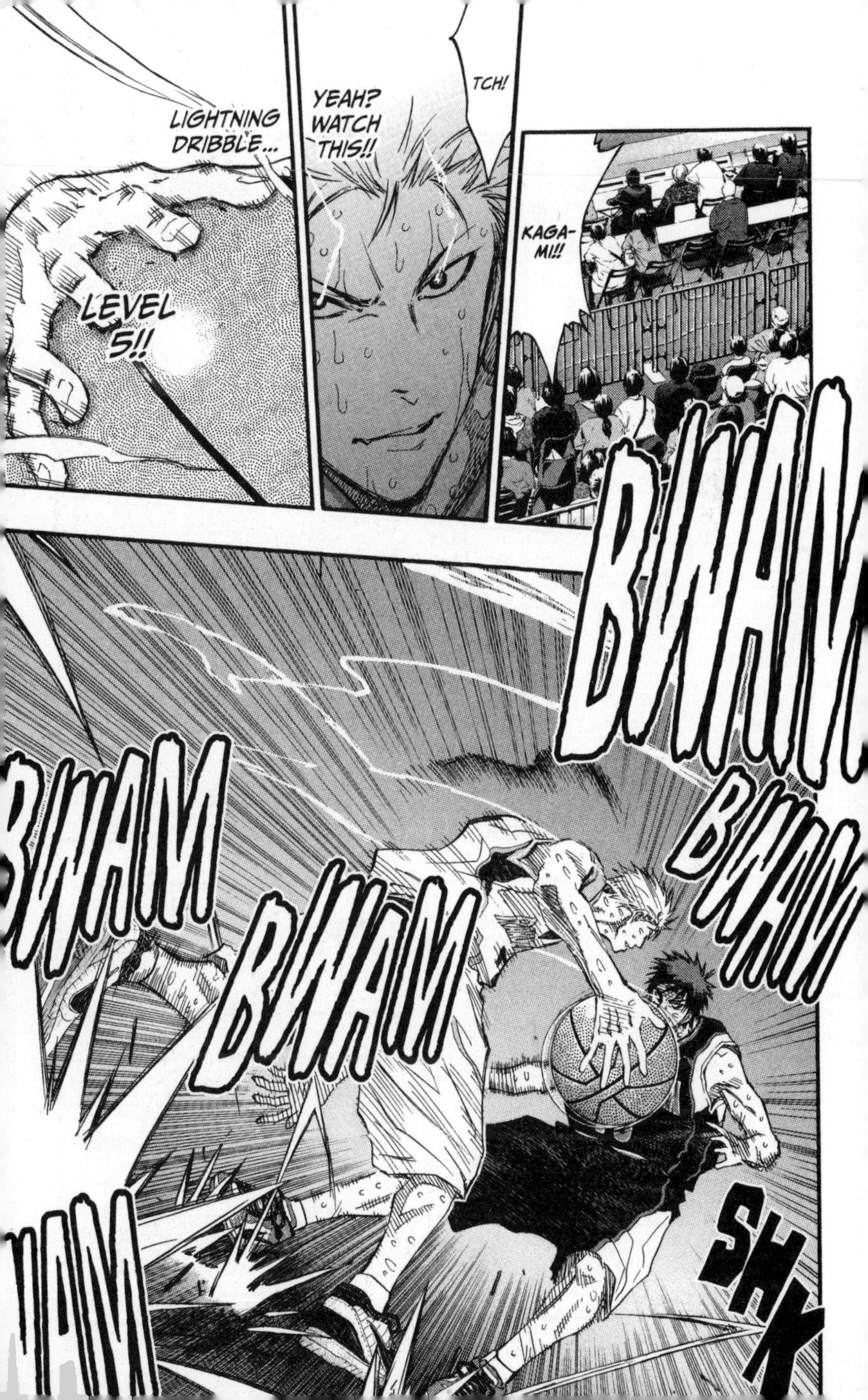
KAGA-
MI!!
TCH!
YEAH?
WATCH
THIS!!
LIGHTNING
DRIBBLE...
LEVEL
5!!
BWAM
BWAM
BWAM
BWAM
SHK

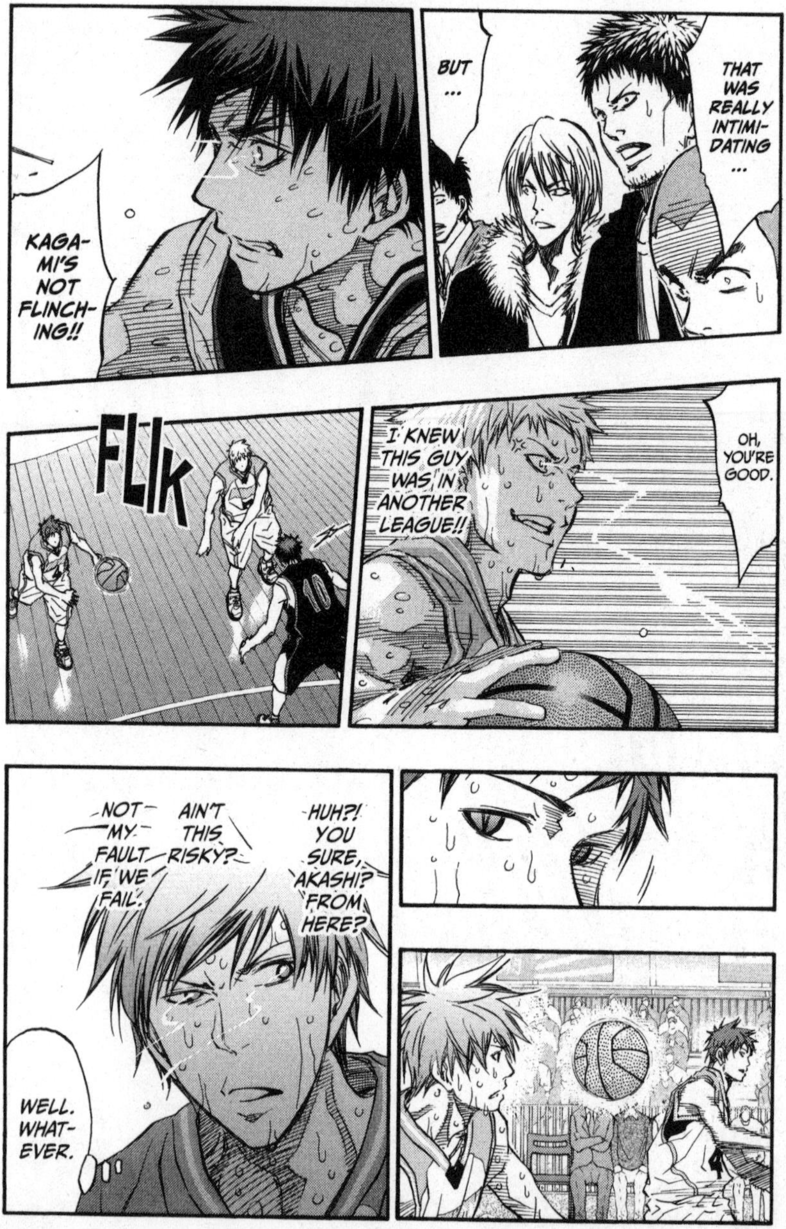
THAT WAS REALLY INTIMIDATING ...
BUT ...
KAGAMI'S NOT FLINCHING!!
OH, YOU'RE GOOD.
I KNEW THIS GUY WAS IN ANOTHER LEAGUE!!
FLIK
HUH?! YOU SURE, AKASHI? FROM HERE?
AIN'T THIS RISKY?
NOT MY FAULT IF WE FAIL.
WELL. WHATEVER.

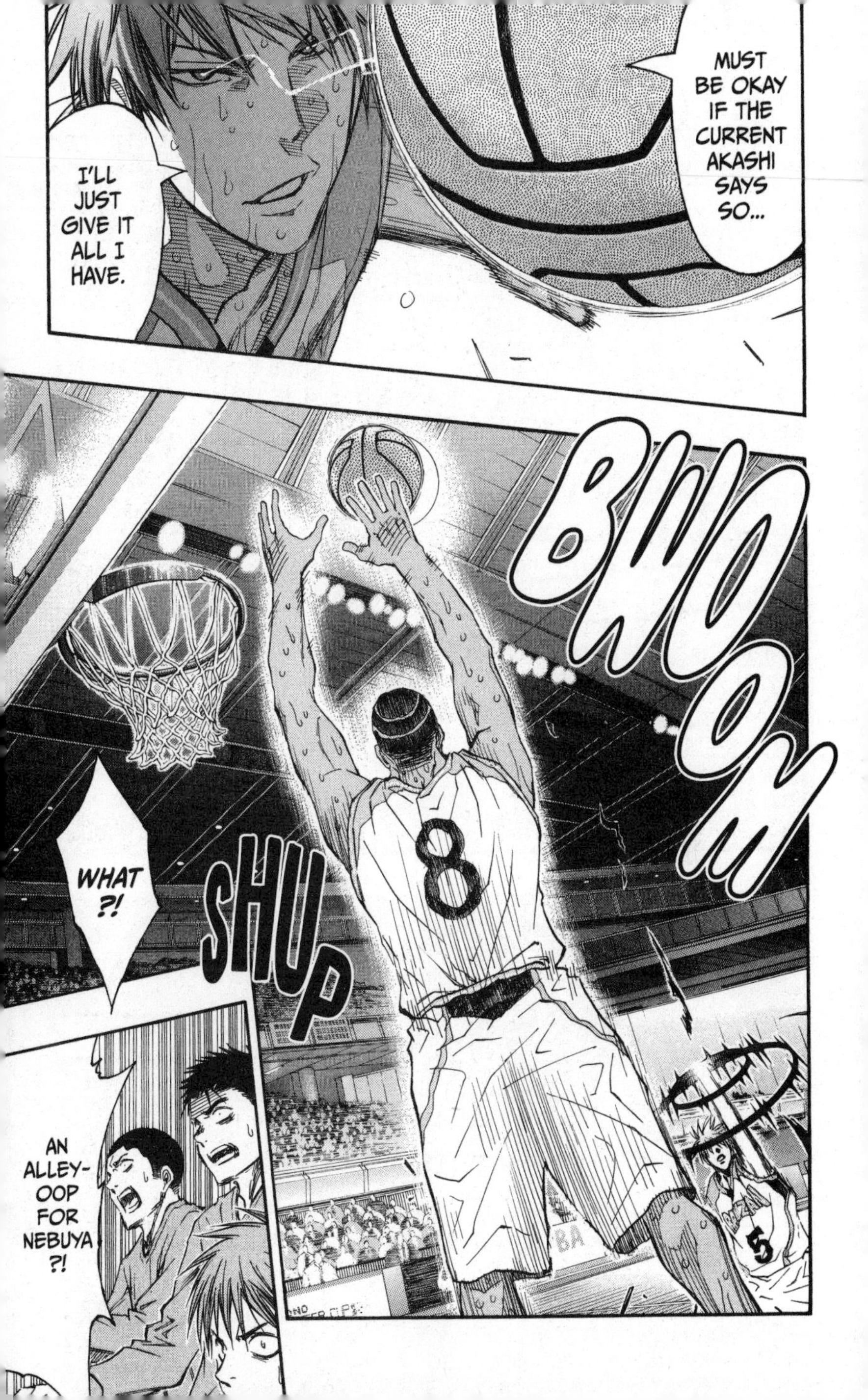
MUST BE OKAY IF THE CURRENT AKASHI SAYS SO...
I'LL JUST GIVE IT ALL I HAVE.
BWOOM
SHUP
WHAT?!
AN ALLEY-OOP FOR NEBUYA?!

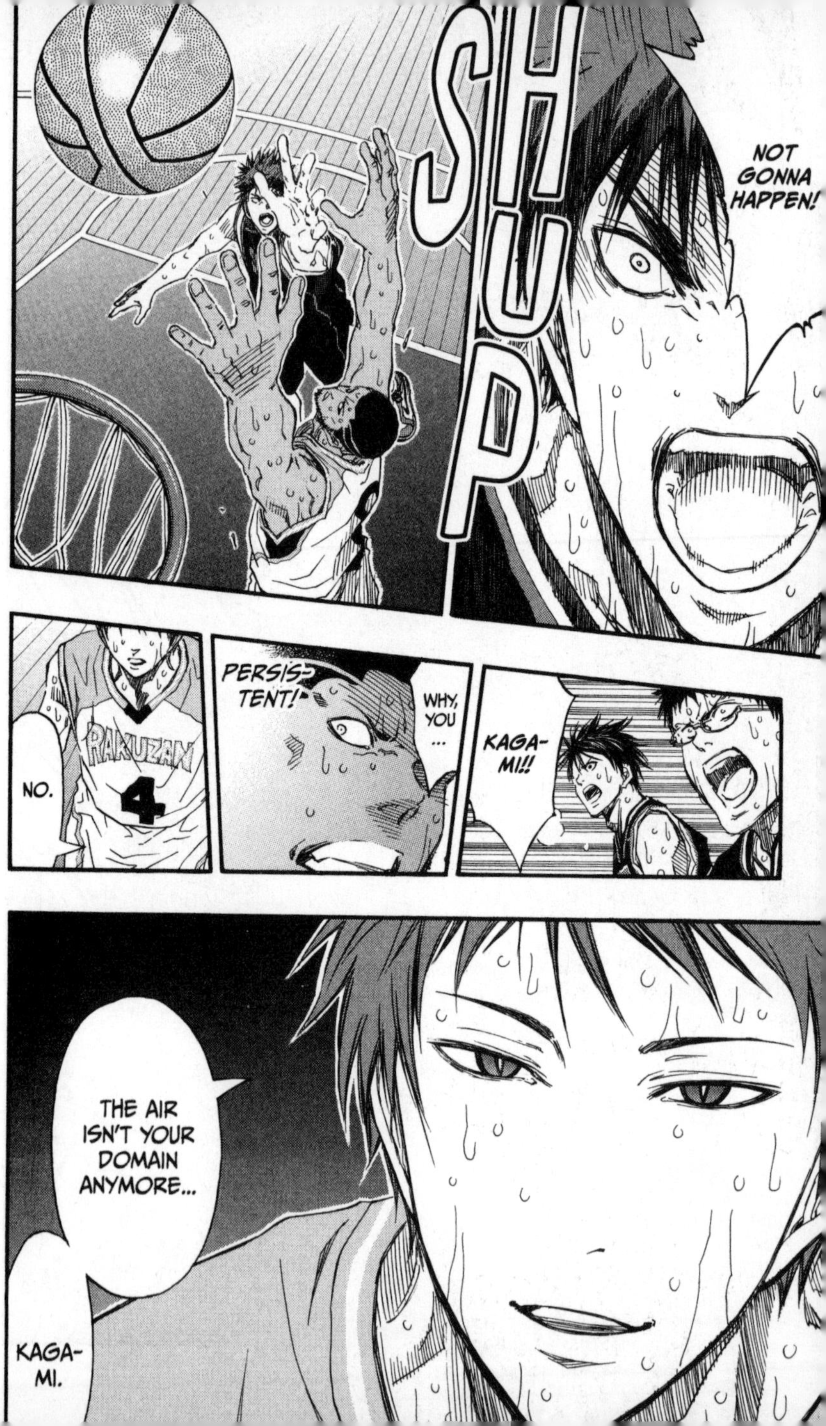
NOT GONNA HAPPEN!
SHUP
KAGA-MI!!
WHY, YOU ...
PERSIS-TENT!
NO.
THE AIR ISN'T YOUR DOMAIN ANYMORE...
KAGA-MI.

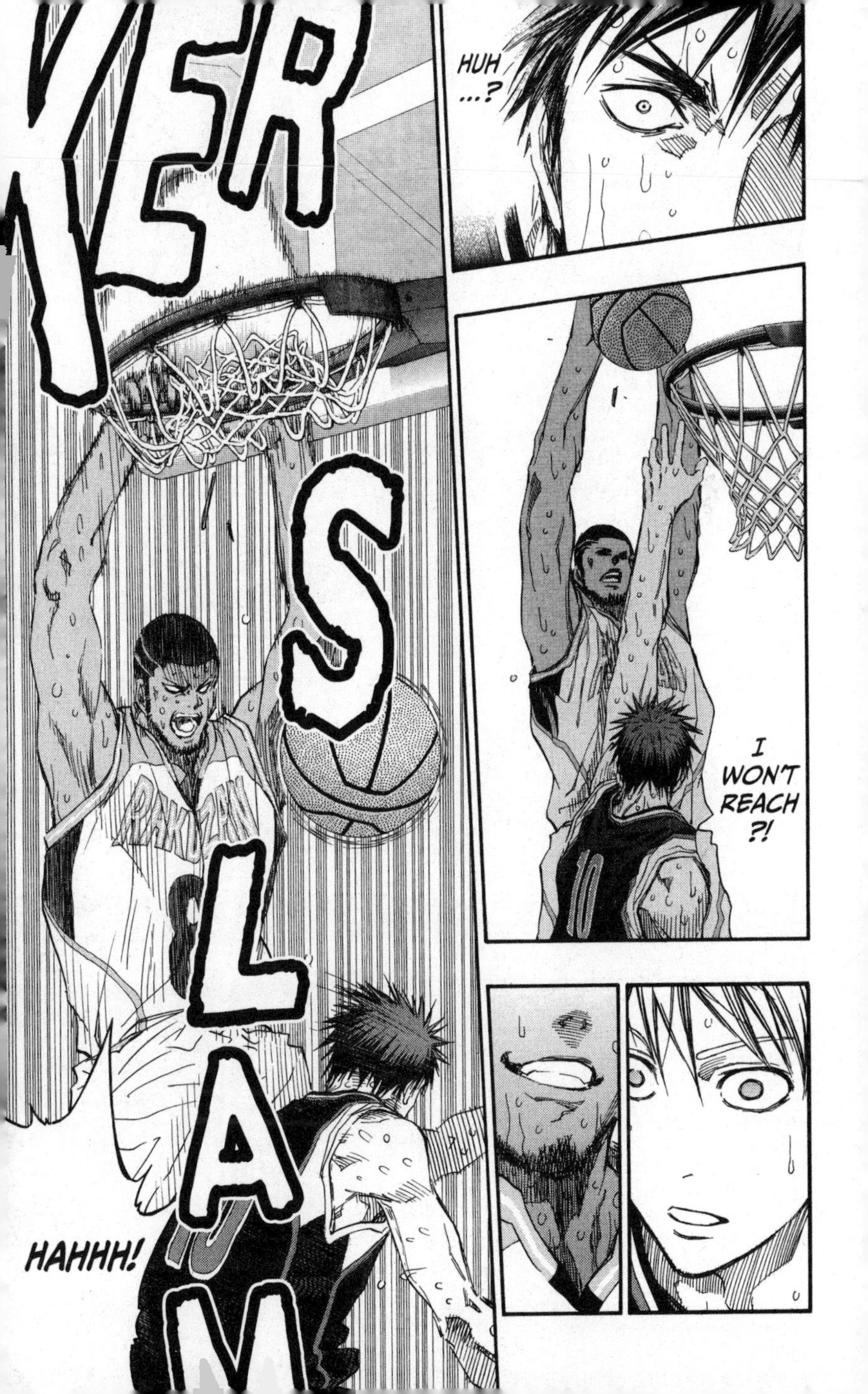
HUH ...?
I WON'T REACH ?!
SLAM
HAHHH!

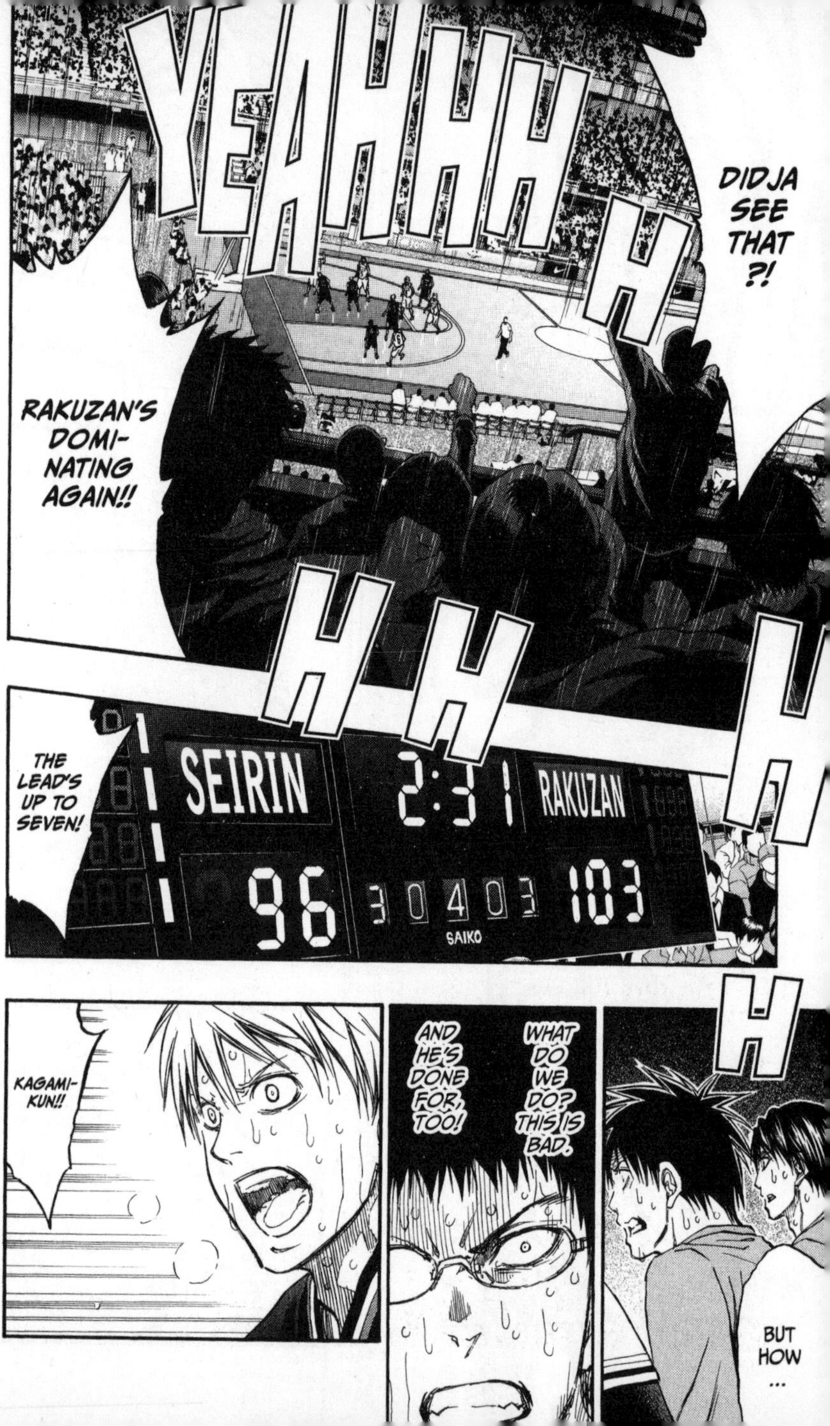
YEAHHHHHHHHHH
DIDJA SEE THAT?!
RAKUZAN'S DOMINATING AGAIN!!
THE LEAD'S UP TO SEVEN!
SEIRIN
2:31
RAKUZAN
96
103
SAIKO
BUT HOW...
WHAT DO WE DO? THIS IS BAD.
AND HE'S DONE FOR, TOO!
KAGAMI-KUN!!

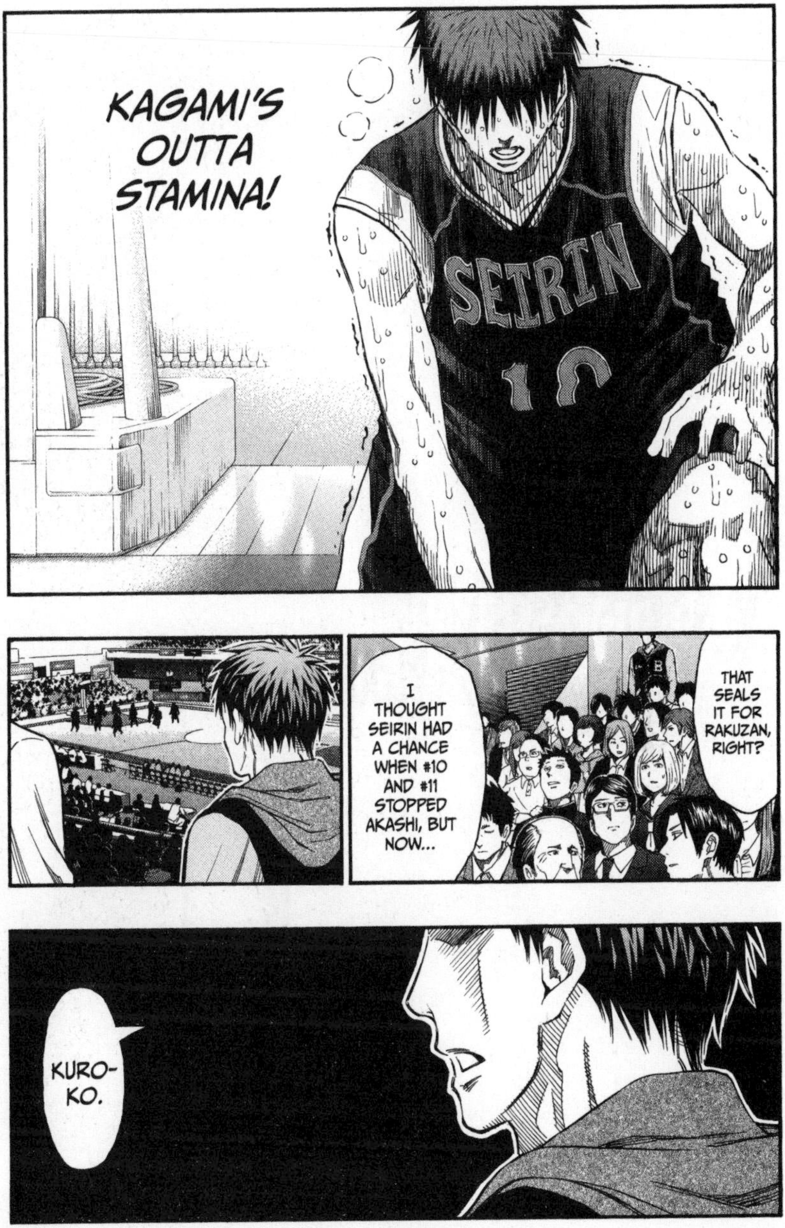
KAGAMI'S OUTTA STAMINA!
SEIRIN 10
THAT SEALS IT FOR RAKUZAN, RIGHT?
I THOUGHT SEIRIN HAD A CHANCE WHEN #10 AND #11 STOPPED AKASHI, BUT NOW...
KURO-KO.

KUROKO'S BASKETBALL BLOOPERS

TAKE 7

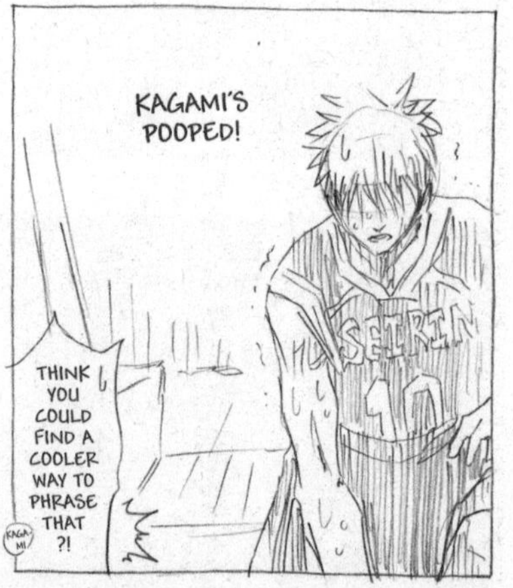
KAGAMI'S POOPED!
THINK YOU COULD FIND A COOLER WAY TO PHRASE THAT?!
KAGAMI

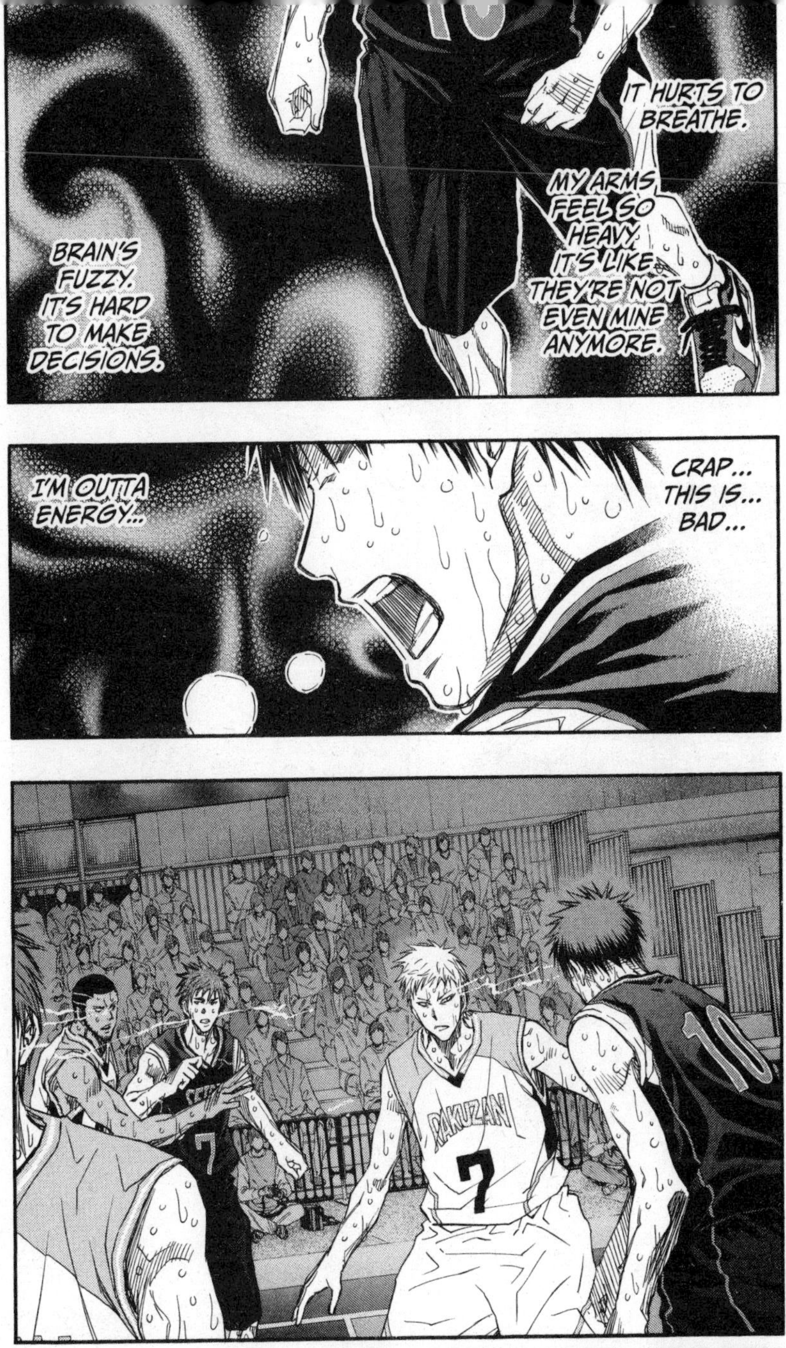
IT HURTS TO BREATHE.
MY ARMS FEEL SO HEAVY. IT'S LIKE THEY'RE NOT EVEN MINE ANYMORE.
BRAIN'S FUZZY. IT'S HARD TO MAKE DECISIONS.
CRAP... THIS IS... BAD...
I'M OUTTA ENERGY...
RAKUZAN
7

269TH QUARTER: DON'T GIVE UP!!

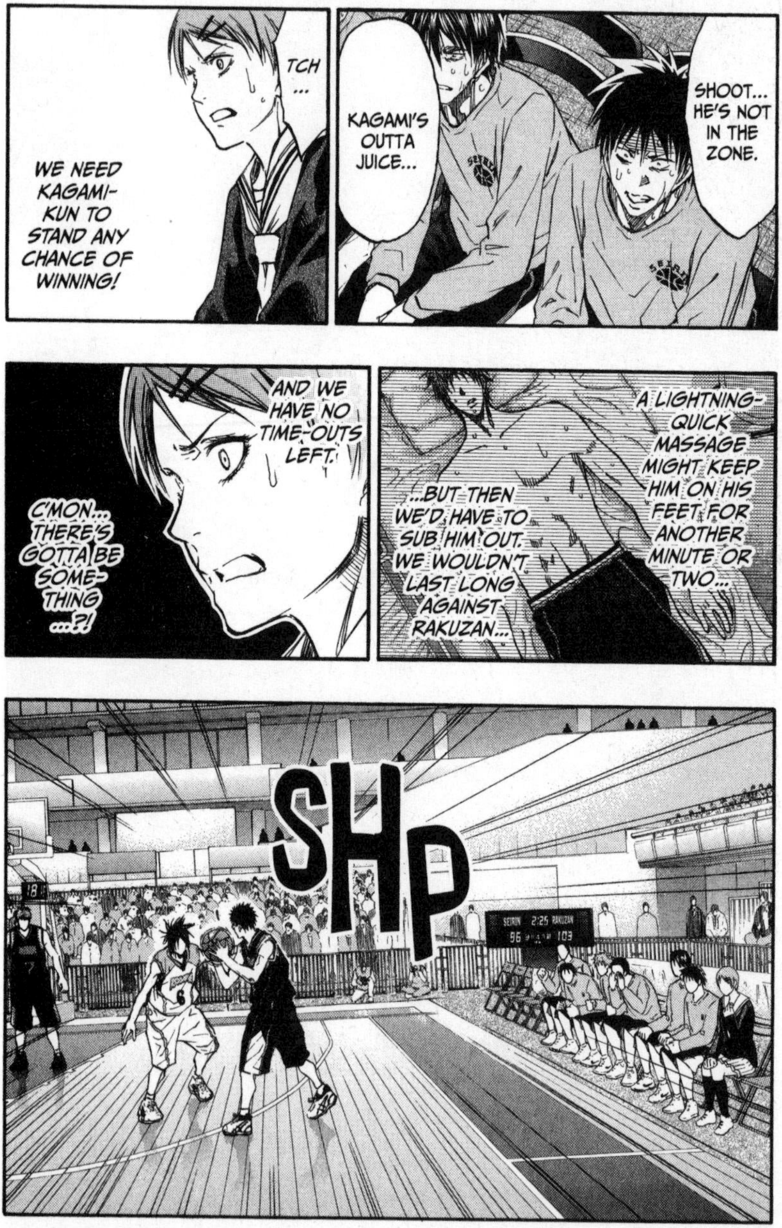
SHOOT... HE'S NOT IN THE ZONE.
KAGAMI'S OUTTA JUICE...
TCH...
WE NEED KAGAMI-KUN TO STAND ANY CHANCE OF WINNING!
A LIGHTNING-QUICK MASSAGE MIGHT KEEP HIM ON HIS FEET FOR ANOTHER MINUTE OR TWO...
...BUT THEN WE'D HAVE TO SUB HIM OUT. WE WOULDN'T LAST LONG AGAINST RAKUZAN...
AND WE HAVE NO TIME-OUTS LEFT.
C'MON... THERE'S GOTTA BE SOME-THING ...?!
SHP
SEIRIN 2:25 RAKUZAN
96 103

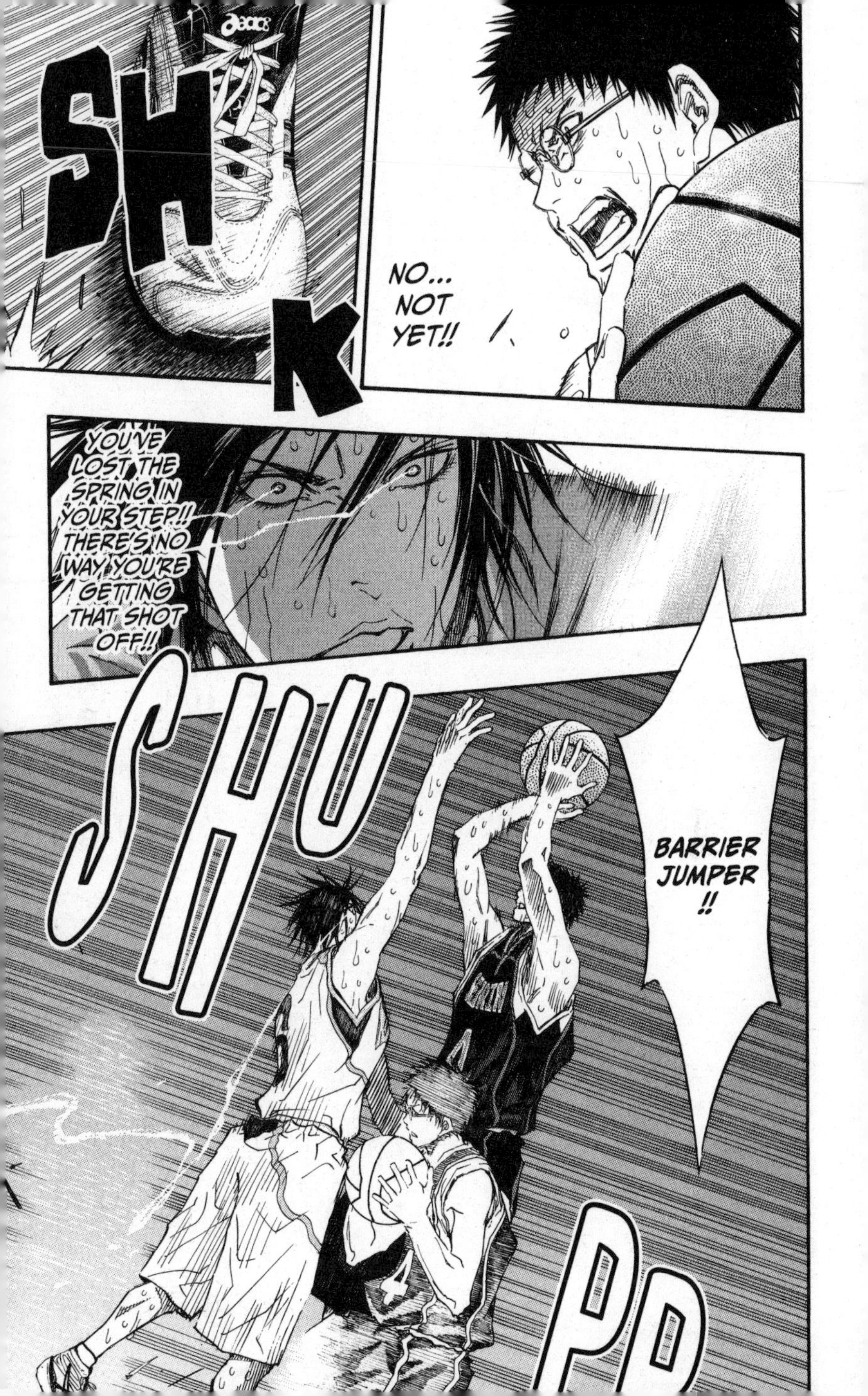
NO... NOT YET!!
SHK
YOU'VE LOST THE SPRING IN YOUR STEP!! THERE'S NO WAY YOU'RE GETTING THAT SHOT OFF!!
BARRIER JUMPER !!
SHUPP

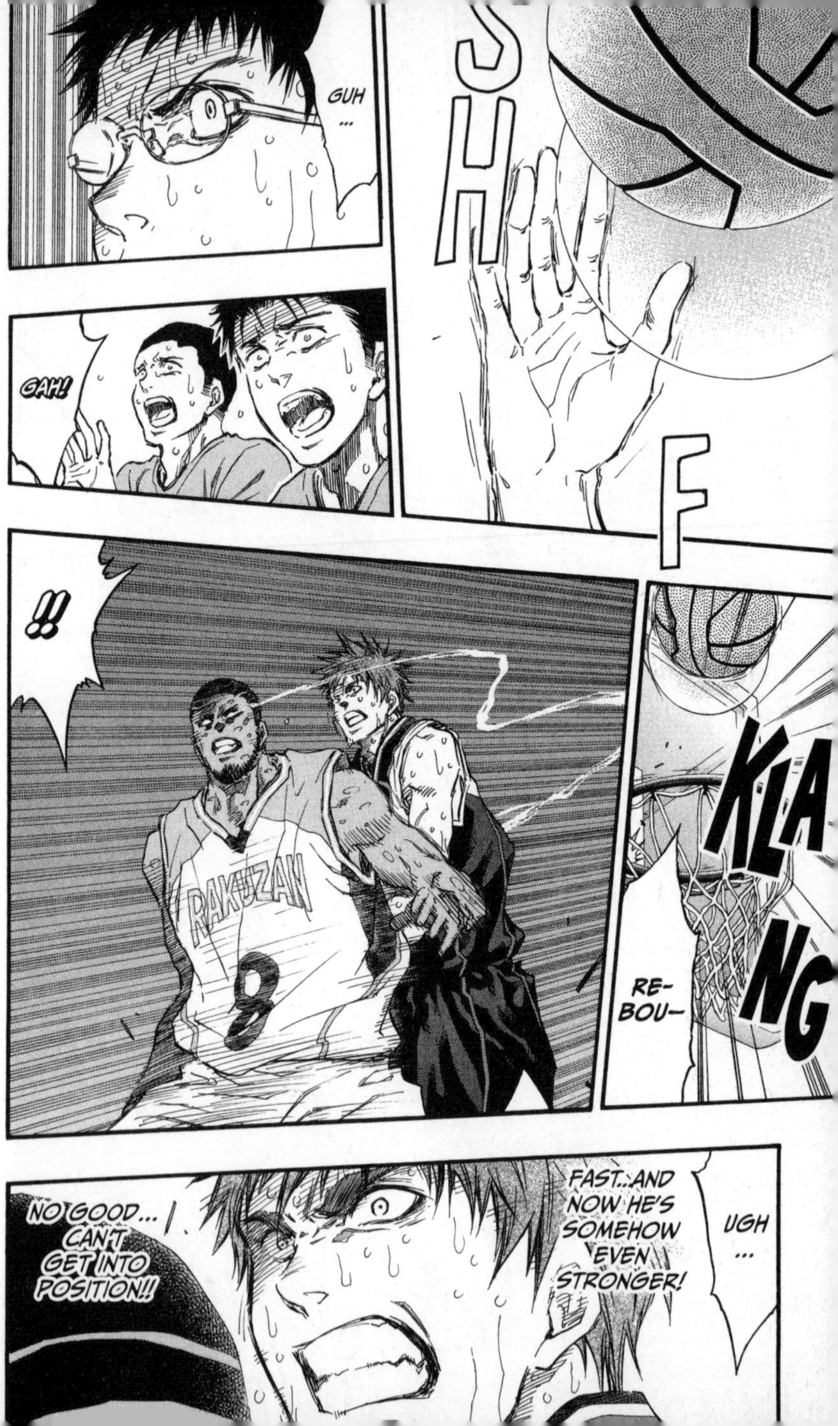
SHF
GUH ...
GAH!
KLANG
RE-BOU—
!!
UGH ...
FAST... AND NOW HE'S SOMEHOW EVEN STRONGER!
NO GOOD... CAN'T GET INTO POSITION!!

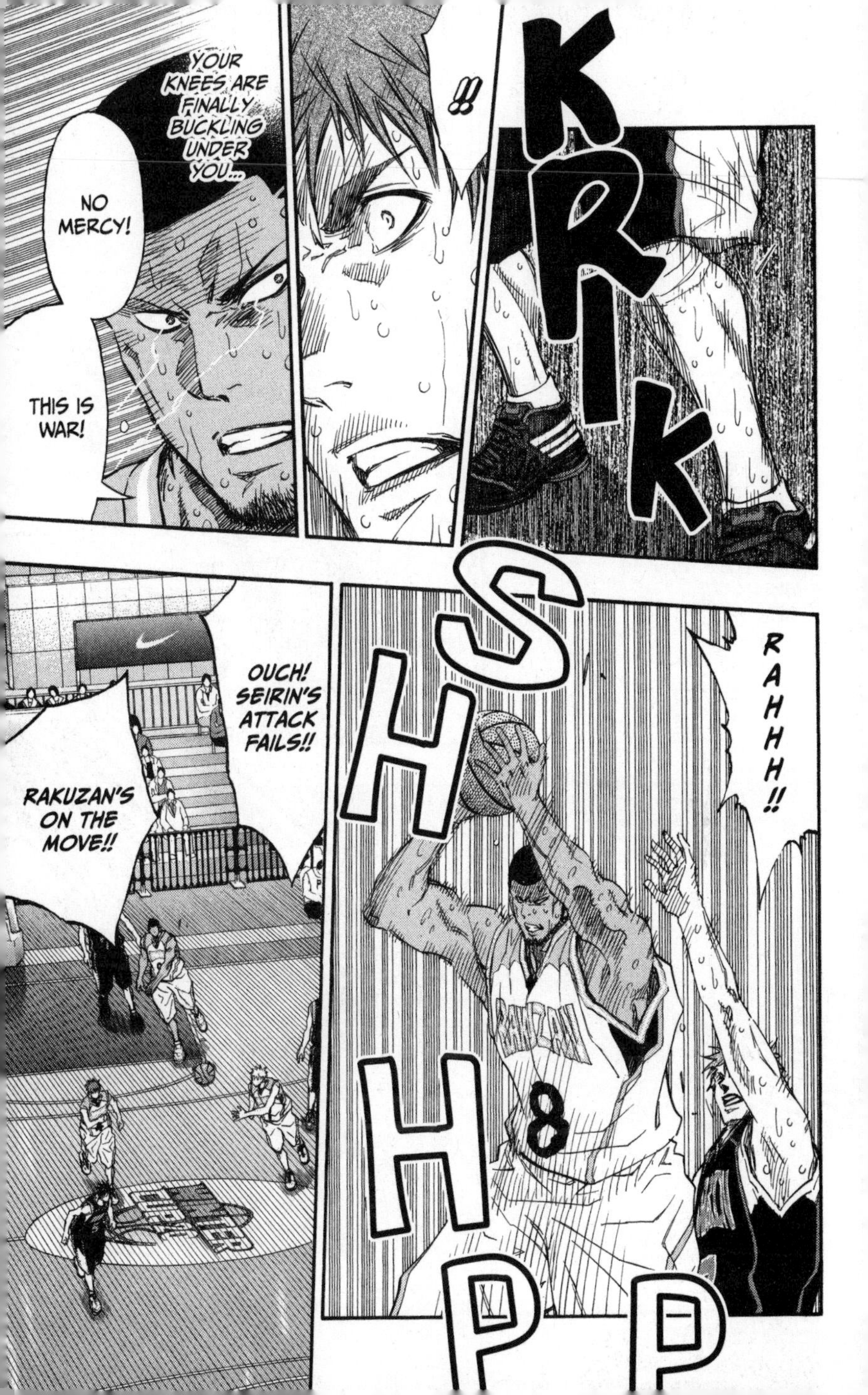
KRIK
!!
YOUR KNEES ARE FINALLY BUCKLING UNDER YOU...
NO MERCY!
THIS IS WAR!
RAHHHH!!
SHHPP
OUCH! SEIRIN'S ATTACK FAILS!!
RAKUZAN'S ON THE MOVE!!

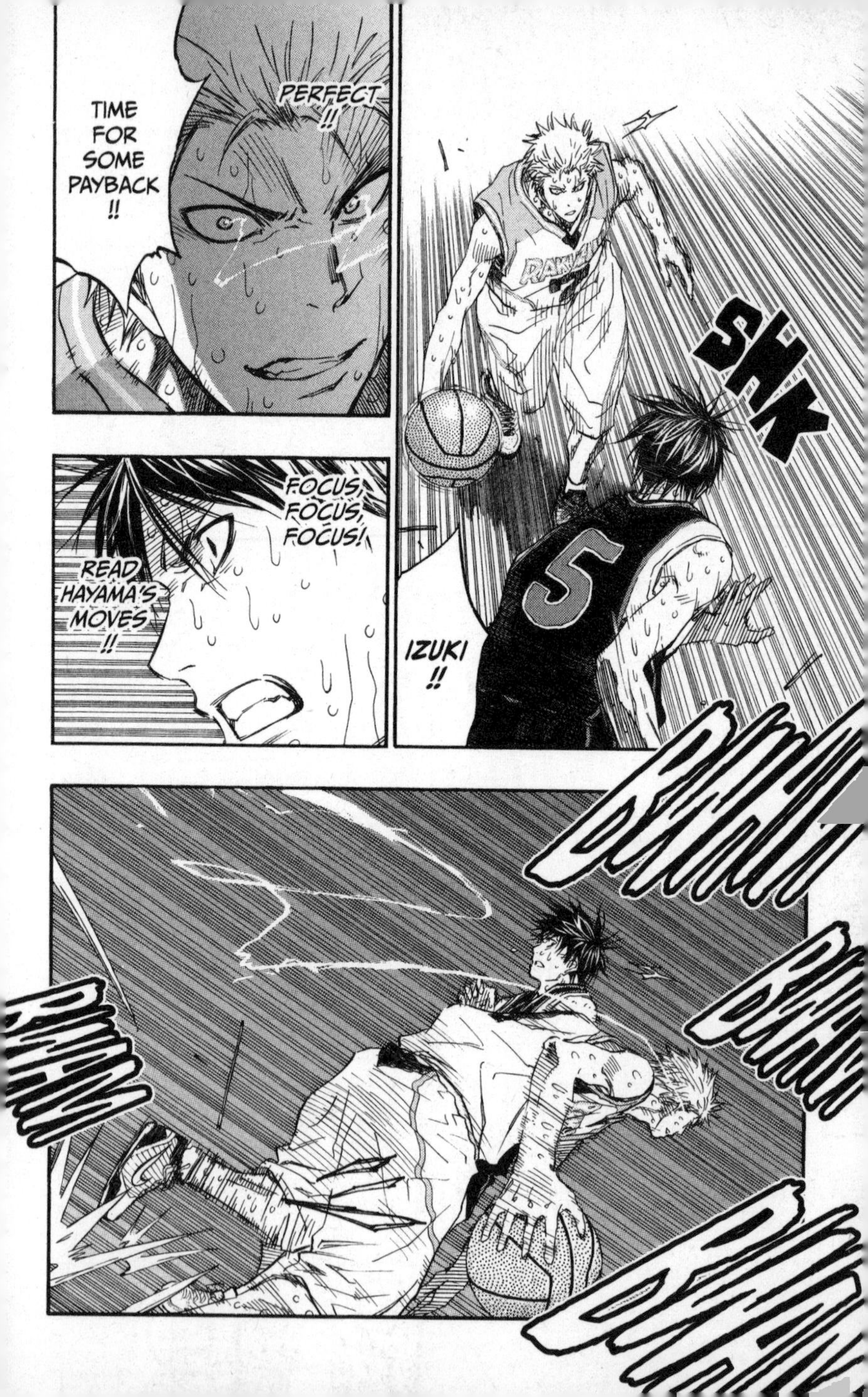
SHK
IZUKI!!
PERFECT!!
TIME FOR SOME PAYBACK!!
FOCUS, FOCUS, FOCUS!
READ HAYAMA'S MOVES!!

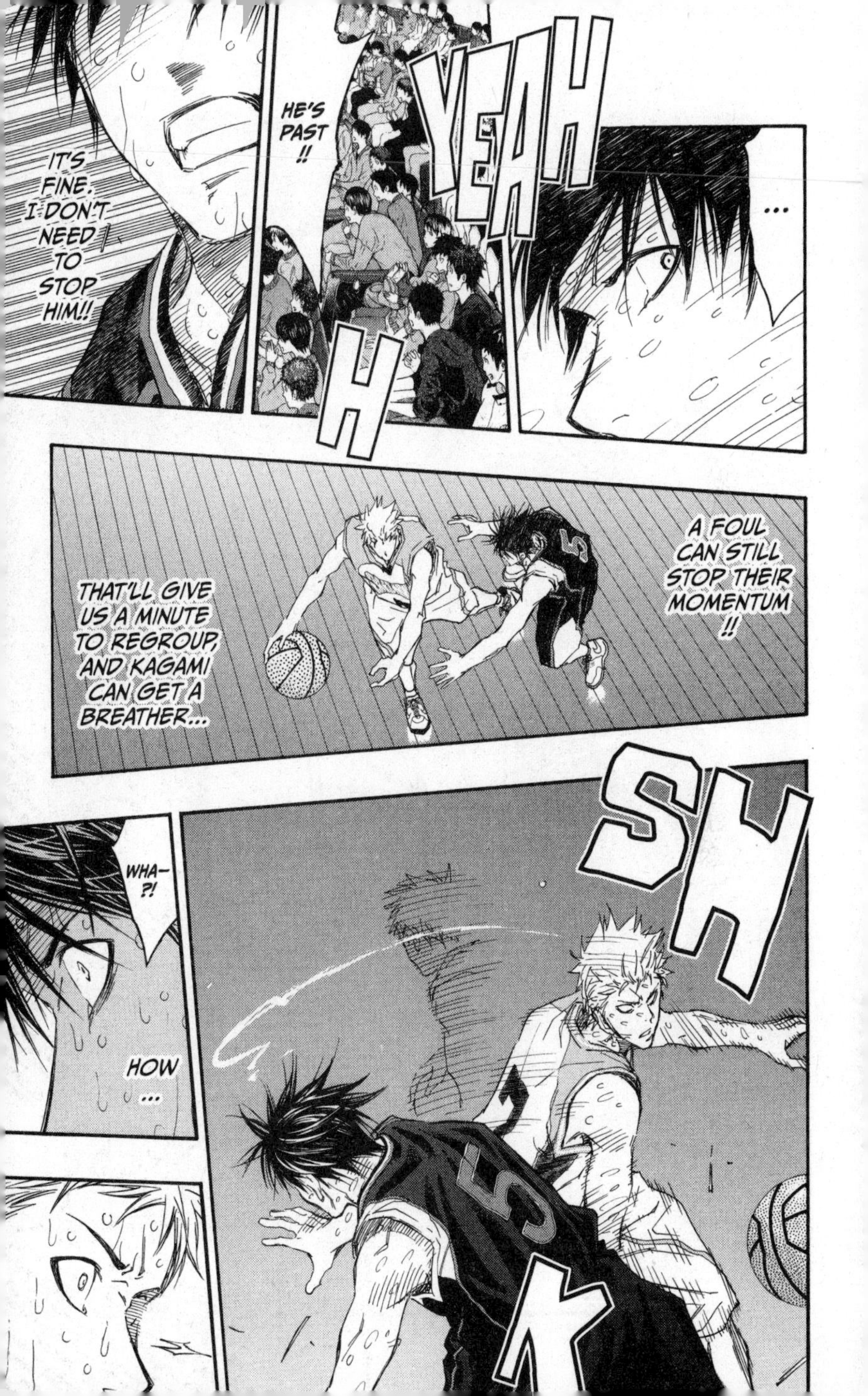
...
HE'S PAST !!
YEAH
H
IT'S FINE. I DON'T NEED TO STOP HIM!!
A FOUL CAN STILL STOP THEIR MOMENTUM !!
THAT'LL GIVE US A MINUTE TO REGROUP, AND KAGAMI CAN GET A BREATHER...
SH
H
K
WHA- ?!
HOW ...

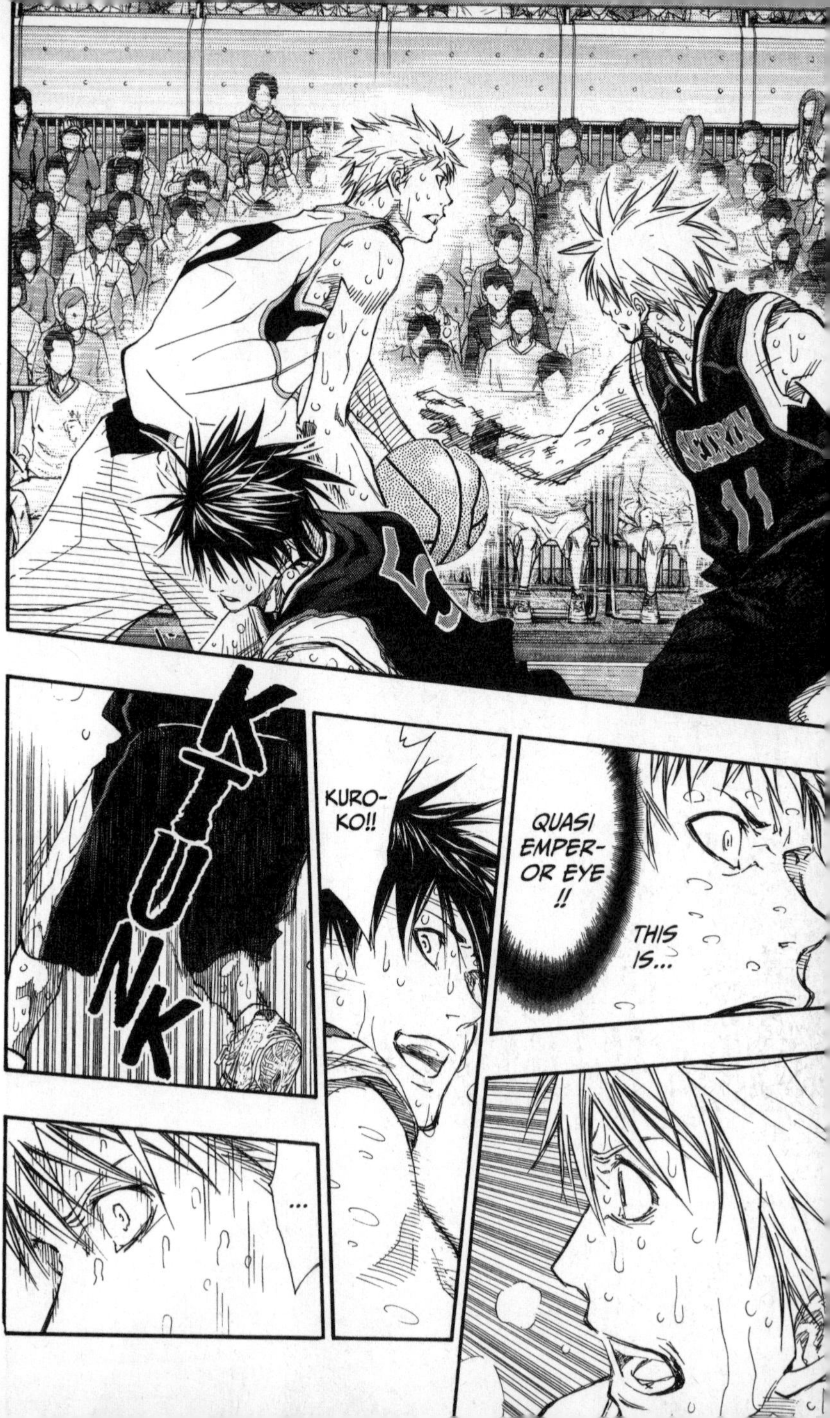
SEIRIN
11
THIS IS...
QUASI EMPER-OR EYE !!
KURO-KO!!
KTUNK
...

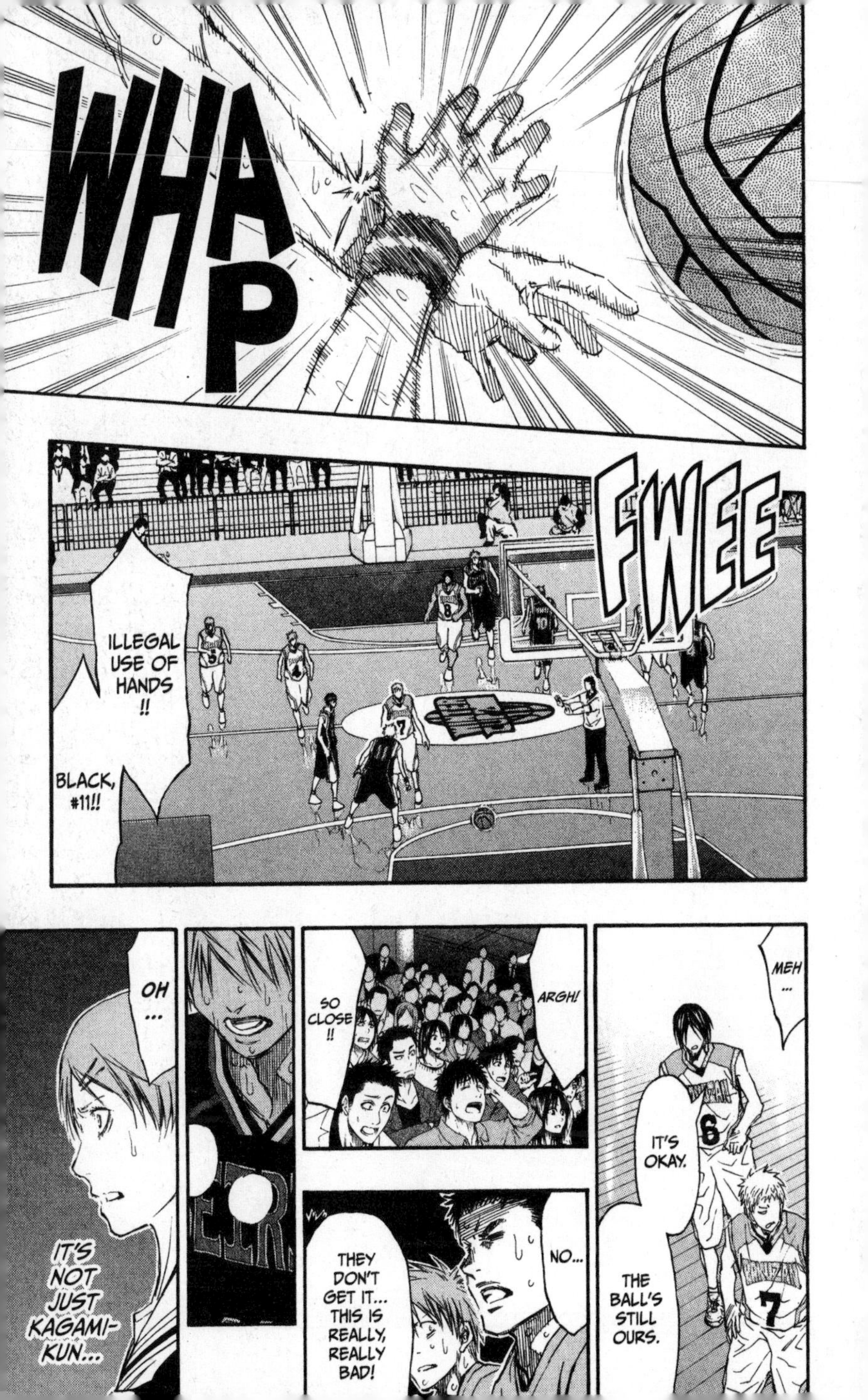
WHAP
FWEE
ILLEGAL USE OF HANDS!!
BLACK, #11!!
MEH...
IT'S OKAY.
THE BALL'S STILL OURS.
ARGH!
SO CLOSE!!
NO...
THEY DON'T GET IT... THIS IS REALLY, REALLY BAD!
OH...
IT'S NOT JUST KAGAMI-KUN...

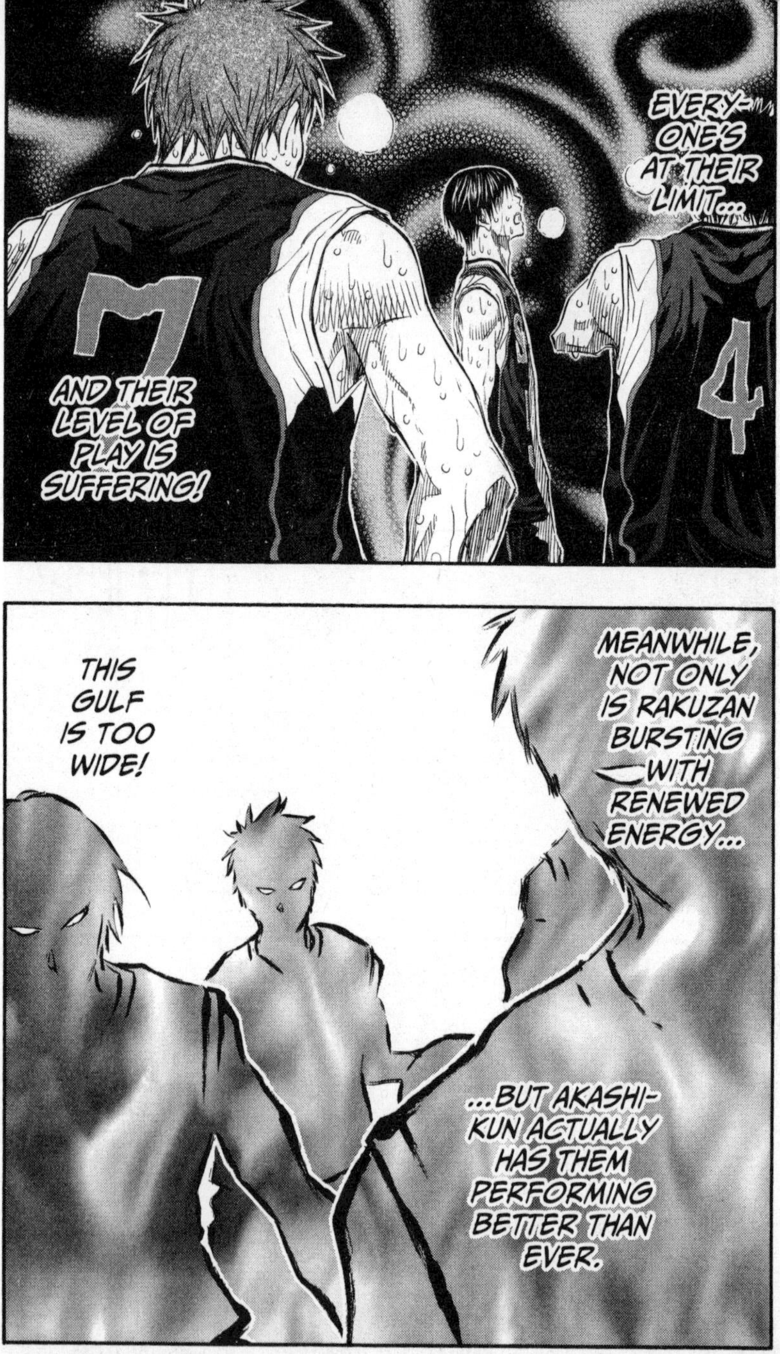
EVERY-ONE'S AT THEIR LIMIT...
AND THEIR LEVEL OF PLAY IS SUFFERING!
MEANWHILE, NOT ONLY IS RAKUZAN BURSTING WITH RENEWED ENERGY...
...BUT AKASHI-KUN ACTUALLY HAS THEM PERFORMING BETTER THAN EVER.
THIS GULF IS TOO WIDE!

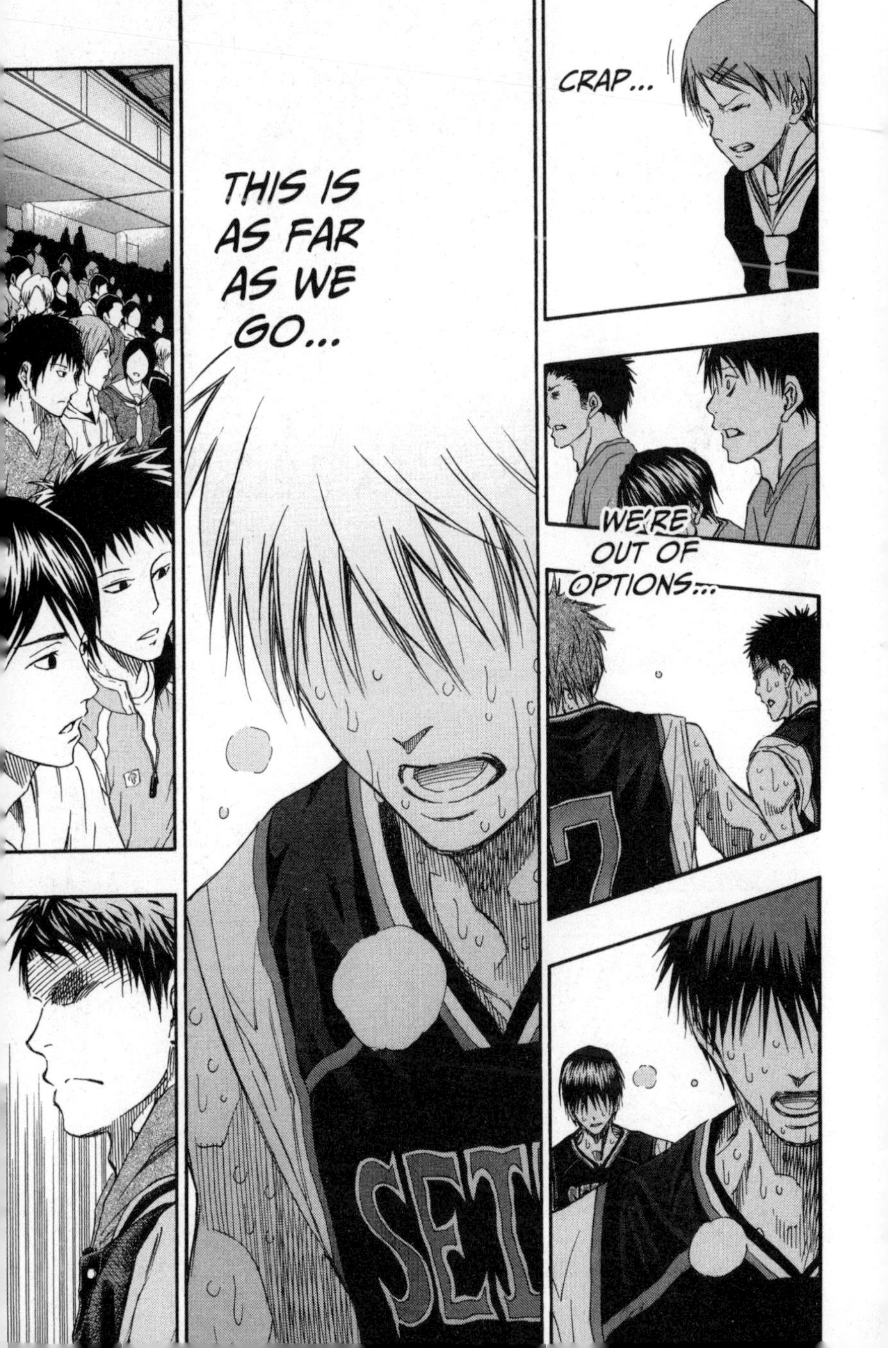
CRAP...
WE'RE OUT OF OPTIONS...
THIS IS AS FAR AS WE GO...

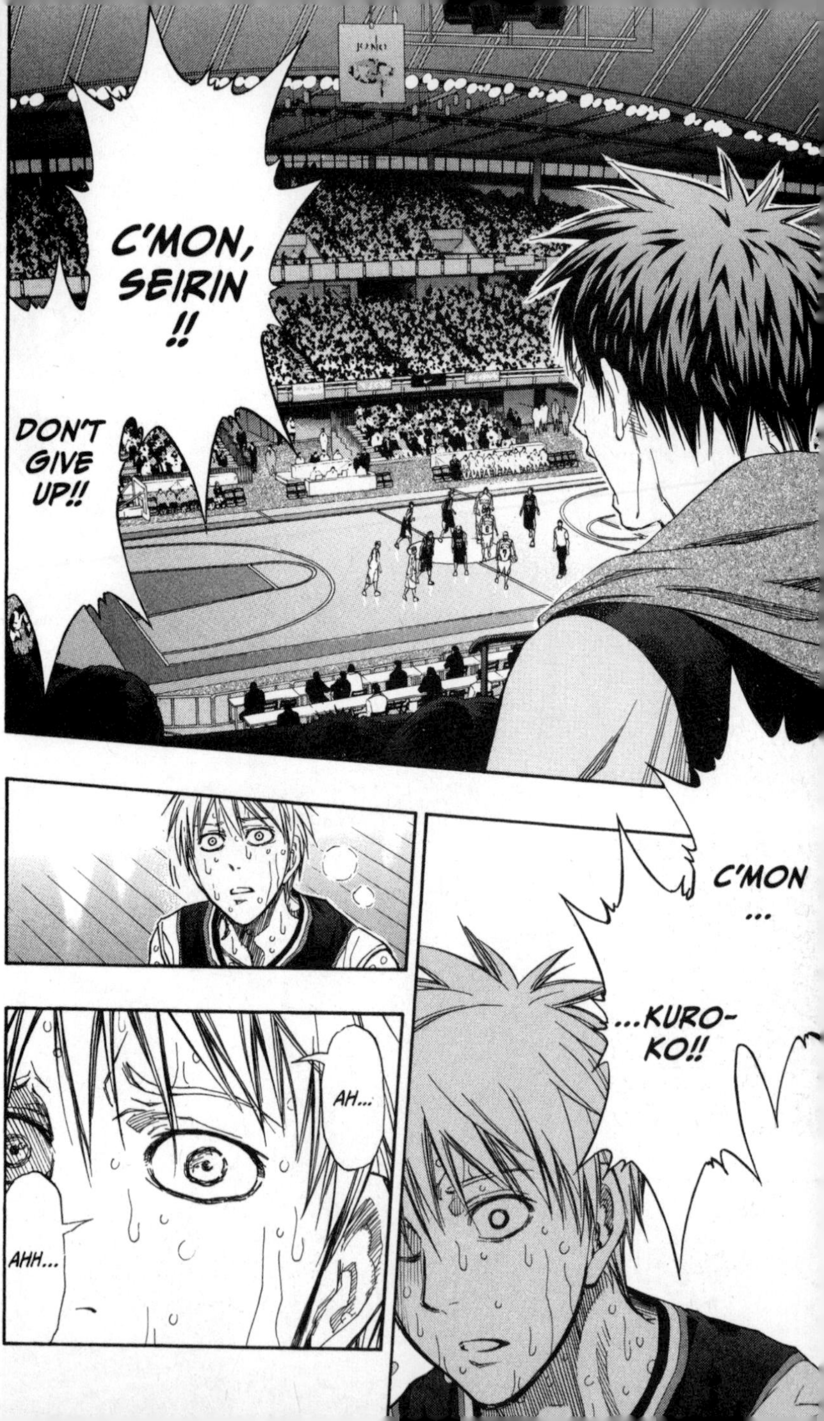
C'MON, SEIRIN!!
DON'T GIVE UP!!
C'MON...
...KURO-KO!!
AH...
AHH...

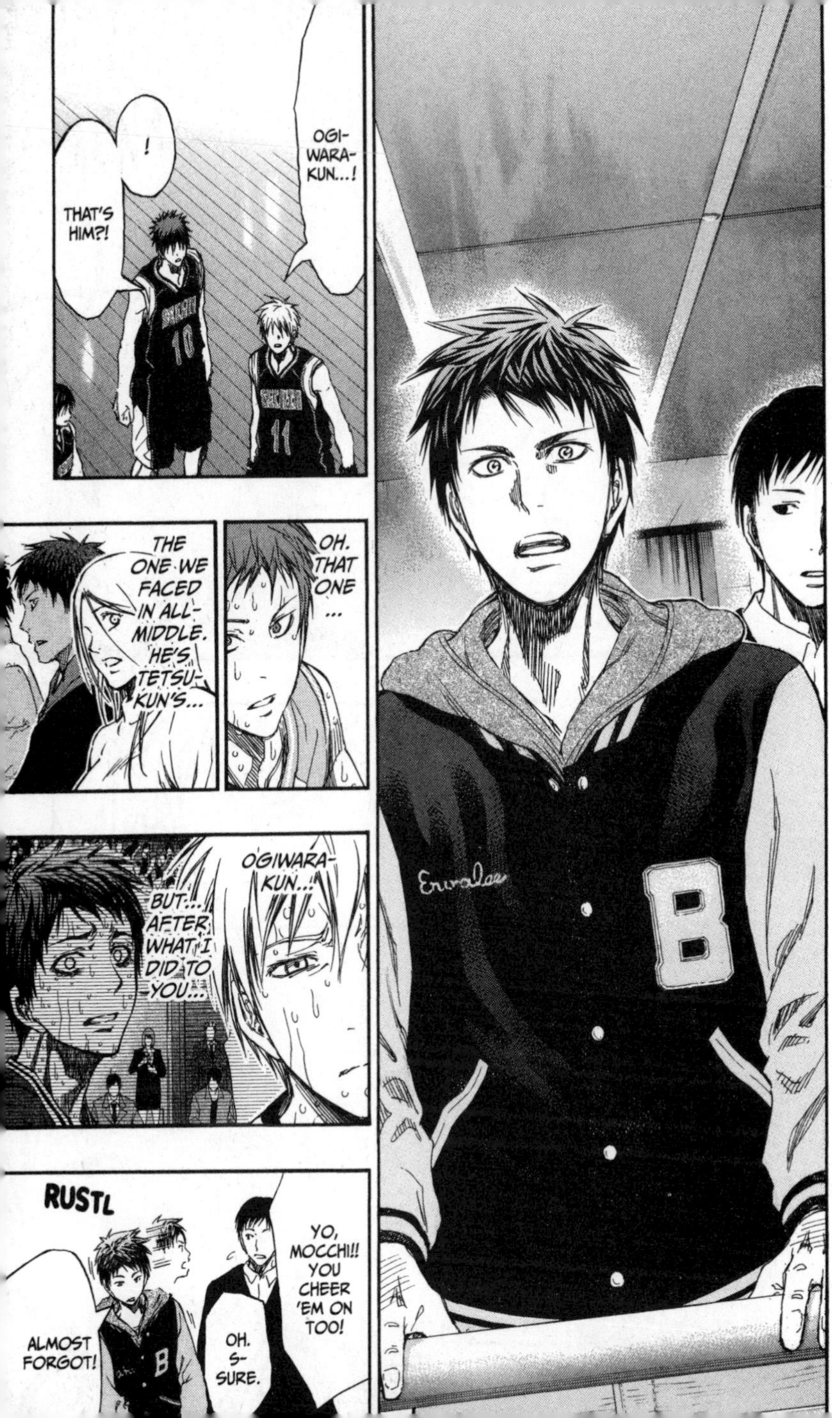
OGI-WARA-KUN...!
!
THAT'S HIM?!
OH. THAT ONE ...
THE ONE WE FACED IN ALL-MIDDLE. HE'S TETSU-KUN'S...
OGIWARA-KUN...!
BUT... AFTER WHAT I DID TO YOU...
YO, MOCCHI!! YOU CHEER 'EM ON TOO!
RUSTL
OH. S-SURE.
ALMOST FORGOT!

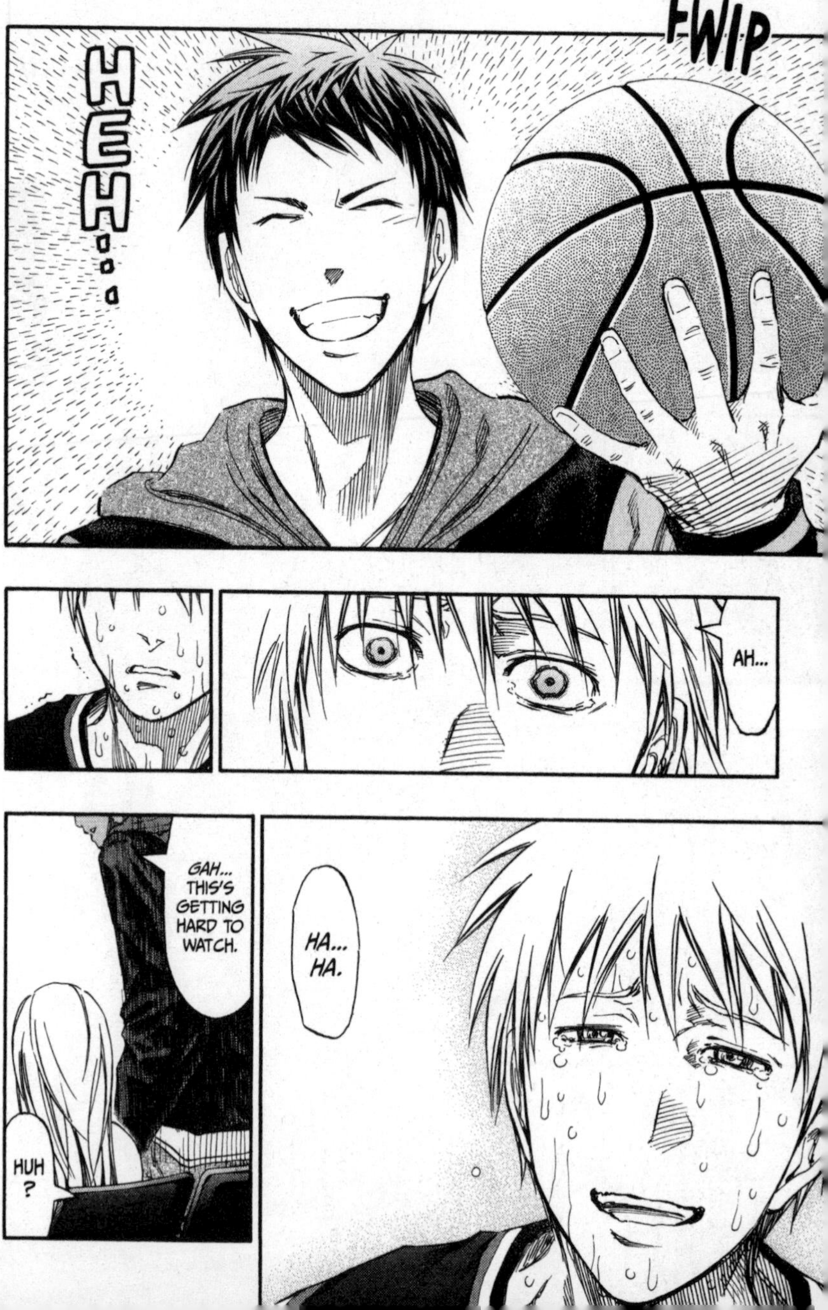
FWIP
HEH...
AH...
HA... HA.
GAH... THIS'S GETTING HARD TO WATCH.
HUH ?

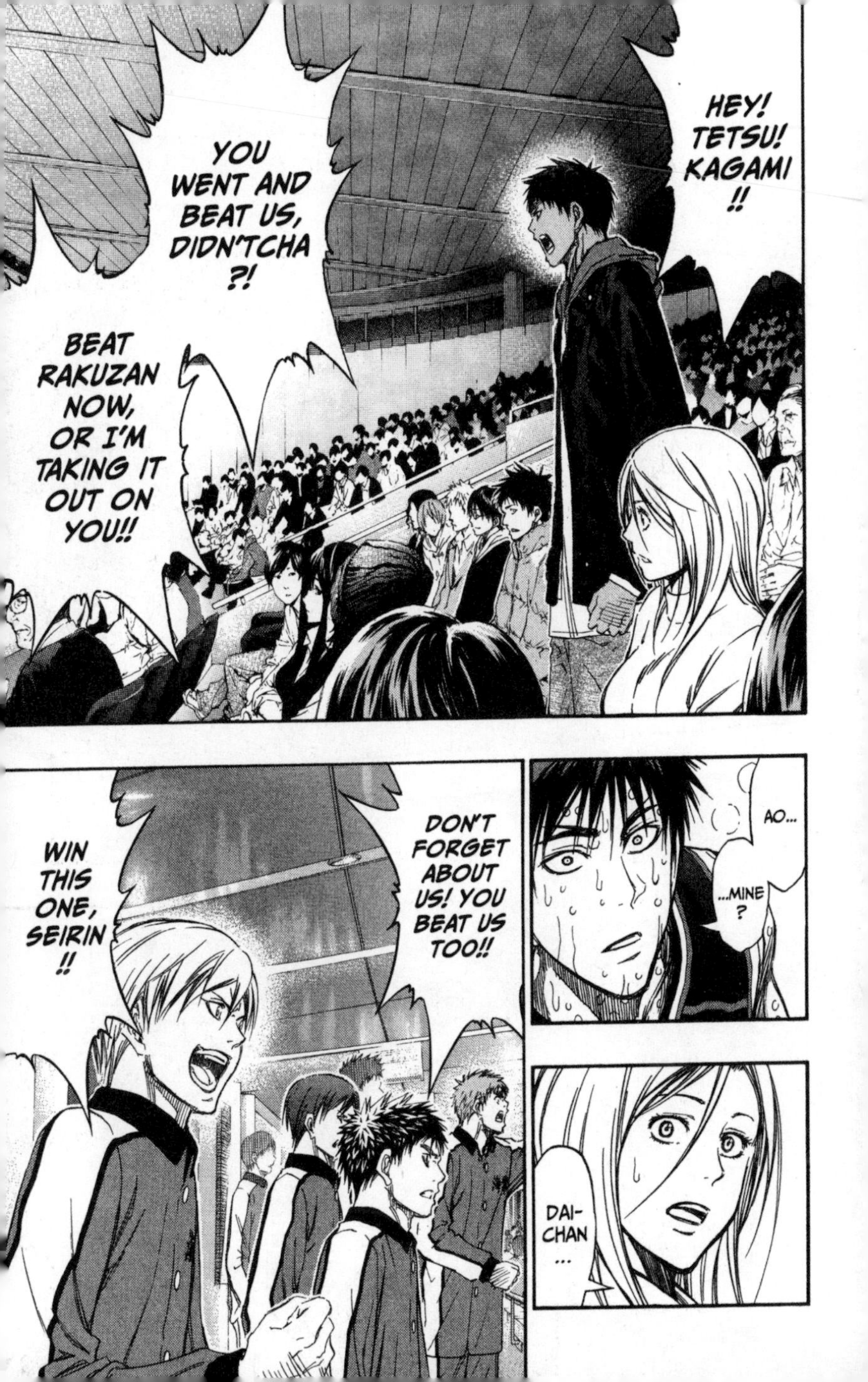
HEY! TETSU! KAGAMI!!
YOU WENT AND BEAT US, DIDN'TCHA?!
BEAT RAKUZAN NOW, OR I'M TAKING IT OUT ON YOU!!
AO...
...MINE?
DAI-CHAN...
DON'T FORGET ABOUT US! YOU BEAT US TOO!!
WIN THIS ONE, SEIRIN!!

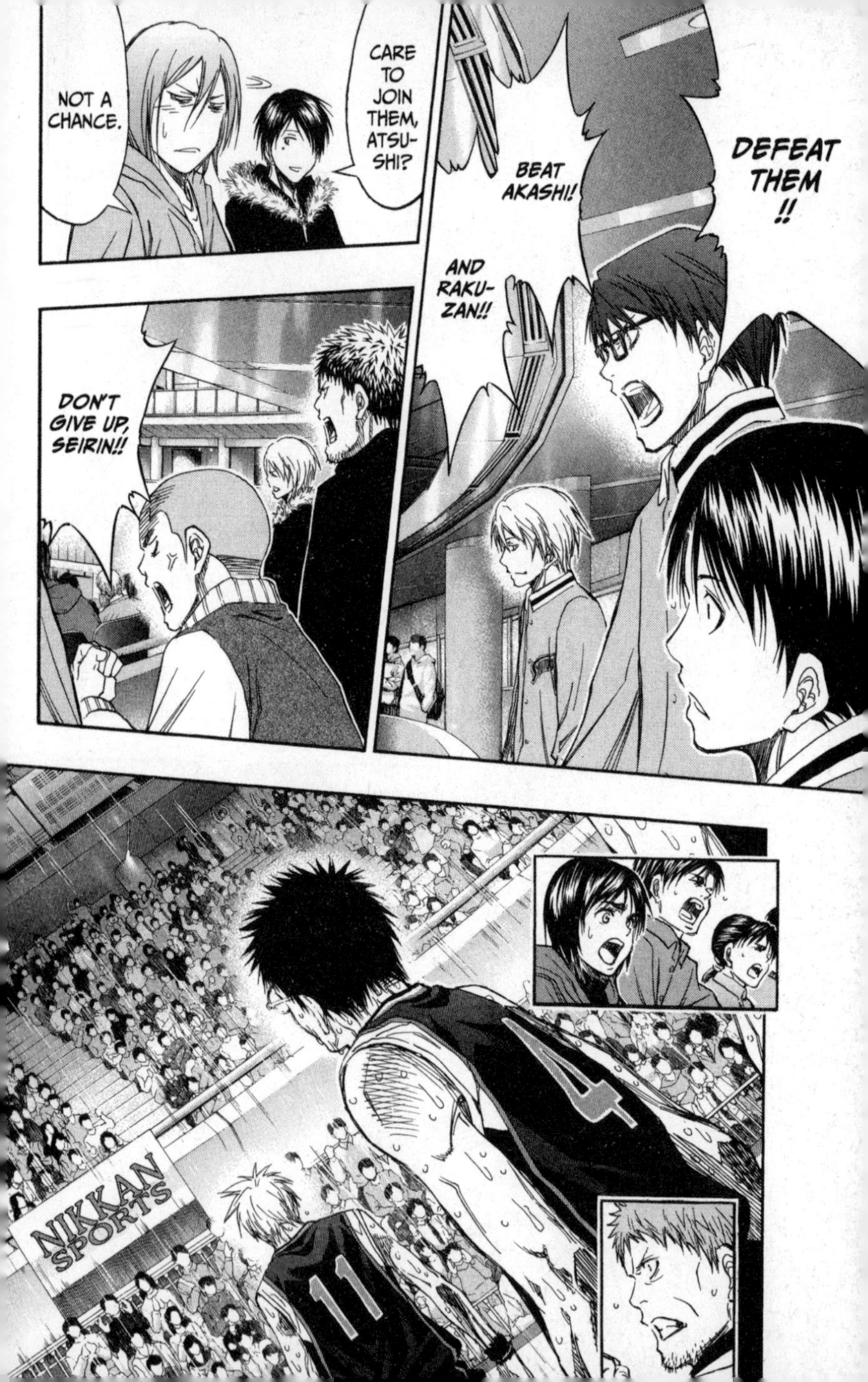
DEFEAT THEM!!
BEAT AKASHI!
AND RAKUZAN!!
CARE TO JOIN THEM, ATSU-SHI?
NOT A CHANCE.
DON'T GIVE UP, SEIRIN!!
NIKKAN SPORTS

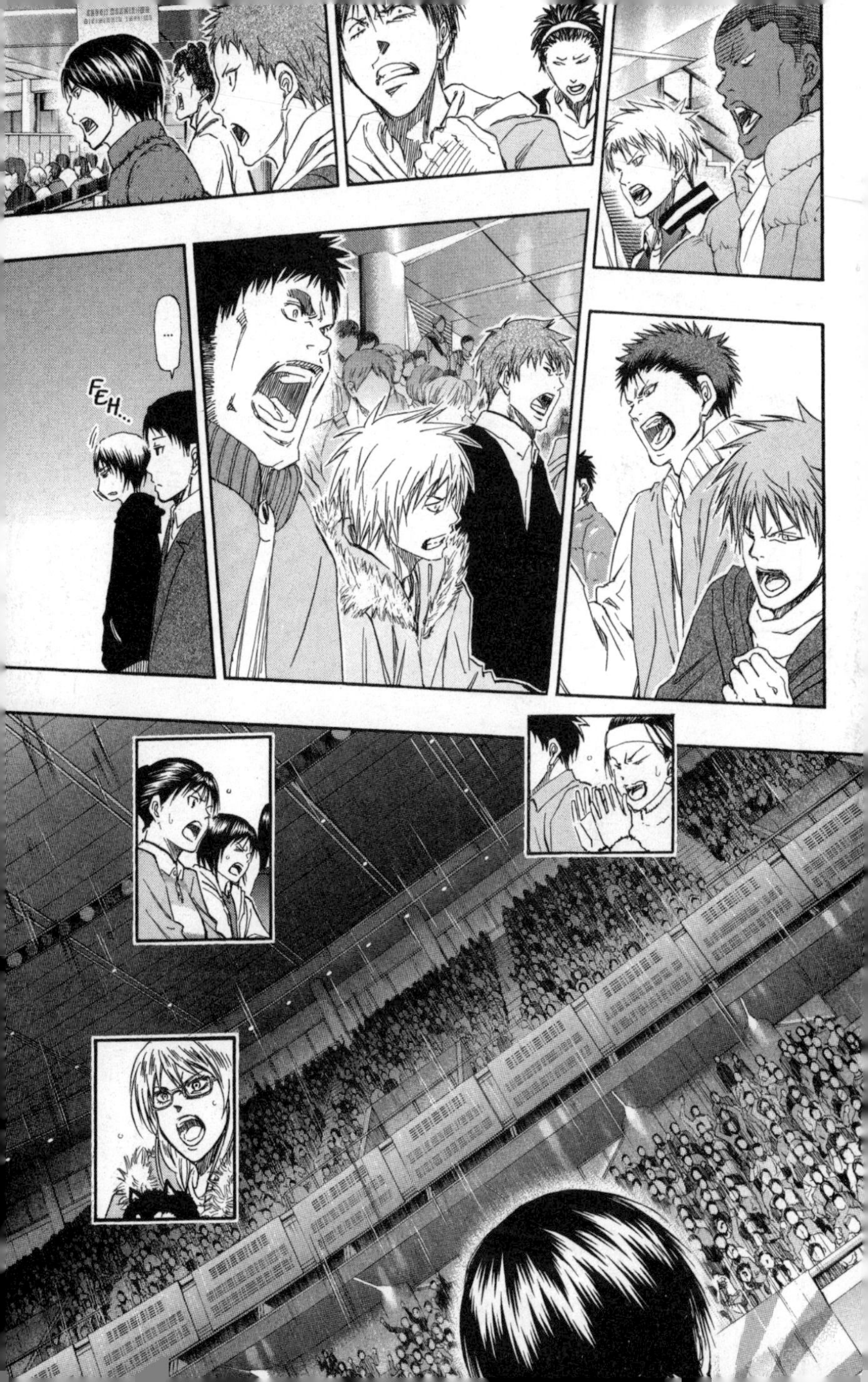

...
FEH...

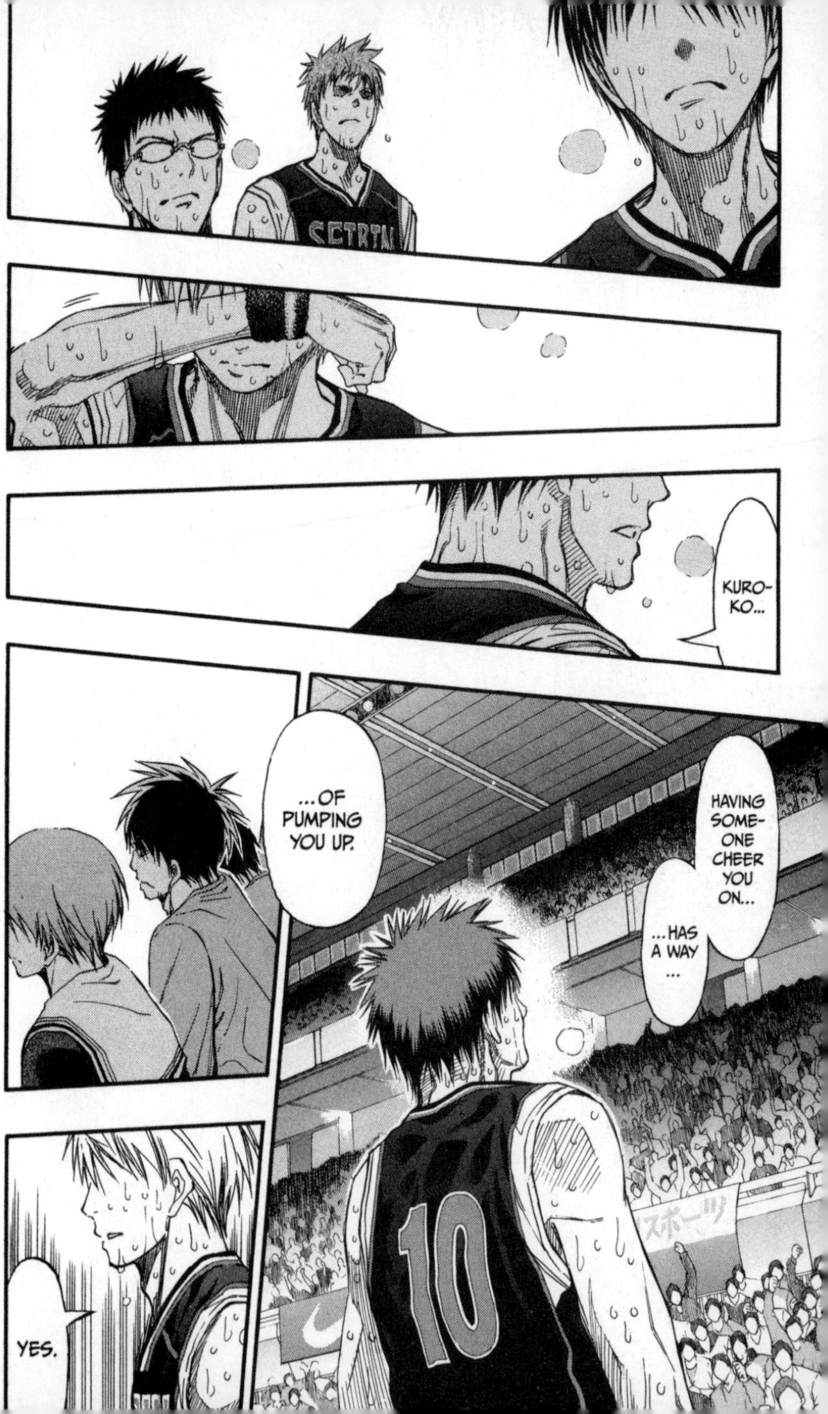
KURO-KO...
HAVING SOME-ONE CHEER YOU ON...
...HAS A WAY ...
...OF PUMPING YOU UP.
スポーツ
YES.

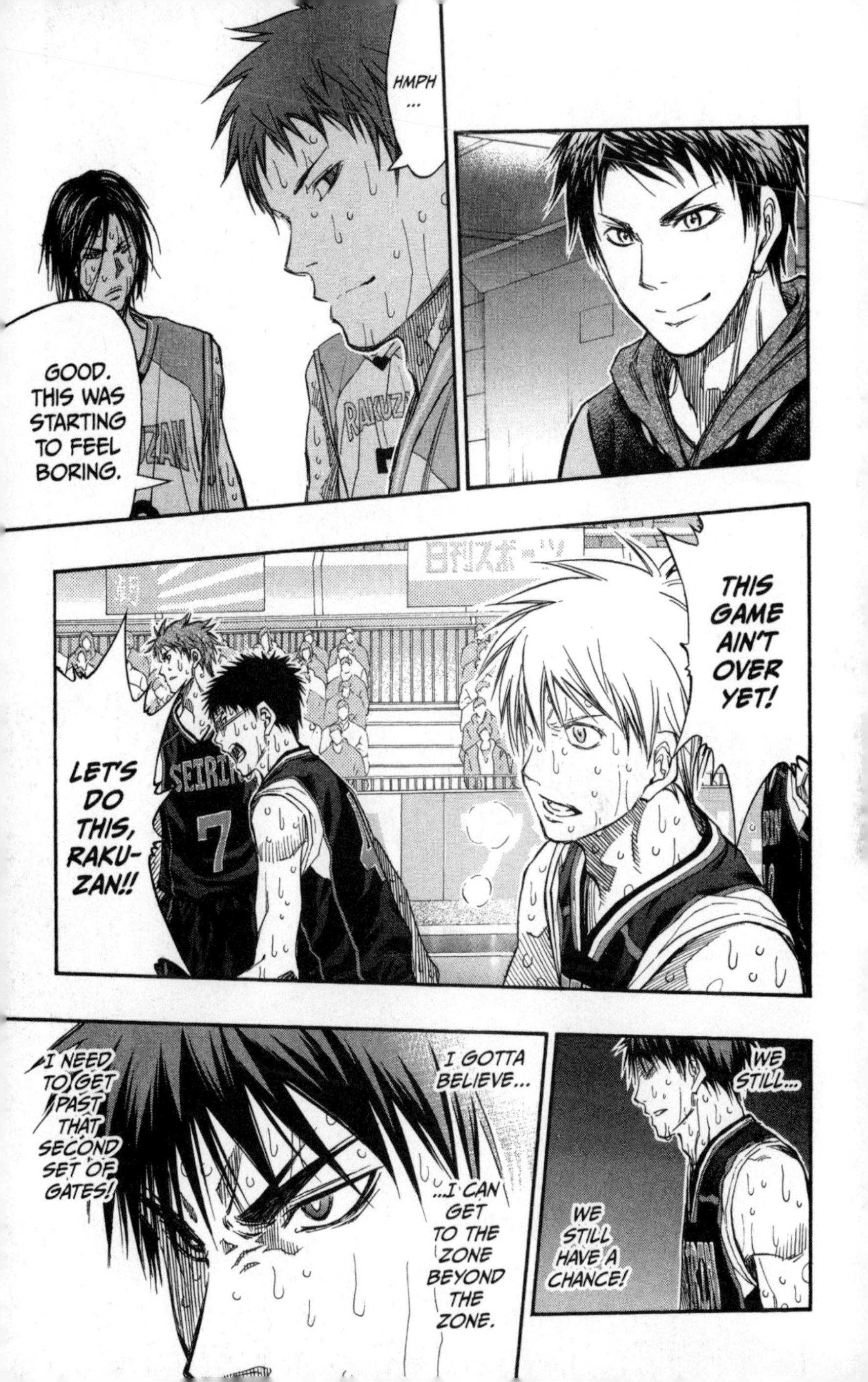
HMPH ...
GOOD. THIS WAS STARTING TO FEEL BORING.
THIS GAME AIN'T OVER YET!
LET'S DO THIS, RAKUZAN!!
WE STILL...
WE STILL HAVE A CHANCE!
I GOTTA BELIEVE...
I NEED TO GET PAST THAT SECOND SET OF GATES!
...I CAN GET TO THE ZONE BEYOND THE ZONE.

KUROKO'S BASKETBALL Q&A
W/ HALFWAY-DECENT ANSWERS

Q. WHO'S MORE POPULAR WITH THE LADIES? KISE-KUN OR HIMURO-SAN?
(SAME BIRTHDAY AS HIMURO-SAN from OSAKA)

A. PARDON ME IF THIS SOUNDS CRASS, BUT HIMURO'S GOT QUALITY, WHILE KISE HAS QUANTITY.

KUROKO'S BASKETBALL BLOOPERS
TAKE 10

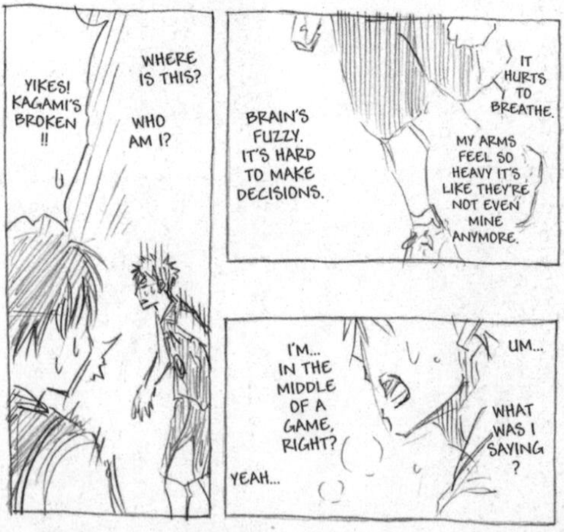
IT HURTS TO BREATHE.
MY ARMS FEEL SO HEAVY IT'S LIKE THEY'RE NOT EVEN MINE ANYMORE.
BRAIN'S FUZZY. IT'S HARD TO MAKE DECISIONS.
UM...
WHAT WAS I SAYING ?
I'M... IN THE MIDDLE OF A GAME, RIGHT?
YEAH...
WHERE IS THIS?
WHO AM I?
YIKES! KAGAMI'S BROKEN !!

270TH QUARTER: IT WAS YOU

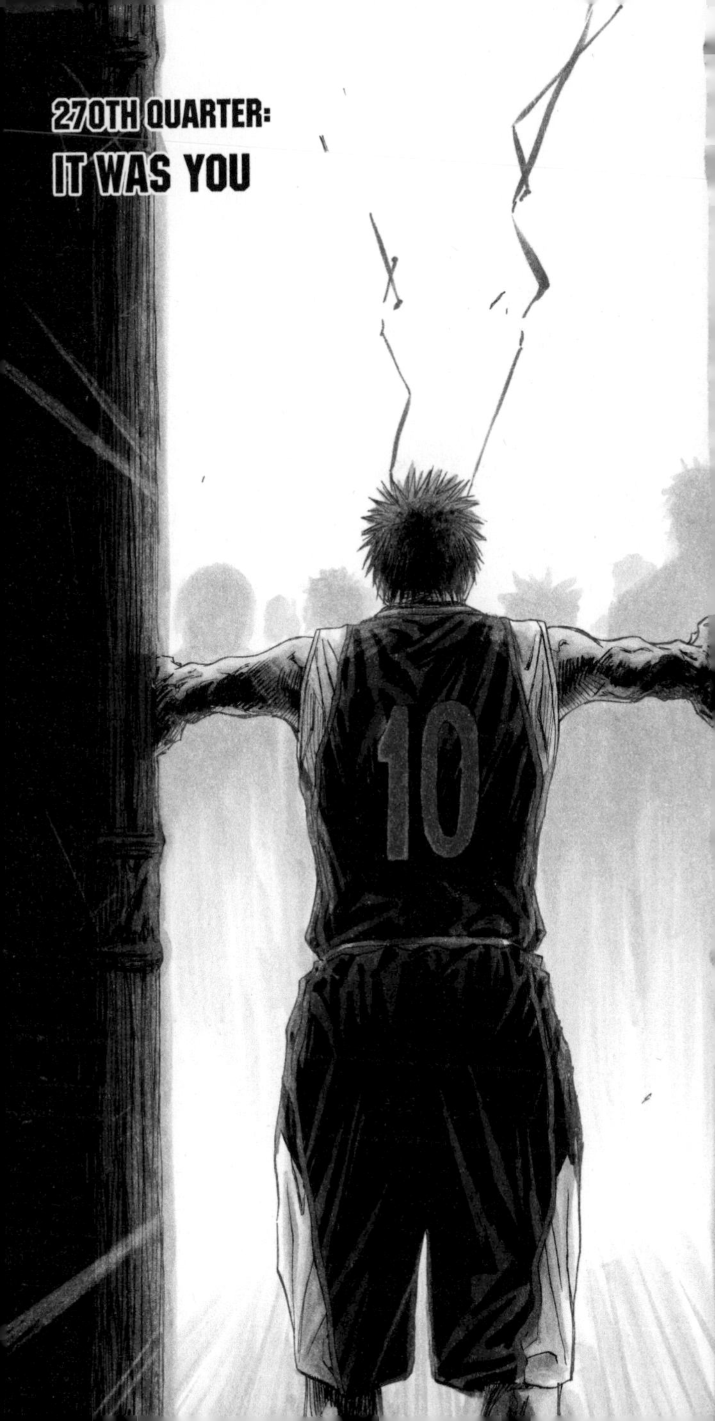

Kuroko's **BASKETBALL**

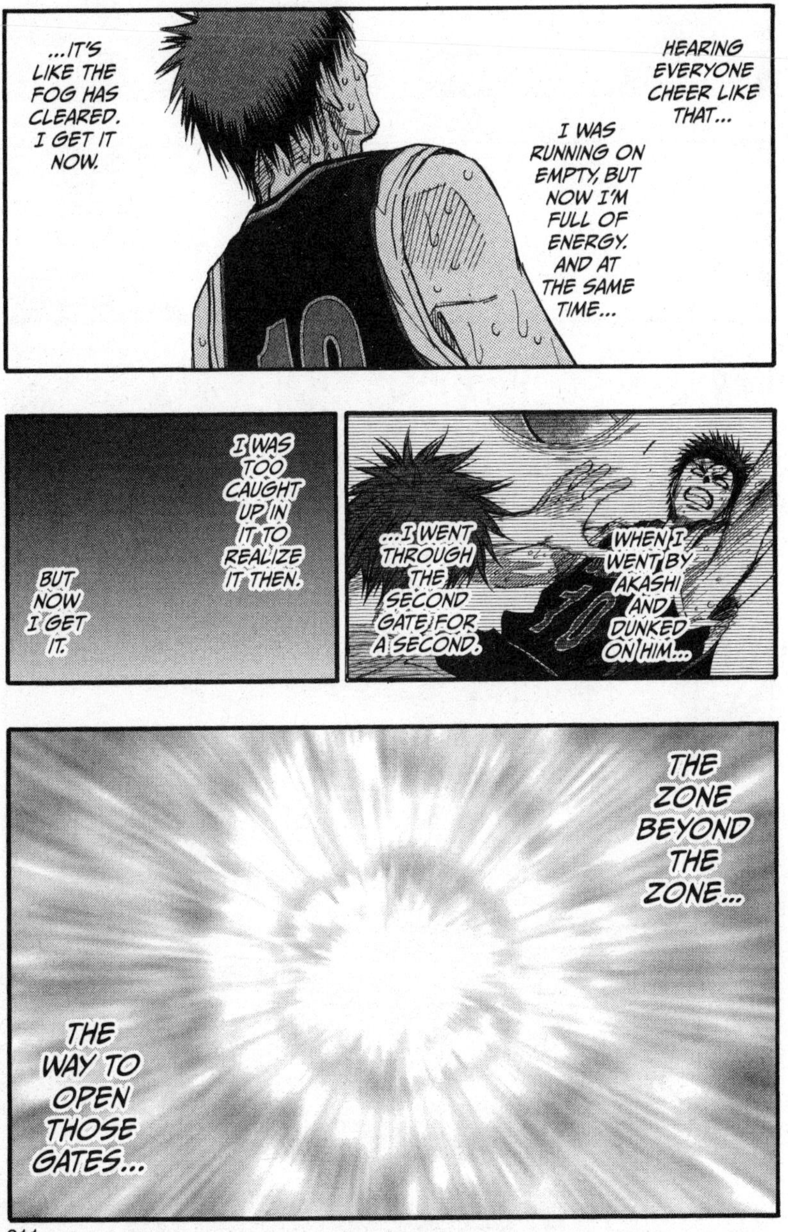
HEARING EVERYONE CHEER LIKE THAT...
I WAS RUNNING ON EMPTY, BUT NOW I'M FULL OF ENERGY. AND AT THE SAME TIME...
...IT'S LIKE THE FOG HAS CLEARED. I GET IT NOW.
WHEN I WENT BY AKASHI AND DUNKED ON HIM...
...I WENT THROUGH THE SECOND GATE FOR A SECOND.
I WAS TOO CAUGHT UP IN IT TO REALIZE IT THEN.
BUT NOW I GET IT.
THE ZONE BEYOND THE ZONE...
THE WAY TO OPEN THOSE GATES...

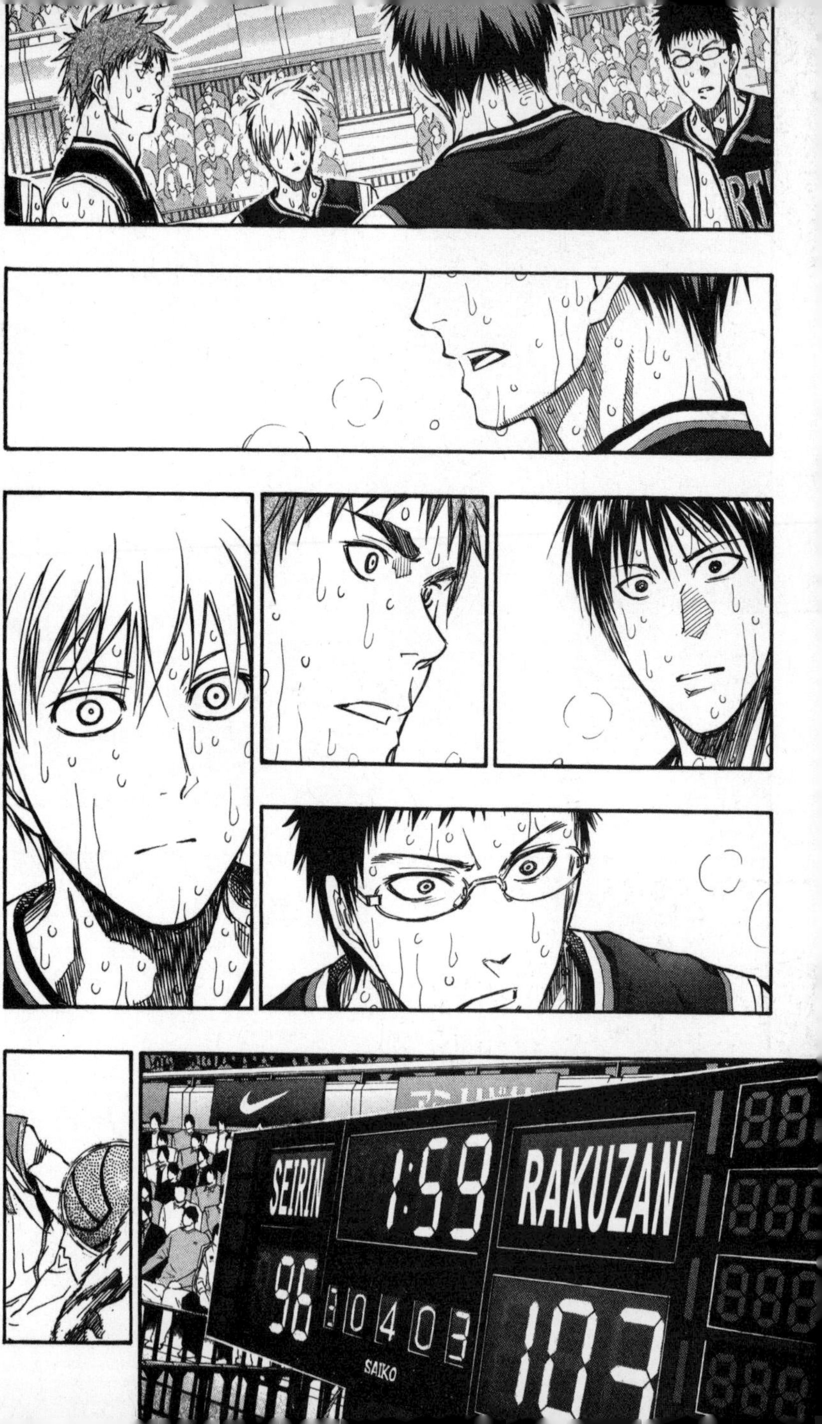
SEIRIN
1:59
RAKUZAN
96
103
SAIKO

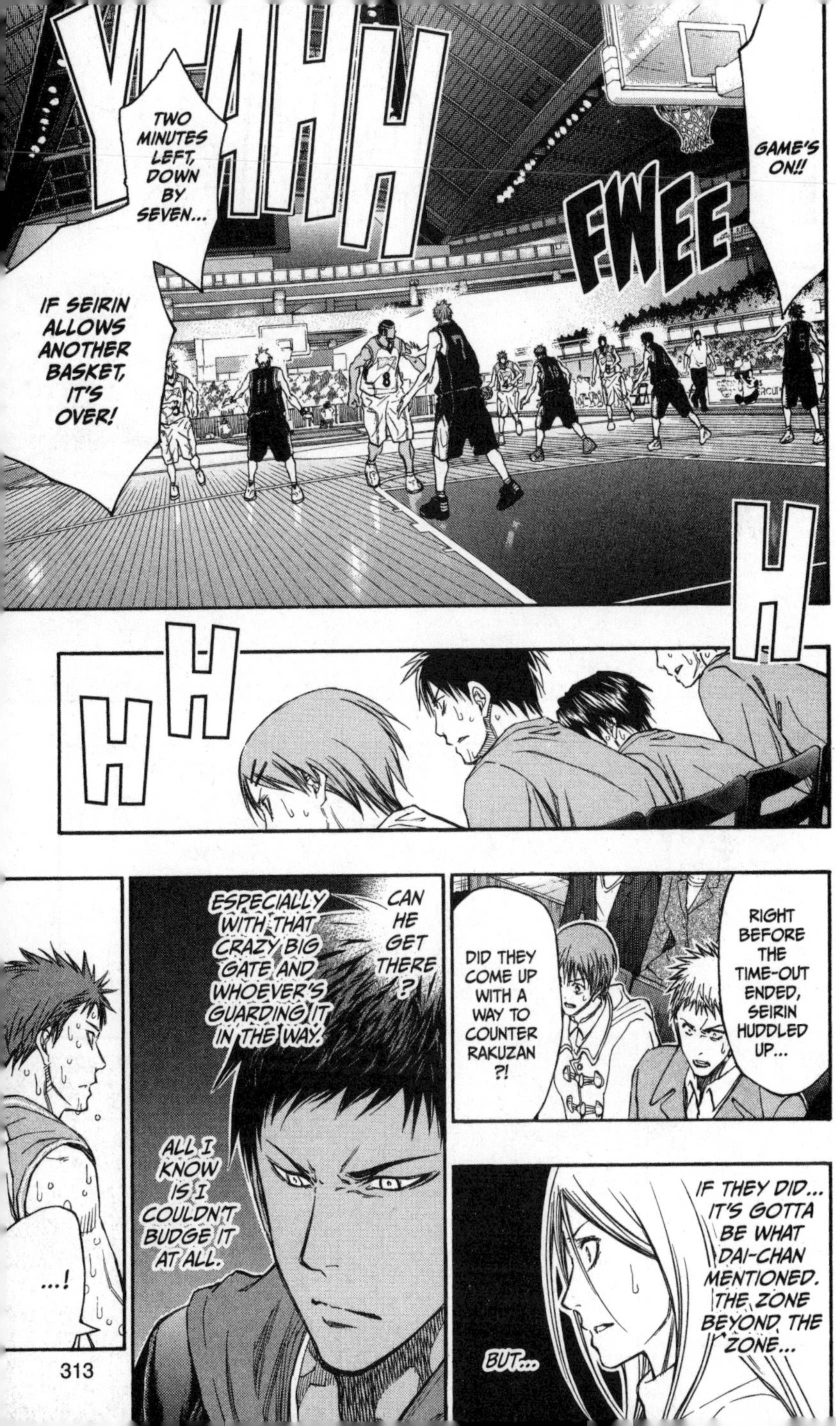

YAHH
GAME'S ON!!
FWEE
TWO MINUTES LEFT, DOWN BY SEVEN...
IF SEIRIN ALLOWS ANOTHER BASKET, IT'S OVER!
HHH
RIGHT BEFORE THE TIME-OUT ENDED, SEIRIN HUDDLED UP...
DID THEY COME UP WITH A WAY TO COUNTER RAKUZAN?!
IF THEY DID... IT'S GOTTA BE WHAT DAI-CHAN MENTIONED. THE ZONE BEYOND THE ZONE...
BUT...
CAN HE GET THERE?
ESPECIALLY WITH THAT CRAZY BIG GATE AND WHOEVER'S GUARDING IT IN THE WAY.
ALL I KNOW IS I COULDN'T BUDGE IT AT ALL.
...!

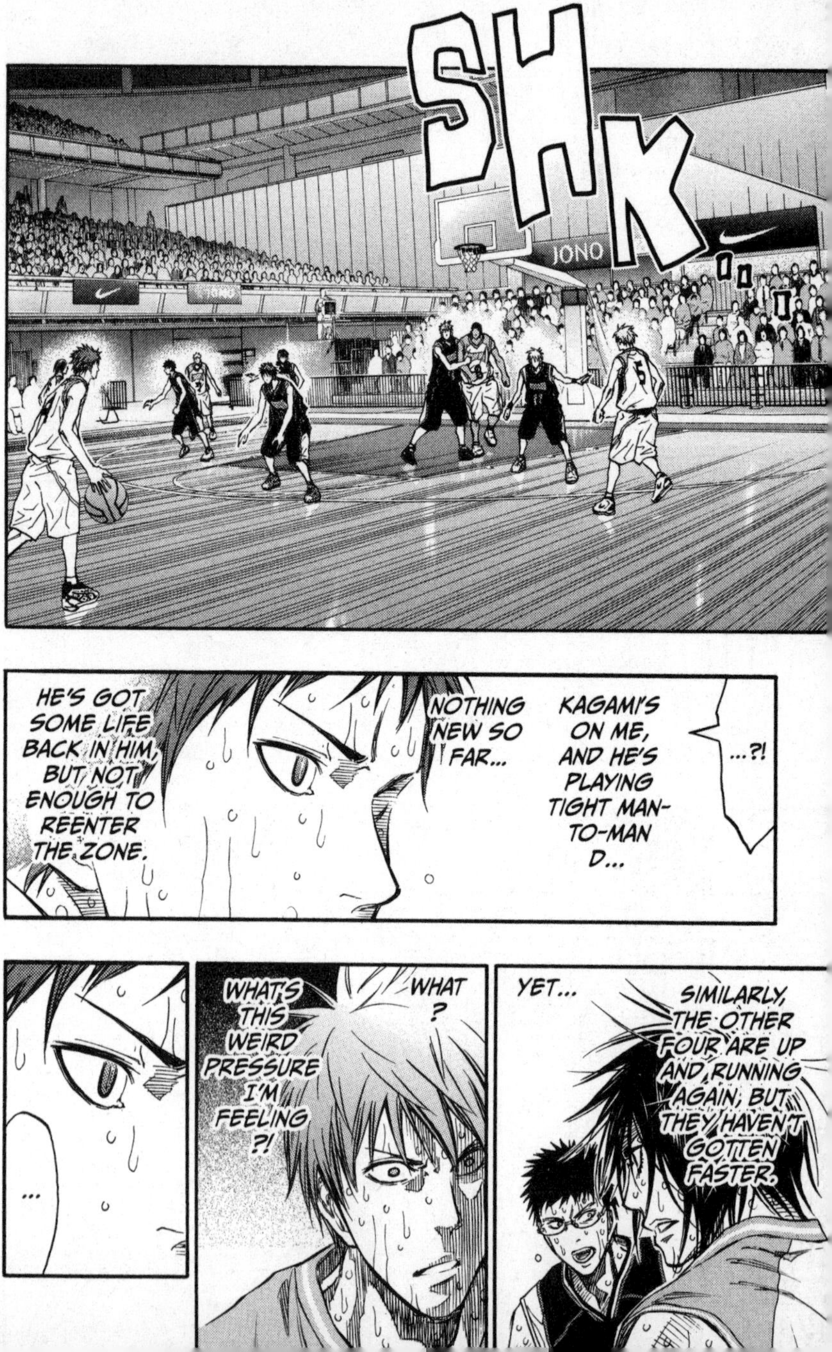
SHK
JONO
...?!
KAGAMI'S ON ME, AND HE'S PLAYING TIGHT MAN-TO-MAN D...
NOTHING NEW SO FAR...
HE'S GOT SOME LIFE BACK IN HIM, BUT NOT ENOUGH TO REENTER THE ZONE.
SIMILARLY, THE OTHER FOUR ARE UP AND RUNNING AGAIN, BUT THEY HAVEN'T GOTTEN FASTER.
YET...
WHAT?
WHAT'S THIS WEIRD PRESSURE I'M FEELING?!
...

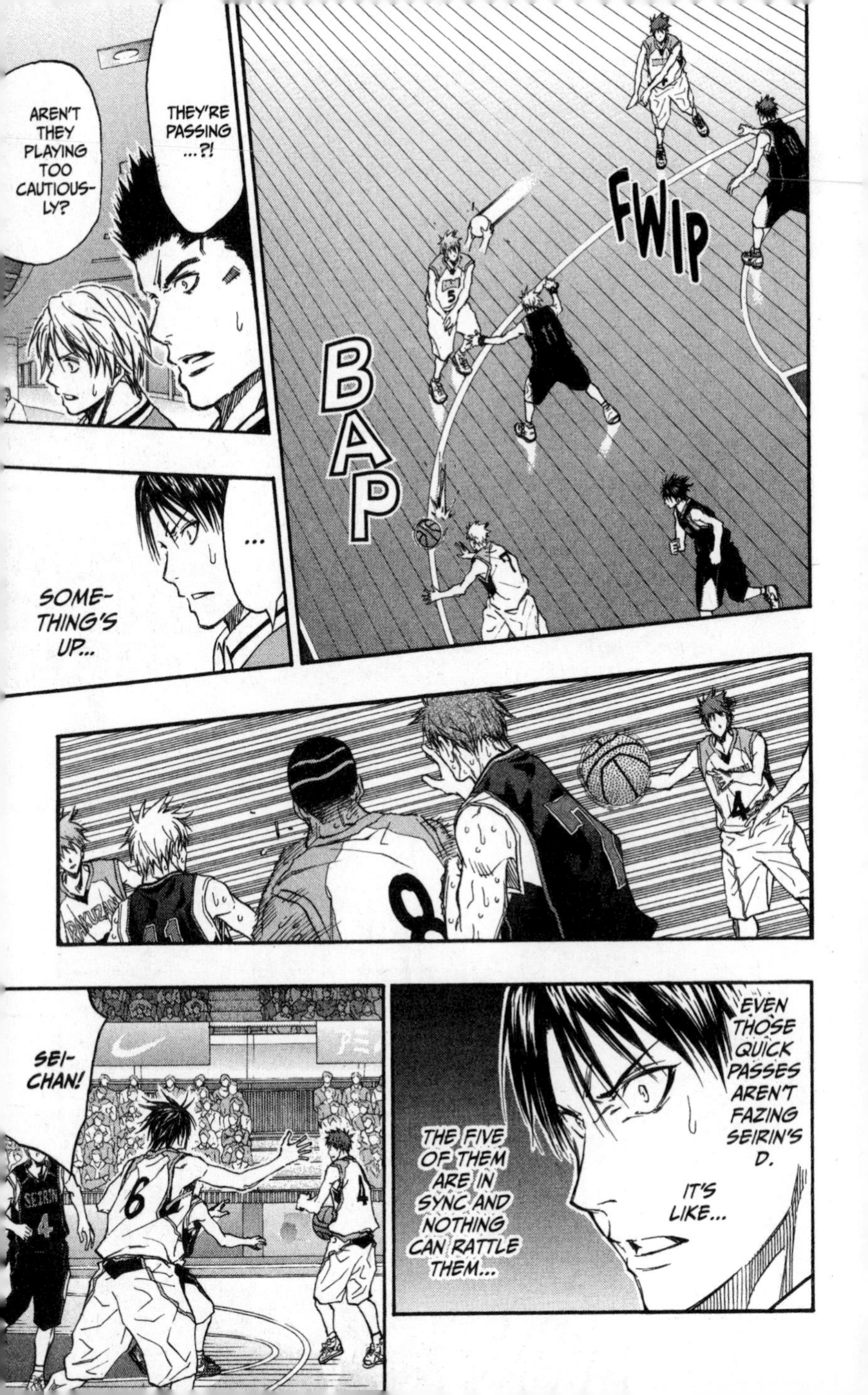
FWIP
BAP
THEY'RE PASSING ...?!
AREN'T THEY PLAYING TOO CAUTIOUS-LY?
...
SOME-THING'S UP...
EVEN THOSE QUICK PASSES AREN'T FAZING SEIRIN'S D.
IT'S LIKE...
THE FIVE OF THEM ARE IN SYNC AND NOTHING CAN RATTLE THEM...
SEI-CHAN!

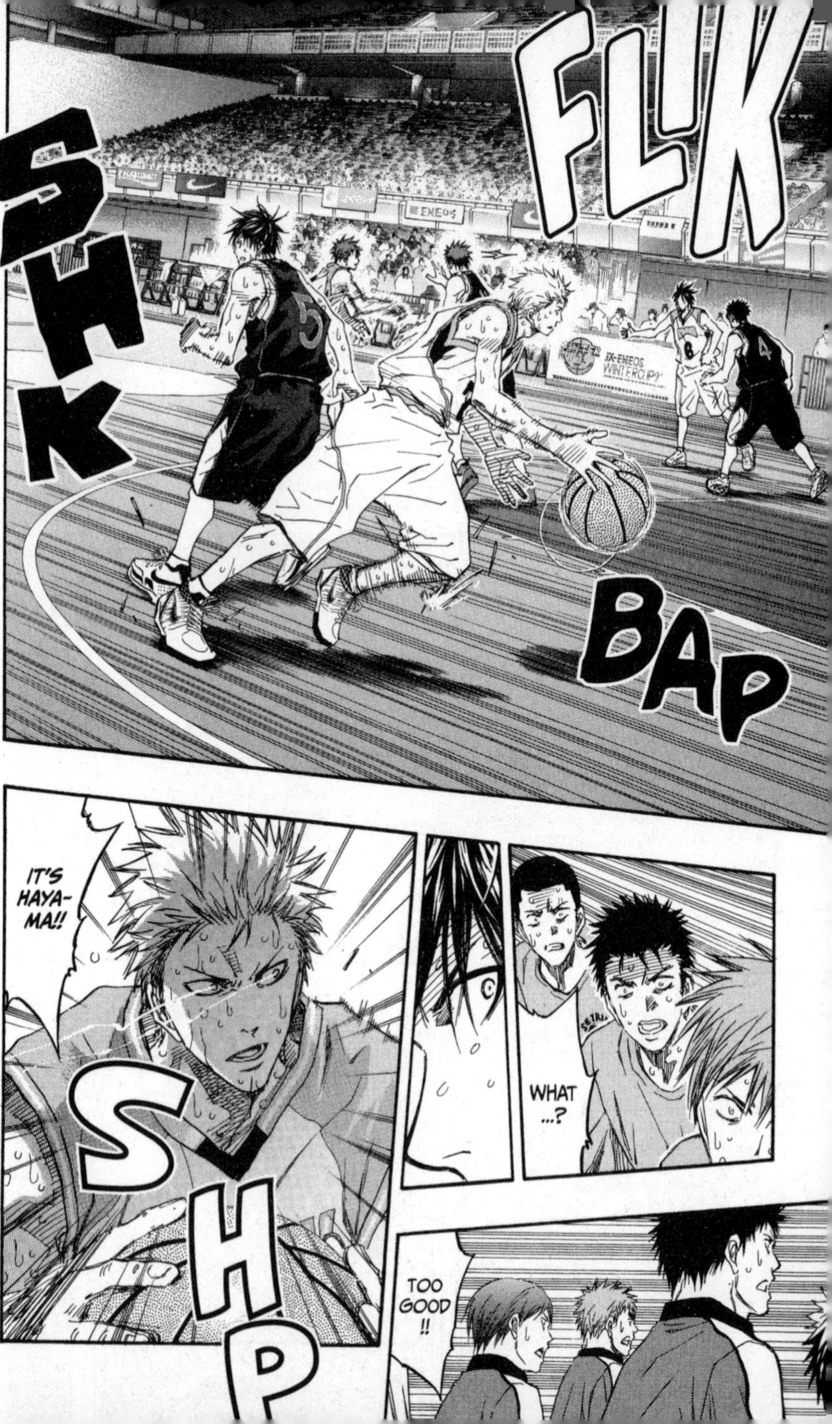
FLK
SHK
BAP
WHAT ...?
TOO GOOD !!
IT'S HAYA-MA!!
SHP

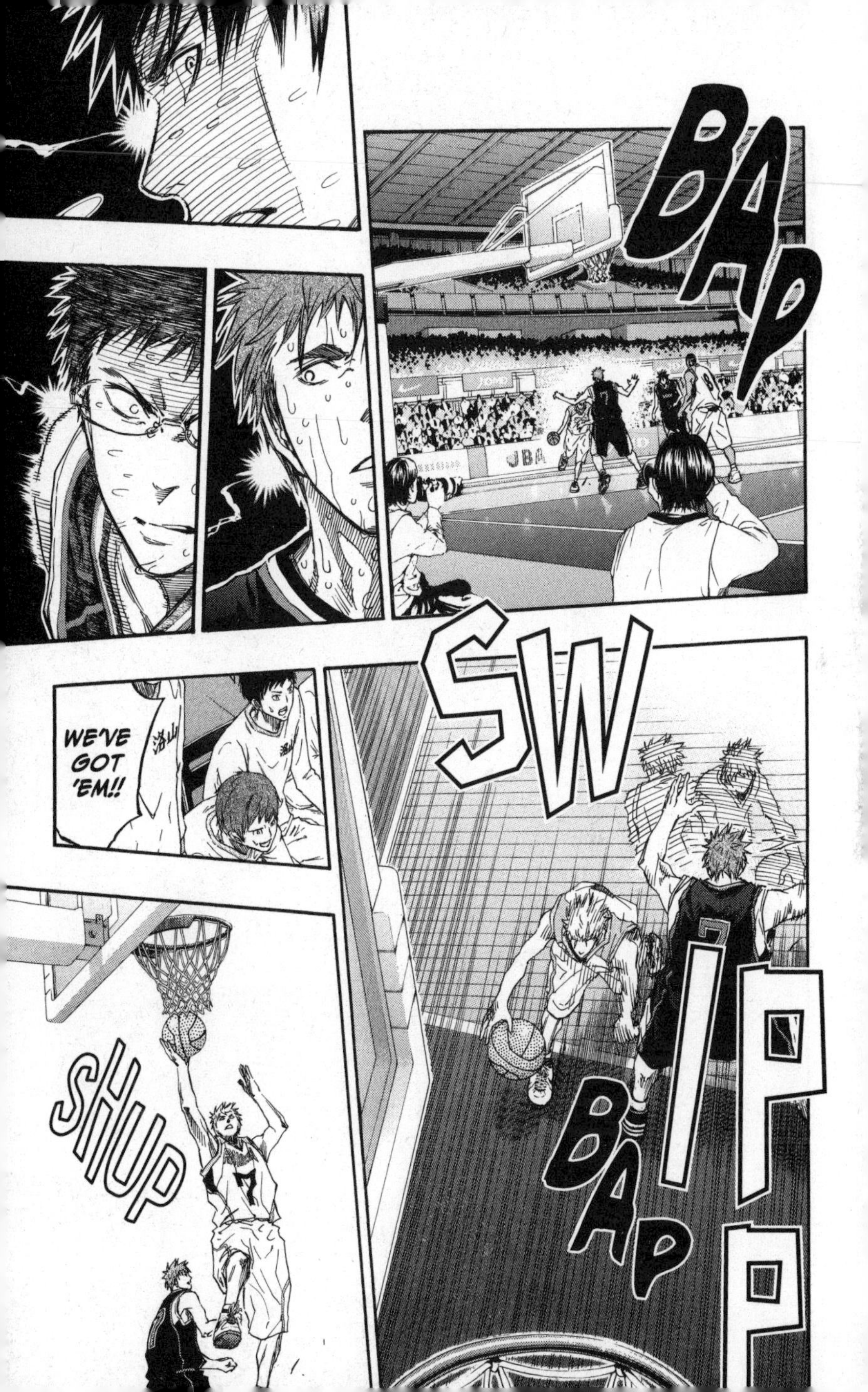
BAP
SWIP
BAP
WE'VE GOT 'EM!!
SHUP

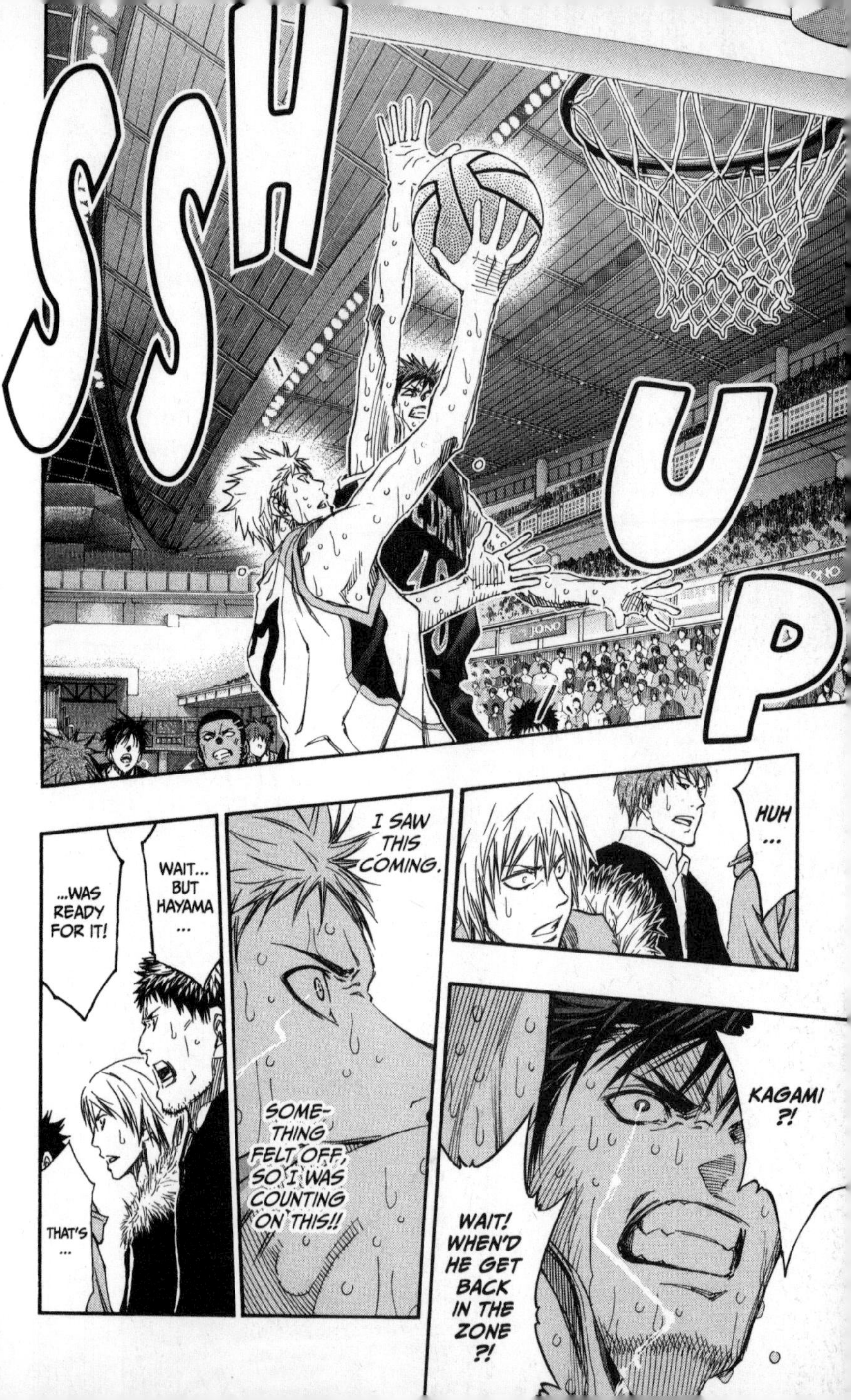
SSHUP
HUH ...
KAGAMI ?!
WAIT! WHEN'D HE GET BACK IN THE ZONE ?!
I SAW THIS COMING.
SOME-THING FELT OFF, SO I WAS COUNTING ON THIS!!
WAIT... BUT HAYAMA ...
...WAS READY FOR IT!
THAT'S ...

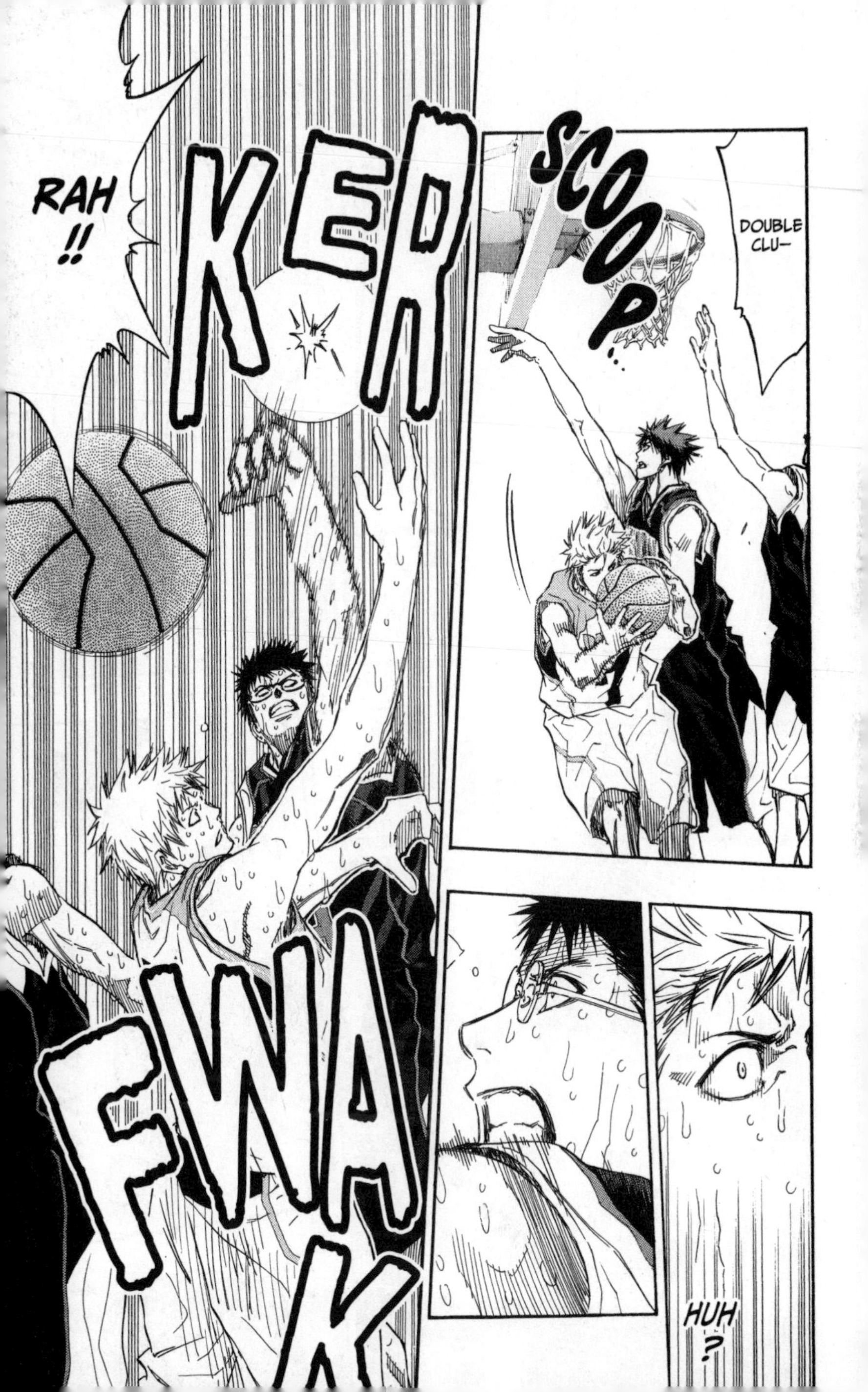
SCOOP...
DOUBLE CLU—
HUH?
RAH!!
KER
FWAK

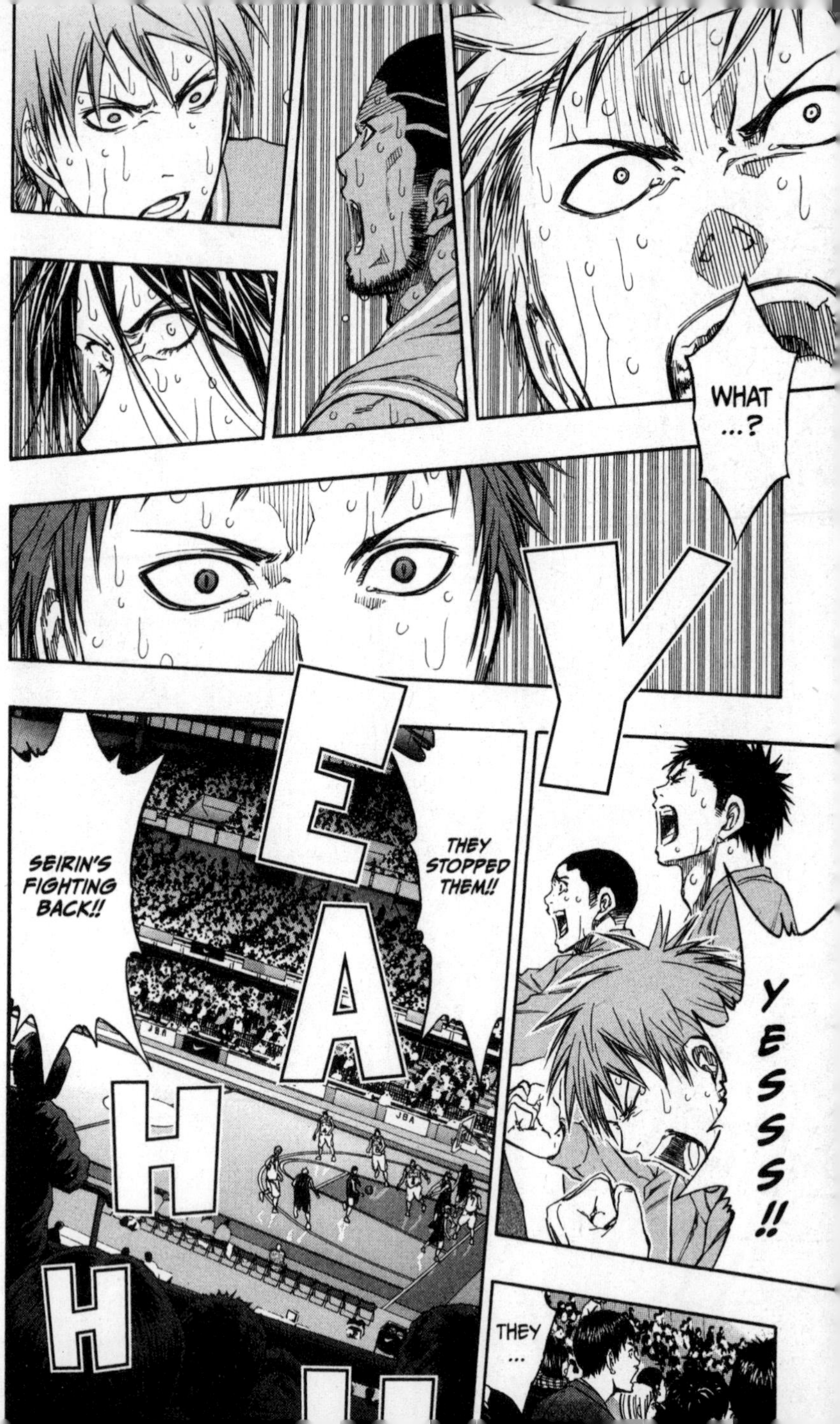

WHAT ...?
YEAHH
YESSS!!
THEY STOPPED THEM!!
SEIRIN'S FIGHTING BACK!!
THEY ...

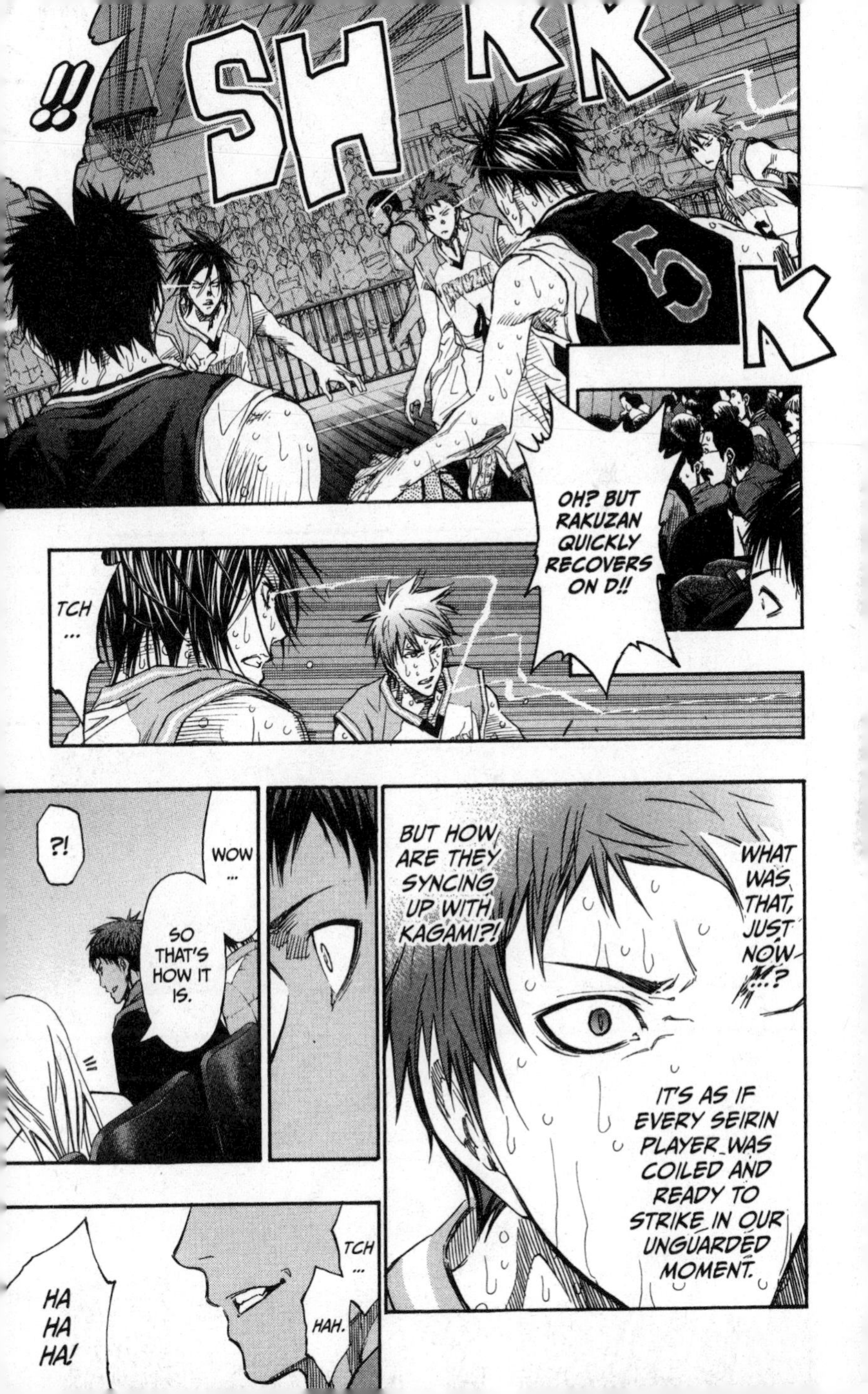
SHKKK
!!
OH? BUT RAKUZAN QUICKLY RECOVERS ON D!!
TCH ...
WHAT WAS THAT, JUST NOW...?
IT'S AS IF EVERY SEIRIN PLAYER WAS COILED AND READY TO STRIKE IN OUR UNGUARDED MOMENT.
BUT HOW ARE THEY SYNCING UP WITH KAGAMI?!
WOW ...
SO THAT'S HOW IT IS.
?!
TCH ...
HAH.
HA HA HA!

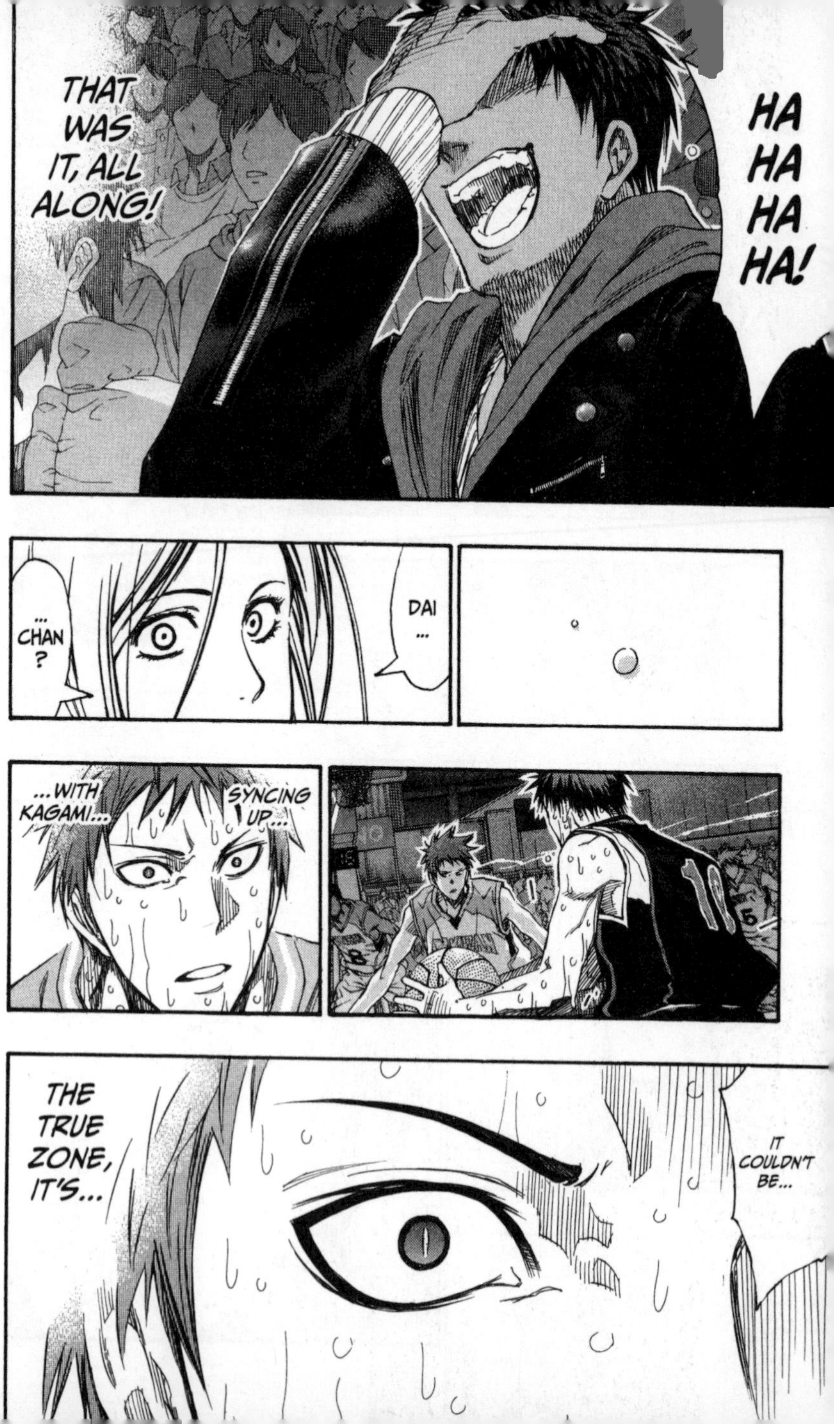
HA HA HA HA!
THAT WAS IT, ALL ALONG!
DAI...
...CHAN?
SYNCING UP...
...WITH KAGAMI...
IT COULDN'T BE...
THE TRUE ZONE, IT'S...

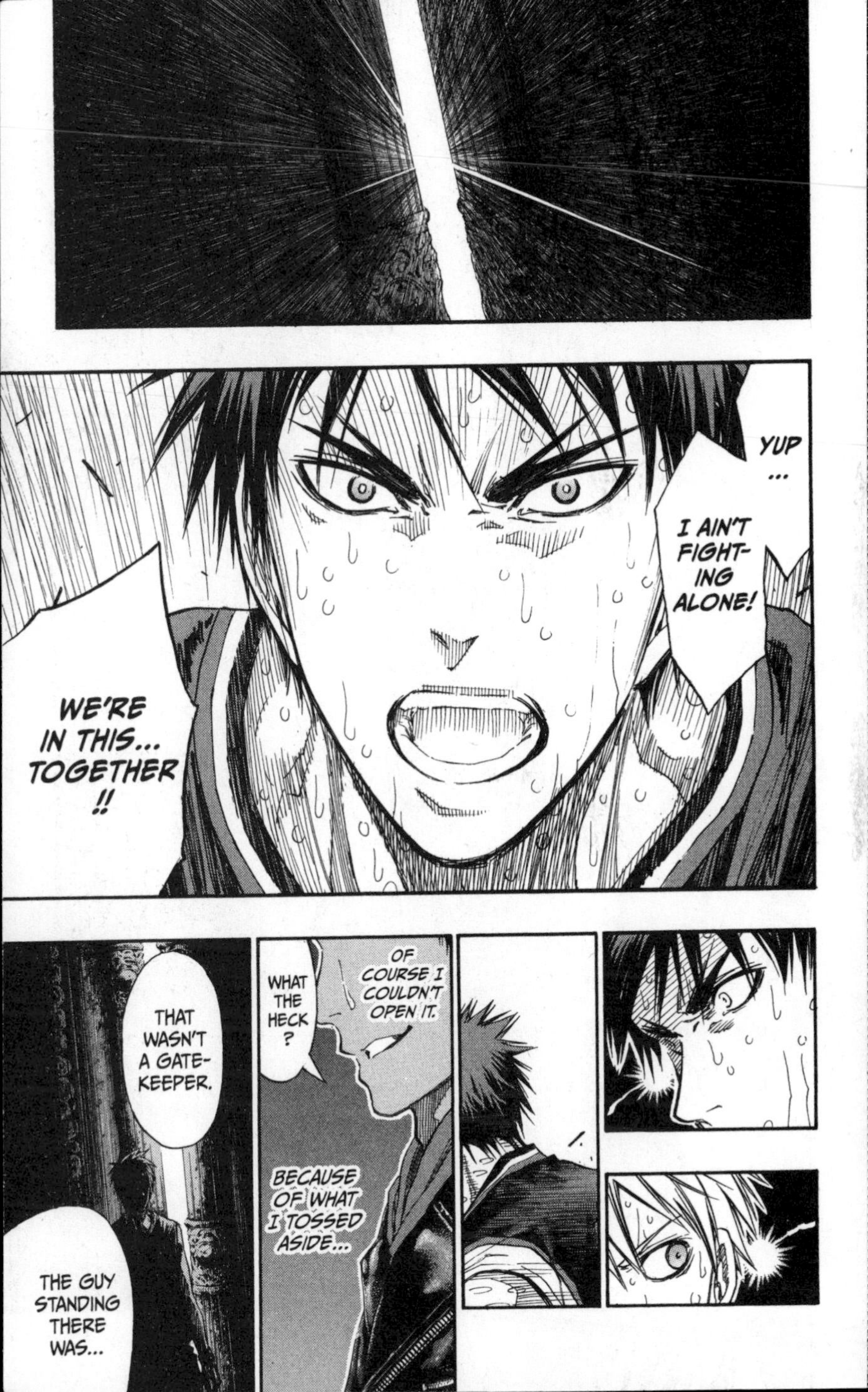
YUP ...
I AIN'T FIGHTING ALONE!
WE'RE IN THIS... TOGETHER!!
OF COURSE I COULDN'T OPEN IT.
WHAT THE HECK?
BECAUSE OF WHAT I TOSSED ASIDE...
THAT WASN'T A GATEKEEPER.
THE GUY STANDING THERE WAS...

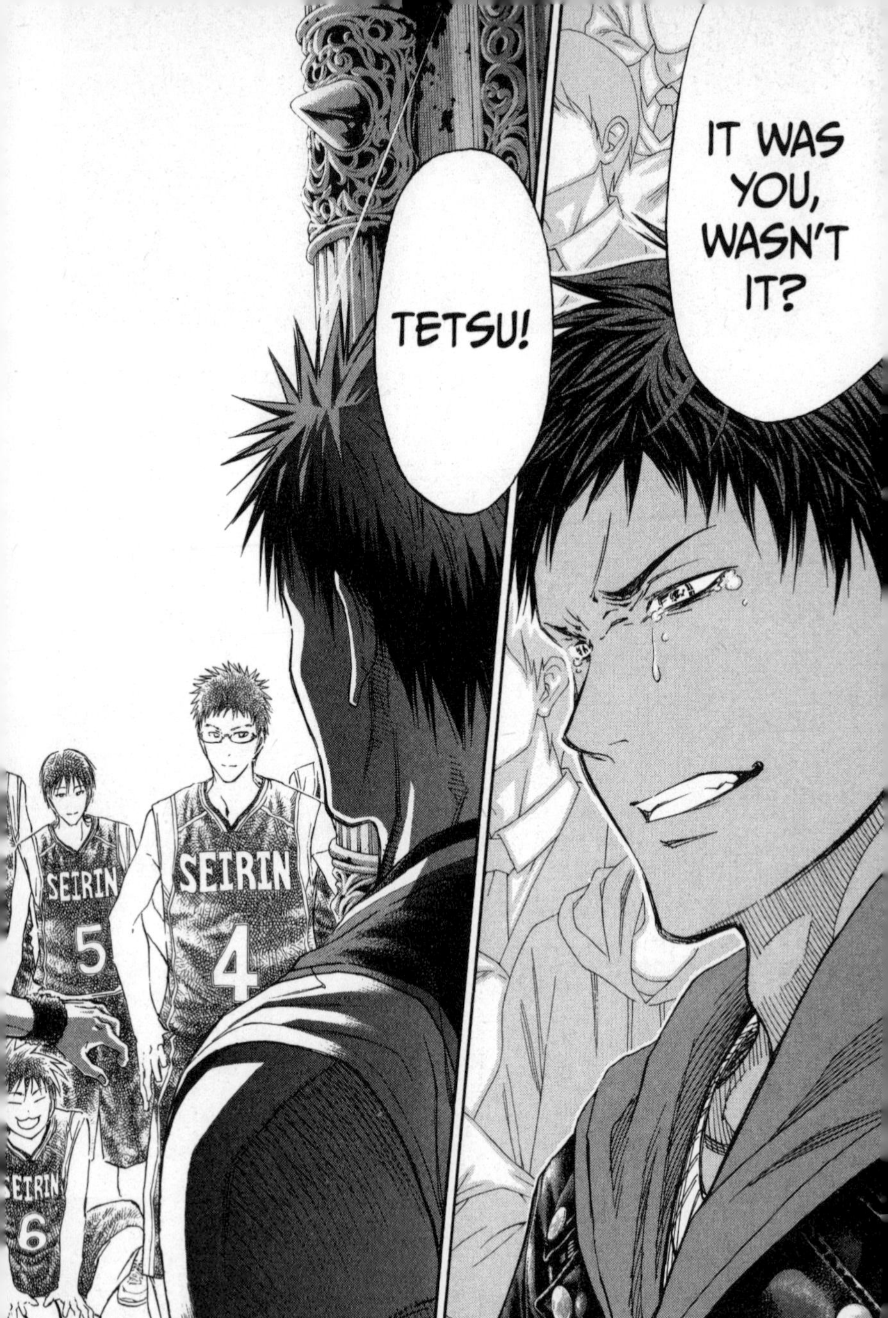
IT WAS YOU, WASN'T IT?
TETSU!
SEIRIN
5
SEIRIN
4
SEIRIN
6

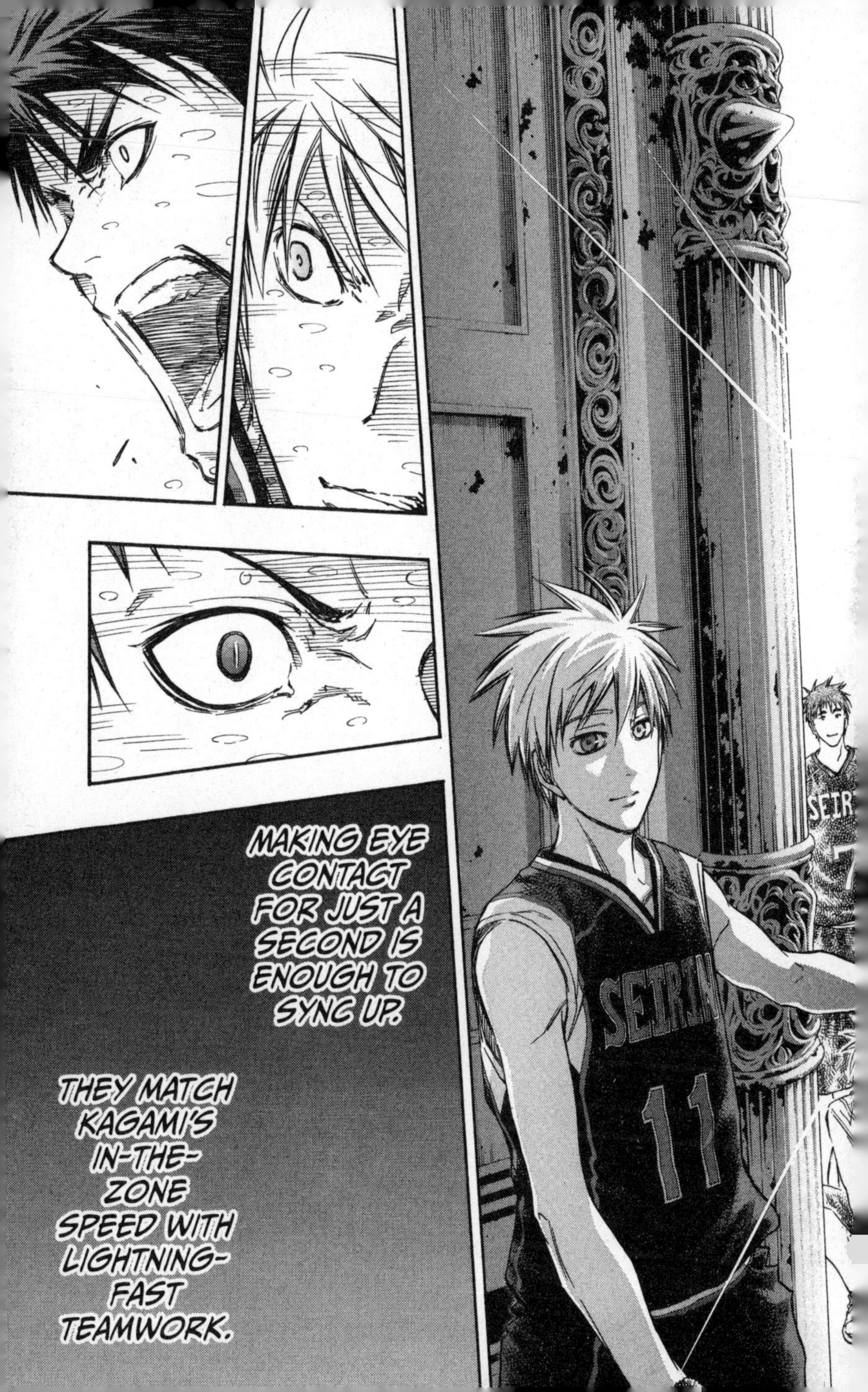
MAKING EYE CONTACT FOR JUST A SECOND IS ENOUGH TO SYNC UP.
THEY MATCH KAGAMI'S IN-THE-ZONE SPEED WITH LIGHTNING-FAST TEAMWORK.
SEIRIN
11
SEIR
7

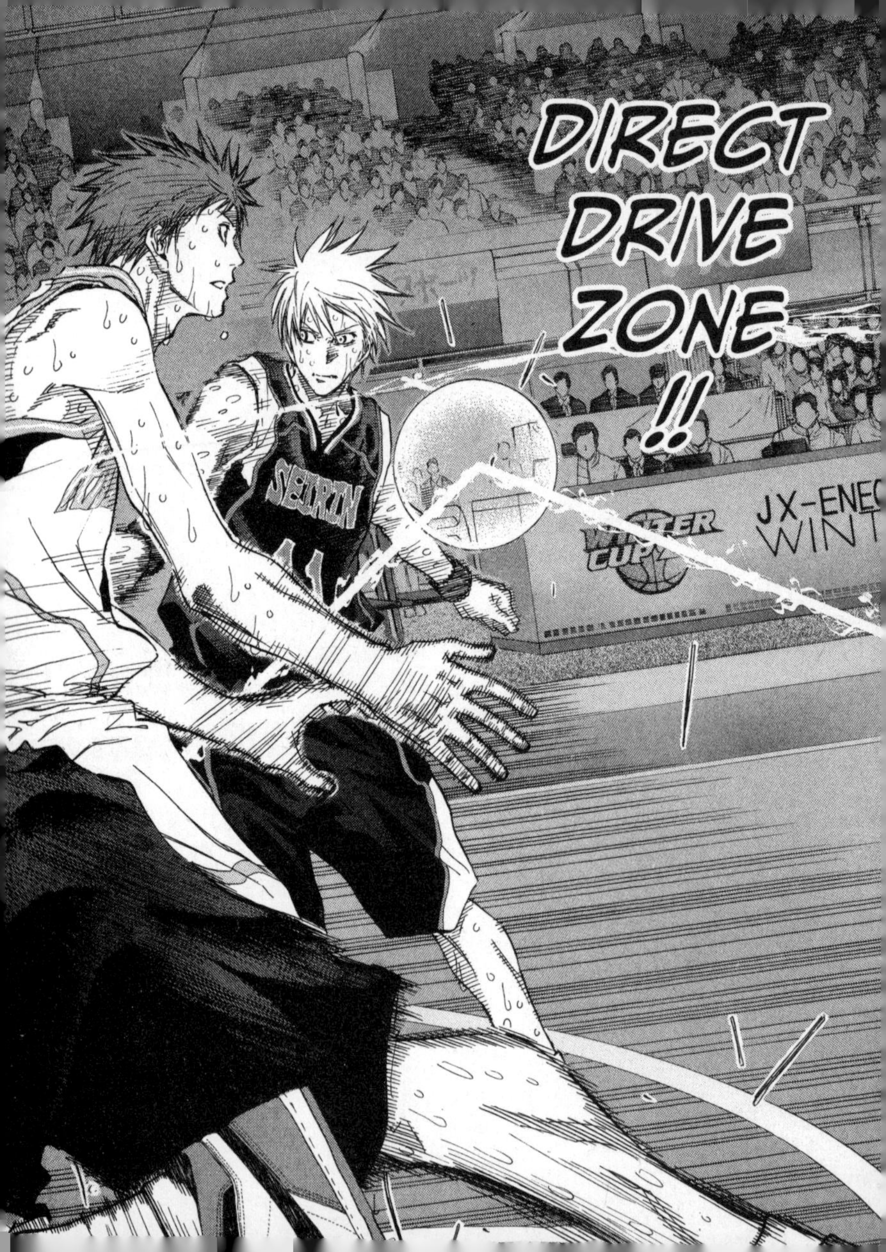
DIRECT DRIVE ZONE!!
SEIRIN
JX-ENEC
WINTER CUP
WINT

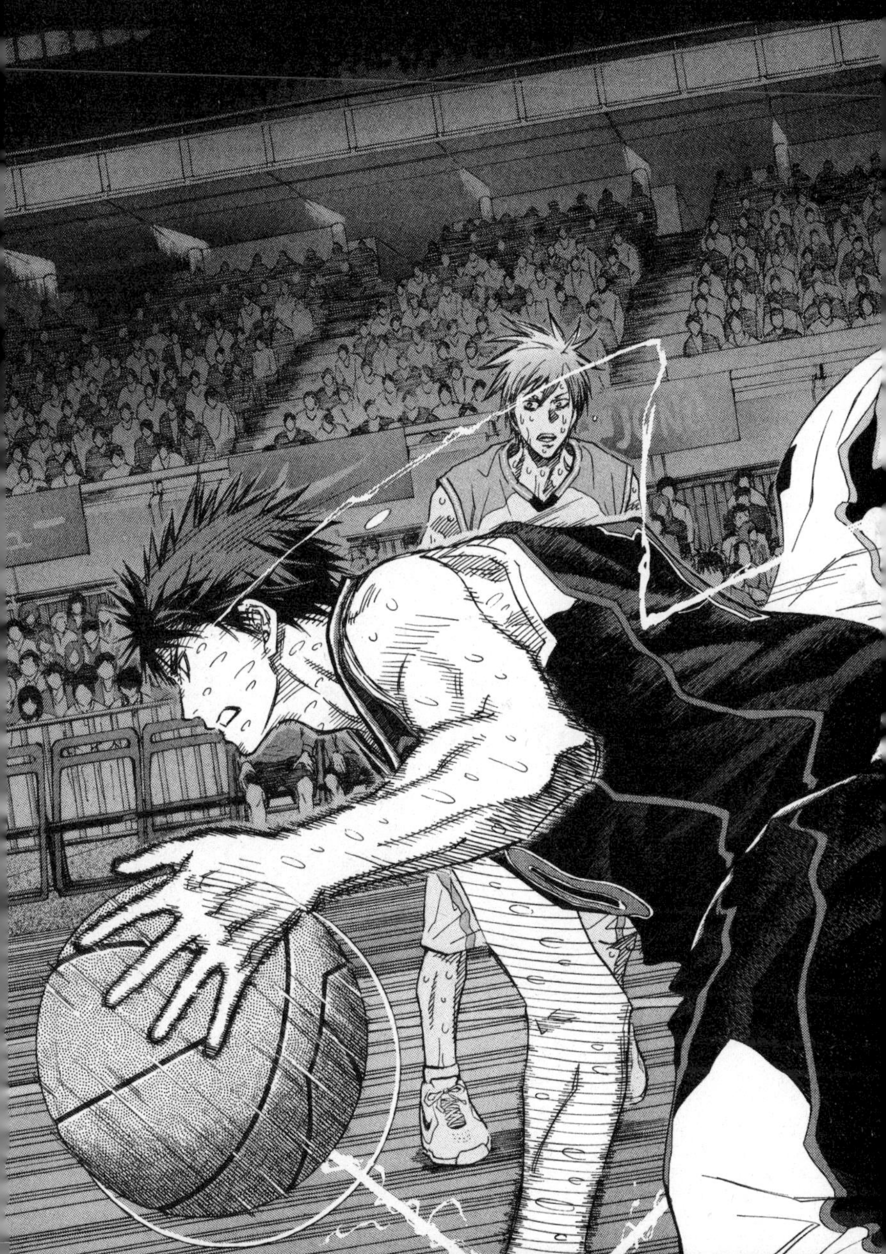

KUROKO'S BASKETBALL BLOOPERS

TAKE 4

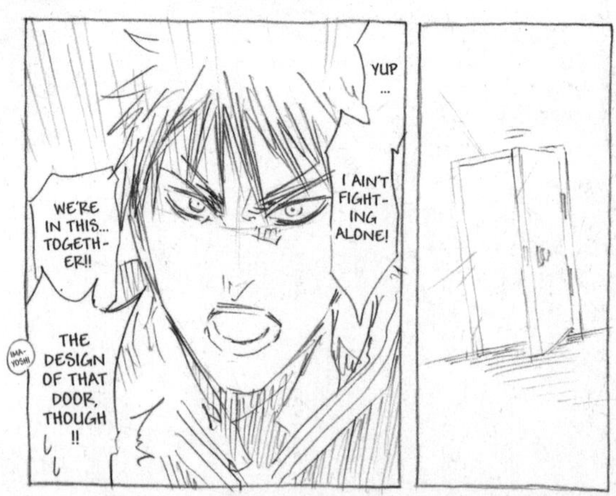
YUP ...
I AIN'T FIGHTING ALONE!
WE'RE IN THIS... TOGETHER!!
IMA-YOSHI
THE DESIGN OF THAT DOOR, THOUGH!!

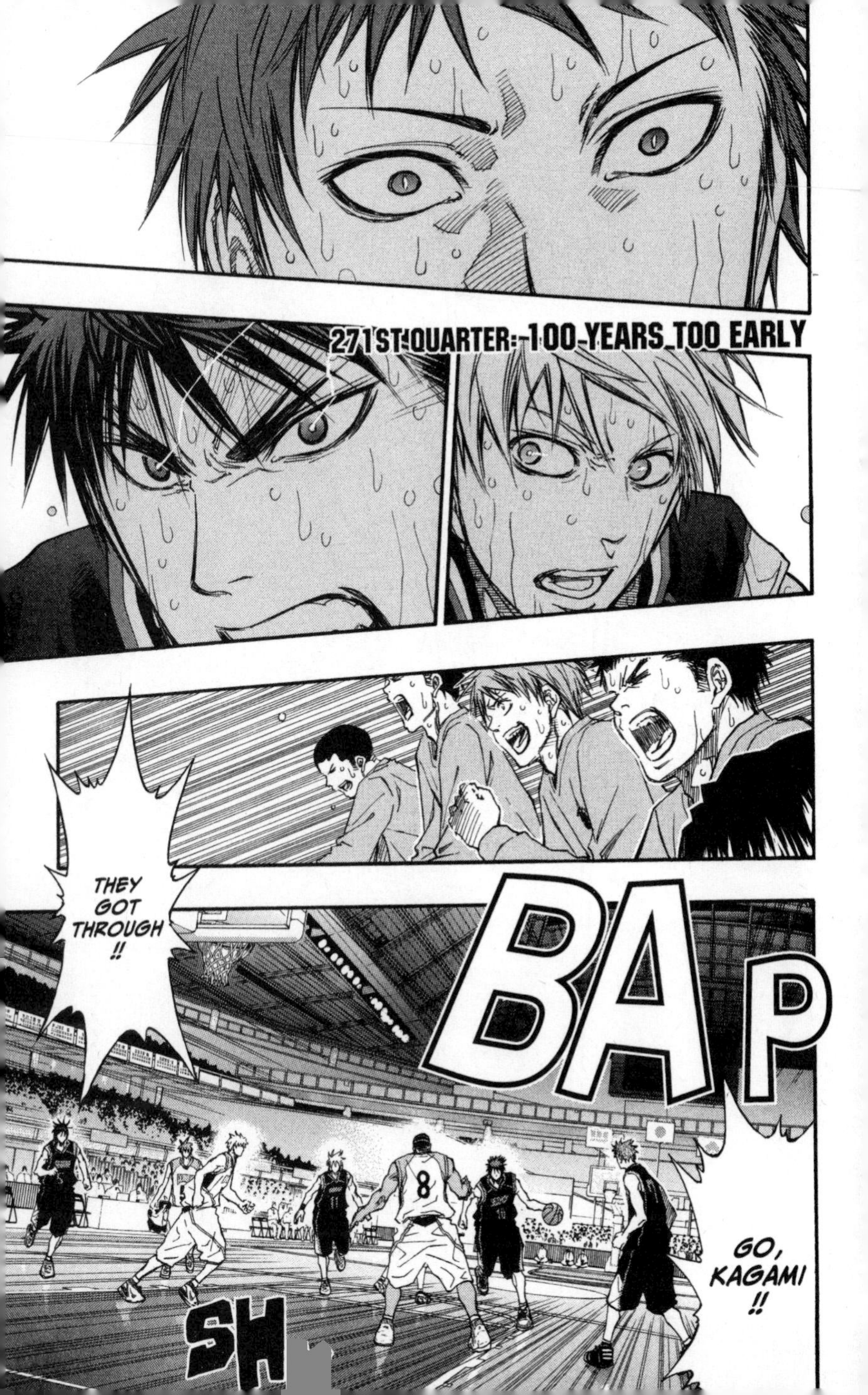
271ST QUARTER: 100 YEARS TOO EARLY
BAP
THEY GOT THROUGH !!
GO, KAGAMI !!
SH

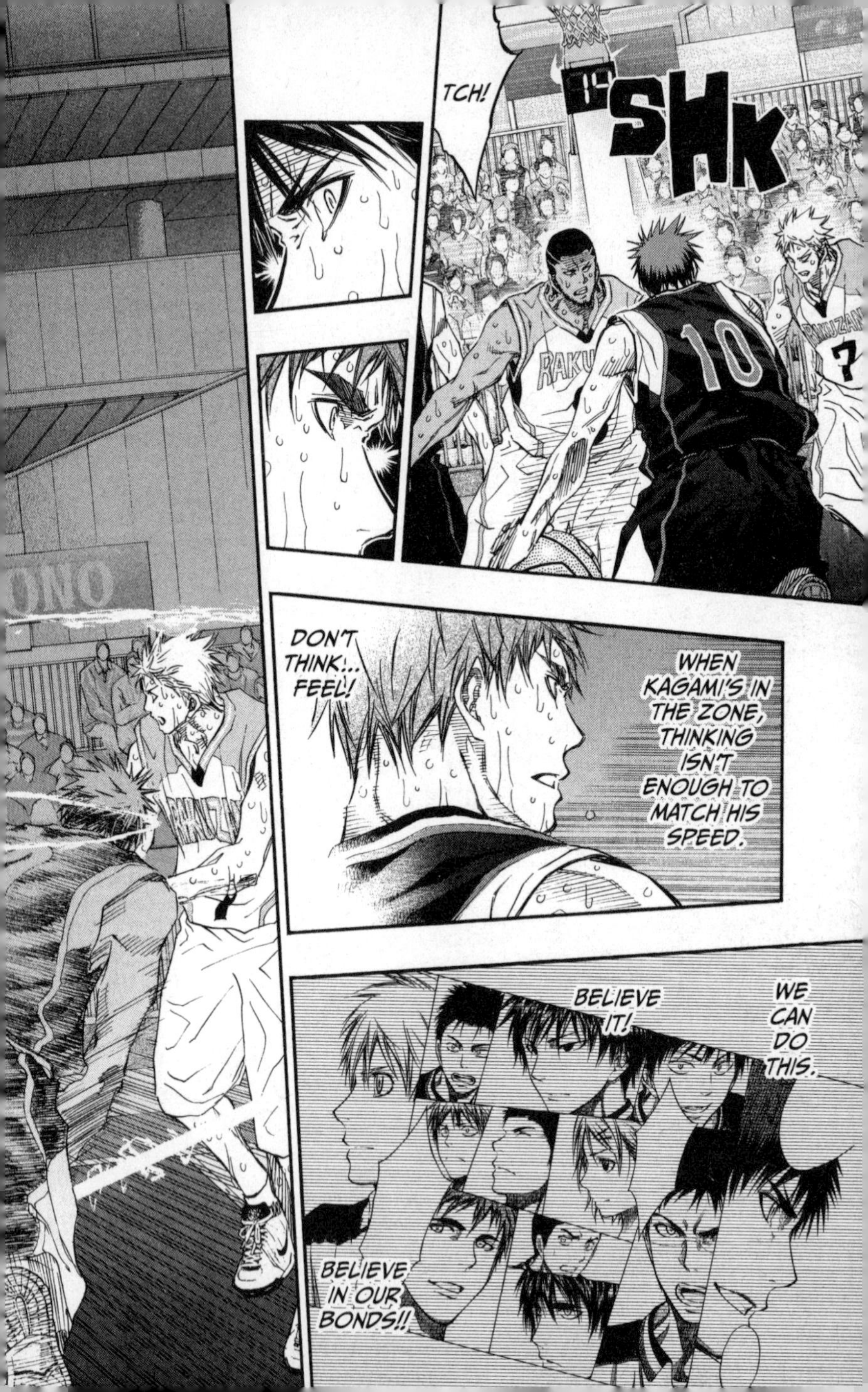
SHK
TCH!
DON'T THINK... FEEL!
WHEN KAGAMI'S IN THE ZONE, THINKING ISN'T ENOUGH TO MATCH HIS SPEED.
WE CAN DO THIS.
BELIEVE IT!
BELIEVE IN OUR BONDS!!

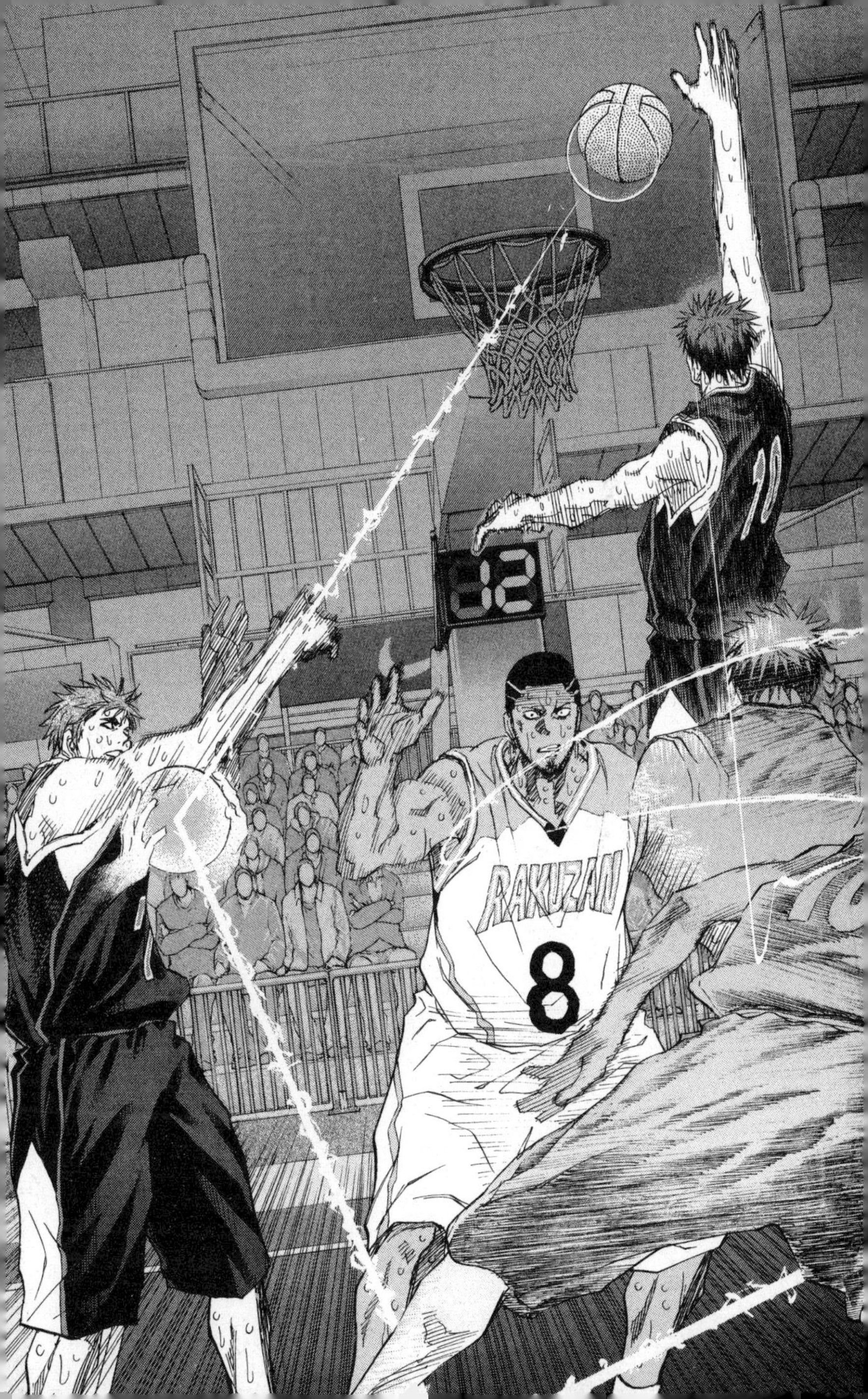
RAKUZAN
8

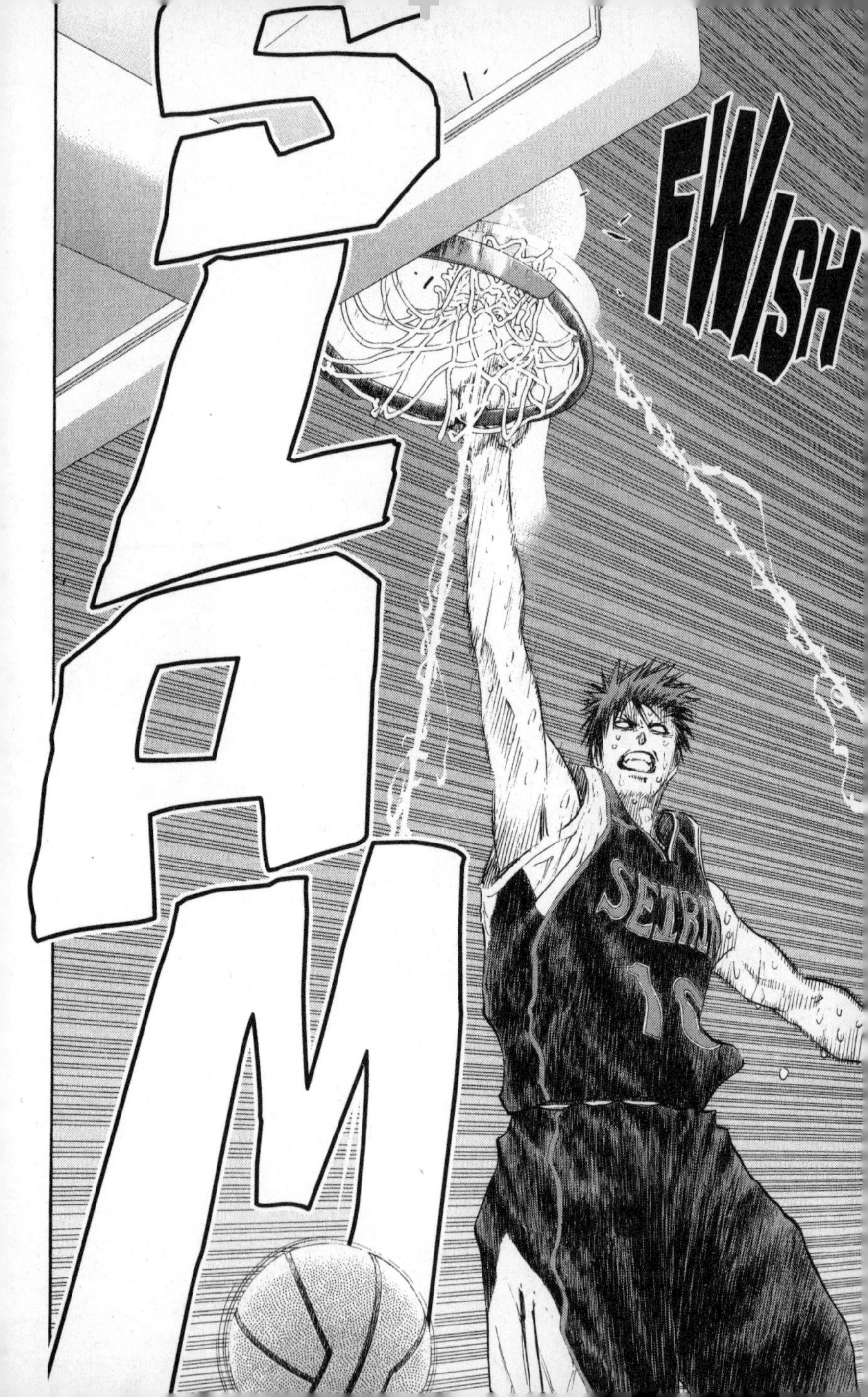
FWISH
SLAM

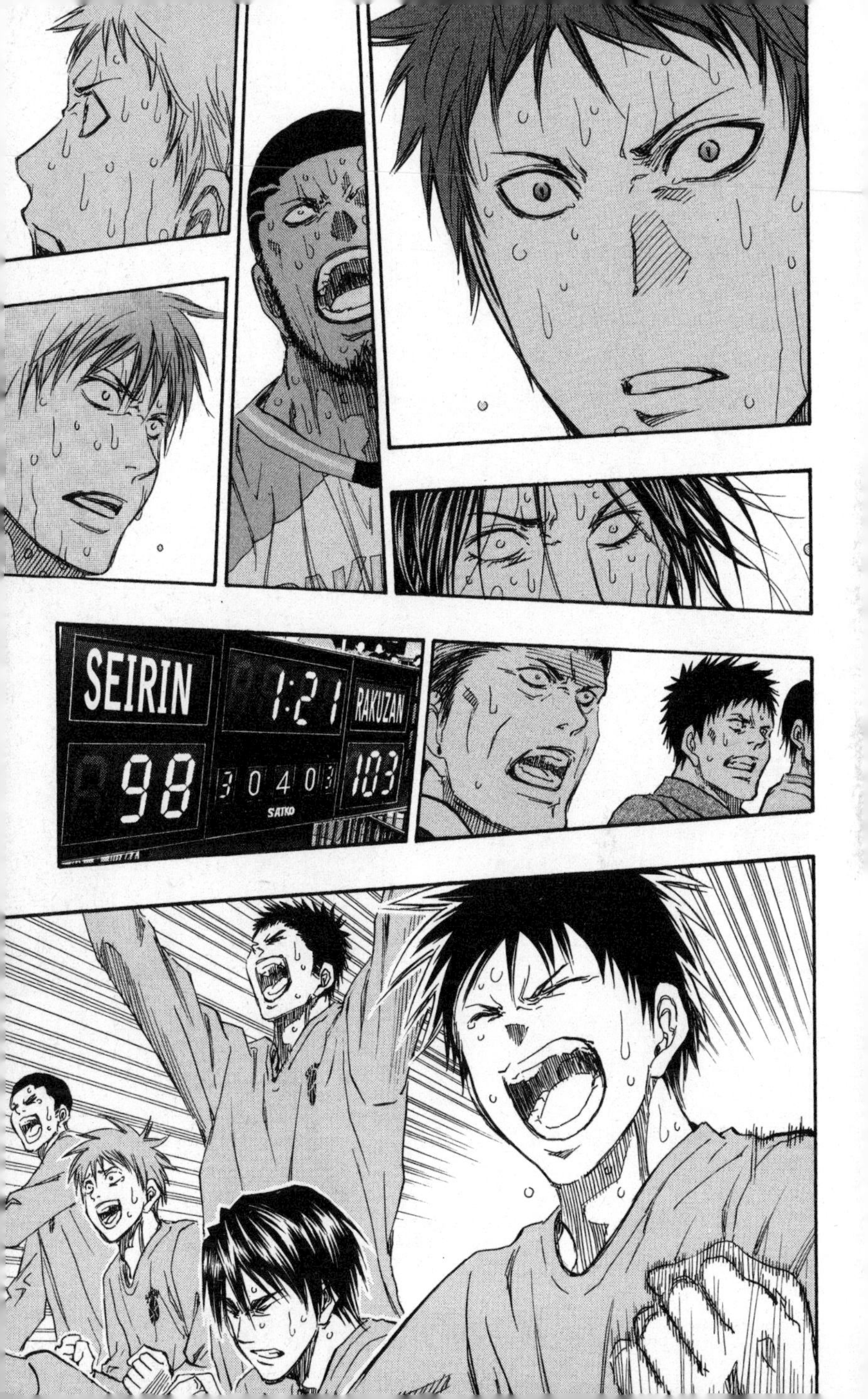
SEIRIN
1:21
RAKUZAN
98
3 0 4 0 3
103
SATKO

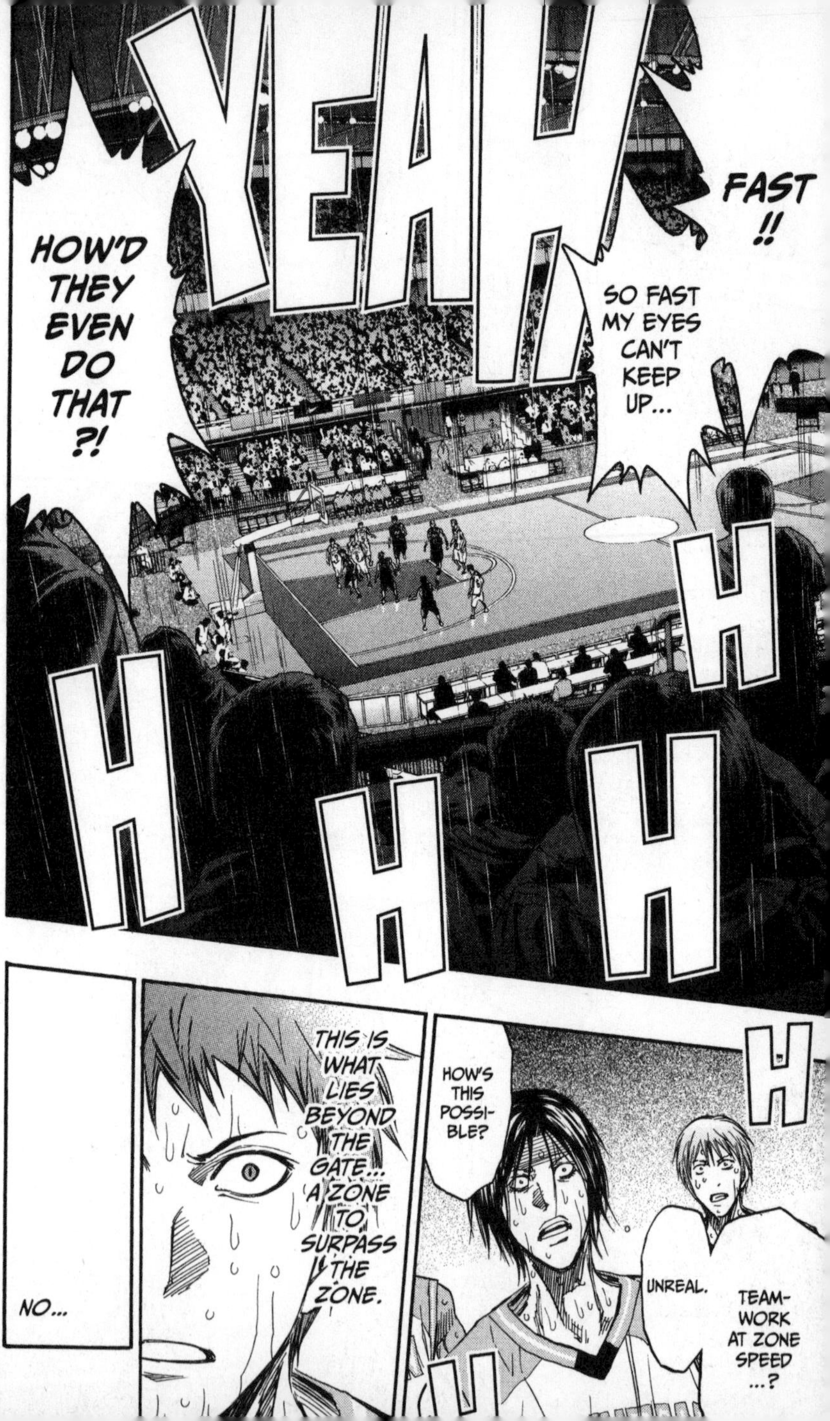
FAST!!
SO FAST MY EYES CAN'T KEEP UP...
YEAH
HOW'D THEY EVEN DO THAT?!
HHHHH
H
TEAM-WORK AT ZONE SPEED...?
UNREAL.
HOW'S THIS POSSI-BLE?
THIS IS WHAT LIES BEYOND THE GATE... A ZONE TO SURPASS THE ZONE.
NO...

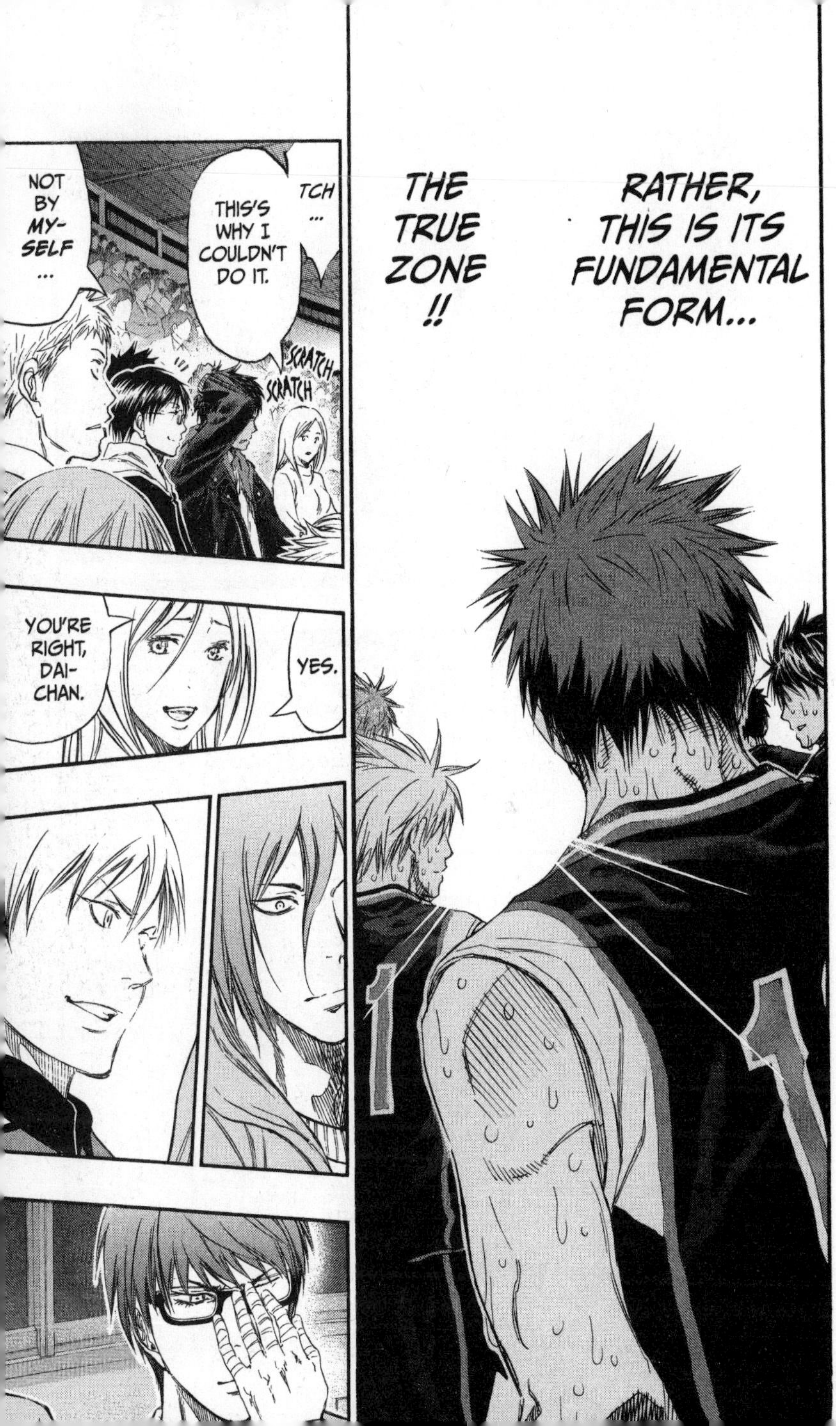
RATHER, THIS IS ITS FUNDAMENTAL FORM...
THE TRUE ZONE !!
TCH ...
THIS'S WHY I COULDN'T DO IT.
NOT BY MY-SELF ...
SCRATCH
SCRATCH
YES.
YOU'RE RIGHT, DAI-CHAN.

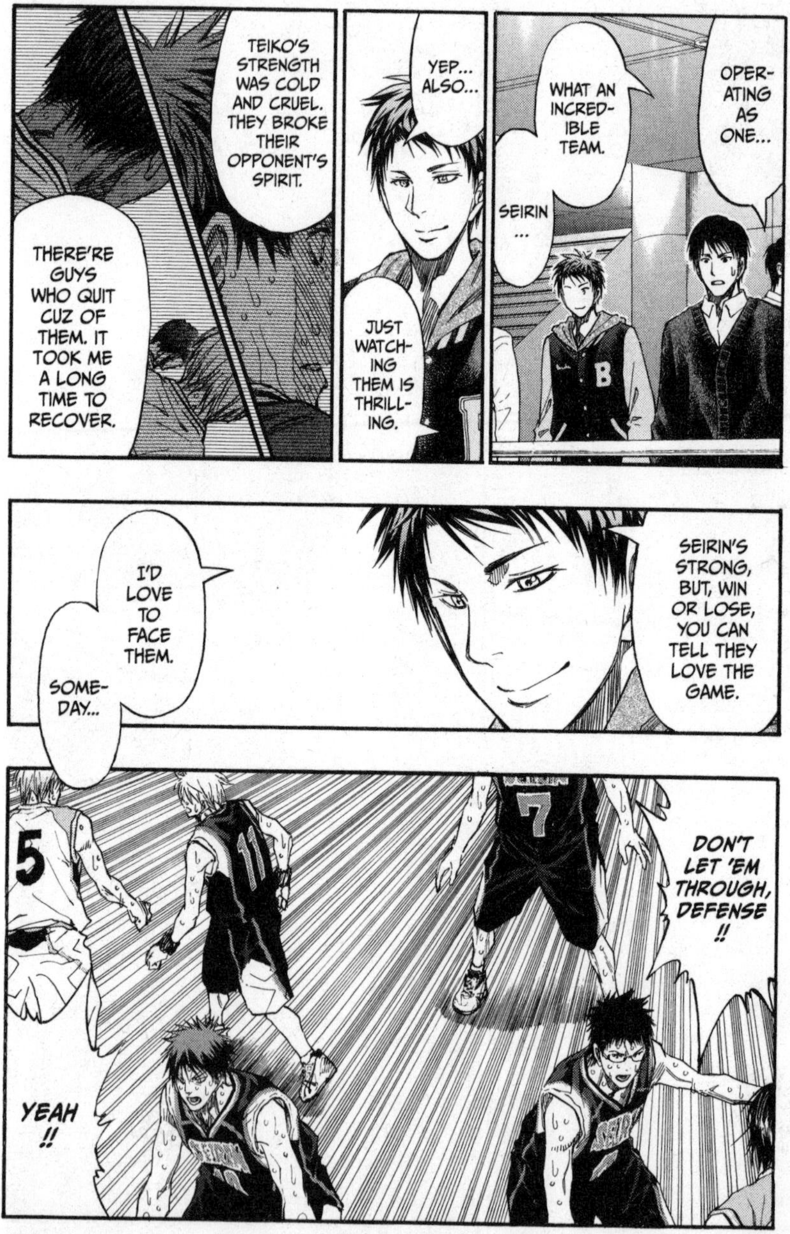
OPERATING AS ONE...
WHAT AN INCREDIBLE TEAM.
SEIRIN...
YEP... ALSO...
JUST WATCHING THEM IS THRILLING.
TEIKO'S STRENGTH WAS COLD AND CRUEL. THEY BROKE THEIR OPPONENT'S SPIRIT.
THERE'RE GUYS WHO QUIT CUZ OF THEM. IT TOOK ME A LONG TIME TO RECOVER.
SEIRIN'S STRONG, BUT, WIN OR LOSE, YOU CAN TELL THEY LOVE THE GAME.
I'D LOVE TO FACE THEM.
SOMEDAY...
DON'T LET 'EM THROUGH, DEFENSE!!
YEAH!!

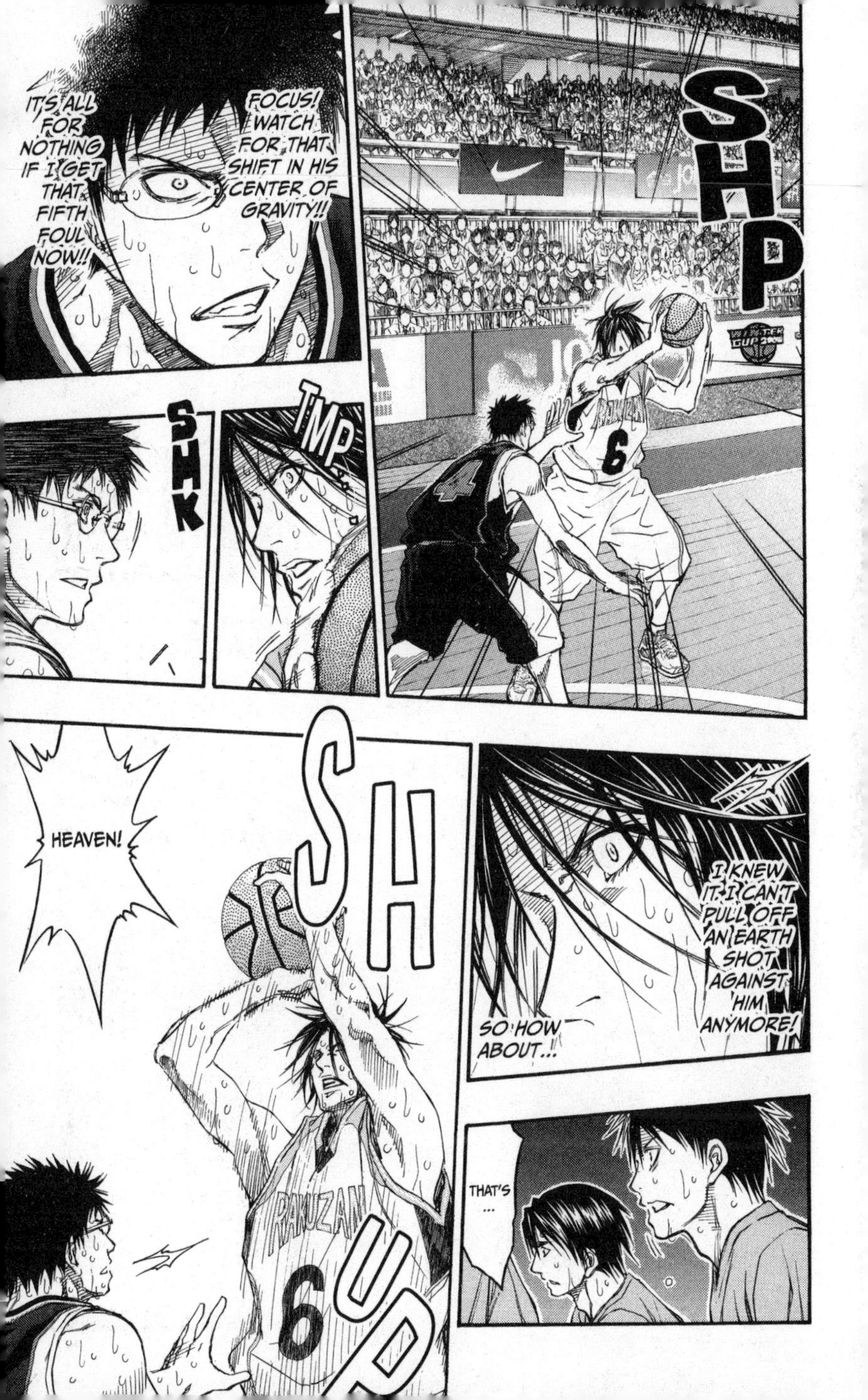
SHP
FOCUS! WATCH FOR THAT SHIFT IN HIS CENTER OF GRAVITY!!
IT'S ALL FOR NOTHING IF I GET THAT FIFTH FOUL NOW!!
TMP
SHK
I KNEW IT. I CAN'T PULL OFF AN EARTH SHOT AGAINST HIM ANYMORE!
SO HOW ABOUT..!
THAT'S ...
SH
HEAVEN!
UP

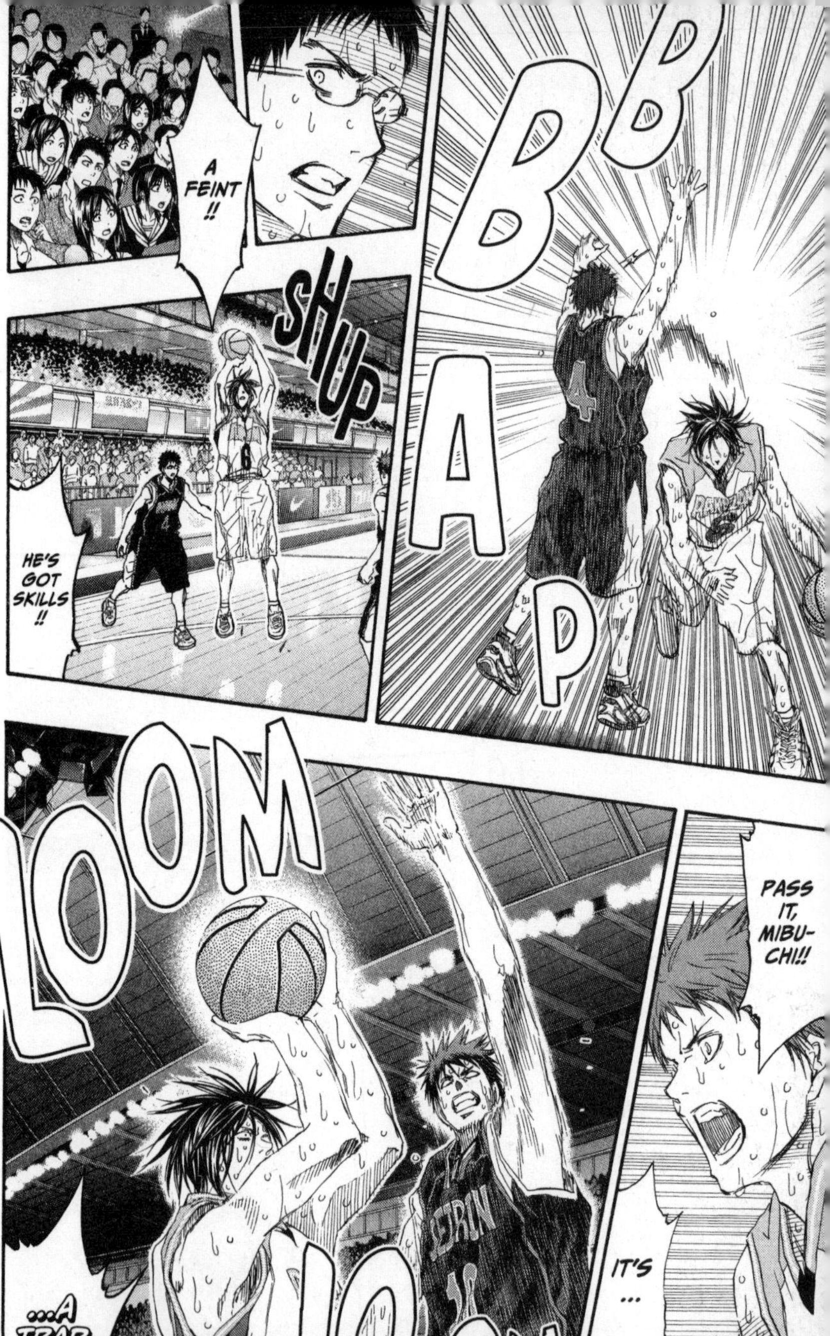
BBAP
A FEINT!!
SHUP
HE'S GOT SKILLS!!
PASS IT, MIBU-CHI!!
IT'S...
LOOM
...A TRAP!!
LOOM

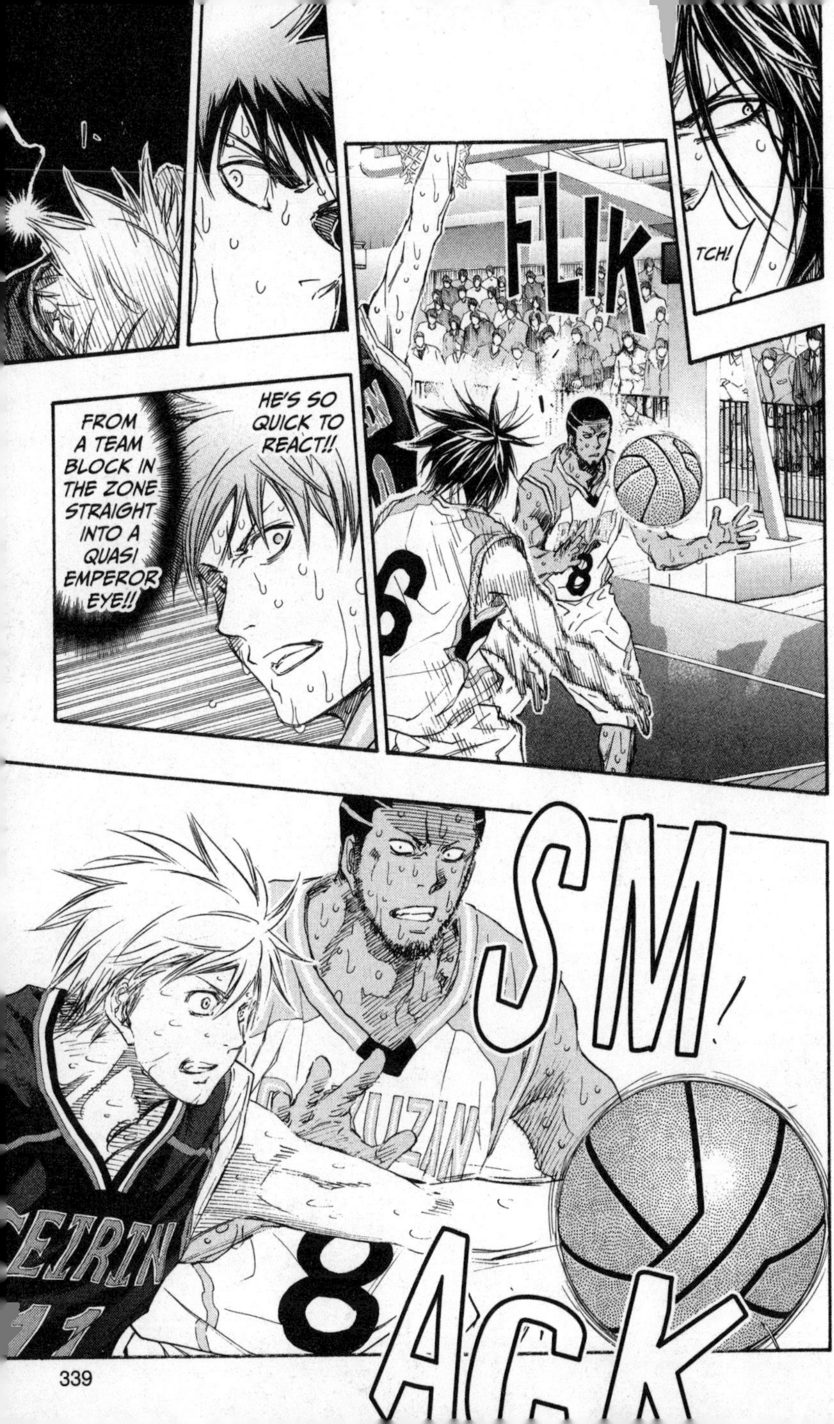
TCH!
FLIK
HE'S SO QUICK TO REACT!!
FROM A TEAM BLOCK IN THE ZONE STRAIGHT INTO A QUASI EMPEROR EYE!!
SMACK
SEIRIN

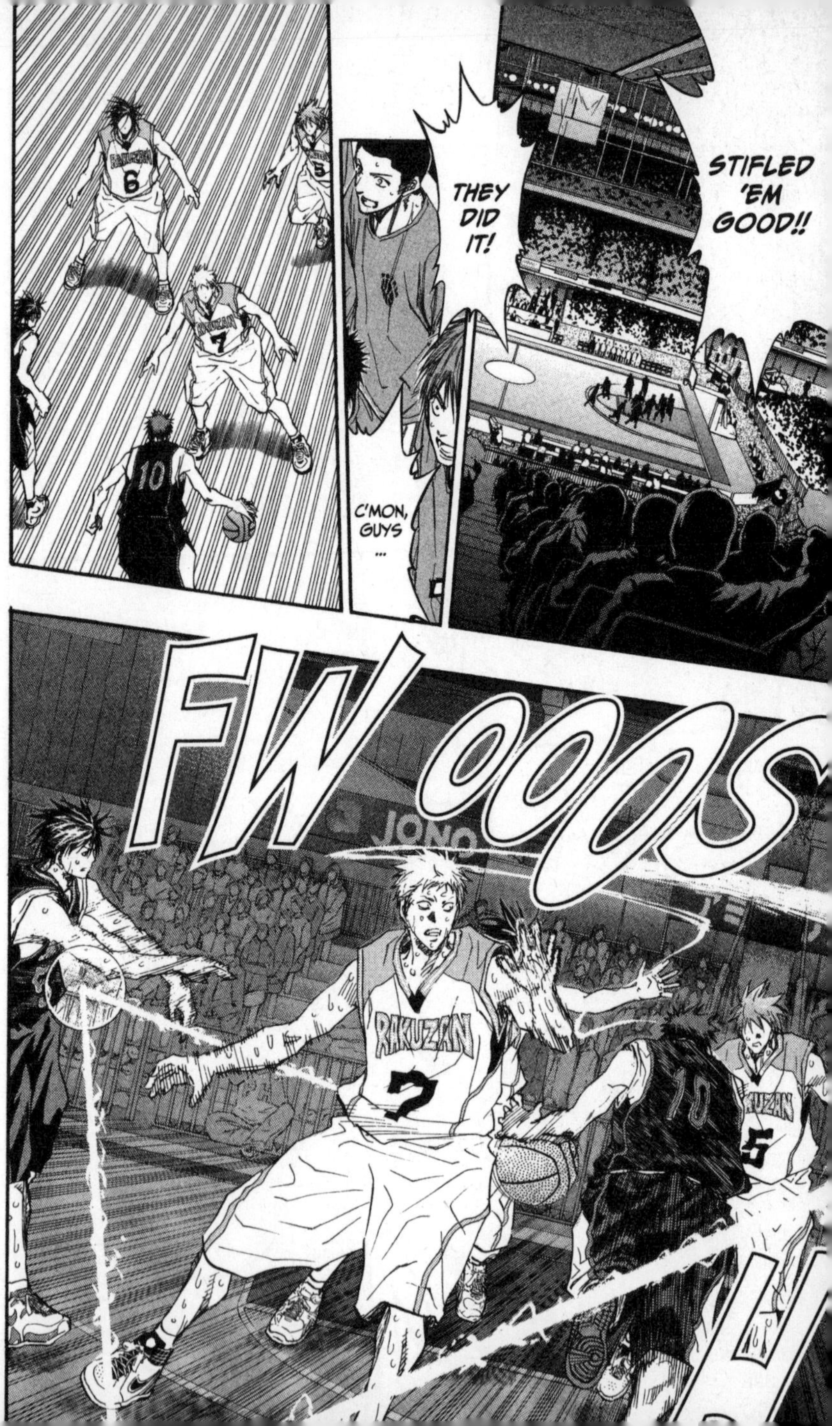
STIFLED 'EM GOOD!!
THEY DID IT!
C'MON, GUYS ...
FWOOOS

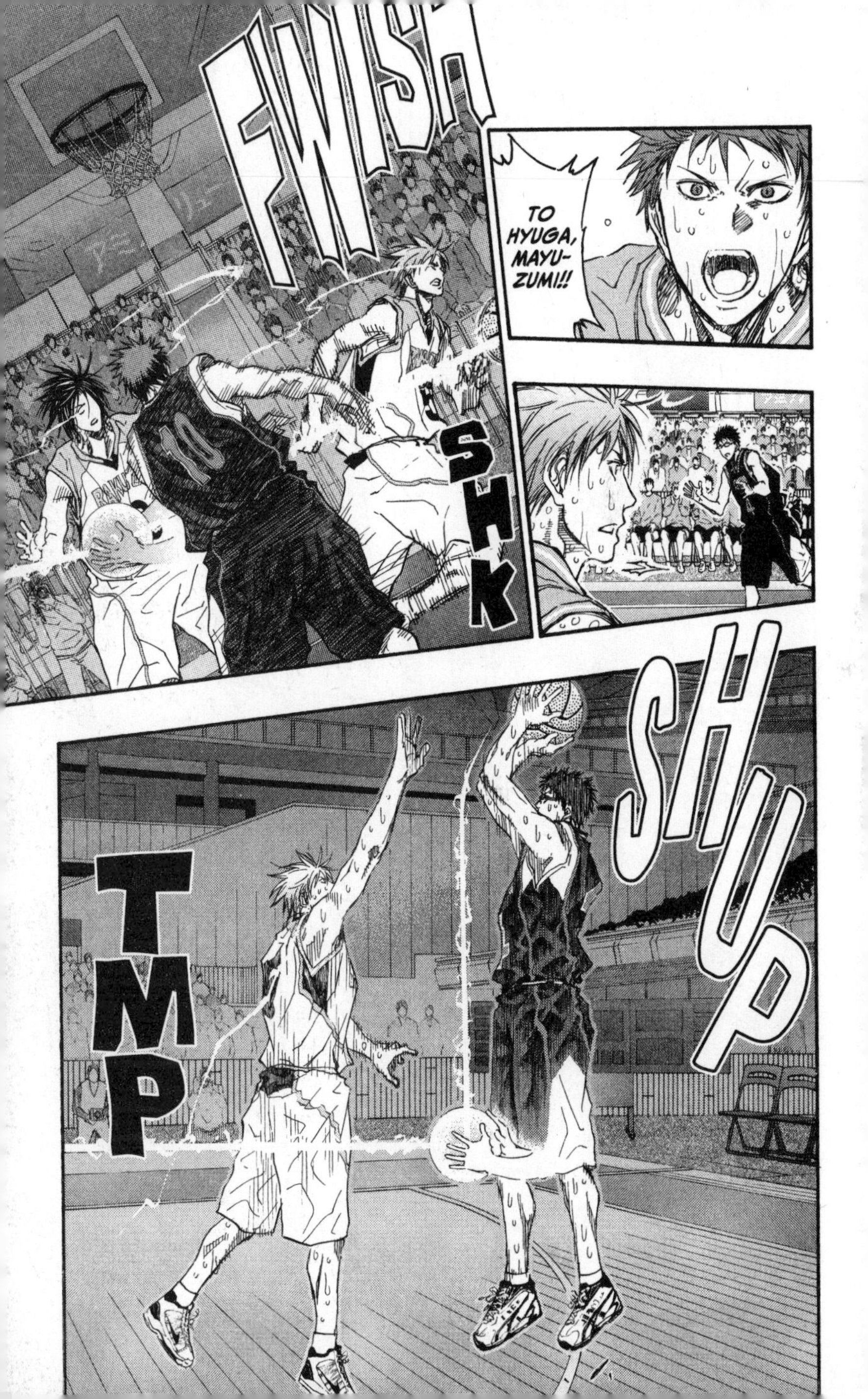
TO HYUGA, MAYU-ZUMI!!
FINISH
SHK
SHUP
TMP

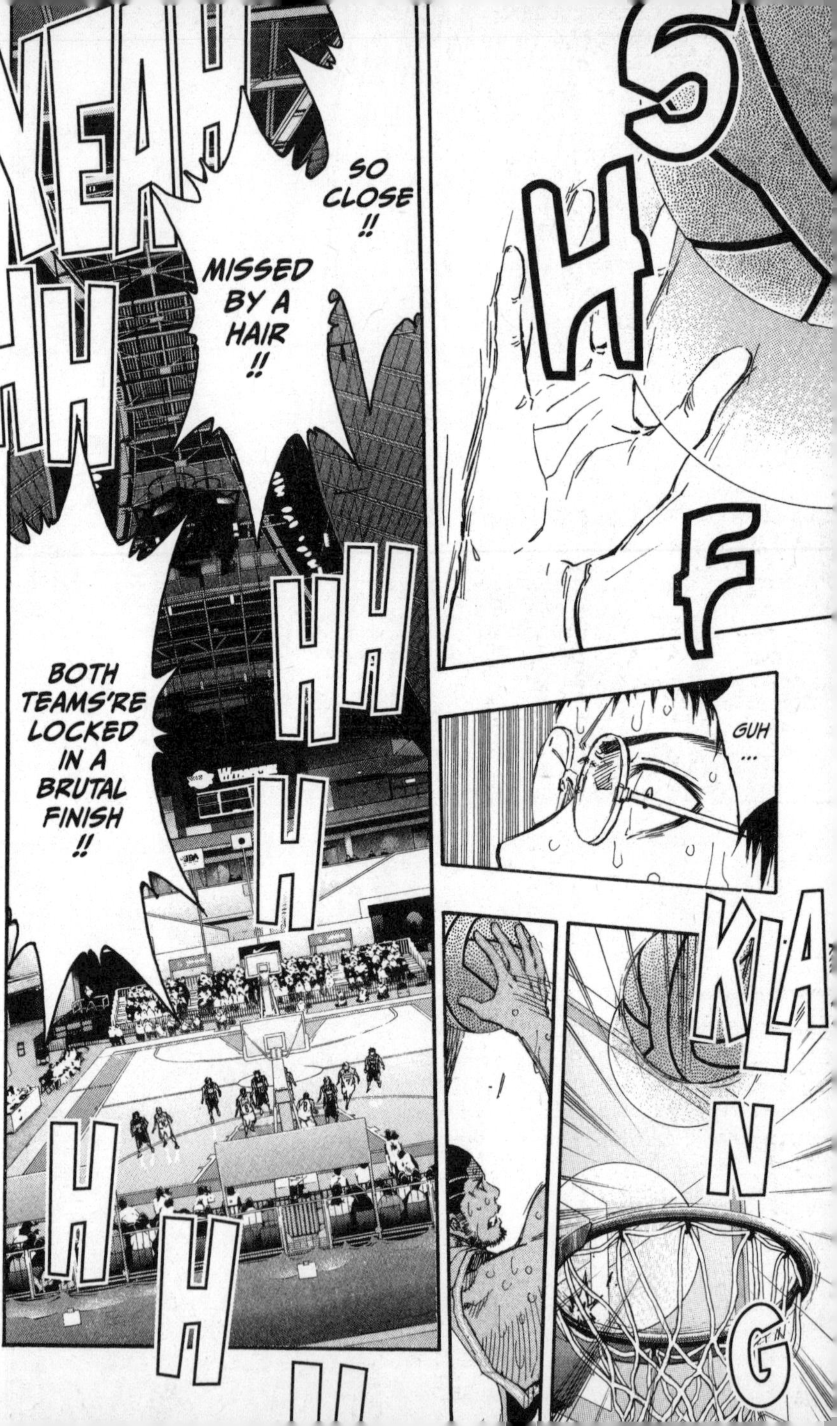
SHF
GUH ...
KLANG
YEAHHHHHH
SO CLOSE !!
MISSED BY A HAIR !!
BOTH TEAMS'RE LOCKED IN A BRUTAL FINISH !!

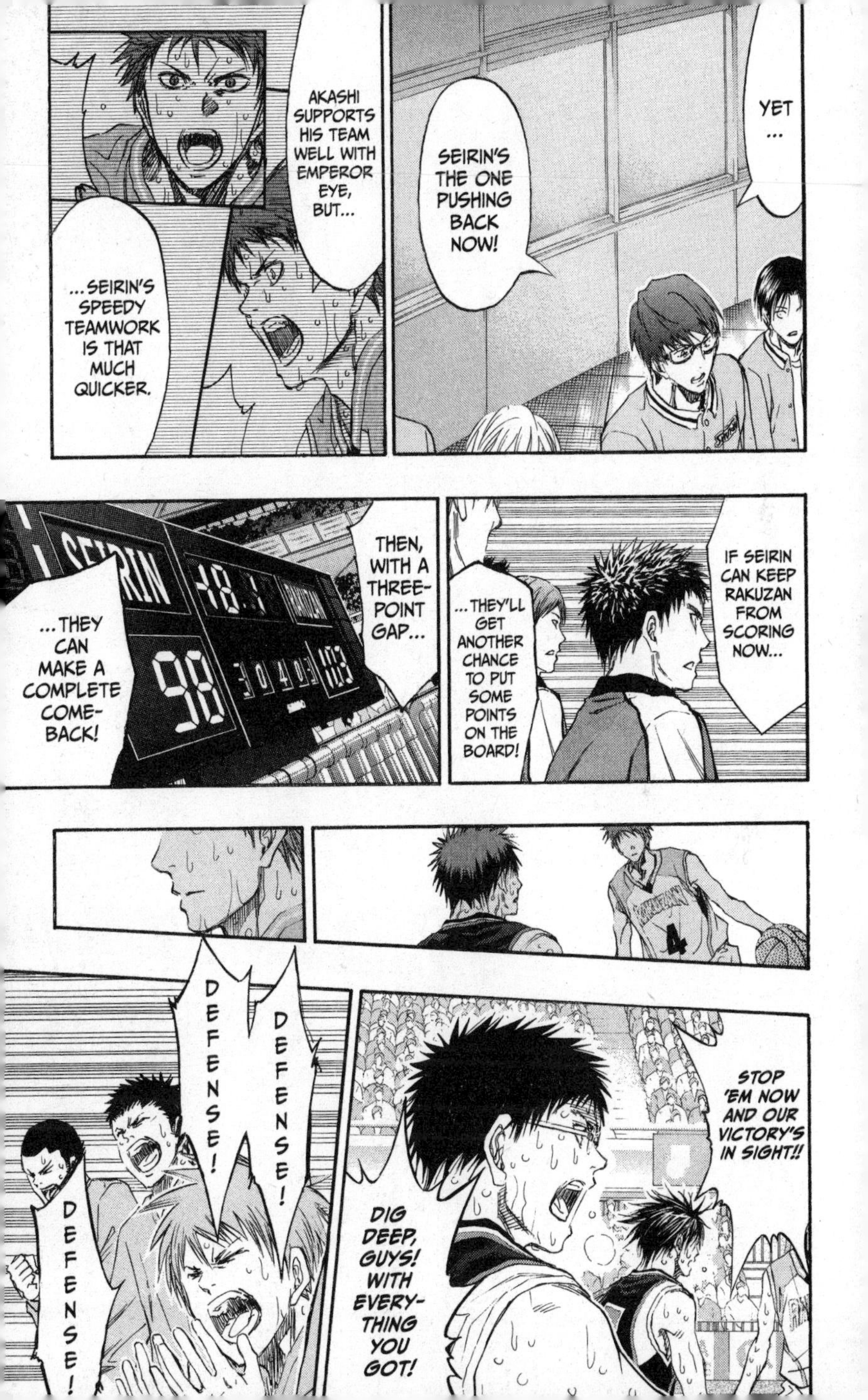
YET ...
SEIRIN'S THE ONE PUSHING BACK NOW!
AKASHI SUPPORTS HIS TEAM WELL WITH EMPEROR EYE, BUT...
...SEIRIN'S SPEEDY TEAMWORK IS THAT MUCH QUICKER.
IF SEIRIN CAN KEEP RAKUZAN FROM SCORING NOW...
...THEY'LL GET ANOTHER CHANCE TO PUT SOME POINTS ON THE BOARD!
THEN, WITH A THREE-POINT GAP...
SEIRIN
98
...THEY CAN MAKE A COMPLETE COME-BACK!
STOP 'EM NOW AND OUR VICTORY'S IN SIGHT!!
DIG DEEP, GUYS! WITH EVERY-THING YOU GOT!
DEFENSE!
DEFENSE!
DEFENSE!

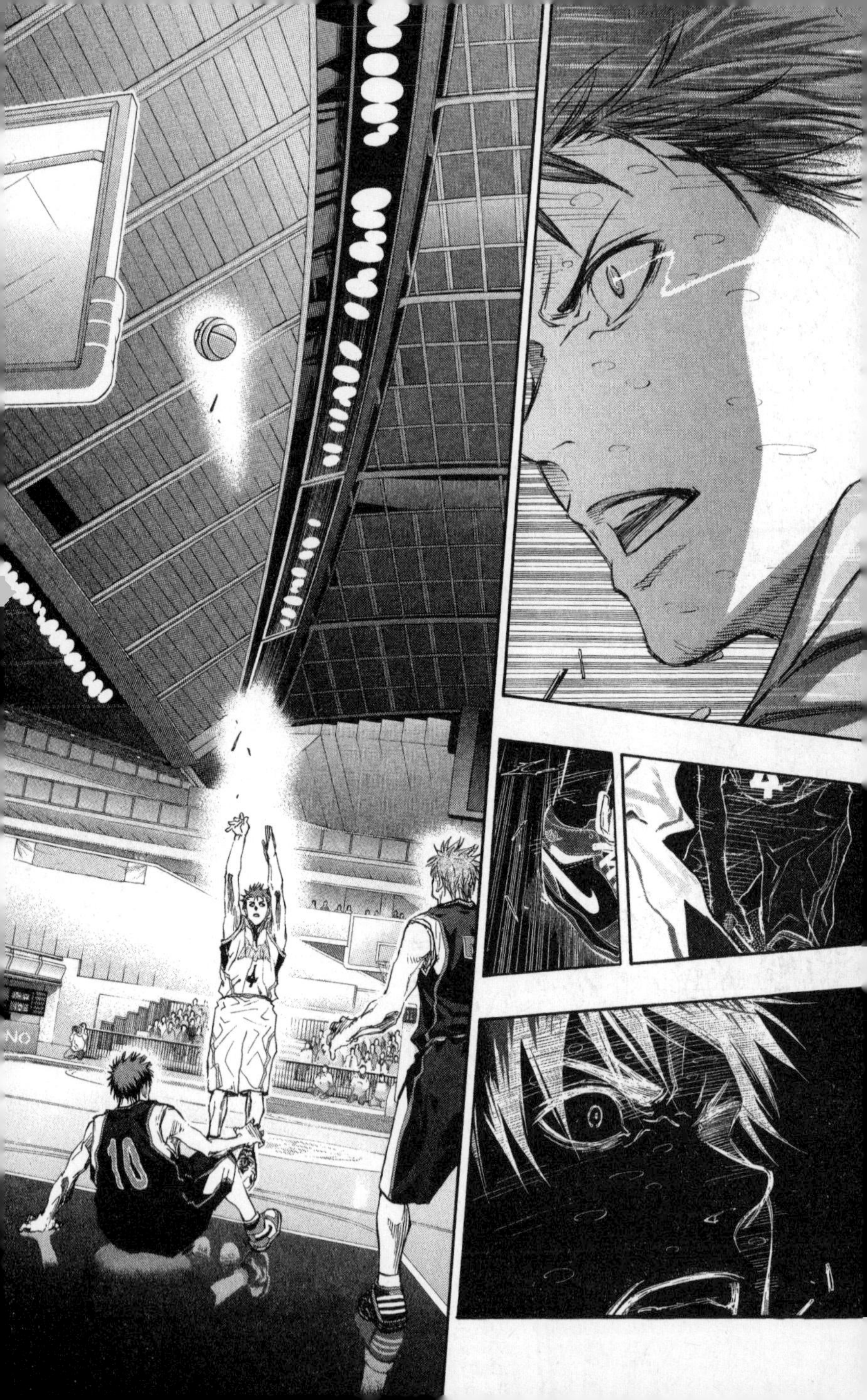

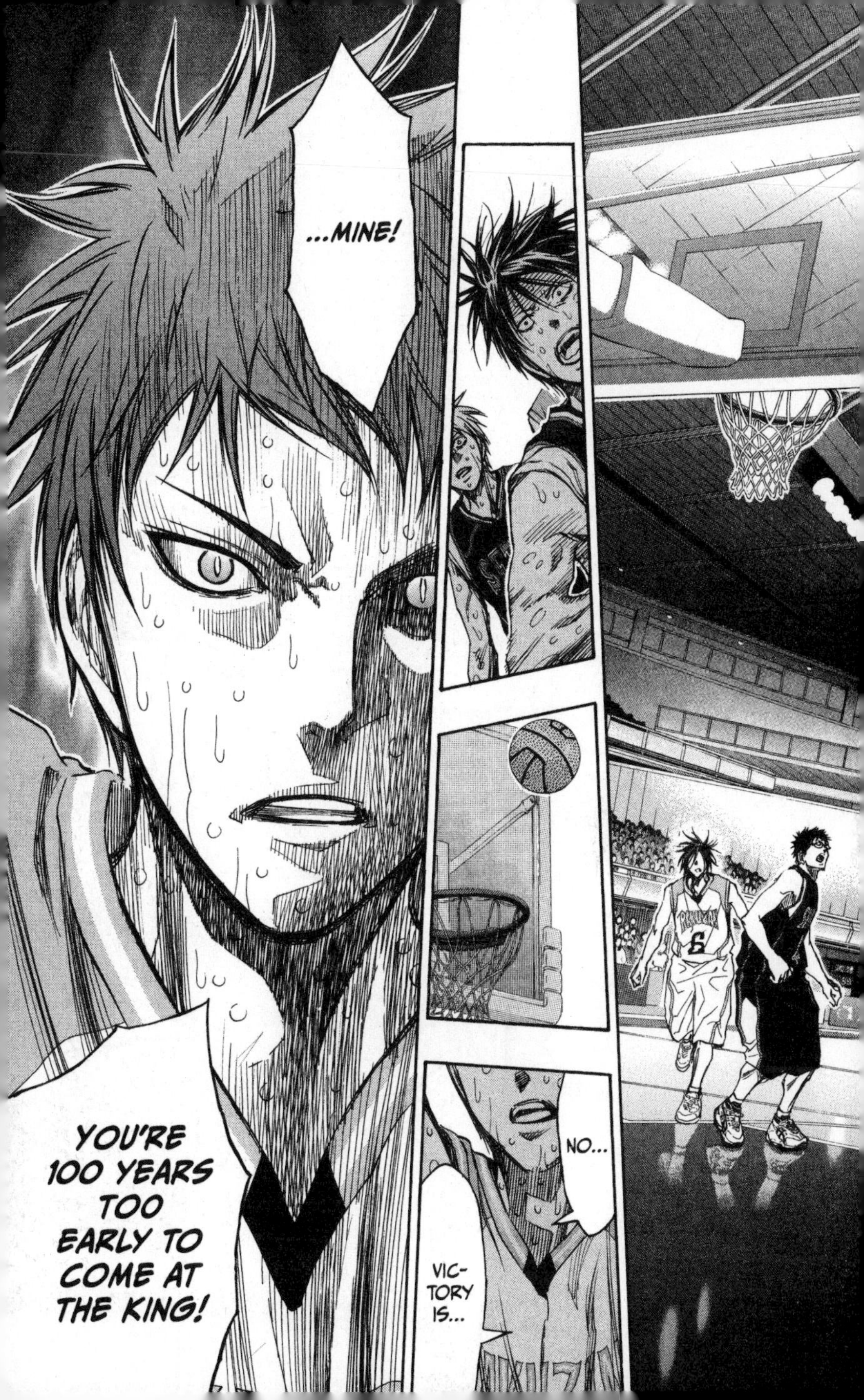
NO...
VIC-TORY IS...
...MINE!
YOU'RE 100 YEARS TOO EARLY TO COME AT THE KING!

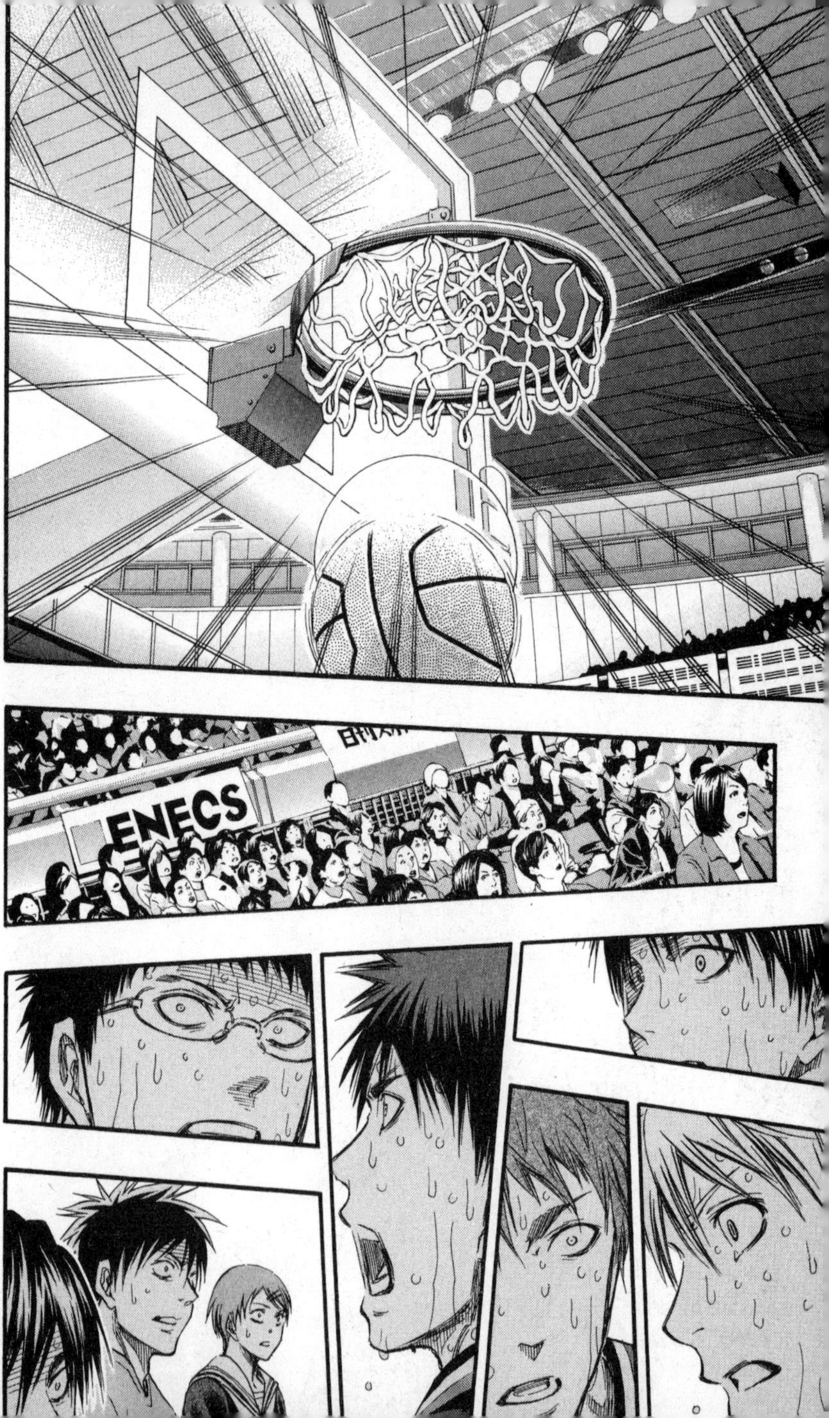
ENECS

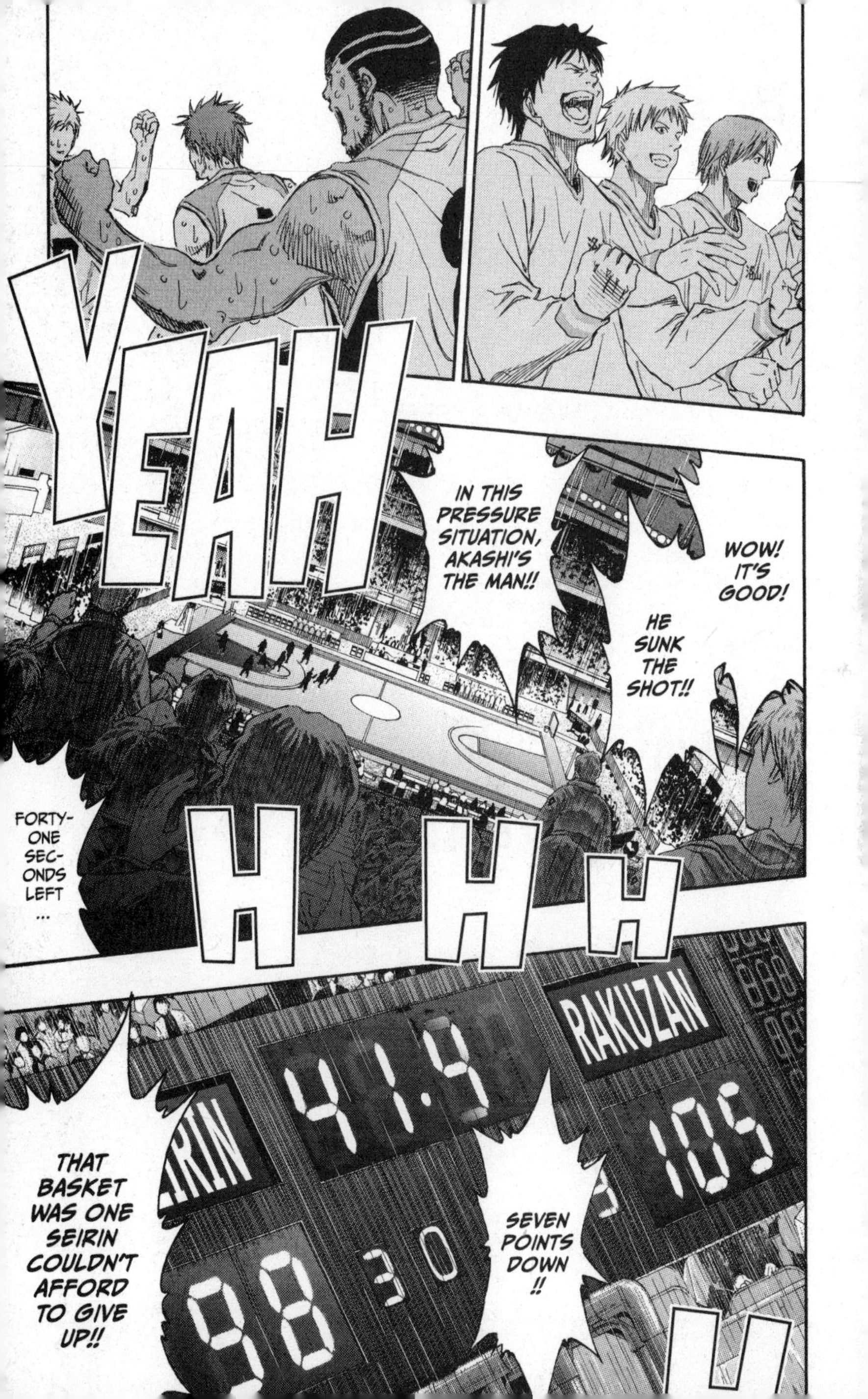
YEAH
WOW! IT'S GOOD!
HE SUNK THE SHOT!!
IN THIS PRESSURE SITUATION, AKASHI'S THE MAN!!
H H H
FORTY-ONE SEC-ONDS LEFT ...
RAKUZAN
41.4
105
IRIN
98
30
SEVEN POINTS DOWN !!
THAT BASKET WAS ONE SEIRIN COULDN'T AFFORD TO GIVE UP!!

KUROKO'S BASKETBALL Q&A (W/ HALFWAY-DECENT ANSWERS)

Q. RIKO AIDA (THE COACH) CALLS THE BOYS (ON TEAM SEIRIN) "XXX-KUN," BUT KIYOSHI IS THE ONLY ONE SHE CALLS BY HIS FIRST NAME, TEPPEI. WHY IS THAT?

(HAL from SHIZUOKA PREFECTURE)

A. BECAUSE THEY ONCE DATED EACH OTHER FOR A HOT MINUTE.

KUROKO'S BASKETBALL BLOOPERS (TAKE 8)

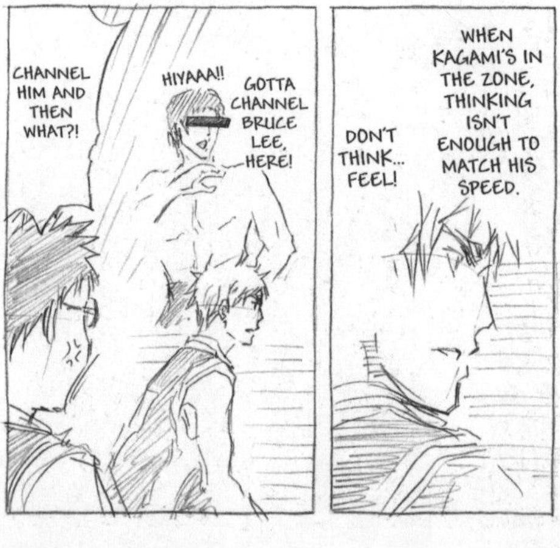
WHEN KAGAMI'S IN THE ZONE, THINKING ISN'T ENOUGH TO MATCH HIS SPEED.
DON'T THINK... FEEL!
GOTTA CHANNEL BRUCE LEE, HERE!
HIYAAA!!
CHANNEL HIM AND THEN WHAT?!

272ND QUARTER: ALL ON THE LINE!!

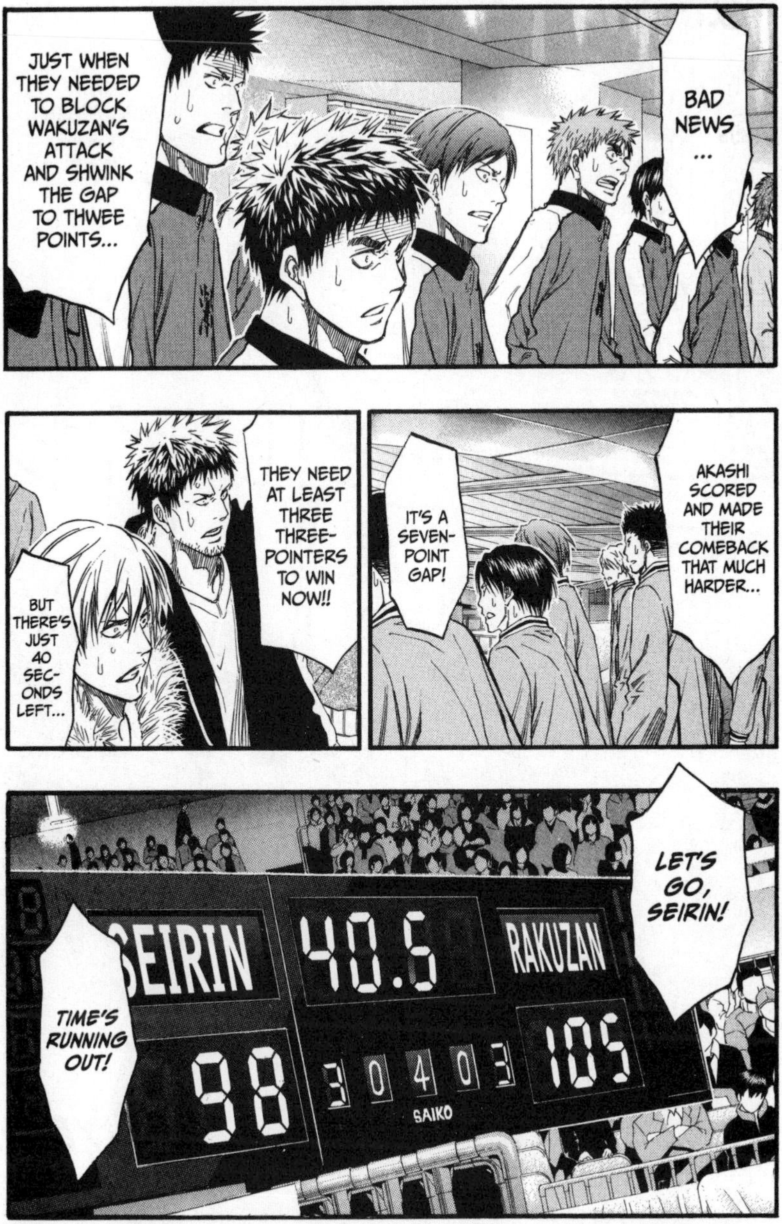
BAD NEWS...
JUST WHEN THEY NEEDED TO BLOCK WAKUZAN'S ATTACK AND SHWINK THE GAP TO THWEE POINTS...
AKASHI SCORED AND MADE THEIR COMEBACK THAT MUCH HARDER...
IT'S A SEVEN-POINT GAP!
THEY NEED AT LEAST THREE THREE-POINTERS TO WIN NOW!!
BUT THERE'S JUST 40 SEC-ONDS LEFT...
LET'S GO, SEIRIN!
SEIRIN
40.5
RAKUZAN
98
105
SAIKO
TIME'S RUNNING OUT!

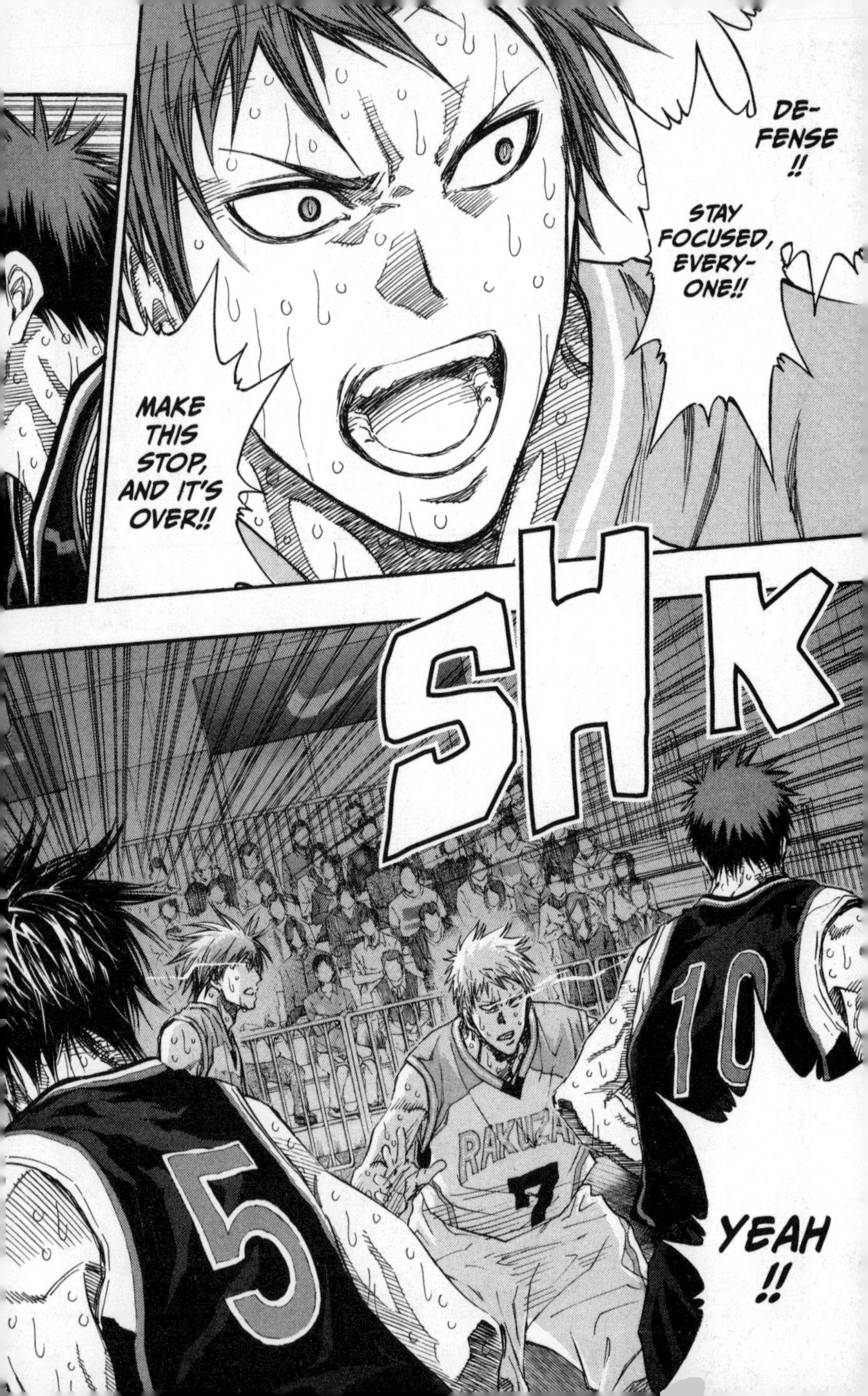
DE-FENSE!!
STAY FOCUSED, EVERY-ONE!!
MAKE THIS STOP, AND IT'S OVER!!
SHK
YEAH!!

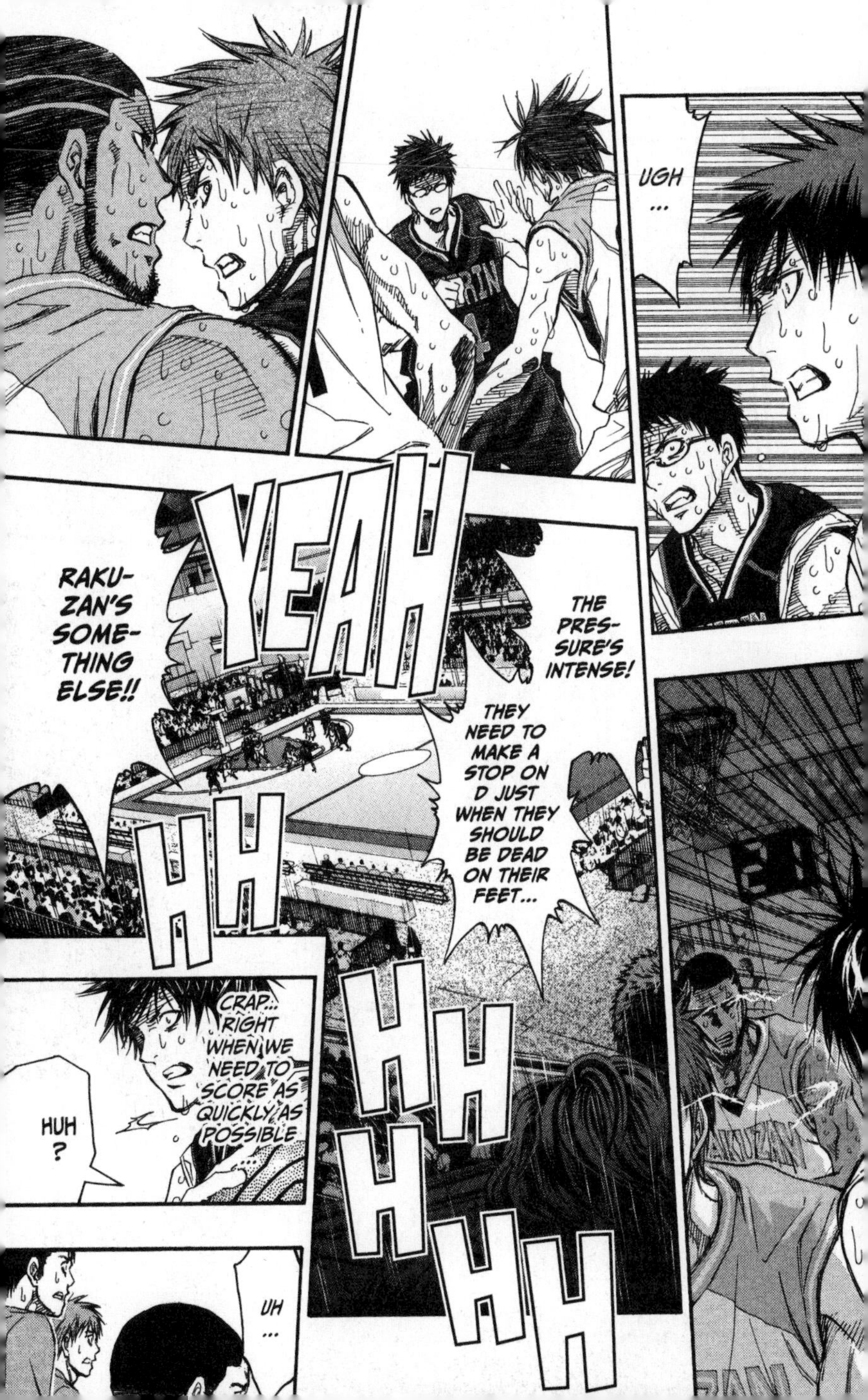
UGH ...
THE PRES-SURE'S INTENSE!
RAKU-ZAN'S SOME-THING ELSE!!
YEAHHHHHHHH
THEY NEED TO MAKE A STOP ON D JUST WHEN THEY SHOULD BE DEAD ON THEIR FEET...
CRAP... RIGHT WHEN WE NEED TO SCORE AS QUICKLY AS POSSIBLE...
HUH ?
UH ...

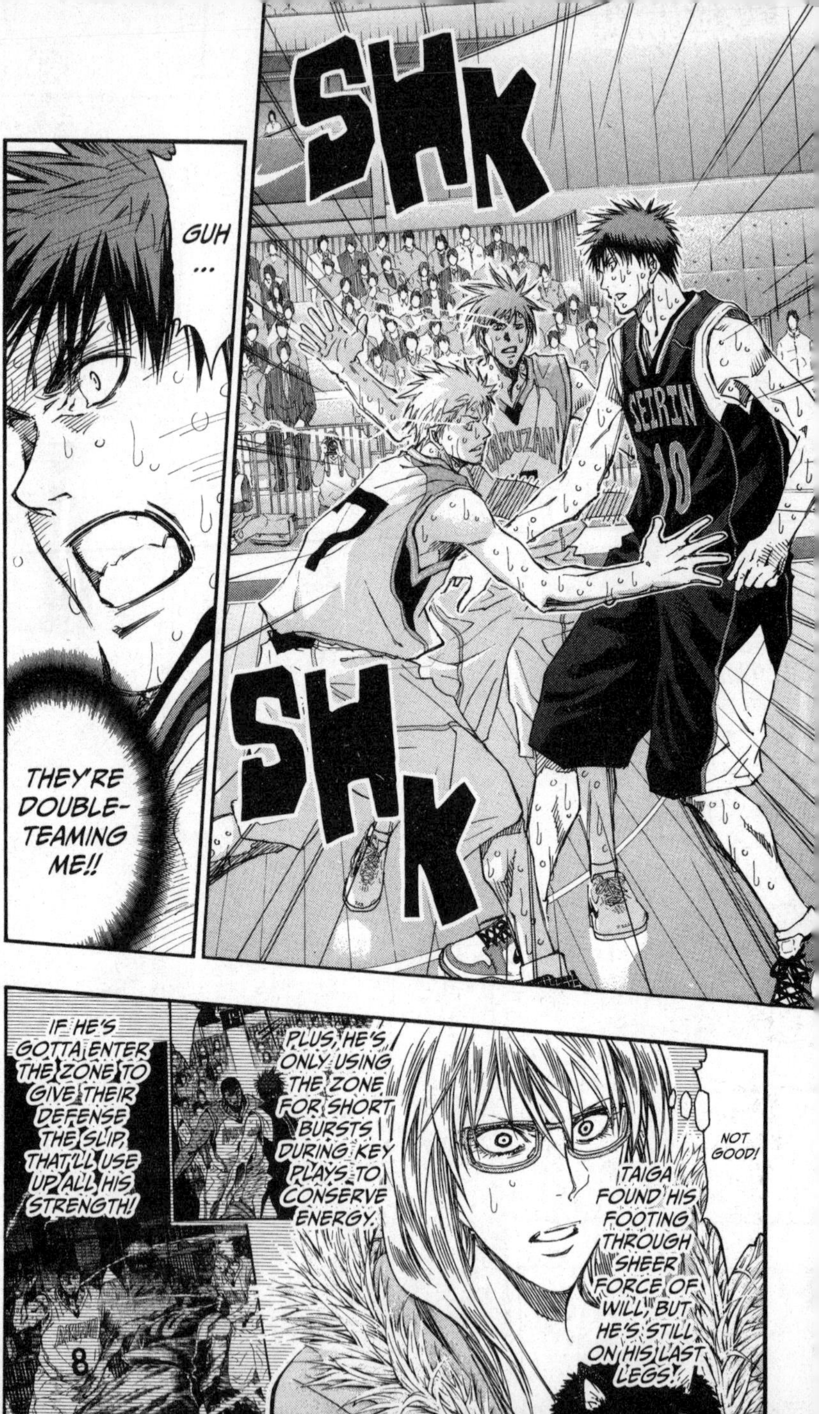
SHK
SHK
GUH ...
THEY'RE DOUBLE-TEAMING ME!!
NOT GOOD!
TAIGA FOUND HIS FOOTING THROUGH SHEER FORCE OF WILL, BUT HE'S STILL ON HIS LAST LEGS!
PLUS, HE'S ONLY USING THE ZONE FOR SHORT BURSTS DURING KEY PLAYS TO CONSERVE ENERGY.
IF HE'S GOTTA ENTER THE ZONE TO GIVE THEIR DEFENSE THE SLIP, THAT'LL USE UP ALL HIS STRENGTH!

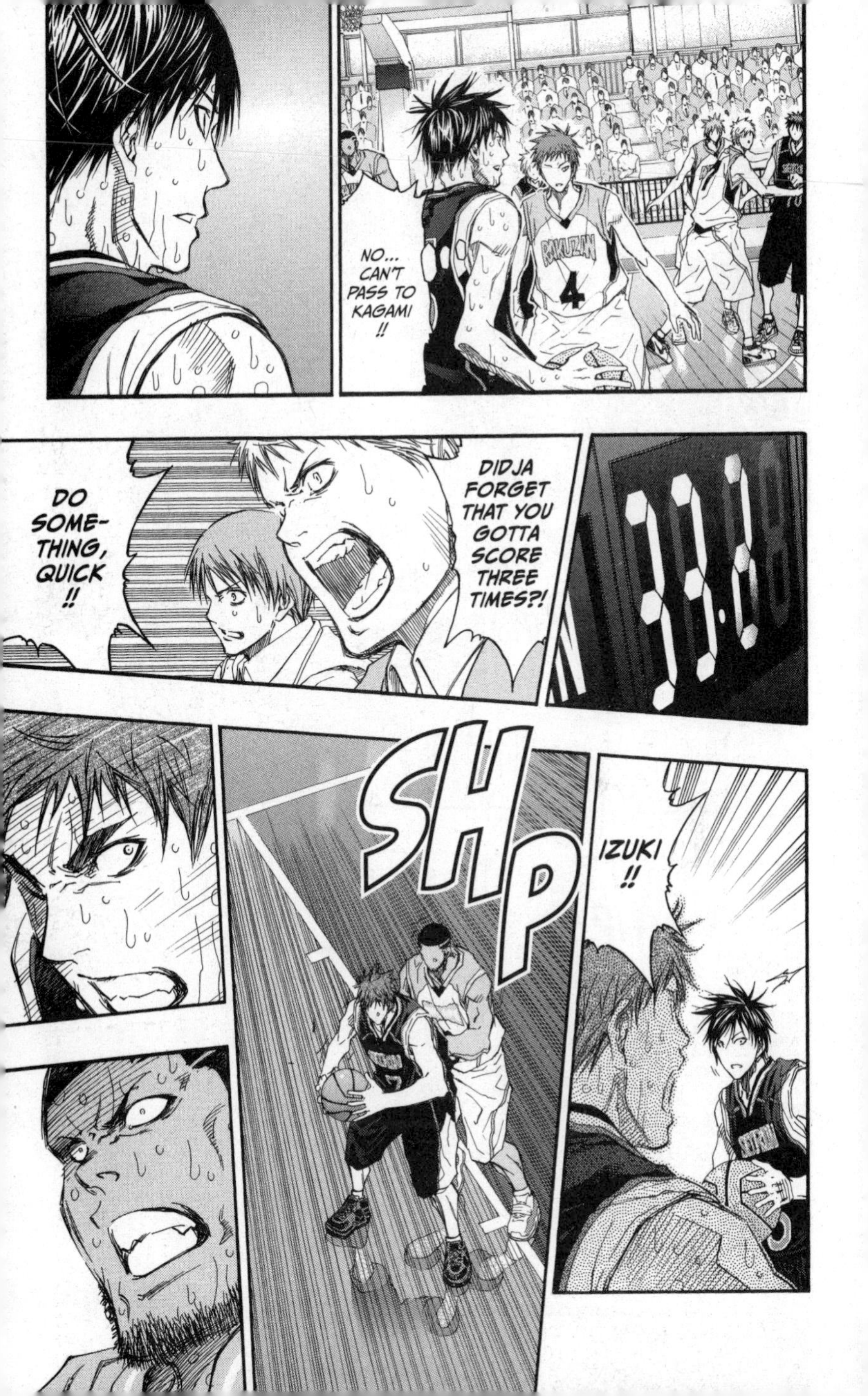
NO... CAN'T PASS TO KAGAMI !!
DIDJA FORGET THAT YOU GOTTA SCORE THREE TIMES?!
DO SOME-THING, QUICK !!
IZUKI !!
SHP

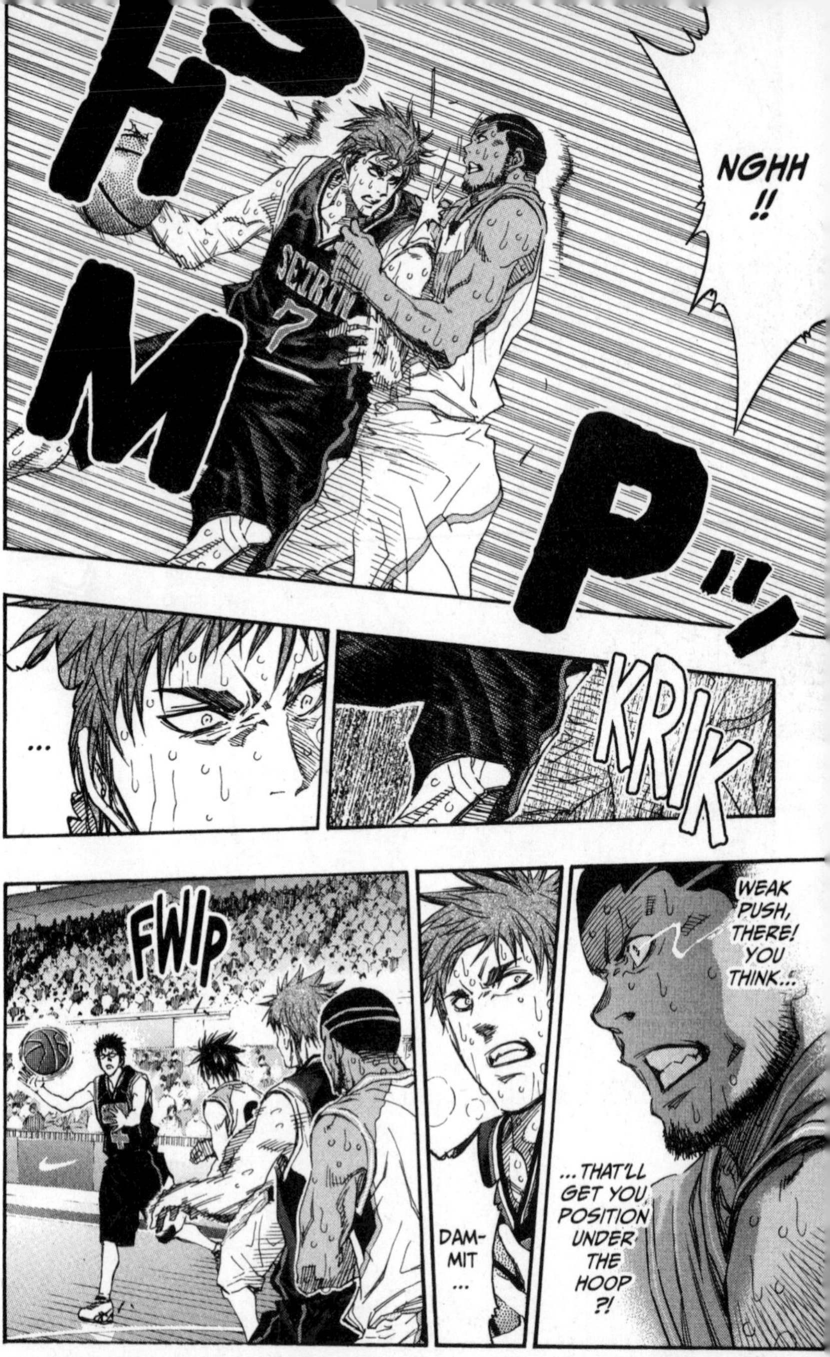
NGHH !!
HMP
KRIK
...
WEAK PUSH, THERE! YOU THINK...
...THAT'LL GET YOU POSITION UNDER THE HOOP ?!
DAM-MIT ...
FWIP

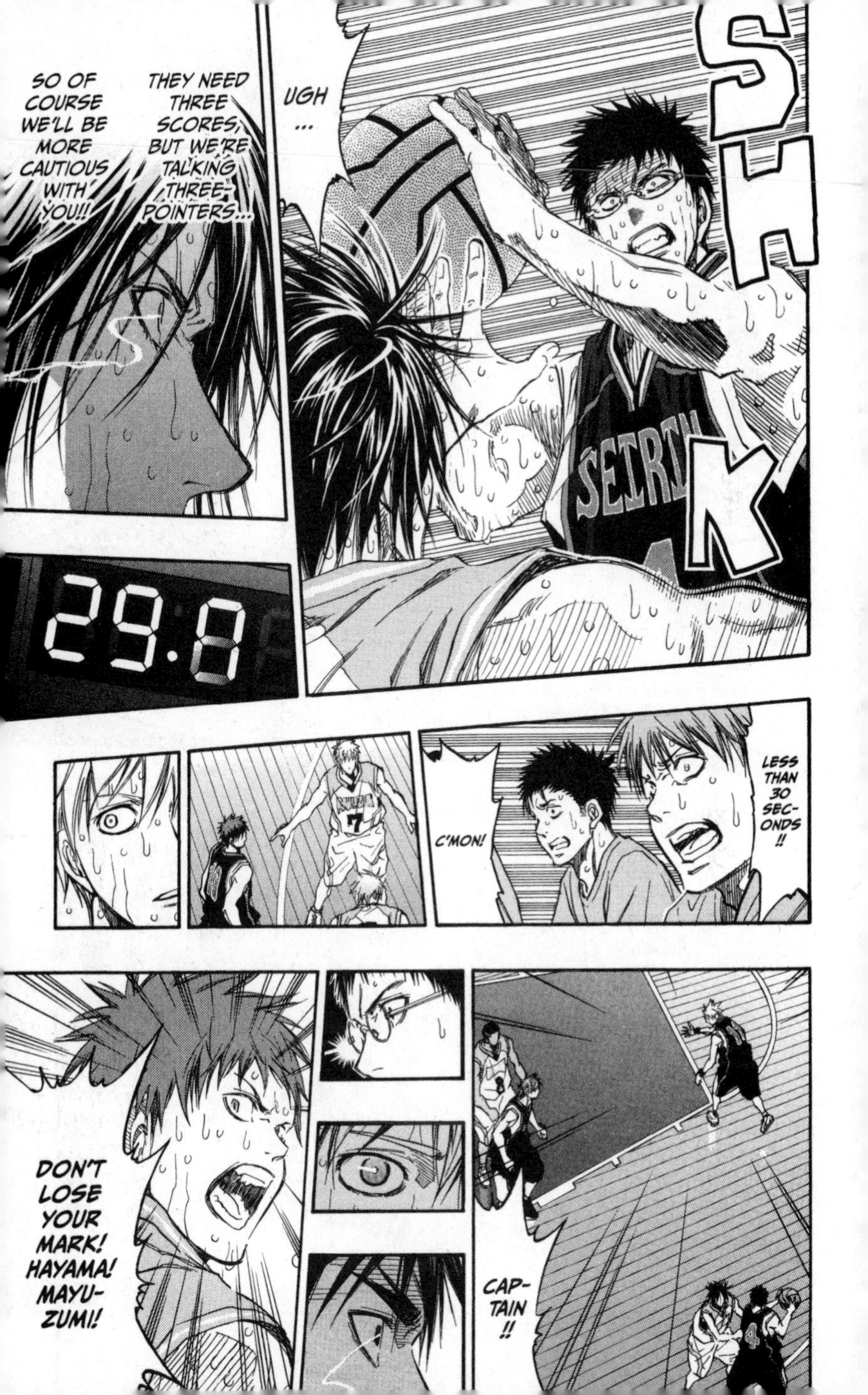
SHK
UGH ...
THEY NEED THREE SCORES, BUT WE'RE TALKING THREE-POINTERS...
SO OF COURSE WE'LL BE MORE CAUTIOUS WITH YOU!!
LESS THAN 30 SECONDS!!
C'MON!
CAPTAIN!!
DON'T LOSE YOUR MARK! HAYAMA! MAYUZUMI!

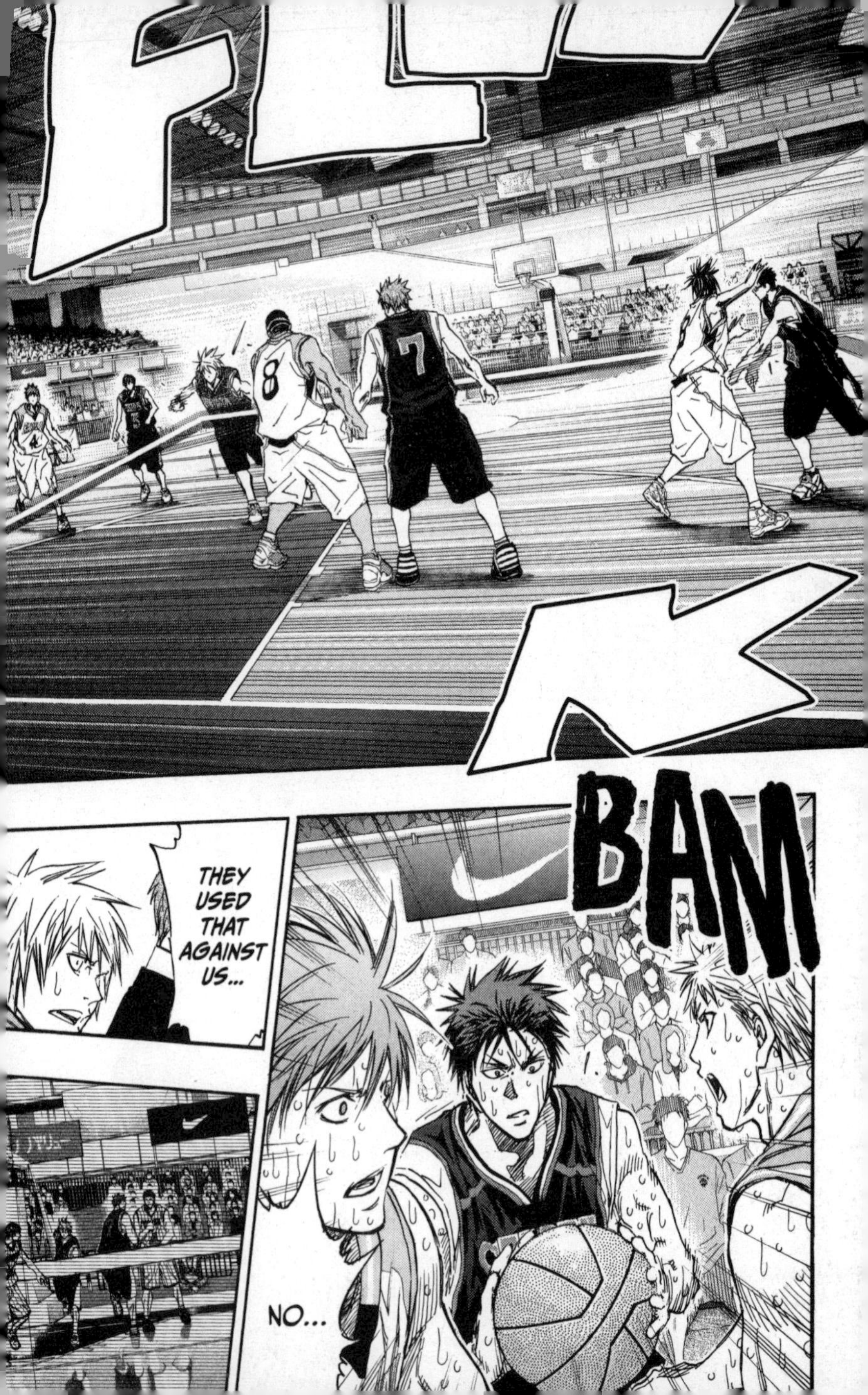
BAM
NO...
THEY USED THAT AGAINST US...

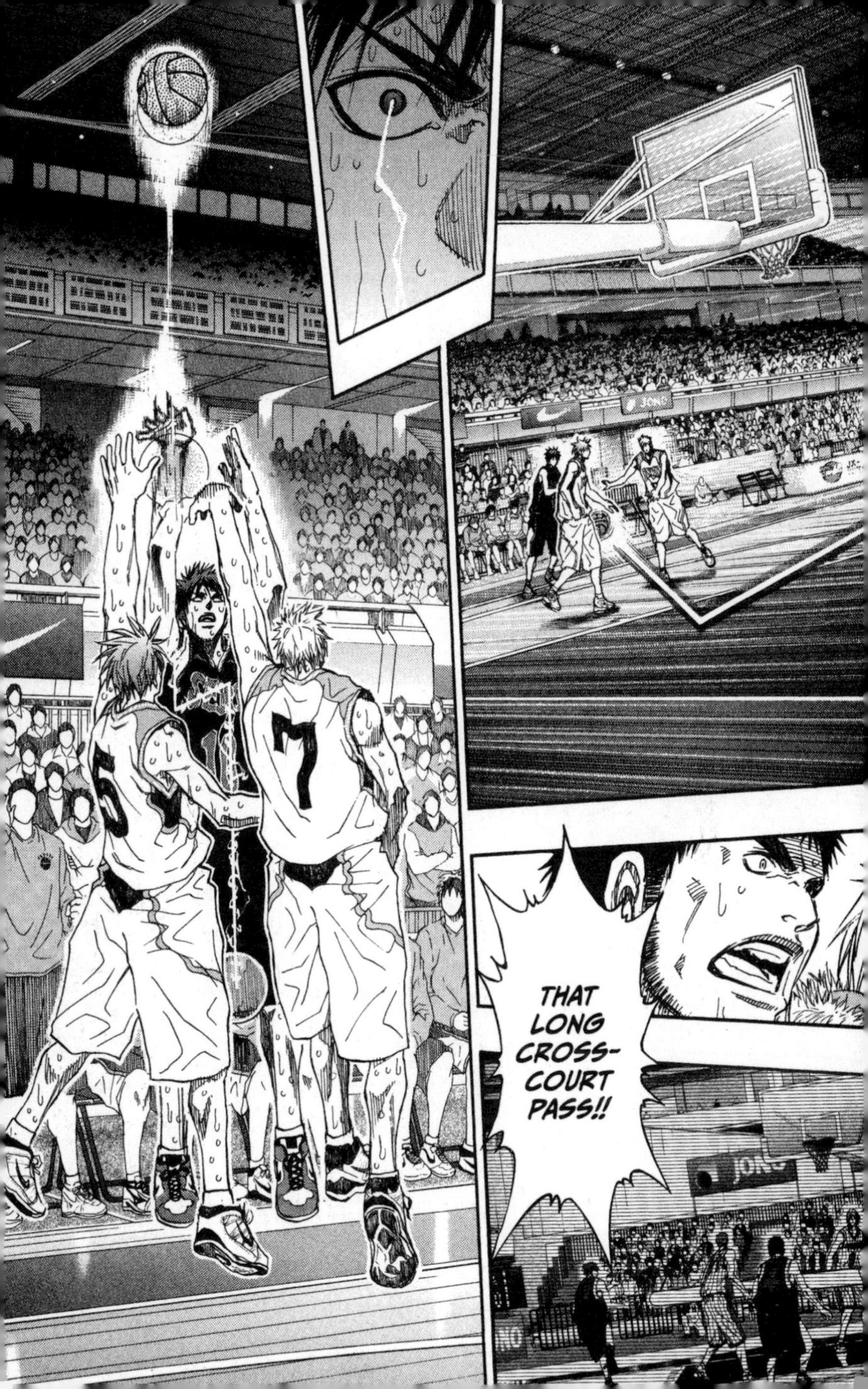
THAT LONG CROSS-COURT PASS!!

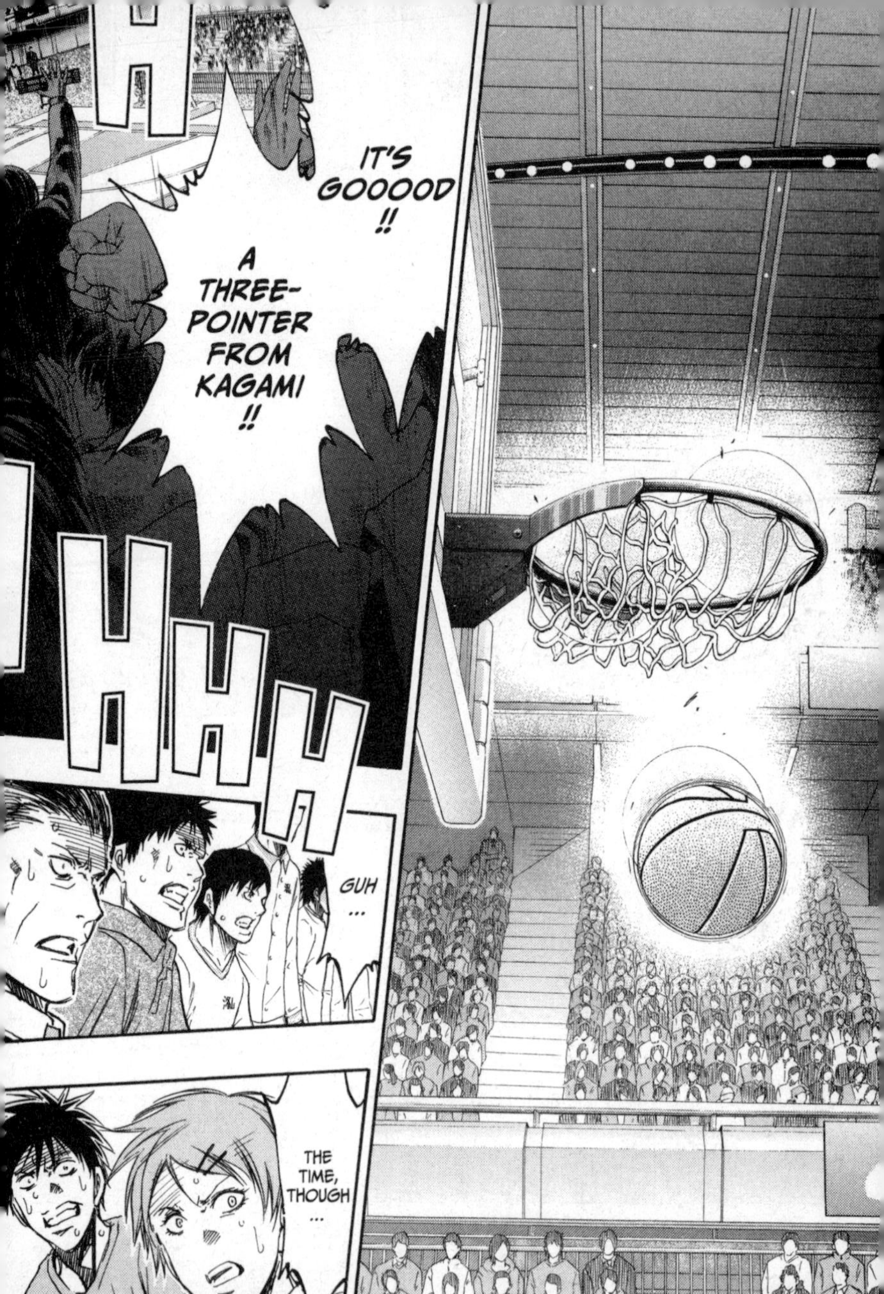
IT'S GOOOOD!!
A THREE-POINTER FROM KAGAMI!!
GUH...
THE TIME, THOUGH...

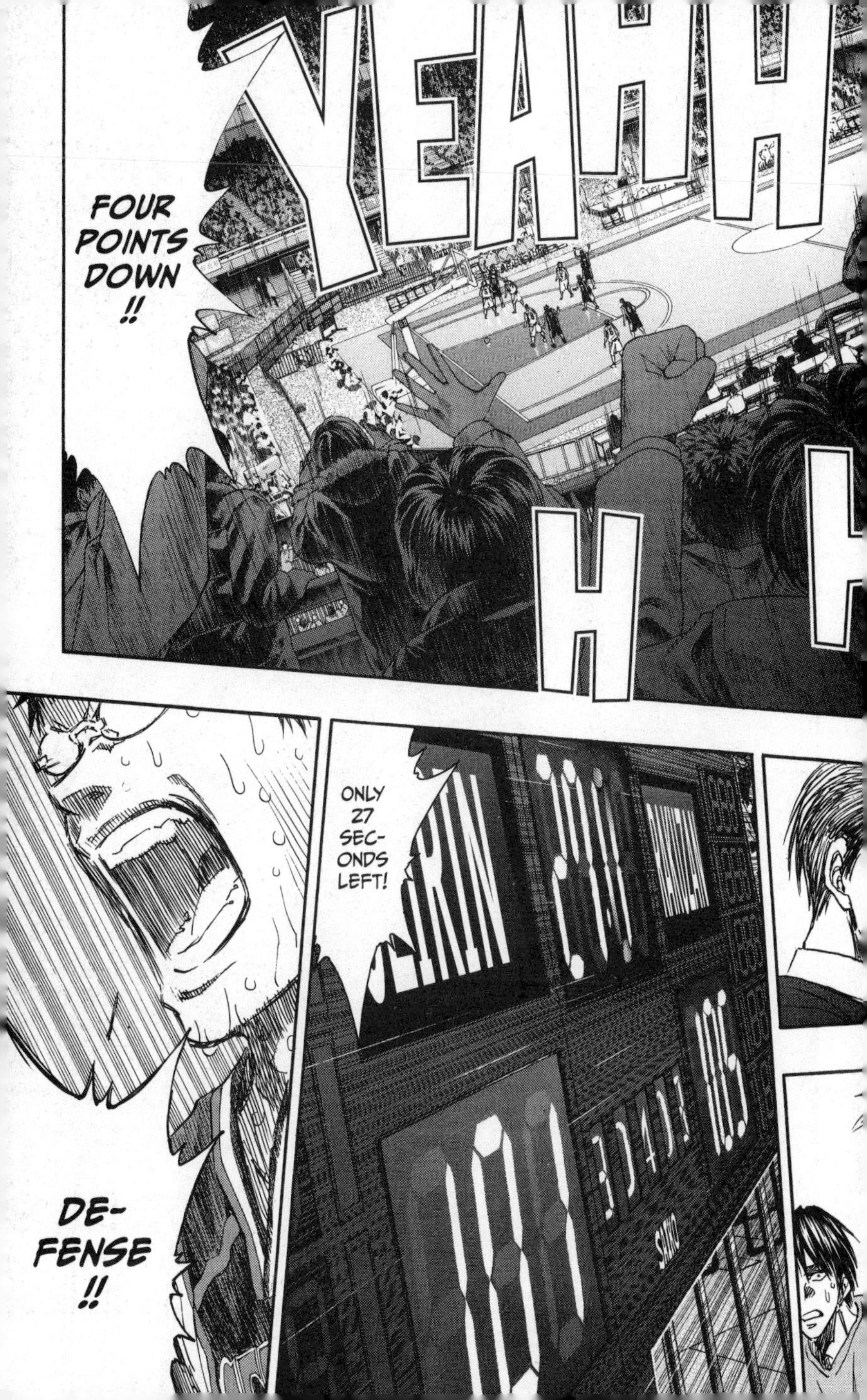
YEAHHH
FOUR POINTS DOWN!!
ONLY 27 SECONDS LEFT!
DEFENSE!!

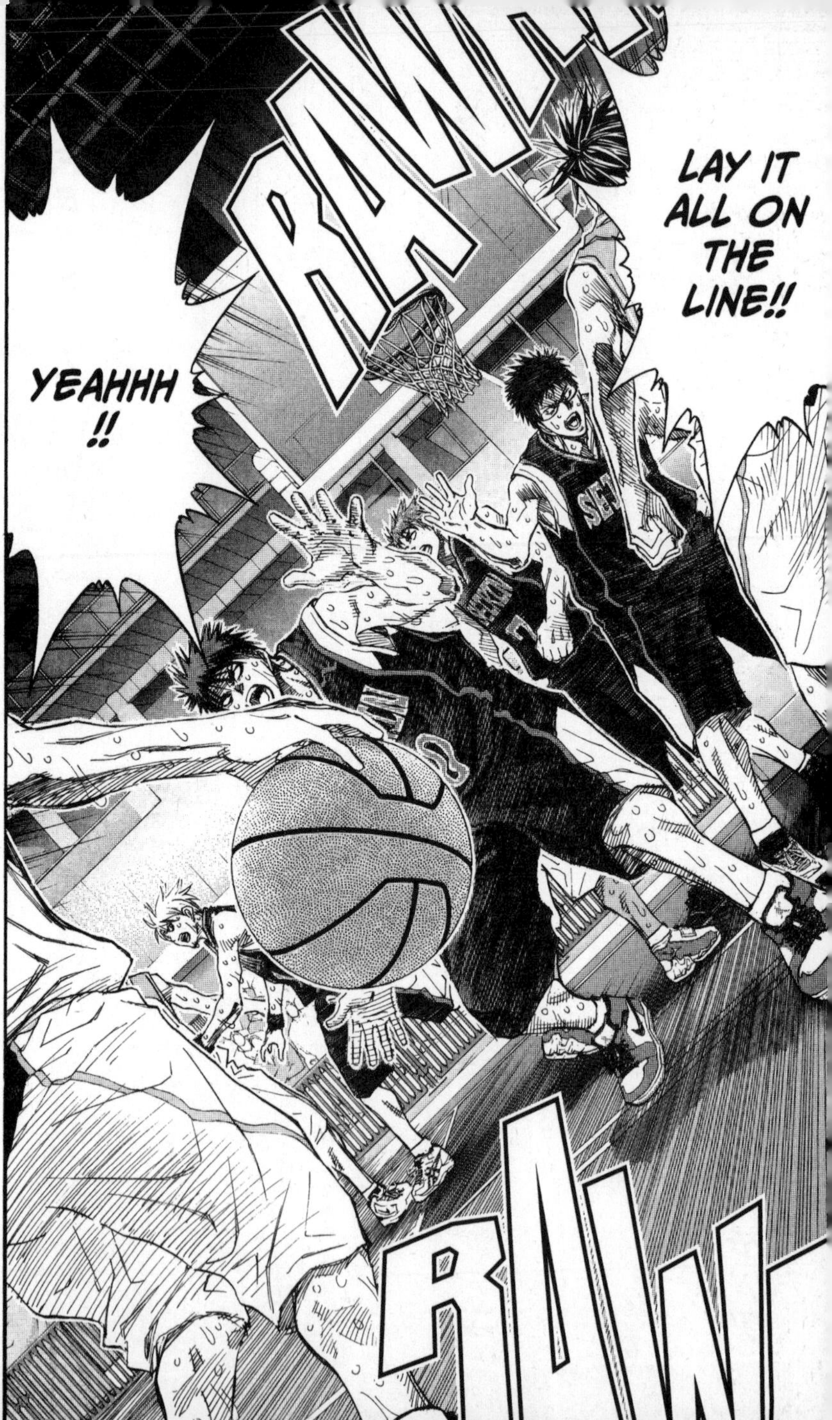

LAY IT ALL ON THE LINE!!
YEAHHH!!

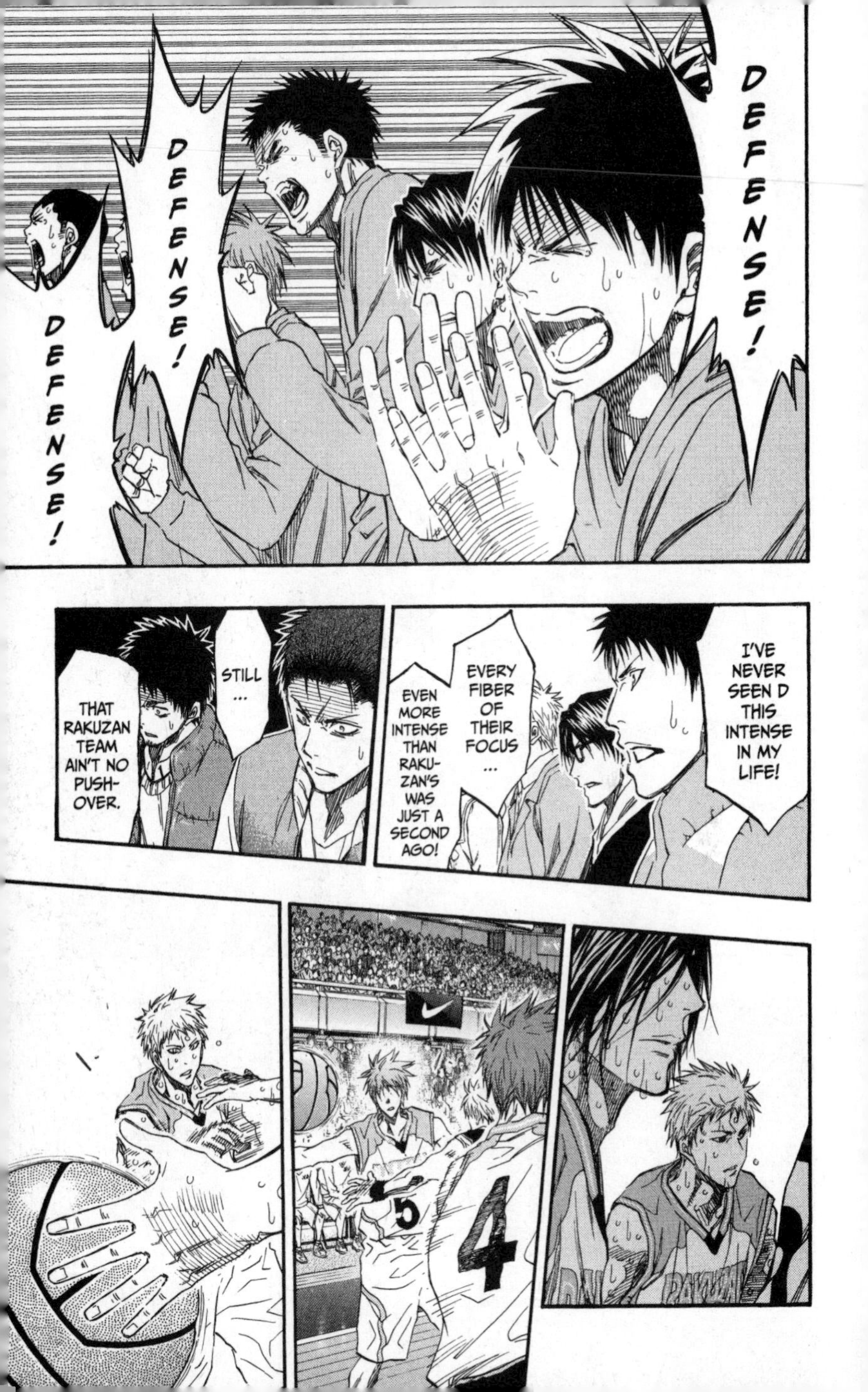
DEFENSE!
DEFENSE!
DEFENSE!
I'VE NEVER SEEN D THIS INTENSE IN MY LIFE!
EVERY FIBER OF THEIR FOCUS ...
EVEN MORE INTENSE THAN RAKU-ZAN'S WAS JUST A SECOND AGO!
STILL ...
THAT RAKUZAN TEAM AIN'T NO PUSH-OVER.

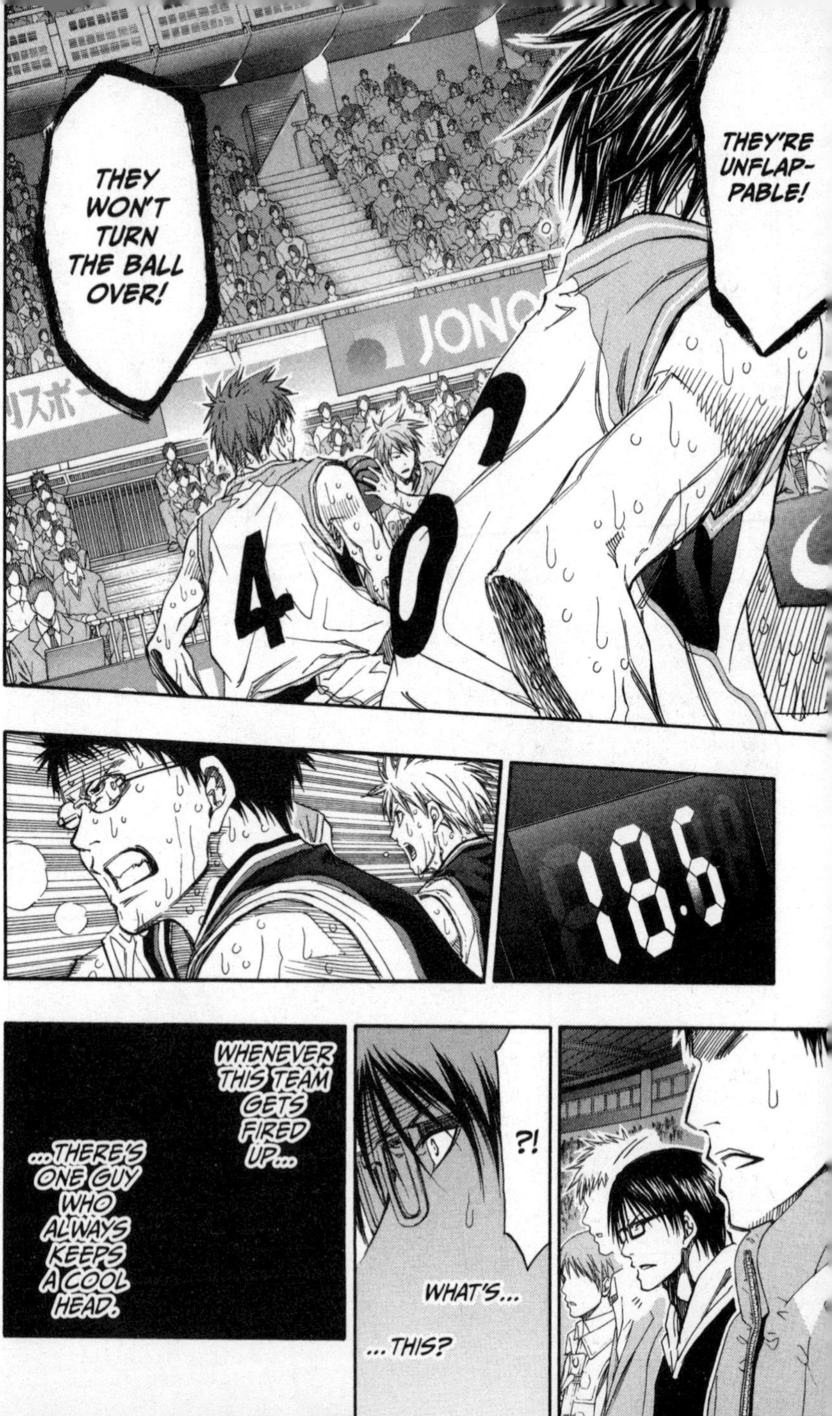
THEY'RE UNFLAP-PABLE!
THEY WON'T TURN THE BALL OVER!
18.6
?!
WHAT'S...
...THIS?
WHENEVER THIS TEAM GETS FIRED UP...
...THERE'S ONE GUY WHO ALWAYS KEEPS A COOL HEAD.

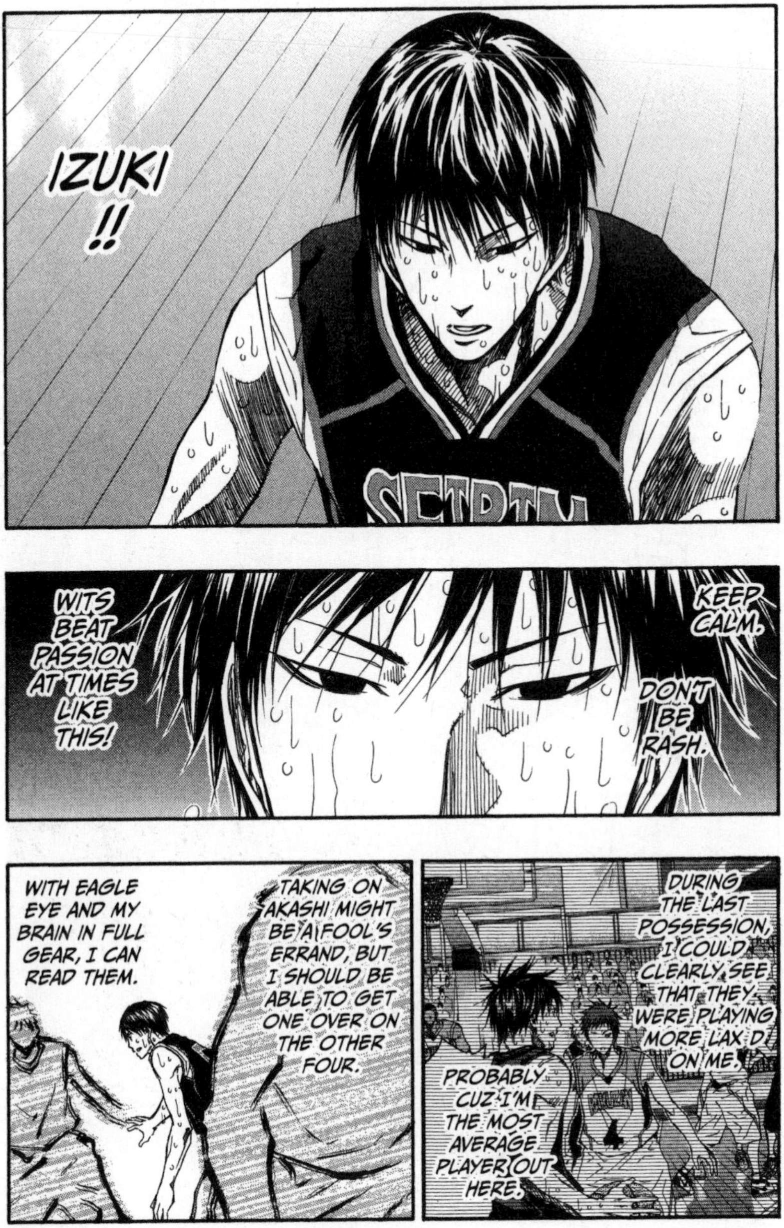
IZUKI !!
KEEP CALM.
DON'T BE RASH.
WITS BEAT PASSION AT TIMES LIKE THIS!
DURING THE LAST POSSESSION, I COULD CLEARLY SEE THAT THEY WERE PLAYING MORE LAX D ON ME.
PROBABLY CUZ I'M THE MOST AVERAGE PLAYER OUT HERE.
TAKING ON AKASHI MIGHT BE A FOOL'S ERRAND, BUT I SHOULD BE ABLE TO GET ONE OVER ON THE OTHER FOUR.
WITH EAGLE EYE AND MY BRAIN IN FULL GEAR, I CAN READ THEM.

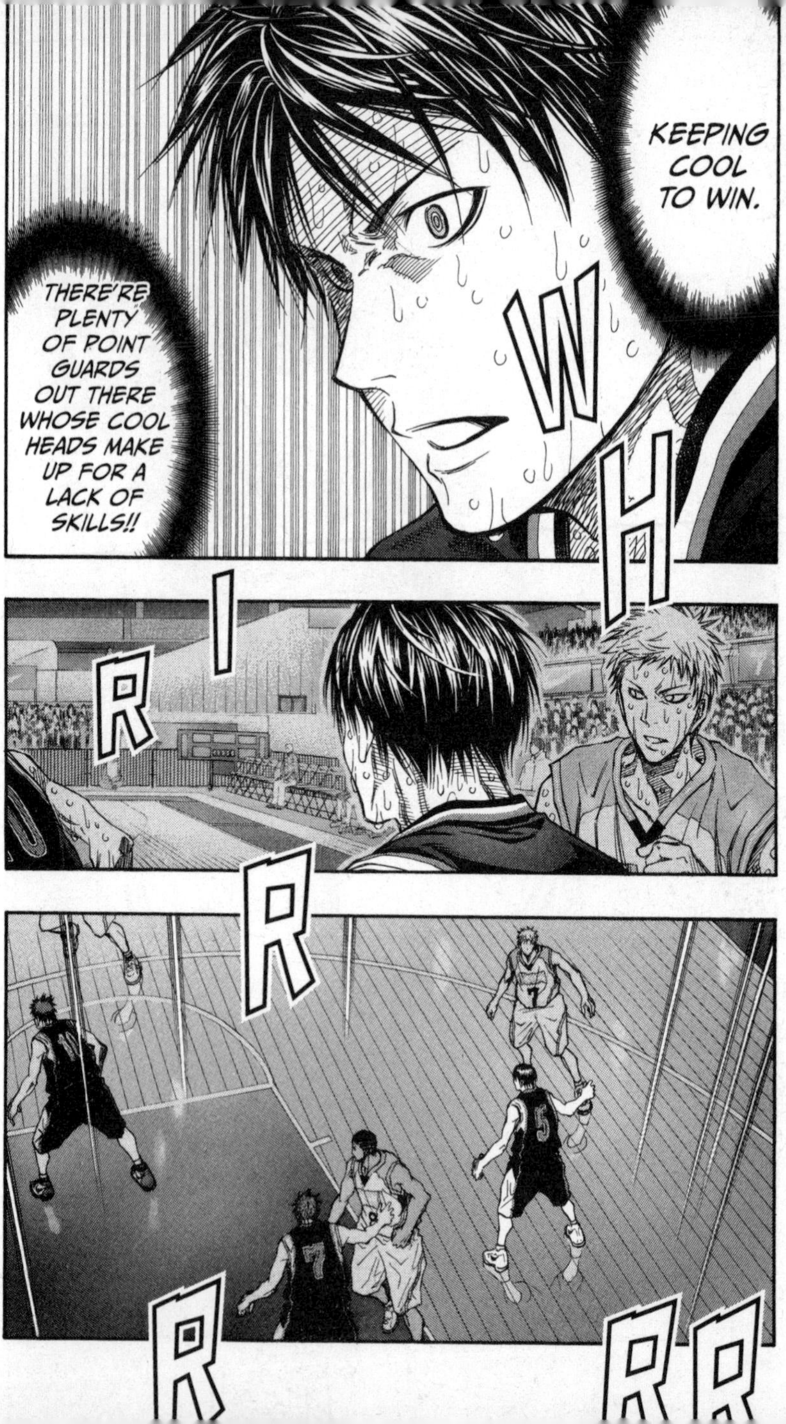
KEEPING COOL TO WIN.
THERE'RE PLENTY OF POINT GUARDS OUT THERE WHOSE COOL HEADS MAKE UP FOR A LACK OF SKILLS!!
WHIRRRRR

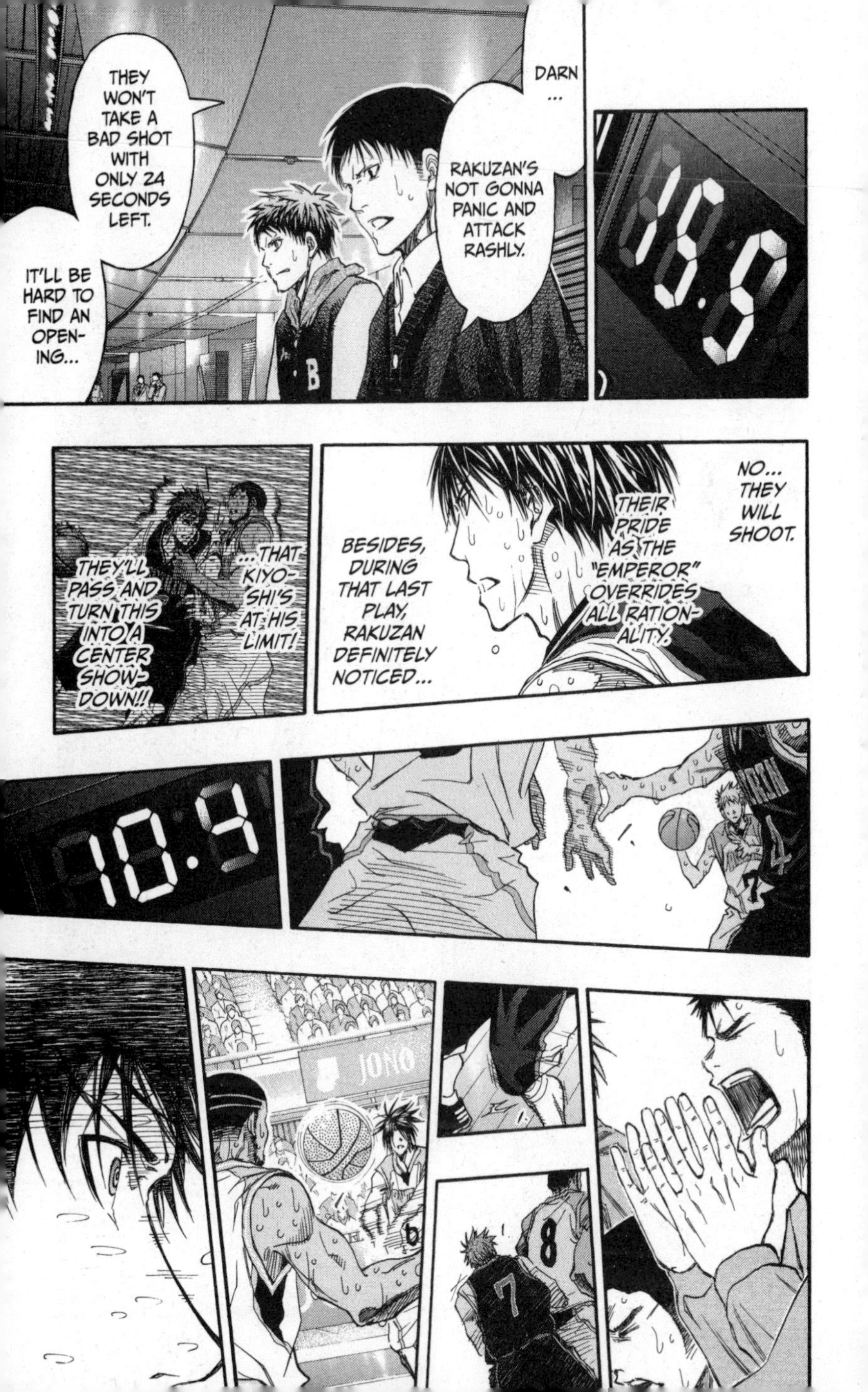
DARN...
RAKUZAN'S NOT GONNA PANIC AND ATTACK RASHLY.
THEY WON'T TAKE A BAD SHOT WITH ONLY 24 SECONDS LEFT.
IT'LL BE HARD TO FIND AN OPEN-ING...
NO... THEY WILL SHOOT.
THEIR PRIDE AS THE "EMPEROR" OVERRIDES ALL RATION-ALITY.
BESIDES, DURING THAT LAST PLAY, RAKUZAN DEFINITELY NOTICED...
...THAT KIYO-SHI'S AT HIS LIMIT!
THEY'LL PASS AND TURN THIS INTO A CENTER SHOW-DOWN!!
JONO

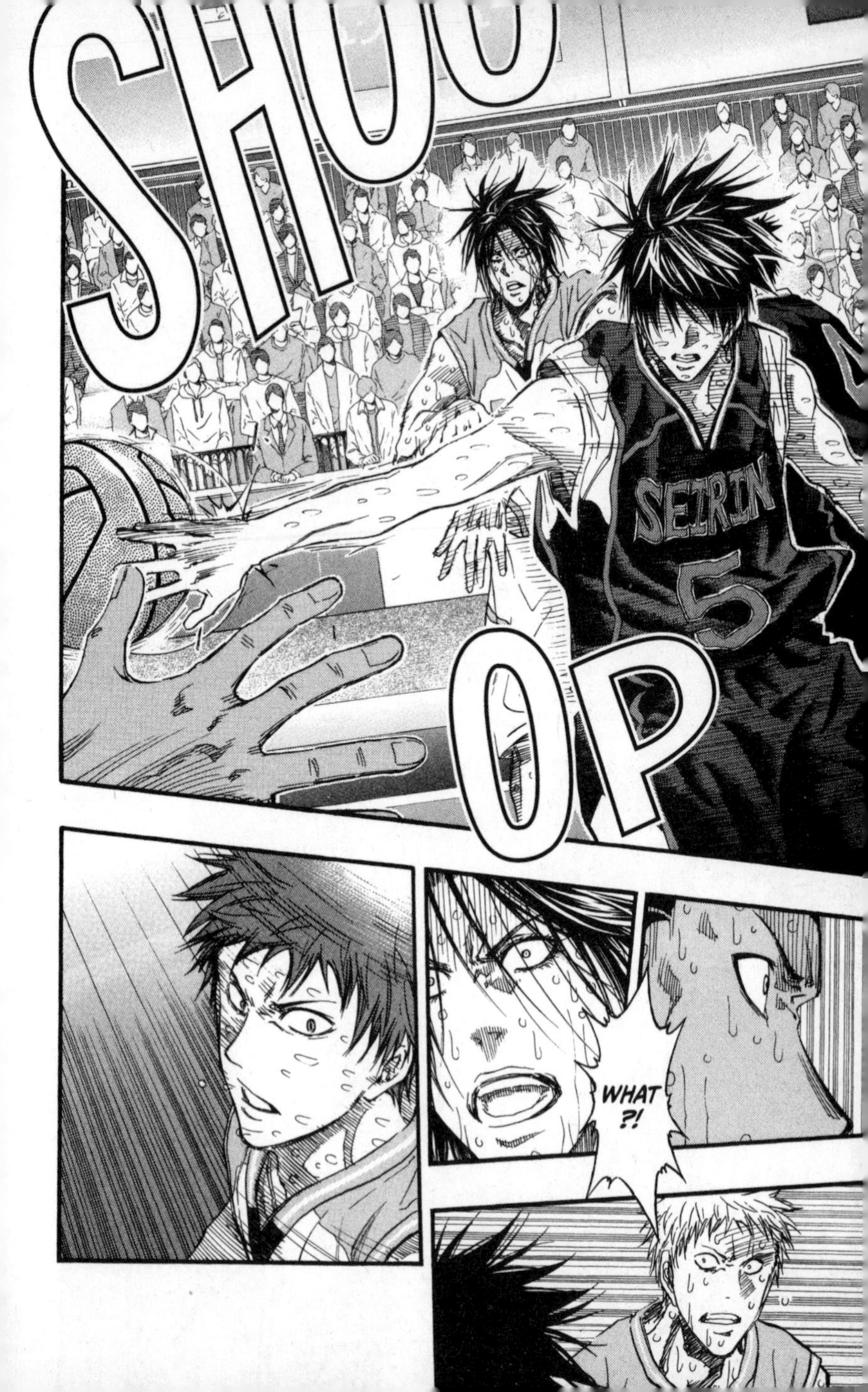
SHOO
OP
SEIRIN
5
WHAT
?!

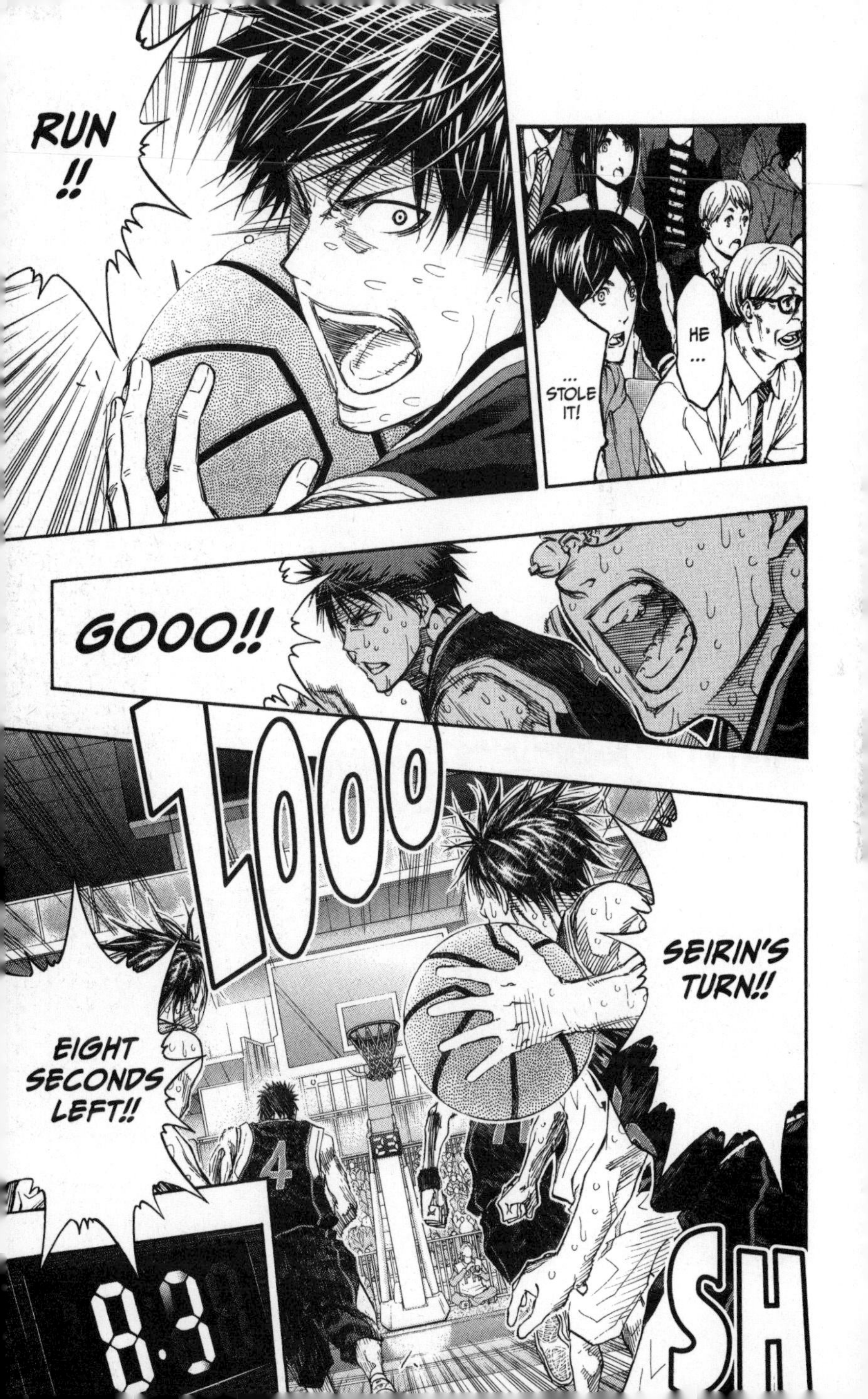
HE ...
... STOLE IT!
RUN !!
GOOO!!
SEIRIN'S TURN!!
EIGHT SECONDS LEFT!!
8.3
SH

KUROKO'S BASKETBALL BLOOPERS TAKE 6

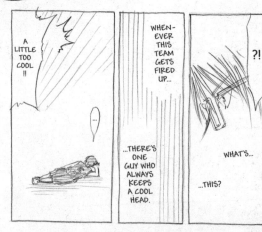

?!
WHAT'S...
...THIS?
WHEN-EVER THIS TEAM GETS FIRED UP...
...THERE'S ONE GUY WHO ALWAYS KEEPS A COOL HEAD.
A LITTLE TOO COOL !!
...

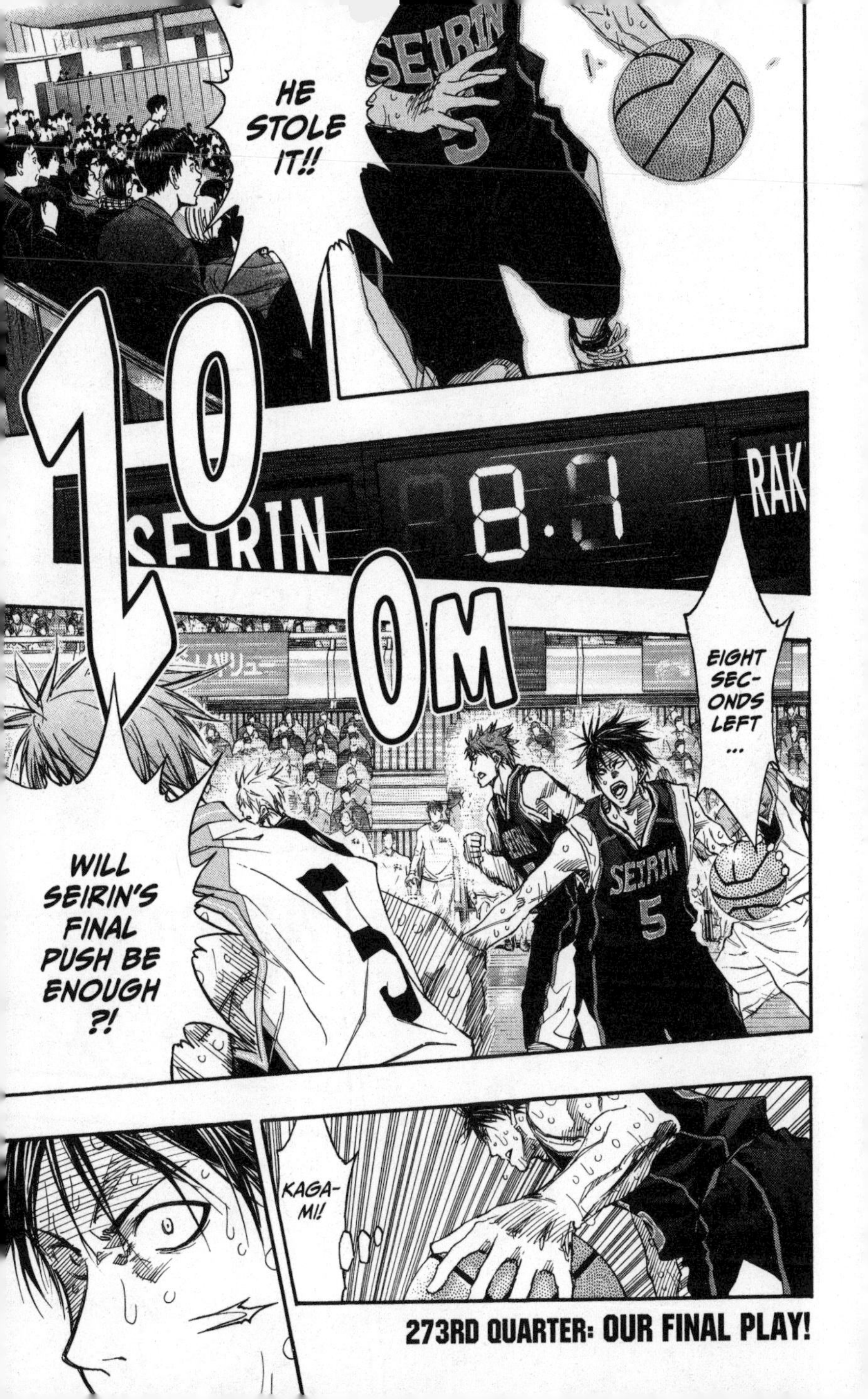
SEIRIN
5
HE STOLE IT!!
RAK
8.1
SEIRIN
EIGHT SECONDS LEFT...
SEIRIN
5
WILL SEIRIN'S FINAL PUSH BE ENOUGH?!
KAGA-MI!
273RD QUARTER: OUR FINAL PLAY!

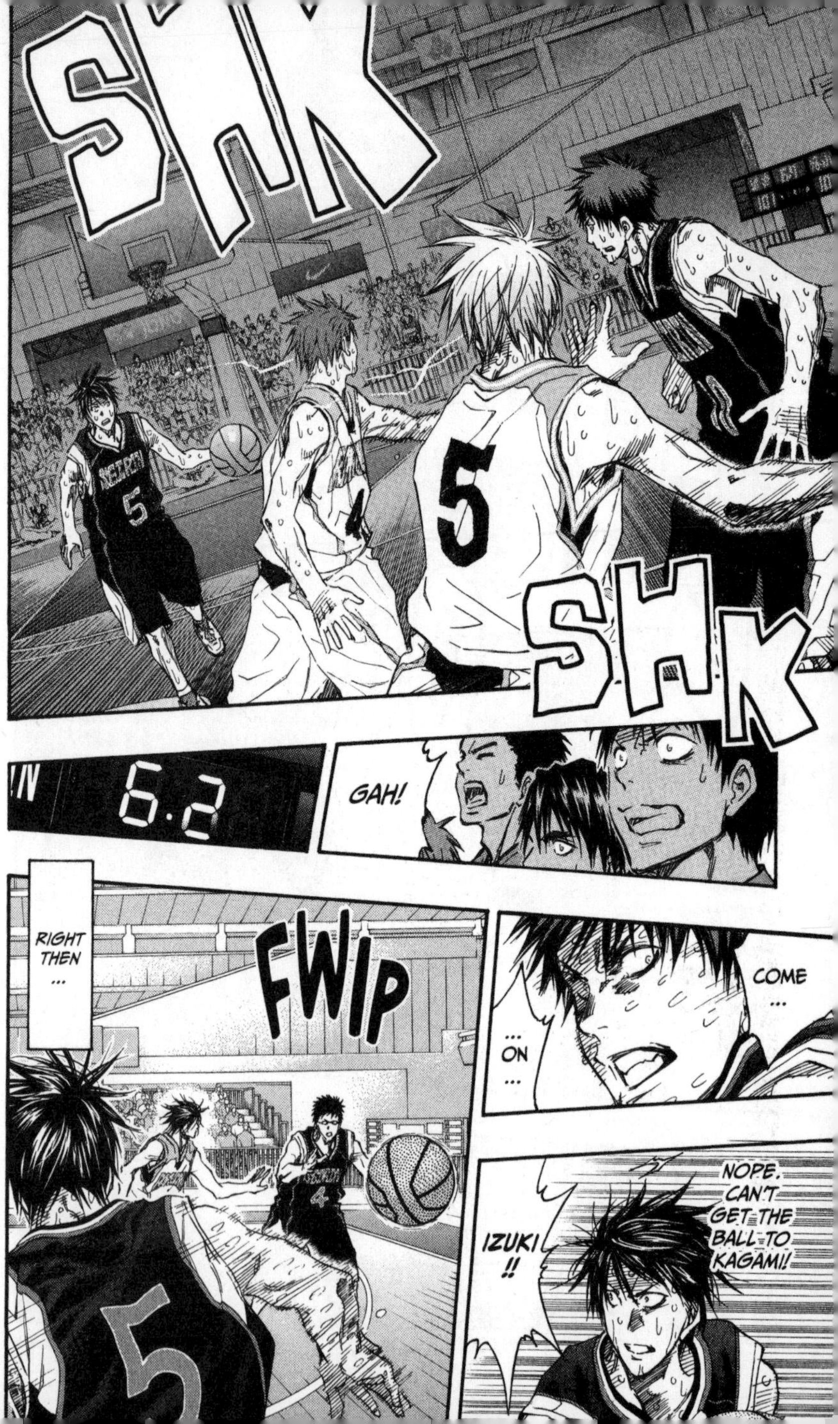
SHK
SHK
GAH!
6.2
COME ...
... ON ...
NOPE. CAN'T GET THE BALL TO KAGAMI!
IZUKI !!
RIGHT THEN ...
FWIP

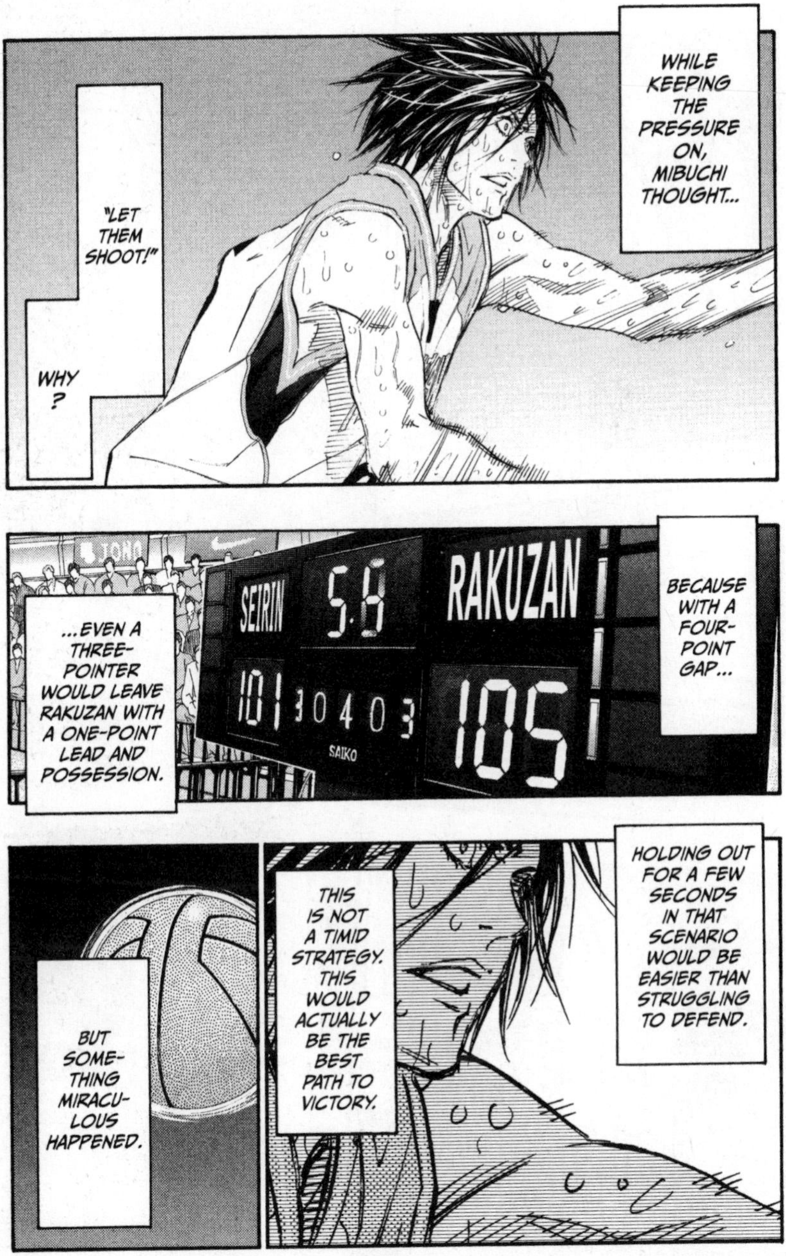
WHILE KEEPING THE PRESSURE ON, MIBUCHI THOUGHT...
"LET THEM SHOOT!"
WHY ?
BECAUSE WITH A FOUR-POINT GAP...
RAKUZAN
5.8
SEIRIN
105
101
SAIKO
...EVEN A THREE-POINTER WOULD LEAVE RAKUZAN WITH A ONE-POINT LEAD AND POSSESSION.
HOLDING OUT FOR A FEW SECONDS IN THAT SCENARIO WOULD BE EASIER THAN STRUGGLING TO DEFEND.
THIS IS NOT A TIMID STRATEGY. THIS WOULD ACTUALLY BE THE BEST PATH TO VICTORY.
BUT SOMETHING MIRACULOUS HAPPENED.

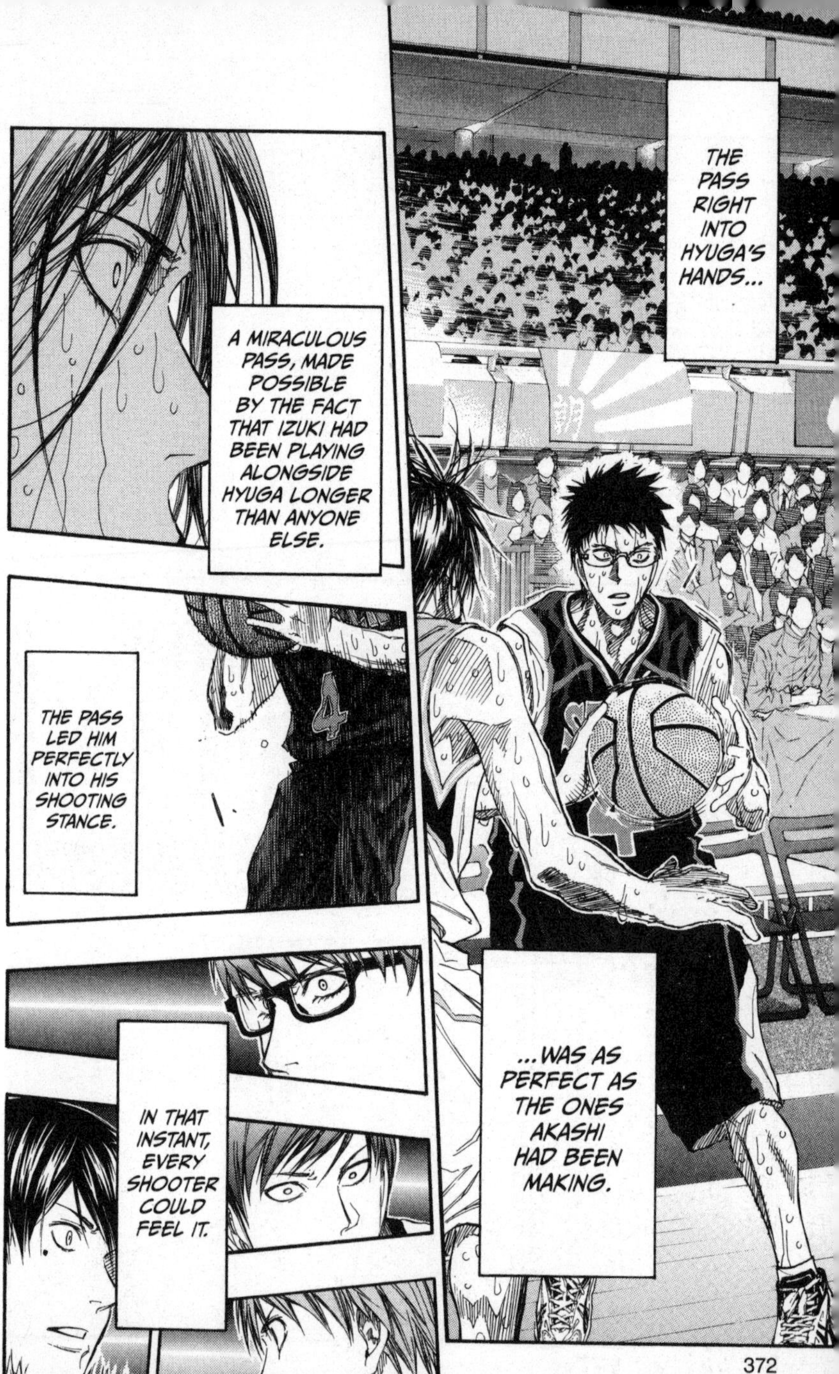
THE PASS RIGHT INTO HYUGA'S HANDS...
...WAS AS PERFECT AS THE ONES AKASHI HAD BEEN MAKING.
A MIRACULOUS PASS, MADE POSSIBLE BY THE FACT THAT IZUKI HAD BEEN PLAYING ALONGSIDE HYUGA LONGER THAN ANYONE ELSE.
THE PASS LED HIM PERFECTLY INTO HIS SHOOTING STANCE.
IN THAT INSTANT, EVERY SHOOTER COULD FEEL IT.

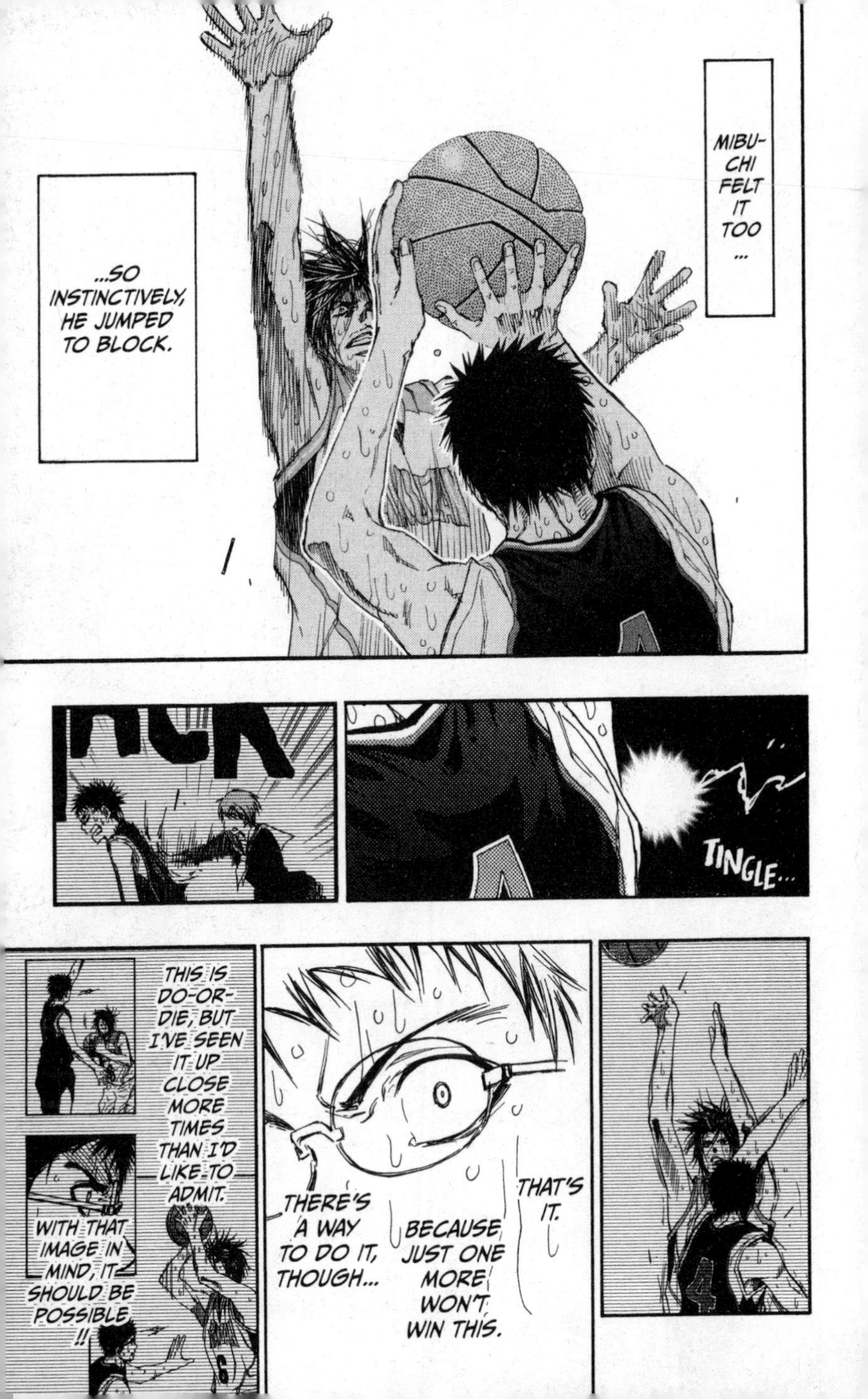
MIBU-CHI FELT IT TOO...
...SO INSTINCTIVELY, HE JUMPED TO BLOCK.
TINGLE...
THAT'S IT.
BECAUSE JUST ONE MORE WON'T WIN THIS.
THERE'S A WAY TO DO IT, THOUGH...
THIS IS DO-OR-DIE, BUT I'VE SEEN IT UP CLOSE MORE TIMES THAN I'D LIKE TO ADMIT.
WITH THAT IMAGE IN MIND, IT SHOULD BE POSSIBLE!!

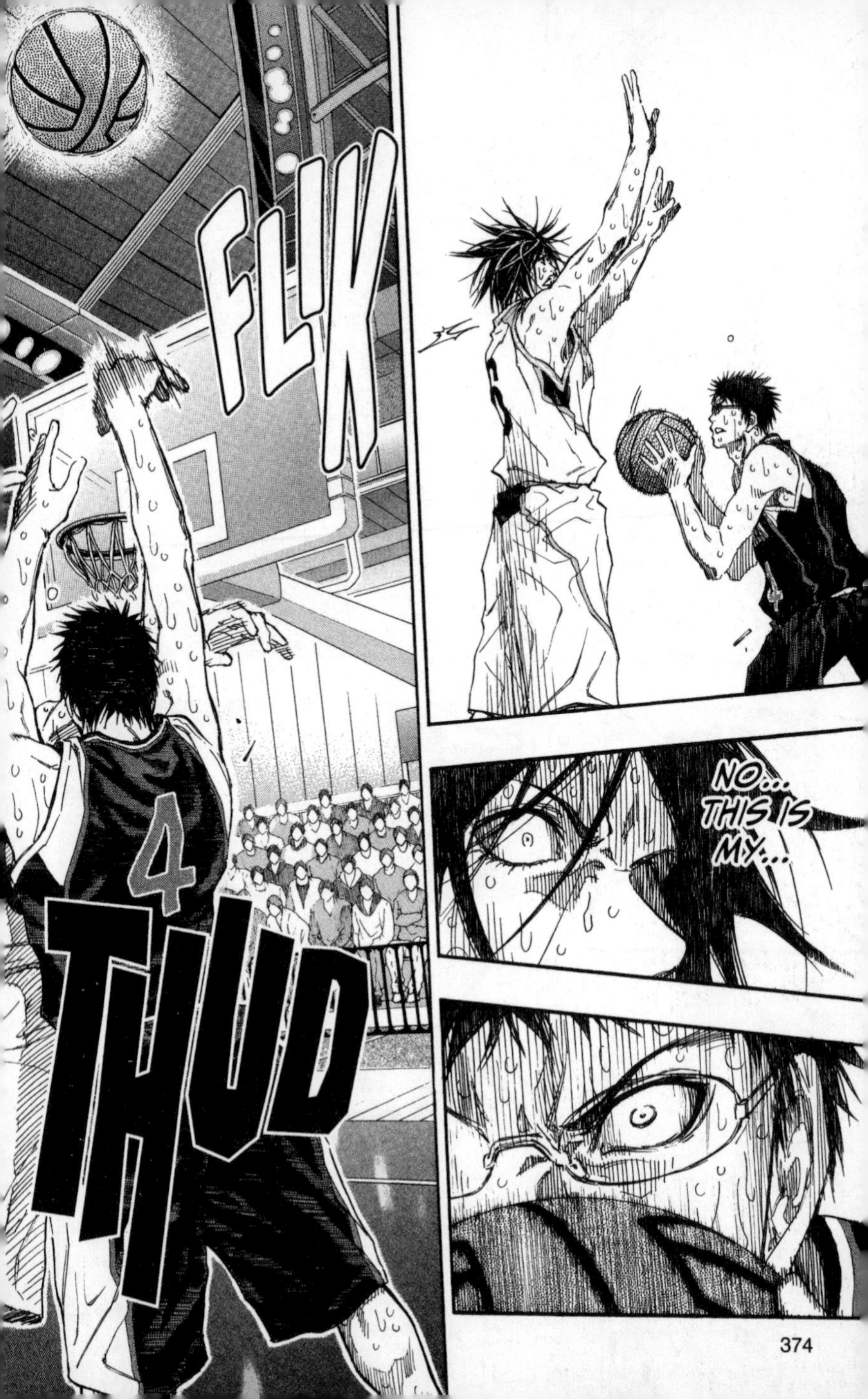
NO... THIS IS MY...
FLIK
THUD

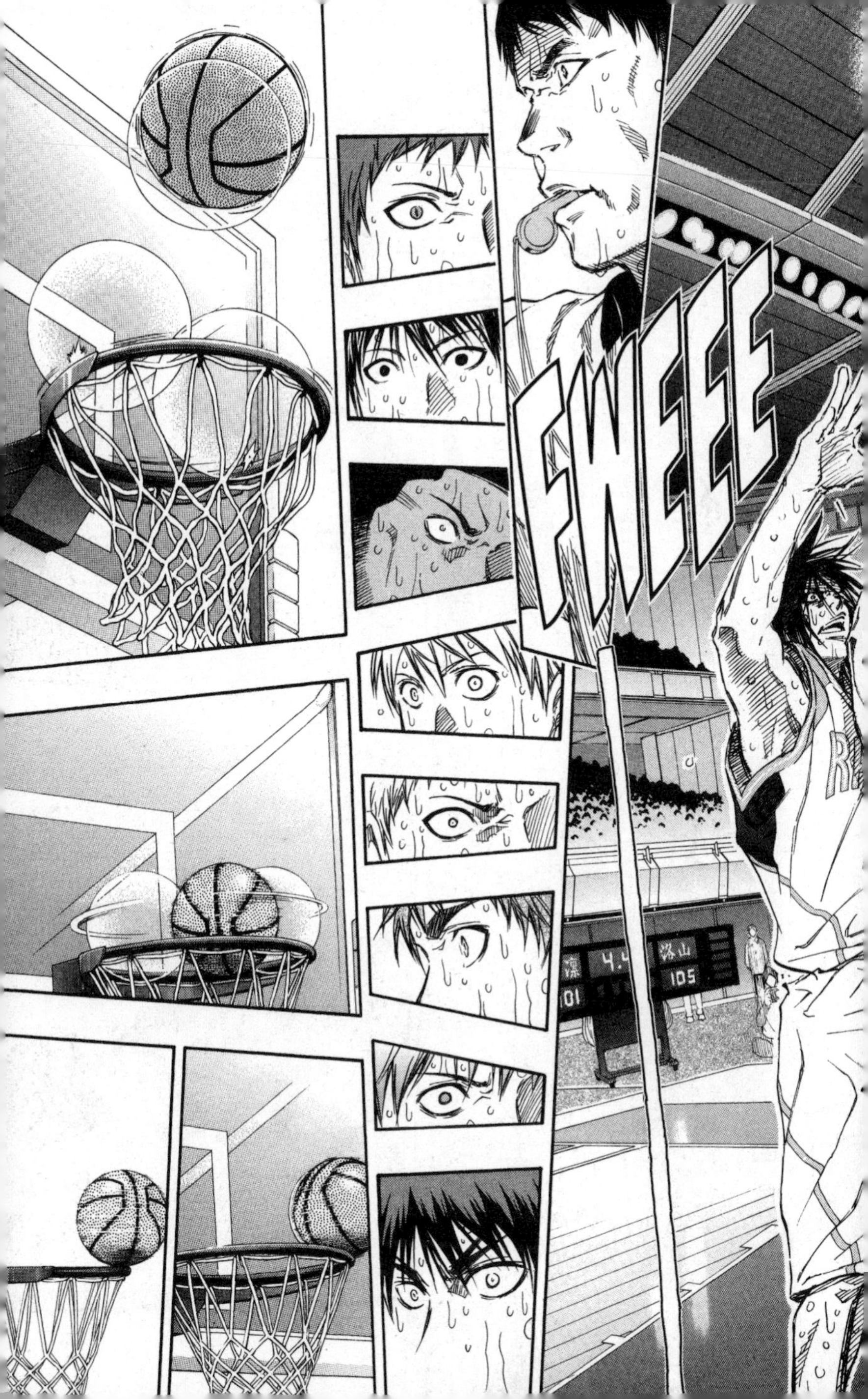
FWEEE
洛山
105

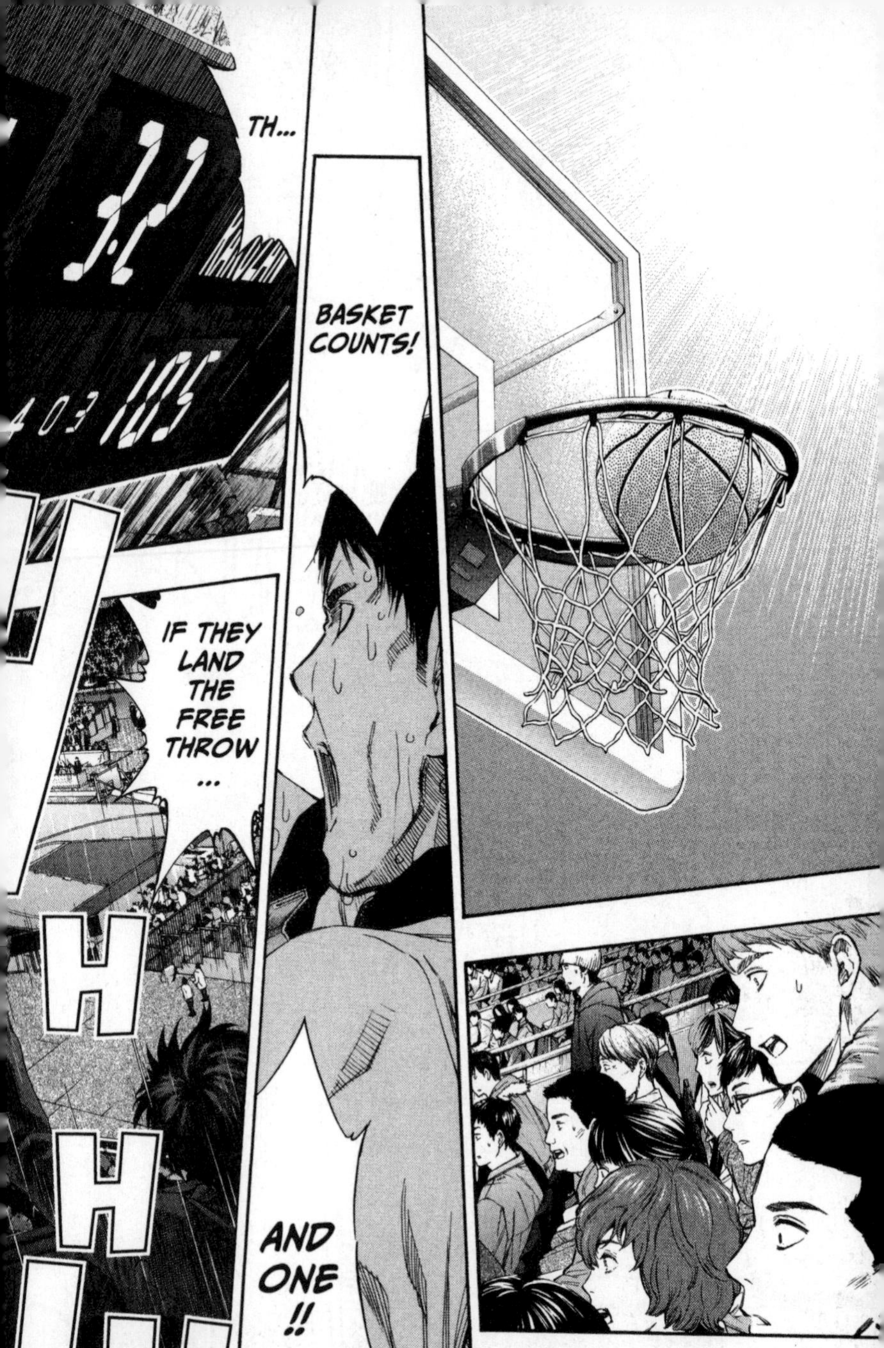

TH...
BASKET COUNTS!
AND ONE!!
IF THEY LAND THE FREE THROW...

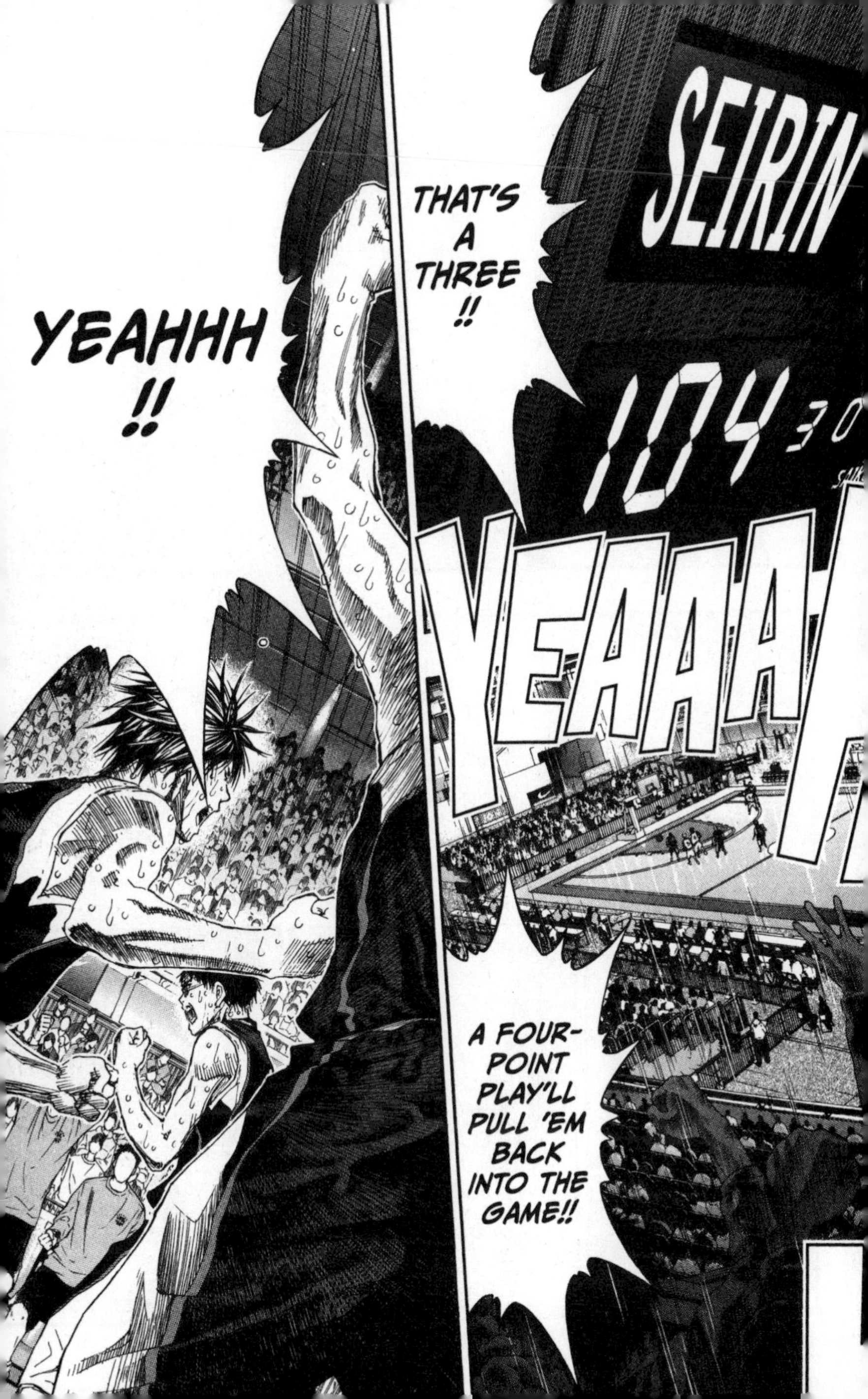
SEIRIN
104
THAT'S A THREE!!
YEAA
A FOUR-POINT PLAY'LL PULL 'EM BACK INTO THE GAME!!
YEAHHH!!

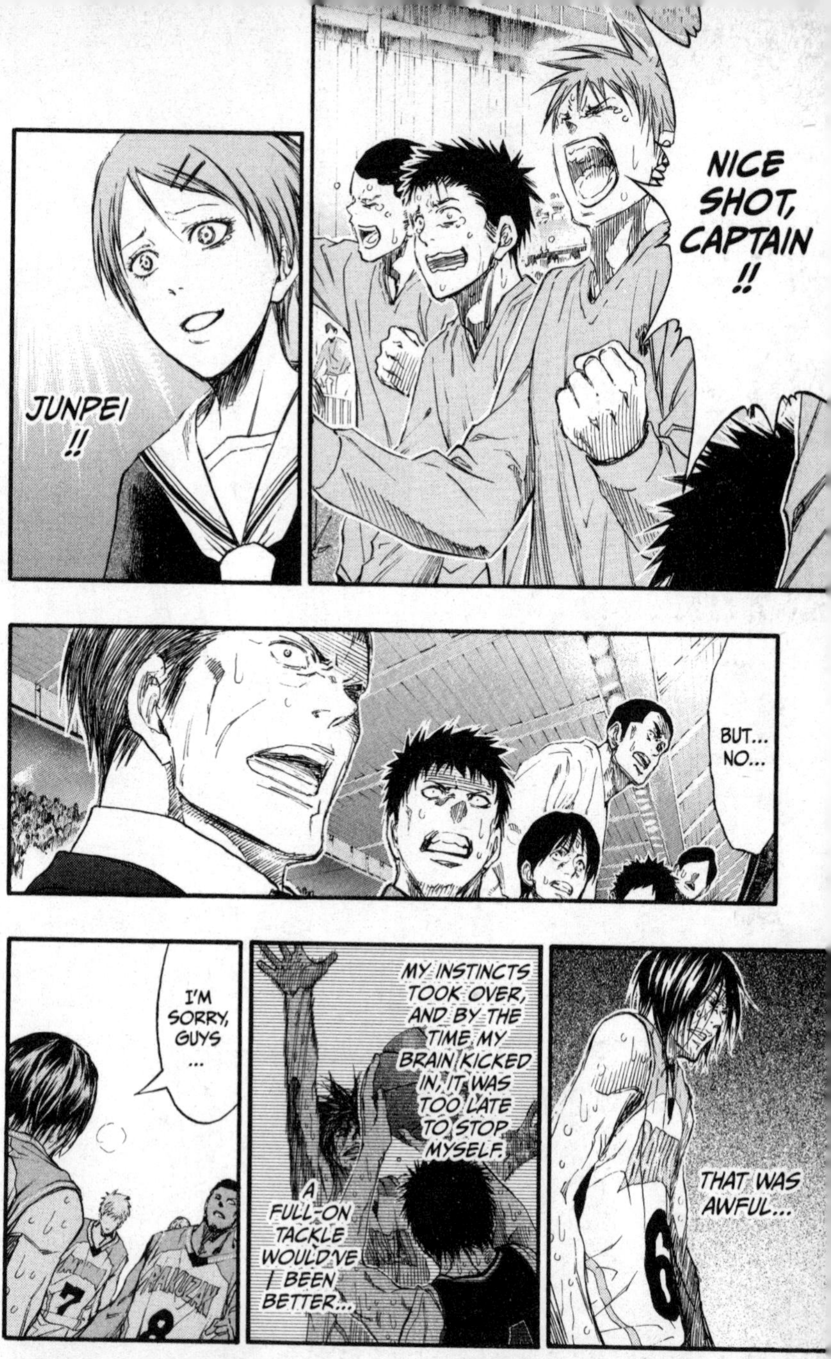
NICE SHOT, CAPTAIN!!
JUNPEI!!
BUT... NO...
THAT WAS AWFUL...
MY INSTINCTS TOOK OVER, AND BY THE TIME MY BRAIN KICKED IN, IT WAS TOO LATE TO STOP MYSELF.
A FULL-ON TACKLE WOULD'VE BEEN BETTER...
I'M SORRY, GUYS ...

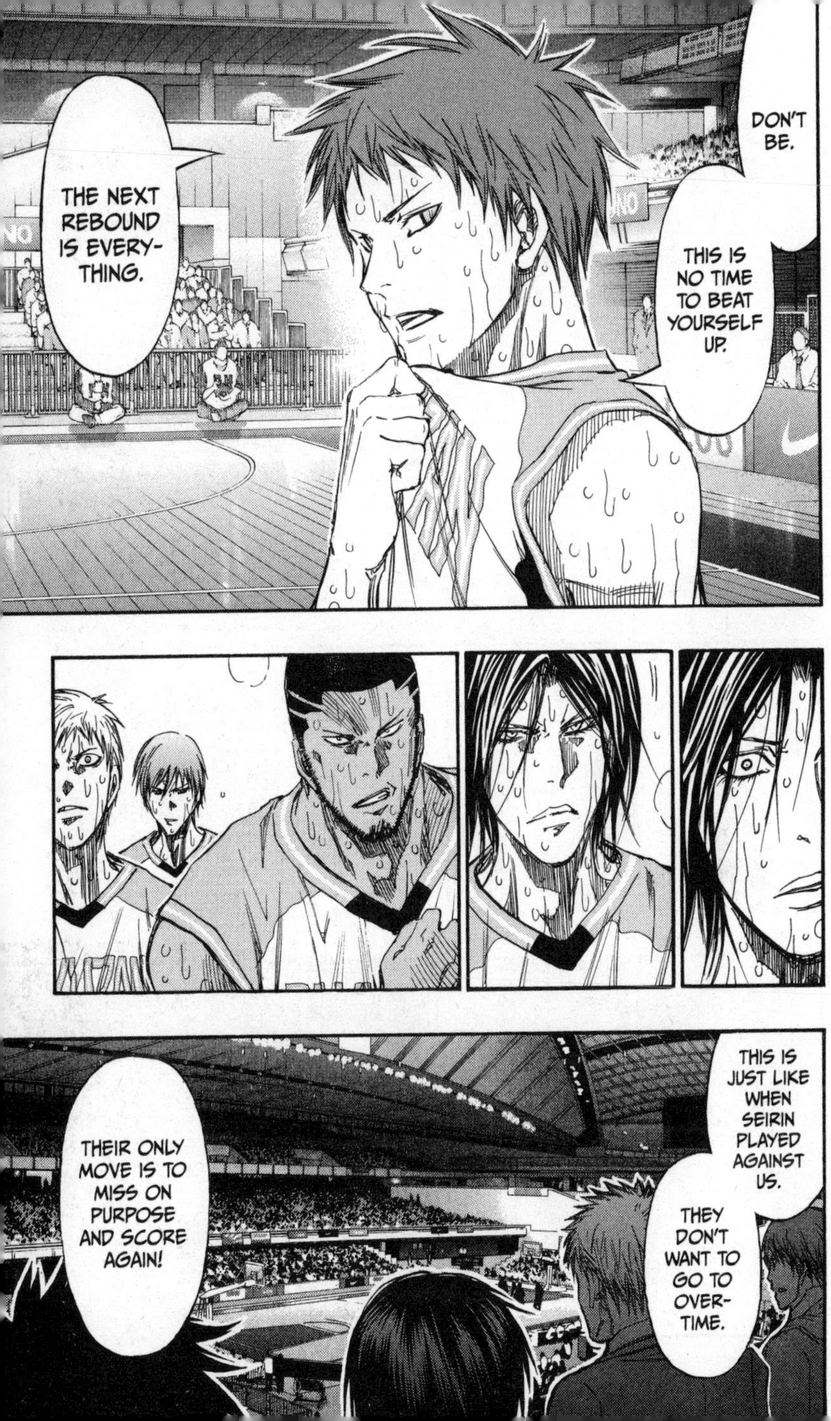
DON'T BE.
THIS IS NO TIME TO BEAT YOURSELF UP.
THE NEXT REBOUND IS EVERYTHING.
THIS IS JUST LIKE WHEN SEIRIN PLAYED AGAINST US.
THEY DON'T WANT TO GO TO OVERTIME.
THEIR ONLY MOVE IS TO MISS ON PURPOSE AND SCORE AGAIN!

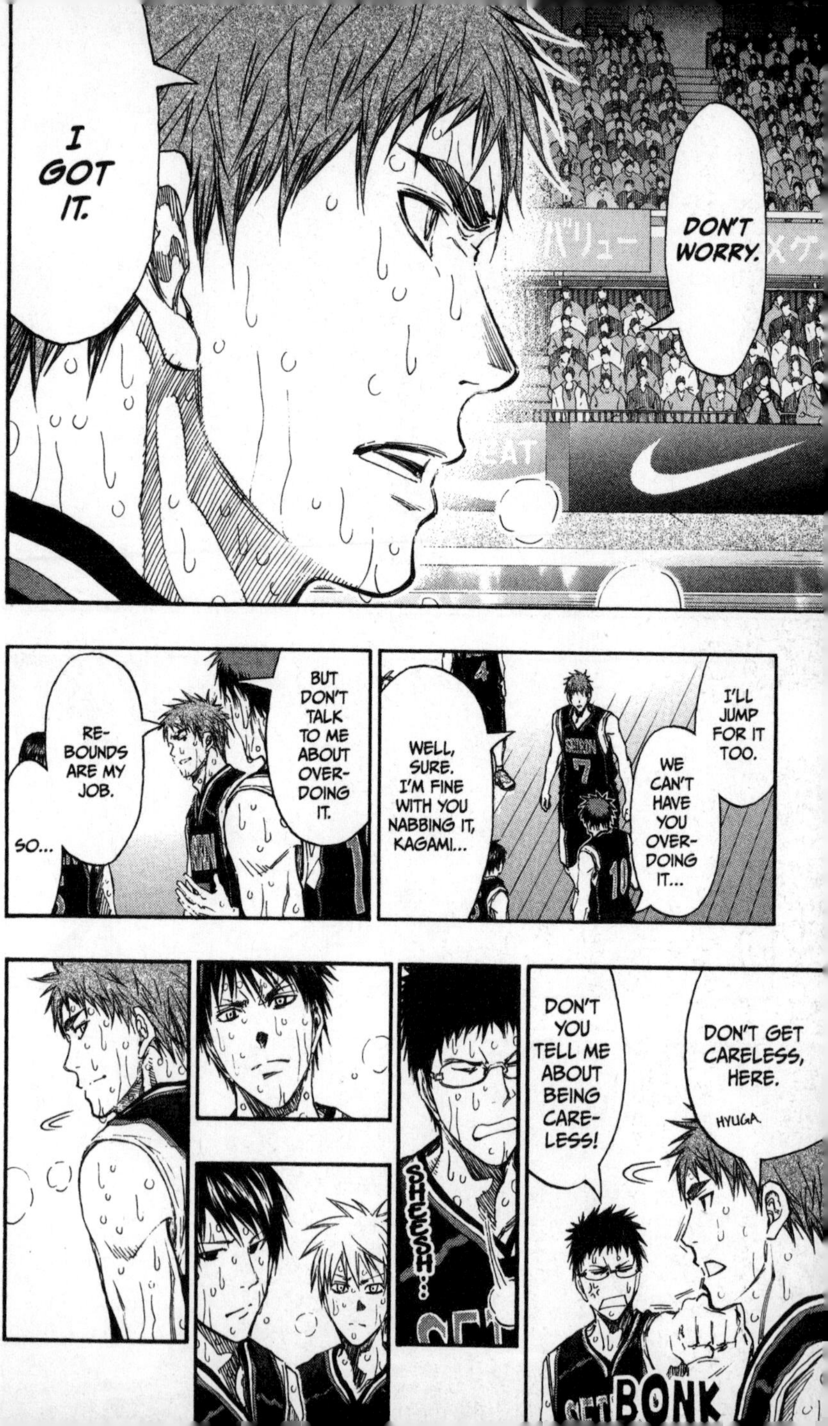
DON'T WORRY.
I GOT IT.
I'LL JUMP FOR IT TOO.
WE CAN'T HAVE YOU OVER-DOING IT...
WELL, SURE. I'M FINE WITH YOU NABBING IT, KAGAMI...
BUT DON'T TALK TO ME ABOUT OVER-DOING IT.
RE-BOUNDS ARE MY JOB.
SO...
DON'T GET CARELESS, HERE.
HYUGA.
DON'T YOU TELL ME ABOUT BEING CARE-LESS!
BONK
SHEESH...

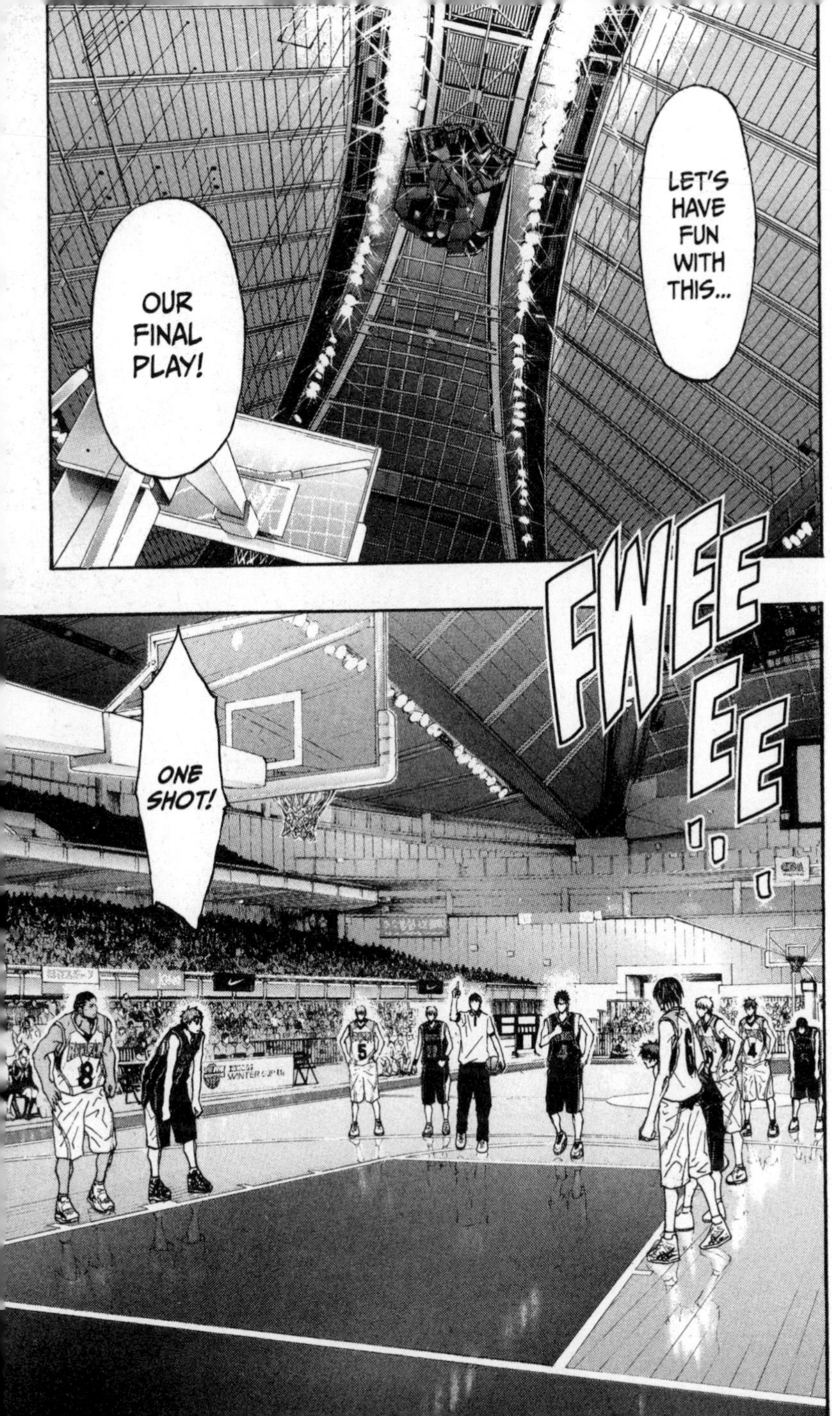
LET'S HAVE FUN WITH THIS...
OUR FINAL PLAY!
FWEEEE
ONE SHOT!

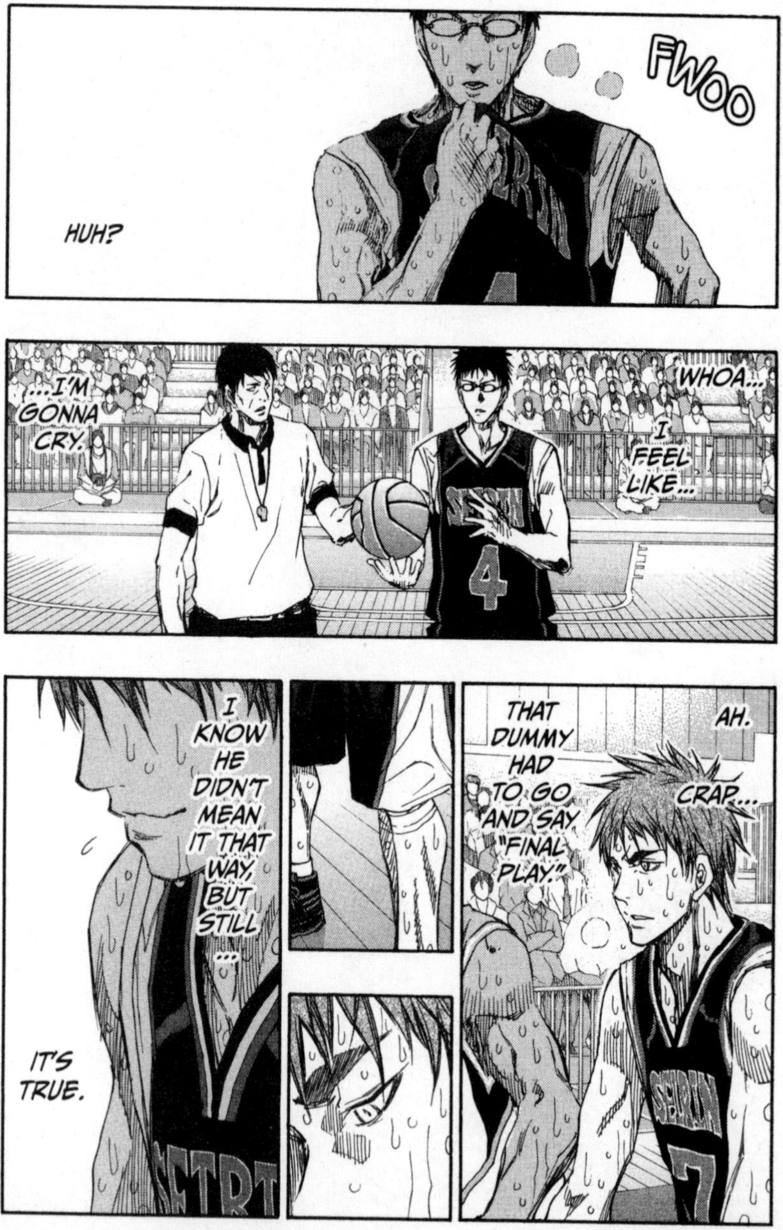
FWOO
HUH?
WHOA... I FEEL LIKE...
...I'M GONNA CRY.
AH. CRAP...
THAT DUMMY HAD TO GO AND SAY "FINAL PLAY."
I KNOW HE DIDN'T MEAN IT THAT WAY, BUT STILL...
IT'S TRUE.

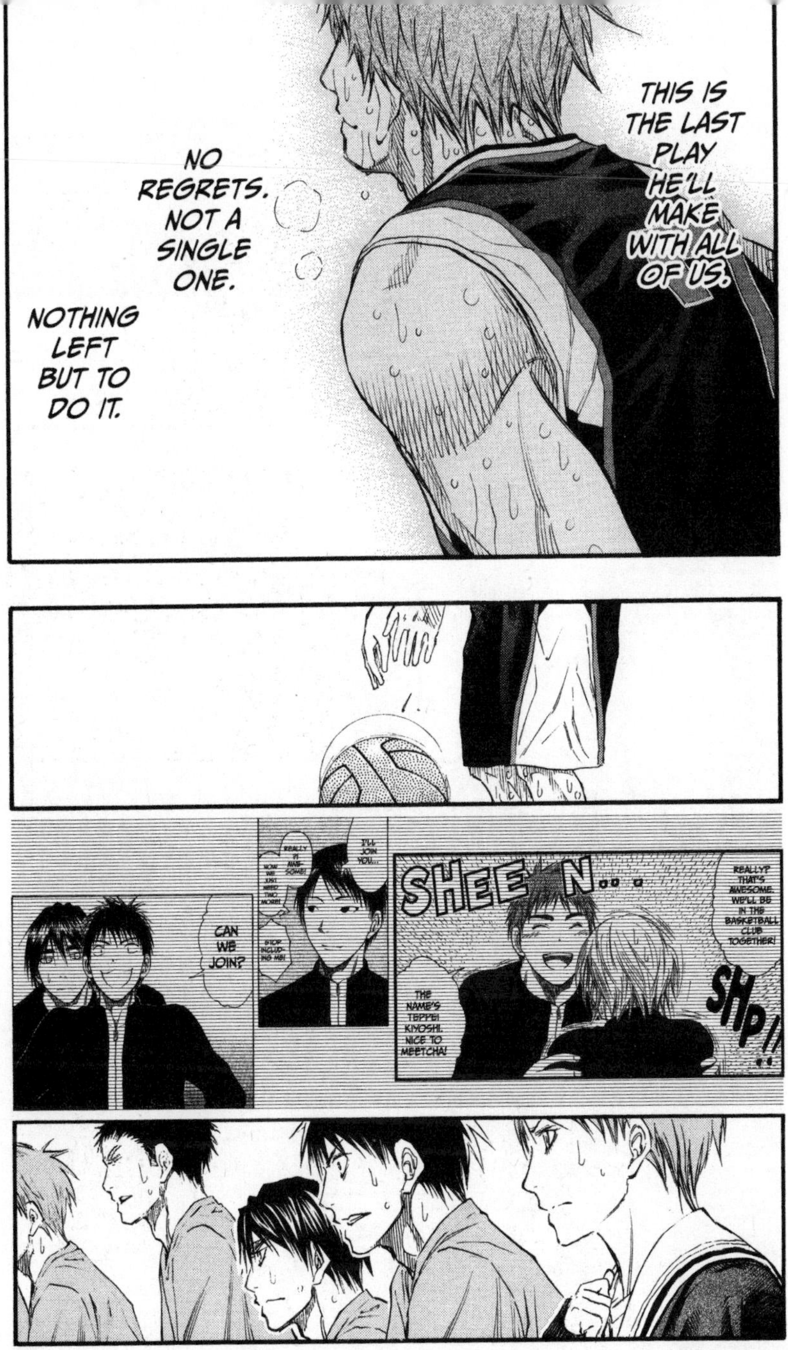
THIS IS THE LAST PLAY HE'LL MAKE WITH ALL OF US.
NO REGRETS. NOT A SINGLE ONE.
NOTHING LEFT BUT TO DO IT.
SHEE N...
REALLY? THAT'S AWESOME. WE'LL BE IN THE BASKETBALL CLUB TOGETHER!
SHP!!
THE NAME'S TEPPEI KIYOSHI. NICE TO MEETCHA!
I'LL JOIN YOU...
REALLY?! AWESOME!
NOW WE JUST NEED TWO MORE!
STOP INCLUDING ME!
CAN WE JOIN?

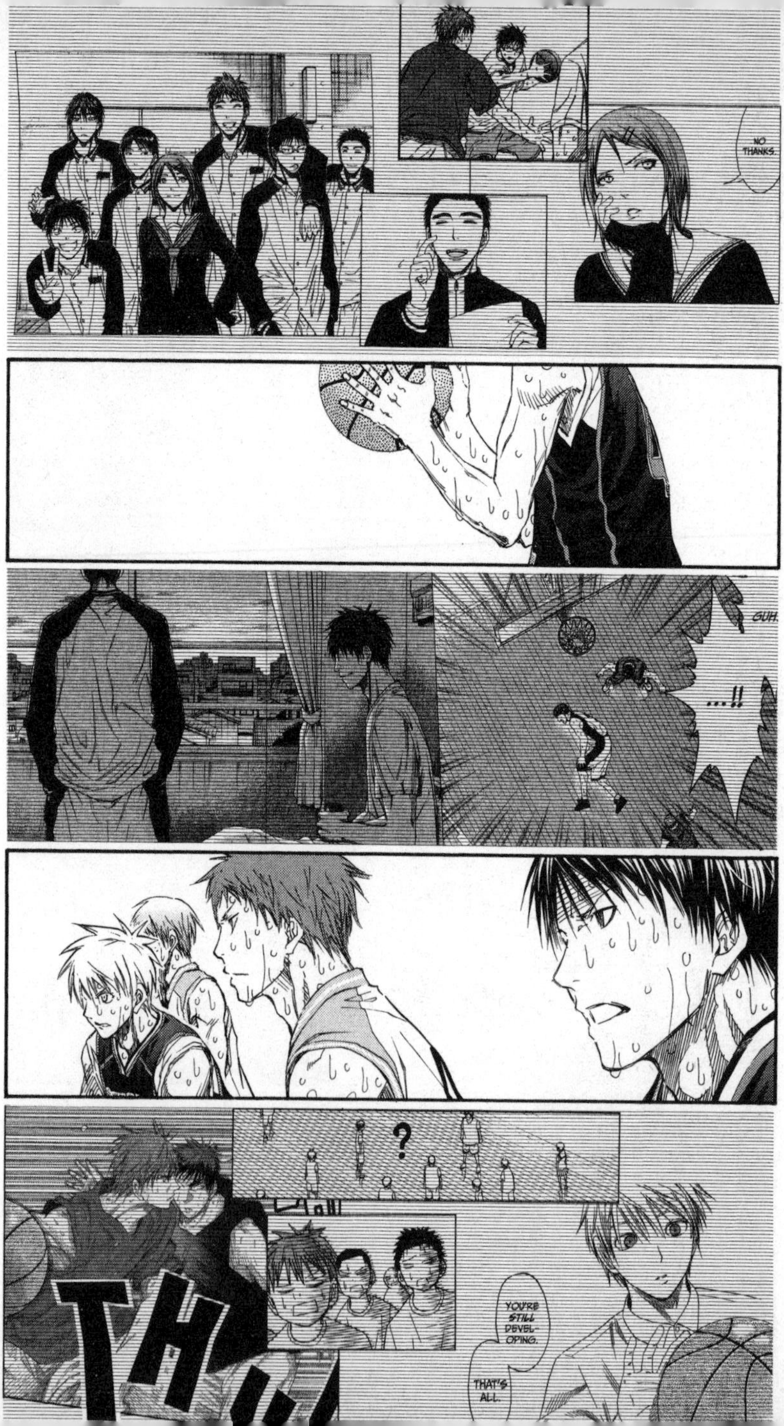
NO THANKS.
GUH.
...!!
?
YOU'RE STILL DEVEL-OPING.
THAT'S ALL.
TH...

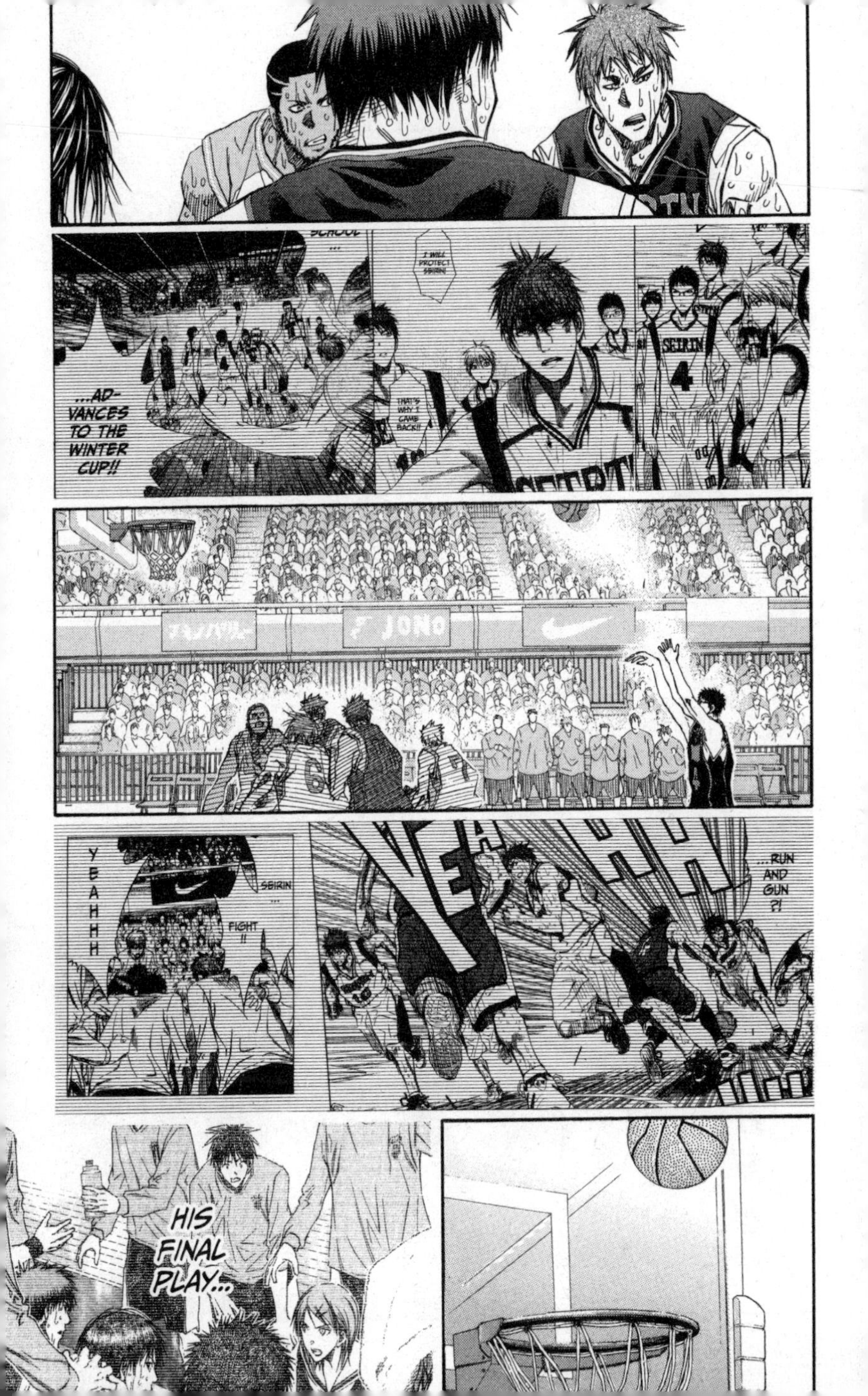

I WILL PROTECT SEIRIN!
THAT'S WHY I CAME BACK!!
SCHOOL ...
...ADVANCES TO THE WINTER CUP!!
JONO
...RUN AND GUN?!
YEAHHH
SEIRIN ...
FIGHT!!
HIS FINAL PLAY...

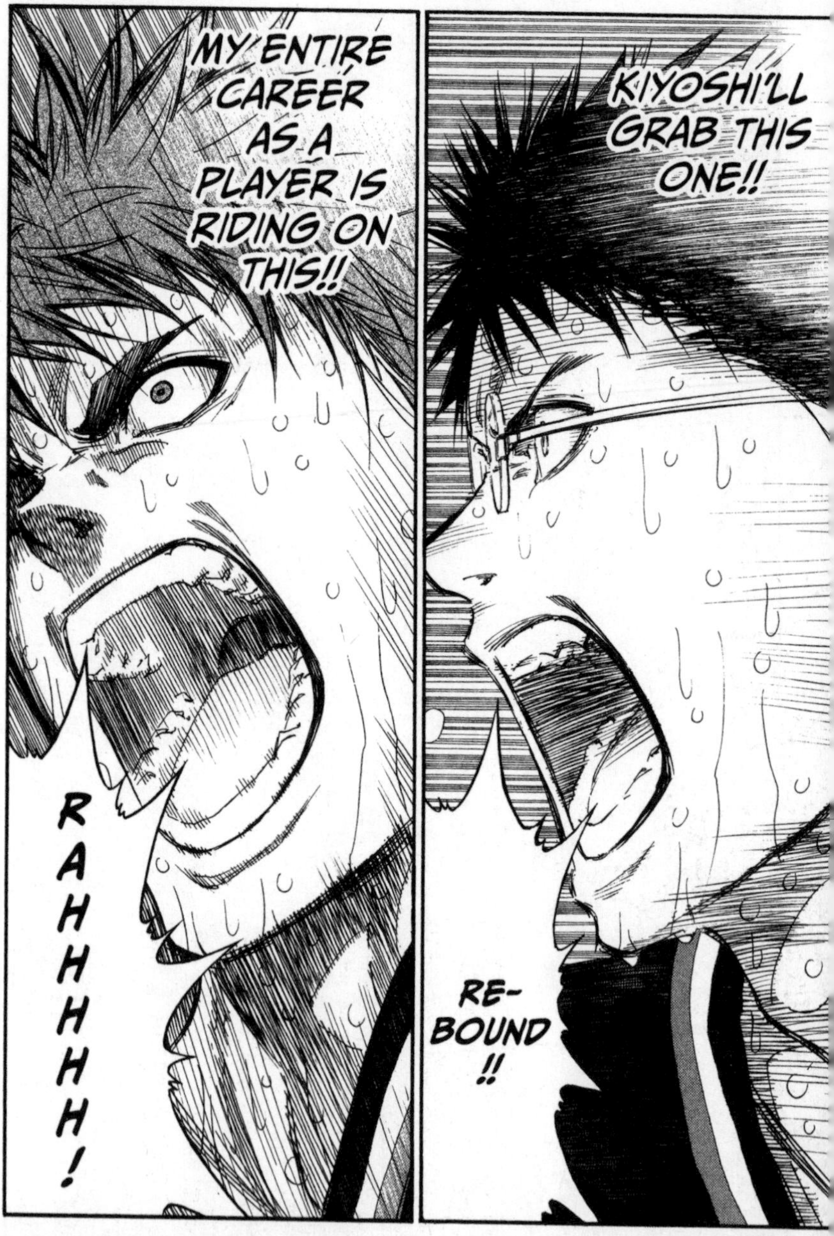
KIYOSHI'LL GRAB THIS ONE!!
RE-BOUND!!
MY ENTIRE CAREER AS A PLAYER IS RIDING ON THIS!!
RAHHHHHH!

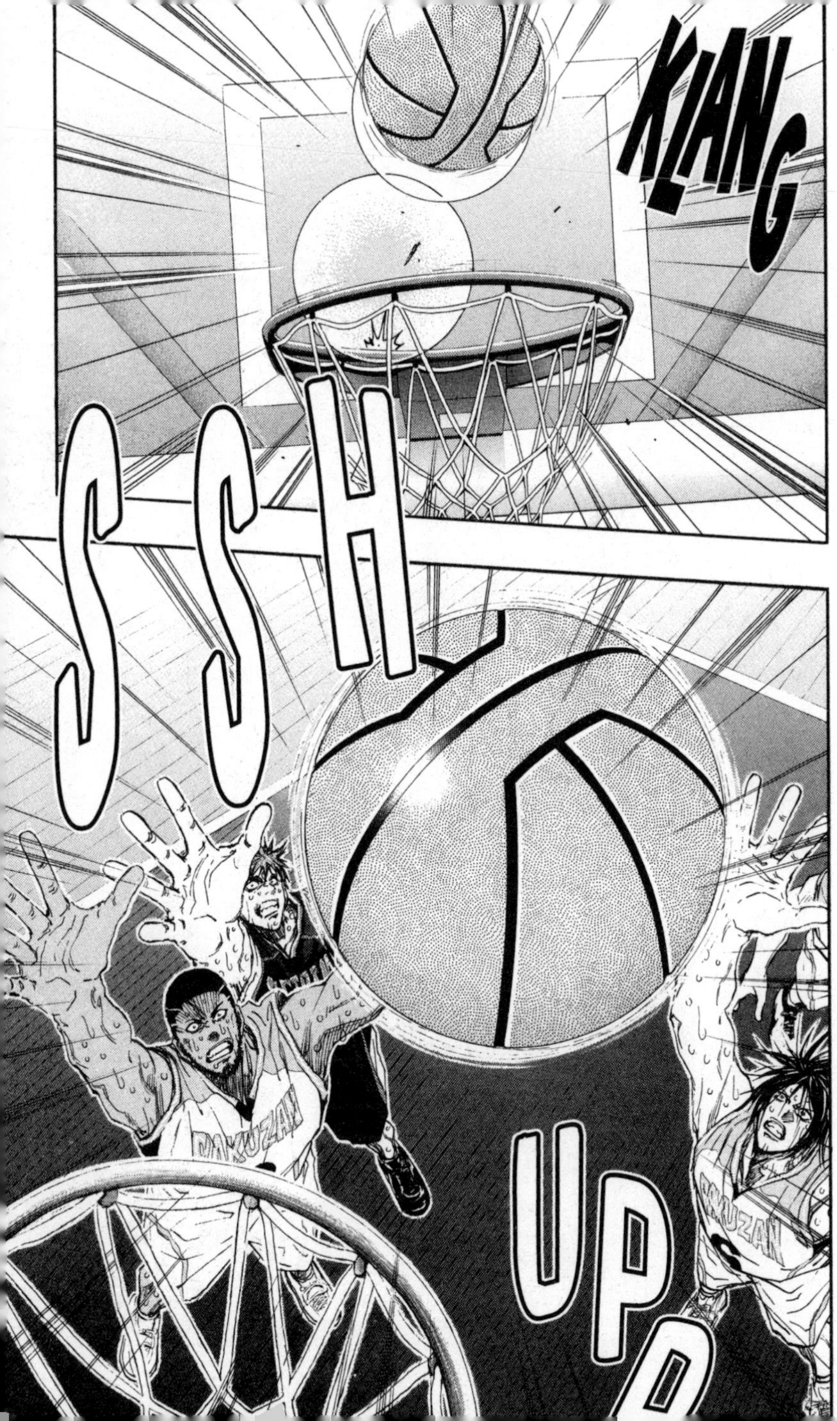
KLANG
SSH
UP

KUROKO'S BASKETBALL Q&A
W/ HALFWAY-DECENT ANSWERS

Q. BESIDES THE ONES FEATURED IN BLOOPERS AND LIGHT NOVELS, WHAT OTHER LIES DID FUKUI TELL LIU?
(YUNA from HOKKAIDO)

A. "IN JAPAN, SHORTER PEOPLE ARE MORE HIGHLY REGARDED THAN TALL PEOPLE."
(I SHOULD MENTION, THOUGH, THAT MOST OF THE TIME FUKUI TEACHES LIU ABOUT JAPANESE CULTURE IN EARNEST. THE LIES AND TEASING ONLY HAPPEN SOMETIMES)

KUROKO'S BASKETBALL BLOOPERS
TAKE 1

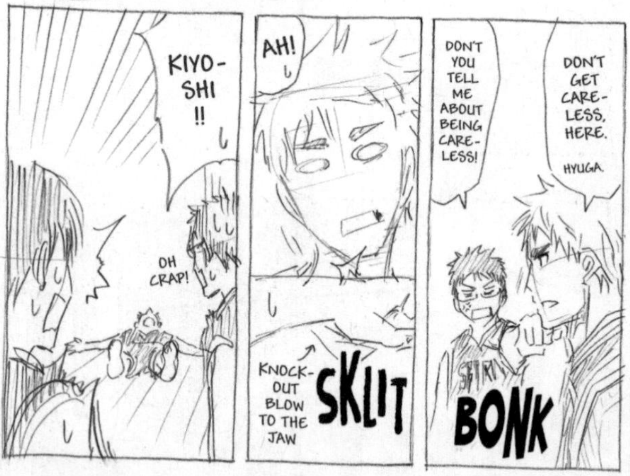
DON'T GET CARELESS, HERE.
HYUGA
DON'T YOU TELL ME ABOUT BEING CARELESS!
BONK
AH!
KNOCKOUT BLOW TO THE JAW
SKLIT
KIYOSHI!!
OH CRAP!

274TH QUARTER: TIME'S UP

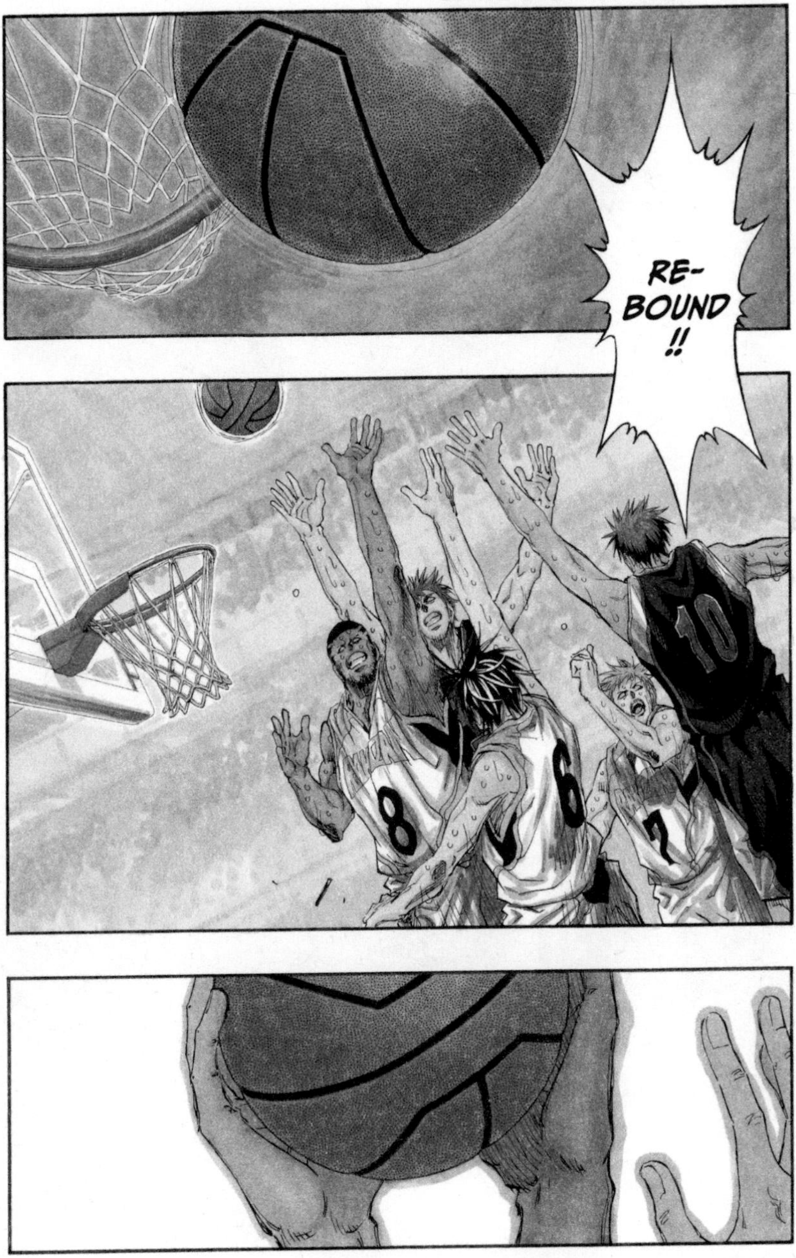
RE-
BOUND
!!

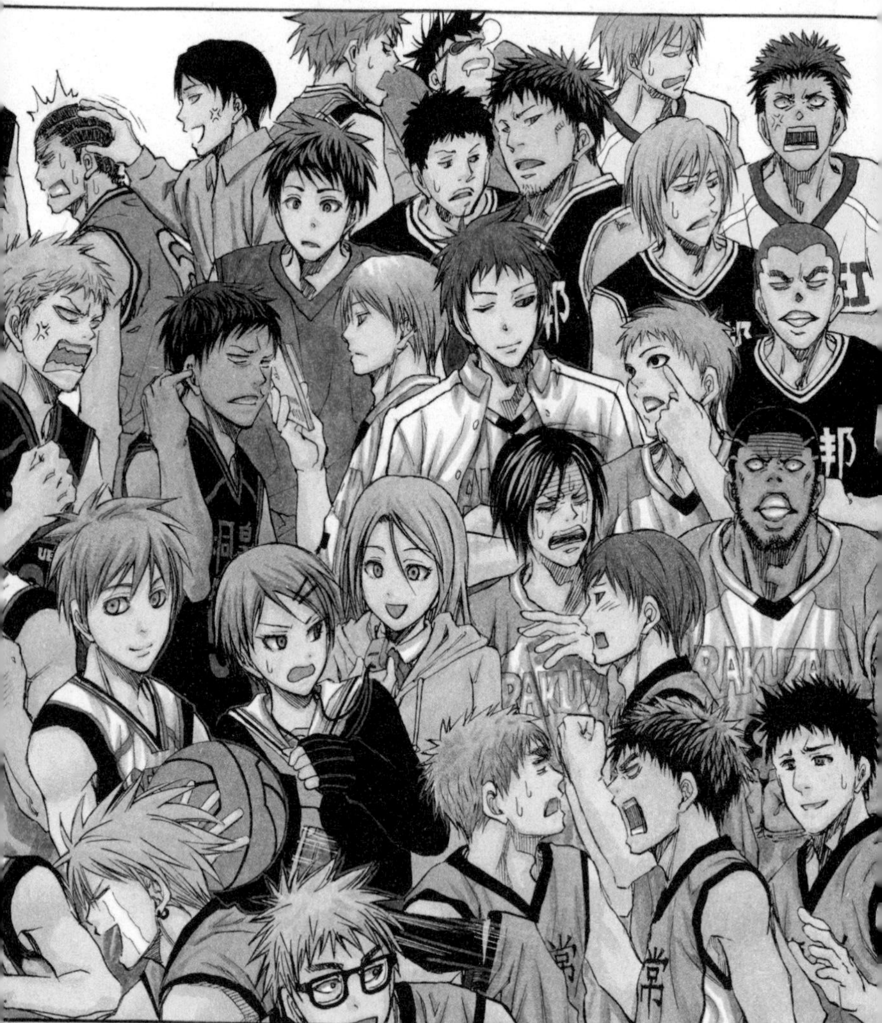

274TH QUARTER: TIME'S UP

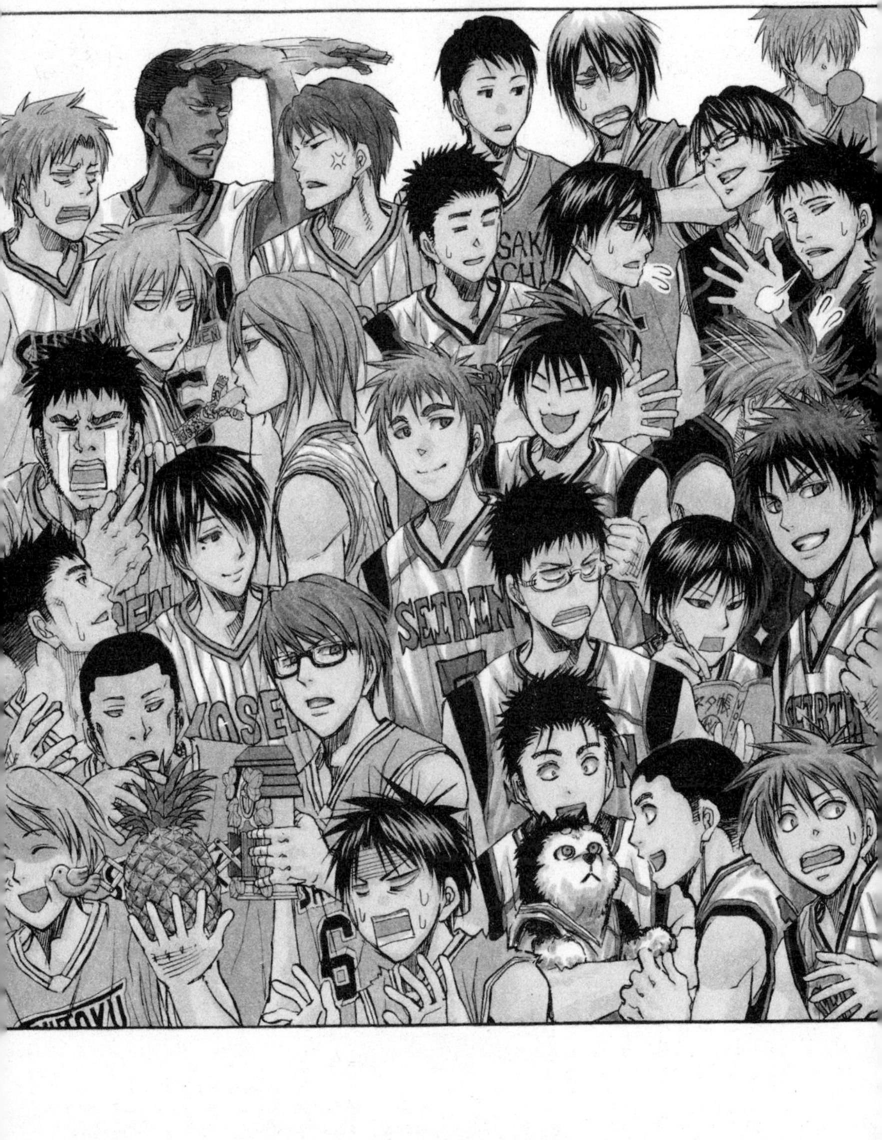
SEIRIN

Kuroko's BASKETBALL

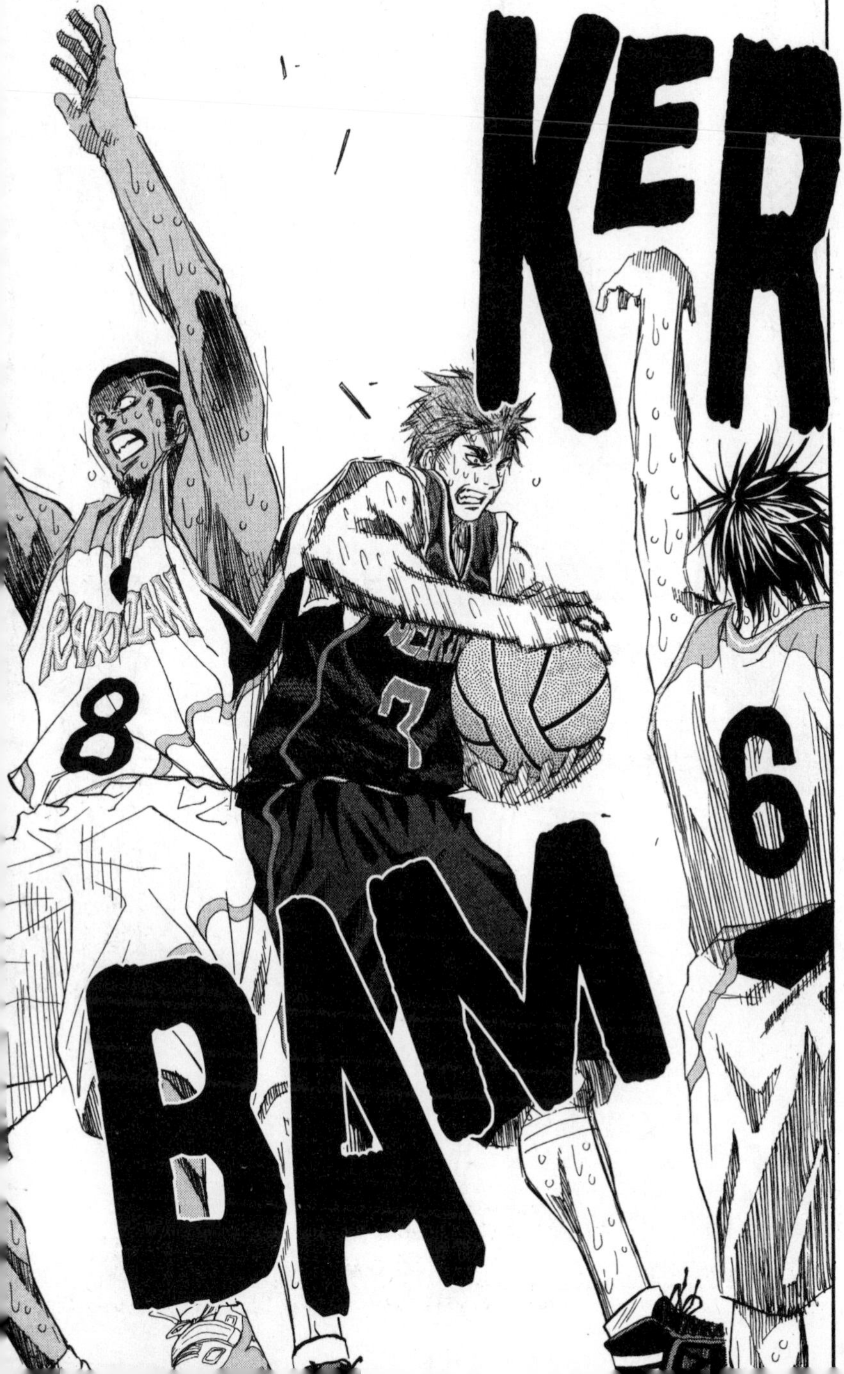
KER
BAM

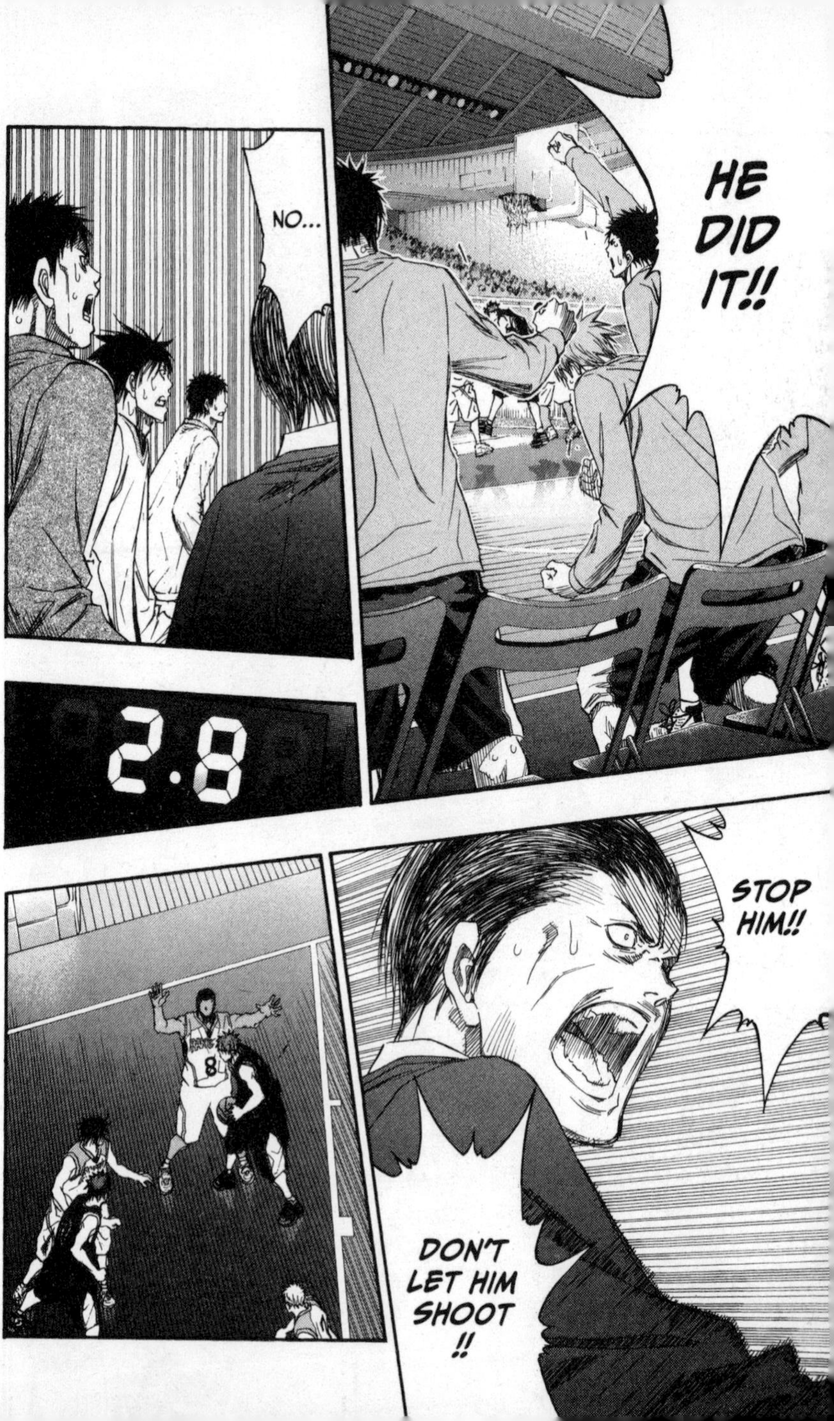
HE DID IT!!
NO...
2.8
STOP HIM!!
DON'T LET HIM SHOOT !!

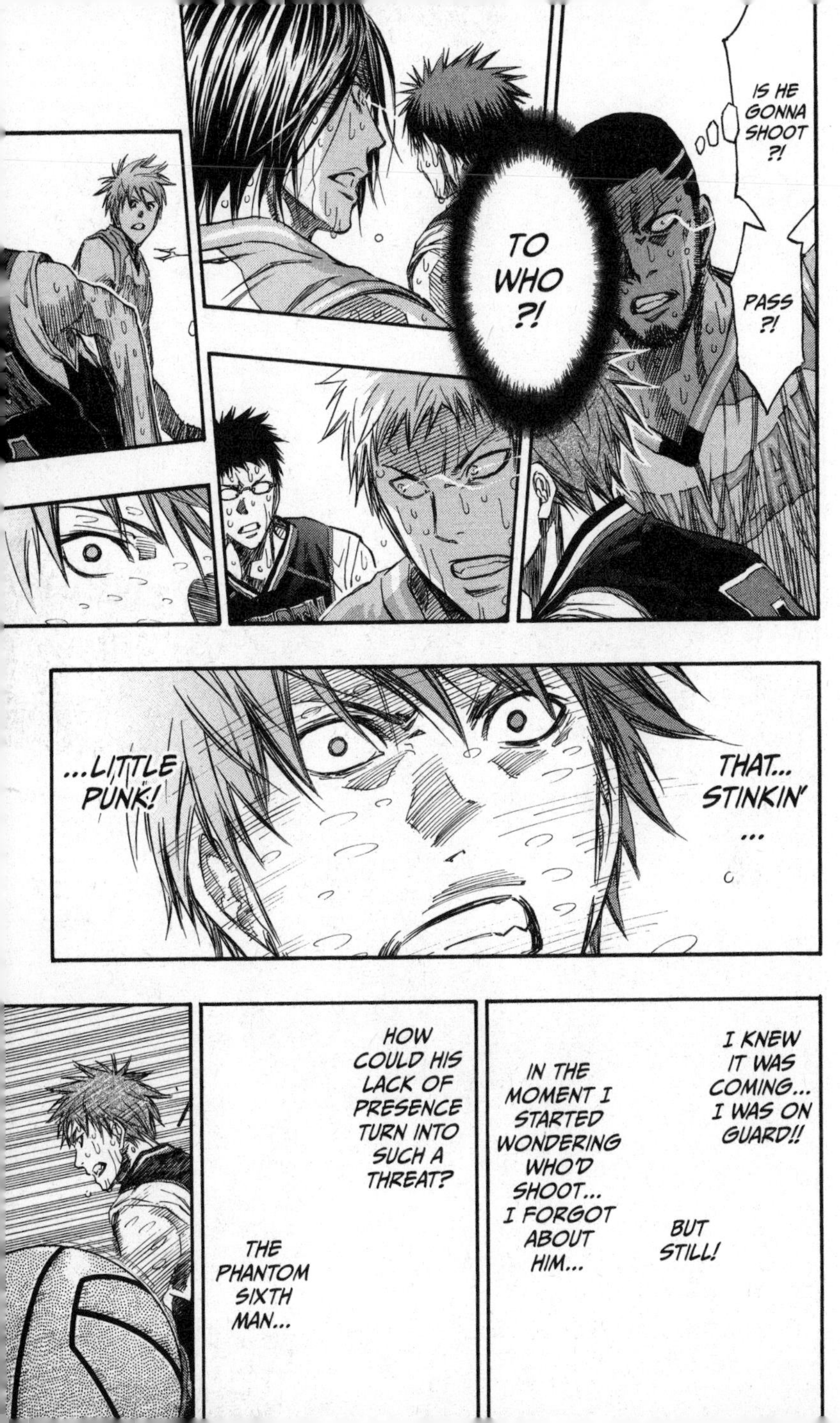
IS HE GONNA SHOOT ?!
PASS ?!
TO WHO ?!
THAT... STINKIN' ...
...LITTLE PUNK!
I KNEW IT WAS COMING... I WAS ON GUARD!!
BUT STILL!
IN THE MOMENT I STARTED WONDERING WHO'D SHOOT... I FORGOT ABOUT HIM...
HOW COULD HIS LACK OF PRESENCE TURN INTO SUCH A THREAT?
THE PHANTOM SIXTH MAN...

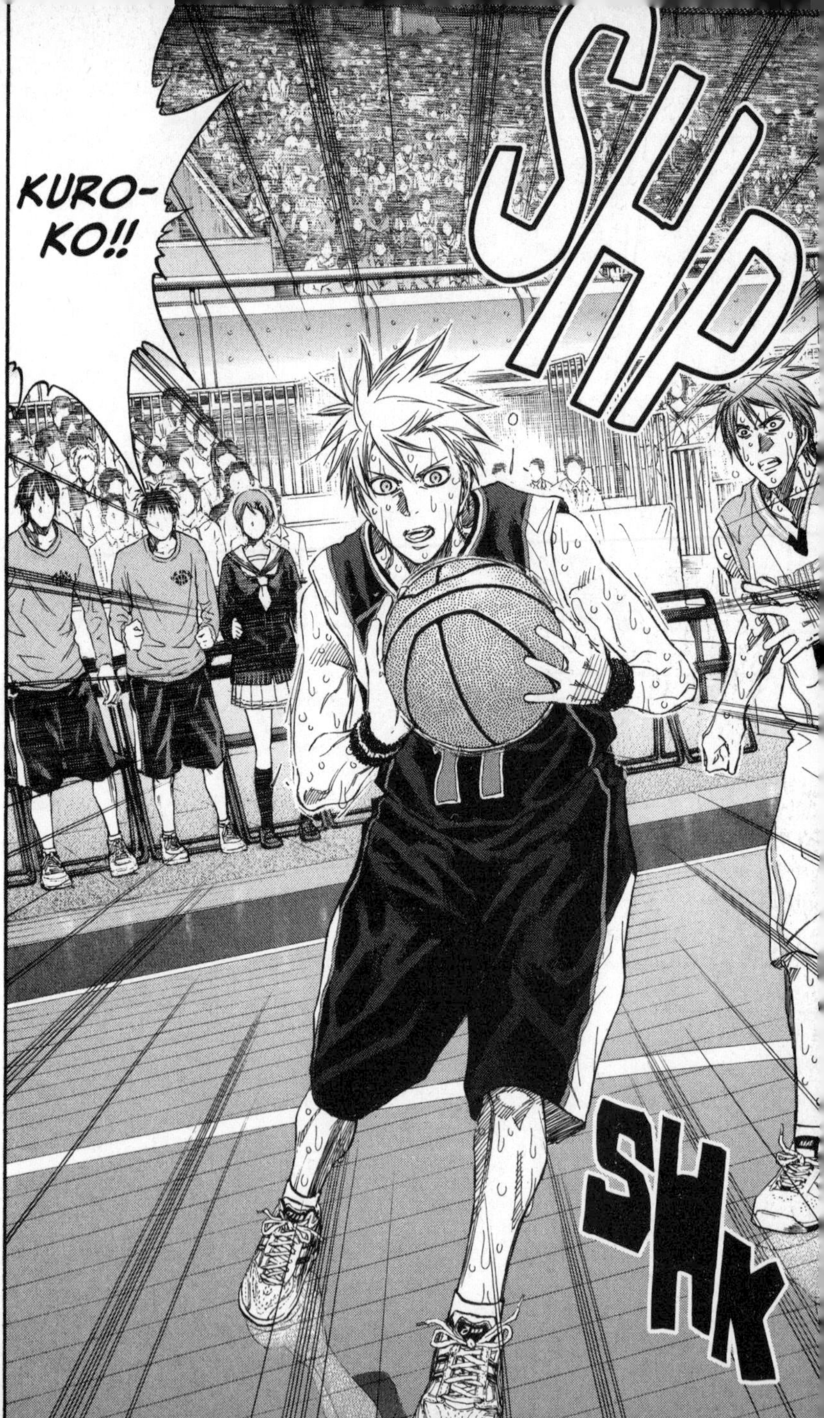
SHP
KURO-
KO!!
SHK

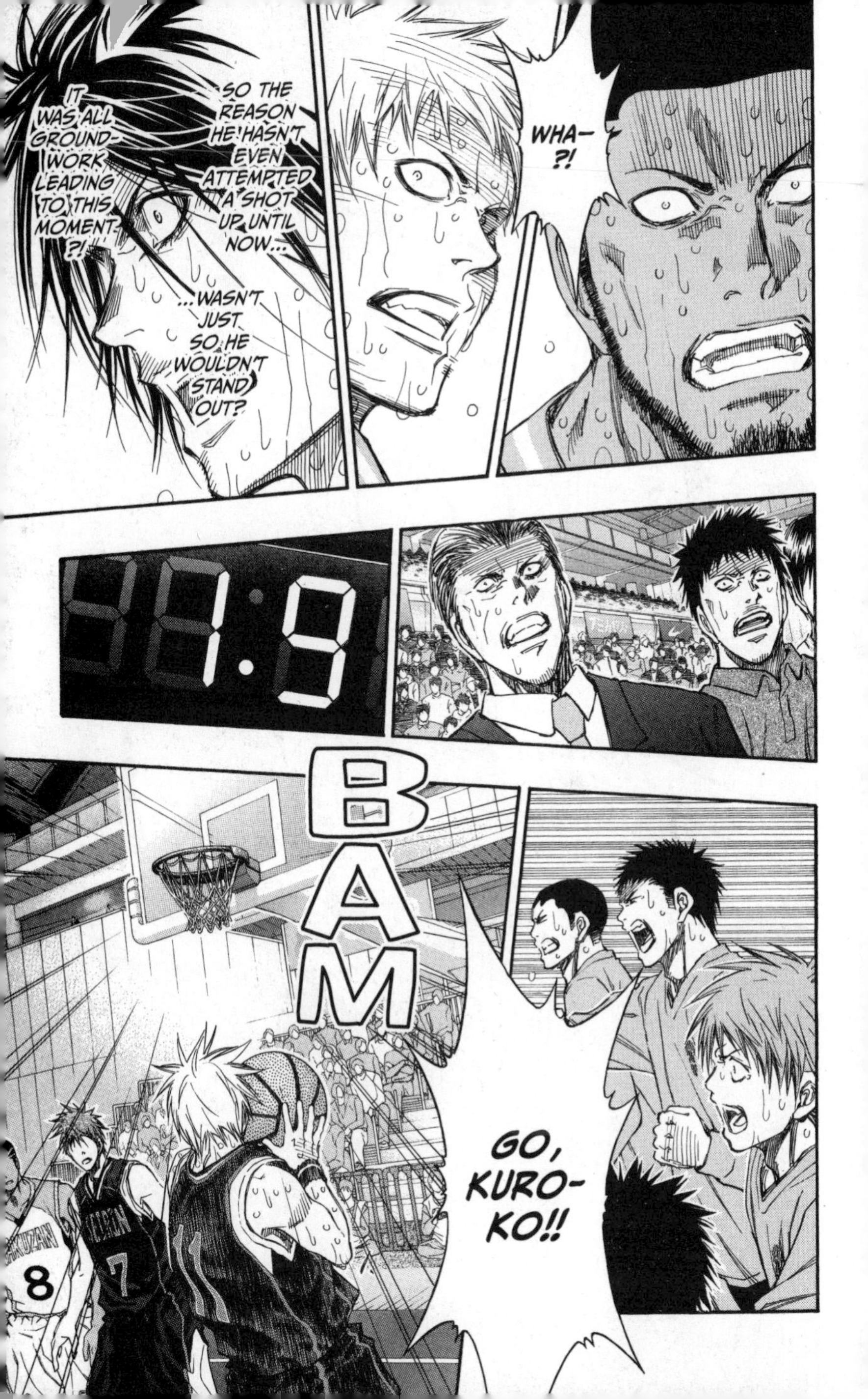
WHA-?!
SO THE REASON HE HASN'T EVEN ATTEMPTED A SHOT UP UNTIL NOW...
...WASN'T JUST SO HE WOULDN'T STAND OUT?
IT WAS ALL GROUNDWORK LEADING TO THIS MOMENT?!
GO, KUROKO!!
BAM

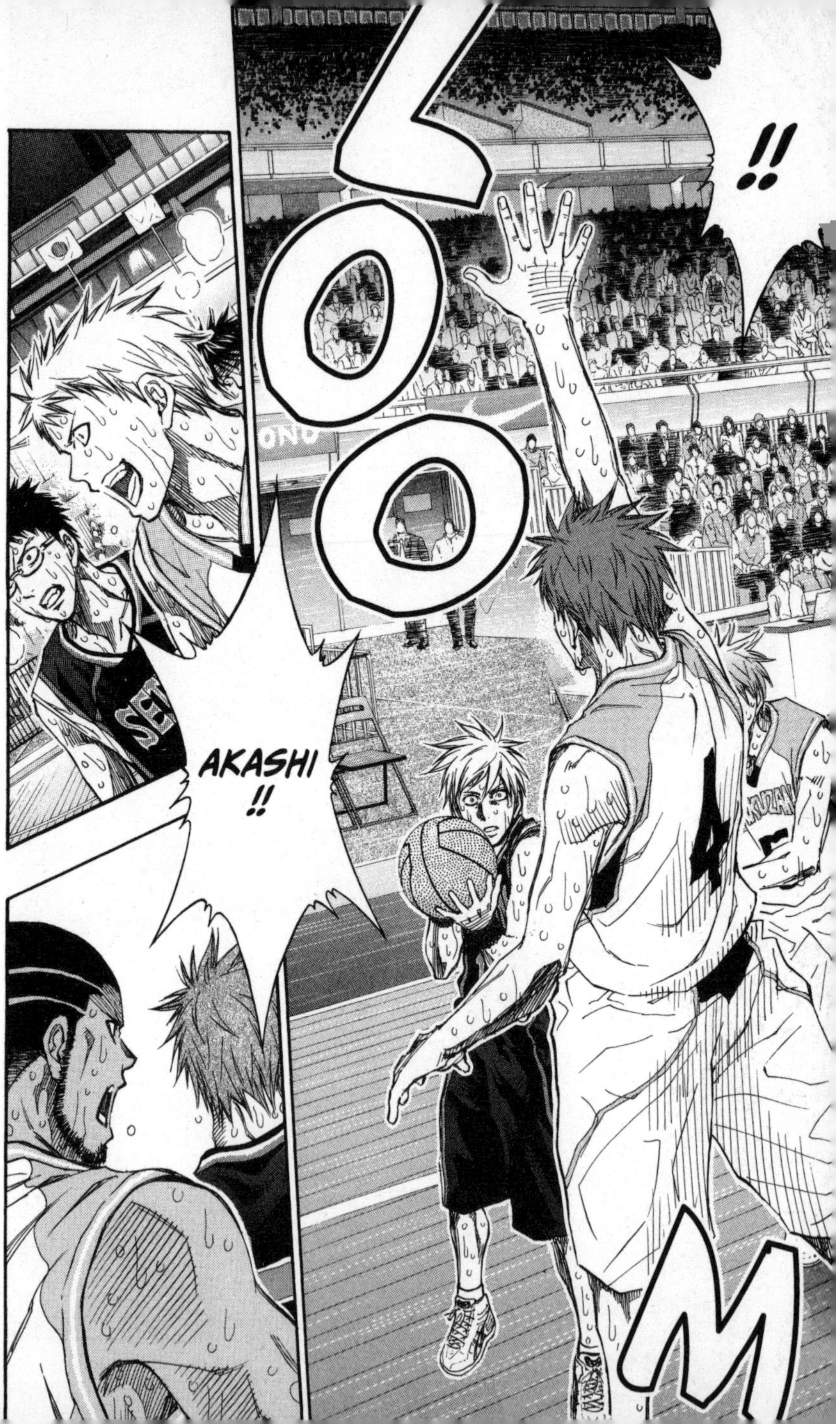
!!
AKASHI
!!

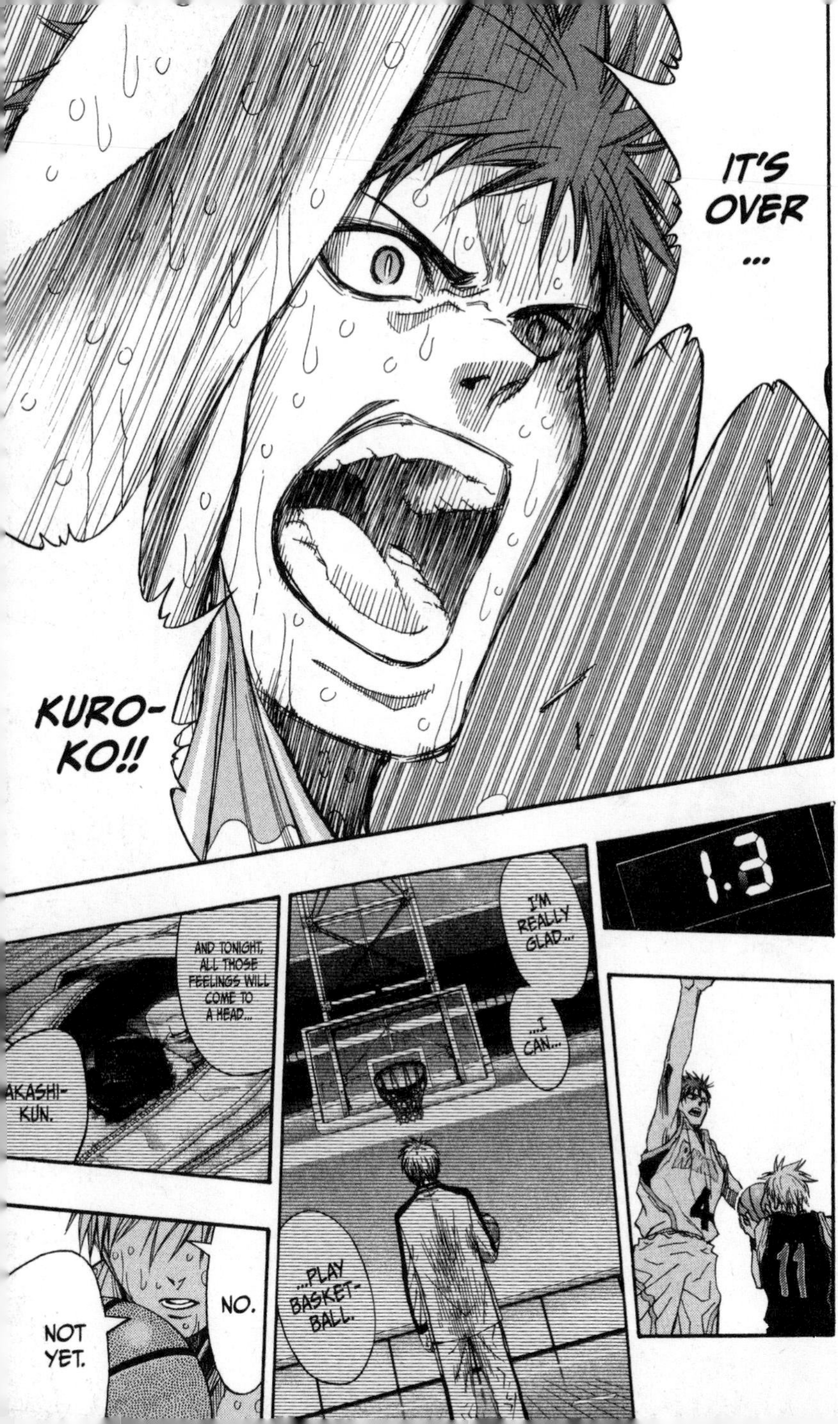
IT'S OVER ...
KURO-KO!!
1.3
I'M REALLY GLAD...
...I CAN...
...PLAY BASKET-BALL.
AND TONIGHT, ALL THOSE FEELINGS WILL COME TO A HEAD...
AKASHI-KUN.
NO.
NOT YET.

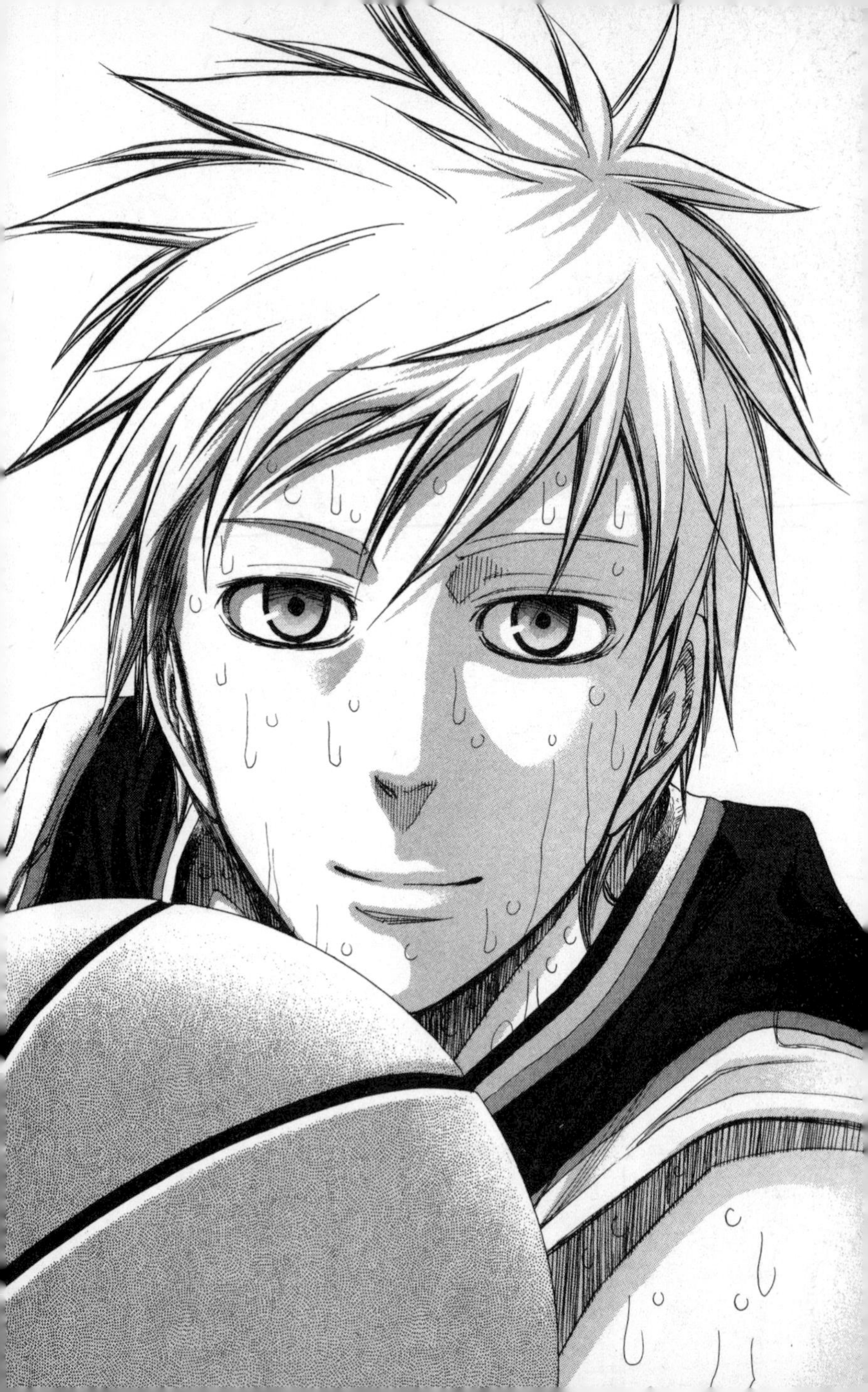

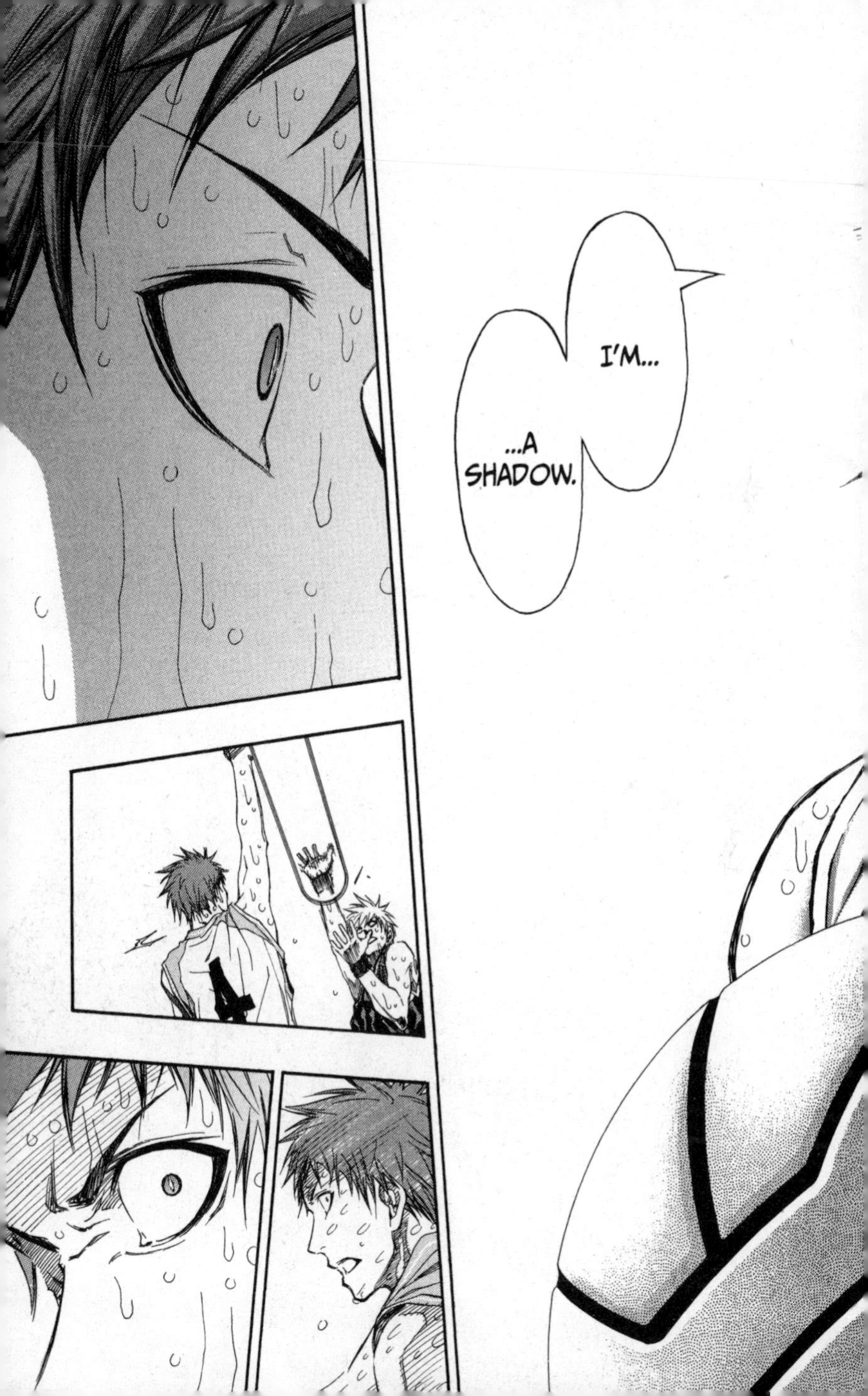
I'M...
...A SHADOW.

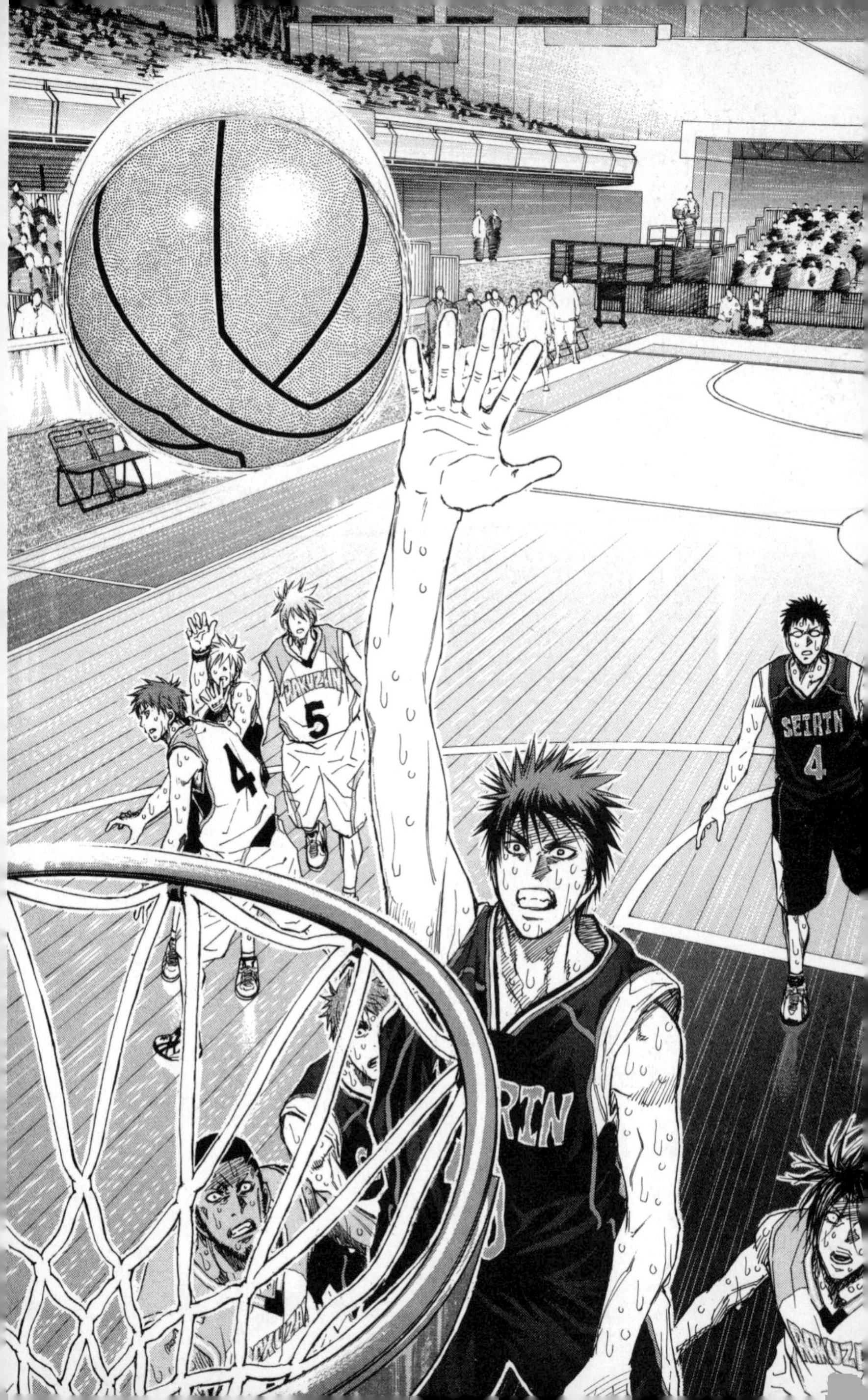

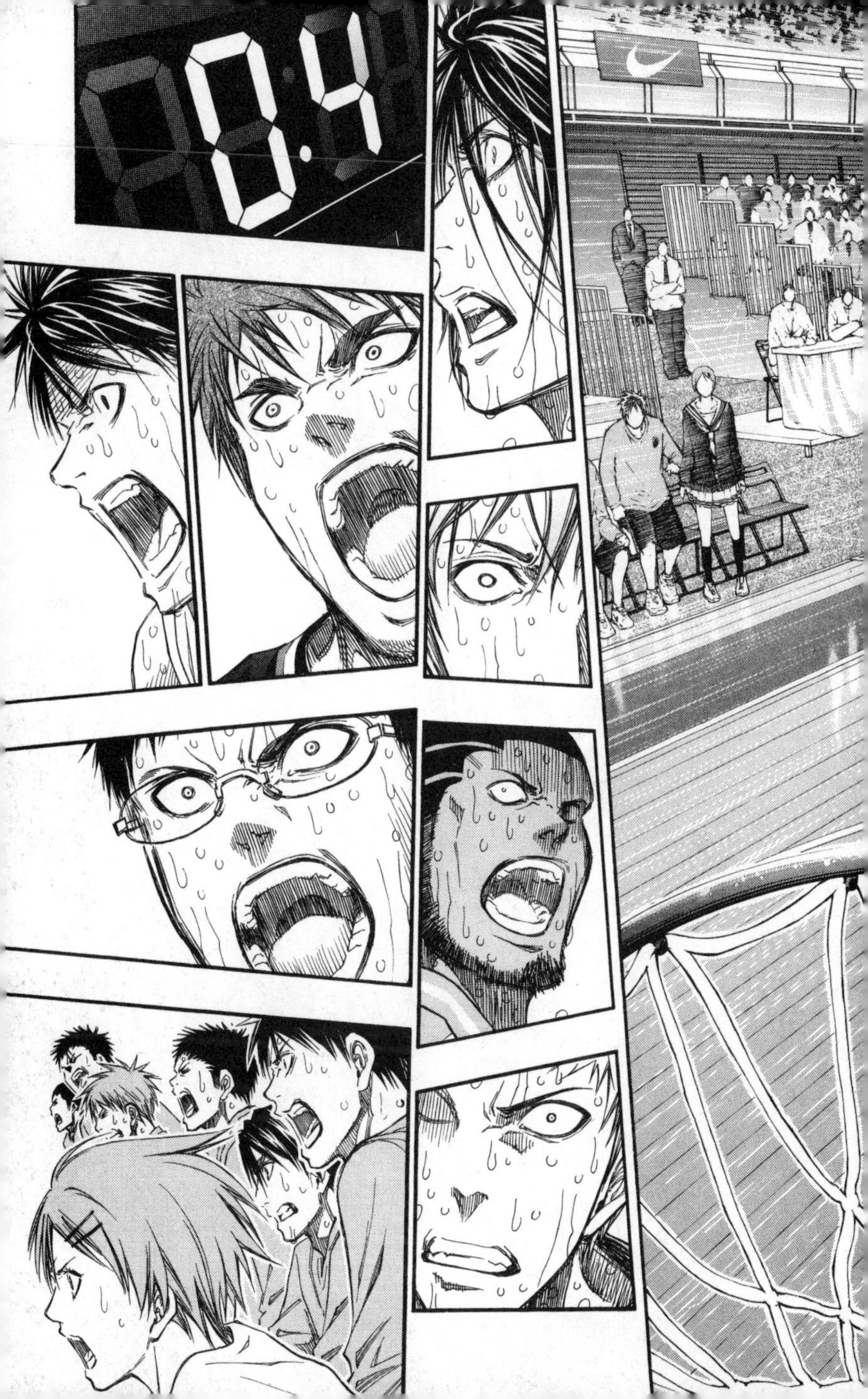
0.4

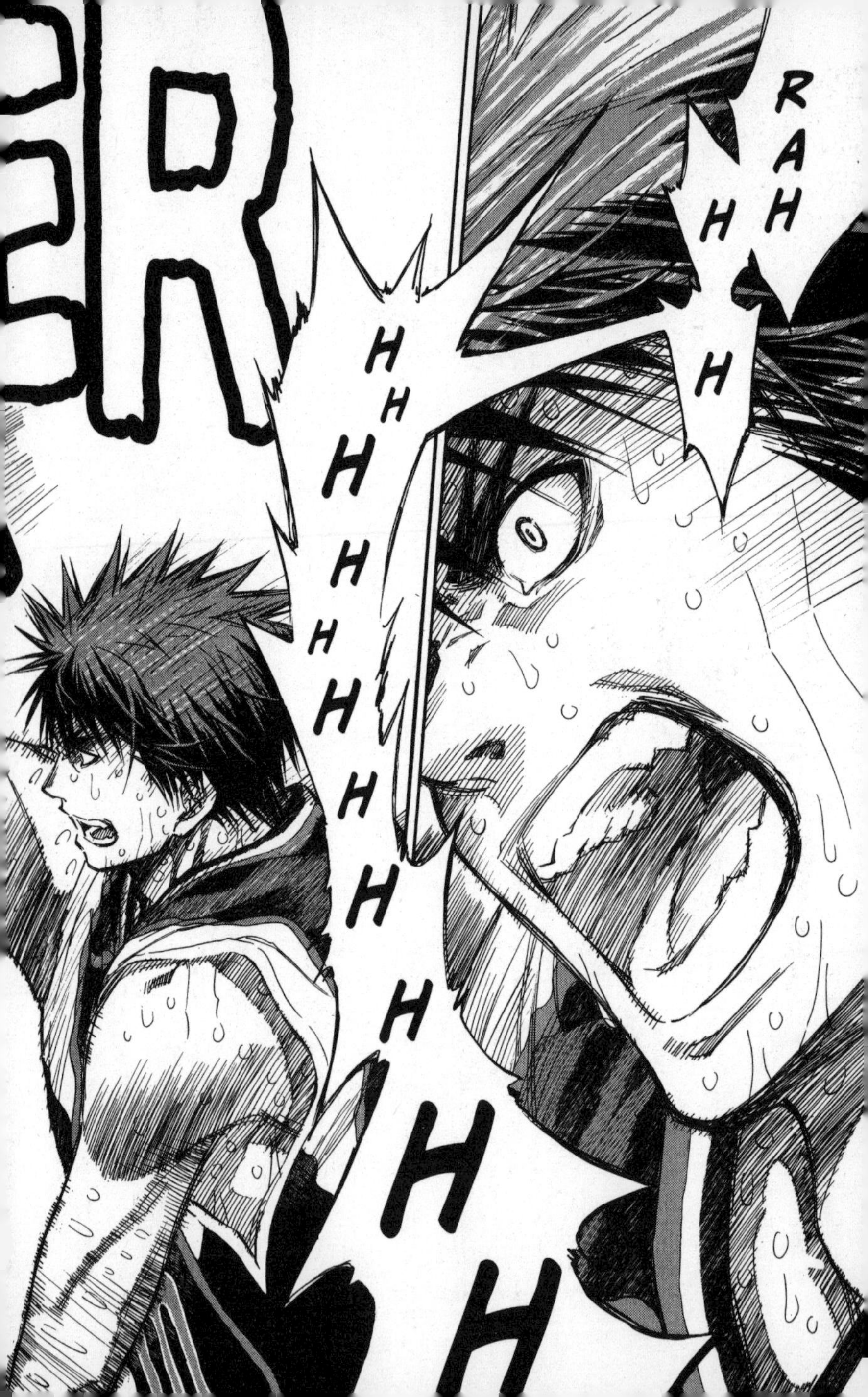
RAHHH
HHHHHHHHHHH
R

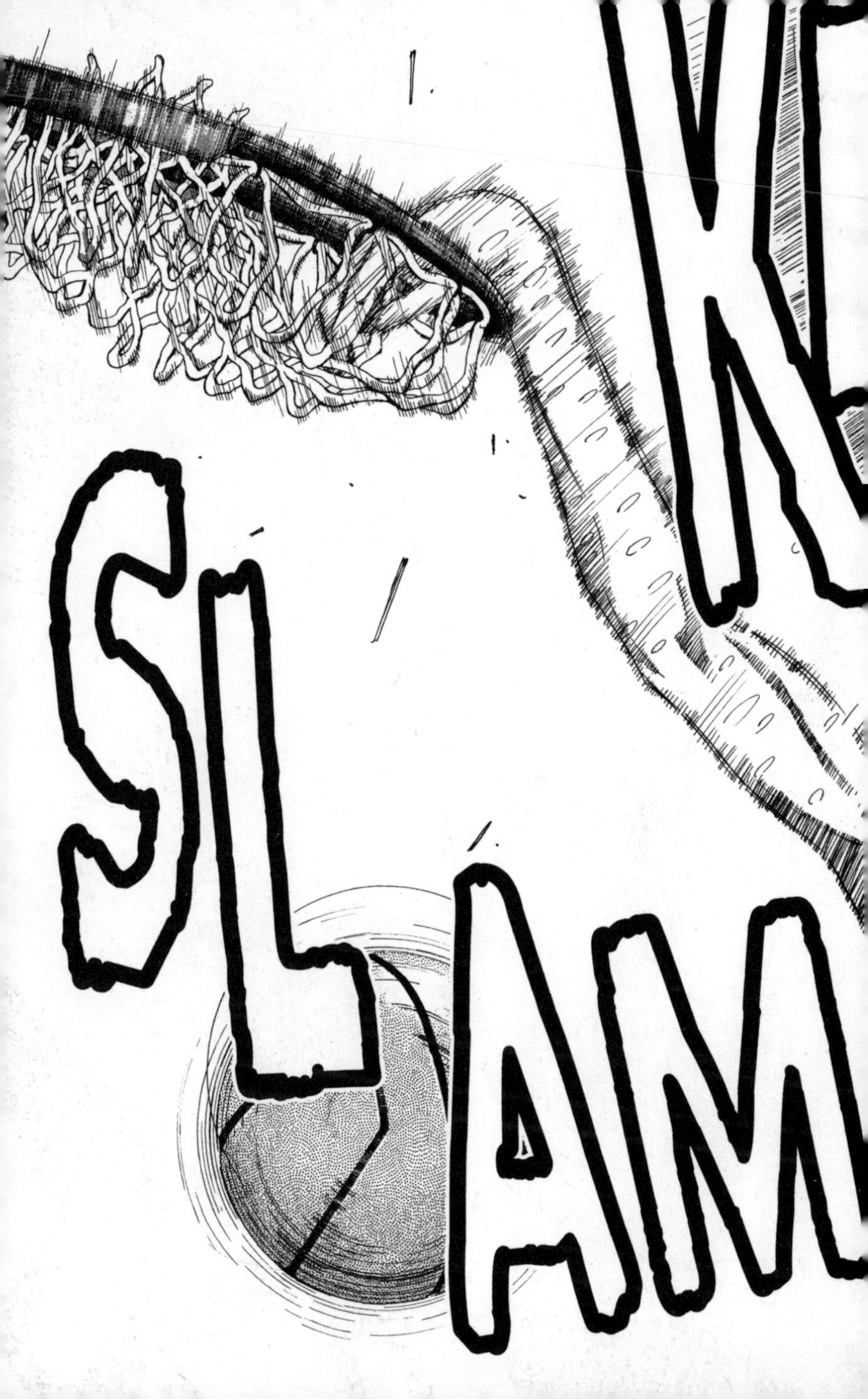
SLAM

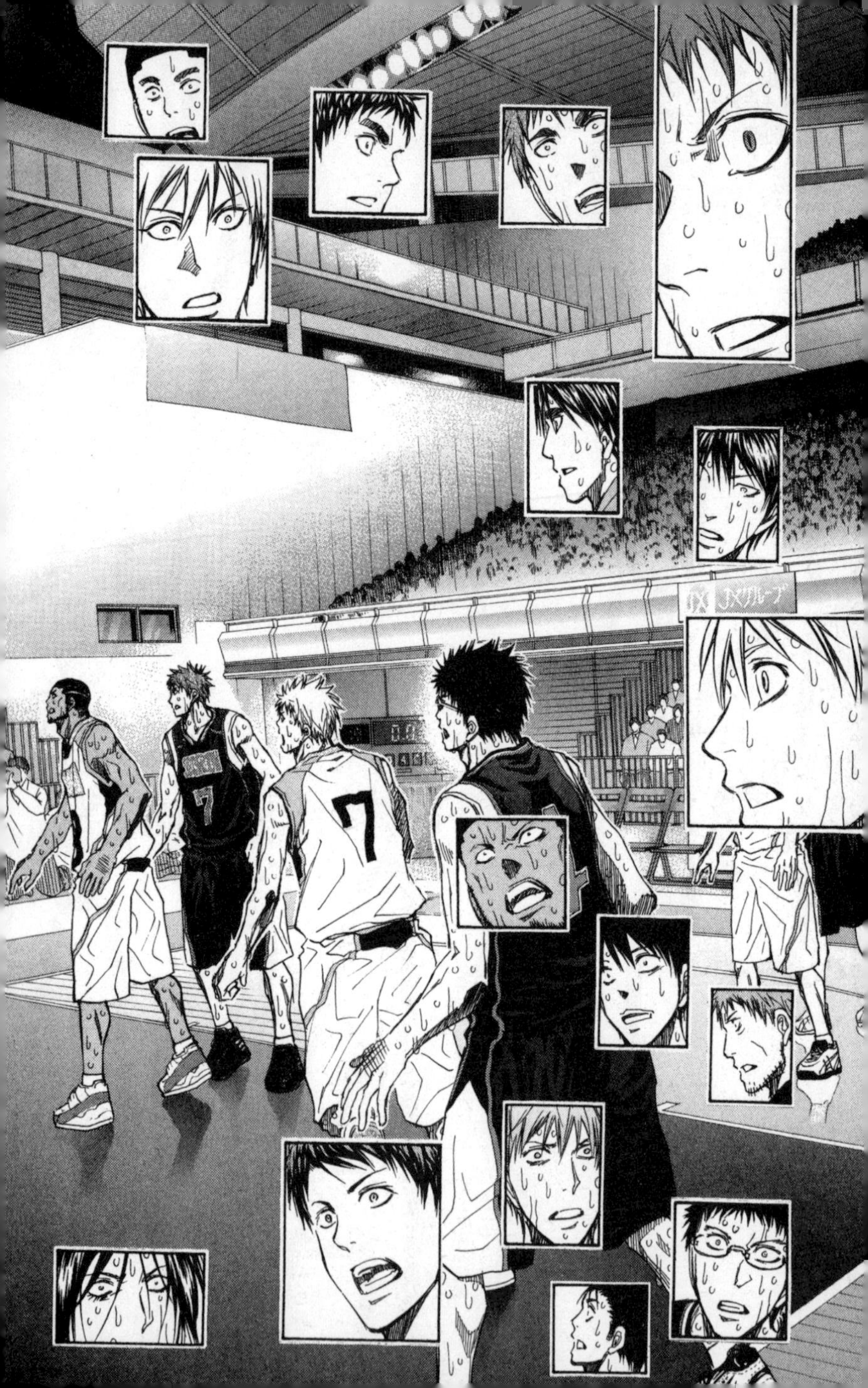

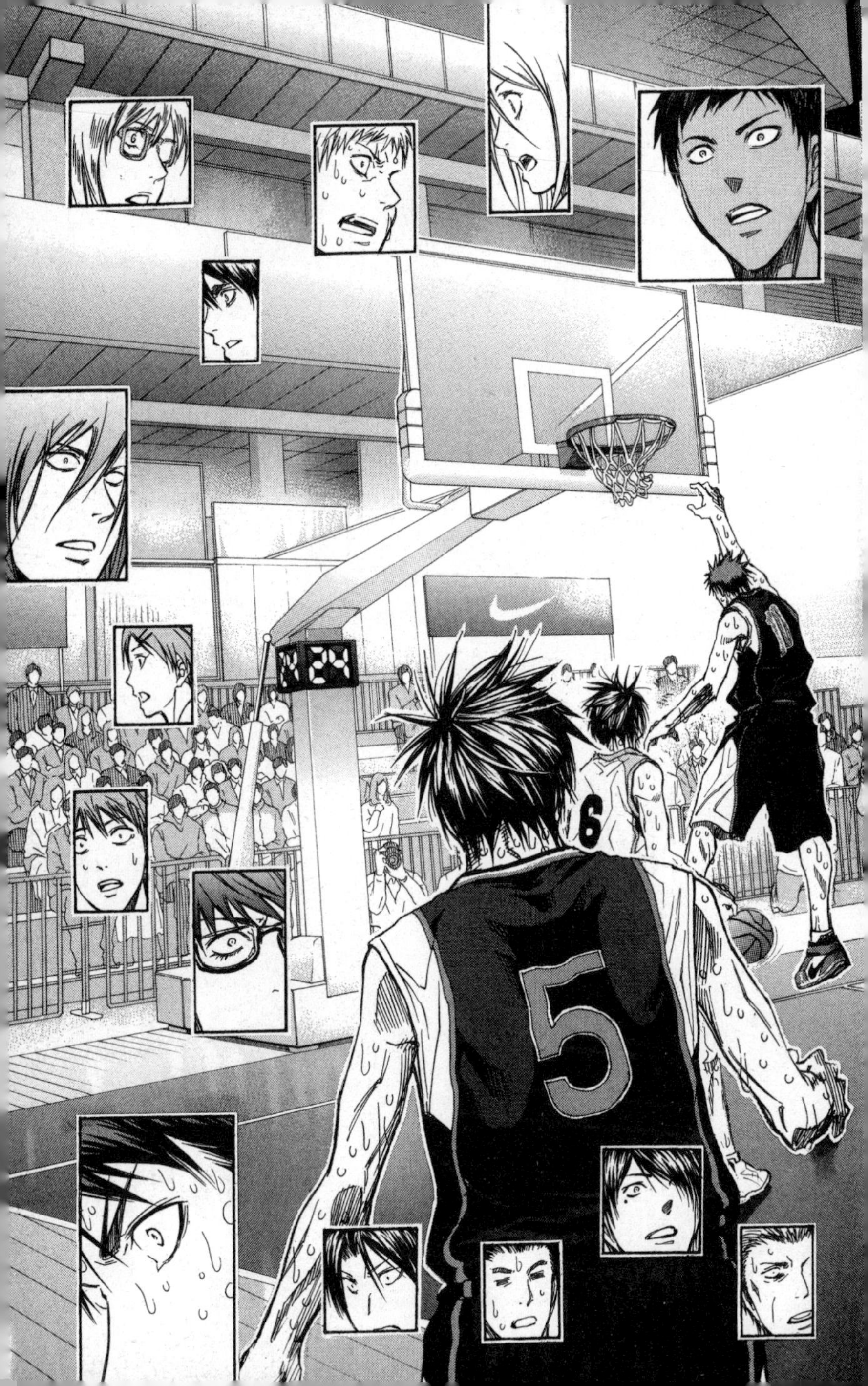

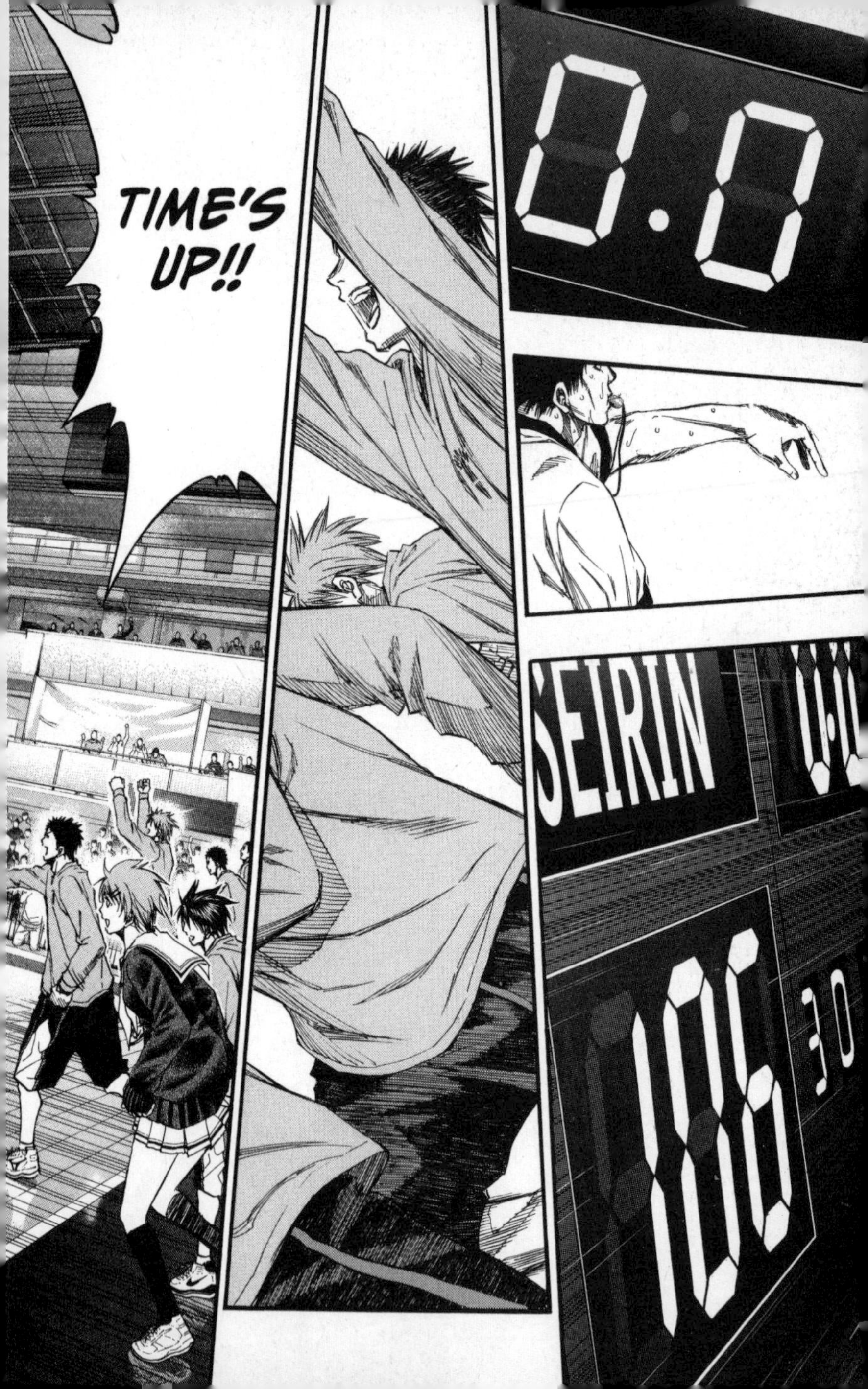
0.0
SEIRIN
106
TIME'S UP!!

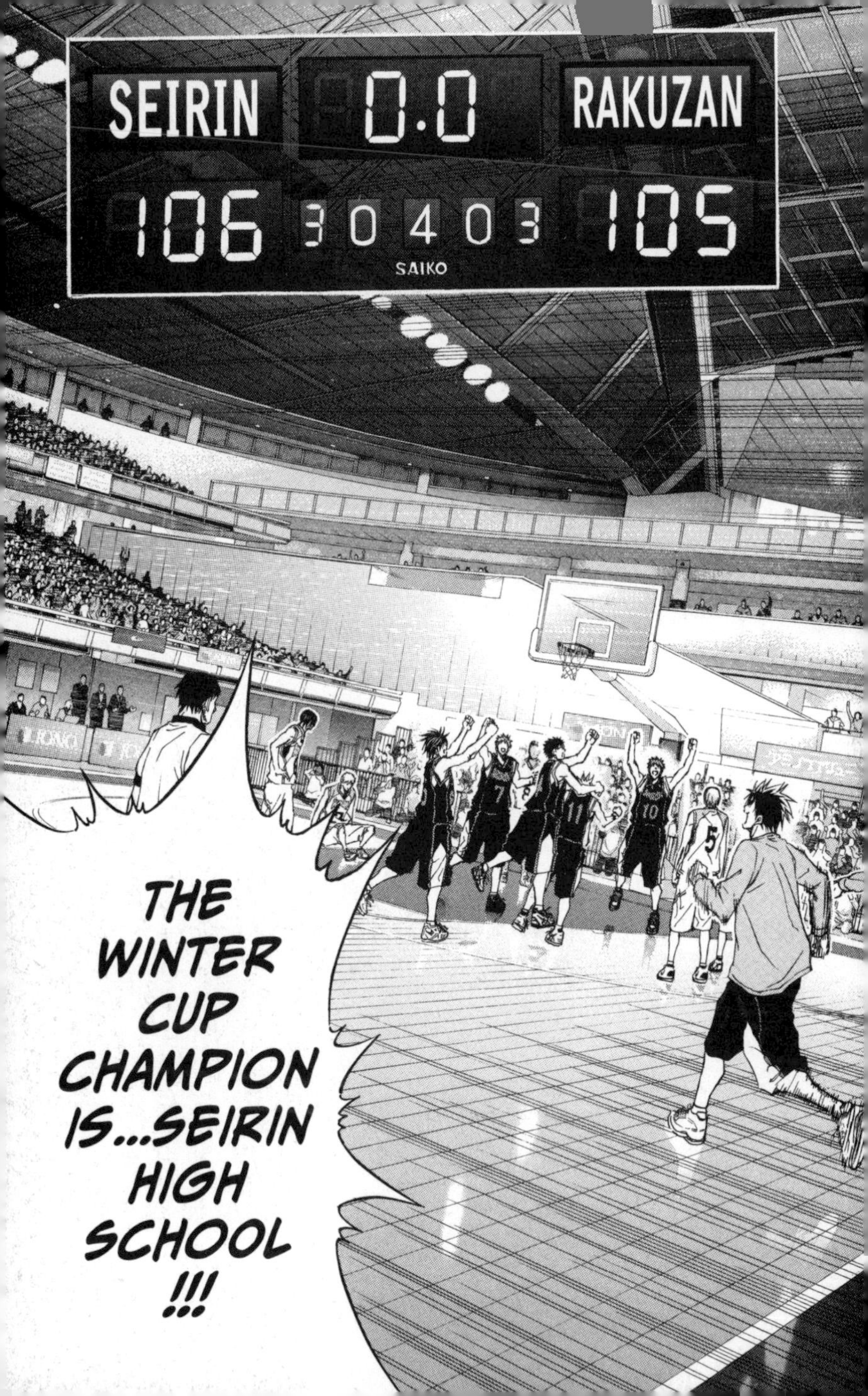
SEIRIN
0.0
RAKUZAN
106
3 0 4 0 3
105
SAIKO
THE WINTER CUP CHAMPION IS...SEIRIN HIGH SCHOOL!!!

THEY WON!

WOO-HOO!

EVEN THE AUTHOR

sHp

FINAL QUARTER: TIME AFTER TIME

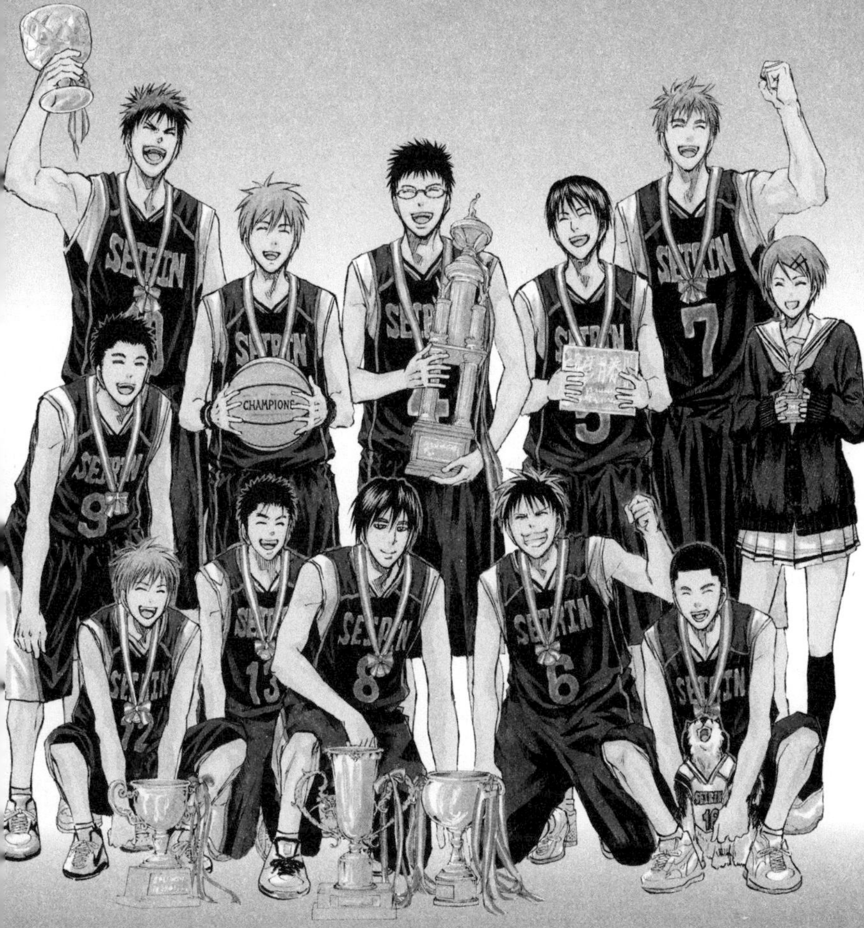
CHAMPIONE

Kuroko's BASKETBALL

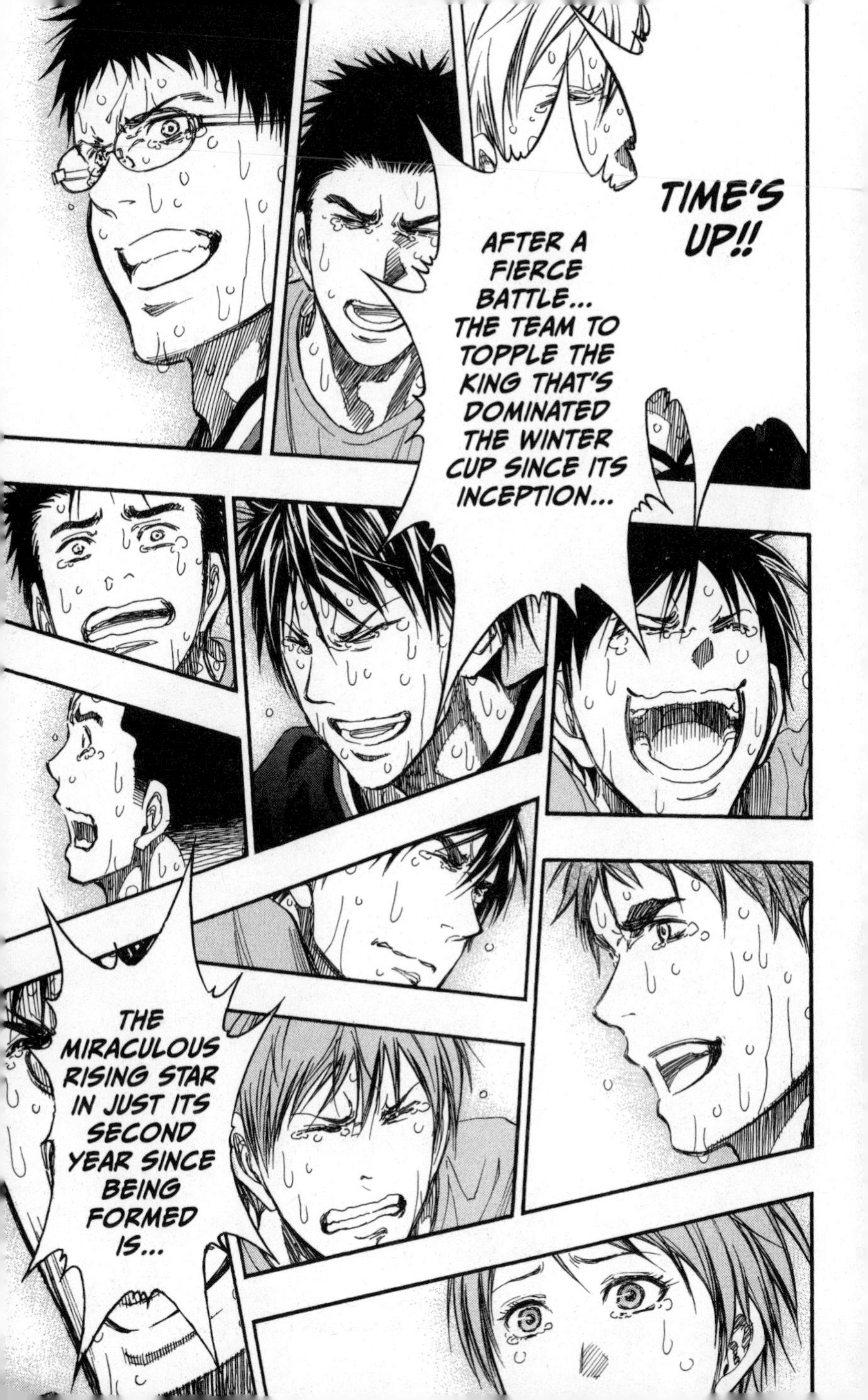
TIME'S UP!!
AFTER A FIERCE BATTLE... THE TEAM TO TOPPLE THE KING THAT'S DOMINATED THE WINTER CUP SINCE ITS INCEPTION...
THE MIRACULOUS RISING STAR IN JUST ITS SECOND YEAR SINCE BEING FORMED IS...

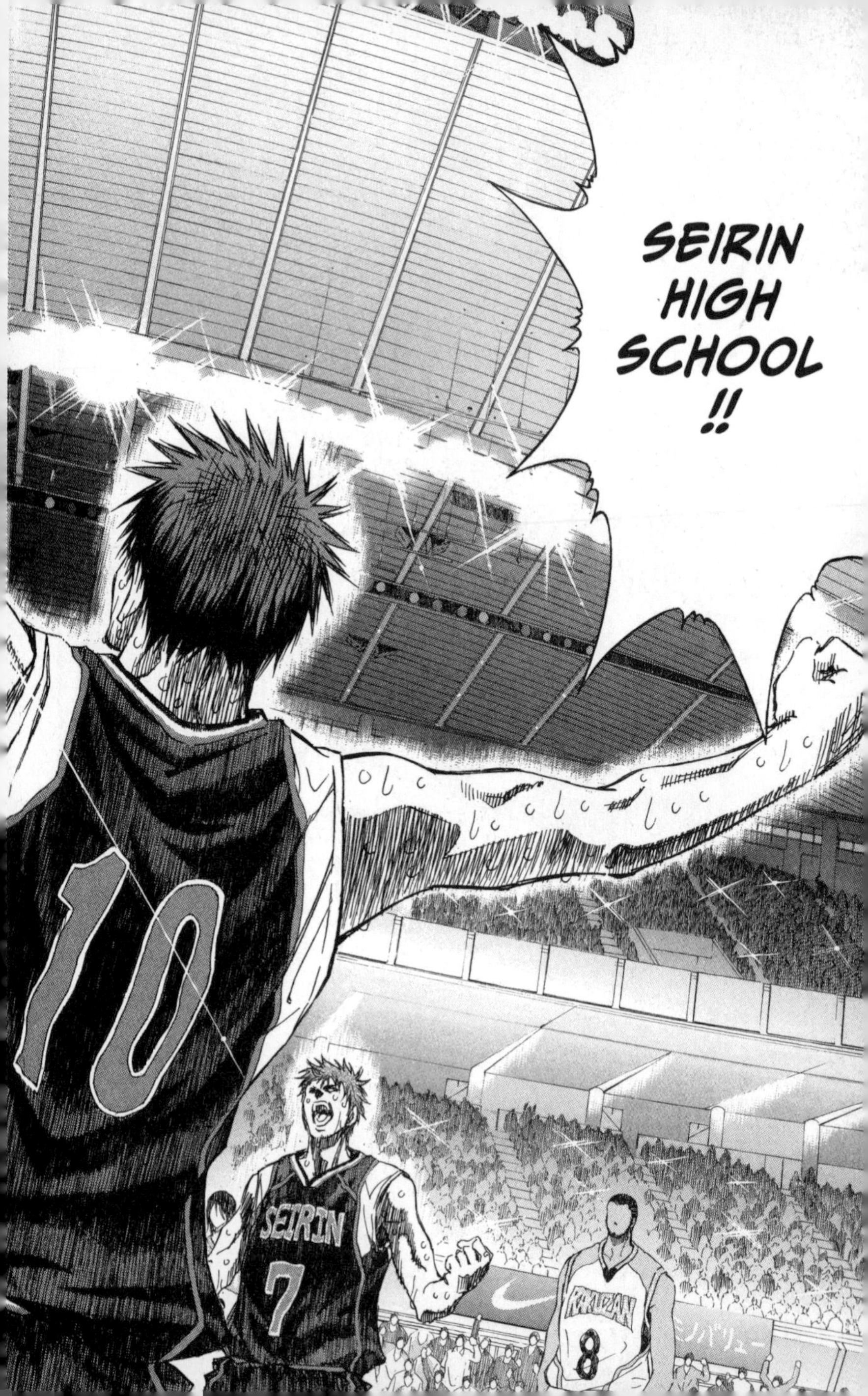
SEIRIN HIGH SCHOOL !!
10
SEIRIN
7
RAKUZAN
8

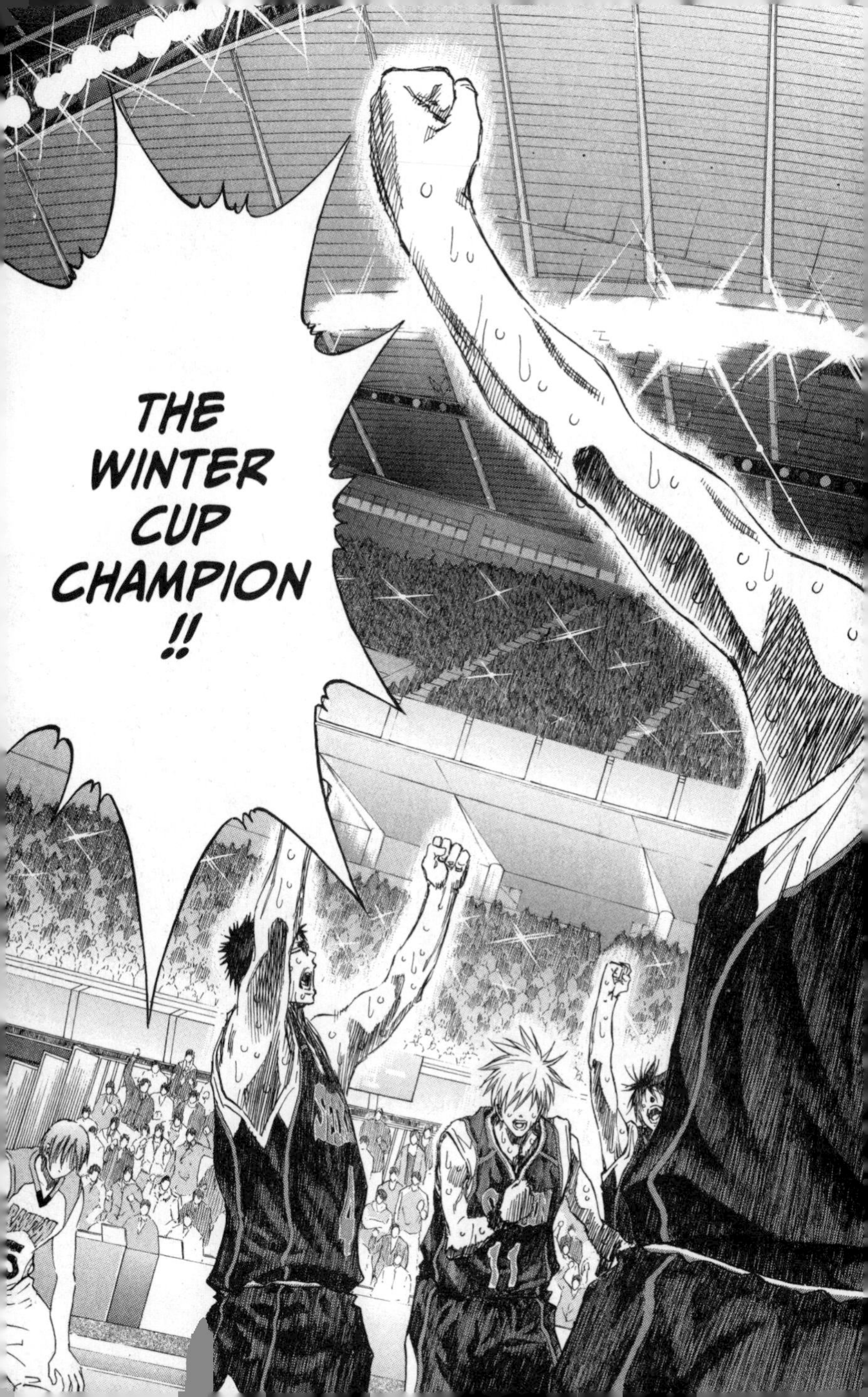
THE WINTER CUP CHAMPION !!

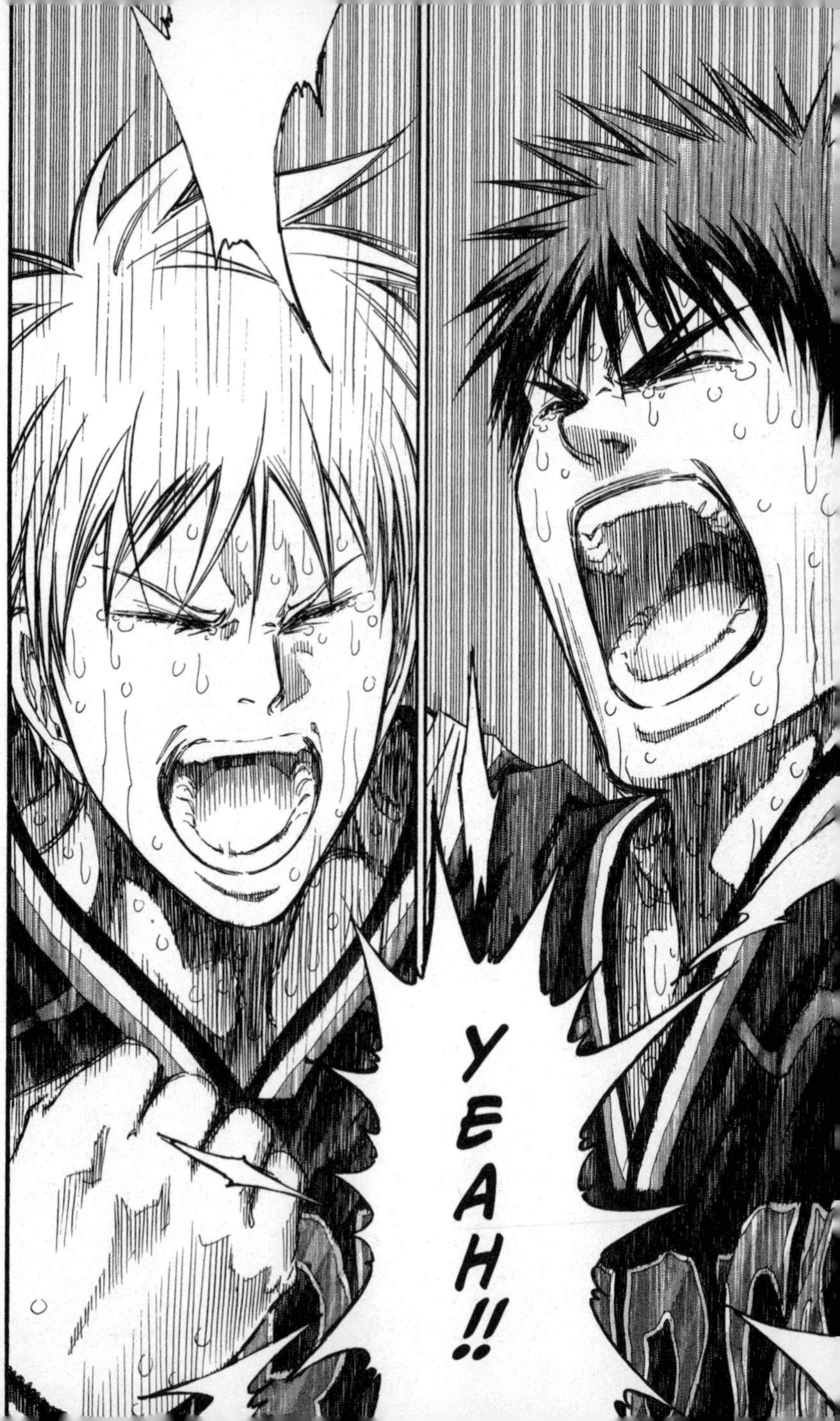
YEAH!!

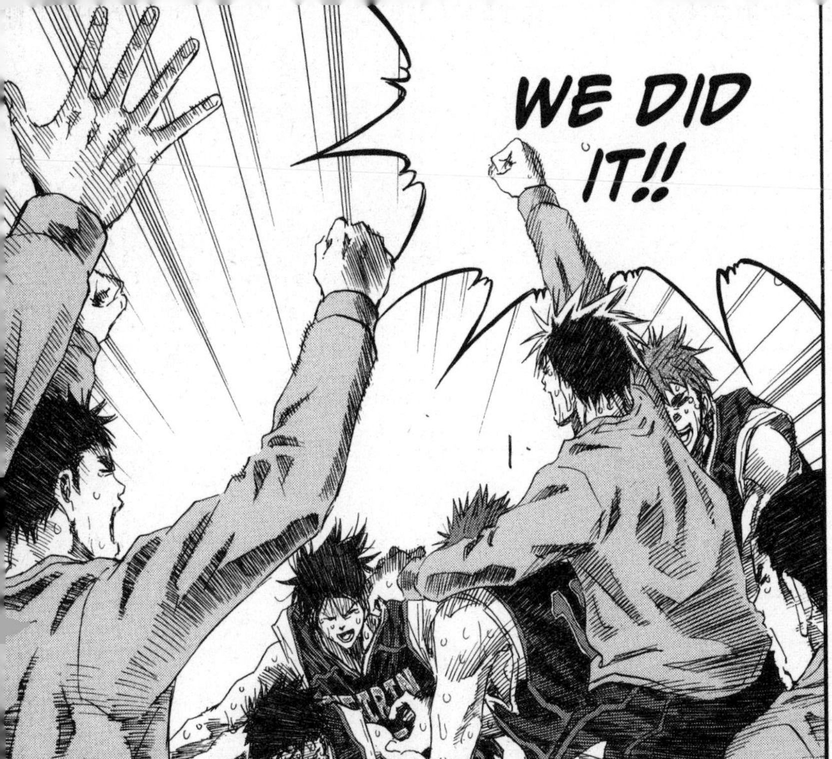
WE DID IT!!
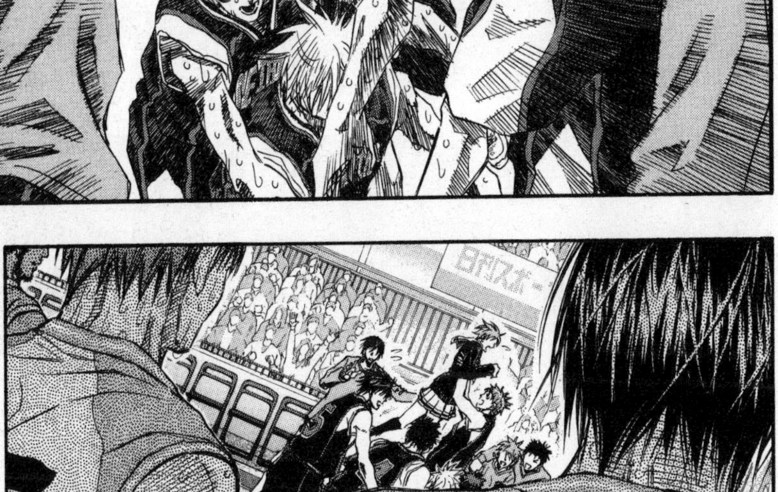

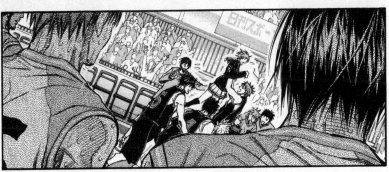

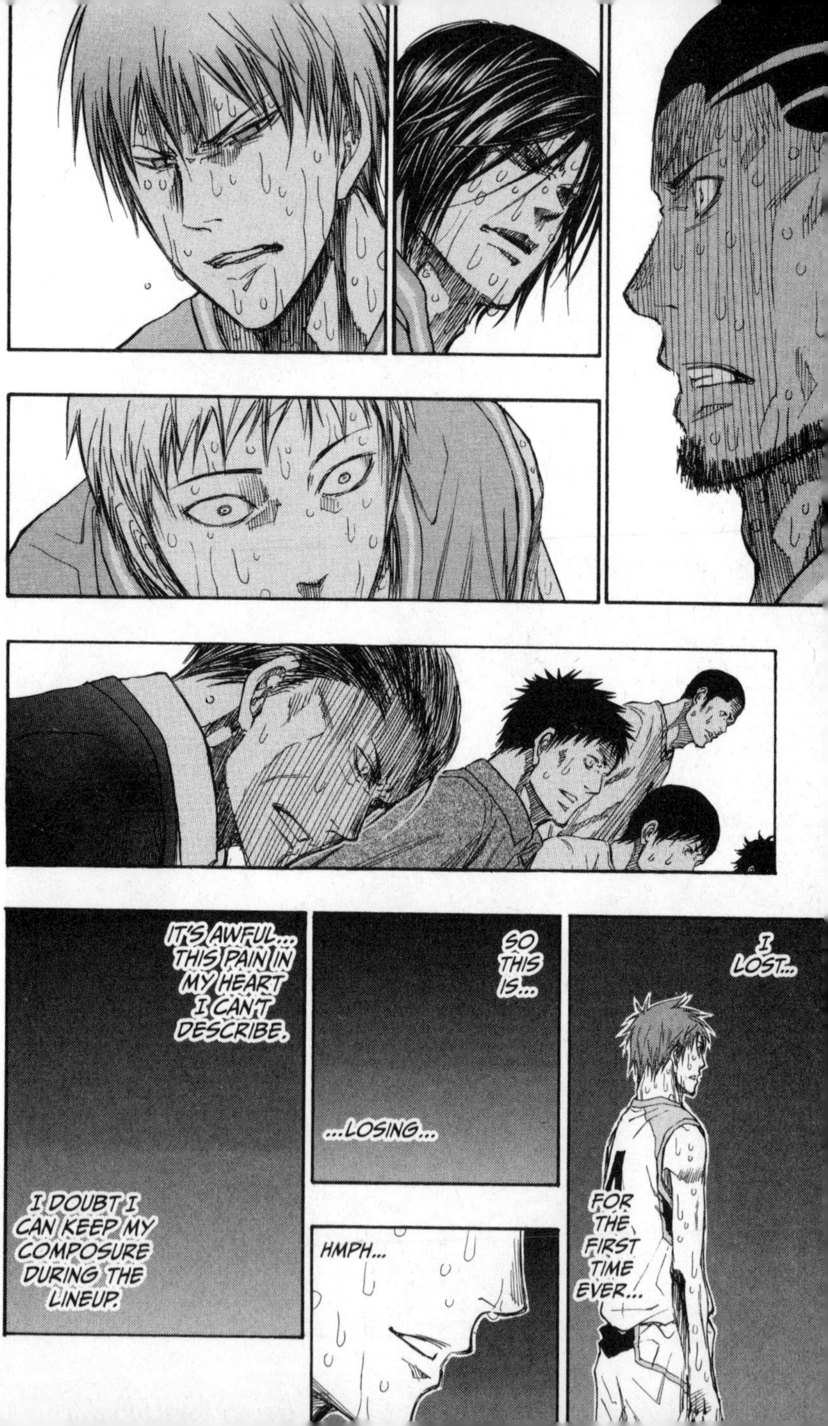
I LOST...
FOR THE FIRST TIME EVER...
SO THIS IS...
...LOSING...
HMPH...
IT'S AWFUL... THIS PAIN IN MY HEART I CAN'T DESCRIBE.
I DOUBT I CAN KEEP MY COMPOSURE DURING THE LINEUP.

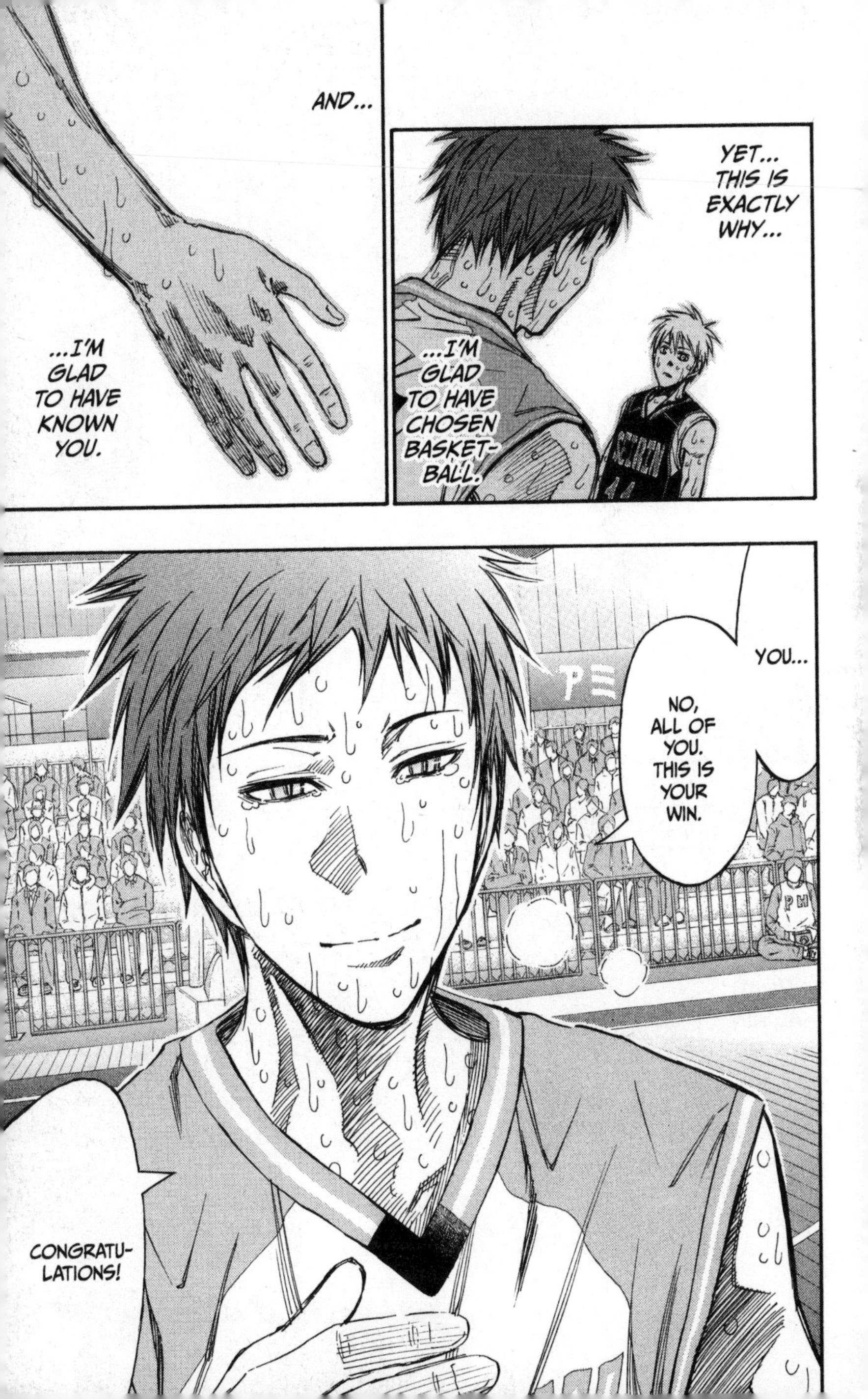
YET... THIS IS EXACTLY WHY...
...I'M GLAD TO HAVE CHOSEN BASKET-BALL.
AND...
...I'M GLAD TO HAVE KNOWN YOU.
YOU...
NO, ALL OF YOU. THIS IS YOUR WIN.
CONGRATU-LATIONS!

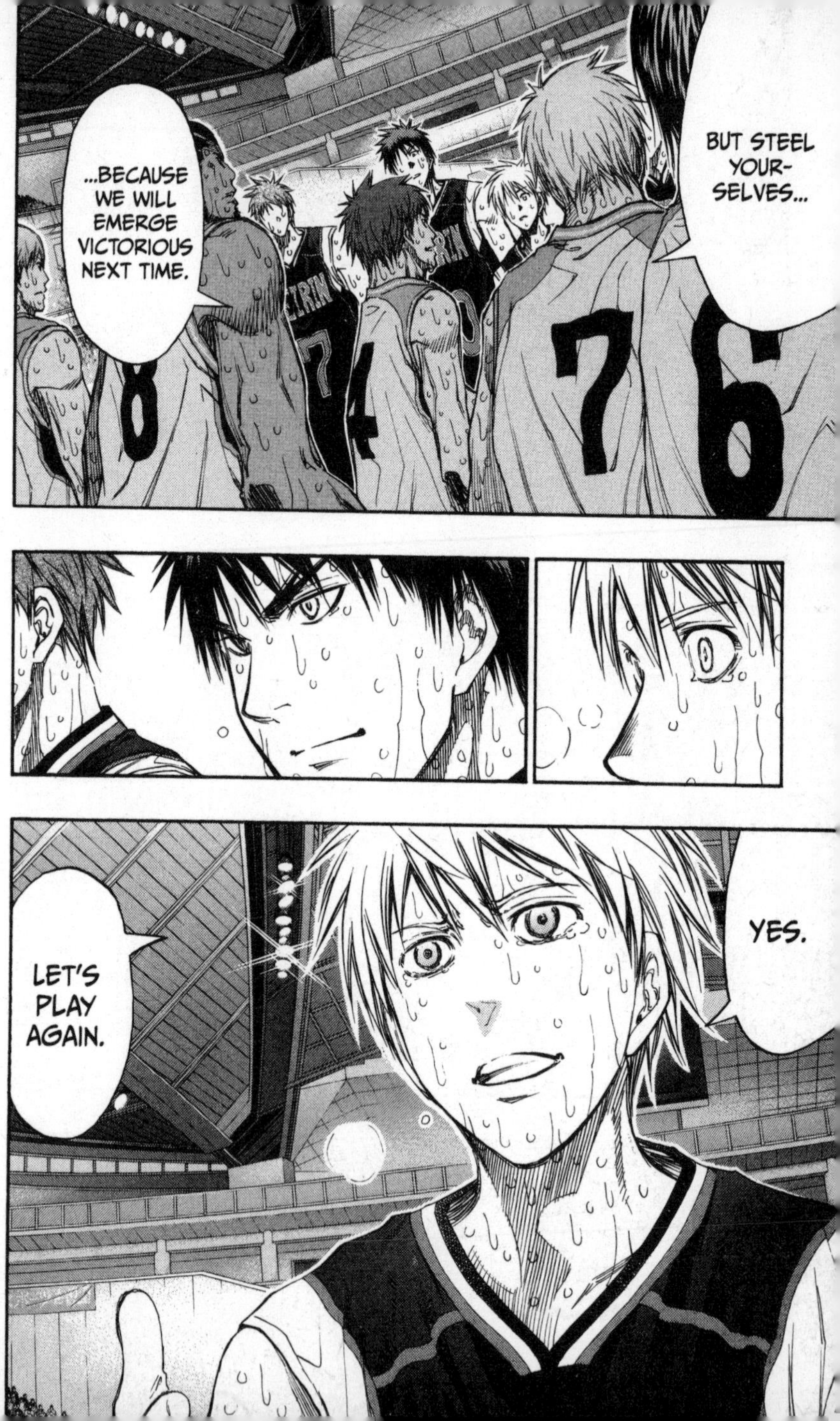
BUT STEEL YOUR-SELVES...
...BECAUSE WE WILL EMERGE VICTORIOUS NEXT TIME.
YES.
LET'S PLAY AGAIN.

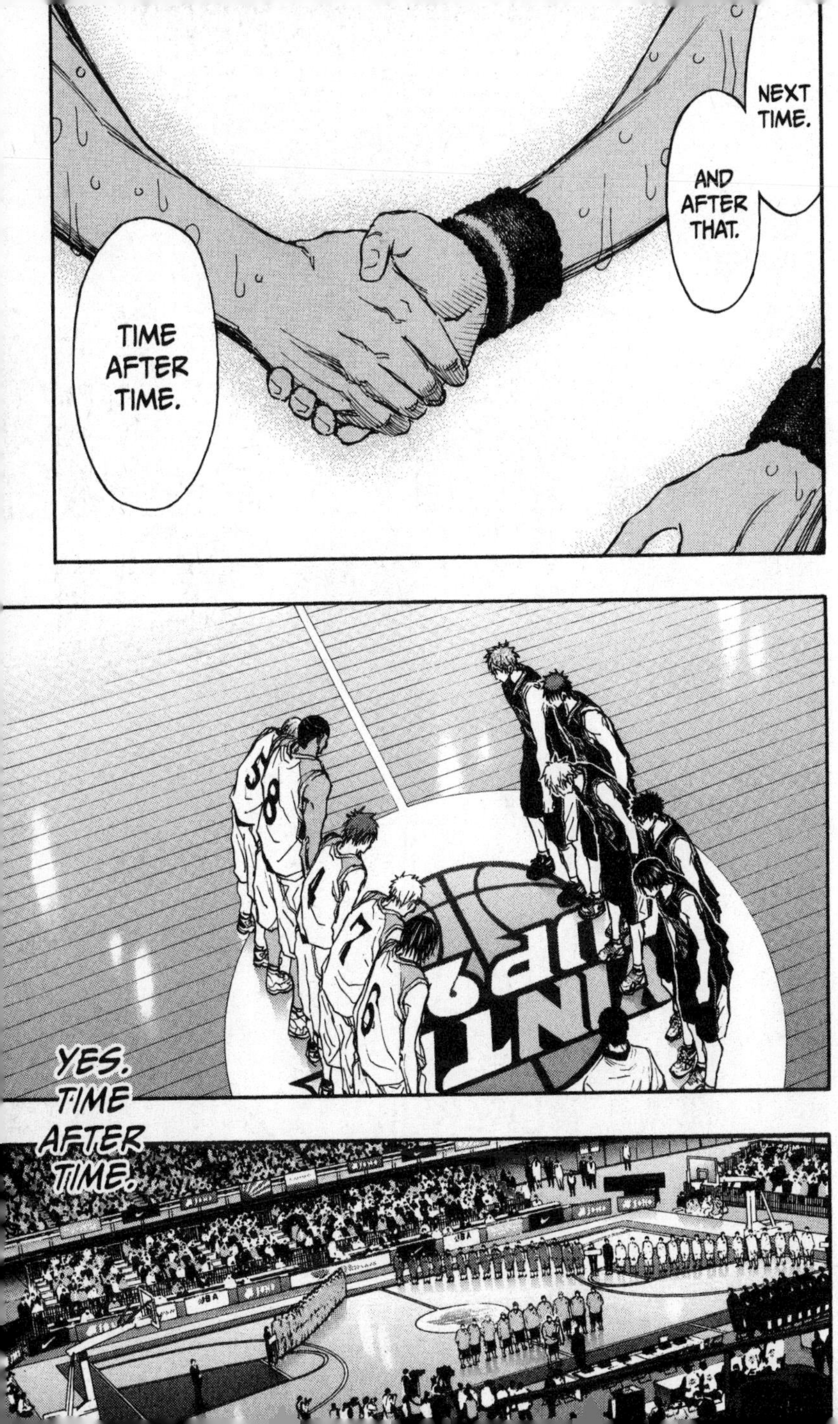
NEXT TIME.
AND AFTER THAT.
TIME AFTER TIME.
YES. TIME AFTER TIME.

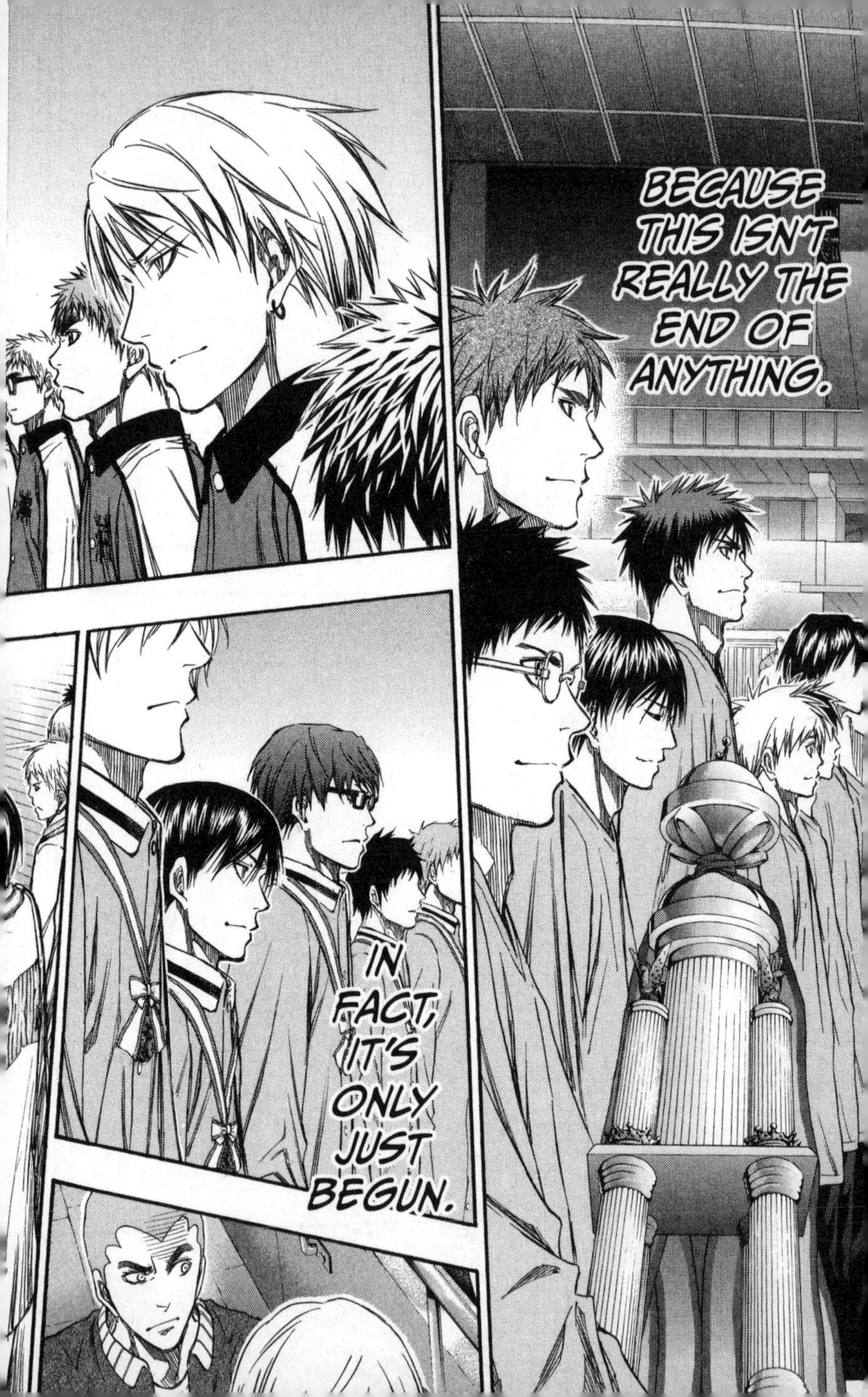
BECAUSE THIS ISN'T REALLY THE END OF ANYTHING.
IN FACT, IT'S ONLY JUST BEGUN.

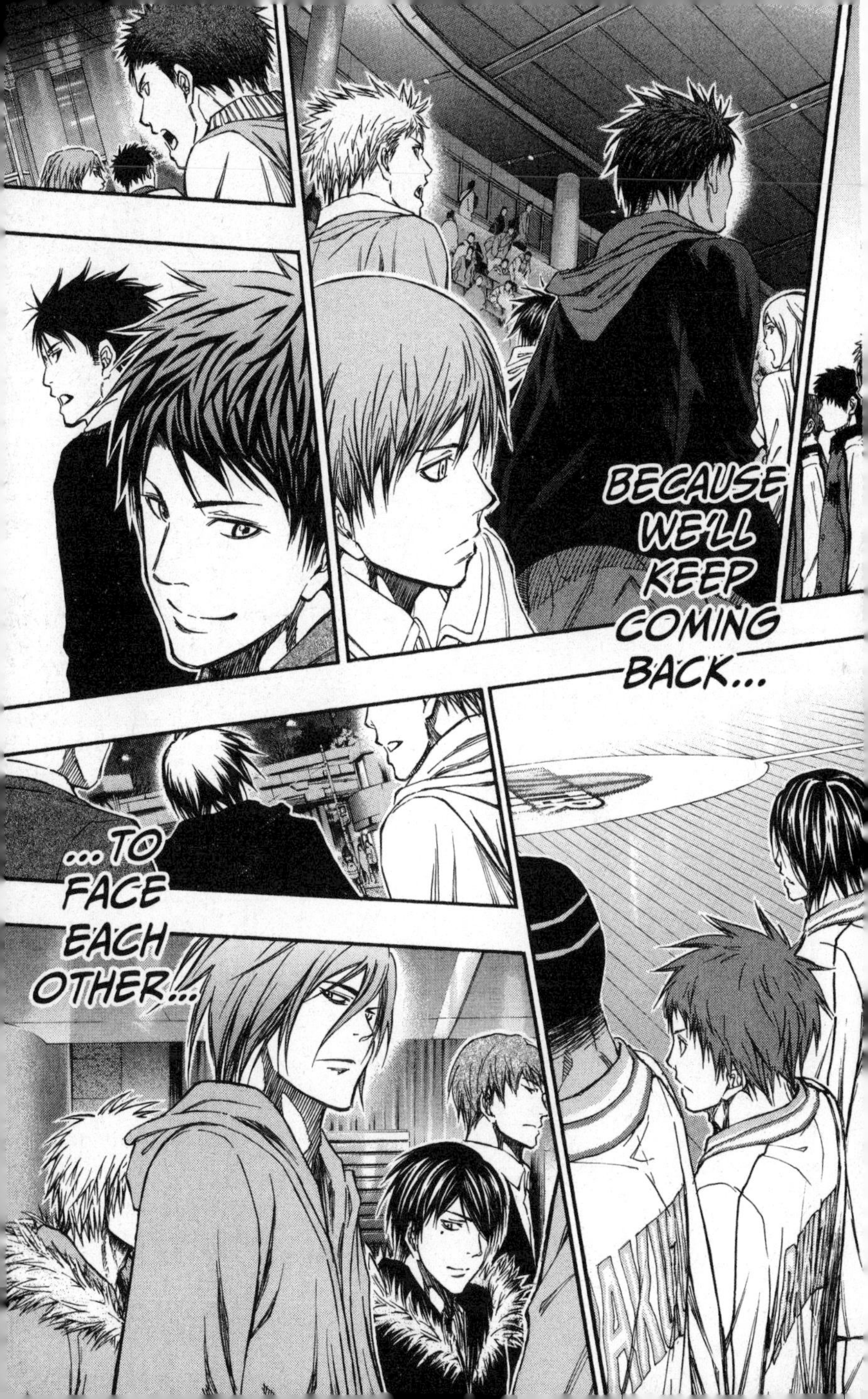
BECAUSE WE'LL KEEP COMING BACK...
...TO FACE EACH OTHER!...

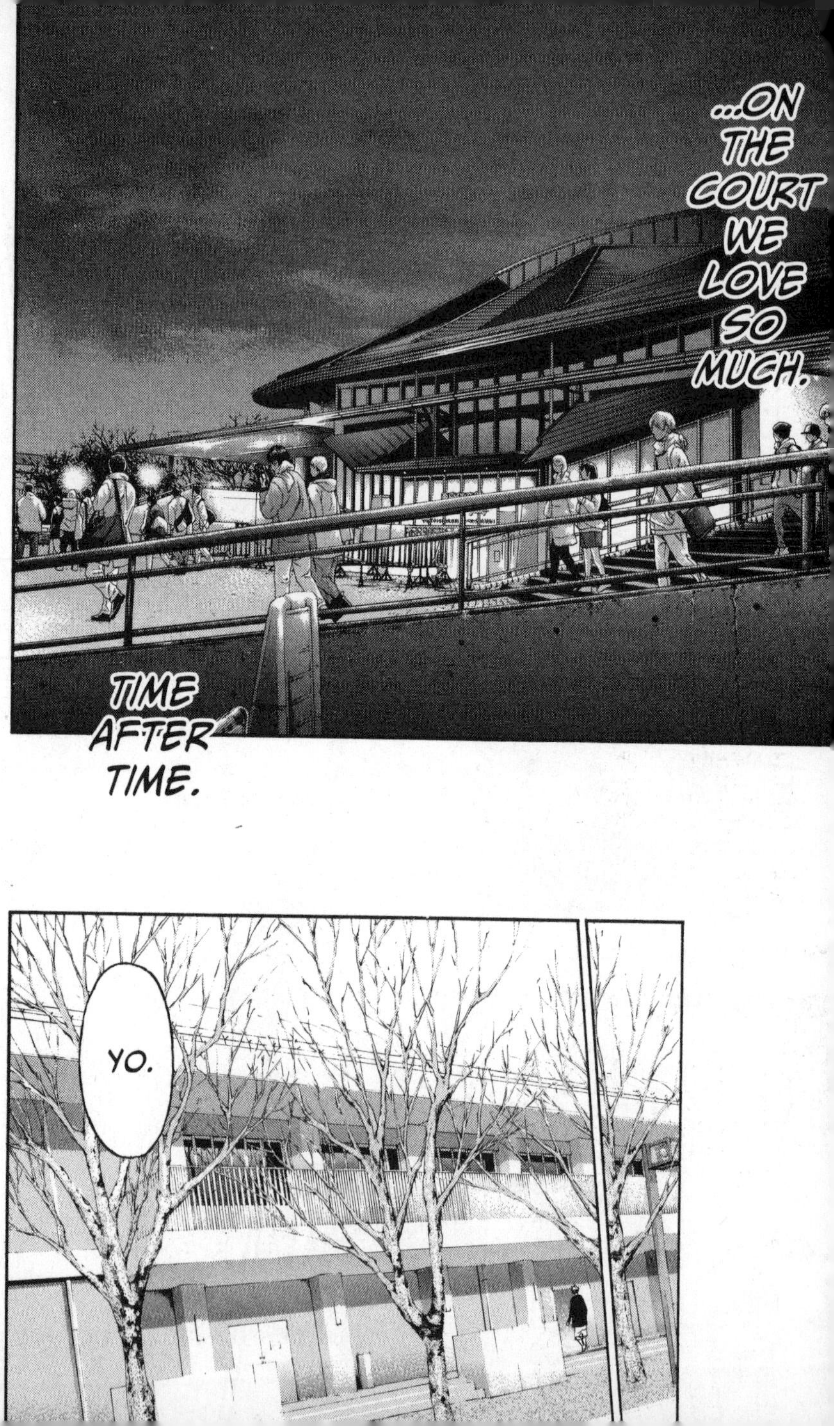
...ON THE COURT WE LOVE SO MUCH.
TIME AFTER TIME.
YO.

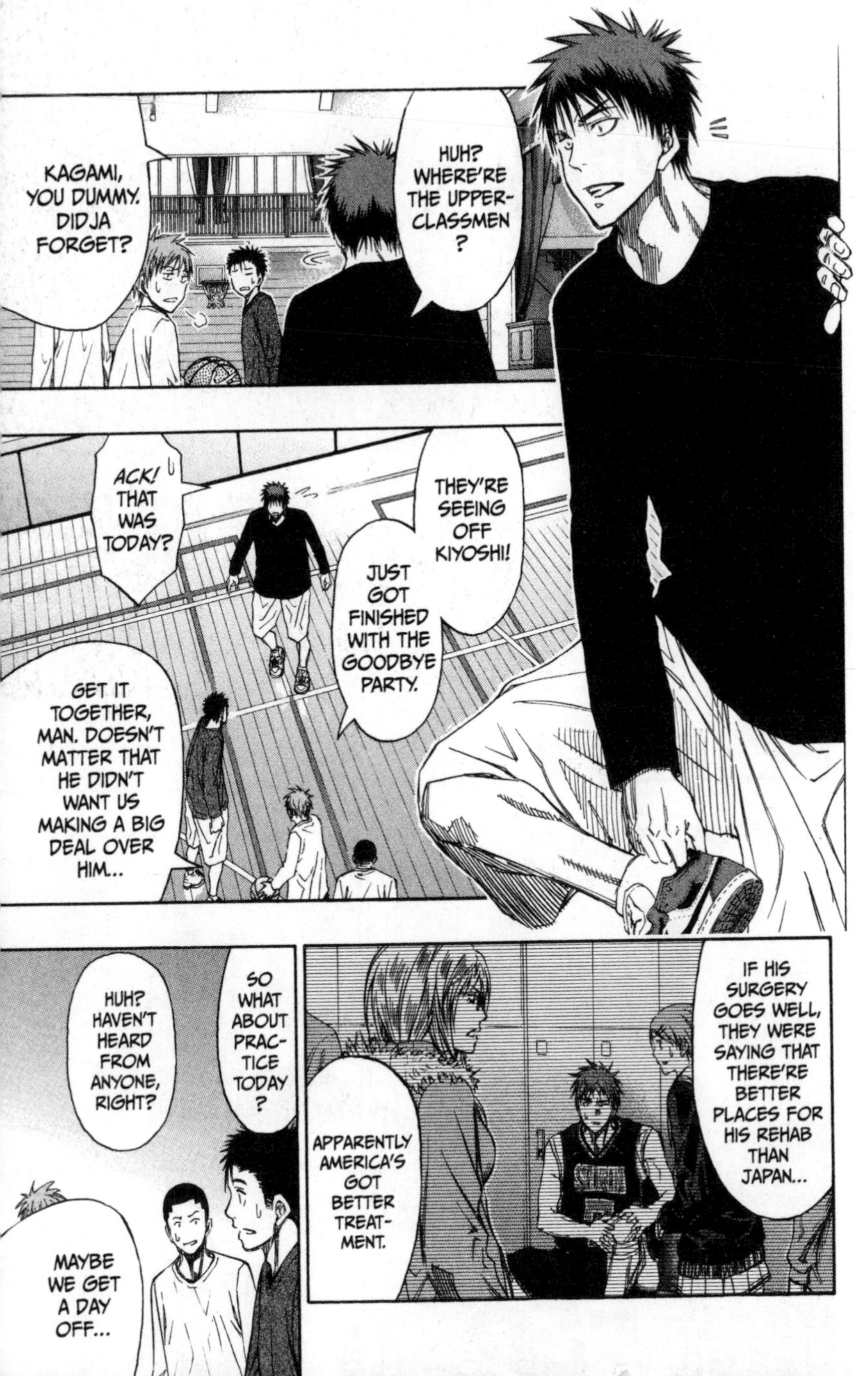
HUH? WHERE'RE THE UPPER-CLASSMEN?
KAGAMI, YOU DUMMY. DIDJA FORGET?
THEY'RE SEEING OFF KIYOSHI!
JUST GOT FINISHED WITH THE GOODBYE PARTY.
ACK! THAT WAS TODAY?
GET IT TOGETHER, MAN. DOESN'T MATTER THAT HE DIDN'T WANT US MAKING A BIG DEAL OVER HIM...
IF HIS SURGERY GOES WELL, THEY WERE SAYING THAT THERE'RE BETTER PLACES FOR HIS REHAB THAN JAPAN...
APPARENTLY AMERICA'S GOT BETTER TREAT-MENT.
SO WHAT ABOUT PRAC-TICE TODAY?
HUH? HAVEN'T HEARD FROM ANYONE, RIGHT?
MAYBE WE GET A DAY OFF...

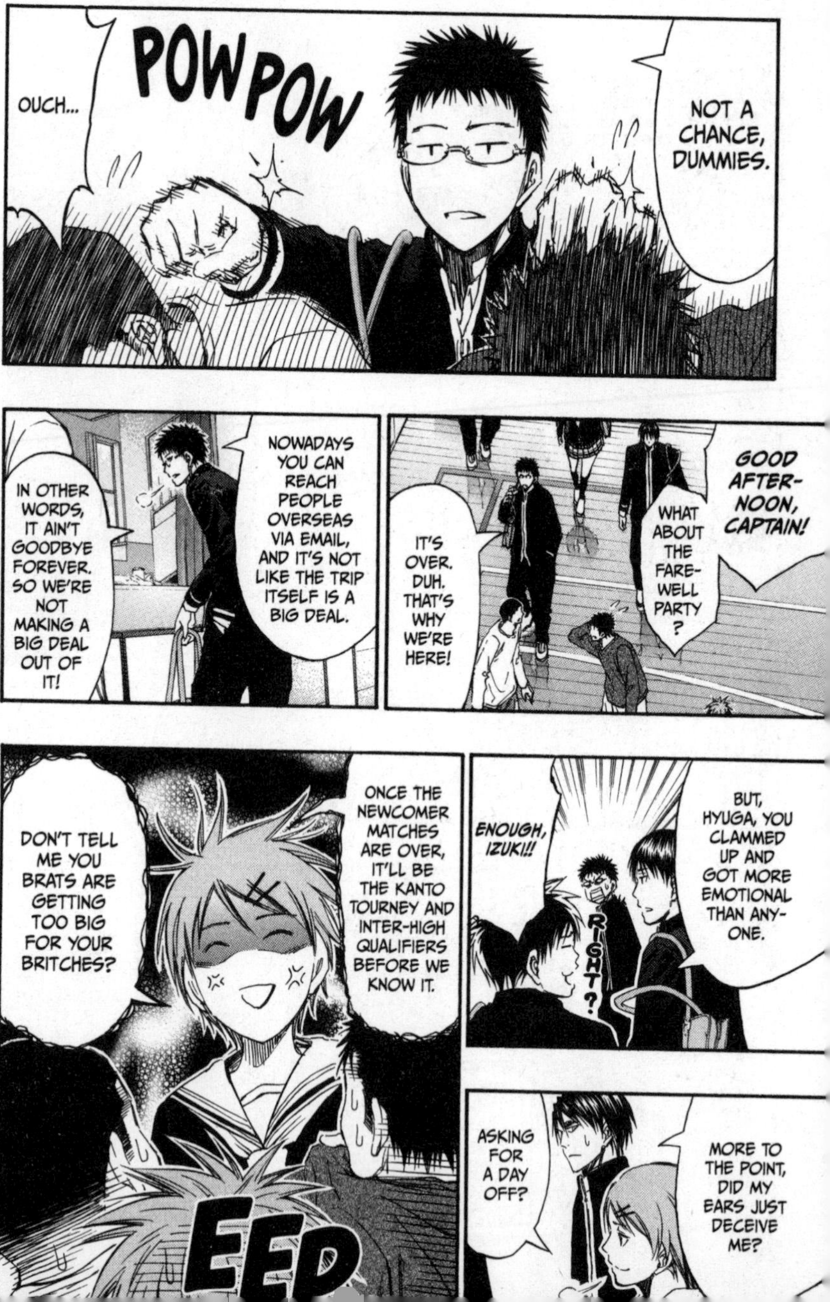
NOT A CHANCE, DUMMIES.
POWPOW
OUCH...
GOOD AFTERNOON, CAPTAIN!
WHAT ABOUT THE FAREWELL PARTY?
IT'S OVER. DUH. THAT'S WHY WE'RE HERE!
NOWADAYS YOU CAN REACH PEOPLE OVERSEAS VIA EMAIL, AND IT'S NOT LIKE THE TRIP ITSELF IS A BIG DEAL.
IN OTHER WORDS, IT AIN'T GOODBYE FOREVER. SO WE'RE NOT MAKING A BIG DEAL OUT OF IT!
BUT, HYUGA, YOU CLAMMED UP AND GOT MORE EMOTIONAL THAN ANYONE.
RIGHT?
ENOUGH, IZUKI!!
MORE TO THE POINT, DID MY EARS JUST DECEIVE ME?
ASKING FOR A DAY OFF?
ONCE THE NEWCOMER MATCHES ARE OVER, IT'LL BE THE KANTO TOURNEY AND INTER-HIGH QUALIFIERS BEFORE WE KNOW IT.
DON'T TELL ME YOU BRATS ARE GETTING TOO BIG FOR YOUR BRITCHES?
EED

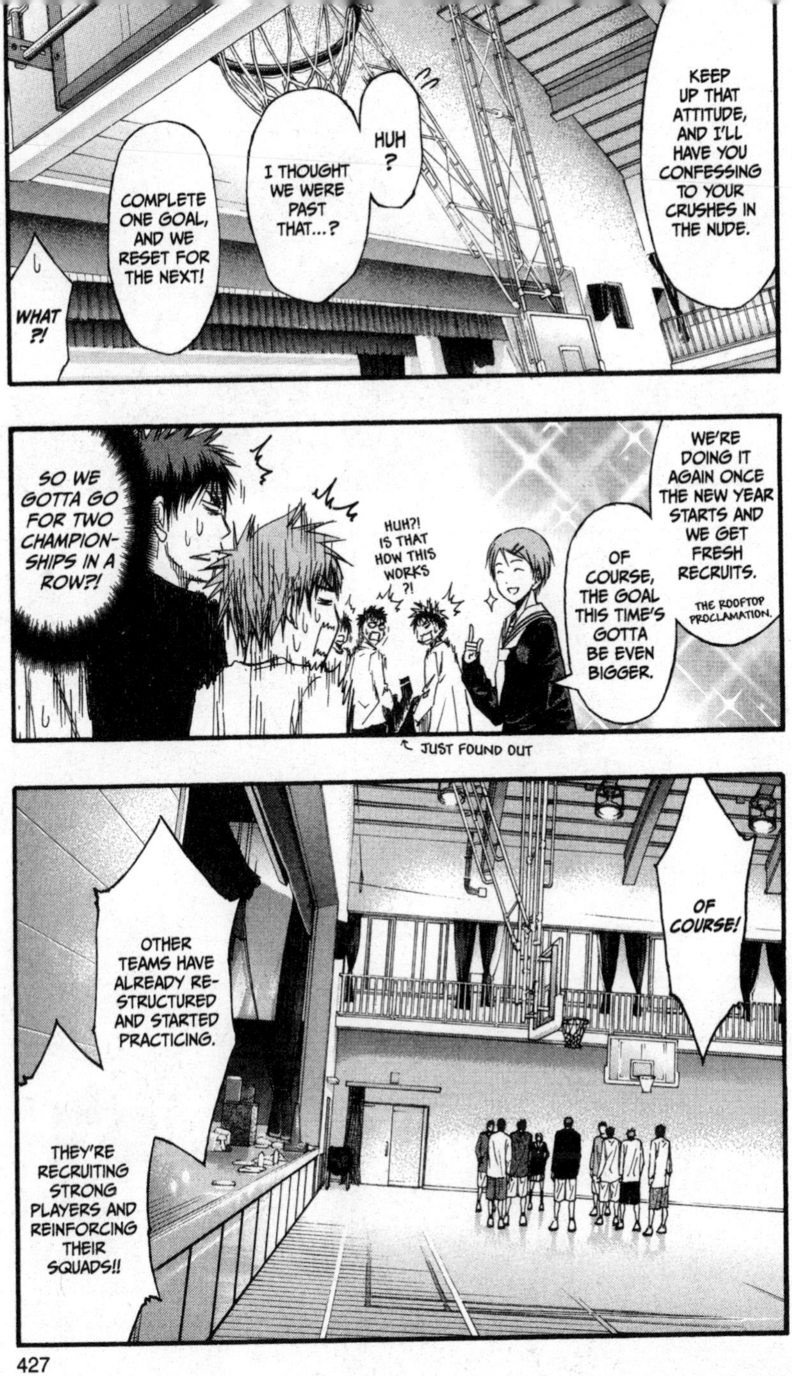
KEEP UP THAT ATTITUDE, AND I'LL HAVE YOU CONFESSING TO YOUR CRUSHES IN THE NUDE.
HUH?
I THOUGHT WE WERE PAST THAT...?
COMPLETE ONE GOAL, AND WE RESET FOR THE NEXT!
WHAT?!
WE'RE DOING IT AGAIN ONCE THE NEW YEAR STARTS AND WE GET FRESH RECRUITS.
THE ROOFTOP PROCLAMATION.
OF COURSE, THE GOAL THIS TIME'S GOTTA BE EVEN BIGGER.
HUH?! IS THAT HOW THIS WORKS?!
SO WE GOTTA GO FOR TWO CHAMPIONSHIPS IN A ROW?!
JUST FOUND OUT
OF COURSE!
OTHER TEAMS HAVE ALREADY RESTRUCTURED AND STARTED PRACTICING.
THEY'RE RECRUITING STRONG PLAYERS AND REINFORCING THEIR SQUADS!!

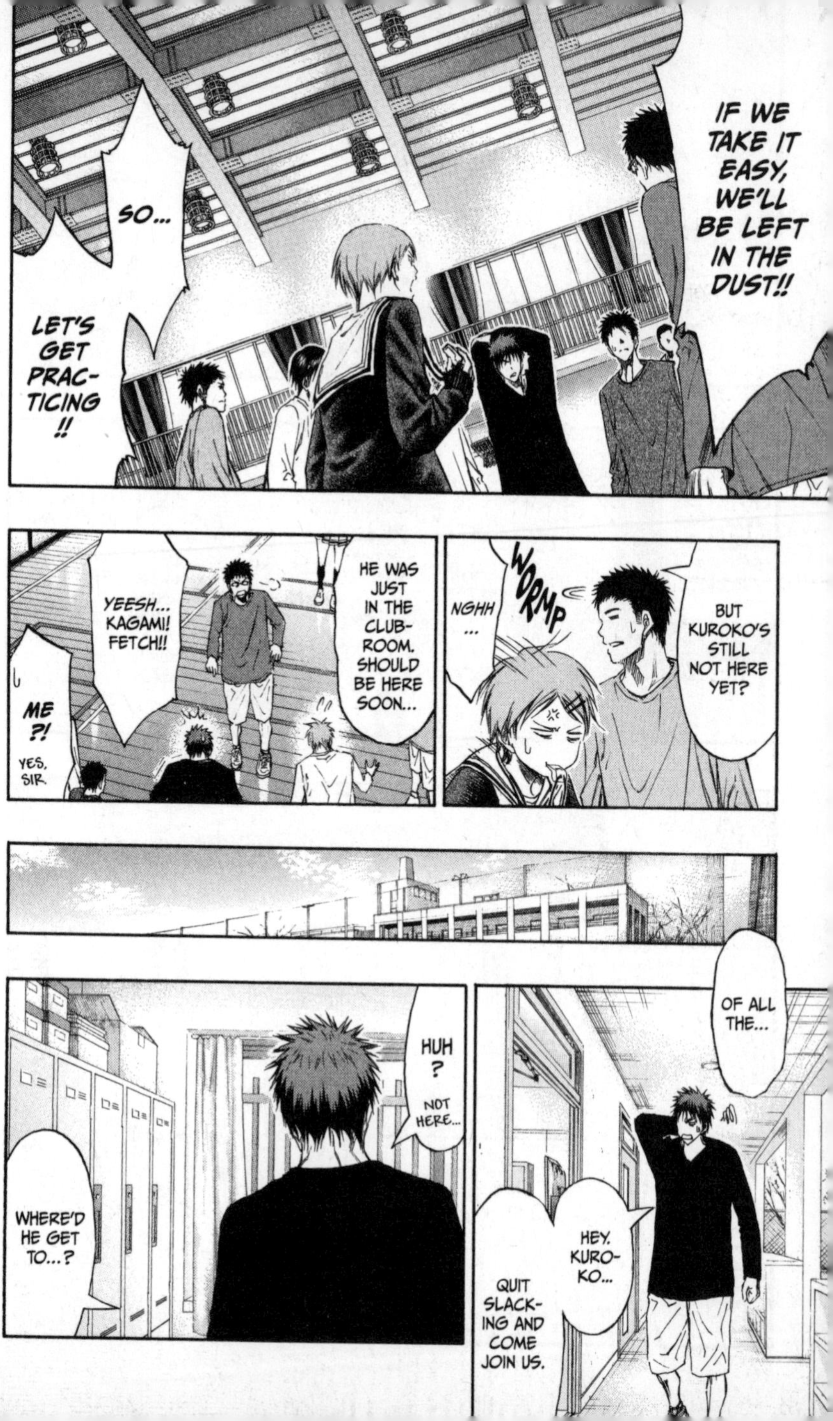
IF WE TAKE IT EASY, WE'LL BE LEFT IN THE DUST!!
SO...
LET'S GET PRACTICING!!
BUT KUROKO'S STILL NOT HERE YET?
WORMP
NGHH...
HE WAS JUST IN THE CLUB-ROOM. SHOULD BE HERE SOON...
YEESH... KAGAMI! FETCH!!
ME?!
YES, SIR.
OF ALL THE...
HEY. KURO-KO...
QUIT SLACKING AND COME JOIN US.
HUH?
NOT HERE...
WHERE'D HE GET TO...?

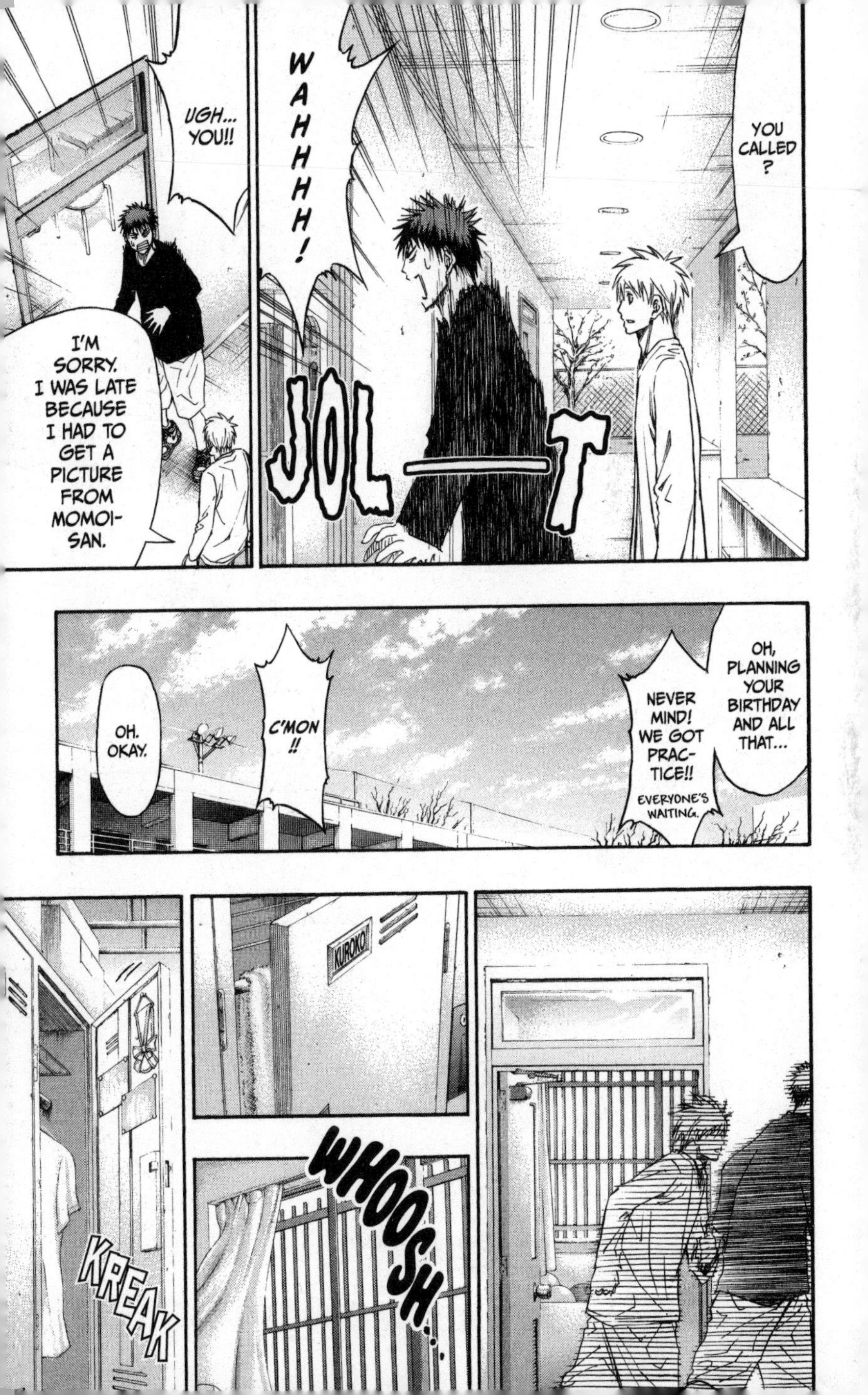
YOU CALLED?
WAHHHHHH!
JOL—T
UGH... YOU!!
I'M SORRY. I WAS LATE BECAUSE I HAD TO GET A PICTURE FROM MOMOI-SAN.
OH, PLANNING YOUR BIRTHDAY AND ALL THAT...
NEVER MIND! WE GOT PRAC-TICE!!
EVERYONE'S WAITING.
C'MON!!
OH. OKAY.
KUROKO
WHOOSH...
KREAK

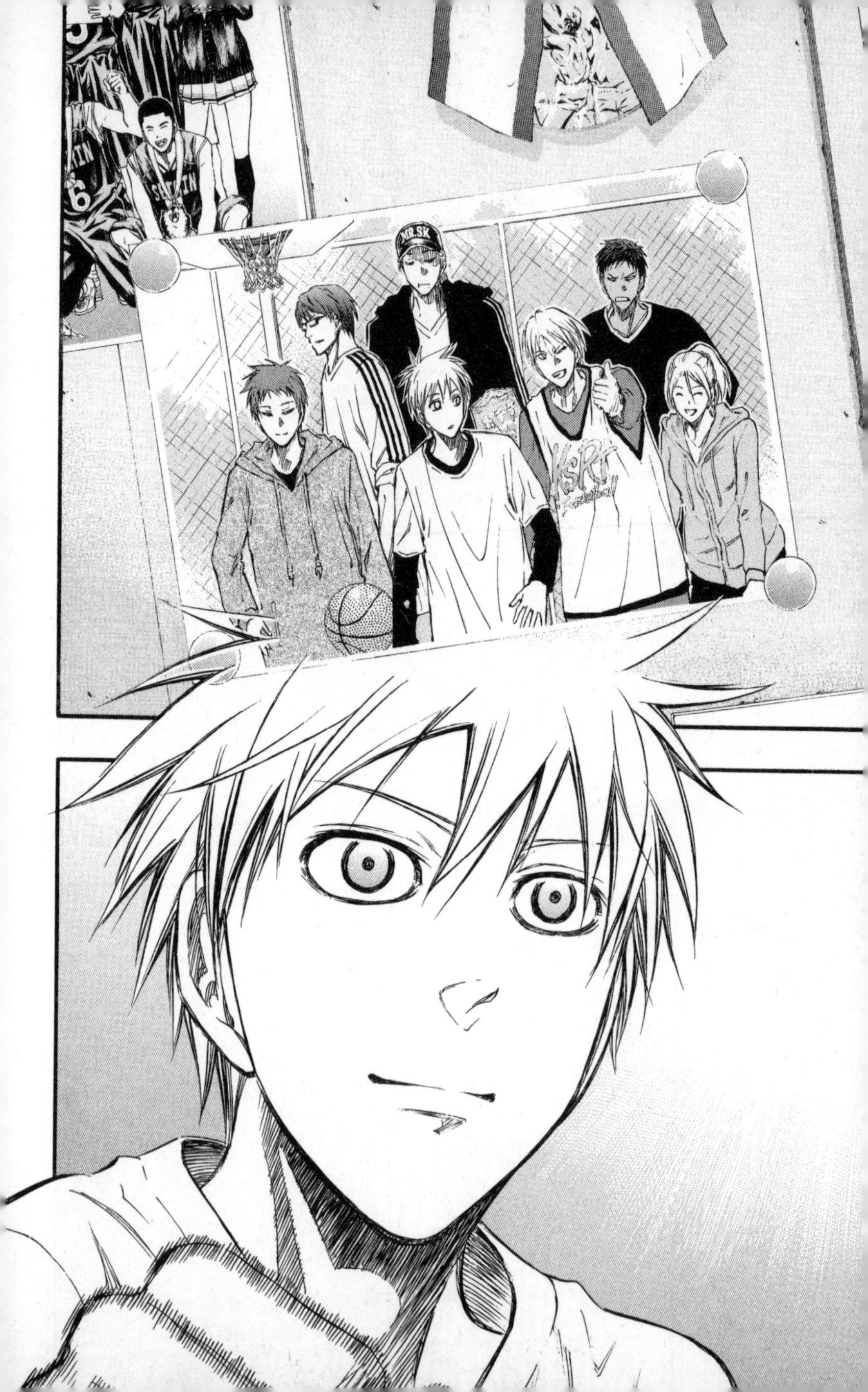
MR.SK

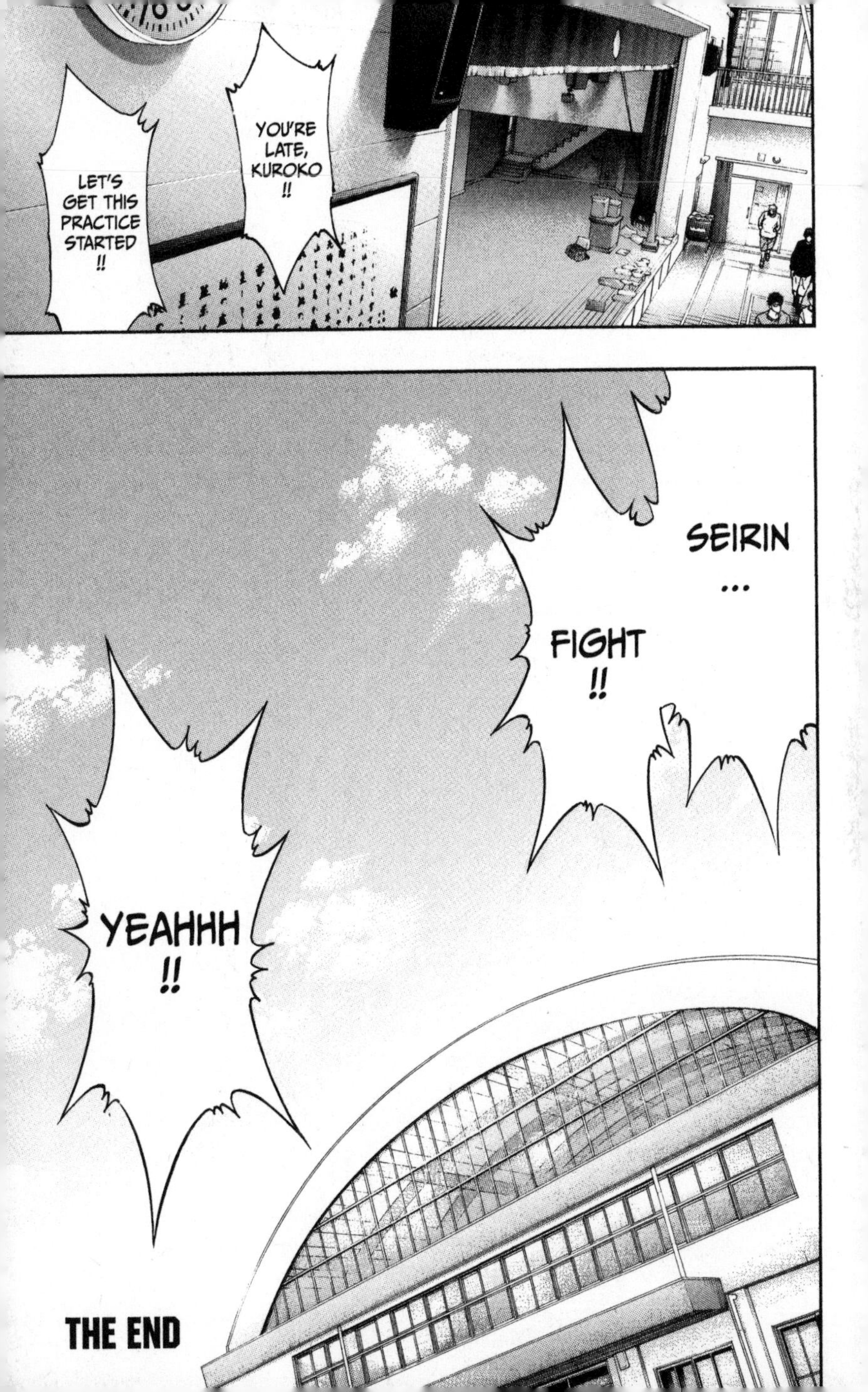
YOU'RE LATE, KUROKO!!
LET'S GET THIS PRACTICE STARTED!!
SEIRIN... FIGHT!!
YEAHHH!!
THE END

UNTIL
WE
MEET
AGAIN.

Afterword

Despite my lack of skill, I have put everything into writing this series. Naturally, I'm as attached to this as anyone could be, which is why I ended it. That is to say, because this felt like the best ending for this particular story. From our protagonist Tetsuya Kuroko's perspective, this tale represents only a fraction of his high school career. As for other characters, it's just one part of their lives. Their futures may hold even more heated battles. More painful times they have to endure. Whatever the story, though, what I can say for certain is that they'll keep playing basketball in earnest and living their lives to the fullest.

In my own life, there's barely any challenge I've taken on and succeeded in, start to finish.

I've developed something of a complex about it, and at times I've thought about how finishing this story was a way of overcoming that. But in practice, it hasn't given me some massive boost of self-confidence—if anything, it's made me reflect on how I never could have done this all by myself.

The afterwords in my published works are always somewhat one-note, like this, and I sometimes worry that I'm too self-conscious or am being too hard on myself, but to not say these things in the end would be a failure to recognize their importance. So if you'll allow me, this is how I need to end it.

To my ever-supportive staff, the editorial department at *Weekly Shonen Jump*, all other related parties and the dedicated readers who've stuck with us to the very end— thank you so much!

—Tadatoshi Fujimaki

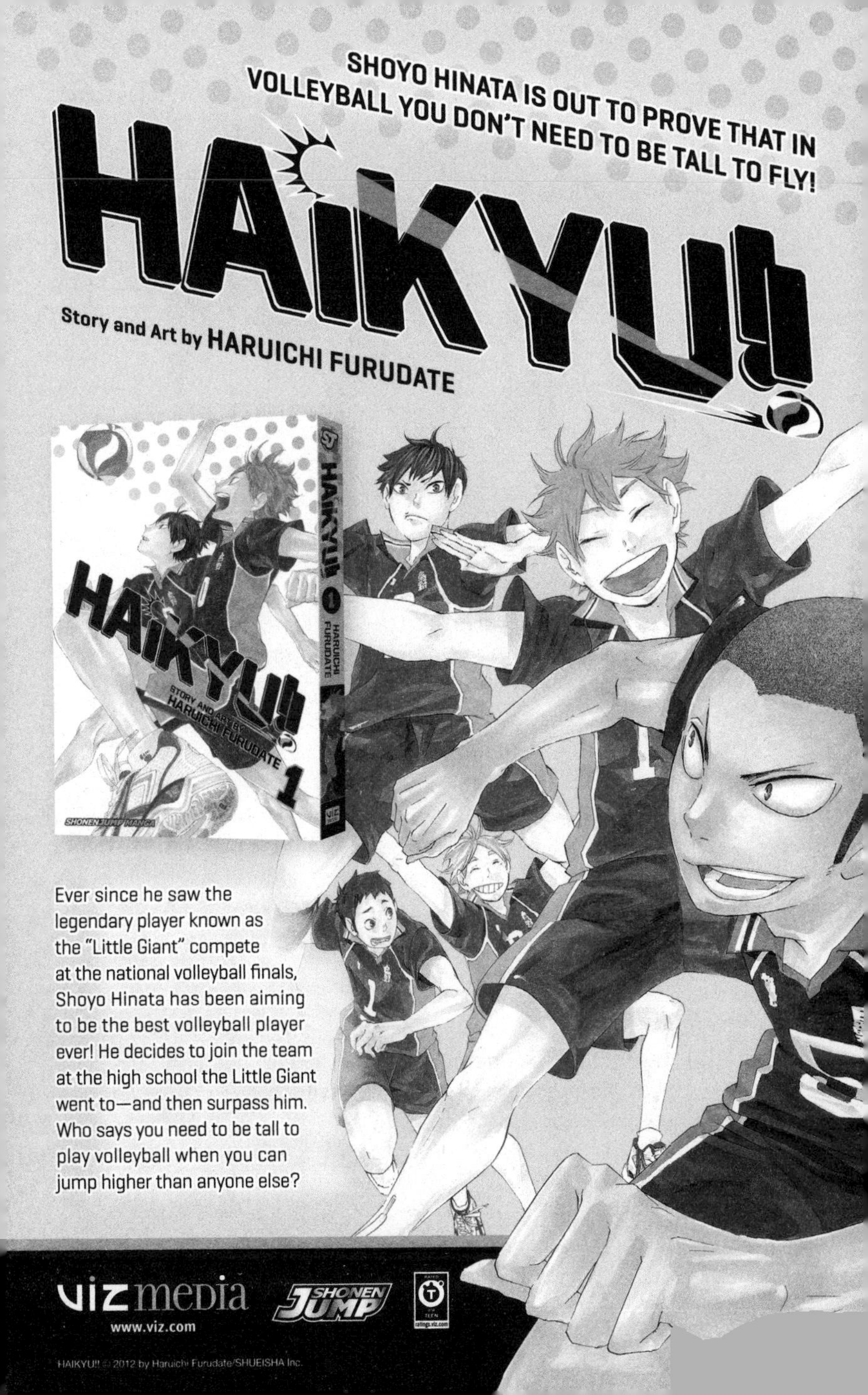

SHOYO HINATA IS OUT TO PROVE THAT IN VOLLEYBALL YOU DON'T NEED TO BE TALL TO FLY!
HAIKYU!!
Story and Art by HARUICHI FURUDATE
HAIKYU!! 1 HARUICHI FURUDATE
STORY AND ART BY HARUICHI FURUDATE
1
SHONEN JUMP MANGA
Ever since he saw the legendary player known as the "Little Giant" compete at the national volleyball finals, Shoyo Hinata has been aiming to be the best volleyball player ever! He decides to join the team at the high school the Little Giant went to—and then surpass him. Who says you need to be tall to play volleyball when you can jump higher than anyone else?
viz media
www.viz.com
SHONEN JUMP
RATED T TEEN ratings.viz.com
HAIKYU!! © 2012 by Haruichi Furudate/SHUEISHA Inc.

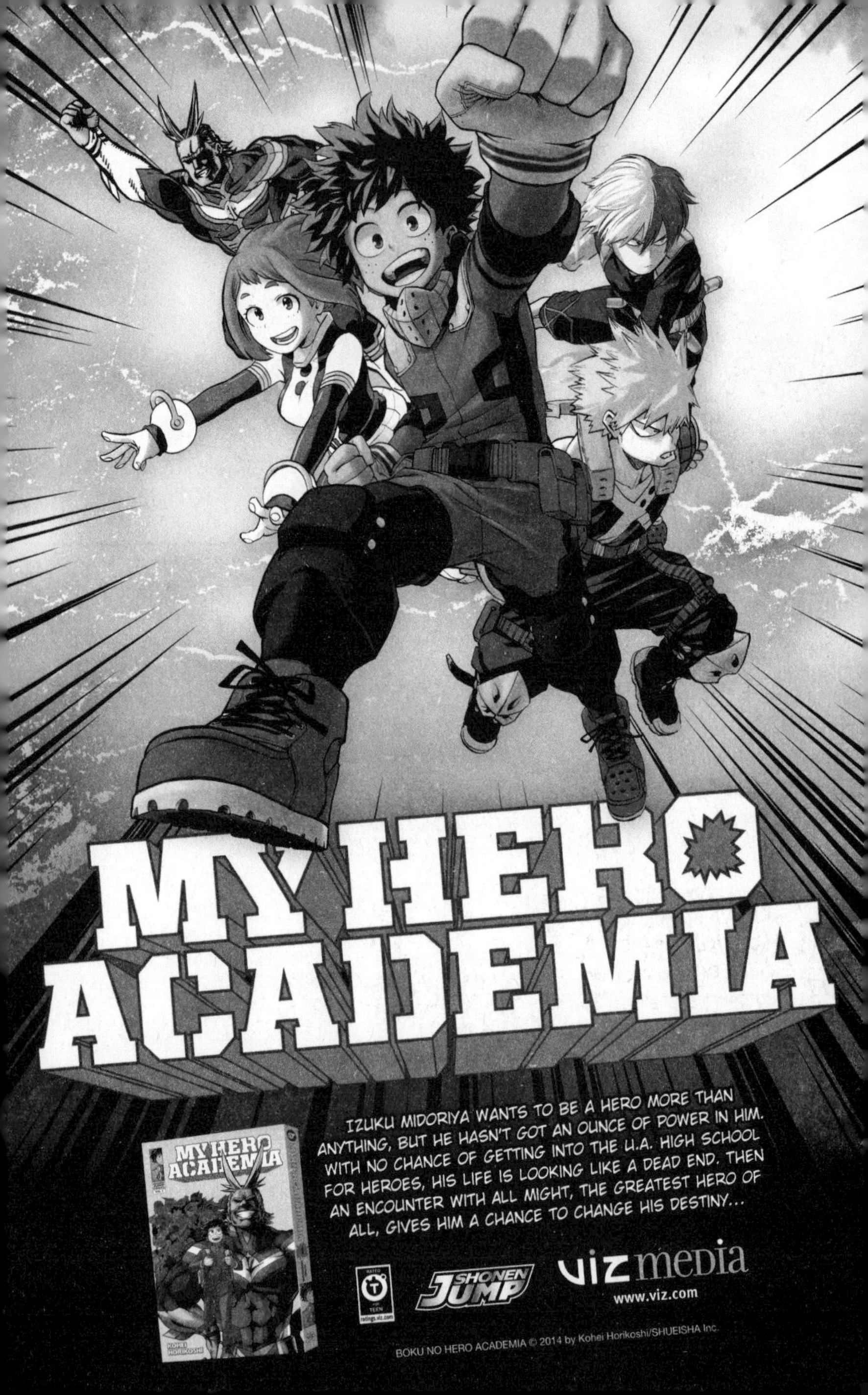
MY HERO ACADEMIA
IZUKU MIDORIYA WANTS TO BE A HERO MORE THAN ANYTHING, BUT HE HASN'T GOT AN OUNCE OF POWER IN HIM. WITH NO CHANCE OF GETTING INTO THE U.A. HIGH SCHOOL FOR HEROES, HIS LIFE IS LOOKING LIKE A DEAD END. THEN AN ENCOUNTER WITH ALL MIGHT, THE GREATEST HERO OF ALL, GIVES HIM A CHANCE TO CHANGE HIS DESTINY...
MY HERO ACADEMIA
KOHEI HORIKOSHI
SHONEN JUMP
viz media
www.viz.com
BOKU NO HERO ACADEMIA © 2014 by Kohei Horikoshi/SHUEISHA Inc.

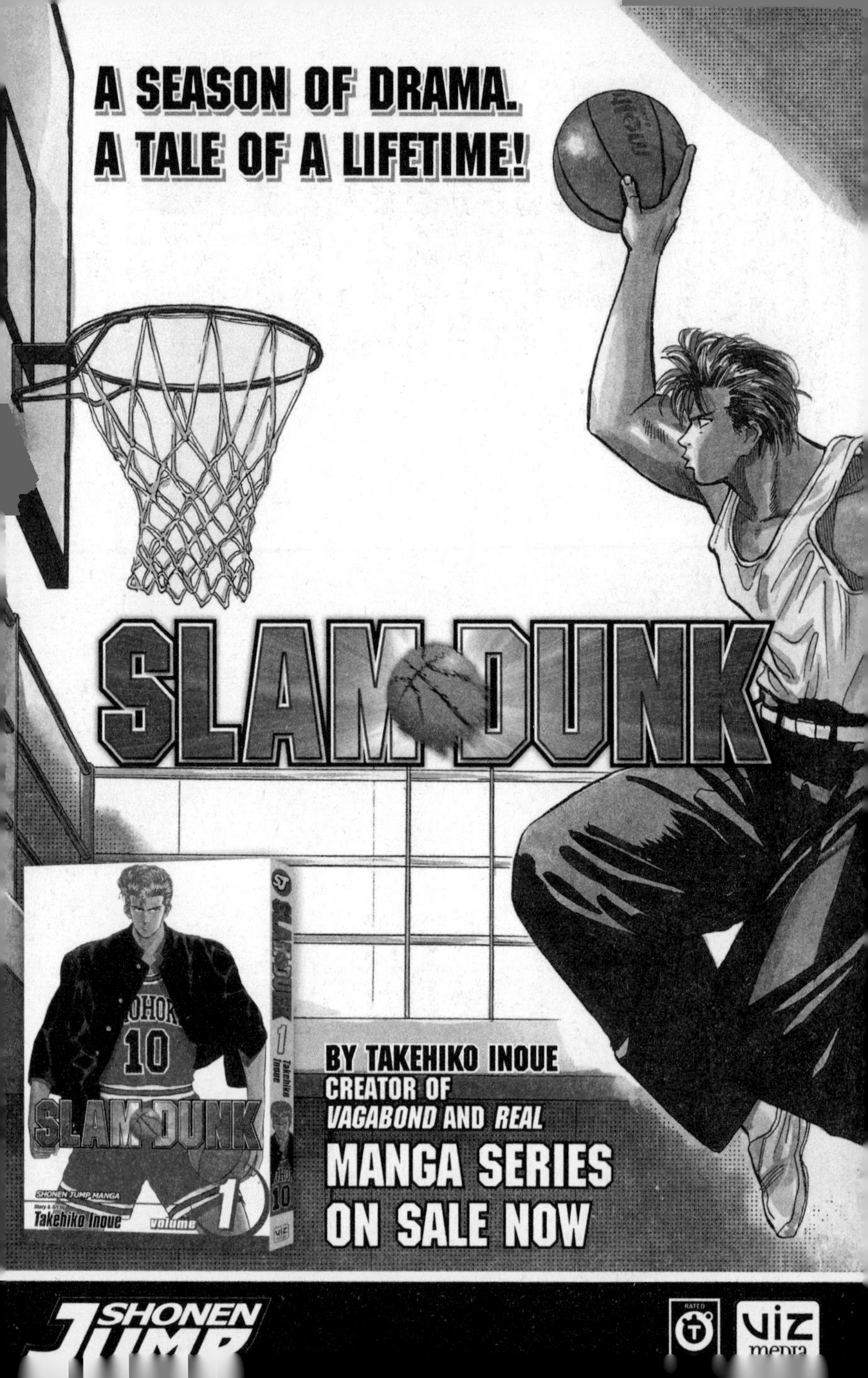
A SEASON OF DRAMA.
A TALE OF A LIFETIME!
SLAM DUNK
10
SLAM DUNK
SHONEN JUMP MANGA
Takehiko Inoue
volume 1
SLAM DUNK 1 Takehiko Inoue
BY TAKEHIKO INOUE
CREATOR OF
VAGABOND AND *REAL*
MANGA SERIES
ON SALE NOW
SHONEN JUMP
RATED T
viz media

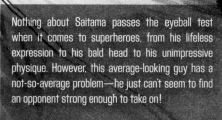

THE ACTION-PACKED SUPERHERO COMEDY ABOUT
ONE MAN'S AMBITION TO BE A HERO FOR FUN!

ONE-PUNCH MAN

STORY BY
ONE | ART BY
YUSUKE MURATA

Nothing about Saitama passes the eyeball test
when it comes to superheroes, from his lifeless
expression to his bald head to his unimpressive
physique. However, this average-looking guy has a
not-so-average problem—he just can't seem to find
an opponent strong enough to take on!

Can he finally find an opponent who can go toe-to-toe
with him and give his life some meaning? Or is he
doomed to a life of superpowered boredom?

RATED
TEEN
ratings.viz.com

SHONEN JUMP

VIZ media
www.viz.com

YOU'RE READING THE WRONG WAY!

KUROKO'S BASKETBALL reads from right to left, starting in the upper-right corner. Japanese is read from right to left, meaning that action, sound effects and word-balloon order are completely reversed from English order.

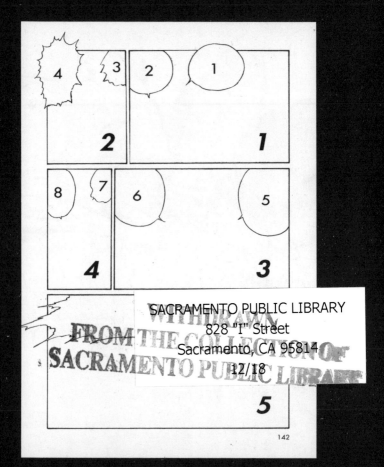

FLIP IT OVER TO GET STARTED!